# THE BOOK OF WINE

solera dry

NORMAN BEZZANT

A QUARTO BOOK

Published by Chartwell Books Inc.,
A Division of Book Sales Inc.,
110 Enterprise Avenue
Secaucus, New Jersey 07094

ISBN 0-89009-939-1



Reprinted 1988



This book was designed and produced by
Quarto Publishing Limited
The Old Brewery
6 Blundell Street
London N7 9BH

**Senior Editor** Stephen Paul
**Art Editor** Marnie Searchwell

**Editor** Paul Barnett
**Designer** Patrick Nugent

**Photography** The photography in this book was specially commissioned and carried out with the help of the vineyard owners and the wine-makers on the estates.
**Photographers** Colin Maher
Jon Wyand
Michael Freeman

**Illustrators** Chris Forsey
Elly King
Anne Savage
Norman Weaver

**Picture Researcher** Anne-Marie Ehrlich

**Paste up** Dave Evans

**Art Director** Alastair Campbell
**Editorial Director** Jim Miles

Typeset by AB Consultants, London
Color origination by Hong Kong Graphic Arts Limited, Hong Kong
Printed by Leefung Asco Printers Limited, Hong Kong

# CONTENTS

# COUNTRIES AROUND THE COMMON MARKET

# NORTH AMERICA

# SOUTHERN HEMISPHERE

# SOCIAL AND AFTER DINNER DRINKS

# WINE AND THE CONSUMER

# FOREWORD

*The Book of Wine* is written specifically for intelligent wine-drinkers; it anticipates their reasonable questions and answers them lucidly. Not all books — certainly not all wine books — are serious. Many people regard wine as a light subject and, in terms of pleasure and relaxed enjoyment, probably it is. Therefore, many have written lightly — though often pleasingly — but not thoroughly, on the subject. Nowadays however, more people, worldwide and in growing numbers, are drinking wine; many want to learn about it and their best way, short of really extensive travel which many cannot afford, is to read about it. When they read they want to be informed; not superficially nor partially, but thoroughly; yet at the same time, not heavily but readably.

These demands Norman Bezzant meets admirably. He was until lately a consultant to the Wine and Spirit Education Trust, which is responsible for the training of beginners — of all ages — in the British wine trade; and joint author of its two major text books. You will find those two works on the shelves, not only of the Trust's former students, but of the most thoughtful readers of the subject.

Was another wine book needed? Are there not enough wine books already? The author answers that question himself — "Aided by new materials, technology and research, a revolution in viticulture and vinification has come about in the last 25 years, and a new and exciting generation of wine-lovers has shown its appreciation". The subject itself is so much larger than it was — consider merely the growth and extent of the 'new worlds' of wine here in North America and in Australasia — that the book which covers it all has to be much bigger than those of even twenty years ago.

In this book, all the myriad wines of the world, as well as spirits and liqueurs, are dealt with informatively and interestingly; so is tasting, the matching of wines with foods, service, storage and mixing. Thus the most demanding students may find the information they want; there is reference to every major factual aspect of the subject; and quiz-makers will find it a godsend. (What is the origin of "Médoc"?)

Quite aside from matters of fact and history, Norman Bezzant writes, too, with a human understanding of wine and its drinkers. To quote from his own book: "Wherever nature has provided the right climate, human beings have cultivated grapes and converted them to wine. These drinks can bring to many of the more civilized experiences of life a conclusion that is at once subtle, mellow and deeply satisfying". Above all, he never loses sight of his purpose — "Knowing not only what one is drinking but where it comes from, its ingredients, and how it is made adds greatly to its enjoyment".

# INTRODUCTION

This book has been written for the consumer, without whom there would be no industries producing wines, spirits and liqueurs, nor any distributing and selling trades making them available. The consumer may or may not be an expert in the field of fermented and distilled drinks, but with few exceptions he or she wants to know more about them, where and how they are made, and the specific purpose of each. Worldwide, thousands of books have been written on these subjects, from those dealing in depth with the products of one country to those content to take the reader on a wine tour through beautiful scenery. What is certain is that the two covers of one book cannot contain it all.

*The Book of Wine* does the next best thing. Chapters on every country in the world having a recognizable wine industry deal with their habitat, history, customs, methods, wine regions, regulations and products, and each is illustrated profusely. Other chapters deal with the techniques of viticulture, vinification and distillation; grain and fruit spirits and liqueurs; the infrastructure of the world's wine and spirit industries; and advice on the purchase of drinks and their storage, use and serving in the home.

The reader will also find a glossary of wine terms as well as a comprehensive index. To save time, the index should always be consulted first, for the glossary headings are indexed, and the reader may instead be referred direct to a page in the text.

Amassing the contents of this book and producing it quickly enough to be up-to-date on publication has been the work of many experts. The gratitude of the publishers and author are due to all of them. In particular the help of the following is specifically acknowledged: Grahame McKenzie, chairman of Trustees, and David Burroughs, lately director of the Wine and Spirit Education Trust, UK; Frank H. Stone, founder, and Dr. John Postilio Jr., Director of Studies, of the Wine and Spirit Education Centers, Georgia, USA; Hugh Johnson and his publishers Mitchell Beazley, for permission to use "Hugh Johnson's Wine Companion" for reference purposes; Leon Adams, author, and publishers McGraw-Hill (USA) and Sidgwick & Jackson (UK) for permission to use "The Wines of America" within the scope of the US Copyright Act of 1976; David Robson, former château proprietor and wine-maker in Bordeaux, for instant answers to the author's innumerable queries; Michael Olivier and Achim Von Arnim (wine-maker) of Boschendal (SA); Michael Back of Backsberg (SA); Paul de Villiers of Landskroon (SA); Janie Momberg and Annie Johnson of Neetlingshof (SA); Bill and Margot Bailey for guiding the photographer around all the Cape vineyards and wineries; and Chris Backwell of Standard Bank.

# VINE, GRAPE AND WINE

Almost everyone has some idea of the eternal battle with nature waged by every grower of grapes. It is no greater nor less than the struggle sustained by every grower of agricultural or horticultural crops, but with one important difference: the high degree of risk arising from the vulnerability of the grape.

The vineyard chief—the French use the term *vigneron*—may lose the crop (and that means his or her whole year's income) for any one of a number of reasons. The weather is not just a risk-factor but a group of risk-factors—heat, wind, rainfall, hail and drought—each of which requires the *vigneron*'s vigilance and anticipation during some part of the calendar year. The *vigneron* cannot abolish them, of course, but in some instances he or she can prevent them from damaging the vineyard. Then there are pests, parasites, fungal diseases, viruses and physiological disorders: again each is a category of threats, rather than a single threat. Some dangers menace the vine, others the grape, and every one has a known method or methods of preventive treatment.

Coping with all this is only a part of the *vigneron*'s job: his (there are as yet few female *vignerons*) program will include fertilization, propagation, training, pruning and the harvesting of the grapes at vintage; each item on the list covers a multitude of tasks, to say nothing of the management and administration involved in each. Additionally, the *vigneron* may also be the wine-maker.

As though it were not enough that he should be an expert viticulturist, the *vigneron* must, to manage a winery, be an expert also in viniculture, for the winery demands the knowledge and attention of an accomplished physicist and chemist, capable of carrying the battle of the vineyard into what is virtually a commercial laboratory. Here there is being created for sale a commercial product in the making of which all measurements, be they of temperature, specific gravity, volume, time, potential alcohol or acidity (and there are many more), are critical. Many of these measurements vary according to the product being made—as for red, white or rosé wine, sparkling wine or fortified wine—and each of these has many variations, as for instance in the grapes used, methods adopted and the customs of the region or country.

In the opening chapters of this book it is possible to give only an outline story of the functions and methods necessary to accomplish the tasks mentioned above and some others that are equally important; in later chapters we shall discuss exceptions to the rules more fully.

The Comte Alexandre de Lur Saluces, owner of Château d'Yquem in Bordeaux, continues the family tradition of producing supreme-quality sweet Sauternes. This illustration of vines at Yquem *(right)* is a grim reminder that the kings and beggars of the wine industry share the risks of winter — and many other hazards.

# VINEYARD, VINE AND GRAPE

**The Soil ♦ Propagation and Training of the Vine ♦ The Vine ♦ Genus and Species ♦ The Grape ♦ The Vineyard Year**

There is a popular misconception that wine starts with the grape. Perhaps this is not so much misconception as hyperbole, for the grape is an end-product in itself—a product of the artfulness of nature and the genius of mankind.

At the most fundamental level, nature is concerned with our world's distance from the Sun, its rotation, its revolution and seasons, its continents and oceans. Within the continents are mountains and plains, rivers and valleys, forests and lakes; above them is the atmosphere, variations in whose barometric pressure create cyclones and anticyclones, and beneath them is the soil. All geographic features affect the climate in different parts of the world: coastlines, mountains, plains and forests all help to vary the weather conditions to give us sunshine, clouds, winds, rainfall and drought. These worldwide influences create huge areas designated according to their climatic regimes, such as the pacific, maritime, continental and mediterranean climates.

One factor of especial importance to the winemaker is the strength of the received sunlight. The illustration (*above right*) shows how this limits wine production to the wine-bands, which together comprise a comparatively small area of the world's land surface. The prospective vineyard-owner must therefore choose a site where sufficient energy from the Sun will be enjoyed. Ideally it should have a southeastern aspect (in the northern hemisphere) to get the most benefit from the rich ultraviolet rays of the morning sun; it should be in or close to a river valley, but not so low as to suffer cold damage from standing water or frost; conversely, it should not be too high up on the hillsides, where winds may damage the vines. Preferably it should be away from forest lands, although in Bordeaux the forests of the Landes actually protect the Médoc and Graves regions from southwesterly salt winds, and in Alsace the vines are unaffected by the neighboring Black Forest.

Next the viniculturist must study the topography and microclimate of his chosen site. Climate is the first feature to consider, for the vine-grower needs an average yearly temperature of 14°C to 15°C (57-59°F), ranging from a winter minimum of 3°C (37°F) to a summer maximum of 22°C (72°F). During the eight months of active growth, starting in March, an average of six or seven hours of sunshine every day is desirable, but this ideal is not always obtainable—and, indeed, the parameters for sunshine necessarily vary between regions and between countries, for the width of the belt between latitudes 30° and 50°, north or south, is no less than 1,400km (870mi). Moreover, the vine will not flower at temperatures below 15°C (59°F). The essential is to have sufficient summer heat to bring the vine to flowering and fruition, as well as enough late summer heat to mature the grape internally. Near the cool limits of the wine-bands, therefore, growers harvest as late in the year as possible.

Study of the microclimate is a matter for each individual vineyard-owner, for here we are concerned with the immediate effect of the elements on a site that may be as small as two hectares (5 acres)—or even less. Weatherwise, the microclimate is a matter not of overall regional conditions but of the eccentricities of the vineyard site—shaded corners that may miss the sun or attract mist or fog; exposed areas where the vine-leaves may need protection from the sun at its hottest; low-lying areas, or areas of river marshland, that may collect standing water or be subject to frost and fog; abnormal periods of sunshine or rainfall; and the all-important character of the soil, which alone may dictate the species of vine to be planted.

Vineyards have three bad-weather enemies: frost, wind and hail. The diagram *below right* shows one of several methods for combating frost. High winds can carry off pollen, thus reducing the effectiveness of fertilization by bees and consequently the number of flowers that will produce grapes, and causing *coulure* (see page

*WINE PRODUCTION AROUND THE WORLD*

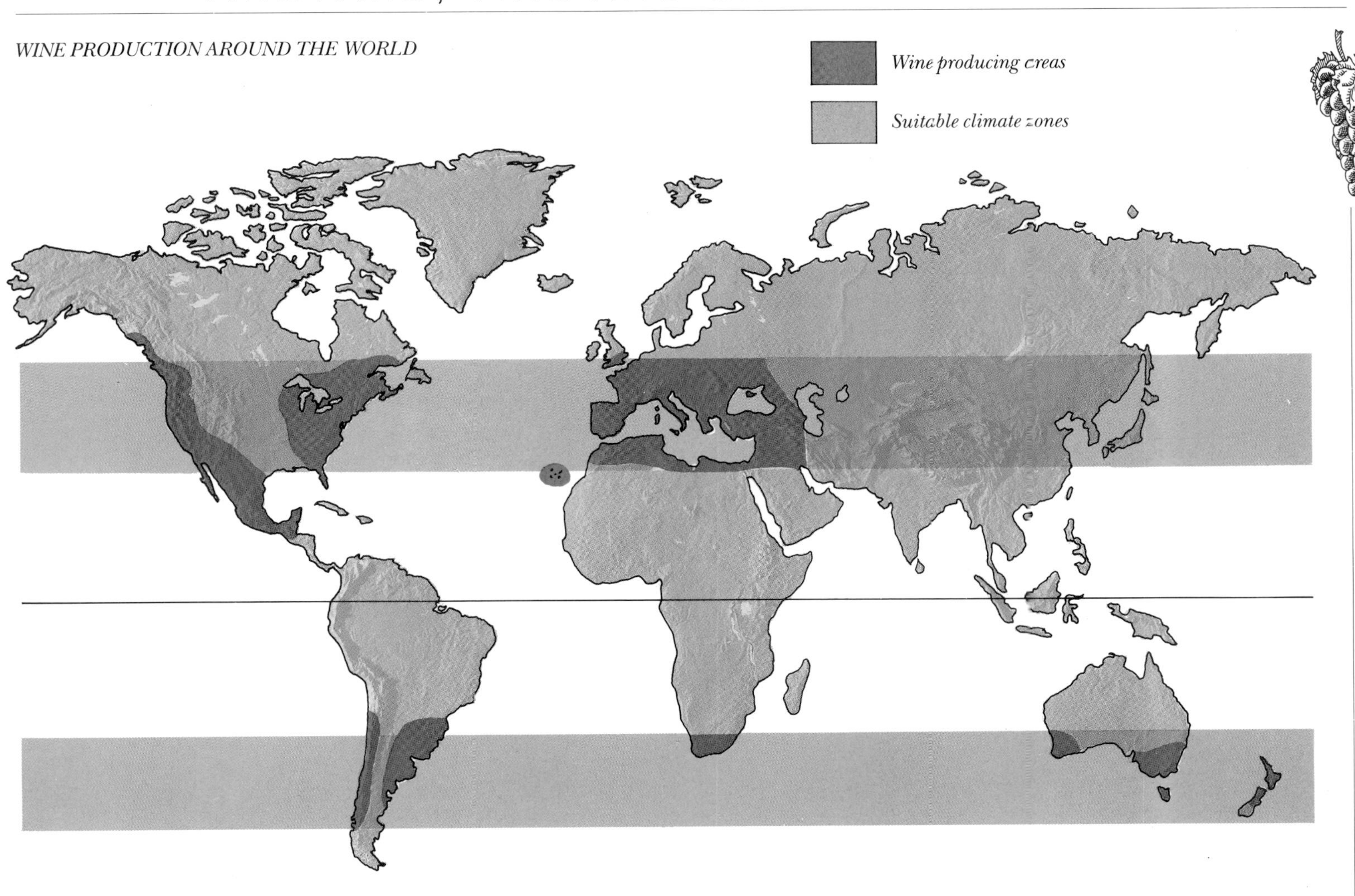


The wine-producing areas of the world *(above)*. The vine must be cultivated in one or other of the wine-bands that encircle the world: they lie between latitudes 30° and 50° north and south, where weather conditions are normally ideal. Nearer the equator, the sun is too hot to give the vine the winter rest it needs to regain strength for the growing season; and at latitudes greater than 50° there is insufficient heat in the sunlight to insure that the grapes ripen fully every year.

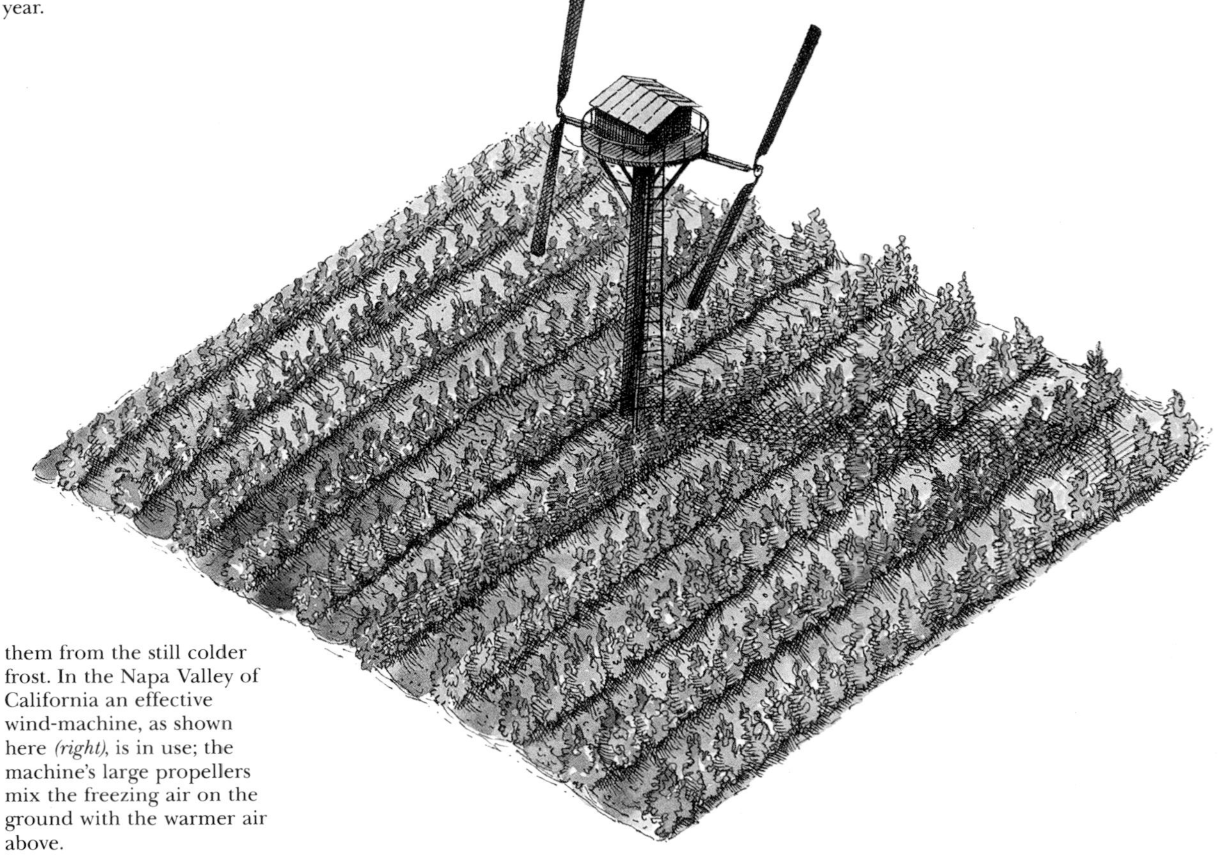

Many devices have been used to protect the vines from frosts. In Europe, fires in "smudge pots" were lit in the vineyards with only limited success. Successive hard winters nearly brought ruin to Chablis until water was sprayed on the vines to form ice, which protected them from the still colder frost. In the Napa Valley of California an effective wind-machine, as shown here *(right)*, is in use; the machine's large propellers mix the freezing air on the ground with the warmer air above.

24). Even once the grapes have appeared, hail and high winds can be as damaging, stripping many grapes from the vine. Hail may break the skins, so that the grapes are discolored and molds are able to form, with the result that the wine made from them is tainted with *goût de grêle* and off-odor. Although rain is needed during the winter and the first days of spring, after that it may cause humid conditions which encourage the vine to rot, while rain just before harvest can be a disaster.

## THE SOIL

The other element of paramount importance to the vine-grower is soil, of which there are an almost infinite number of variations. The map *seen below* shows the major tectonic plates of our planet's surface, interactions between which are directly or indirectly responsible for the wide diversity of soil types. ("Tectonic" simply refers to distortions or changes of our planet's crust as a result of forces within or beneath it.) Soil is made up of disintegrated rocks, organic material, minerals, water and air; plate-tectonic processes play the cardinal role in determining the composition of the "rocks" component in this list (as well as a more indirect role in determining the other components).

Rocks are of three types: igneous, metamorphic and sedimentary.

Igneous rocks are those derived directly from our planet's mantle, the molten layer beneath the crust: this molten material reaches the surface in several ways, the most dramatic of which is its explosive eruption from a volcano, as lava. Volcanoes are found at the margins of plates, either where material from the mantle is welling up to form new stretches of the "conveyor belts" on which the continents are carried around (these margins, most of which are in the oceans, are called constructive), or where one plate is being forced under another at a destructive margin (e.g., an ocean trench) to make room for the material emerging at a constructive margin elsewhere. The famous "Ring of Fire" around the Pacific is the best known example of the latter process in action.

Metamorphic rocks "start life" as either igneous or sedimentary rocks, but for one reason or another, usually connected with plate tectonics, they are forced beneath the surface of the planet and there undergo conditions of heat and pressure. On their reappearance at the surface they are quite different from their original forms; for example, metamorphosis transforms limestone into marble.

Sedimentary rocks are formed when existing rocks are weathered and/or eroded, the resulting particles being transported (usually by water) and then deposited in distinct strata—typically when a body of water for some reason disappears, usually as a result of large-scale tectonic action. Sedimentary rocks often contain organic remains, too, some of which may be preserved in the form of fossils. Typical sedimentary rocks are limestones and shales, eroded particles of the latter forming the clays found in many soils.

So we can see how great is the effect on soils of plate-tectonic activities. Climatic considerations also play a major part: we have already referred to erosion and weathering. The photographs (*right*) illustrate six types of soil variation.

It has often been said that the poorest soils make the best wine, but this is an oversimplification and not always true. Soil normally regarded as fertile is rich in nitrogen, which gives the high growth factor necessary for agricultural crops; but the vine, which is on the borderline between agricultural and horti-

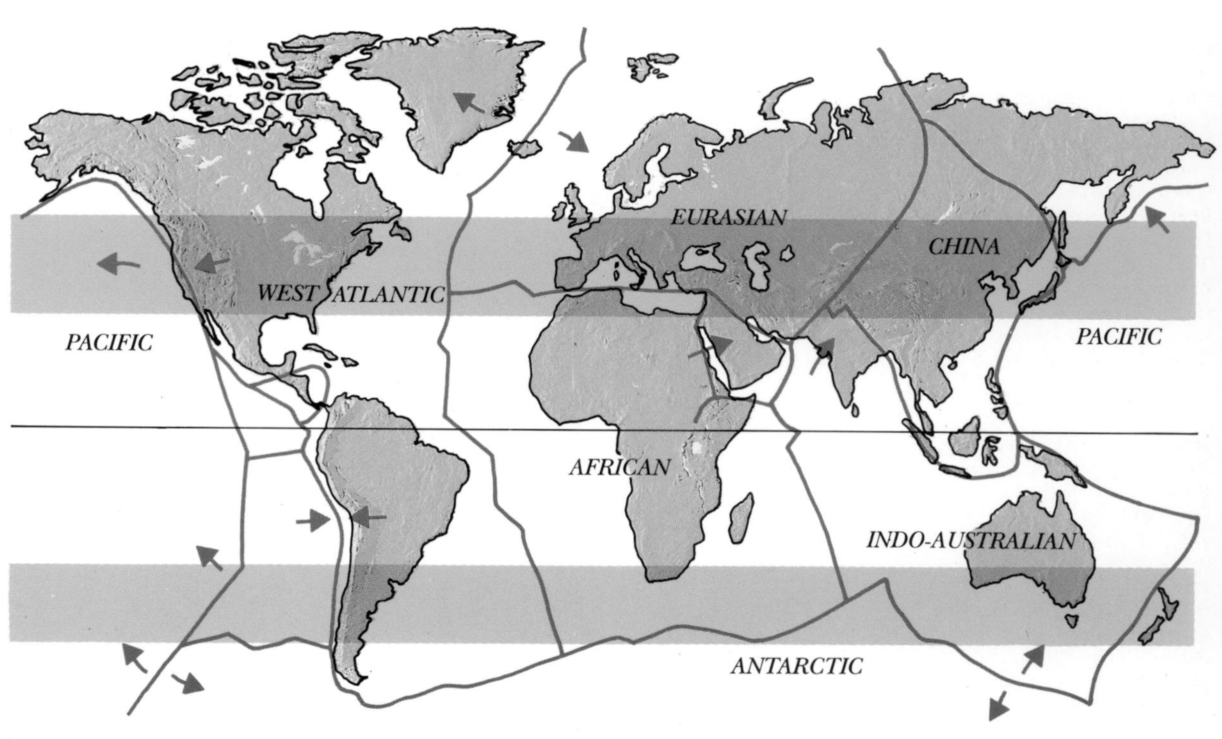


Soil-types result from the constant movement of the tectonic plates making up the world's surface *(right)*. The most dramatic activity centers in the zones where there is collision or lateral friction between them. In the distant past large landmasses have sunk into the oceans to emerge once more with overlays of sedimentary soil. Glaciation has had effects, too. The irresistible forces of nature have also thrown up mountain ranges, generating high subterranean temperatures and pressures, and thus creating volcanic rocks that break down slowly into igneous soil. Alluvial soils have formed as a result of the erosion of the canyons, gorges and valleys through which rivers flow. Extreme pressure and heat also cause rocks to change their character.

**Douro** *(top left).* The fortified wine marketed as Port comes only from grapes grown in Portugal's Upper Douro region. The soil here is derived from schist, a soft crystalline rock that splits and crumbles, outcropping in a mountainous environment composed almost entirely of granite.

**Rheingau** *(top right).* At the western end of Germany's famous Rheingau region slaty soils persist at the foot of steep hills. To the east, the soil turns from slate to quartzite and loess at Schloss Johannisberg, and then to red sandy loam. At Rheingau's eastern end, the soils vary from vineyard to vineyard.

**Rhône** *(center left).* The soils in the northern Rhône region are from granite and schist, interspersed with lime and iron mixtures. In the south the soils are varied, but are mainly of sand and clay with outcrops of limestone. Glaciers have left beds of large round stones, noticeable especially here at Châteauneuf-du-Pape.

**Médoc** *(center right).* The Grands Crus of the Médoc occupy the best positions above the Gironde, where the gravelly mound bordering the river is highest above the alluvial deposits along the banks. The gravel pebbles *(cailloux)* store the sun's heat to ripen the grapes by night, and provide good drainage.

**Champagne** *(bottom left).* Soil is all-important in Champagne, where its quality determines the individual vineyard ranking. The principal soil is belemnitic and oolitic limestone, covered by a thin layer of Tertiary deposits. The chalk contains the precise minerals needed for Champagne as well as caves for almost unlimited underground cellarage.

**Jerez** *(bottom right).* The Palomino grapes thrive on the white *alberiza* soil of Jerez, which contains up to 75% pure chalk. This bakes in the sun, retaining subsurface moisture and reflecting intense heat to ripen the grapes. *Barro,* a darker, chalky clay soil, is planted with grapes that produce coarser sweetening wines.

cultural plants, hungers rather for various minerals—minerals which will in due course give noble qualities to the wine. These minerals, usually present only as trace elements in rocks and soils, include boron, cobalt, copper, iodine, manganese, molybdenum, nickel, selenium, vanadium and zinc. Certainly these elements affect the taste and aroma of the eventual wine, and enological research into these and other properties of individual minerals continues, especially in Europe, North America and Australia.

The work of converting virgin soil into a vineyard can be arduous in the extreme. In Europe many, if not most, vineyards are sited in river valleys whose slopes defy the use of mechanical equipment. Terraces may have to be built, rock may have to be blasted away, or soil may need to be shifted in vast quantity. Moreover, these jobs may largely have to be achieved by hand. In certain areas of the USA, Australia and elsewhere there is space for bigger vineyard units, so that mechanization is economically and physically viable. Land in such regions can be cleared and leveled rapidly, and new soil, if required, can be imported, so that the vines may be planted out within a matter of a month or two of commencement of operations. In Europe it may be desirable first to prepare the soil and then to clear it with a cover crop; one or two years may elapse before the vines go down.

The large-scale creation of new vineyards is a matter for the future, but of course there is a wide range of fine wines available to us today. For these we are mostly indebted to the heritage of hundreds of years' husbandry of the great vineyards of the world, and to the ever-improving skills of the wine-makers. To such an extent has the science of enology burgeoned in recent years, however, that vineyards created in California (and elsewhere in North America), Australia, New Zealand and South Africa during the last 25 years are now producing noble wines whose quality challenges that of Europe's best.

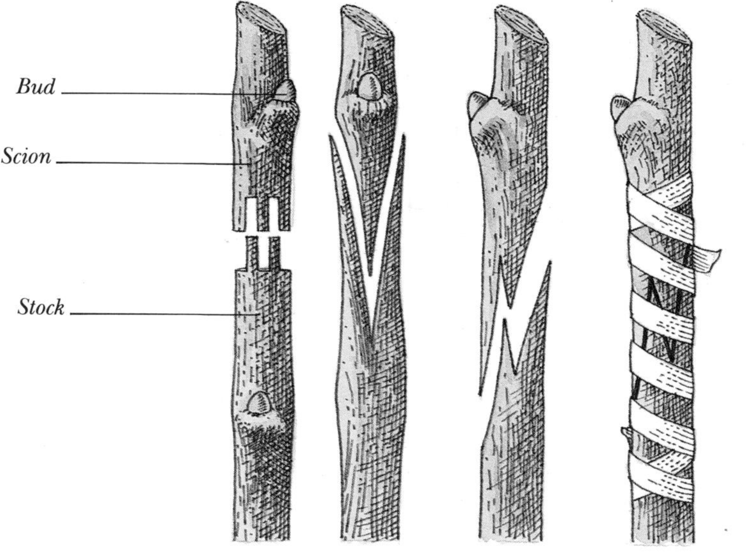


Three principal styles of grafting *(above)*. Following the arrival of the *Phylloxera* louse the vineyards of Europe were ravaged and almost completely destroyed. Grafting European *V. vinifera* scions onto resistant American rootstocks was the answer — and usually still is. Another method is "field-budding", where a resistant rootstock is first planted in its permanent position and then, when it buds, a bud is cut off and a scion is "budded-on" in its place. A US variant of this is "T-budding", cutting off an old vine close to the ground and budding on a scion that will produce grapes in two years' time. An important development in California is "mist propagation", an assembly-line method of producing many thousands of vines in heated greenhouses from a single plant in one year.

# PROPAGATION AND TRAINING OF THE VINE

Mankind has learned to its cost that the vine has to be protected from the scourges of nature. In any event, the working life of a vine for wine production is no longer than 30-40 years at most, and so there is a perennial demand for new vines, and systematic propagation is necessary. The obvious answer has a snag: vines *will* grow readily from grape pits, but unfortunately the new vine will not necessarily be the same as the one that bore the grape, because cross-pollination by bees can give rise to mutations. The first alternative to be devised was grafting, a technique which can of course be applied to practically any genus of plant although most readily to trees, bushes and vines, and which provided the answer when most of the world's vineyards were destroyed by phylloxera in the closing decades of the nineteenth century. The diagram *below left* explains three of the internationally accepted patterns of grafting employed in the vineyard industry. There are several other methods of grafting and propagating vines; and quite recently mist propagation, a method that may well become the most used of all in the foreseeable future, has been developed in California.

From the moment the two-year-old vine takes its place in the vineyard, and thereafter from year to year, its growth must be controlled. This involves two things: training and pruning. The differences between these, as well as some examples of the initial training styles that can be adapted for particular climates, microclimates and the contours of individual vineyards, are illustrated and described in the diagram *right*.

# THE VINE: GENUS AND SPECIES

So far we have talked about the vine as though it produces grapes suitable for wine-making as a matter of course—just so long as the *vigneron* brings those grapes safely to maturity. But the grapevine is by no means so obliging. The genus

STYLES OF VINE TRAINING

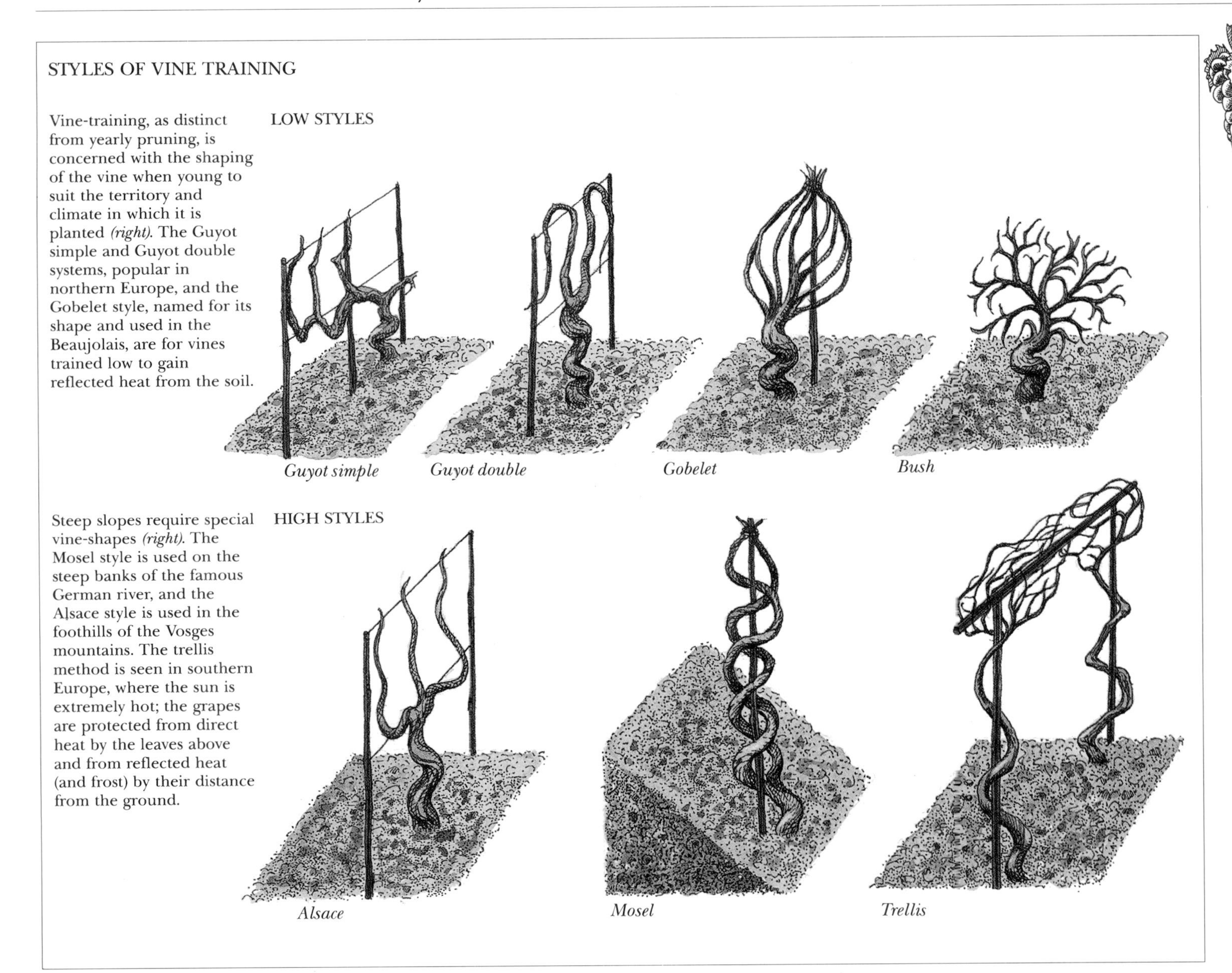


Vine-training, as distinct from yearly pruning, is concerned with the shaping of the vine when young to suit the territory and climate in which it is planted *(right).* The Guyot simple and Guyot double systems, popular in northern Europe, and the Gobelet style, named for its shape and used in the Beaujolais, are for vines trained low to gain reflected heat from the soil.

Steep slopes require special vine-shapes *(right).* The Mosel style is used on the steep banks of the famous German river, and the Alsace style is used in the foothills of the Vosges mountains. The trellis method is seen in southern Europe, where the sun is extremely hot; the grapes are protected from direct heat by the leaves above and from reflected heat (and frost) by their distance from the ground.

*Vitis*, which belongs to the botanical family Vitaceae, is the only one of real significance to the wine-maker; *Vitis vinifera* is the species from which all the world's great vines, and hence their wines, have been derived. *V. vinifera*, "the wine-bearing vine," is said to have originated in the Caucasus and spread throughout Europe and Asia, but the most favorable conditions for its growth are to be found around the Mediterranean.

From the genus or subgenus *Euvitis* came the American species, including *E. labrusca* in the east, *E. riparia, E. berlandieri* and *E. rupestris* in the centre, and *E. californica* and *E. arizonica* in the south. Although these American species have greater resistance to heat, cold and pests, they also have an unpleasant pungency in their juice and in the resultant wine; such wines became known as "fox wines," and the planting of these vines has been banned in many regions.

The Spaniards took *Vitis vinifera* from Europe to Mexico, from where it spread to California—and flourished. In the eastern states, however, it is only recently that a method of growing *V. vinifera* has been discovered, and the better wines made there in the past were the product of hybridization of labrusca with vinifera vines.

## THE GRAPE

And so to the end-product—the grape. The diagram (*see page 22*) shows the different constituents of the grape and the contribution that each makes to the qualities of the wine; in addition, there are the yeasts on the surface of the grape, which are essential to its wine-making function. Some constituents required for the making of red wine are unnecessary for—indeed, must be avoided in—the making of white wine. There are the pits, which in wine-making must not be crushed lest the pungent oils embitter the product. The methods of separation of such constituents are described in the following chapter.

The diagram (see page 26) illustrates part of the viticultural "philosophy" of the Boschendal wineries at Paarl in South Africa. The grape starts life without sugar but strong in acid. As the sugar develops the concentration of the acid is progressively and proportionately reduced to a point of perfect balance. However, if the grape is allowed to overripen after its full sugar-in-

WHITE GRAPES

The number of *vitis vinifera* grape varieties now being used around the world is constantly increasing. Those illustrated here and on pages 26-7 have been selected either because of their widespread success in the soils and climates of many countries or because of their individuality in giving character to the quality wines of one region.

Character in a wine does not depend solely upon the grape, however: consider what noble rot does to a grape such as the Riesling, given the right weather sequence. These Riesling grapes from the Rheingau *(below)* have turned from a light misty green to bronze while shriveling in the heat of the late summer sun. They will be selected individually to produce Trockenbeerenauslese, one of the rarest of German wines.

The Aligoté grape plays second fiddle to Chardonnay in Burgundy's famous côtes, but this is no dishonor. The commune of Bouzeron in the Chalonnais has its own appellation for Aligoté; it makes wine for drinking within three years.

Chenin Blanc is the dominant grape of the Loire region: Vouvrays and other excellently balanced wines of Touraine are made from it. Further down river the Chenin Blanc remains the chief grape until beyond Anjou, where the Muscadet takes its place.

GRAPE ANATOMY

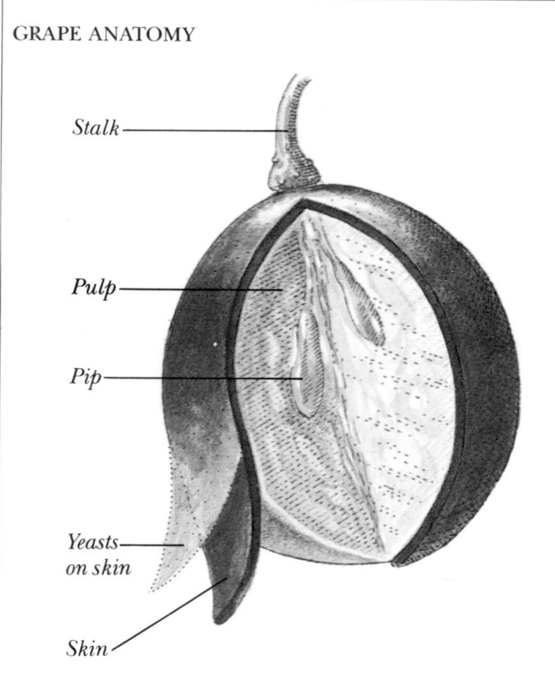


The anatomy of the grape proves that nature can show Man a thing or two when it comes to wrapping ingredients in a perfect package *(above)*. Inside the skin is a pulp which contains sugar, fruit acids, pectins, and water. On the outside of the skin are some 100,000 wine yeasts (*Saccharomyces ellipsoideus*) together with 10,000,000 wild yeasts, and about 100,000 bacteria, principally *Acetobacter*. It only remains for human beings to open the package and all the ingredients for wine-making start to work. It is not *quite* so simple, however: without Man's intervention the end product would be water!

Malvasia is an important grape in Iberia today. It started as Monemvasia in native Greece, and in France is the Malvoisie. It is used in the Riojas and elsewhere in Spain, and also for Port. Its sweet heavy wines reached England in the seventeenth and eighteenth centuries as Malmsey.

Chardonnay, now grown in five continents, gives white Burgundy wines a texture and strength almost equal to that of the reds; in addition, it produces more vintages. The wines are rich and well balanced, with a long finish.

The Chasselas, known in Germany as the Gutedal, in Switzerland as the Fendant, and in California as the Chasselas Doré, produces light fruity wines with a delicate bouquet. They are low in acid and best drunk young The Chasselas is possibly Europe's best table grape.

The Gargenega is the main grape for the wines of Soave, in Veneto. The Soaves are the most popular of all Italian wines, light and easy to drink when young. The grapes are partly dried for the richer Recioto di Soave.

The off-white, almost pink, Gewürztraminer grape was originally used only in Alsace, but has become immensely popular in Germany and other European countries as well as in North America. Its wine is unsubtle but delicious in flavor and aroma.

The small white Muscat de Frontignan, otherwise known as Muscat Blanc and Moscato Canelli, is the best of several Muscats being used for the sweet dark wines of Roussillon (Frontignan), the dry Muscats of Alsace and the Italian sparkling Asti Spumante.

The Trebbiano Toscano, known as the Ugni Blanc in France, is common in central Italy. This white Tuscan grape is blended into the red Chianti: elsewhere it is used almost to exclusion in several DOC wines of the region, both still and sparkling.

alcohol potential has been produced, only a minimal amount of acid will remain, and the wine produced will be flat and quite unacceptable to the serious wine-drinker.

Photographs of 20 of the world's most noble vinifera grapes are given (see pages 22-23 and see pages 26-27), with a short description of their characteristics, the types of wine made from them, and the regions in which they are principally grown. More about each will be discovered in following chapters (see the Index).

# THE VINEYARD YEAR

In established vineyards the year's cycle finishes, as it has always done, with the vintage or harvesting of the grapes. According to the latitude and the kind of wine into which the grapes are to be made, the date of harvesting may be anywhere from the end of September to early November (in the ensuing discussion all our dates refer to the northern hemisphere). After tidying up, a new year's cycle begins, and the first task of the *vigneron* is to prepare the vines for the winter ahead. Soil must be plowed up to give protective cover to their roots and grafts; a mulch of compost may be added to provide additional protection and nourishment.

By December the vineyard is prepared to face the frosts (preferably light ones), which kill disease and enable the vines to rest. Early in the new year, hard pruning begins (it is essential that it be done at this time, when the sap has withdrawn from the cane; the longer pruning is delayed the later the vine will flower—although this may have the advantage of saving the flowers from being killed by a late frost); unwanted growth is removed to leave only a few buds on selected canes, from which the new grape-bearing shoots will develop.

In spring any excess buds are removed and the new spurs are carefully trained with ties. Any mulch that was spread in November is plowed under, and the soil that was plowed up to protect the roots is plowed away again. Young vines of two years' growth are planted out in April, both to replace any winter casualties and, in certain years, for the gradual replanting of the vineyard.

As the atmosphere gradually warms up, the vineyard needs rain to guarantee good growth. In order to avoid the risk from late frosts, fires may be lit in the vineyard to keep the air moving, or fans may be used. In California, growers have developed a German method of combating frost: they spray water onto the vines, where it freezes and so protects them from the frost, which is colder than this icy layer.

The vines come into leaf as April turns into May, and flower a month later. Then the grower's yearly battle with pests and diseases begins. Insects, funguses and viruses put up the most sustained and determined attack on the vine, while the depredations of birds and the sapping of strength by weeds are not to be underestimated. The diagram (*right*) deals with a number of these pests and diseases, and with the known methods of countering them.

Once the vine flowers, mild weather is needed for about two weeks to enable pollination to proceed fully and effectively; the dangers from wind, rain and late frosts persist, and may result in *coulure*, whereby the diminutive green berries fail to form, so that the grape crop is reduced or even entirely eliminated. With luck, however, the bees will have been able to complete their task of pollination by about the end of June. Then the critical period of 100 days begins, leading up to the vintage at the end of September. During this time, mild rain is needed to swell the grapes, while workers in the vineyards labor with chemical sprays to inhibit mildew and other diseases, and with insecticides to kill pests—above and below the ground. Several treatments may be necessary, especially in humid conditions.

In many regions, the date of vintage, when grape harvesting begins, is controlled, and it varies from year to year according to the weather conditions and their consequences; in Europe the vintage may take about four weeks. The bunches of grapes are carefully pared from the vine with knives or clippers and gathered in baskets. These are discharged with infinite care into tubs, special containers, or tipper-trucks for removal to the first-year *chai*, where wine-making begins. In California and elsewhere a mechanical method of collecting the grapes by shaking them from the vine is now in almost universal use (see the illustration *left*). This method of harvesting is enjoying growing acceptance and acclaim on both sides of the Atlantic and in the southern hemisphere.

The mechanical harvester already crops most of the vineyards in the United States, and will soon be used almost universally where reasonably flat ground permits *(below)*. The big machine straddles a row of vines which it gathers in beneath it. There, a number of flexible arms and paddles shake the grapes from the vines onto conveyor belts that carry the grapes up each side of the machine. Transverse belts then carry them over the next row of vines, and down a chute (with a fan to remove leaves) into a hopper-trailer, which moves along the adjacent alleyway at the same speed as the machine. The robot can harvest up to 16ha (39½ acres) in 24 hours.

## PESTS AND DISEASES

Parasites add to the many enemies of the vineyard. In Europe two birds in particular, the thrush and ortolan, plunder the vineyard, taking grapes whole or leaving them damaged.

The almost invisible *Phylloxera vastatrix* aphid wiped out most of the vineyards of Europe and elsewhere during the last quarter of the nineteenth century. Affected vineyards have to be uprooted, the vines burned, and the soil sterilized with carbon disulfide before the long process of recovery can begin. The fat white Cockchafer grub gnaws at the surface roots of the vine, and may be killed with sprays having arsenic and nicotine bases. Eelworms (nematodes) are, in fact, second only to *Phylloxera* as a vine enemy. The threadlike worms puncture the root of the vine, forming calluses and killing the vine. There is no cure – only the same treatment as for *Phylloxera*.

There are three other significant pests: the Meal moth *(Pyralis)*, whose caterpillars eat the emergent vine shoots; the caterpillars of the Grape-berry moth *(Cochylis* and *Eudemis)*, which feed on the grape blossom and newly formed fruit; and *Altise*, a beetle that feeds on the vine leaves. The treatment for all three is as for the Cockchafer grub.

Six fungal diseases affect the vine. Powdery mildew *(Oidium tuckerii)*, native to the USA, swept through Europe in the 1850s. It lodges on the young shoots, covering them with a white deposit; later the grapes split, rot and dry up. Treatment is by sulfur spraying during blossoming, and dusting the flowers with sulfur. Downy mildew *(Peronospera)*, also from the USA, reached Europe via South Africa in 1878. It attacks the vineleaf in conditions of high humidity, and affects the grapes in the same way as Powdery mildew. Copper- and zinc-based sprays will arrest it, and will also deal with Black rot, another North American fungus, which appears as black spots on the leaves and shrivels the fruit. The same sprays are effective for Anthracnose, a European disease that stains both leaf and fruit: the grape-stains turn into holes. *Botrytis cinerea* may attack the vine-leaves and grapes in humid weather, leaving a grey mold on the fruit; in this form it is known as Grey rot, or *Pourriture grise*, and will spoil the wine. Normal vineyard hygiene will prevent its occurrence. The beneficent form of botrytis, *Pourriture noble*, occurs when humid conditions are followed by hot weather. The filaments of the fungus pierce the grape-skins, seeking water for nourishment; the grapes shrivel and turn golden-brown, concentrating their sugar, some of which is converted to glycerine, giving the luscious flavor to Sauternes, Tokay, and Trockenbeerenauslese.

The Fan leaf virus *(Court noué)* turns the vine-leaf yellow. The vine degenerates and must be grubbed up, and the vineyard disinfected. The physiological disorder *Chlorosis* occurs when excess chalk prevents certain vines from assimilating iron: they then lack chlorophyll. Applying ferrous sulfate helps, but choice of the right vine is more important. Finally, *Coulure* results when bad weather interrupts pollination: many berries remain green and hard, so that the yield is dramatically reduced. There is no cure.

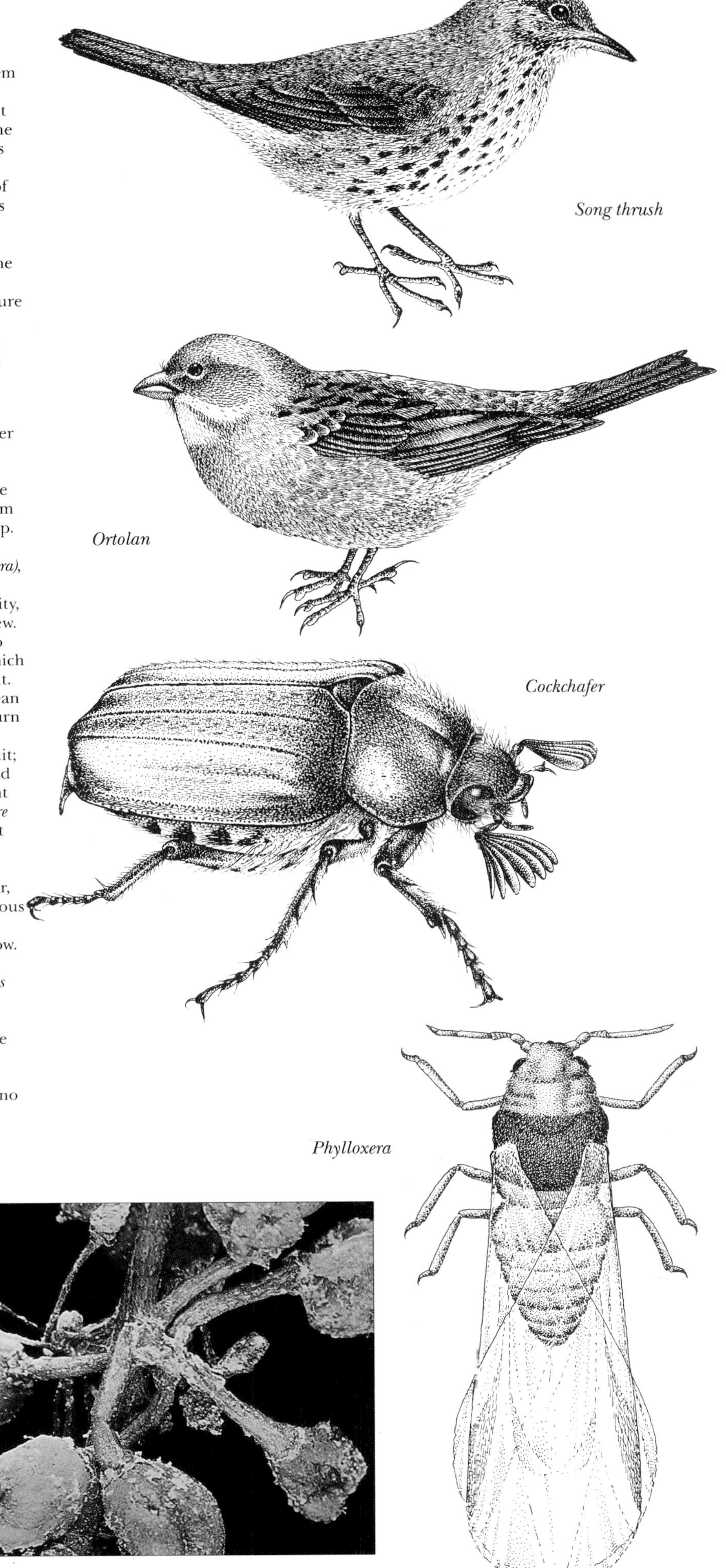

*Song thrush*

*Ortolan*

*Cockchafer*

*Phylloxera*

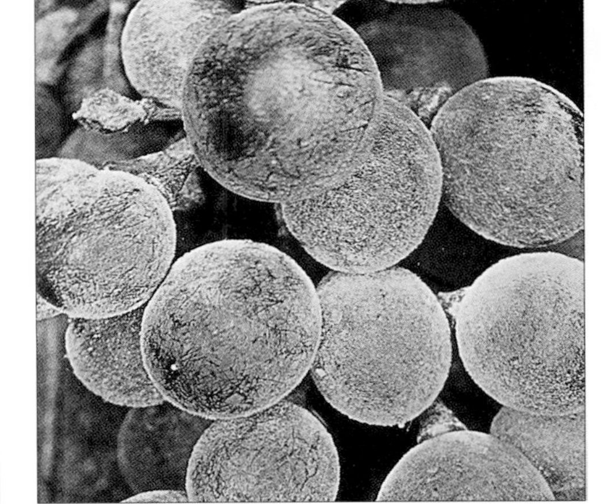

*Oidium*

*Mildew*

## BLACK GRAPES

By "black" grapes we here refer also to those with a red or brown skin.

The perfect black grape is the Cabernet Sauvignon, shown here. Originally the grape of the Médoc, its outstanding qualities have spread its use to the majority of the world's important wine regions. The small dark grapes ripen late and give heavy tannin and an aroma likened to blackcurrants. In Bordeaux, Cabernet Sauvignon is often blended with Merlot. The wine is slow to mature and benefits from long aging in oak and bottle.

### RIPENESS

This is how Achim von Arnim, of the Boschendal vineyards in the Cape, sees the secret of balance in wine *(below)*. He says that "grapes of ideal ripeness look after themselves". The grape when green is bitter, with little sugar or acid. Ideal ripeness is reached when maximum potential alcohol and maximum acidity are present. "TA" — total acidity.

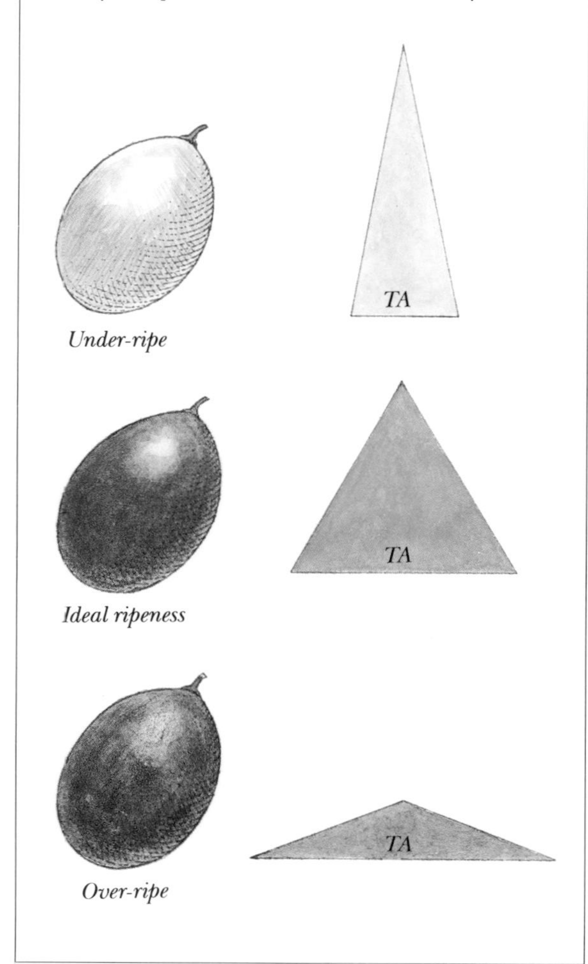

Related to Cabernet Sauvignon, Cabernet Franc is grown in Bordeaux, especially in St Emilion, where it shares the major role with the Merlot. It is planted also in the Loire valley, where it is the quality black grape of Touraine.

Merlot, the blue-black grape of Bordeaux, softens and rounds off the harsher wine from Cabernet Sauvignon in the Médoc and Graves districts. Its use is spreading: the vine is already common in Italy and Switzerland, and is gaining ground in California.

The Sangiovese supplies 70% of the grapes for the production of Chianti. The wine is ruby in color, deepening to garnet with age. Fairly dry and slightly tannic, Chianti is velvety smooth and well balanced with an odor of violets or irises.

Canaiolo Nero and its white Bianco sister are the handmaidens of Tuscany. Nero supports Sangiovese in the production of Tuscany's most famous red wine, Chianti. With the introduction of white grapes into Chianti blends, the dark Canaiolo is invaluable.

Gamay is the mandatory vine for Beaujolais, which has a comparatively light color and little tannin. The wines at their best are full and fruity with the unmistakable Gamay nose.

Nebbiolo is the noble grape of Piemonte. When its wine has matured for four years, the aroma is redolent of plums and raspberries. The wine is not blended, but imitates in a gentler way the dominant Barolo of Piemonte.

Pinot Noir is now a ubiquitous grape, doing well throughout most of the world's wine regions. It is primarily the grape of Burgundy and Champagne; the Côte de Nuits grows practically nothing else, and Pinot Noir plantings dominate the Montagne de Reims.

Syrah is the great grape of the northern Rhône, so dark and tannic that a small proportion of the white Viognier is added to lighten it. As it ages, for up to 20 years, it moves steadily closer in quality to the best Médocs.

Zinfandel is California's "own grape"; it may well be related to the Italian Primitivo vine from Apulia. It works to best effect in California, making crisp fruity wines in many styles, but it flourishes also in South Africa and Australia.

# THE MAKING OF WINE

**White Wines ♦ Red Wines ♦ Sparkling Wines ♦ Autovinification ♦ Alcohol Levels**

Wine-making starts with the disciplines that the *vigneron* imposes on the workers in the vineyard and the methods and equipment which they use. The good wine-maker will not accept grapes that are impure—for example, bunches already affected by molds, or contaminated with vine-leaves, soil and stones (in many parts of the world this is nowadays called collectively "MOG — matter other than grapes"). In France and other European countries the size of container in which grapes are brought in is limited so as to avoid crushing the bunches at the bottom and thus starting the process of fermentation before its strict control is possible. Countries vary in their attitudes towards the rival virtues of quality and quantity. The appellation laws of France, for instance, are designed to put quality first, so that the *rendement* (permitted yield of grape juice per hectare) is restricted to 35hl/ha in areas of supreme quality, such as the Haut Médoc, and to 85hl/ha at the other end of the scale, for *vin de pays*. Such thinking is by no means universal, however: Germany allows heavy cropping, and in the USA, where wine production falls far short of consumption, the question of limiting yield has yet even to be considered.

Another element enters the modern wine-making scene. All over the world, to an increasing extent, the producers of grapes are creating cooperative wineries, so that the advantages of having tight control exercised by the old *vignerons*/wine-makers are being lost; at the same time, wine-making is being undertaken on a vast commercial scale at fewer wineries. The cooperative may penalize a grower for sending in contaminated grapes, but there are obviously problems related to which cultivar—or cultivars—is being processed, and vintage wines may give way more readily to shippers' blends.

Whatever the quality or quantity involved, however, the universal objective is to avoid contamination before the process of fermentation is brought under control. This is more difficult than may be imagined, for no catalyst has to be added by wine-makers to start the fermentation process: the grape is a perfect package containing all the necessary ingredients for fermentation to occur naturally.

## WHITE WINES

Grapes may be black, deep blue, red, brown, green or pale yellow in color, yet all of them have a white misty bloom on their skins. This bloom (see below) will start to ferment the jelly-like pulp of the grape as soon as the skin is broken. And, whatever shade the skins may be, this pulp is always the same color; it contains a mixture of glucose, fruit acids, pectins and water, as well as the pips. It follows, obviously, that red wines must get their color from deep-colored grapeskins and cannot be made from white grapes, but the converse is not true, because white wines may be made from black grapes, so long as the skins are removed early in the process of fermentation. Champagne provides a perfect example of this, for much of it is made from the black Pinot Noir grape.

The white, waxy, slightly sticky bloom on a grape's surface is composed of a massive number of single-celled organisms deposited there by fruit-flies and other insects or blown there by the breeze. Each single grape attracts roughly ten million wild yeasts, 100,000 wine yeasts, and 100,000 acetobacters (bacteria which can convert alcohol into acetic acid—vinegar). Only the wine yeasts, *Saccharomyces ellipsoideus*, are desirable in wine-making and so the grapes must be brought under controlled fermentation as rapidly as possible. Fortunately the wine yeasts are anaerobic, needing no oxygen to live, whereas the wild yeasts and acetobacters are aerobic (need oxygen). Sulfur dioxide gas is therefore used to shield grapeskins from the air. The diagram (*above right*) shows firstly how the processes of nature, if left to themselves, pursue fermentation to the point where the acetobacters are left to work out their natural cycle, in which they convert the wine first to vinegar and then

Fermentation remained much of a mystery until Pasteur's experiments (*c.* 1857) started the research that has now revealed its secrets *(below)*. Unlike wine yeasts, both wild yeasts and acetobacters need air to live. In natural (uncontrolled) fermentation, the wild yeasts work until the alcoholic strength has reached 4% by volume, at which level they die. The acetobacters, however, continue their work, turning the wine first to vinegar and then to water. In controlled fermentation the wild yeasts and acetobacters are first killed by blanketing the grape-mass with sulfur dioxide, so that the air supply vital to them is shut off. Fermentation stops at 16% vól. alcohol, an alcoholic level which kills the wine yeasts; the chemical process that achieves this end is shown here as a formula. Without the 3% of fractional components, the product would consist of alcohol and pure water and have no taste at all.

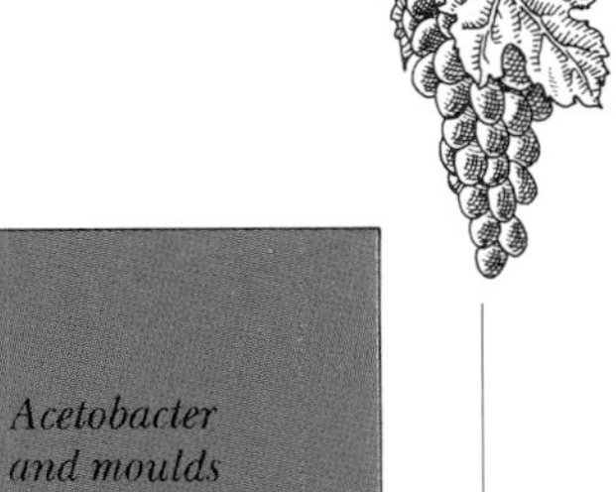

*NATURAL FERMENTATION*

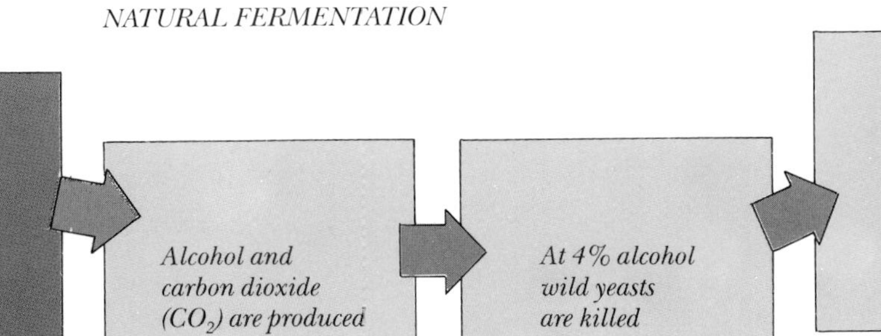

*Wild yeasts start fermentation* → *Alcohol and carbon dioxide ($CO_2$) are produced* → *At 4% alcohol wild yeasts are killed* → *Wine yeasts continue until fermentation is complete* → *Acetobacter and moulds destroy wine*

*CONTROLLED FERMENTATION*

*Sulphur dioxide is added to must before fermentation starts* → *Wild yeasts and acetobacter destroyed* → *Wine yeasts control fermentation* → *Fermentation continues at temperatures between 5°C and 30°C...* → *...until either all sugar is converted to alcohol, or alcohol reaches 16% and kills wine yeasts*

*ALCOHOLIC FERMENTATION*

*GRAPE SUGAR (Glucose)* + *YEAST* = *ETHYL ALCOHOL (Ethanol)* + *CARBON DIOXIDE*

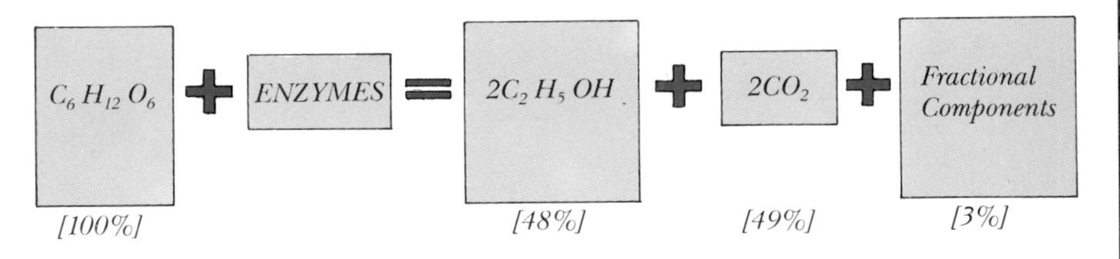

$C_6H_{12}O_6$ + *ENZYMES* = $2C_2H_5OH$ + $2CO_2$ + *Fractional Components*

[100%] [48%] [49%] [3%]

The packing of grapes into a vaslin horizontal press *(right)*. This is essentially a batch-process; prior to the invention of the dejuicer, the grape-mass had to be pressed many more times by the moving plates than is necessary today.

WHITE WINE PRODUCTION

Flowchart showing the essential stages involved in the production of white wine. Of course, the precise details of the process used vary from winery to winery. For example, every piece of equipment and machinery shown exists in countless different forms and variations, so that almost every single one of the world's thousands of wineries will have a unique ensemble of equipment: such variations are in size, shape, design, materials and mechanisms — i.e., in any aspect of the production process whereby an alteration may improve the characteristics of the individual wine. Note that the pieces of equipment shown in the flowchart are not rendered to scale and that, while pipes are shown connecting them, the product is at some stages in the process semi-solid, and so incapable of being passed through anything like a pipe. Finally, for reasons of space, details of all ancillary items — such as pumps, motors and driving gear — have been omitted.

Further information relevant to that given in the explanatory captions can be found in the text on pages 32 and 36.

**3** When the dejuicer is loaded the lid is sealed and $SO_2$ is pumped in under pressure. This presses out the juices, kills the wild yeasts and acetobacters, and prevents oxidation.

**1** Grapes are first fed into a crusher which exerts sufficient pressure to break the skins. Often black grapes, particularly the Pinot Noir, are used for white-wine production.

**2** The grapes with their skins and stalks go forward to the dejuicer in batches. The grapes are fed round a wire-mesh cylinder where their juice *(vin de goutte)* is extracted.

**7** The remaining grapeskins, with their pips and stems, are removed and dried to be distilled.

**6** The grapeskins, pips and stalks left in the dejuicer are removed and fed into a press to extract the remaining juice. This must is also run off into the settling tank.

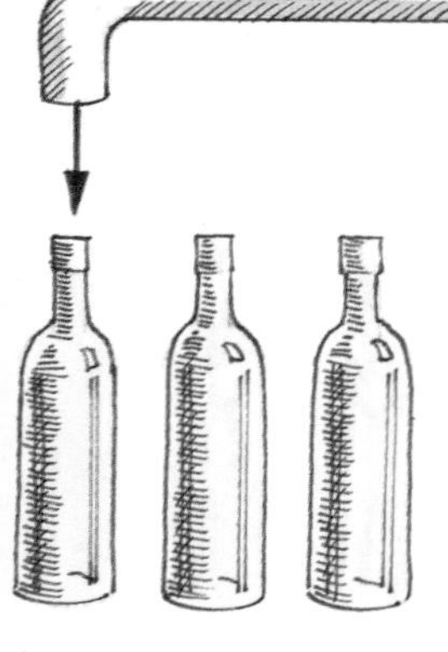

**19** Wine is a living thing, and will continue to mature in storage, whether in tank, cask or bottle. The alcohol, fruit acids, pectins, tannins and other substances present in wine as trace elements will continue to react upon each other until the wine is finally consumed. Because of this constant change, a young wine does not and cannot taste like an old wine. Tartrate crystals that often form on the cork inside a bottle of white wine are a good sign: they indicate quality and several years' maturation in the bottle.

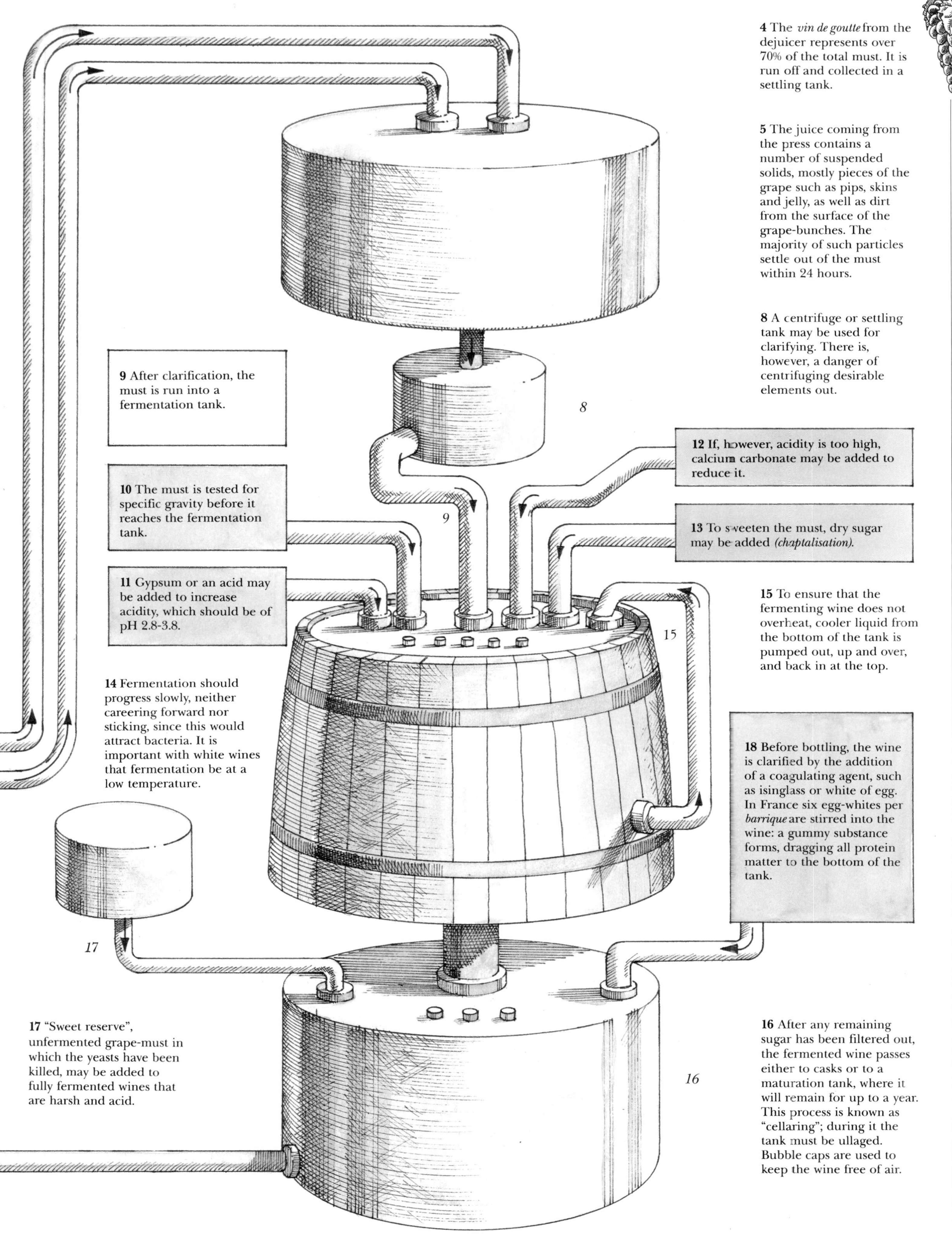


**4** The *vin de goutte* from the dejuicer represents over 70% of the total must. It is run off and collected in a settling tank.

**5** The juice coming from the press contains a number of suspended solids, mostly pieces of the grape such as pips, skins and jelly, as well as dirt from the surface of the grape-bunches. The majority of such particles settle out of the must within 24 hours.

**8** A centrifuge or settling tank may be used for clarifying. There is, however, a danger of centrifuging desirable elements out.

**9** After clarification, the must is run into a fermentation tank.

**10** The must is tested for specific gravity before it reaches the fermentation tank.

**11** Gypsum or an acid may be added to increase acidity, which should be of pH 2.8-3.8.

**12** If, however, acidity is too high, calcium carbonate may be added to reduce it.

**13** To sweeten the must, dry sugar may be added *(chaptalisation).*

**14** Fermentation should progress slowly, neither careering forward nor sticking, since this would attract bacteria. It is important with white wines that fermentation be at a low temperature.

**15** To ensure that the fermenting wine does not overheat, cooler liquid from the bottom of the tank is pumped out, up and over, and back in at the top.

**18** Before bottling, the wine is clarified by the addition of a coagulating agent, such as isinglass or white of egg. In France six egg-whites per *barrique* are stirred into the wine: a gummy substance forms, dragging all protein matter to the bottom of the tank.

**17** "Sweet reserve", unfermented grape-must in which the yeasts have been killed, may be added to fully fermented wines that are harsh and acid.

**16** After any remaining sugar has been filtered out, the fermented wine passes either to casks or to a maturation tank, where it will remain for up to a year. This process is known as "cellaring"; during it the tank must be ullaged. Bubble caps are used to keep the wine free of air.

to water; and secondly how the wild yeasts and acetobacters may be destroyed by the use of sulfur dioxide in controlled fermentation.

The chemical conversion also shown in the diagram (see page 29) is responsible for the production of fractional compounds, amounting to 3% of the total, during the fermentation process. These compounds include total acids, esters and aldehydes, or secondary substances; and terpenes, essential oils and other tertiary substances present in minimal quantities. For the presence of these we should be truly grateful, for without them the wine would be just a mixture of ethyl alcohol and water, and would have no taste at all.

White wines rely considerably upon the fruity flavors from the fractions contained in the grape jelly; in wine-making the objective therefore is to free this jelly without absorbing excessive flavors from the skins. The diagram (see page 30) shows how the grapes are fed into a crusher as soon as possible after they have been gathered from the vineyard. In the production of white wine the stalks are retained during the whole pressing process, because they help to break up the grape mass, which becomes increasingly sticky and heavy as the pectins and sugars are released. The crusher exerts just enough pressure to break the grapeskins, and it is in this form that grapes and their stalks go forward for pressing. For more robust white wines the grapes, before they enter the dejuicer, may be held in their juice in a tank at low temperature for about 24 hours, as this helps the process of maceration in which certain elements are extracted from the grapeskins. (This applies only to white grapes; the skins of black grapes would yield unwanted color.)

In the modern winery the dejuicer is rapidly becoming the primary means of freeing the grape juice. Two functions are combined within this device: the force that squeezes the grapes is applied by sulfur dioxide gas injected under pressure, and the gas at the same time kills the wild yeasts and acetobacters and protects the juice from oxidation. The majority of the grape juice is released as free-run must *(vin de goutte)*; this practice has great advantages, for the subsequent period for which the grapes, skins and pits (a mixture internationally called "marc," but in English "pomace") have to be pressed in the horizontal press (see diagram *below*) is shortened. This is advantageous not only because the pressed wine (*vin de presse*) receives more tannin from the grape pits each time the plates of the horizontal press are brought together, but also because the laborious work of refilling the press (a batch process) is reduced. There are, of course, several types of dejuicer and horizontal press—and in cooperative wineries a continuous mincing process may be used instead of the horizontal press to produce pressed wine, although this is detrimental to quality. So, while the flowchart (see page 30) illustrates the essential stages of white-wine development, it should be borne in mind that no equipment is in universal use; even the materials of which fermentation and other tanks are made vary, to include wood, tile-lined concrete and, increasingly, stainless steel.

The free-run must, being of superior quality, is processed separately from the pressed must when intended for *Premiers* and *Deuxièmes Crus* wines or for appellations of superior quality, to conform with *règlement* mandates. Otherwise, however, the free-run and pressed musts are piped together to a settling tank before being centrifuged so that suspended solids can be separated out. Even the practice of centrifuging (or filtering through very fine screens) is now being questioned and often eliminated on the grounds that desirable elements of flavor and aroma are removed during the process.

When people talk of a wine as being well balanced they are referring, whether they know it or not, to the ratio between its acid and sugar strengths, and it is worth noting that acidity is measured not so much by the strength as by the

The vaslin horizontal press, used for the extraction of the remaining 15% of white wine or fermented red wine from the marc *(below)*. The press is batch-fed through a lid at its top-center, the grape-pulp being packed in as tightly as possible. Through the center of the press runs a reversible steel Archimedean screw driven by a motor. The screw is contrathreaded from its middle to its ends (i.e., to the right of center the thread is right-handed, and to the left of center it is left-handed). Two solid plates, threaded onto the screw, are thus repeatedly drawn to the center and back to the ends of the machine, pressing the grapes as they meet. Between the two plates are four hoops linked together by chains. The chains dangle into the pulp as the plates come together, and stretch as they separate, thus breaking up the sticky pulp.

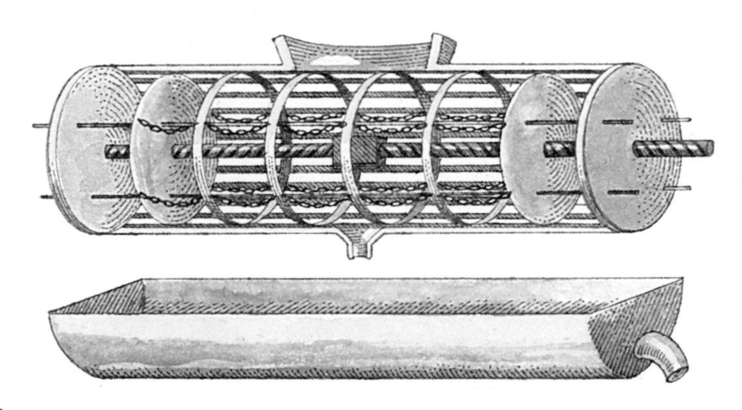

During the first three months of cellaring *(top)* a sediment is thrown; this consists mostly of dead yeast cells that decompose and would, if left, damage the wine. The casks are therefore "racked" by pumping the wine carefully off its lees, and are thereafter topped up regularly.

A moment of total concentration at Château Climens in Barsac *(above)*. A sample of uncleared wine (not yet fined) is being studied by owner Lucien Lurton. The exceptional quality of the Climens wine has earned it the title of "First Lord of Barsac".

A load of grapes is brought to the Domaine Clair Daü *chai* at Marsannay-la-Côte in the Côte d'Or *(right)*. Aligoté grapes are being fed directly into a hopper *en route* to a crusher. Clair Daü is the largest family-owned *domaine* in the Côte d'Or, with 27ha (67 acres) of vineyards, mainly in the north.

Domaines Viticoles Schlumberger have 130ha (321 acres) of vineyards in the Haut-Rhin; half their yearly yield of 80,000 cases is exported. Here a skip of Gewürztraminer grapes is being filled in the vineyard *(below)*.

A huge cask used for maturing "late-gathered" wines at the Riquewihr headquarters of Hugel et Fils *(bottom)*. The Hugel brothers specialize in these wines, which they call "Sélection des Grains Nobles," equivalent to *Beerenauslese Prädikat*.

Shining rows of bubble caps in the bungs of these casks at Château d'Yquem show that the wine is in the process of maturation *(above)*, which will take three and a half years. It will be racked every three months and topped up twice weekly. Some 22% of the total volume is lost by ullage. *Maître de chais*, Guy Latrille, has drawn a sample of Sauternes, for the tasting of sweet wines needs care; their sediment does not settle in the usual way, and they need fining twice during their cask-life.

quantity of acid content, whereas sugar is measured solely in terms of the quantity of its alcohol potential. The living grape itself runs through a cycle of acid and sugar development, with the acids reaching their maximum early and then declining while the sugars develop slowly to their maximum in the late-summer and autumn sun. There is therefore a *right* time to harvest the grape, when the balance between the two is perfect for the type of wine which it is intended to make. The acidity is measured in terms of pH, the technical definition of which need not concern us here; grapes for wine—indeed, the grape must and the finished wine itself—should have a pH reading in the range 2.8-3.8. The sugar content is measured by use of a hydrometer or a hand-held refractometer; the former device gives a specific-gravity (SG) reading and the latter a reading in degrees Baumé (France), Oechsle (Germany) or Brix (USA). (The required SG of must for German white wines is 1,047, equivalent to 47° Oechsle—see pages 120-121.)

As the must for a particular white wine approaches the fermentation tank, both acidity and sugar strengths have to be checked, and either or both adjusted if necessary. Failure to check acidity may affect the wine's acceptability and even render it unsalable. Normally acidity may be increased by adding gypsum or tartaric acid, or decreased by adding calcium carbonate (chalk). Chaptalisation, the addition of sugar, is allowed in France only for the purpose of increasing the wine's alcohol potential, not for sweetening it. Sugar levels can instead be adjusted by adding concentrated grape must. Another point is that there are laws in many countries specifying the minimum alcoholic strength; it is essential for the winemaker to find out and if necessary adjust the alcohol potential of the must before fermentation.

Fermentation starts dramatically, and the temperature rises. As the wine yeasts are sensitive to heat it is essential that temperatures are maintained between the minimum of 5°C (41°F) and the maximum of 30°C (86°F), the range within which these yeasts will do their work. If the temperature of the must goes outside the range—up or down—the fermentation will stop, or "stick," and may refuse to restart, especially if the temperature has risen high enough for the sugars to undergo chemical reactions (in which case, anyway, the wine will have been ruined). To keep within the range, the fermenting must may need to be cooled in hot countries or gently warmed in cold ones. The diagram (see page 31) shows the method known as "pumping over," whereby cooler must from the bottom of the vat is pumped out, up and back into the top where the heat is greatest.

During fermentation, quantities of carbon dioxide are produced, bubbling to the surface. A series of bubble caps (valves) in the top of the tank let the gas out without letting air in, and can be adjusted to regulate the pressure under which fermentation proceeds; this is known as *macération carbonique*.

After the first two days the violent fermentation subsides, although the wine will continue to ferment for a further period of about four weeks, depending on the type of wine being made. When fermentation is complete the wine is piped from the fermentation tank and any residual sugar is filtered out; it then passes to a separate tank for a maturation period of between six and twelve months. (Because white wines lack the tannin derived from the grape-skins and stalks, this period of maturation is shorter than for red wines—see page 37.) The wine is clarified (fined) by the addition of one of several coagulating agents; this agent first forms a film on the wine's surface and then slowly falls through the wine collecting impurities as it goes down; sediment from the bottom of the fermentation and maturation vats goes with the marc to be dried or distilled. After fining, still, light white wines may be bottled; they will continue to mature, and will improve during aging. Heavy, rich white wines—from, for example, Chardonnay or Sauvignon Blanc grapes—are matured at temperatures between 15°C and 25°C (59-77°F); they may be fermented as well as matured in barrels.

## RED WINES

Red-wine production has points of similarity with white-wine production, but a number of differences, too—as may be deduced from the diagram on pages 38 and 39.

For red wine the skins of black grapes are essential but the stalks are not, and so the crusher combines the function of destalking with the primary task of gently breaking the skins: a pulp of grapes in their skins therefore goes forward immediately to the fermentation tank. The tank itself is different: it is designed to take a fixed charge of grape pulp, which is fed into it through a wide-bore pipe and down through a screen; this screen becomes submerged as soon as sufficient free-run must runs clear of the grapes. Sulfuring, together with the correction of acidity and alcohol potential, takes place immediately, as in white-wine production.

Fermentation begins at once, and the wild yeasts and acetobacters are killed instantly by sulfur dioxide. As carbon dioxide is generated during controlled fermentation, bubbles of the gas trapped in the skins raise them towards the surface of the free-run must that is already being released from the broken grapes. The weight of the grape pulp decreases as the glucose jelly is converted to alcohol, and gradually all the mass of grapeskins and pits is carried up to form a "cap of skins" that presses up against the submerged screen. The object now is to extract maximum color from the skins, and so the cap of skins has to be agitated as much as possible. Must from the base of the tank is therefore "pumped over" onto the surface under pressure; assisted also by gravity, it necessarily forces its way back down through the cap of skins into the lower part of the tank. For the production of rosé, early free-run must is drawn off before the skins darken the color of the must too much. This must is as yet not fully fermented, and will need to be passed separately through the remaining stages of the wine-

Robert Revelle, *maître de chais* at Château Lafite, stands like a colonel before the marshaled lines of casks in the huge cellars *(above right)*. The casks here are waiting for new wine in January; according to custom at Lafite, all new wine goes into new casks.

The nowadays relatively rare process of treading the grapes is seen in the Domaine Louis Latour *chais* at Aloxe-Corton, Burgundy *(left)*. This takes place in the initial stages of fermentation of red wine to keep the *chapeau* in contact with the wine.

At Château Latour in the Médoc, *maître de chais* Jean Malbec supervises the fining and casking of wine from a fermentation tank *(right)*. Latour was the first Médoc château to install stainless-steel tanks (1964), and in 1985 there are some 20 of them.

## RED WINE PRODUCTION

Flowchart illustrating the production of red wine; the explanations and comments given on page 30 in connection with the white-wine flowchart are all applicable equally to this chart. All variants on standard wine-making methods, such as those for Champagne, fortified wines and many others, will be found in ensuing chapters; the reader should consult the Index.

This apparatus *(top)* automatically monitors the level of sulfur dioxide gas displacing air above the must in the fermentation tank. The sulfur dioxide serves three important purposes, as explained opposite.

A stream of must from the bottom of the fermentation tank has been 'pumped over' and is seen *(above)* re-entering its top, at once cooling and agitating the must and drawing color from the skins.

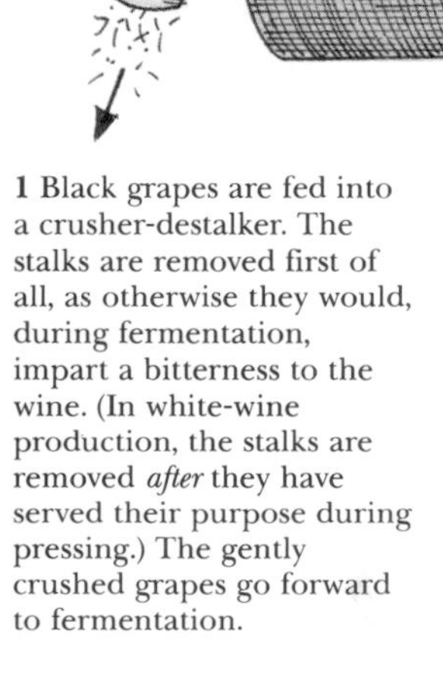


**1** Black grapes are fed into a crusher-destalker. The stalks are removed first of all, as otherwise they would, during fermentation, impart a bitterness to the wine. (In white-wine production, the stalks are removed *after* they have served their purpose during pressing.) The gently crushed grapes go forward to fermentation.

**2** A charge of grapes is fed deep into the fermentation tank to a level below a wire-mesh screen; the charge is sufficient for the level of the must to rise above the screen.

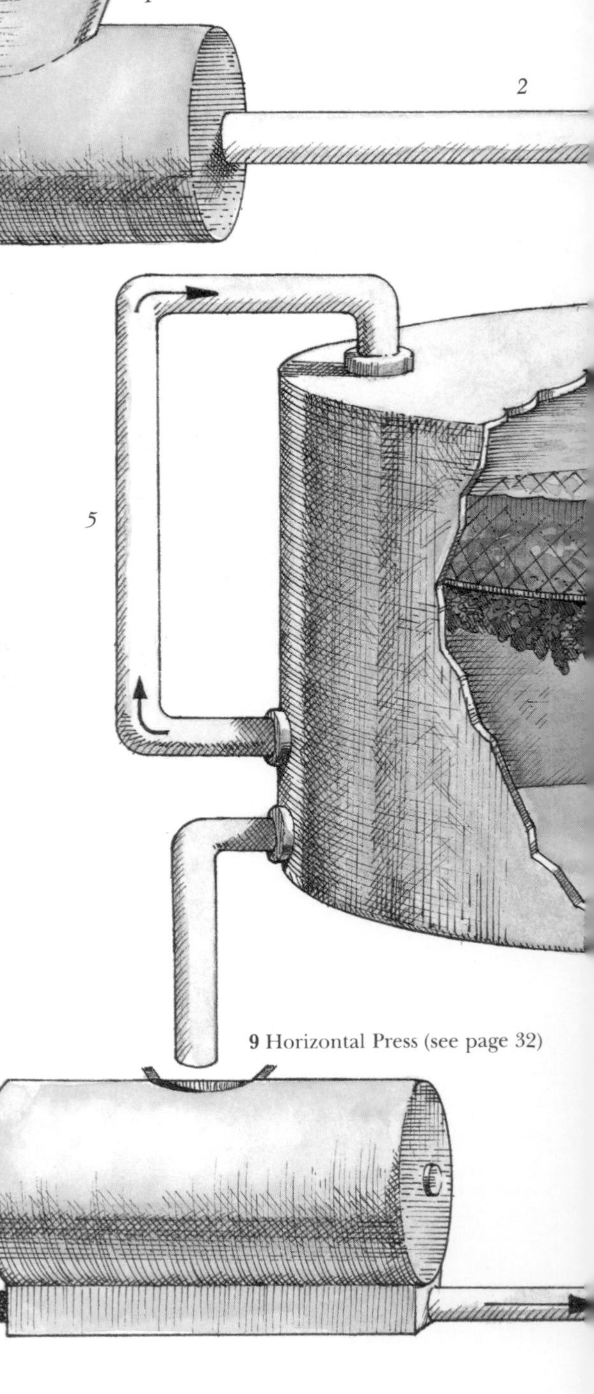


**5** "Pumping over" provides temperature-control and, by directing a pressured stream onto the *chapeau émergé*, keeps the skins moving and extracts their color.

**9** Horizontal Press (see page 32)

**10** At this stage the remaining grapeskins and uncrushed pips are removed, dried, and sent for distillation.

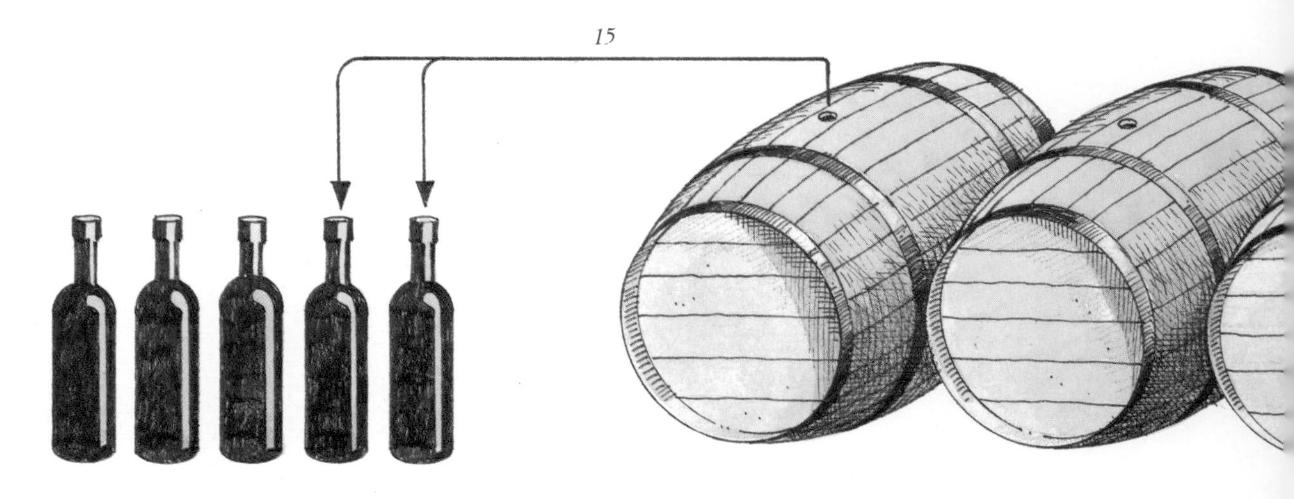


**15** In the spring following vintage, there usually occurs a malolactic fermentation caused by bacteria converting malic acid in the wine into lactic acid, with the release of bubbles of $CO_2$ (carbon dioxide). This "rounds off" the sharpness of the wine's acidity and improves its ultimate flavor. The wine has to be racked off its lees every three months during maturation. Good-quality red wines may age for up to three years in barrel, and after a further three years in bottle may be ready for drinking.

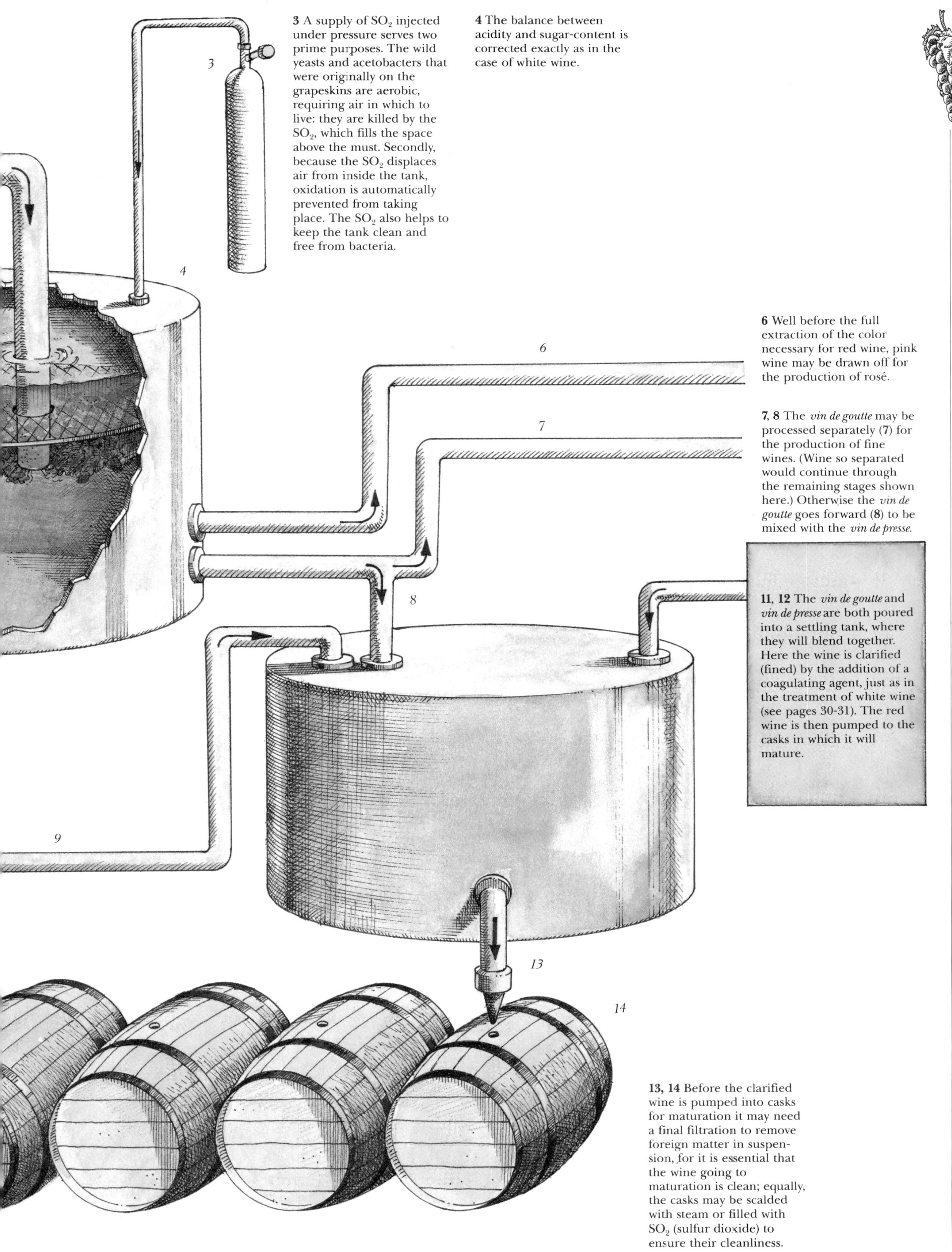


**3** A supply of $SO_2$ injected under pressure serves two prime purposes. The wild yeasts and acetobacters that were originally on the grapeskins are aerobic, requiring air in which to live: they are killed by the $SO_2$, which fills the space above the must. Secondly, because the $SO_2$ displaces air from inside the tank, oxidation is automatically prevented from taking place. The $SO_2$ also helps to keep the tank clean and free from bacteria.

**4** The balance between acidity and sugar-content is corrected exactly as in the case of white wine.

**6** Well before the full extraction of the color necessary for red wine, pink wine may be drawn off for the production of rosé.

**7, 8** The *vin de goutte* may be processed separately (**7**) for the production of fine wines. (Wine so separated would continue through the remaining stages shown here.) Otherwise the *vin de goutte* goes forward (**8**) to be mixed with the *vin de presse.*

**11, 12** The *vin de goutte* and *vin de presse* are both poured into a settling tank, where they will blend together. Here the wine is clarified (fined) by the addition of a coagulating agent, just as in the treatment of white wine (see pages 30-31). The red wine is then pumped to the casks in which it will mature.

**13, 14** Before the clarified wine is pumped into casks for maturation it may need a final filtration to remove foreign matter in suspension, for it is essential that the wine going to maturation is clean; equally, the casks may be scalded with steam or filled with $SO_2$ (sulfur dioxide) to ensure their cleanliness.

making process. (Nor is this the only method of producing rosé—see Index.)

Fermentation continues until the required color and tannin have been drawn from the skins, at which time it will still not necessarily be complete. The free-run wine, or *vin de goutte*, is now run off from the bottom of the tank, and the cap of skins or marc will settle on the tank bottom; the marc is shoveled out through a hatch at the foot of the tank, for feeding into a horizontal press. Free-run wine accounts for some 85% of the yield and *vin de presse* from the marc for the remaining 15% or so. The *vin de presse*, which is much stronger in tannin, may or may not be blended with the *vin de goutte*; the latter will certainly be used unblended for superior grades of wine. After pressing, the marc is dried and goes for distillation.

The resulting wine is now fed into a tank for clarification (fining and filtering), and is then cellared in large casks or barrels to complete fermentation and to age, usually for about three years. During the first few months of maturation the wine will throw a sediment of yeast-cells that have either died through a lack of sugar on which to feed or been killed by excessive alcohol. If such yeast-cells are not removed, an off-flavor will develop in the wine. The wine must therefore be racked off its lees by transfer from one cask to another: to avoid disturbing the lees, this is done by pumping air into the full cask. Racking should be repeated every three months. The casks need also to be regularly topped up, or ullaged, to replace wine lost through the pores of the wood or by evaporation into the atmosphere. As red wines age in cask or barrel in the presence of oxygen, many beneficial reactions occur between their remaining secondary and tertiary constituents.

An important difference from the processing of white wines is that in the production of red wines secondary or malolactic fermentation is encouraged. This fermentation is now known to be caused by bacteria feeding on malic acid in the wine and converting it to lactic acid, with carbon dioxide bubbles as a by-product. Malolactic fermentation can be made to occur during the first (yeast) fermentation or during cellaring in the spring following vintage. In the latter case the correct bacteria and a cellar temperature of around 20°C (68°F) are necessary. The wine does not retain any sparkle, but its smoothness and stability are improved by a tempering of its acid strength and sharpness.

The gleaming red-painted oak fermentation tanks at Château Palmer in the Margaux commune of the Haut Médoc banish any thought of lack of hygiene *(right)*. While other châteaux have turned to steel for reasons of cleanliness and temperature-control, the use of wood is retained at Palmer as an aid to the quality of the wine.

Château Branaire-Ducru has an estate of 65ha (161 acres) in St Julien, the smallest appellation of the finest Médocs. The wines, here maturing in the first-year cellar *(above)*, are renowned for their flavor and fragrance and typify the wines of St Julien.

After *vin de goutte* and *vin de presse* have been extracted, only the marc remains to be taken from the horizontal press. Here *(left)*, marc at Château Branaire-Ducru is being manhandled into a truck. It will be dried and then distilled to make *eau-de-vie-de- marc.*

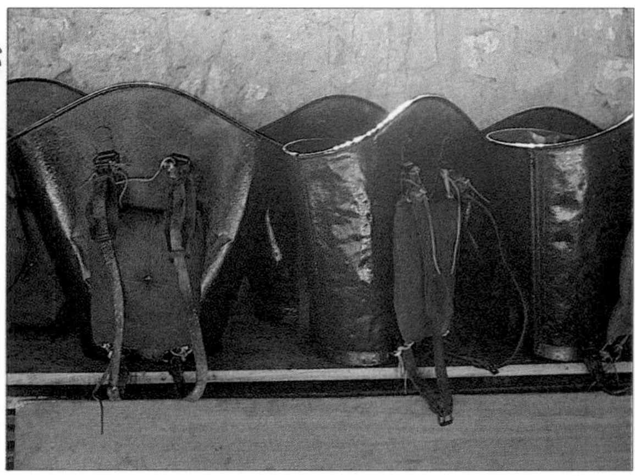

These receptacles *(above)*, in use at Château Palmer, are strapped onto the backs of pickers in the vineyards. They are much used almost everywhere in the Bordeaux region.

Les Forts de Latour is the second quality wine made at Château Latour — that is, after the small quantity of *grand vin* that ranks first. Les Forts throws a heavy deposit in the bottle *(right)*.

Michel Roland, *maître de chais* at Château Leoville Las-Cases, in St Julien, is racking new wine *(inset)*. Infinite care is taken in drawing the wine from its cask by suction, to avoid disturbing the lees.

A sample of grape-pulp *(below)* is being tested as part of the rigorous process of protecting the superb wines from Château Leoville Las-Cases.

For many years Raoul Blondin *(below right)* has been *maître de chais* of Château Mouton Rothschild. Here he checks a sample of wine for color during its first year.

# SPARKLING WINES

Champagne must be made by the *méthode champenoise* (see pages 86-89), but this is not the case for every type of sparkling wine, although the bottle shape and size, the muzzled cork and all the gold wrappings and labels may suggest that what you are buying is Champagne in all but name and provenance. The high cost of Champagne spurred Eugène Charmat to develop in 1910 a cheaper way of producing a similar (although inferior) product. The sealed-tank or Charmat process, which is carried out under sustained pressure from beginning to end, is used to this day. Still wine is run into a first tank and artificially aged by heating for 12 to 16 hours, after which it is cooled and pumped into a second tank where yeast and sugar are added, the resulting fermentation lasting for 10 to 15 days. After being pumped into a third tank the wine is clarified by refrigeration and filtered before bottling: a continuous flow of good sparkling wine results.

The bubbles or sparkle, however, last only for a limited period. To improve this the transfer method was developed; this process, too, is completed under pressure. The secondary fermentation takes place as for Champagne in the bottle but, instead of *remuage* and careful *dégorgement*, the bottles are cooled and opened, so that the wine, now clouded by rising sediment, can be sucked through a filter and rebottled. The transfer method may not be employed in the making of any AC wine in France, but is used for quality-wine production in all five wine-producing continents.

The carbonation method of producing sparkling wine is the simplest, cheapest and most unsatisfactory. The still wine is cooled to a low

Of the four ways to make wine sparkle *(right)*, the *méthode champenoise* is the most complicated and by far the most labor-intensive and expensive. This is due to the processes of *remuage* and, applied after secondary fermentation has taken place in the bottle, *dégorgement*. The Charmat (sealed-tank) method artificially ages the wine by heating, after which yeast and sugar are added to cause a further fermentation; the sparkling wine is clarified by refrigeration and filtered before bottling. The whole process is conducted under pressure.

The *cuve close* or transfer method came next; the natural malolactic fermentation takes place in the bottle as for Champagne, but the bottles are then cooled and opened. The wine, clouded by its rising sediment, is sucked out, filtered and rebottled.

The carbonation method (used also for many mineral waters) is done by simply injecting carbon dioxide into a sealed vat, where bottling is done under pressure.

| | 2nd Fermentation and maturation | Clearance of sediment |
|---|---|---|
| Champagne method | In bottle | Remuage and degorgement |
| Tank method | In tank | Filtration |
| Transfer method (cuvé close) | In bottle | Vatting under pressure, then filtration |
| Carbonation | Carbon dioxide ($CO_2$) injected into chilled vat of still wine, which is then bottled under pressure. | |

temperature in a closed vat, on the outside of which a frost forms. Carbon dioxide gas is injected into the vat, and the wine is then bottled, always under sustained pressure. The bubbles will last for an even shorter time than in wines produced by the Charmat process.

## AUTOVINIFICATION

The processes of making Port and Sherry and their essential differences are explained on pages 165-169 and 156-161. Radical changes have been made in pressing grapes for Port, however. Although the original treading of grapes in the *lagar* is still retained as a premium by one or two *lagares*, the process has been mechanized and updated by the use of a crusher-destalker, from which the broken grapes and skins pass to a syphon vat called an autovinifier (see illustrations *right*). Each time the upper trough is filled, the color extracted from the skins may be gauged, until the desired shade is obtained.

## ALCOHOL LEVELS

When the Sikes hydrometer (see page 324) was adopted in the late nineteenth century, the strength of alcohol in drinks was measured for duty on a Proof scale running from 0° Proof for pure water to 175° Proof for pure alcohol, one unit on the scale being known as a "degree Sikes." Subsequently, however, most countries have enforced for duty purposes the use of the "percentage alcohol by volume" system, running from 0% for pure water to 100% for pure alcohol. Joseph-Louis Gay-Lussac (1778-1850), the famous French chemist, first introduced this system, with the percentages being measured at a temperature of 15°C (59°F). More recently, the Organisation Internationale de Métrologie Légale (OIML) have adopted a virtually identical system in which the percentages are, however, measured at a temperature of 20°C (68°F): the differences in percentages recorded are negligible for all practical purposes other than the calculation of duty payable (the diagram *below right* shows the relative figures for each scale). It is a useful *aide-mémoire* to have in mind that, taking rough average figures in each case,

5% is the alcohol level in beers,
5% × 2 = 10%, the alcohol level in light wines,
10% × 2 = 20%, the alcohol level in fortified wines, and
20% × 2 = 40%, the alcohol level in liquors.

Obviously each of these four classes of alcoholic drinks has its own minimum/maximum range of alcoholic strengths.

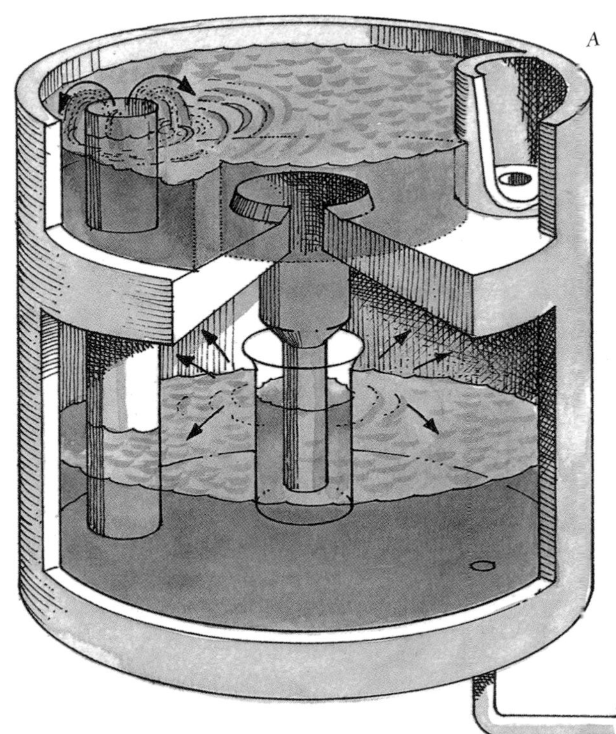


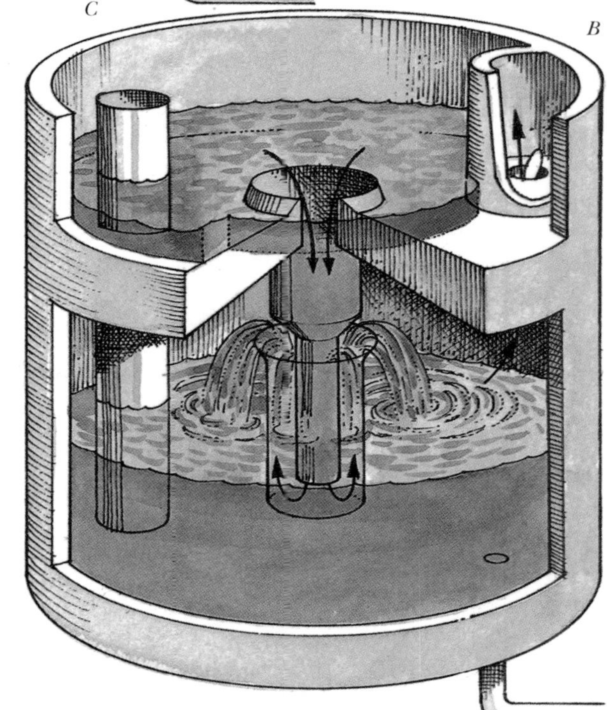


The autovinifier has largely, although not entirely, replaced the *lagar* as the equipment used to press grapes for Port. After going through a crusher-destalker the grape-pulp is fed (in batches) into the autovinifier and the top is sealed. The hydraulic valve (A) is first closed. A central shaft with vanes (not shown) rotates, bringing the cap of skins into the center where an Archimedean screw on the lower end of the shaft forces it down into the lower chamber. It is then forced by hydraulic pressure with the wine up the tube (C) to float on the surface in the upper chamber once more. The hydraulic valve is then opened (B), letting the free-running wine descend; and the cycle is repeated. Each time the upper chamber is filled, the wine may be assessed for color.

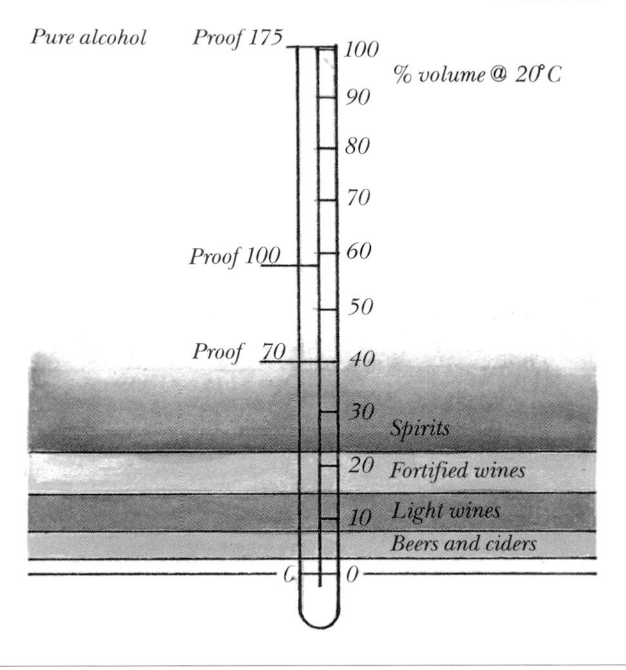


The relative figures of the Sikes Proof scale, the US Proof scale, and the Gay-Lussac and OIML scales, which are today internationally more current. The Sikes Proof scale runs from 0 for pure water to 175 for pure alcohol. The US Proof scale runs from 0 to 200, two of its divisions being equivalent to one on the Gay-Lussac scale. The Gay-Lussac and OIML scales each run from 0 to 100. The Gay-Lussac system calculates the volume of alcohol in a sample at 15°C (59°F), whereas the OIML calculation is done at 20°C (68°F).

# WINES OF THE EUROPEAN COMMUNITY

Vineyards of the beautiful Castell'in Villa in the heart of Tuscany *(below)* were laid down in 1968 by Riccardo and Coralia Pignatelli della Leonessa. From the 60ha (150-acre) estate some 4,000hl (106,000gal) of Chianti Classico is produced each year, about half being sold in bottle. Coralia is the winemaker.

When the EEC was formed in 1957-58 a commission was set up to govern its affairs. In addition to its political, financial and other group responsibilities, the objectives of the Community included the development of resources and the protection of trade and the consumer. As one result, certain laws of individual member countries were amalgamated and rationalized to produce so-called EEC Regulations and Directives, and these continue to be issued to meet the exigencies of a changing scene. Regulations apply jointly to all member countries, while Directives apply to only one (or, exceptionally, to an individual or company within it). It then becomes the responsibility of a member country to amend its own laws, where necessary, to accommodate the Regulation or Directive. Such edicts may be issued either by the Commission or by the Council of Ministers of the member states, and may be enforced by the Community's Court of Justice.

However, as each country has a differing political and economic situation and its own laws and customs, the Commission or Council may grant to a member country a Derogation that effectively negates the force of all or part of a Regulation or Directive binding that country. Nevertheless, it remains the overall intention that each member state should comply with the common standards of the Community so far as possible and in its own terms.

Many Regulations and Directives affect the industries concerned with the making, packaging, distribution and selling of wines. In 1985, only six members of the EEC — France, Germany, Italy, Luxembourg, Greece and the UK — had wine industries. But the entry of Spain and Portugal into the EEC was finally resolved in March 1985, to take effect from the beginning of 1986; both have therefore been treated as members of the EEC in this volume. (So far no controls affecting the spirits industry have been formulated, although much debate has been and still is being given to it.) The controls over wine industries within the EEC affect vineyard areas and vinestocks; vineyard and winemaking practices; the quality of EEC and imported wines and their minimum prices; bottle and other sizes, and the measures of wine they must contain; and labeling and advertizing.

This is not to say that these wine industries had done nothing to improve and standardize their products in earlier days. France, whose wine laws were taken as the pattern for the whole Community, had classified the wines of the Médoc in 1855, and in 1932 set up the Institut National des Appellations d'Origine ("INAO"), with a countrywide network of officials, to regulate quality. This was followed by the setting up of the Office National Interprofessional des Vins de Table, to regulate producers of *vin ordinaire*.

Italy had a *vinattieri* or guild of wine merchants in Florence in the Middle Ages, and by the eighteenth century her agricultural academies were teaching viticulture and vinification. In the 1930s district *consorzi* were appointed by Royal Decree to delimit geographic areas; though it had its limitations, the *consorzio* system was the first step towards order in the industry.

Germany's wine industry, started by the Romans, survived under monastery control until the vineyards were secularized by Napoleon III in 1803. Only the large Domaine Vineyards remained intact, and the mandatory handing down of all other vineyards in equal shares to descendants resulted in a patchwork of diminutive vineyards (the vast majority under half a hectare in size), with uncoordinated practices in viticulture and vinification. Membership of the EEC pointed the way, and the resulting West German wine laws of 1971 have created a manageable and satisfactory system for the future. Through it all, the white wines of Germany have remained delectable and supreme in their class.

Luxembourg had established a *Marque Nationale* for quality wines in 1935. Greece, in preparation for her entry into the Common Market, evolved her own system of fundamental vineyard and wine controls during the 1970s; in this way she anticipated acceptable standards for her exports while remaining faithful to Retsina and young country wines for drinking at home. The diminutive wine industry of England formed the English Vineyard Association in 1967; few vineyards have as yet evoked the Association's optional seal of quality which in 1978 it was empowered to grant.

The Spanish Ministerio de Agricultura introduced its "Statute of Vines, Wines and Spirits" in 1970, delegating to some 20 regional *consejos* power to regulate and administer a new system of Denominaciones de Origen, roughly parallel to the French AC and Italian DOC systems. In Portugal the Junta Nacional do Vinho in Lisbon is already responsible for the control of all wines other than port, which is controlled by its own official Instituto in Oporto. The Junta has already demarcated seven regions, including the port region. Both these newcomers to the EEC are therefore well prepared to fit into the Community control pattern.

# FRANCE

**Bordeaux ♦ Other Wines of the Southwest ♦ Burgundy ♦ Jura Savoie ♦ Côtes du Rhône ♦ Provence ♦ Languedoc ♦ Roussillon Val de Loire ♦ Champagne ♦ Alsace**

The wines of France have qualities that set them above those of all other countries. Here climate and soil, with vines to suit them bred for 2,000 years, combine to produce wines that are forever emulated, rarely equaled, but never surpassed.

Many of the reasons for this may be seen by looking at the physical map of France. She has the advantage of maritime, mediterranean and continental climates. From the Massif Central, the Pyrénées, Cévennes and Alps, the Jura and Vosges mountains, great rivers cut their way down to water France's fertile plains. On the way, every soil important to the vine-grower may be found. And her vineyards lie between latitudes 43°N and 50°N, so that there is the warmth to produce every type of wine from full reds to dry whites. Add to all this the skills of her wine-makers, who benefit from experience handed down through a hundred generations, and the answer is complete: the wines of France have an unmistakable character, style and finesse of their own.

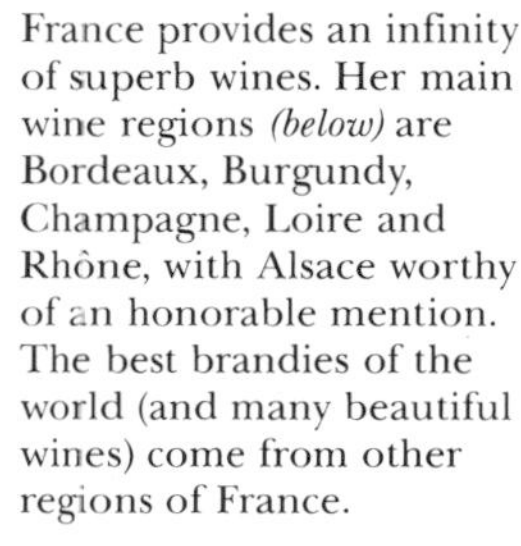

France provides an infinity of superb wines. Her main wine regions *(below)* are Bordeaux, Burgundy, Champagne, Loire and Rhône, with Alsace worthy of an honorable mention. The best brandies of the world (and many beautiful wines) come from other regions of France.

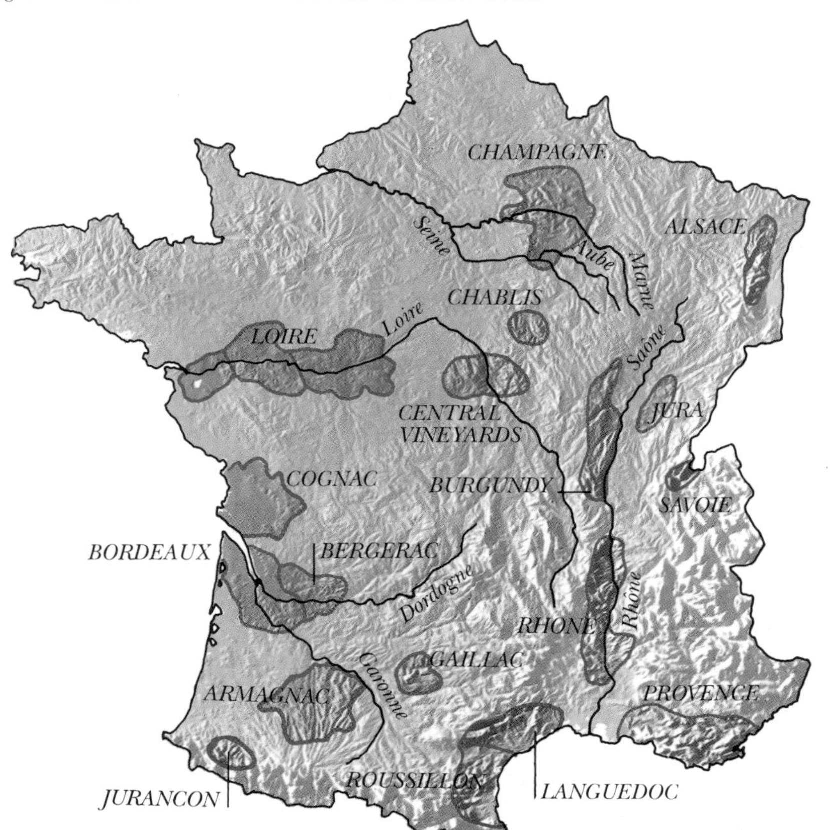


The main wine regions lie in two great arcs: a southerly sweep starting with Bordeaux in the west and running anticlockwise through Jurançon, Roussillon to Languedoc, to the Rhône and up to Burgundy; and a northerly sweep running clockwise from the Loire in the west to Champagne, Chablis and Alsace. The regions of the southern arc, where the greatest of France's red wines and many superb white wines are made, are here treated before the northerly regions, which specialize in white wines. So great is the variety of French wines that comparisons between them can be invidious and even somewhat boring; therefore no attempt is made here to put the regions in an order of precedence. However, Bordeaux is the largest and most important wine region in the world, and this surely provides a good enough reason to start there.

## BORDEAUX

The Bordeaux region officially covers the Department of the Gironde, with the exception of the dunes on its Atlantic seaboard. Within it there are 2,000 châteaus of varying size and importance; between them they average a production of some 2¾ million hl (25 million cases) of Appellation Contrôlée (AC) wine annually; of this about two-fifths is exported. Two-thirds of total production is of red and rosé wine, and one-third white. No Vin Délimité de Qualité Supérieure (VDQS) wine is produced in the region, but 2½ to 3 million hl of table wine is produced, of which two-thirds is white. Red-wine production is concentrated in the north of the region, which has higher rainfall; in the south, drier conditions help the development of benevolent botrytis, more favorable to the ripening of white grapes for the sweet wines of the upper Garonne.

The basic AC Bordeaux Rouge requires at least 10% alcohol by volume, and the strengths of other ACs of the region vary up to a maximum of at least 13% for Sauternes. Strict control of AC wines in Bordeaux requires analysis as well as tasting by the INAO. There are about 40 Appellations Contrôlées within the Bordeaux region, the basic two being AC Bordeaux and AC Bordeaux Supérieur, each subdivided into red and white wines, and to one or other of which all classified châteaus are entitled. The other ACs apply to districts and communes within the region—communes being areas, usually around a town or chief village, in which a number of châteaus are grouped.

Equally strict is the control of grape varieties within the region. The permitted black varieties are Cabernet Franc and Cabernet Sauvignon, giving strength to Bordeaux red wines; Malbec, giving color; Merlot, giving softness; Carmenere; and Petit Verdot. The permitted white grapes are the heavy croppers Sauvignon (not to be confused with the black Cabernet Sauvignon) and Semillon, with Muscadelle and Merlot Blanc. Almost all wines made in the region are blends, although the proportion of each permitted grape may vary from château to château. Wines that are château-bottled may vary somewhat from year to year but have a promise of better quality—especially in good years—than the regional wines blended by Bordeaux shippers to produce consistency. These regional wines must *ipso facto* be less than the best, but conforming to type have the ability to "follow themselves."

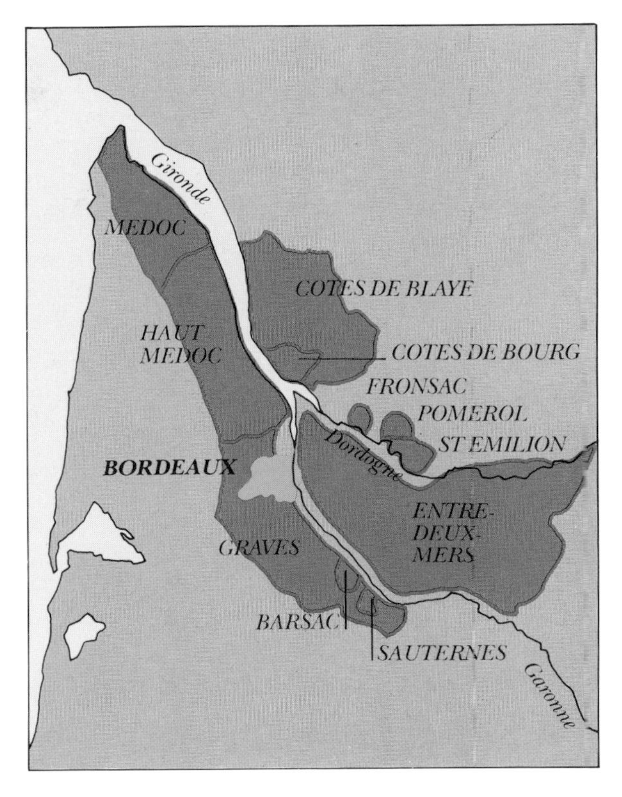


Bordeaux was the first region of the world to perfect claret: fading with age to garnet, the wine has perfect balance and finesse. But Bordeaux has other claims to fame — including the sweet whites of Sauternes and the unique reds of Pomerol and St Emilion.

## THE MEDOC

The peninsula north of the port of Bordeaux on the left bank of the Garonne and Gironde is the most important district in the region. The clarets of the Médoc are acclaimed everywhere as the greatest red wines of the world, and are produced on a strip of land 130km (81 mi) in length and 25km (15½ mi) wide which is almost surrounded by water (hence "Médoc," "in the middle of the water," from the Latin *in medio aquae*). The finest wines are made in the Haut-Médoc on a strip 3km (nearly 2 mi) wide along the river banks.

The oldest bottles in the cellars of Château Lafite *(above)* in the Médoc; they date from the end of the eighteenth century, and are recorked at intervals.

The 1855 Classification of the Médoc châteaus has been modified under the AC system so that, in the six leading communes, only the four Premiers Crus Classés and 14 Deuxièmes Crus Classés may be quoted on the label. The original third, fourth and fifth Grands Crus now rank as Crus Grands Bourgeois (41 châteaus) or Crus Bourgeois (68 châteaus). The four Premiers Crus Classés are Château Lafite-Rothschild, Château Latour, Château Margaux and Château Mouton-Rothschild—the order is alphabetical, according to a decree of 1973. (The only other Premier Cru for red wine in the Bordeaux region is Château Haut-Brion, in the Graves, which should therefore head the list.) The two great communes of the Haut-Médoc are Pauillac, having three of these Premiers Crus and two Deuxièmes Crus Classés, and Margaux, having Château Margaux and five Deuxièmes Crus Classés. Next come St Julien, with five Deuxièmes Crus Classés, and St Estèphe, with two.

The steepest slope in the Lafite vineyards reveals quartz fragments *(left)* among the smaller gravel pebbles *(cailloux).*

| | Lafite | Latour |
|---|---|---|
| CS | 70% | 75% |
| CF | 5% | 10% |
| M | 20% | 10% |
| PV | 5% | 5% |

CS Cabernet Sauvignon
CF Cabernet Franc
M Merlot
PV Petit Verdot

The blends of black grapes used by these and other leading châteaus vary slightly, containing 70-85% Cabernet Sauvignon, 5-20% Merlot, 5-10% Cabernet Franc, and up to 5% Petit Verdot. The differences between the resulting wines are considerable, as is illustrated perfectly by a comparison between Lafite and Latour. The blends are as shown in the table. Lafite has 10% more of the Merlot, which gives softness to the wine, while Latour substitutes 10% more of the Cabernets to give strength, a heavy tannin content and an intense flavor of blackcurrants. The two resulting wines represent the extremes of the Médoc clarets. Lafite, being gentle and light, is quicker to mature, while the heavier but deeply satisfying Latour needs to mature very slowly in oak. Lafite more nearly matches the supreme Margaux in this respect, while Latour is reminiscent of the equally slow-maturing Mouton-Rothschild.

But the high quality of these wines is not solely a result of the blends of grapes. The four Premiers Crus Classés occupy the best sites on the gravel mounds (little over 30m (about 100ft) in height) that border the river banks, and thus avoid the alluvial soil below and enjoy the best of the deep gravel over limestone above it. Pebbles in the gravel retain the sun's heat, which is radiated back during the night onto the vines—in the Médoc they are for this reason trained low in the Guyot Simple style.

North of Haut-Médoc the peninsula on the left bank of the tidal Gironde tapers off to the Pointe de Grave. This area, the Lower or Bas-Médoc, does not have the same reputation for fine clarets, for two principal reasons. The soil is heavier with clay (although sand gives some relief) and the mounds are smaller and fewer. Moreover, there is less protection from the salt

Candlelight in the cellars of Château Latour *(above left)* reveals the heavy deposit in the bottom of a bottle of claret.

The pallid light of the fall sun *(left)* on Château Latour after the harvest.

Lafite is one of only two châteaus in the Médoc that make their own *barriques* *(top)* (the other is Margaux). Here the year's product awaits the new season's wine.

Château Latour was the first great Médoc château *(above)* to install stainless-steel vats, in which control of fermentation temperatures is comparatively simple

Powdered chalk is sprayed in the vineyards of Château Branaire-Ducru *(above)*, St Julien. Nutrients such as chalk and Bordeaux mixture are applied in Spring.

*Décuvage* at Château Margaux *(center left)*. This is the process of taking wine off its lees during its maturation in large oak casks.

The imposing Château Margaux *(above)*, which gives its name to the commune. The vineyards are planted mainly with Cabernet Sauvignon.

An old vine at Château Margaux *(above right)* that has become unproductive and has therefore been uprooted. The soil will be left to rest for up to eight years.

The forest of the Landes *(right)*, which shelters the vineyards of Bordeaux from driving salty Atlantic gales.

winds of the Atlantic. The main town in the area is Lesparre, and the principal communes are Bégadan, St Yzans, Prignac, Blaignan, St Christoly and Ordonnac. Classified châteaus enjoy the AC Médoc. Showplace of the Bas-Médoc is Château Loudenne, in St Yzans, the property that has belonged to Gilbey-Vintners for more years than any other British-controlled property in the Médoc. Here the late and sadly missed Martin Bamford MW set up an invaluable museum of vineyard and wine-making artifacts for posterity.

The Premiers Crus Classés of the Médoc are for near-millionaires and their financial betters, but the Appellations Contrôlées Haut-Médoc, Médoc, AC Bordeaux, and AC Bordeaux Supérieur have among them clarets of great character that are within easier reach of the wine-lover.

## GRAVES

The stones and gravel brought by glaciers from the Pyrénées during the Ice Age gave its name to the district of Graves, the land lying along the left bank of the Garonne. Under the gravel is a subsoil of ironstone with clay or chalk. Graves runs north from Langon for 64km (40mi) to the fringes of the Médoc, north of the city of Bordeaux. It varies in width but averages about 18km (11mi).

The wines of Graves were omitted from the 1855 Classification, but in 1953 and again in 1959 the best vineyards were classified, and as a result there are seven Crus Classés for red wines, two for white wines, and seven for both red and white. The star of them all is the world-famous Château Haut-Brion, whose red wine had anomalously been included in the 1855 Médoc Classification, and whose white wine, omitted in error from the 1959 Graves Classification, was classified in the following year.

Although resembling the lighter clarets of the Médoc, the best Graves red wines, from vineyards now within the city of Bordeaux (as a result of encroachment) and just south of it, have more body, but are drier and less crisp, and share the *goût de terroir* imparted by the gravel throughout the district. Noticeable, however, are the different proportions of the same vines used for these red wines. In the Graves the Merlot provides an average 35% of the blend, against 20% in the Médoc, and this is balanced with less Cabernet Sauvignon. Hence the red Graves wines have more softness and mature more quickly. The good white wines, with their characteristic delicate and fruity flavor, are made from an average of 60% Sauvignon Blanc and 40% Semillon, although these proportions are reversed for the best of all white Graves, Château Laville-Haut-Brion,

The entrance to Château Lafite *(left)*, which is dwarfed to some extent by the huge *chai* seen to its left. In all, the château has some 1.4ha (3½ acres) of building space, including the chateau itself, the *chai*, storage, and quarters for 70 workers.

Craft of the cooper *(top)* at Château Lafite. The oak staves are assembled individually, then winched together as the hoops are hammered on.

The *chai* at Château Lafite *(above)*. The sign at the approach to the winery reads *"Montez doucement."*

A bottle of the 1877 vintage of Château La Mission Haut-Brion *(right)* has survived from one of the last pre-phylloxera years. It is one of an extensive collection of old wines carefully catalogued and stored in numbered bins at the Château.

Château La Mission Haut-Brion and its vineyards *(far right)* have slowly been engulfed by the city of Bordeaux. But benefit results: the ambient temperature is raised by the proximity of the city's population and buildings, and the city protects the vineyards from icy north winds.

The original Haut-Brion estate *(below)* was split when Dame Olive de Lestonnac died in 1630, willing a portion to the clergy of Bordeaux. In 1698 the Order of Lazarites built the small chapel now attached to the château.

which—at its price—should be left to mature before being drunk.

The vineyards below the Crus Classés are ungraded, and the better châteaus lie in the communes of Portets, Leognan, St Pierre-de-Mons, Toulenne and Martillac. The largest commune, Portets, is midway between Bordeaux and Langon, and its reputation for red wine is growing, according to Hugh Johnson: he rates Château Rahoul as the leader of the commune. Here winemaker Peter Vinding-Diers has taken over the adjacent Château Domaine La Grave to control a property of about 27ha (67 acres), producing some 7,500 cases of red wine and 850 of white each year.

Generally the reds and whites of Graves are good value for money and have often matured fully at the time of purchase.

## SAUTERNES AND BARSAC

The enclave of Sauternes is cut out of Graves along the left bank of the Garonne just north of Langon. Its microclimate is exceptional, in that the vineyards are mostly on north-facing hills of gravel and limestone, and enjoy misty falls which encourage botrytis, or noble rot, in the grapes. The Ciron, a small tributary of the Garonne, flows through the enclave, separating Barsac (to its south) from the other four communes of Sauternes. Barsac has its own AC but also may use the AC Sauternes label.

The magic of these sweet white wines lies in the natural chemistry that noble rot brings about. The shriveled grapes, picked separately late in the year, are pressed five times. They have already lost moisture on the vine and so their sugar content has increased. The *Botrytis*

A reminder of La Mission Haut-Brion's ecclesiastical past *(main picture)* hangs above the stairway of the aging *chais*.

An old vine grows in soil typical of the gravel from which the name "Graves" derives. The grapes are Merlot.

A traditional wooden vertical press, still in use at Haut-Brion. It is as efficient as a mechanical press, but more labor-intensive.

A conical tub used in the Haut-Brion vineyards carries the insignia of the Order of Lazarites.

The Château d'Yquem vineyards *(main picture)* are planted with 80% Semillon and 20% Sauvignon grapes.

Semillon grapes at Château d'Yquem affected by noble rot.

Pierre Mesher, *régisseur* at Château d'Yquem. Only at Yquem is Sauternes left to mature in the wood for three years.

Before château-bottling at Yquem, Sauternes matures in *barriques* that allow carbon dioxide to escape but do not let air (oxygen) in.

*cinerea* mold now increases the pectins and glycerins during fermentation, which is stopped only when the alcohol content reaches 13 or 14%, and 12% of the sugar remains unconverted; fermentation takes place in new oak *barriques*. The thick syrup-like wine has been called "golden nectar"—deservedly.

Made from about 75% Semillon and 25% Sauvignon Blanc, with occasionally a little Muscadelle, Sauternes are prohibitive in their cost of production. To add to the costs of picking and of new barrels there are the loss of volume, the period of maturation, and the depredations of frost, thunder and hail as winter approaches.

Château d'Yquem was the sole "First Great Growth" of the 1855 Sauternes Classification. It remains in a class of its own, and today there are 11 Premiers Crus and 12 Deuxièmes Crus in the district. Many Bourgeois properties abound in the district. Sauternes is ideal at the end of a meal with dessert or fruit, and may even be served instead of either. The owner of Château d'Yquem would have you take it with certain seafoods, too.

Sauternes failing to reach 13% alcohol by volume is declassified to AC Bordeaux. In store, Sauternes must be kept at a constant temperature; exposed to air or light it maderizes rapidly.

The small district of Cérons is immediately north of Barsac on the left bank of the Garonne. Using the same grapes as for Sauternes, Cérons produces wines sometimes affected by noble rot, and AC Cérons, for white wine only, requires 12.5% alcohol by volume. Failing this, the wine is declassified to AC Bordeaux.

## EAST OF THE GARONNE

Along a narrow strip on the right bank of the Garonne, from north of Bordeaux city south to Langon, lie the vineyards entitled to AC Premières Côtes de Bordeaux. Following the pattern of Graves, more red wines are produced in the north while sweet white wines become predominant towards the south. Permitted grapes for red wines are the same as for the Médoc, and for white wines the same grapes are permitted as for Sauternes. Loupiac and Ste Croix-du-Mont, in the little enclave opposite Barsac, are sweet wines similar to the best Sauternes, though not of the same quality—as is reflected in their price. Loupiac, Ste Croix-du-Mont and St Macaire (close to the right bank, east of Langon) each has its own AC for sweet white wine.

## ENTRE-DEUX-MERS

The lower reaches of the Garonne and Dordogne rivers, which at their confluence become the Gironde, form a shape reminiscent of the swallow—*hirondelle* in French—and it is from *hirondelle* that the Gironde derived its name. Much of this area is occupied by Entre-deux-Mers ("between two waters"), the largest district of the Bordeaux region, which features gravel *under* clay topsoils. Entre-deux-Mers is relatively thinly planted except in the north, where the red wines make no claim to greatness and are entitled only to AC Bordeaux or AC Bordeaux Supérieur. The white wines have slowly changed over in style from cheap sweet varieties to dry firm wines that make excellent carafe drinking when chilled, and have AC Entre-deux-Mers. There are no great vineyards in this district, and a number of cooperatives convert much of the harvest to wine.

On the left bank of the Dordogne are two widely separated enclaves, Graves-de-Vayres, opposite Libourne, and Ste-Foy-Bordeaux. As the name suggests, the gravel soil of Graves-de-Vayres contrasts with the surrounding clay. Here wines more like those of Pomerol and St Émilion are produced, although the quantity is minimal and the red wine, hard when young but quick to mature, is far superior to the white. Ste-Foy-Bordeaux adjoins Bergerac, to the northeast of Entre-deux-Mers, and here—no doubt because of the chalky clay soil—the white wines have good class and the red is not so good. They share AC Ste-Foy-Bordeaux.

## NORTH OF THE DORDOGNE AND GIRONDE

Opposite Entre-deux-Mers, on the hills sloping down to the right bank of the Dordogne, are three districts blessed by the wine-lover and known throughout the world for their red wines. Farthest east is St Émilion with its capital Saint-Émilion, the oldest and probably the most beautiful wine town of all France, raised from the soft limestone of the hills that hem it in—indeed, its stone quarries of the past have become wine cellars of today. St Émilion hugs the Dordogne bank all the way to Libourne, the second port of the Bordeaux region. Pomerol, separated from the Dordogne by Sables St Émilion and running up to the Barbanne river, is a much smaller district even when its subdistricts, the Lalande and Néac, are included. About the same size as Pomerol, across the river Isle to its west, is Fronsac, a third red-wine district.

Separated from Fronsac by some 100km (62mi) are Bourg, at the confluence of the Dordogne and Garonne, and Blaye, stretching some 20km (12½mi) north of Bourg to Cognac country and about the same distance to the east.

### St Émilion

The climate here tends to become continental rather than maritime, giving hotter summers and harder winters. Behind the hilly country, where the wines are "côtes," is a plateau where, confusingly, the wines are "graves." Château Ausone, supreme château on the côtes, grows vines above its limestone cellars; the other Premier Grand Cru château, Château Cheval Blanc, is out on the graves. Many *chais* in St Émilion are underground, for there is no risk of flooding.

The Cabernet Franc (here called Bouchet) and Merlot are the principal vines used, each varying between 60% and 30% of the blend at

St Émilion viewed from Château Ausone *(right)*, which stands high on the limestone escarpment that surrounds the town. Ausone has a cellar cut out of the limestone under the growing vines.

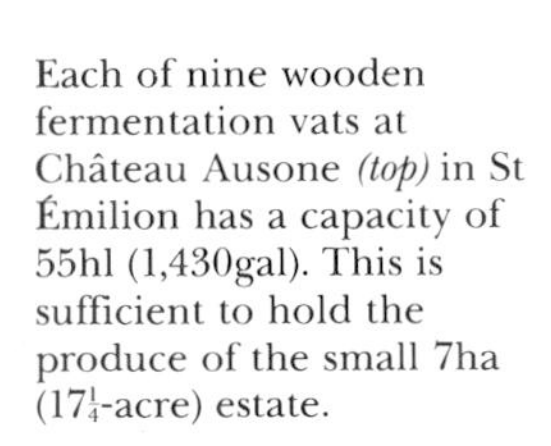

Each of nine wooden fermentation vats at Château Ausone *(top)* in St Émilion has a capacity of 55hl (1,430gal). This is sufficient to hold the produce of the small 7ha (17¼-acre) estate.

The red wines of St Émilion have a long aging period in the cellars of Château Ausone. Until recently these bottles of the 1975 vintage *(above)* occupied cellar space.

The slope of the vineyards of Ausone is clearly seen *(right)*. The vines planted are Cabernet Franc (Bouchet) and Merlot in about equal quantities.

New wine at Ausone is transferred to new barrels *(far right)* in February; the bunghole then remains at the top for three months. Thereafter the wine is racked seven times before bottling.

A 40-year-old Merlot vine *(left)* at Château Ausone. The Bordeaux custom was to retain vines for their full lifecycle, and it is only in the last 10 years that whole sections of the vineyard have been uprooted and rested before replanting.

The owner and chief cellarman of Château Figeac *(right)* racking wine in the fifteenth-century cellars. The wine has run from one cask to the point where great care is needed to stop the flow before the lees are disturbed.

At Château Magdelaine in St Émilion a typical bunch of Merlot grapes *(below left)* has reached ripeness. The Bordeaux districts north of the Dordogne are dedicated to the production of fine red wines, made principally from Cabernet Franc (Bouchet) and early-ripening Merlot grapes.

Gaston Vaissier, *maître de chais* of Château Cheval Blanc *(left)*, which stands with Ausone at the head of the St Émilion Classification of 1954; Cheval Blanc is much the bigger estate, with 41ha (101 acres) of vineyards.

According to the present owner, Thierry Manoncourt, this part of the Château Figeac vineyards *(below)* was originally planted by the Romans. Having exceptionally gravelly soil, the estate is planted with 35% each of Cabernet Sauvignon and Cabernet Franc and 30% Merlot.

different châteaus, while Cabernet Sauvignon is not unusual, at levels up to 25% and occasionally more. The soil in the côtes is essentially limestone or clay, with overlays of gravel and sand, and, as might be expected, the plateau in the hinterland is mainly gravel. The variation is marked in the wines, which are lighter in the côtes and firmer in the graves.

Five communes have the right to add their names to the district Appellation St Émilion. All the wines were classified in 1955. After Ausone and Cheval Blanc, there are 10 Premiers Grands Crus Classés, 72 Grands Crus Classés, and about 150 Grands Crus, followed by long lists of principal and lesser châteaus. The wines have something of the Médocs about them; although stronger and lighter in tannin, they mature more quickly, bringing them to a satisfying fruity sweetness.

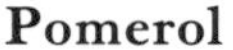

**Pomerol**

More and more connoisseurs are discovering the red wines of Pomerol. They share the grape varieties used in the Médoc and St Émilion, and the soils of Pomerol are not noticably different; the wine, however, is. It enjoys the sturdiness of the St Émilions and the subtlety of the Médocs, plus a velvety fatness (*gras*) unusual in Bordeaux. But Pomerols also have a taste born from the iron lying in the clay subsoil, and more Merlot is used in the grape blends than in St Émilion, at the expense of Cabernet Franc: Château Pétrus, the best vineyard in the district, uses 95% Merlot and only 5% Cabernet Franc (Bouchet). Pomerols mature in oak barrels and, although ready to drink at five years, improve for far longer. There has been no official classification of the Pomerols, but all judgments from the experts place Château Pétrus in a supreme class of its own, parallel with Margaux, Haut-Brion and d'Yquem.

Château Pétrus in Pomerol *(top)* proclaims its past religious associations, although neither its wine nor its wine history were important until a gold medal was unexpectedly won at the Paris Exhibition of 1878.

The wines of Château Pétrus are made from Merlot grapes *(middle)* with only a fraction (5%) of Cabernet Franc added. Pétrus wines are superbly different from other wines of the Pomerol.

Preparing for harvest *(above)* on the 11.5ha (28½-acre) estate of Château Pétrus. The vehicles are hooded (against rain, which can affect the alcohol yield by half a per cent), and are equipped to act as crushers.

Across the river Barbanne lies Lalande de Pomerol, a commune that now includes the smaller Néac to its east. Although they have an unaccountably different taste that devalues them slightly, the wines produced by several of the châteaus compare well with good Pomerols. Château Bel Air is the leading property.

**Fronsac**

Set within the Côtes de Fronsac are the Côtes Canon-Fronsac, rather after the style of the Italian "classico" areas, where the best wines are made. Situated in the fork of the Isle and Dordogne rivers, Côtes de Fronsac occupies the rim of the Canon hills. The height of this bluff overlooking the Dordogne opposite Vayres saved the district from the freeze that destroyed Pomerol, most of St Émilion and many other districts in 1956. The wines are heavy and meaty, yet attractive after aging in the bottle for a few years; they are made with the vines used by the neighboring districts but with some Malbec added. The soil of Canon-Fronsac is lighter, with more limestone, and this accounts for its excellent wine quality. The two ACs are for red wine only.

**Bourg and Blaye**

The district of Bourg is almost surrounded by the much larger district of Blaye, yet touches the bank of the Gironde for a few kilometers, just where the Dordogne flows into the Garonne. There are six ACs: Bourg, Bourgeois, and Côtes de Bourg; and Blaye, Côtes de Blaye and Premières Côtes de Blaye. It cannot be said that any of the red and white wines produced in the two districts have much distinction. Bourg makes equal quantities of reds and whites; the reds are fuller-bodied than those of Blaye, and are reckoned to be superior.

The Appellations of Blaye overlap the same area, and simply indicate quality. AC Blaye applies to both red and white wine, and AC Côtes de Blaye only to white wine. 15% of AC Premières Côtes de Blaye are white wines and the remainder are red. This classification specifies that only noble grapes may be used; the dry to semi-sweet white wines are superior to those of Bourg.

Although none of these wines merits superlatives (good or bad) they are fairly priced, and it may be that their elegant neighbors in the Bordeaux region make us think less of them than we should.

## OTHER WINES OF THE SOUTHWEST

### BERGERAC, MONBAZILLAC AND CÔTES DE DURAS

Bergerac, in the Department of Lot-et-Garonne adjacent to Bordeaux, originally produced only

white wines; but more recently the Cot (Malbec) grape has been planted with Cabernet Sauvignon to produce wine that bears comparison with average to good claret. At 10% vol. alcohol, and cheaper than the Bordeaux reds, it is well worth while. The Dordogne runs east-to-west through the region, and in the northeast, in the district of AC Pécharmant, are found the best reds. Here a preponderance of the Cot gives a wine light in bouquet but complete in character, at a strength of 12% vol. alcohol. Generally, the soil of Bergerac is sandy clay with gravel subsoils and some iron. The better white wines, from Sauvignon and Semillon grapes, are to be found in the northwest corner of the region, where some limestone persists. The AC districts are Montravel and Haut-Montravel.

Within this region and south of the Dordogne is AC Monbazillac, where sweet long-lasting white wines of high alcohol content approaching the quality of Sauternes are produced—and sold at a lesser price. Another AC, Rosette, has a light slightly sweet wine with a Muscat flavor. Both can be found and are worth seeking.

Côtes de Duras is tucked in between Entre-deux-Mers, Ste-Foy-Bordeaux and Bergerac; on its southern border is the river Dropt. Here the soil is sandy with some lime, and, although the AC extends to white wines, the main production is red from the Bordeaux grape varieties. The resulting wines are similar to those of Entre-deux-Mers.

## MARMANDAIS AND CÔTES DE BUZET

Côtes de Marmandais VDQS has not yet achieved AC ranking; it lies along the river Garonne, but just beyond the Bordeaux border. Here red wines are made from the Bordeaux grape varieties, in roughly the proportions used in the Médoc, to produce a plausible claret. The white wines from the Sauvignon and Semillon grapes give a wine of average Bordeaux quality. Produced by many small growers, the grapes are converted at two local cooperatives and marketed through UNIDOR at Monbazillac.

A little further up the Garonne and to its south are the Côtes de Buzet, now elevated to AC from VDQS. The soil—of gravel, chalk and clay—is good for red-wine production, and the hard work of a generation has improved these clarets noticeably. Some white wine, both sweet and dry, is also made, conversion of grapes to wine mostly being done at the Damazan Cooperative.

## CAHORS, FRONTON AND GAILLAC

In the valley of the Lot, an agreeable fruity red wine is made from the Auxerrois grape — a thick-skinned variety of Malbec grown on rocky limestone and gravel. (The old "black wine of Cahors," made by long fermentation and boiling of the must, is now history.) Elevated these days to AC Cahors, the wine may be slightly chilled and is ready for drinking after as little as two years.

The Côtes du Frontonnais, another wine region of southwest France, lies between the Garonne and Tarn rivers. The AC wines here are made principally from Negrette (another variety of Malbec) with Cabernets, Syrah and Gamay to balance. The soil is sandy, contributing to full-blooded red wines which are rich in both color and alcohol. Pech-Langlade is the best property.

A little over 30km (19mi) to the east are the age-old vineyards of Gaillac in the Department of Tour Tarn. Now that the Sauvignon, Merlot, Syrah and Gamay vines have been brought in, only two of the indigenous grapes, the white Mausac and the black Brocol, survive in quantities worth mentioning here. The white wines are still and dry, or, when retained on their lees and bottled under pressure, are marketed as sparkling Gaillac Perlé with the AC Gaillac Mousseux. The red wines are fair but unspectacular and, like the whites, are for drinking young.

## WINES OF THE PYRÉNÉES

Good wines are to be found in the Pyrenean foothills in the Departments of Pyrénées Atlantiques, Hautes-Pyrénées and Landes. The soils turn from sand in the plain to sandstone in the hills.

## MADIRAN

Madiran, in the Vic-Bilh hills, survived phylloxera in the nineteenth century only to sink into obscurity in the 1950s; since then it has produced one of the finest red wines (some say *the* finest) in the southwest. Originally made solely with Cabernets, AC Madiran is today made mainly from Tannat, a small grape high in tannin and related to the Malbec, with one or both of the Cabernets added. From sharp beginnings, Madiran matures into a claret of great character and smooth texture. Also from Madiran come the sweet or dry white wines of AC Pachérenc-du-Vic-Bilh (Pachérenc is the local name for the white Manseng grape, and Vic-Bilh the name of the village).

## JURANÇON

South of Pau are produced the strong white wines of AC Jurançon; according to the year, these may be sweet or medium dry. They have a distinct yet elusive flavor which has been likened variously to peaches, camomile, mangos, cinnamon, carnations and guavas. The grapes are Gros and Petit Manseng, with some Courbu. Spring frosts can cause havoc and the vines are accordingly trained up stakes some 2m (6ft) in height, from which the shoots are spread laterally after the bulk of the danger is past.

Worthy of mention are the AC Vins de Béarn from the valley of the Gave de Pau, which take their name from the province. They may be red, white or rosé and are piquant (to complement their own sauce Béarnaise) yet velvety. The same velvety texture is noticeable in the wines

of Tursan VDQS in the Department of Landes, the whites being made from Picpoul, Manseng and Courbu grapes, and the reds from Malbec and Tannat. AC Iroulèguy, from the commune of St Etienne-de-Baïgorry, is mainly red wine, produced in the deep Pyrenean valleys in one of the most idyllic settings imaginable.

# BURGUNDY

On the map the wine region of Burgundy all looks so simple. The isolated district of Chablis, east of Auxerre, is separated from Dijon by roughly 120km (75mi), but from Dijon to Chalon-sur-Saône the world-renowned districts of the Côte d'Or and the Chalonnais are clustered, and in line due south the districts of the Mâconnais and Beaujolais follow the river Saône to its confluence with the Rhône at Lyon. And that's it—until you discover, for instance, that the Beaujolais is not, nor ever was, in Burgundy, and that no one has yet found a logical reason for including it now. It has its own *Comité*, or governing body, but so has the Chalonnais, and perhaps both need one since the north of the Beaujolais overlaps the Chalonnais which *is* in Burgundy! The whole region is fraught with anomalies and exceptions to the generally accepted rules and methods that apply elsewhere in France. This mostly results from her history.

The vineyards of Burgundy date from time out of mind—long before the Roman invasion of Gaul. From the seventh century the vineyards were given to the Church by the kings and later by the dukes of Burgundy. It was the monasteries that founded the great vineyards such as Clos-de-Vougeot, and Cluny in the Mâconnais.

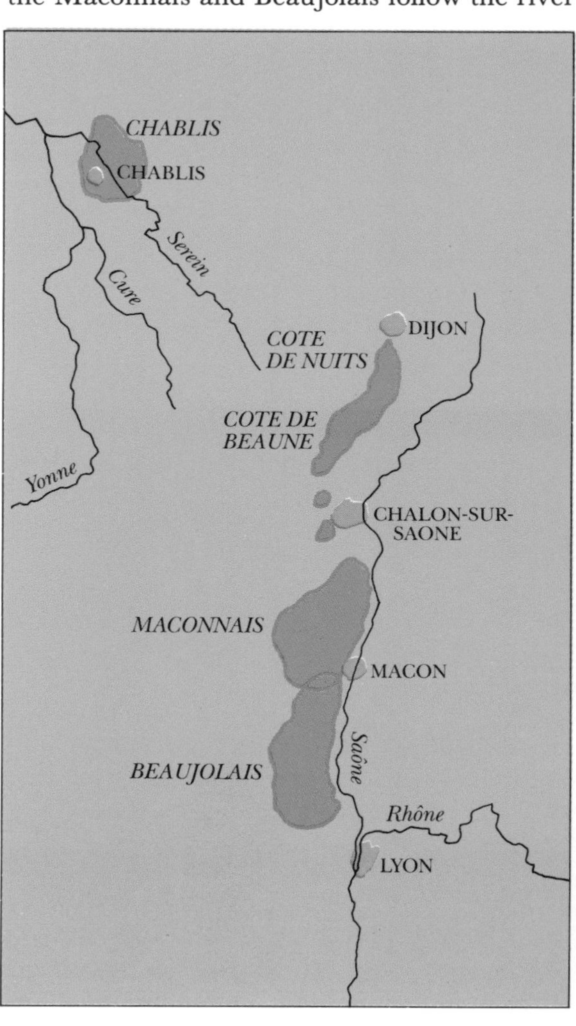


The vineyards of Burgundy *(above)* were there long before the Roman occupation. Later, the vineyards were controlled and cultivated by the Church, on lands given first by the kings of Burgundy and then by the Duchy. The Church founded great vineyards such as Cluny, Clos-de-Vougeot and Clos-de-Tart.

The Pinot Noir, the grape of Burgundy *(above right)*, is responsible for all the best Côte d'Or red wines; they have a memorable flavor and an aroma of oak and fruit. The grapes illustrated were grown on the famous Louis Latour property at Beaune, founded in the eighteenth century and owned and managed by Latours since 1867. Three-quarters of their product is Domaine wine.

The Louis Latour domaine at Aloxe-Corton encircles a large purpose-built winery. Included in the domaine are 40ha (100 acres) in Corton and Aloxe-Corton; of this 10ha (25 acres) are for Corton-Charlemagne, far the best-known Latour white wine, made from the Chardonnay *(right)*. A big firm white that needs to age, Corton-Charlemagne and other Chardonnays have built a fine reputation for white Burgundy vintages.

Les Grenouilles is a small Grand Cru property *(above)* that produces some of the best Chablis made today: Paul Droin keeps his Grands Crus from Grenouille Vaudesir, Les Clos and Valmur in cask for at least a year. When Napoleon III visited Auxerre in 1866, Droin's great-grandfather made him a gift of some of this estate wine.

Chablis is made exclusively from the Chardonnay grape, and the wine it produces is classically pale with a steely bouquet, dry and with great finesse. An old vine is seen *(right)* trained low in the Guyot simple style which suits the natural conditions of latitude, height, slopes and microclimate in Chablis.

The industry had a well ordered and progressive existence that was rationalized to some extent by Nicholas de Rodin. In the fifteenth century he built the Hospices de Beaune, the institution that has acted ever since as an index, through its auctions, to the current year's prices of Burgundy wine.

But with the French Revolution came tragedy: the great vineyards were split up and sold to the *citoyens* in small plots, and neighboring plots could produce widely different qualities of wine. The French have now had 200 years to restore order from the chaos that followed—the last 18 under the aegis of the EEC. The resulting classificatory system is good, but nevertheless essentially very complicated.

There are five appellations, to one or more of which all growers in the region are entitled (provided, of course, that the standards are met). Each specifies a maximum crop in hectolitres per hectare and a minimum degree of alcohol.

AC Bourgogne specifies a maximum crop of 50hl/ha and 10% vol. alcohol for reds and rosés, or 10.5% for white wines. The grapes must be Pinot Noir for red wines and Chardonnay or Pinot Blanc, or a blend of these, for white wines. The important exceptions are that Beaujolais must use the Gamay Noir, not Pinot Noir, and in Chablis the local grapes Cèsar and Tressot are admitted.

AC Bourgogne Passé-tout-grains for reds and rosés also specifies a maximum crop of 50hl/ha, but with a minimum alcoholic strength of 9.5% vol. At least one third of the blend must be Pinot Noir and the balance Gamay.

AC Bourgogne Aligoté is for white wine from the Aligoté grape, optionally with Chardonnay added. The critical figures are 50hl/ha and 9.5% vol.

The little-used AC Bourgogne Grand Ordinaire (or AC Bourgogne Ordinaire) specifies 50hl/ha and 9% vol. for red and rosé, and 9.5% vol. for white wines.

A fifth appellation, AC Crémant de Bourgogne, applies only to red, white and rosé wines that have been made sparkling by the champagne method.

Throughout Chablis and the Côte d'Or, every vineyard is ranked by its appellations, and at the head of the list are about 30 Grands Crus; they are described simply as "Le"—for example, Le Chambertin, Le Corton, Le Montrachet and Les Musigny (for both red and white wine). Surviving from the nineteenth century are classifications where village names precede the Grand Cru name, such as AC Gevrey-Chambertin, AC Aloxe-Corton and AC Puligny-Montrachet. In Chablis the name of the commune may precede the Grand Cru in much the same way.

Next come the Premiers Crus—parcels of land in the best vineyards of the Premiers Crus communes. These communes occupy practically all of the narrow strip of hillside—perfect for soil and aspect—running through the Côte d'Or. Vineyards on the surrounding land, above and below this strip, may take the name of commune and vineyard, but on the label the vineyard name must be in letters not more than half the size of the name of the village or commune holding the Appellation Contrôlée. Vineyards on inferior land within the Côte d'Or are not allowed their village name, only the appropriate Bourgogne basic classifications.

## CHABLIS

The wine region of Chablis lies so far north that frost has been its greatest enemy. Had it not been for the merchants of Beaune, Chablis might well have disappeared entirely after the invasion of phylloxera. Marketing centered on Beaune, and Chablis became synonymous with the best of white Burgundy; but time and again the vineyards were wrecked by spring frosts, and Chablis remained rare. The old smudge pots placed in the vineyards for heat were unequal to their task. Then, some 20 years ago, the system of using sprinklers in the vineyards was introduced, so that ice formed on the vine and its young shoots and thereby protected them from frost. From an area of a mere 400ha (1,000 acres) at their lowest ebb, the vineyards today have increased to over 1,600ha (4,000 acres). The crops are guaranteed and, with the old risk beaten, investment has been attracted to assure vineyard husbandry at its best.

Chablis village *(above)* has all the charm of rural France. Through the village the river Serein flows peacefully north to join the Yonne, which in turn flows into the Seine.

A typical Burgundian *cave* at Domaine Armand Rousseau *(right)* in the Côte d'Or at Gevrey Chambertin. Here is a long line of *"bouteilles en piler et tonneaux."*

Chablis, made only from the Chardonnay grape, is a pale wine with great finesse; it is light, dry and crisp, with a fruity flavor and earthy bouquet. The district centers on the town of Chablis and the vines run in rows up and down the hills. The Grands Crus, or best of Chablis, are huddled in an area of 100ha (250 acres) immediately to the east of the town: they are Blanchots, Bourgros, Les Clos, Grenouilles, Les Preuses, Valmur and Vaudésir. After these come the Premiers Crus, some 25 in number, producing wine occasionally difficult to distinguish from the Great Growths. Mostly they lie in the commune of Chablis or in neighboring Chichée, Fleys, Fyé, Milly and Poinchy. Lower down the AC scale is Petit Chablis, a class restricted in quantity, coming from the fringe areas of the vineyards. The rest is Chablis Villages of which much is sold in barrel. The minimum alcohol content is 9.5% vol.; the best is fermented slowly and needs at least three years (improving up to 15 years) in the bottle.

## CÔTE DE NUITS

The Côte de Nuits runs from Marsannay, just south of the defunct Côte de Dijon, down to the communes around Nuits St Georges, 19km (12mi) away. The N74 road from Dijon to Beaune runs right through the vineyards, some 15km (9½mi) from the upper reaches of the Saône to the east.

Here the names of each of eight villages breathe something of the magic of Burgundy wine at its best. They are Marsannay-la-Côte, Fixin, Gevrey-Chambertin, Morey-St-Denis, Chambolle-Musigny, Vougeot, Flagey-Échézaux and Vosne-Romanée. The wine produced is almost entirely red, and made from the mandatory Pinot Noir, to which a little Chardonnay may be added. (Exceptionally, the Grand Cru vineyard Les Musigny makes also Grand Cru white Burgundy—otherwise "Les" would be "Le;" full-bodied with a wonderful bouquet, these white Burgundies are unforgettable.) The soil is a red clay, containing chalk, pebbles and lava, with a high mineral content; the subsoil is a flinty clay with iron and more chalk. Three official classifications raise the quality wines of the Côte above the regional classifications already mentioned. These require for Grands Crus harvests not exceeding 30hl/ha and 11.5% vol. alcohol for red wine and 12% for white. (For Gevrey-Chambertin 32hl/ha is permitted.) For the Premiers Crus the relevant figures are 35hl/ha with 11% vol. alcohol for reds and 11.5% for whites; and for commune wines they are 35hl/ha with 10.5% vol. alcohol for reds and 11% for whites.

Gevrey, like other villages in the Côte d'Or, has added to its name that of its finest vineyard, Chambertin. It has nine Grands Crus, headed

The soil at Chambertin *(above left)* in the Côte de Nuits. The best of the wines are made in the north where the soil has a suitable consistency and mineral content to give the red wines fullness and great finesse.

Picking Pinot Noir, the required grape of Burgundy *(center left)*, in the vineyard of Louis Latour at Aloxe-Corton Les Chaillots. The long baskets, a Burgundy feature, are emptied directly into a destalker in the *chai*.

Chaptalisation *(center right)* is done by dissolving sugar in some fermenting must and then returning it to the fermentation vat. It is illegal to dissolve the sugar in water instead, as this would affect the wine's alcoholic strength.

*Ouillage*, or the topping-up of barrels of wine during the early stages of maturation *(above right)*, to compensate for evaporation.

Alain Roumier, *régisseur* of the Domaine Comte de Vogüé *(left)*, which ranks among the finest of all Burgundy estates; it has been in the family since 1450. Of the 12ha (29½ acres) of vineyards, three-fifths are in Le Musigny.

All the 8ha (19¾ acres) of vineyards of Domaine Henri Gouges *(right)* are in Nuits-Saint-Georges itself, and the estate is the acknowledged specialist concerning this famous wine.

The commune of Gevrey in the Côte de Nuits has added the name of its finest vineyard, le Chambertin, to its own. Clos St Jacques *(below)* is one of the larger Premiers Crus vineyards, with over 6ha (15 acres).

Close-les-Porrets *(below left)* is one of the largest properties in the commune of Nuits St Georges. Henri Gouges has an unparalleled reputation for the powerful red Porret wines.

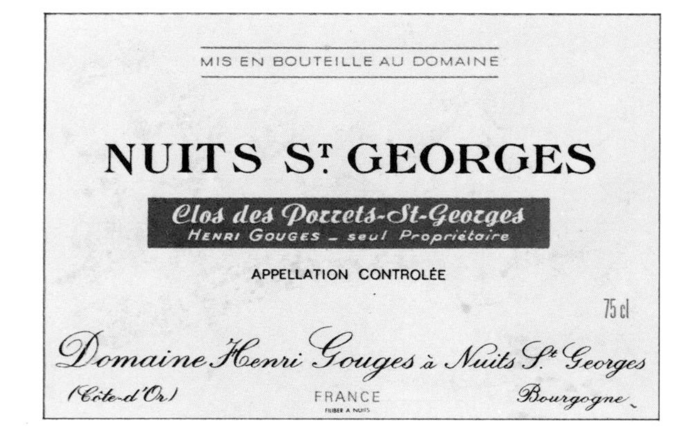

by Le Chambertin and Chambertin-Clos-de-Bèze; the other seven attach "Chambertin" *after* the vineyard name. Next comes Morey-St-Denis with four Grands Crus: two of them, Bonnes Mares and Clos-de-Tart, extend into Chambolle-Musigny. In the village of Vougeot is the walled vineyard of Clos-de-Vougeot where over 50 owners vinify their wine separately, resulting in some qualitative variation of the wine going to market. To its south is Flagey-Échézaux which, despite its two Grands Crus, is often included with its neighbor Vosne-Romanée, which has four diminutive Grands Crus of its own, producing wines of velvety softness and strong bouquet. Every Grand Cru of the Côte de Nuits lies in its northern half: to the south the soil lacks the consistency and minerals needed for the very best. All share the practice of using barrels of Troncois oak which helps to give a woody flavor and increased tannin to the wines.

South of Vosne-Romanée is Nuits St Georges, the largest commune of the Côte de Nuits. St Georges is the only Premier Cru vineyard in all the Côte d'Or to have its name adopted for the commune—a singular honor. Included in AC Nuits St Georges is another Premier Cru, Prémeaux, which shares a reputation with St Georges for wines often needing 10 years' maturation to shake off a raw and boisterous youth and emerge as worthy bestsellers. Nuits St Georges is the trading center for the whole of the Côte de Nuits.

South of Nuits there is just one Premier Cru, the Clos des Langres at the southern tip of the Côte. The wines of the intervening villages, Comblanchien, Corgoloin, Prémeaux and Prissey (once known as "vins fins de la Côte de Nuits") share with those of Brochon, Fixin and Marsannay in the north the right to the AC Côte de Nuits Villages; additionally, Fixin and Marsannay have their own appellations.

## CÔTE DE BEAUNE

The northern extremity of the Côte de Beaune cannot be missed; it is the rounded Montagne de Corton, capped with trees and having vineyards on all sides except the north. The region runs down to Santenay in the southwest, and a list of the world-famous wines made here would be an exercise in name-dropping equal only to one for the Côte de Nuits.

The 25km (15½mi) sweep of the Côte de Beaune depends to a great extent upon its soil for the variety of its wines. In the Beaune and Pommard districts there is a hard rock base covered with a thin layer of earth, with a white marl sometimes appearing. There is more of this marl in the Côte de Meursault, where the soil becomes ideal for white-wine production. At the foot of the slopes the soil starts to turn grey, and an element of oolitic limestone rich in iron gives superb light red wines; higher up the slopes, the clay content increases to give beautifully balanced red wines which are of great finesse yet full and rich.

The village of Aloxe, which has added the name of Corton, lies on the favored southeast slope of the mountain, where there grows an abundance of Pinot Noir to produce Grands Crus red wines that are strong and full with great bouquet. Chardonnay covers the higher regions and the west, producing white wines of great fruitiness and steely strength or "backbone." Grands Crus AC Corton is for red and white wines and AC Corton Charlemagne is for white only.

The valleys of Pernand-Vergelesses and Savigny-lès-Beaune lead down to the city of Beaune through Ladoix-Serrigny and Chorey-lès-Beaune. The town is memorable as the walled city where the Hospices de Beaune were founded; it is also today the center of the Côte de Beaune wine industry. The district of Beaune has about 35 Premiers Crus vineyards, but no Grands Crus. Beaune produces red wines which bear the vineyard name, whether or not Premier Cru, and some white. The AC for these white wine is Côte de Beaune with AC Côte de Beaune Villages for the less famous red wines.

South of Beaune, the AC commune of Pom-

Vineyards in La Tâche *(right)* at Vosne-Romanée, the property neighboring and owned by Romanée Conti. The soil must be protected because, although 200 years ago fresh loam used to be brought up from the Saône valley by the Prince de Conti, this is now prohibited.

At the Domaine de la Romanée Conti, a bunch of Pinot Noir grapes *(below)* has reached the stage of perfect balance between acid and potential alcohol.

A demonstration of grafting *(below right)*, using the whip and tongue pattern (otherwise known as the English graft), at the Romanée Conti vineyard.

mard begins: here the wines, all red, have deep color, a full fruitiness, and last well. Just south is Volnay, a small village with a small vineyard and steep slope; this slope includes the Premier Cru AC Les Santenots in the AC commune of Meursault. The wines of Meursault are fruity and crisp with the long "finish," or aftertaste, that stands for quality. With bottle-age the Meursault turns deep gold in color and develops a rich bouquet, but there is no age at which these wines are not exceptional.

So too—perhaps even more so—are their neighboring wines, the Montrachets, which have five Grands Crus AC vineyards for white wines in the communes of Puligny and Chassagne (which attach their names), at the southern extreme of an area of loess soil which is perfect for white wines. The wines of Montrachet are simply the best that Chardonnay can produce. Chassagne Montrachet turns ably to red-wine production in its southern vineyards.

Close by are the Marange vineyards, which produce full-bodied red wines, soft in texture, that sell as Côte de Beaune Villages, and white wines as AC Bourgogne Blanc.

Bouchard Père et Fils are the proud owners of one hectare (2½ acres) of vines in Le Montrachet. Chardonnay grapes are being gathered *(above)* for making their superb Puligny Montrachet wine.

On a cask in the cellars of the Domaine Ampeau in the Côte de Beaune, a silver *tastevin* and wines *(left)* are set out in preparation for expert tasting. The *tastevin* was especially designed for examining wine in dark cellars.

In the Côte de Beaune, it does not take a bottle of wine as long as you might think to look old. Bottles of 1964-vintage Meursault *(bottom left)* at the Domaine Ampeau are unaffected by a white fungal growth.

The 250-year-old firm of Bouchard Père et Fils have nearly 200 acres of Grands Crus and Premiers Crus within their Domaine. The cellars of the old Beaune fortress *(left)* hold huge stocks of famous wines.

Part of the 4ha (10 acres) of Grèves Vigne de l'Enfant Jesus *(right)*, one of Bouchards' most important vineyard holdings in Beaune Premiers Crus.

Claude Bouchard *(below)*, of Bouchard Père et Fils, relaxes for a moment to prove that modern developments in Burgundy can have their enjoyable as well as their demanding aspects. Bouchards are the largest single vineyard owner in Burgundy.

Michel, son of Robert Ampeau *(right)*, is busy pruning (the *taille préparatoire*) while the vines sleep after the harvest. The bush has already been trained to Guyot-simple shape.

Tidying up the vines after pruning *(far right)* is essential because foliage often obscures the operative's view: a bad cut could leave space where an unwanted bud might shoot. The Meursault soil is in the center of a patch of loess, favoring white-wine production.

In the cellars of Domaine Ampeau at Meursault Robert Ampeau *(right)* is topping up casks of new white wine to avoid oxidation. Robert and his son Michel do nearly all the work necessary out on their 10ha (25-acre) estate and in the *chai* and cellar.

## THE CÔTE CHALONNAISE

In the region stretching 25km (15½mi) south of Chalon-sur-Saône are the small districts of Rully, Mercurey, Givry, and Montagny. Their soil is similar to that in the Côte de Beaune, but more fertile and hence somewhat inferior for great wine production. The wines vary and lack any common regional characteristics, although all are made from Pinot Noir, or Pinot Blanc and Chardonnay.

Rully produces red and white wines in equal quantities, the reds being thinner than those of Mercurey and the whites having a freshness that makes them the best in the region. Mercurey produces more wine than all the rest of the region, 90% being an interesting clear red with an attractive steely *goût de terroir*, best for drinking between two and seven years after bottling. Givry also produces mostly red wines, but they are fuller and keep longer. Montagny's wine is all white and, if it has 11.5% vol. alcohol or more, warrants Premier Cru AC; it has more body and less finesse than those of Rully. The communal ACs call for 35hl/ha in Mercurey and 40hl/ha in the other three communes. The red wines must have a minimum of 10.5% vol. alcohol, and the white wines 11%.

Between Rully and Chalon-sur-Saône is the village of Bouzeron, enjoying AC Bourgogne Aligoté de Bouzeron for a very fine crémant wine.

The Domaine de la Renarde, at Rully in the Chalonnaise, is a new property owned by Jean-François Delorme, an enologist and *negoçiant*. Here Chardonnay grapes are unloaded into a trailer.

## THE MÂCONNAIS AND BEAUJOLAIS

The Côte Mâconnaise runs down from Tournus, first through a range of limestone hills and valleys and then on to a point just south of Mâcon; a dramatic change in character occurs between Cluny and Mâcon, where the limestone valleys give way to the enormous granite rocks that dominate the scene deep into the Beaujolais. North of Mâcon, the red-wine area of the AC Mâcon Villages contains some 40 villages which may insert their village name; for example, AC Mâcon-Viré Villages. With the other red wines of the Mâconnais, all made now from Pinot Noir grapes, they share AC Mâcon (or AC Mâcon Supérieur, if they have enough alcohol) and AC Mâcon Passe-tout-grains if mixed with the Gamay grape. The Mâcon reds have improved noticeably since the *macération carbonique* method was adopted.

The change to igneous rock marks the beginning of the district with the best villages for white wines. Made entirely from Chardonnay grapes, they are classified AC Mâcon Blanc and AC Mâcon Blanc Supérieur. These white wines are greatly superior to the reds. The full-bodied Pouilly-Fuissé takes its name from two villages in the delimited area: a high alcohol content distinguishes it from the lighter wines of Chablis and the Côte de Beaune. ACs for the smaller Pouilly-Loché, Pouilly-Vinzelles and the larger Pouilly St Veran were added some 15 years ago. St Veran is a group of seven villages, some of which may also sell their wine as Beaujolais Blanc.

The soil in Haut-Beaujolais is essentially granite with an overlay of schist; it gives Gamay, the Beaujolais grape, the chance to show its full range of qualities. Although Beaujolais wine of the summer's harvest may be sold *en primeur* or *nouveau* after November 15 each year, the best of Grands Crus Beaujolais are not bottled until the following March. They are full and fruity, with the unmistakable Gamay nose. It is usually a scramble to complete fermentation of the *nouveau* by November 15 and, although Beaujolais Cru may be sold after December 15, the finest Crus prefer to ignore this opportunity and guard their reputations.

Nine communes—the Beaujolais Crus—have their own ACs: they are St Amour, Juliénas, Chénas, Moulin-à-Vent, Fleurie, Chiroubles, Morgon, Brouilly, and Côte de Brouilly. The minimum alcohol level for AC Beaujolais is 9% vol. and for AC Beaujolais Superior 10% vol. The Grands Crus are stronger—they must be over 10% vol.—but no other figure is decreed by law except that the alcoholic strength must be declared on the label.

In the Bas-Beaujolais, the area south of Villefranche-sur-Saône, the soil is once more of limestone; here about half of Beaujolais' total production of around 13 million cases per year is made; mostly this is red wine which lacks the finer qualities of those from the villages in the north.

Every hill in France seems to be a challenge to her vineyards. At Fleurie *(above)* in the Beaujolais they climb up to the chapel of La Madonne. Fleurie is perhaps the most popular Beaujolais cru, and most Fleurie wine is consumed before it has had a chance to mature.

Fermentation tanks in Julienas *(right)*, the northernmost cru of the Beaujolais. These wines tend to be strong in color and vigor, and are more suited for drinking with meals than on their own merits. Julienas has some 500ha (1,360 acres) under vines and produces one-third of a million cases each year.

The Gamay grapes of Beaujolais *(main picture)* have nothing very noble to offer, but they make a wine that has the edge and young juicy flavors that truly quench the thirst. As a result, Beaujolais has been able to build an export business in *primeur,* or new season's wine, that during the 1980s has become an international vogue.

Côtes de Brouilly is one of the smallest crus of the Beaujolais; the wines are said to develop a strong scent of violets after two or three years in bottle. An operative *(below)* empties *marc* from a fermentation tank.

A close-up of the hatch through which the *marc* is removed *(bottom)* after fermentation of the wine has been completed. The *marc* is then dried and sent away for distillation.

A cellar-tasting of Beaujolais has just been arranged on an upturned cask *(inset left),* complete with beaker, glass, hydrometer, thermometer and *tastevin.*

Filling a horizontal press *(inset right)* at Mt Bessy in Brouilly. Gentler than the old vertical press, the horizontal (or vaslin) press has many varied designs, and increasingly its work is being lightened by prior use of a dejuicer to free the *vin de goutte.*

## JURA

The valley of the Saône broadens considerably near its source: 25km (15½mi) to the west is the Côte d'Or and 50km (31mi) to the east are the Jura mountains, famed for their (Jurassic) oolitic limestone. On their western foothills the Côtes du Jura produce a variety of wines, of which several are unique. The vineyards are disjointed and spread over an area some 15km (10mi) wide and 70km (44mi) from north to southwest, roughly parallel with and opposite to the Côte de Nuits and Côte de Beaune. The climate is continental, with cold winters and hot summers, the latter marred by rain and hail that fortunately give way to sun in September and October.

The best red wines are made in Arbois and the surrounding villages of Salins, Montigny, Pupillin and Poligny. Above the regional AC Côtes du Jura is the superior AC Arbois, which has a higher alcohol content. The grapes are the Poulsard, almost rosé in color, with a little Trousseau to give body, fermented on their skins for the production of rosés; for the much smaller-scale production of red wines, Pinot Noir is added. Chardonnay (locally the Melon d'Arbois) is used for white wines, of which the best come from the village of l'Etoile, further south. AC l'Etoile is for white wine only, much of it being made crémant by the *méthode champenoise*.

Wine from the local Savagnin grape may be used to top up white wines in the barrel, but is famed rather when used alone for *vin jaune*. This is produced in open, aged barrels where a yeast *flor* (similar to that in Sherry) develops on and covers the surface; it matures thus for a minimum of six years, becoming yellow as it oxidizes. It is an acquired taste, and is better with nuts or cheese than as an aperitif. The lengthy production process is, of course, reflected in the wine's relatively high price. The commune of Château-Chalon has its own AC for *vins jaunes*.

Sadly, *vin de paille*, a local specialty made by concentrating the grape juice before fermentation, is disappearing. The grapes are laid out in bunches on mats of straw (*paille*) to dry out for this purpose.

### BUGEY AND SEYSSEL

These two small districts lie south of the Côtes du Jura and across the mountains. Bugey VDQS makes some red and rosé wine, but the white wine from the Roussette (or Altesse) grape is worth noting and may be called Roussette du Bugey. Smaller is the AC district of Seyssel, making water-white still and sparkling wines, the latter by the *méthode champenoise*. The vineyards straddle the Rhône valley, where the soil is sandy clay with flints that impart a flavor to these excellent dry whites.

## SAVOIE

In the Savoie and Haute Savoie a few scattered vineyards may be found in the alluvial plain to the south of Lac Léman. AC Crépy, for white wine only, is made from the Chasselas grape and produces a light fruity wine. AC Vins de Savoie applies to the whole region for red, white and rosé wines. Most are white; the best are those from Château Ripaille, at Thornton-les-Bains, and some from south of Chambéry, using the Roussette grape. Here alpine herbs and fruits are often added to make the renowned dry Chambéry Vermouth.

## CÔTES DU RHÔNE

The most important region in the South of France is the Côtes du Rhône. The river runs between overhanging granite rocks due south from Lyon and broadens into a wider, flatter valley before reaching Avignon, 200km (125mi) to the south. The Rhône wines lack the subtlety of the clarets of Bordeaux or the Burgundies to their north, taking their character rather from the rugged terrain from which they spring: hence they are big, heady, sturdy wines, pungent and slow to mature.

With the important exceptions of AC Clairette de Die, a crémant wine made from the Clairette grape at Die on the river Drôme, and another crémant, AC St Péray, the wines of the Rhône are predominantly red, and may be recognized for strength, and to a certain extent for quality, by their labels. "AC Côtes du Rhône," given without qualification, requires 10.5% vol. alcohol. If "Côtes du Rhône" is followed by the name of a Department (as, for example, "Côtes du Rhône-Ardèche"), it is of *lesser* quality, and only 9.5% vol. alcohol is needed. However, when "Côtes du Rhône" is followed by the name of one of the three better communes, Cairanne, Chusclan or Laudun, not less than 12% vol. alcohol must be present, and these wines when mature will be excellent.

The climate varies from a temperate continental one in the north, with cold winters and warm summers, to a mediterranean climate, with cool winters and hot summers, in the south; according to Professor Philip Wagner there *are* only two viticultural seasons, winter and summer, in the south of France. From Montelimar southward the mistral brings cold air down from the glaciers of the Alps into the low plains; it can generate a wind force of 50-60km per hour (31-37mph)—a threat to all but the sturdiest vines, which accordingly are mostly trained wigwam-fashion on three poles. The steep slopes of the north require terracing and maintaining by hand. The soil in the north is typical of the surrounding valley—granite and schist, but with some iron and lime; in the south, clay and sand prevail, with outcrops of limestone.

## NORTHERN RHÔNE

Most northerly of the Rhône vineyards is AC Côte Rôtie, on its right bank; this vineyard reputedly makes the finest of all the Rhône reds. Heavy in tannin (like most wines from the north Rhône), the wine is astringent and heady with a strong bouquet. To moderate this power and to add finesse to the wine, white Viognier grapes are added to 80% Syrah grapes. The Rôtie wines are deep crimson in color, fading to "onion skin" during their long maturation of 10 to 20 years. The vineyard is divided into the Côte Brune, which has soil reddened with iron oxide, and the Côte Blonde, whose soil is pale with lime. The legend that this came about after an earlier *vigneron* gave one half to his brunet daughter and the other to his fair daughter is less than convincing.

A few kilometers south, at Condrieu, again on the right bank, Viognier is planted unblended to produce a fine white wine of considerable finesse. Château Grillet, a diminutive vineyard within Condrieu, has its own AC and must, by definition, be rare. It is a full-bodied white wine with much finesse. Hugh Johnson finds the wines of Condrieu superb for drinking young, although they have been claimed to last well.

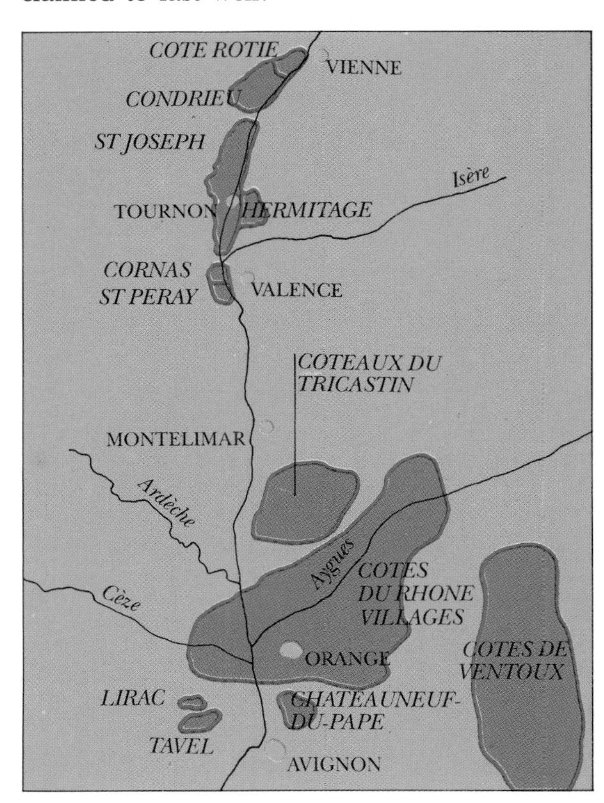


The Rhône valley *(above)* is divided by a vineless strip 40km (25mi) long, where the Drôme and Rhône meet. In the north, Condrieu produces fine whites, and Hermitage the red Syrahs.

The Château des Fines Roches vineyards in the huge Châteauneuf-du-Pape estate in the Rhône valley *(right)*. Fine Roches is the headquarters for several other properties on the estate. Seen here are the renowned large oval stones with the castle beyond.

Société Louis Mousset has nearly 250ha (615 acres) of estates in the Châteauneuf-du-Pape, where the Château des Fines Roches *(right)* is but one of their properties.

Hosing down a stainless-steel fermentation tank *(far right)* at the Château des Fines Roches. This young property is already held to produce one of the best Châteauneuf-du-Pape appellation wines.

At Hermitage La Chapelle, pressed wine is pumped into a lined concrete vat *(right)*. The thick mass of *vin de presse* will rest and clarify before being added to the *vin de goutte*.

A charge of grapes and their skins has been fermented *(center right)*, and both the running and pressed wines have been drawn off.

The *maître de chai* at the Hermitage La Chapelle property of the Paul Jaboulet Ainé company *(above)*. The *maître de chai* is responsible for all cellarwork, and is a man of many skills.

The vineyard at Hermitage La Chapelle. The vines have been trained in Gobelet fashion *(left)*, and as they grow older the foliage and grapes slowly move from the original planting position.

At the southern end of Tournon, the hill of Hermitage *(right)* overlooks the Rhône from the east. Young Syrah vines are each trained around a single stake to give protection from the strong mistral winds.

For some 50km (30mi) from Condrieu the commune of AC St Joseph stretches along the same bank of the river, with a number of vineyards producing variable red wines from the Syrah grape. These are fruity, with less "backbone" than those of Hermitage: they have a fine ruby color and are ready for drinking after four or five years in the bottle. White wines are made in lesser quantity: a number of grapes, including Roussanne and the productive Marsanne, give golden white wines that age well without too much oxidation; they are included in AC St Joseph.

On the left bank, opposite Tournon, are the vineyards of the famous Hermitage, almost surrounding the little town of Tain-l'Hermitage. Red wines made from unblended Syrah grapes, grown here on the granite soil, are full-bodied with vigor, yet have a delicacy and softness in maturity. They age well and their fragrance has been likened to that of iris-roots. About three-quarters of Hermitage wines are red. The vineyards cover over 300ha (740 acres) and are all south-facing, those at the top of the hill giving the best wines; here three white wines rank as first growths—Les Bressards, Le Méal and Les Greffieux. Ten second-growth white wines include Chante Alouette. These white wines, from Roussanne and Marsanne grapes grown on sand and schist, last even longer than the red wines, and are eminently drinkable at 10 years. They are fruity yet dry, and develop a golden tinge as they mature without oxidizing. The wines of the surrounding Crozes-Hermitage compare rather with those of St Joseph than with Hermitage growths; they are lighter in color and harder than Hermitage reds, and have a slight *goût de terroir*. Red-wine output far exceeds that of white wines.

On the right bank, below St Joseph and opposite the confluence of the river Isère with the Rhône, is Cornas, where AC wines heavy in tannin are made from the Syrah grape. The soil is granite sand heaped with beds of large stones. The larger and better known district of St Péray is next to Cornas. AC St Péray Mousseux is exclusively for a fine sparkling wine made by the *méthode champenoise*. This does not quite match the quality of the crémants from the Loire, but it is strong and has plenty of flavor.

### SOUTHERN RHÔNE

The vineyards of the southern Rhône produce a massive volume of wine each year, exceeding that of all Burgundy and not far short of all Bordeaux. As a consequence, vinification in the south is largely entrusted to huge cooperatives that have the equipment—and money—to convert and age the product. These vineyards are separated by 50km (31mi) from those of the North Rhône, and the mediterranean climate brings on strong wines for drinking young, almost all of them reds and rosés. Recently Rhône *primeur*, parallel in some respects to Beaujolais *primeur*, has become popular for daily drinking.

AC Côtes du Rhône is the basic appellation for the region, permitting up to 52hl/ha, with a minimum of 11% vol. alcohol. But many years of endeavor by the growers in four leading vineyards, Cairanne, Chusclan, Gigondas, and Laudun, eventually resulted in a red wine of up to 42hl/ha, with a minimum of 12% vol. alcohol. A number of communes followed their example and, subject to obligatory tasting, AC Côtes-du-Rhône-Villages was granted to them all in 1967. Eleven villages included in this AC lie in the hilly area known as les Baronnies, six of which are entitled to VDQS Haut Comtat, while five may add their names to AC Côtes du Rhône. One of the original villages, Gigondas, now has its own AC for red and rosé wines, made with a maximum of 65% Grenache blended with other Côtes-du-Rhône grapes; the most important black vines in the southern region are Carignan, Cinsault, Mourvèdre and Picpoul.

Just north of these villages is AC Coteaux de Tricastin, a district with 12 villages making red wine, and in the hills to its west is Côtes de Vivarais VDQS for red and rosé wines. Here five villages may add their name if their wine has 11% vol. alcohol instead of 10%. Some 60 villages on the slopes of Mont Ventoux enjoy AC Côtes de Ventoux for light red and rosé wines from the Grenache and Carignan vines.

In 1309 Pope Clement V set up his court at Avignon. He is best remembered, in secular terms, as the first occupant of Châteauneuf-du-Pape, a castle on the Rhône between Avignon and Orange. The wines predated the Romans and are certainly the best known from the Rhône; they remain worthy of their reputation. At 12% vol. alcohol the wines are full-bodied but deceptively soft. The vineyard is renowned for the large stones which store heat from the sun. Eight grapes are used in combination: 40-60% Grenache, giving finesse and mellowness; 10-30 % Syrah for strength, color and bouquet; 20% Cinsault, Mourvèdre or Vaccarèse for viscosity; and 10% Clairette, Terret or Picpoul for volume and lightness.

Another famous name here is Tavel, opposite Châteauneuf on the Rhône, where AC rosé wines from the Grenache are vinified with Clairette and Bourboulenc to produce an astringent rosé of minimum 11% vol. alcohol, although often nearer 13%. To the north of Tavel lies AC Lirac, where the red wine is superior to the rosé and white wines are also produced.

## PROVENCE

Provence is the most easterly of the three French wine regions which blanket the Mediterranean coast. In the center is Languedoc, and running down to the Spanish border is Roussillon: Languedoc and Roussillon are also known collectively as the Midi. In many ways Provence

is an extension of the southern Rhône region, starting south of Avignon, and running east from the Rhône to the Italian border, hemmed in by mountains and sea. Sand and granite with outcrops of limestone cover the region. Except where mechanical harvesting machines have necessitated vine-training on wires by the Guyot method, bush cultivation is standard. This is because the mistral is a particular danger in Provence. High vines prepared for the harvesting machines have to be planted in line with the prevailing wind.

There are eight districts in the region, four having their own ACs. The smallest, AC Palette, close by Aix-en-Provence, has only one vineyard, Château Simone. Here the *méthode ancienne* is rigorously adhered to: 20 traditional grapes in the classic proportions are processed under ancient conditions, with the must and wine never touching metal. During three years' maturation in hogsheads the wine is blended and racked, and before bottling it is fined with casein. The resulting wine is full and fruity, deep in color, and will keep for 30 or 40 years. AC Palette is expensive but worth the money.

Nearer Marseilles is AC Cassis, producing a good white wine, slightly sweet and with a high alcohol content, from Clairette, Ugni Blanc and Oeillade grapes. AC Bandol, east of Cassis, produces mostly red wines, light in color though heavy in alcohol and having a bouquet of violets. They are said to resemble Bordeaux rather than Rhône wines. AC Bellet, almost 100km (62mi) to the east, is tucked in the Alpine valleys behind the Côte d'Azur. Unspectacular red, white and rosé wines are made here from local grape varieties.

## VDQS DISTRICTS

Côtes-de-Provence is contained between the river Argens, to its north, and the coast from Toulon to St Raphael, with a northwesterly bulge towards Aix; the area should not be confused with the more important VDQS Coteaux d'Aix-en-Provence, which lies in a triangle between Avignon, Marseilles and Aix. Côtes-de-Provence produces an excellent rosé made from a blend of Carignan, Cinsault and Grenache grapes, in addition to red wines.

The Coteaux d'Aix-en-Provence makes principally a good red wine, at one time with the Carignan grape alone but latterly with the Cabernet Sauvignon added to give more finesse and bouquet to a strong wine. Two small districts northeast of the Coteaux are Côtes-de-Lubéron and Coteaux de Pierrevert. The former produces sound red, white and rosé wines in the Rhône tradition, and the latter, from a group of 40 villages, produces a fresh white wine from Ugni Blanc and Clairette grapes.

COTES DU LUBERON
COTEAUX DE PIERREVERT
BELLET
Durance
Verdon
NICE
CANNES
AIX
CASSIS
MARSEILLE
COTES DE PROVENCE
TOULON
BANDOL
COTEAUX D'AIX EN PROVENCE

The Provence wine region *(above)* blankets France's Mediterranean coast from the mouth of the Rhône to the Italian border: it is bounded in the north by the valleys of the Durance and its tributaries and, above Nice, by those bordering the Estéron, Var and Vésubie. Several good VDQS districts (the most important is Coteaux d'Aix-en-Provence) produce quality white, rosé and red wines.

La Gaude, standing above Cannes *(above right)*, is reputed to have been named by Caesar himself. When tasting the local wine he is alleged to have smacked his lips saying, *"Gaudeamus."*

The *paysage de Provence (right)*. Most wine from this region is fresh, clean, palatable rosé.

The *village perché* of Saignon *(above)*, towering on the cliffs above the Provence coastline of the Mediterranean.

The vineyards of the hilly country south of the Provence Alps are watered by rivers flowing to the southwest *(right)*.

# LANGUEDOC

Languedoc, like Roussillon, has a variety of different soil conditions that succeed in varying the wines noticeably. The river valleys with their rich soils are planted with massive vineyards, previously of Aramon vines; these are latterly being replaced with Carignan. The plains, of clay over gravel (which surfaces in large pebbles), produce quality wines from Carignan, Grenache and Picpoul grapes. The soil in the hills and moorland is limestone or schist under a thin topsoil, and is ideal for vines. The sedimentary igneous sand from the Rhône has formed dunes along the coast that need fertilizing to be suitable for wine-making, but this can be and is being done. While *Vitis vinifera* grows happily in this sand, the *Phylloxera* louse cannot penetrate it.

There are three AC districts in Languedoc (from "langue d'oc," a group of medieval French dialects; a few enthusiasts in the area still use the archaic "oc" instead of "oui"). AC Clairette de Bellegarde, from within the Costières du Gard just west of the Rhône, is a golden wine from the Clairette grape, well perfumed and often used as base wine for Vermouth. AC Clairette du Languedoc, found to the west of here, is a sweet white wine developing "rancio"—an acquired taste. AC Fitou, once called Corbières-Maritimes, produces full red wines, dark, pungent and heady, that must have 75% Carignan and Grenache grapes in the blend. Fitou, a district of nine communes, makes one of the best wines to be found in the whole of the Midi.

Several VDQS districts produce sound, drinkable wines—mainly red—that vary considerably from district to district. Costières du Gard VDQS, southwest of Avignon, produces rugged red wines, redolent of the stony hillside where they are made; a little white and rosé wine is also produced. The main grapes are Mourvèdre, Terret Noir and Grenache. Coteaux du Languedoc VDQS contains some 75 villages in the area between Nimes and Narbonne in the Cévennes. Though red, white

The mistral, cold air from the Alps, sweeps down into the plains of Provence, gathering speeds of up to 60kph (37½mph). For protection, vines are trained in bush fashion *(below)*.

and rosé wines are made, few of the villages are licensed to produce more than two of them. Fragrant red wines come from St Chinian, the principal subdistrict. Minervois and Corbières VDQSs centre on Lézignan-Corbières. The red wine of Minervois is paler and has more finesse than the reds of Corbières; the latter start with a bitterness that goes with age.

## ROUSSILLON

The corner of France next to the Spanish border is its hottest, so that here grapes are chosen primarily for their sweetness. Though red, white and rosé wines are made in Roussillon, they are regarded as unimportant compared with the large production of Vins-Doux-Naturel and Vins-de-Liqueur—fortified wines that are dealt with in Chapter 18 (see page 328).

The region of Roussillon includes the districts of Banyuls, Côtes d'Agly, Côtes du Roussillon, Maury, and Rivesaltes in the Departments of Pyrénees-Orientales and Aude. All make white wines, AC Maury using Grenache and others mostly the Muscat, which gives a flavor of sultana raisins. The outstanding wine of the region is AC Collioure from the Spanish border, a robust red wine blended mostly from Mourvèdre, Grenache Noir and Carignan grapes. Collioure obtained its AC in 1949. Côtes du Roussillon, Caramany and Latour-de-France, nearer the Cévennes, obtained their appellations in 1977.

At Limoux, in the limestone hills of the upper Aude river, sparkling wines are made as AC Blanquette de Limoux. Originally the Blanquette (or Mauzac) grape was used exclusively, but recent changes in AC rules permit Chardonnay and Chenin grapes to be used, taking longer to mature but giving a longer life to the wine, which is made by the *méthode champenoise*. The Mauzac grape is used for AC Vin de Blanquette, a semi-sparkling wine made by the *méthode rural*: the wine is bottled before the first fermentation is complete, so that a slight sparkle without sedimentation results in the bottle. AC Limoux is delimited for a small quantity of white wine, also from the Mauzac grape.

## VAL DE LOIRE

The Loire, 1,020km (634mi) in length, is the longest river in France. From its source in the Cévennes the stripling river flows north for about 300km (190mi) to Nevers before reaching fertile plains which are watered also by many tributaries, including the Cher, Indre, Vienne, Layon, and Sèvre. It is along the Loire from the Bay of Biscay to Nevers, and along these tributaries, that the four wine districts of the Loire are based.

### NANTAIS

The vineyards here are nearly all devoted to white-wine production; they border the Loire almost to its mouth opposite St Nazaire, and stretch up-river to within 30km (19mi) of Angers. In the west, on a bed of clay over granite and helped by a mild climate, the Muscadet grape ripens in mid-September, giving its name to the district and the wine made exclusively from it. Having a low natural acidity, the new wine is left in barrels on its sediment (*sur lie*) after fermentation, and is racked into bottles without fining in late March or April. The resulting wine can vary from dry and sharp to a more fruity and full flavor, but the percentage volume of alcohol is low. Exceptionally, therefore, and perhaps wisely, AC Muscadet decrees a minimum degree of alcohol for each vintage.

Muscadet is superb with a number of seafood dishes, and is best drunk young, although some producers are now allowing longer periods of maturation to create a longer-lasting wine. Within the area of the general appellation are two superior ACs, Muscadet-des-Coteaux-de-la-Loire, spanning the river, and Muscadet-de-Sèvre-et-Maine, a little lower downstream, opposite Nantes; the latter produces the best of the Nantais wine.

In the Nantais are the extensive vineyards of Gros-Plant-du-Pays-Nantais VDQS, south of Nantes, where a sharp and fresh white wine is made from the Gros Plant (Folle Blanche) grape; and Coteaux d'Ancenis VDQS, a small strip along the north bank of the Loire within the Coteaux-de-la-Loire, making red and rosé wines, from Gamay and Cabernet Sauvignon, together with a little white wine from the Chenin Blanc.

### ANJOU-SAUMUR

The vineyards of this district lie south of the Loire—with the single exception of Anjou-Coteaux-de-la-Loire, which spans the river west of Angers. The soil here turns from schist in the west to limestone in the east; famous underground caves have been quarried in this limestone, which is also ideal for the delicious white wines of Saumur—both still and crémant. AC Anjou covers the whole district, for both white and red wines. The whites are mainly from the Chenin Blanc (locally Pinot de la Loire), with a little Chardonnay or Sauvignon and Pineau d'Aunis. Red wine from the Gamay has its own AC Anjou-Gamay.

Rosé wines made from Cabernet grapes alone have AC Cabernet-d'Anjou-Rosé or AC Cabernet-de-Saumur-Rosé, according to subdistrict. These rosés are finer and sweeter than AC Rosé-d'Anjou, which is made from Cabernet Franc and Cabernet Sauvignon, with the addition of Pinot d'Aunis, Gamay, Cot, and Groslot, and is a medium-dry rosé, light pink in color.

AC Anjou-Coteaux-de-la-Loire, mainly north

of the river, makes dry and medium-dry white wines with considerable finesse from the Chenin Blanc grape. The little commune of Savennières, contained in Anjou-Coteaux-de-la-Loire, produces a white wine of superior quality, owing much of its flavor to a bank of volcanic debris from the Massif Central: the four vineyard slopes are Château d'Epire, Clos-du-Papillon, Coulée de Serrant and La-Roche-aux-Moines.

Two tributaries run into the Loire opposite Angers, the Layon and Aubance, on the sides of which vines are grown. Each has its AC—Coteaux-du-Layon and Coteaux-de-l'Aubance. Here sweeter white wines than those of Savennières are produced. In the Layon vineyards of Quarts-de-Chaume and Bonnezeaux, *pourriture noble* occurs so that fine sweet wines matching those of Sauternes result.

Saumur, 40km (25mi) east of Angers, has limestone soil which contributes to fine still and sparkling AC wines. Here also is AC Saumur-Champigny, which specifically covers robust, full-red wines with a heavy bouquet made from Cabernet grapes.

## TOURAINE

The vineyards of Touraine are far enough from the sea for the climate to change subtly from maritime towards continental, and the ability of the soil to store heat becomes increasingly important. In the better districts clay and limestone cover a tufa chalk subsoil; the tufa is a lime, boiled by volcanic action, which has high mineral content and holds water—an ideal soil for the needs of Touraine. As a bonus, the tufa provides natural caves for the wine cellars.

The general delimited area of Touraine produces red, white, rosé, semi-sparkling and sparkling AC wines in a vineyard area of nearly 50,000ha (120,000 acres); its production approaches 10 million hectoliters of wine annually, including some internationally known varieties. Best of them is the white Vouvray from the Chenin Blanc grape, produced in a small district north of the Loire above Tours. Vouvray is often made crémant (which implies the *méthode champenoise*), but otherwise reaches the market as a full though delicate dry still wine, said to have a taste of quince, and aging quite rapidly. On the southern bank of the Loire, at Montlouis, similar wines but somewhat lighter in character are made, also from the Chenin Blanc grape.

The red wines of Touraine—they are the best reds produced on the Loire—come from the eastern districts of AC Bourgueil, to the north of the Loire, and AC Chinon to its south, surrounding the town of Chinon. The famous commune of AC St Nicholas-de-Bourgueil produces the best of these reds from the Cabernet Franc grape; they have a distinct raspberry taste and age well, although they may also be drunk young. The wines from Chinon, a district divided by the river Vienne, are lighter and have a perfume of violets.

From the Chenin Blanc grape comes the superb sparkling Saumur wine of the Loire, made by the *méthode champenoise*. The vital task of *remuage* is here performed manually by the expert *remueur*, who can turn up to 30,000 bottles in one day.

## LOIR

The Coteaux du Loir lie 25km (15½mi) to the north of Tours, outside the delimited Touraine district (this is le Loir, a tributary, flowing into la Loire at Angers). Notable here is AC Jasnières, made from the Chenin and Pineau d'Aunis grapes to give a fruity dry white wine.

## CENTRAL VINEYARDS

Two subdistricts of this isolated region share the best reputation: they are Pouilly-sur-Loire and Sancerre. Pouilly borders the right bank, and opposite is Sancerre, running down to the left bank from the chalky Collines du Sancerrois; both are 40km (25mi) north of Nevers. Making up the region are three other districts running in a line a little south of due west from Sancerre; they are Meneton-Salon, Quincy and Reuilly, the most westerly.

Both Pouilly and Sancerre have concentrated on the Sauvignon Blanc grape for their white wines, described as spicy and green, slightly smoky, and with a distinct aroma of gunflint; this aroma has added the "fumé" to the AC Pouilly-Blanc-Fumé (not to be confused with AC Pouilly-Fuissé, named for the Mâconnais village). The international reputation of these Loire-style wines has caused some Bordeaux wine-producers to concentrate more on the Sauvignon rather than blending it with the Semillon grape. AC Pouilly-Blanc-Fumé ages within one to two years whereas the stronger AC Sancerre needs three. AC Pouilly-sur-Loire is permitted for wines made with a proportion of the more neutral Chasselas grape added giving a pale wine for early consumption.

Sancerre produces also red and rosé wines from Pinot Noir grapes; these are good although they are thinner than those from southern France and do not last so well.

The AC districts of Quincy, on the Cher, and Reuilly, on the Arnon, produce pleasant white wines from the Sauvignon grape; although strong in alcohol and with a fine bouquet, they do not age satisfactorily. Good reds and rosés are produced from the Pinot Noir on a small scale at Reuilly and Meneton-Salon; in fact, one property at Meneton-Salon regularly takes gold medals for its dry rosés. These wines reach Paris, but rarely leave France.

# CHAMPAGNE

Here, in the most northerly wine region of France, everything is different. Within the delimited 25,000ha (62,000 acres) of AC Champagne there are over 5,000 vineyards, yet relatively few growers vinify their grapes. Instead they sell them mostly to the "Houses" (internationally known shipping firms who also own one-fifth of the vineyard area) or to cooperatives, who make and blend the wines. Even the method of pricing the grapes is unique.

Since there is an obvious conflict of interest between seller and buyer, a Comité Interprofessionel du Vin de Champagne (CIVC) was set up in 1942 to lay down a price per tonne for grapes on a sliding scale related to quality. The scale runs down from a quality rating of 100% to one of 75% for individual growths within the main districts of Montagne de Reims, the Marne Valley, and Côte des Blancs. One price is fixed for the best growths, which are given 100% rating, and other prices are calculated as percentages of this. Separate ratings for black and white grapes may be changed from year to year by the CIVC, and a producer's wine is rated for quality by the loaded average rating of the grapes used. There are ten 100% ratings for black grapes (four in Montagne de Reims and six in the Marne Valley), and three for white grapes (one in Montagne de Reims and two in the Côte des Blancs).

Grape varieties are controlled and restricted to two black grapes—Pinot Noir and Pinot Meunier—and two white—Chardonnay and the Petit Meslier (the latter is not so much in use); Pinot Noir is early-ripening and susceptible to frost, while Pinot Meunier compensates as a late-ripener; Chardonnay bears heavier crops

A bunch of Pinot Noir *(below right)*, the classic grape of Champagne, grown at Sillery.

Chardonnay grapes *(below far right)* from the Côte des Blancs. Blanc de Blancs, from a *cuvée* of Chardonnay grapes only, has more subtlety and less firmness than traditional Champagne.

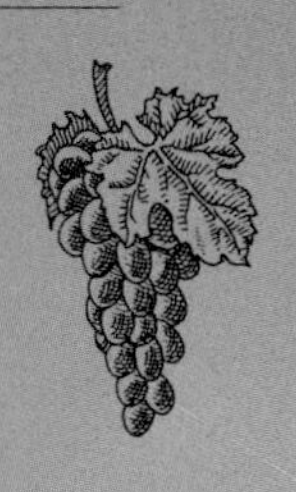

Under the Montagne de Reims is a catacomb of cellars in which much of the production and maturation of Champagne is done. Here a Gallo-Roman chalk cave is used by Veuve Clicquot-Ponsardin to store Champagne after the first fermentation *(left)*. In the Clicquot cellars are some 25 million bottles, representing four years' production.

Some 70% of the grapes used for the annual production of Bollinger Champagne come from their own 140ha (345 acres) of vineyards *(main picture)*, mainly above Ay on the Montagne de Reims. These vineyards of Pinot Noir vines are rated as a 99% growth.

This wine, being nosed in the Krug cellars, is not a finished Champagne but a sample of a blending wine or taken from an in-house experiment. Henri, of the fifth generation of Krugs, is in charge of the cellars.

than Pinot Noir and ripens later, but dislikes frost even more. A third white grape, the Arbanne, is permitted in the delimited vineyards of the river Aube, to the south.

The thin soil surface is mostly a mixture of silica and clay which drains well and consequently dries out and packs down hard. The subsoil is Kimmeridge chalk, in depth sufficient not only to water the vines but to provide caves for the processing and storage of Champagne; the temperature some 30m (100ft) below ground is constant at 4°C (39°F), which is ideal for these purposes. One of the Houses is said to own 17.5km (11mi) of these caves. Cold winters are experienced between the 49th and 50th parallels, but long summers with an average temperature of 10°C (50°F) are just sufficient to bring the grapes to full ripeness. The chalk retains the sun's heat, particularly in the many white limestone pebbles that break through the surface.

Viticulture in Champagne has a unique feature, for the thin surface soil needs to be topped up every three or five years, and in the years between actually requires manure to provide nitrogen. The vines are planted about halfway up on the so-called Montagne de Reims, which varies in height from only 300m to 600m (1,000-2,000ft). Most of the vineyards face south or southeast, but those in the Côte des Blancs face east, and Verzeney, a 100% growth, faces north. Pruning—which must be done by one of three methods, the Taille Chablis, Cordon de Royat, or Guyot (either Simple or Double)—takes place from March into April. The cool damp climate brings pests and diseases, and the Chardonnay vine is especially susceptible to *pourriture gris*; frequent spraying is therefore necessary.

The date of harvest can vary from early September to early October, and the permitted yield per hectare is fixed each year according to the fulness of the crop: it may be in the region of 8,000kg/ha (7,000 lb/acre). The vaslin press now used in Champagne varies in volume, but the law says that, from 150kg (330 lb) of grapes, 100 l (26½ gal) of must may be used for making Champagne. The six pressings from that weight give the quantities of must shown in the table. In addition, 10-12 l (2⅔-3¼ gal) of juice (*rebêche*) is pressed for fermentation and distillation for industry. The pomace (pulpy residue) is then processed for the production of eau-de-vie (see pp. *41*, 340.) The better Houses use only the Cuvée and sell the Tailles to smaller converters.

|  |  |
|---|---|
| 1st pressing: 38 l (10 gal) | Vin de Cuvée 75 l (20 gal) |
| 2nd pressing: 22 l (5¾ gal) | |
| 3rd pressing: 15 l (4 gal) | |
| 4th pressing: 8 l (2 gal) | Premières Tailles, 15 l (4 gal) |
| 5th pressing: 7 l (1¾ gal) | |
| 6th pressing: 10 l (2⅔ gal) | Deuxièmes Tailles, 10 l (2⅔ gal) |

A small amount of sulfur dioxide ($SO_2$), a strong oxidant, is added to the juice running from the press; this kills wild yeasts and eliminates any color from the black grapeskins. Then, after the first fermentation, which must produce 9.5% vol. alcohol, there follows the blending of wines from different vineyards. The discovery of this process is attributed to Dom Pérignon, the cellar-master of Hauvilliers some 300 years ago, who realized that the characteristics of wines from different districts were essential to the perfection of the whole—the Montagne giving vinosity and "backbone" to Champagne, the Valée giving it fruit and body, and the Côte des Blancs giving it elegance and finesse.

At this stage, while the wines remain still, the vital question of declaring a vintage must be resolved. This requires keen judgment, for to warrant a vintage year there must be sufficient wine of supreme quality, possibly including the best wine of former years.

Before bottling the blend of still wines, *liqueur de tirage* (cultivated yeasts and sugar) is added and mixed with it in tanks containing paddles. The mixture is then bottled and corked with special crown corks secured with clips (*agrafes*) in preparation for its secondary or malolactic fermentation, during which carbon dioxide ($CO_2$) produced by chemical reaction is dissolved in the wine, making it sparkling. The bottles are then inverted in a *pupitre* and slowly turned and shaken in the process of *remuage* (developed by the Widow Cliquot in about 1800); this gradually brings the sediment down onto the cork. The task of the *remueur* is painstaking and seemingly endless—he turns some 30,000 bottles a day—but the process is now being increasingly mechanized by sizable machines that simulate the hand operation.

After *remuage* the bottles are taken carefully to be stacked *en masse*, the neck of each upturned bottle standing in the hollowed bottom of the one below it. Here the wine ages, "sleeping" as it matures until required; the minimum period of maturation for Champagne is three years.

Eventually the sediment on the cork has to be removed: the bottles are carefully placed in a bath of chilled brine, so that only the wine in the neck of the bottle, containing the sediment,

Close-up of one of the traditional 205-liter (54 gal) oak casks in which all fermentation of Krug Champagne still takes place. Krug specialize in exquisite Grande Cuvée non-vintage Champagne blended from up to 10 vintages and 25 growths.

is frozen. The *degorgeur* must then swiftly but carefully remove the cork so that the ice pellet is ejected by the pressure within the bottle; however great the *degorgeur*'s skill some wine is inevitably lost, and the bottle is replenished with a sweetening *dosage* before recorking and muzzling. Because of the high cost of cork today, Champagne corks are composite, being made mainly of cork chips; but three discs must be glued to the end inserted into the bottle, and the word "Champagne" must then be branded on this end, by law. The side of the cork is waxed for ease of extraction.

The sale of Champagne now runs to nearly 200 million bottles every year, of which a little under two-thirds goes through the hands of merchants, the rest being marketed direct by growers and their cooperatives. Overall, two-thirds of the volume is consumed in France and one-third is exported. The growers have increased their share of the home market slowly but steadily, and this has not only created a stock shortage for export among the great Houses of Champagne, but has pushed the price of grapes up by over 400% in the last 10 years. These two factors have combined to let other French sparkling wines encroach on Champagne's export markets.

During their long history the great Houses of Champagne have survived wars as well as political and national crises—many, including Cliquot, Lanson, Möet & Chandon, Louis Roederer, and Ruinart being established before the French Revolution. The cellars of other great shippers today include Bollinger (at Ay), Perrier-Jouet, and Pol Roger (at Eperney) and Heidseck-Monopole, Charles Heidseck, Mumm, Pommery & Greno, and the incomparable Krug (at Reims).

Subject to the content and quantity of *dosage* added by the *degorgeur*, which may be varied to meet the taste of individual export markets, the styles reaching the consumer are usually marked *Brut* (very dry), *Extra Dry* (dry), *Sec* (slightly sweet), *Demi-Sec* (sweet) and *Doux* (very sweet). Care should be taken to drink Champagne at the right temperature, between 8° and 12°C (46-54°F). If you drink it too cold, there will be noticeably fewer bubbles in the glass; this means that there is excess $CO_2$ still dissolved in the wine—which $CO_2$ will be discomfortingly released inside you.

Not all the wine of the Champagne region goes on after its first fermentation to produce sparkling wine. Much is appropriated for the production of still wines. Among these is AC Rosé-des-Riceys, made from the Pinot Noir in the district of Aube, part of the delimited area for AC Champagne. From the Montagne de Reims comes the white wine of Sillery and the red wine of Bouzy, now sold as AC Coteaux Champenois. The red wine of Bouzy is blended with white wine to make a basic rosé for processing into pink Champagne. It is the *only* rosé in the EEC that may be made by blending red and white wines.

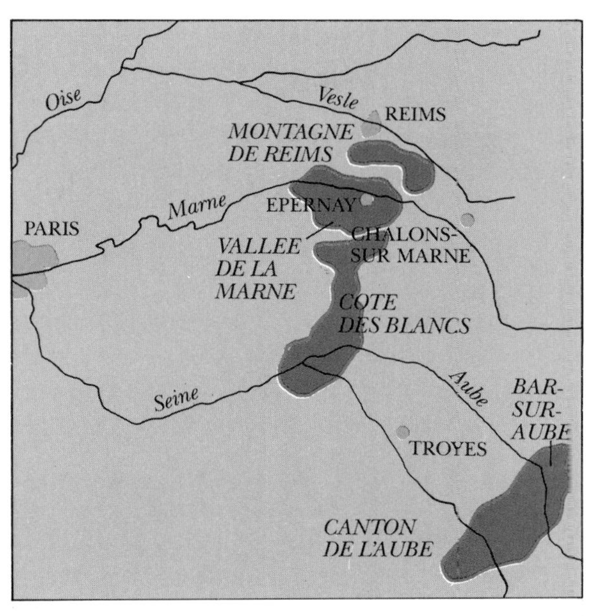


The Champagne region *(left)* has three main districts: Montagne de Reims, Vallée de la Marne, and Côte des Blancs. The vineyards of the Montagne give vinosity and backbone to the blend; those of the Vallée give fruit and body; those of the Côte give finesse and elegance. Wine from the Département of the Aube to the south is also admissible in the blends for Champagne.

This part of the Ruinart caves under the Montagne de Reims *(above)* has been hollowed out in pyramid shapes. Ruinarts make lighter Champagnes once appreciated by Napoleon's Josephine.

Two types of container ready for the harvest *(left)* in Krug's vineyards at Ay and Le Mesnil. The smaller is for grapes as they are cut from the vine, and the larger for collection of the grapes from individual pickers before transportation to the *chai*.

# ALSACE

The two vineyards of Schlumberger in the Haut-Rhin are planted with five different vines: 35% Gewürztraminer, 30% Riesling, and a total of 35% Sylvaner, Pinot Blanc and Chasselas; *(below)* is a ripe bunch of Gewürztraminer.

Bunches of Riesling grapes *(below right)* adopt a symmetrical shape if given space on the vine to do so. Wines from the Riesling are deeply satisfying: the French ones are drier than the equally attractive Rieslings from Germany.

The region of Alsace has a fairy-tale atmosphere, attributable largely to its natural beauty and its medieval architecture. Between the Vosges mountains to the west and the Rhine valley to the east, such is the calm and charm of Alsace that it is hard to credit the wars and political crises that it has weathered unscathed during the last 100 years. Beneath this romantic veneer, beautiful crisp white wines are made today in a modern and uncomplicated way. Historically, these wines were shipped down the Rhine to add body and quantity to the wines of Germany but, since World War II, Alsatian wines have come into their own and gained a worthy reputation all over the world.

The vineyards of Alsace are concentrated along a narrow 110km (69mi) strip halfway between the Vosges mountains and the Rhine. The vineyards are divided between the Departments of the Haut-Rhin and Bas-Rhin, the better properties surrounding Colmar in Haut-Rhin and the picturesque township of Riquewihr, its center. The vineyards are watered by little tributaries running down from the mountains to join the river Ill, which itself runs into the Rhine north of Strasbourg. The soil is a mixture of limestone and silica under a surface of loess. The mountains protect the vineyards from rain for long periods, and shelter them from westerly winds. The climate is essentially continental, with cold winters and hot summers.

There are six noble vines of Alsace, and they are doubly important as the wines are marketed with these grape names, rather than with the name of a village or commune. Riesling (the most mispronounced wine name of all—it should be pronounced "rees-ling") is *the* grape of Alsace, giving wines described as strong yet subtle and gentle; then comes the Gewürz-

The village of Riquewihr *(main picture)* is *the* beauty spot of Alsace. Hugels have been making wine here for almost 250 years; their vineyards look down on the village.

These freshly picked Gewürztraminer grapes on their way to the Hugels *chai (inset left)* have already been tested for sugar and labeled accordingly.

The cellar-master at Hugels *(inset center)* locked in concentration as he deals with records and administrative matters.

This slightly macabre spigot *(inset right)* allows wine to be drawn from a wooden fermentation vat at Hugels' Riquewihr winery. The wine next enters casks that are lined with tartrate crystals to "seed" tartrate-precipitation.

Vineyards in the Haut-Rhin looking south *(far left)*, lie in the rainshadow of the Vosges mountains and have a perfect position for wine-production.

Alsace is virtually one big vineyard, and space is at a premium. The vineyards of Schlumberger *(left)* at Guebwiller run up the foothills of the Vosges mountains at an alarming angle. Viniculture is made possible by an intricate terracing pattern plus much manual labor.

traminer, for clean dry wines which have a fruity and spicy flavor. The four other noble grapes are Pinot Gris (Tokay d'Alsace), Muscat, Pinot Blanc, and Sylvaner, which has the largest production. In addition to the noble grapes there are two grapes used for blending: never mentioned on the label, these are the Chasselas and Knipperlé.

AC Alsace or AC Vin d'Alsace may be used to describe wines made from any permitted grape variety or from a blend of them, with a maximum crop of 100hl/ha. If a grape is stated on the label, the wine must be 100% from Alsace and 100% from the named grape; it must also have a minimum of 8.5% vol. alcohol. AC Alsace Grands Crus wines follow similar disciplines, but must have 10% vol. alcohol for Riesling or Muscat, and 11% for Gewürztraminer or Pinot Gris, and a maximum crop of 70hl/ha. When Grands Crus labels give the name of a vineyard, the grapes must all come from that vineyard. Wines made by blending noble grapes may use AC Alsace Edelzwicker, but the varieties used may not be mentioned on the label.

In Alsace the grape juice may be artificially sweetened with dry sugar before fermentation, to guarantee a minimum of 11% vol. alcohol. Alsace Crémant was authorized in 1976 for wine made by a secondary fermentation in the bottle at a lower pressure than AC Mousseux wines. By the summer of 1985 no Grands Crus for individual vineyards had been granted under the appellation system in Alsace, although this had been discussed.

There are about 24 large estates, but the average vineyard size is little over one hectare (2½ acres), and there are over 9,000 of them. The small grower may be "attached" to a large property which may vinify for him or absorb his crop into its own blends. Alternatively, he may sell into one of the great cooperatives, such as the massive Union Vinicole Divinal, which markets 500,000 cases of wines each year.

Hugel et Fils announce their presence in Riquewihr with this delicate metal hanging sign *(above)* which shows their crest and the date of their foundation. The family have been making wines in Riquewihr since 1639, and today three brothers, Jean, André and Georges, control the business. 80% of their annual sale of 100,000 cases is exported.

The Hugels headquarters *(left)* is on the main street at Riquewihr. The reference to "grands vins" is fully justified: they are late-gathered wines ranging through Regular, Cuvée Tradition, Réserve Personnelle and Vendage Tardive (a big sweet wine) to the very sweet Sélection des Grains Nobles, which is made only in exceptional years.

Picking of the Gewürztraminer grapes *(above)* has just begun in 8ha (19¾ acres) of Hugels' vineyards in the Sporen. These grapes are converted to wine that conforms to the house-style of full, supple wines, fermented well towards dryness, although not fully. Hugels' own plantings are 47% Gewürztraminer, 46% Riesling, 4% Pinot Gris and 3% Muscat.

Bernard Trimbach noses a sample of Riesling *(right)* taken from a maturation tank. Each wine variety is produced by the Trimbachs at three quality levels: vintage (standard level), Réserve, and Réserve Personnelle (the two latter are equivalent to the lower German *Prädikaten* for sweetness). Total annual production is about 65,000 cases, of which 60% are exported.

The headquarters of the family *domaine* and *negoçiant* house of F. E. Trimbach *(below right)* at Ribeauvillé. Trimbachs' pride is their Hunawihr Riesling Clos St-Hune; equally fine is their Gewürztraminer Cuvée des Seigneurs de Ribeaupierre.

The firm of F. E. Trimbach has been trading since 1626, and has a fine reputation for delicate dry wines. They have 12ha (29½ acres) of vines *(top)* at Ribeauvillé (their trading center), Hunawihr and Bergheim, and lease some 15ha (37 acres) in Riquewihr and Mittelwihr; all these plantings are in the Haut-Rhin.

A row of wooden fermentation vats in the Trimbach cellars *(above)* at Ribeauvillé. In front of them and lower down is a row of open *cuves* that will be used for blending the wines as soon as fermentation is complete.

# ITALY

## The Wines of Northern Italy ♦ The Wines of Central Italy
## The Wines of Southern Italy ♦ Sicilia and Sardegna

The average consumption of wine by the Italians—man, woman and child—amounts to about 150 bottles a year, and this accounts for 80% of the country's wine production. Grapes in Italy are grown wherever the land is habitable, and innumerable small growers, each owning one-third of a hectare (¾ acre) or less, produce wine for their own and purely local consumption. In the cities, however, Italians drink the quality wines of Italy. All told, less than 20% of Italian wine is available for export, mostly to Germany but also to France, Switzerland, the USA and the UK. "Strengthening" wines from southern Italy make up a considerable proportion of the wine exported to Germany and France to give body to EEC table wines. Altogether Italy produces between 70 and 80 million hl of wine in an average year, usually exceeding the production of France: no other country competes for the greatest annual production in the world—a somewhat doubtful honor.

Italy, stretching from latitudes 37° to 47° North, is one enormous fragmented vineyard *(below)*; vines grow wherever the rugged mountains permit, from the French Alps and Dolomites in the north down the whole range of the Apennines to the toe of Calabria, in the south.

Italy is about 1,100km (685mi) in length and averages 200km (125mi) in width; the climate changes from continental in the north—where cold winters followed by long hot summers give subtle wines—to mediterranean in central and southern Italy—where winters are warm (except high in the Apennines) and the summers are hot and humid, producing beefy wines with high alcohol content.

Despite the popularity of wine during Italy's long classical history, her wine industry was ragged and fragmentary through the centuries thereafter until the formation of the *consorzio* system in the early 1930s, when some semblance of order began to prevail. Royal Decree proclaimed the constitution of each *consorzio*, giving power to control production in specified districts; but each constitution differed and the system was voluntary, so that many districts had no *consorzio*; each made its own rules determining the boundaries of delimited areas, the permitted vines and the minimum alcoholic strengths. The *consorzi* were also made responsible for implementation of government regulations affecting imports and exports. The system worked only some of the time, but it was a start toward law and order.

In July 1963, the national control of the wine industry according to EEC principles was enforced by the Italian Government, and categories of Denominazione d'Origine were granted by the Ministry of Agriculture for wines of delimited areas made under specified conditions. The categories are Denominazione d'Origine Controllata (DOC) and Denominazione d'Origine Controllata e Garantita (DOCG). (A third, Denominazione d'Origine Semplici, has already been abandoned.) DOCG applies only to a DOC wine bearing a government seal of guarantee, bottled in the delimited area in containers holding less than five liters (1⅓ gal). So far, only a few DOCGs have been

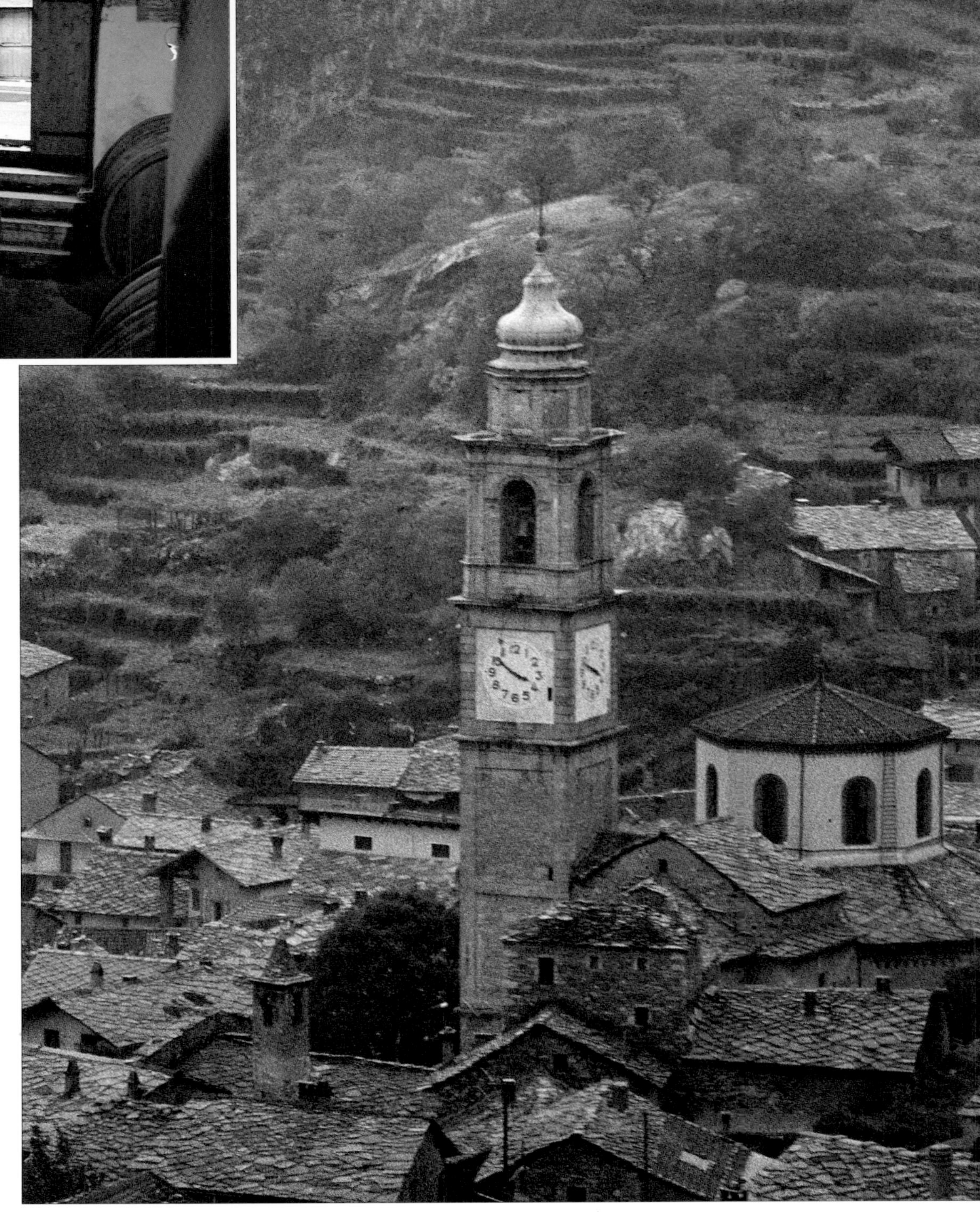

The Nebbiolo *(top)* is the most prolific grape of Piemonte: it is the source of several important Italian wines, including Barolo, Barbaresco and Gattinara. "Nebbia" is the fog that persists in northwest Italy in the fall.

Cellars *(above)* in Carema village on the borders of Piemonte and Valle d'Aosta have to take whatever shape the mountainous location will allow. The Nebbiolo grape, here called the Picotener, is used to produce DOC Carema red wine.

The village of Carema *(right)* in the province of Torina is locked in the precipitous territory of the Pennine Alps. The struggle for vineyard space is clearly demonstrated by the terraces above the village — no wonder the average yearly output of DOC Carema is restricted to some 11,000 cases.

granted. The Presidential Decree for DOC and DOCG status is granted on recommendation from the Ministries of Agriculture and of Industry and Commerce. They in turn are advised by a National Committee of government and wine-industry nominees. The Italians may have been late starters, but now they have added their own uniquely strict laws to enforce fair trading. Offenders may have their wineries or warehouses closed for as much as a year, and details of indictments and penalties must be published in the press.

A considerable number of vines are grown in Italy, many disguising their identity with local names. There is widespread use of Malvasia, Moscato, Sangiovese, Trebbiano, Verdicchio, and Vernaccia vines, while Barbera, Cabernet, Dolcetto, Freisa, Merlot, Nebbiolo, and Pinot are each to be found solely in one region or perhaps two. Italian wines may be named for a large area, a district, a commune or for the sole or principal grape used in their production; for quality wines (qwpsr) a place-name must follow the grape-name.

For a combination of geographic and historic reasons, Italy is divided into *compartimenti* (equivalent to French *provinces*) that are subdivided into *provinci* (equivalent to French *départements*). Customarily the international wine trade designates each *compartimente* as an Italian wine "region," and a group of villages as a "district," equivalent to the French commune.

# THE WINES OF NORTHERN ITALY

## PIEMONTE

Piemonte is the most important wine region of Italy, boasting about twice as many DOCs as Veneto, its nearest rival. Sheltered by the Alps in the north, it lies on the upper plain between the French border and Lombardia. With the notable exception of Asti Spumante, this is red-wine country, where the Nebbiolo and Barbera grapes are all-important.

Of the three wines made from Nebbiolo, the greatest is Barolo, named for the district near the northern extremity of the Apennines in which it is made. Barolo is a full-bodied wine, high in tannin and alcohol, with a superb flavor and a bouquet of tar. After three years it is ready for drinking, but given the chance it will improve for a century, rising in color from deep oriental to brick red. Said to be softer and less austere is Barolo's "younger brother," which takes its name from the neighboring village of Barbaresco, although production extends also to the nearby villages of Treiso and Neive. Ruby-red Barbaresco is fully mature after three years. Around Gattinara, center of the Vercelli

A welcome in stone *(above)* to the village of Carema. Despite the small contribution made by the village, the region of Piemonte is fifth in Italian wine production. Vines other than the Nebbiolo are planted up into the high corners of the Valle d'Aosta.

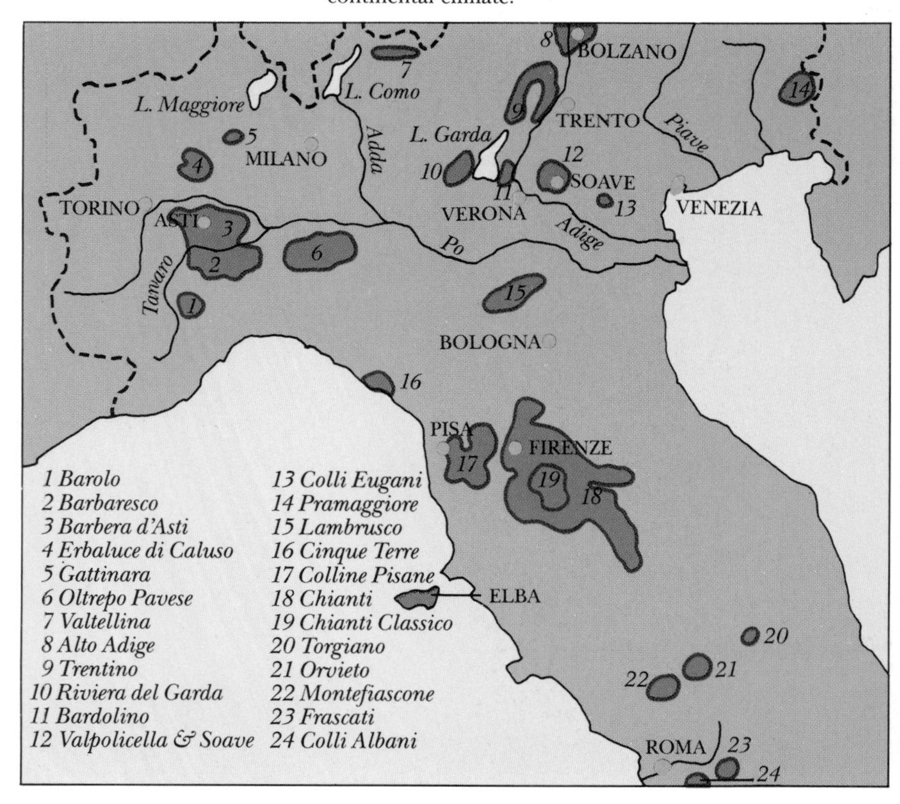


The *compartimenti* of northern and central Italy *(below)* produce the best of the country's red, white, and sparkling wines. South of Lazio and Marche the heat intensifies and the wines become bigger and meatier, losing the delicacy given by the north's gentler continental climate.

Paring Nebbiolo grapes from the vine using a curved blade *(right)* of a type that has been used around the Mediterranean for many centuries. The tall picker has an advantage in reaching grapes on the trellised vines.

province, the Nebbiolo grape (known locally as the Spanna) is blended with other grapes, including the Croatina, to make Gattinara wines; these are less powerful than Barolo, yet superior to other wines simply called by the grape-name with or without a place-name: Nebbiolo d'Alba is perhaps the best known.

Barbera is a noble grape grown in great quantity. Barbera d'Asti is an astringent fruity wine; the place-name indicates that it is DOC. Barbera wines are also made *frizzante* (crémant) and semisweet. The Grignolino grape gives its name to a wine that has been called "the table wine *par excellence* of Piemonte." The wine is bright, light and dry. DOC Asti-Grignolino will mature in two years but is best at three. Several districts around Asti produce, from the Freisa grape, softer wines than Barbera. The better known include those of Asti itself, Chieri to its northwest, and Monferranto to its northeast.

Internationally, Asti Spumante is perhaps better known than any other wine from Piemonte. Its grape is the strong-scented Moscato, small quantities of Pinot and Riesling being added to quell its pungency. The wine is fermented once in a sealed tank, during which time the must is filtered under pressure to eliminate the yeasts while retaining the dissolved carbon dioxide. Some yeast spores remain, however, and they work on residual protein in the must so that the fermentation continues. The filtering under pressure is repeated until no

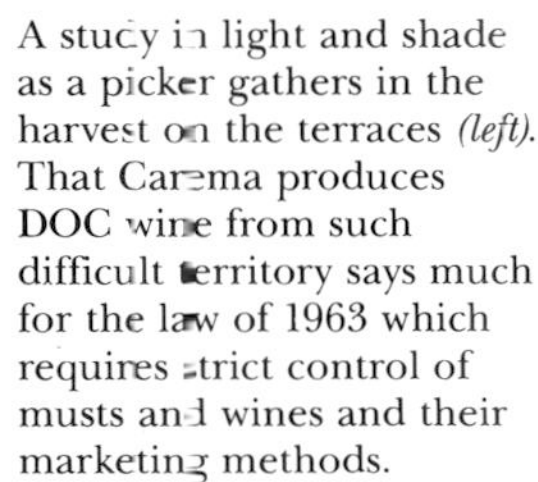

A study in light and shade as a picker gathers in the harvest on the terraces *(left)*. That Carema produces DOC wine from such difficult territory says much for the law of 1963 which requires strict control of musts and wines and their marketing methods.

A close view of the terraces of vines at Carema *(below)* reveals the method of training. The vines grow high onto a trellis which provides a shield from both the direct and the reflected heat of the sun. Moreover, the vines are protected from winter ground-frosts.

The Fontanafredda *(far left)*, just north of the Ligurian Alps, is the prize estate of Piemonte and is now owned by the Monte dei Paschi di Siena Bank. The picture shows the façade of the Hunting Lodge at Cuneo.

The camera explores the detail of the façade at Cuneo *(above left)*. Fontanafredda was founded in 1878 and now has an estate of 100ha (247 acres).

The cellars at Cuneo *(above)*. Winemaker Livio Testa has perfected a Spumante made by the *metodo classico* (French *méthode champenoise*) and marketed as Contessa Rosa.

The vineyards at the Fontanafredda estate *(left)*. The vines planted here include Barbera d'Alba and Dolcetto d'Alba, producing wines named for the vines, according to Italian custom.

"For God, Country and Family" is the motto *(inset)* of Vittorio Emmanuel II, King of Italy, whose son founded Fontanafredda in 1878.

protein remains, so that a sweet sparkling wine with 7.5-9% vol. alcohol results. It is bottled at low temperature under pressure and is sealed with Champagne corks. Both its taste and fragrant bouquet are fugitive, and it must therefore be drunk young.

## VALLE D'AOSTA

The Valle d'Aosta is a small enclave on the northwest border of Piemonte, and is known primarily for its role as Italy's rail and road link with western Europe, then for its skiing resorts, and lastly for its wines. Small vineyards have claimed south-facing sites on the Alpine slopes.

There are two DOCs for red wines: Donnaz, made at the south of the valley from the Nebbiolo grape, has an almond flavor and needs three years to age; Enfer d'Arvier, made from local grape varieties including the Petit-Rouge, is ready after only one year. Valle d'Aosta is not considered an important wine area, partly as a result of its small production. Only those intent on skiing are likely to enjoy these wines as they cannot be found elsewhere.

## LIGURIA

The region of Liguria runs along the Italian coast from France to La Spezia, and backs up to the Alps Maritimes in the west and the Apennines in the east. The port of Genoa is at its center. Ligurian wines are not well known because they are not exported, but a few of them are distinctly better than most of the table wines found farther south.

In the district of La Spezia, steep cliffs rise out of the sea. At their tops are precarious vineyards, of which some can be reached only by boat. Here three local vines, Bosco, Albarolo, and Vermentino, are blended to make the white wines of DOC Cinqueterra, named for five lands that have lost their individuality. Cinqueterra is a dry wine with a subtle flavor.

DOC Rossese di Dolceaqua is red wine with good style produced at the western extreme of the region. Rossese is a local vine valued for its versatility of usage. Also west of Genoa may be found the Vermentino grape, which produces a smooth white wine good for drinking with fish.

## LOMBARDIA

Lombardia, otherwise Lombardy, rises into the Alps to the north and runs down to wet valleys where rice and other crops displace the vine. But there is room for all in this large region of Italy.

Valtellina, the district on the north bank of the Adda river running west into the northern end of Lake Como, produces wines that have a wide reputation abroad. Here, almost on the Swiss border, red wines are made, mostly from the Nebbiolo grape, which is locally called Chiavennasca. The resulting wines are named for five subdistricts of the region—Grumello and Sassella, which are said to be the better, and Fracia, Inferno, and Valgella. When made solely from grapes from its own subdistrict, Valtellina Superiore may be prefixed with its name; for example, Sassella Valtellina Superiore. Such wines have a lively red color, and are fresh, dry and tannic; by law, the wine must spend one of the two years required for maturation in wooden casks. Alcohol varies between 11% and 12% by volume except in the case of Sfursat, which is made from partly dried grapes and attains 14.5% vol. alcohol or more. At four years old, Sfursat may be called *reserva*.

In the southeast corner of Lombardia, six wines from the province of Pavia share the mark DOC Oltrepo; this may be followed by the name of the principal grape—Barbera, Bonarda, Cortese, Moscato, Riesling, or one of several others. DOC Botticino covers a small commune near Lake Garda in the southeast where red wines are made from Barbera, Schiava, Marzemino, and Sangiovese grapes. This is a wine to be drunk young.

Frecciarossa, a vineyard of about 30ha (74 acres) on a hill in the province of Pavia, makes notable but rare white wines from Riesling and Pinot Noir, and red and rosé wines by adding Bonarda di Gattinara, Barbera, and Croattina grapes. These wines are estate-bottled—unusual for Italy—and widely exported. Lombardia also produces Muscat still and sparkling wines, and, in Brescia, two DOC wines, Franciacorto Rosso and Franciacorto Pinot, the red from Barbera, Cabernet, Merlot, and Nebbiolo grapes and the white from Pinot.

## TRENTINO-ALTO ADIGE

This is Italy's most northerly region; Italian and German are common languages. The river Adige rises within a few kilometers of the Swiss border and, after turning east, runs south into Veneto and then east again to flow into the Adriatic 35km (22mi) south of Venice.

The Alto Adige has retained the German vine styles cultivated for white wine before 1919, when it was part of Austria. The wines are mostly made from the Traminer and Riesling grapes and, perhaps logically, find their way to markets in Austria and Switzerland, although they are stronger than the German wines and have a slightly bitter vanilla flavor.

DOC Riesling del Trentino is among the better whites, although not up to the Rieslings of Germany. Terlano wines are greenish-white, taking their name from the local Terlano (Garganega) vine, although not less than 50% Pinot and some Riesling goes into the blend. These white wines come from Trentino, lower down the Adige.

The best red wines come from the northern province of Bolzano. DOC Santa Maddalena is smooth and full in body and deep in color; it has an odor of violets and almonds. DOC Lago di Caldaro, produced on the shores of the diminutive Lake Caldaro—once the Kaltersee—is a garnet-red wine for drinking young; it is made from the Schiave grape but with some Pinot and Lagrein added; the best may be called Classico Superiore.

Cellars at the Istituto Agrario Provinciale San Michele all'Adige *(right)*, the agricultural college at Castel San Michele. Its DOC Castel San Michele is among the best wines of the Trentino-Alto Adige.

This carved caskhead *(above)* in the cellars of Castel San Michele commemorates the first centenary of the Istituto's foundation in 1875. An inscription may be translated as: "Wine of Trento – the brotherhood of life and God."

The vineyards of Castel San Michele *(right)*, north of Trento, are far enough south of the German border to assume a truly Italian identity. The emphasis is already on red wines and the vines are trained in the Italian trellis pattern.

Looking north over the town of Soave *(far right)* from its castle. Mixed crops are becoming rare but individual olive trees such as the ones seen in the vineyards here will no doubt survive until the ends of their natural lives.

The harbor of Bardolino *(right)* on Lake Garda. Bardolino is in the center of the Classico district of DOC Bardolino, a red wine blended from the Corvina, Rondinella and Molinara grapes.

## VENETO

No wines are produced in the strip, 50km (31mi) wide, that runs down from the Austrian border between Trentino-Alto Adige and Friuli-Venezia Giulia. But business starts in earnest when Lake Garda is reached; in fact, nearby Verona is now regarded as the wine center of all Italy. From the province of Verona come Bardolino and Valpolicella, two of the three wines for which Veneto is famous; the third, Soave, is named for a small town 20km (12½mi) east of Verona.

DOC Bardolino starts life with a pale-sherry color which deepens with age to garnet; it is slightly bitter and dry and has 11.5% vol. alcohol. It is made in a group of 16 communes around Bardolino, bordering the southeast corner of Lake Garda: six communes form the inner Classico district. It is blended principally from the Corvina, Molinara, Negrara and Rondinella grapes, and may become acceptably *frizzante* from its remaining sugar. After the wine has aged in the province for a year, measured from January 1 after vintage, it may be described as Superiore.

At Gargagnago *(right)* the firm of Masi, owned by the Boscaini family, has been producing wines for six generations. Winemaker Nino Franceschetti converts Garganega and Corvina Veronese grapes to produce Soave and Valpolicella-Recioto-Amorone wines.

At the Pieropan winery in Soave *(right)*, owner Leonildo Pieropan produces 10,000 cases annually of the finest Soave Classico available, from a total of 15ha (37 acres).

Cantine Pieropan emphasize their name in metal on solid studded wood *(center right)*. Leonildo Pieropan still makes the quality of Soave that won a prize for his grandfather in 1906.

The Cantine Pieropan *(far right)*.

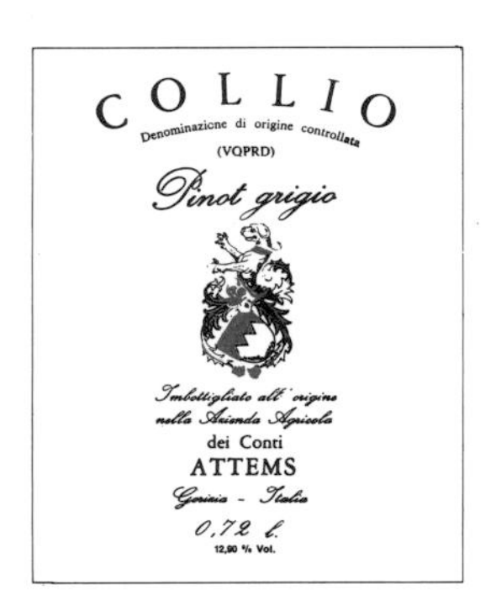


The river Adige flows parallel to Lake Garda and separates the Bardolino district from the Valpolicella vineyards on the hills to its east. Although the vine plantings are almost identical with those in Bardolino, the wines have differing characteristics. DOC Valpolicella is restricted in yield per hectare and must have at least 12% vol. alcohol; it is naturally semidry, with a delicate bouquet and a ''mouth-filling'' texture. It turns slowly from ruby red to garnet. Wines produced at Valpantena, in the center of the district, may add this name to the DOC. DOC Recioto della Valpolicella is made from selected, partly dried grapes picked from the prominent edges of the bunch (the ears or ''recie''), and the wine is thus semisweet; it is delicate with a deep ruby color. When fermented to dryness, Recioto may be called *amarone*; it may also be made sweet or sparkling. Five of the 19 communes have Classico rating.

Like Valpolicella, the fresh white wines of DOC Soave are restricted in yield per hectare and share the description ''Classico'' for wines from the center of the group of communes (of which there are 13 in Soave's case), and ''Superiore'' for wines aged for a full January-to-January calendar year. The subdistrict surrounds Soave, a small town 20km (12½mi) east of Verona; the soil is mostly clay. The Garganega and Trebbiano grapes are used to produce a straw-colored, crisp, dry white wine with a delicate scent and subtle bitterness. There is also a semisweet version, Recioto di Soave, which is light golden in color and has a slightly fruitier flavor.

DOC Colli Euganei wines are produced in the Euganean hills in the province of Padua, halfway between Soave and the Adriatic. Dryish velvety white wines are made principally from the Garganega and Serprina grapes. Red wines from the Merlot grape with some Barbera and Cabernet added are dry to semisweet and have a good body. Both red and white wines must have a basic alcoholic strength of 10.5%, with Superiore at 12%; both may be made sparkling, with up to 12% vol. alcohol according to type.

## FRIULI-VENEZIA GIULIA

At the northeast tip of Italy good wines have been made for thousands of years. In Collio, a small district west of Gorizia, well balanced, dry white DOC Collio Goriziano wines are made, occasionally sparkling. Although the chief grape is Ribolla Gialla, the rule here is that the DOC may add the name of the predominant grape used in its manufacture; the list includes Tokai, Malvasia, Pinot Bianco and Nero. Sauvignon, Traminer, Merlot, and Cabernet. The soil—of marl and sandstone—is ideal for the vines and their resultant wines.

East of Udine, DOC Colli Orientale del Friuli red and white wines are made, notably Merlot di Latisana and Cabernet di Latisana among the reds, Verduzzo and Ribolla among the whites, and the sweeter Picolit, a golden dessert wine—one of the best from Italy.

Bottled at the Acienda Agricole of Conti Attems at Lucinico, this shipment *(below)* of DOC Collio Pinot Grigio (the Rulander of Germany) may reach one of many export markets.

The vines are trained high on the slopes *(right)* of the Conti Attems estate in Collio Gariziano, the best DOC in Friuli-Venezia-Giulia. The Attems family came here from Germany 1,000 years ago, and have survived many wars (and earthquakes!) in the years since.

An orderly vineyard of Merlot grapes *(far right)*. The plastic sheeting is spread over the vines when hail is imminent. The Attems' Merlot and equally full-flavored Cabernet Franc wines are bottled with a little carbon dioxide gas which helps to retain their freshness.

Rows of the local Tokai grape at Conti Attems *(right)*; these are planted horizontally to the slope in order to get the most exposure to the sun.

Vines of Sauvignon Blanc are trained high on wires in the Goriziano vineyards *(far right)*: the resulting wine is crisp and fragrant when young, and can improve with barrel-age to have full flavor and considerable body.

Small is beautiful, when it comes to the quantities of precious wines. At the Conti Attems estate, every capsule for the limited wine output is put on by hand *(above)*.

The Attems insignia *(right)* is reproduced on the label of every bottle leaving the Conti Attems vinery at Lucinico.

# THE WINES OF CENTRAL ITALY

## EMILIA-ROMAGNA

Emilia-Romagna runs east from the Apennines, south of the River Po, into a level plain stretching to the Adriatic. The region is renowned for the gormandizing of its population. Their massive meals are liberally washed down with much of the 10 million hectoliters of red wine the region produces each year. There are, however, a few wines of some pretension; since the EEC had its say, many of the region's vineyards have acquired a twentieth-century look.

Lambrusco is a good wine, named for the grape (which must not be confused with the North American wild grape *Euvitis labrusca*). It has four DOCs: Lambrusco di Sorbara, Lambrusco Grasparossa di Caltevetro and Lambrusco Salamino di Ste Croce, all of which are made near Modena, and Lambrusco Reggiano, made at Reggio-nell-Emilia. All are red, semidry, semisparkling wines which hide in the glass under a disturbing pink froth—which is not to say they taste unpleasant, although they can be too sweet and too bubbly. Carbonation is forbidden.

Sangiovese, which again takes the vine's name, is a dry red wine, sometimes hard and bitter and at other times warm and mellow. The DOC is attributed to Italian enthusiasm rather than quality—or perhaps quantity came into account, for the bulk of Emilia-Romagna's wine production is Sangiovese.

The Trebbiano di Romagna grape gives its name to a dry, straw-colored DOC wine made in an area touching Bologna, Farli and Ravenna provinces. The sparkling version may be dry, semisweet or sweet.

## TOSCANA

The region of Tuscany lies to the south of Emilia-Romagna, on the west side of the Apennines; in this beautiful area wines of great quality are produced. The virtues of the excellent red Chiantis come first to mind (there are no white Chiantis). The matter of interpreting their labels, however, is not simple: not only has the name been plagiarized worldwide, but neighboring producers pirated it and tried to extend the Chianti wine region. Moreover, several vineyards in the inner, classico area are excluded from the *consorzio* because the EEC has restricted the "classico" description specifically to those wines both vinified and bottled within this area.

Seven districts surrounding the classico district are entitled to use the name DOC Chianti followed, respectively, by: dei Colli Fiorentini, Colli Senesi, Colli Aretini, Montalbano, Colli Pisane, Colli Pistoiese, and Rufina (not to be confused with the Tuscan wine firm

This is not "any old vine" but one of *the* old vines of the Biondi-Santi estate at Montalcino *(far left)*. The vine is the Brunello di Montalcino, a noble strain of Tuscany's Sangiovese.

12ha (29½ acres) of these very special old vines at Il Grippo *(above)* produce 2,900 cases of DOC Brunello di Montalcino each year. This is Italy's most valued wine, and has been described as Italy's only Grand Cru. It will last for a century.

Containers full of Sangiovese Grosso grapes *(left)*. Ferruccio Biondi-Santi is credited with having created Brunello di Montalcino wine.

Ruffino). The seven jointly subscribe to Consorzio Putto, and their labels bear the *consorzio* symbol of a white cherub; Consorzio Classico has a black cockerel. Classico wines have a permitted yield of 11.5 tonnes/ha and must have 11.5% vol. alcohol, as against 12.5 tonnes/ha and 11.0% vol. alcohol for other Chiantis. Colli Senesi, the largest Chianti district, is subdivided into vineyards in the Siena hills, on the one hand, and around the towns of Montepulciano and Montalcino, on the other.

Some Chiantis are still made by the old system, in which up to 10% of the grapes, usually Malvasia and Trebbiano, are dried on wicker frames, while the remainder, 70% Sangiovese and 20% Canaiolo Nero, ferment in vats. The dried grapes (*passiti*) are added to restart fermentation. The result is a light ruby-red wine with residual sugar and a distinctive bouquet of violets, or possibly irises. The red will turn to garnet with age; at two years Chianti may be called *vecchio* if it has a strength of 12½% vol. alcohol, for Classico, and 12% for other Chiantis. After three years it may be called *riserva*.

Chianti in the bottle will age well and last for 30 years or more. It is best served at about 15°C (59°F). The handsome *fiasco*, or raffia-covered flask, in which Chianti was originally bottled is now too expensive for normal marketing; in fact, wine does not age well in the *fiasco* and, when found, should be drunk quickly before it deteriorates.

Parts of the vineyards of Castello di Cacchiano *(above)* are relatively flat, and here the Sangiovese (70%), Canaiolo Nero (20%) and residual Malvasia and Trebbiano are grown for blending into DOC Chianti Classico.

The cellars of the twelfth-century estate of Castello di Cacchiano at Monti near Gaiole *(left)*. The description "DOC Chianti Classico" applied to wines from this estate means by definition that both the vineyards and the winery lie within the delimited Chianti Classico region.

The cellars of Castello di Cacchiano *(right)*. In the foreground are huge straw-covered carboys of Chianti Riserva which will be sold after it has aged for three years.

A carved stave *(center)* built into the side of a wooden fermentation vat at Castello di Cacchiano. The capacity in hl is beneath.

A glass stopper *(bottom)* is fitted to the bung of a cask so that carbon dioxide gas may escape without permitting oxidation.

As one looks northeast from the Castello di Cacchiano, a beautiful vista *(main picture)* unfolds, stretching over the Colli Fiorentini hills to the Apennines. The late-afternoon sun brings out in relief some details of the vineyards of the Castello property.

Tuscan wine is by no means limited to Chianti: DOC Brunello di Montalcino, made in the hills south of Siena, is one of Italy's finest red wines. The Brunello grape is a Sangiovese variety and its full-bodied wine will age, it is said, for 50-100 years. The wine must be made and matured for six years in cask in the Montalcino commune to become *riserva*. Rare and costly, this wine should be allowed to breathe for 24 hours before serving. Villa Banfi, founded in 1977 by the US House of Banfi, have a 300ha (740-acre) vineyard at Montalcino concentrating on Brunello and Moscadello wine production, as well as good representative wines from Cabernet Sauvignon and Chardonnay grapes. Ezio Rivella, Italy's leading enologist, is developing Villa Banfi as the model for new-style Italian wines to compete in the international market. The House of Banfi is already the largest US importer of Italian wines.

For at least eight centuries the local nobility have made the wine now called DOC Nobile di Montepulciano around the village of Montepulciano (although "Montepulciano" is also a grape name). The wine comes from the Prugnola Gentile vine—another Sangiovese variety—with some Canaiola, Malvasia and Trebbiano, all planted in a soil of Tertiary-rock origins. It is deep garnet in color, dry and smooth, and has 12% vol. alcohol. It must age in wood for two years before sale, becoming *riserva* after three years and *riserva speciale* after four. It will improve for several decades.

There are no sensational white wines of Tuscany. DOC Bianco Vergine Valdichiana—"virgin white" in color—has 11% vol. alcohol and is crisp and dry with relatively high acidity. Only free-run juice is used, and this helps the pale color.

Dry well balanced wines of a light-straw color are made on the island of Elba from Trebbiano grapes (known locally as Procanico). The Italians are enthusiastic and compare it with Chablis, but there is some optimism involved. DOC Elba covers also a red wine made from Sangiovese grapes.

Unloading grapes from a tipper-trailer at the 38ha (94-acre) vineyards of Badia a Coltibuono at Monti *(below)*. The hills are too steep for vineyards at Gaiole, where the winery is situated, and so the grapes have to be brought from Monti, which is halfway to Siena – hence the large-sized trailer.

The bottle store in the cellars of Badia a Coltibuono at Gaiole *(below)*, showing stocks of 1948 and 1949 Chianti Classico. The buildings of this medieval abbey are now kept in superb condition by the Stucchi-Prinetti family, who have been owners since 1846. Each bottle of Chianti Classico bears the black-cockerel symbol of the Classico *consorzio*.

Time was when bottles were not made by machinery and the variations that resulted were noticeable. Note the elaborate forerunner of the wire muzzle *(right)*. This display is part of a collection at Badia a Coltibuono in the twelfth-century abbey at Gaiole.

The stylish fifteenth-century villa of Vignamaggio at Florence *(below left)*: it has as much historical interest as wine significance, for the Mona Lisa (no less) is reputed to have lived there. Today owner Ranieri Sanminiatelli produces a worthy, if light, DOC Chianti Classico there.

Bringing in the harvest at Castell'in Villa *(bottom right)*, a business founded in 1968 by Riccardo and Coralia Pignatelli della Leonessa. The estate of Castelnuovo Berardenga, Siena, has an area of 60ha (148 acres), from which 4,000hl (106,000gal) of DOC Chianti Classico and 750hl (19,800gal) of white wines are made.

## MARCHE

The vineyards of Marche, on the Adriatic side of the Apennines, are scattered yet produce altogether some two million or more hectoliters of wine each year; most are consumed within the region. A few DOCs have been granted, and the red wines of Marche, although less known, are considered better than the whites. Rosso Conero and Rosso Piceno, made near Ancona, are fruity dry wines very acceptable to local palates and enterprising visitors; they are rarely found abroad. Conero has mostly Montepulciano grapes, with 15% Sangiovese; Piceno has 60% Sangiovese balanced with Montepulciano. Another DOC is Vernaccia di Serrapetrona, a sweet, red sparkling wine from the Vernaccia grape grown in Macerata.

The white wines include DOC Verdicchio dei Castelli di Jesi, a clean dry wine from Ancona cleverly marketed in amphora-shaped bottles; it should be drunk young. The distinctive bottle carries the spirit (not a solecism!) of Italy to many lands. Two other DOCs, Verdicchio di Matelica and Bianchello del Metauro, both named for their chief grape, are crisp, light and dry, and are good with local seafood.

## UMBRIA

Time was when the wines of Orvieto were synonymous with Umbria, but the fashion in wine has had to change with taste; the classic semisweet *abboccato* wine, "dancing with golden lights," although as well made as ever it was, has largely given way to a crisp, refreshing dry wine that has no really exceptional character. Orvieto and its surrounding villages use mainly Trebbiano Toscano with Verdello, Malvasia and Greco grapes to produce the DOC Abboccato. After fermentation to complete dryness, the wine is sweetened with a dried-grape *passito* to produce a full velvety wine with up to 12% vol. alcohol; when, in a good year, a humid fall brings beneficent botrytis, higher strengths are reached in a rich and mellow product which is, sadly, none too stable. The dry white wines more acceptable to the modern market are made principally from Trebbiano grapes and have 13% vol. alcohol. The Orvietos are aged in cellars cut out of the tufa under the city.

DOC Torgiano red and white wines, from the province of Perugia, have been earning a growing reputation. The Rubesco di Torgiano is likened to a first-class Chianti; it is made from Sangiovese grapes blended with Canaiolo, Trebbiano Toscano and Montepulciano. Also from Torgiano, white Torre di Giano, made with Trebbiano and Grechetto grapes, is crisp and fragrant. The recent introduction of Cabernet, Chardonnay and Gewürztraminer vines here gives promise of further developments.

DOC Colli del Trasimeno covers red and white wines from the borders of Lake Trasimeno. The reds are made mostly from Trebbiano Toscano grapes and the whites mostly from Sangiovese. The reds are dry and tannic with a scent of violets, and the whites are fresh with effective acidity.

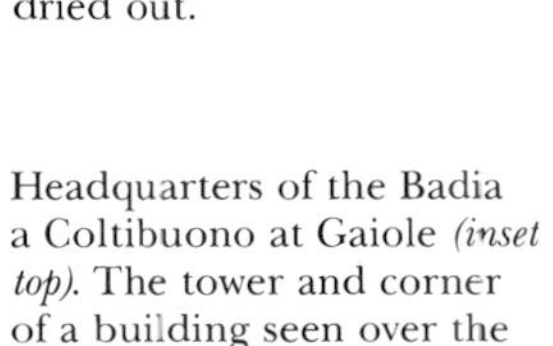

Drying grapes at Badia a Coltibuono for the production of Vin Santo *(far left)*. The grapes are suspended from hooks until two-thirds of the juice has dried out.

Headquarters of the Badia a Coltibuono at Gaiole *(inset top)*. The tower and corner of a building seen over the courtyard roof are part of the twelfth-century abbey.

Vin Santo is made by leaving the ultrasweet juice from the dried grapes in a warm, sealed container *(inset center)* for four years; the wine maderizes, becoming a deep amber color.

Here Vin Santo is put up in the ever-popular raffia-covered bottles *(inset bottom)* — as Chianti used to be until the cost of the bottle became prohibitive.

In the hilltop village of Torgiano *(below)*, Dr Georgio Lungarotti is working wine miracles for Umbria. His Rubesco di Torgiano already has DOC status.

### LATIUM

When in Rome, to adapt the cliché, you should certainly drink the wines of Colli Albani, a DOC covering the general region of the Alban hills, just south of the city, including the two communes of Albano and Aricca and a few surrounding villages. A variety of vines are blended, headed by Malvasia Rossa, Malvasia del Lazio, Trebbiano Toscano, and Bonvino. The wine is straw-colored and semisweet with a refined scent and, at 12.5% vol. alcohol, may be called *superiore*. Frascati is the best known, with Colonna, Marino, Velletri and others all named for their towns. In Rome the one you order may or may not be served, but it doesn't matter much which you find yourself drinking.

Between Rome and Cassino, to its southeast, DOC Cesanese del Piglio, a red wine rather drier than semisweet, is regarded as Latium's best. It is made from Cesanese and Cesanese di Affile grapes. It is a big wine, deep in color, and may range up to 15% vol. alcohol. Affile, a town close to Piglio, produces a very similar wine.

In the north of Latium, near the southeast corner of Lake Bolsena, is the village of Montefiascone, and here a tenuous link with the eleventh century survives by virtue of a wine with the bizarre name "Est! Est! Est!" ("Est" being short for "*vinum bonum est*"). Made then with Muscat but now with Trebbiano grapes, DOC Est! Est! Est! is today slightly more acceptable than the story of its origin, which can be found in many books on Italian wines. The wine is white, dry and tinged with a yellow color. Whatever its keeping qualities, 900 years have done little to justify its superlative name.

## THE WINES OF SOUTHERN ITALY

South of Latium and Marche, the wines of Italy slowly become heavier in alcohol, so that by the time the boot of Italy is reached much of the wine is worthy only to be shipped abroad or up-country as "strengthening" wine. Nevertheless, good wines are to be found and each region has its fair share of DOCs to prove it.

### ABRUZZO AND MOLISE

Abruzzo, east of the Apennines, seems a remote corner of Italy—perhaps because of its inaccessibility and the rolling mountains that stretch out to the Adriatic. Its wine industry is a simple one. There are two grapes, one for white wine and one for red. The name Trebbiano d'Abruzzo tells the whole story; this DOC covers white wines made anywhere in the province. A dry velvety wine, it goes well with Adriatic fish dishes. Similarly, DOC Montepulciano d'Abruzzo is a light red wine, Montepulciano being the name of the grape and nothing to do with the Tuscan town that shares the same name.

The same grapes are used in the little region of Molise—a newcomer to the regions boasting DOCs—to Abruzzo's south. The DOCs, Biferno and Pentro, are for both red and white wines, which are well up to the quality of Abruzzo's.

### CAMPANIA

Campania, commanding a coastline that includes the Bay of Naples and its romantic islands, with Vesuvius standing aloof in the forefront of the Apennines, is renowned for its beauty. The volcanic soil provides an ideal base for the vine and, although good wines are in the minority, they succeed in complementing Campania's natural charms. Lacrima Christi del Vesuvio is produced on the western slopes of the volcano. Perhaps the variety of its production—red, white and rosé in differing qualities—has stopped its good reputation being recognized with a DOC, but that may yet come. The range includes a notable dry, smooth red wine, of full color, and whites ranging from some with a golden tint to the well known pale medium-dry wines with their delicate flavor. Various dubious legends surround the wine's name, "tears of Christ."

Ischian DOC red and white wines are well above average but are not often seen away from the island.

DOC Greco di Tufo, made from Greco di Tufo and Coda di Volpe grapes, reflects the tufa (boiled-limestone) soil of Avellino, 45km (28mi) east of Naples; the wine, some of it sparkling, bears a resemblance to the French Vouvrays, whose vines grow on a similar soil.

Falerno, from Falanghino grapes, is mostly a golden-yellow wine of medium strength and dryness made near the borders of Latium. Red Falerno, from Aglianico grapes, is also made. Today's Falerno wine, despite many claims, can hardly be a descendant of the *Falernum* of ancient Rome, of which both grape and flavor are unknown: the Legions would have had to have been desperate to drink it from their primitive hipflasks in the far-flung corners of the Empire!

### APULIA, BASILICATA AND CALABRIA

Respectively the heel, instep and toe of Italy, these three regions produce some average to good wines and some that fall below those standards.

Apulia's production is the fourth largest in all Italy, only Sicily, Emilia-Romagna and Veneto, in that order, usually producing more. Much of the white wine goes north for conversion into Italian Vermouth, while quantities of the red wine, deep in color and excessive in strength, are exported to France and Germany for blending into EEC table wines. The DOC wines include Castel del Monte, red, rosé (*rosato*) and white; Aleatico, a dark-red strong dessert wine named for its grape; Locorotondo, dry,

strong and white; and Primitivo, another strong red. The Primitivo vine has red stems, sharing this feature with only one other vine—the Zinfandel of California.

Basilicata is bordered by Campania, Apulia, Calabria and the Gulf of Taranto; the vine is the only crop to survive on its poor soil. DOC Aglianico del Vulture, red wine made in the foothills of the dormant volcano Monte Vulture, is Basilicata's best—and, incidentally, one of the best of Southern Italy.

Calabria, at Italy's toe, has little of significance to offer other than the Ciro wines on which, it is said, the Italian Olympic teams have been sustained during training both in the days of ancient Greece and since the modern restoration of the Games. The red and rosé wines come from the Gaglioppo grape; the red registers a minimum 13.5% vol. alcohol. Ciro whites are dry and are made from the Greco Bianco grape.

# SICILIA AND SARDEGNA

Sicily has come up to date at last, and, so far as her wine industry is concerned, has managed to create a benign schism within the EEC-DOC pattern. A large letter Q (for "quality") enclosing the words "Regione Siciliano" is now permitted by way of reinforcement of the DOC system, which has recognized only 5% of Sicilian wines. Three-quarters of the massive yearly production of about 120 million cases is white wine, and of this over three-quarters is produced in the Cantini Sociali (cooperatives). The best wines are Regaleali and Corvo, from the west, near Palermo; and Etna Blanco, made in the province of Catania from the Carricante grape.

The most famous Sicilian wine is the fortified Marsala, created by two Englishmen, Woodhouse and Smith, in 1773. *Vino cotto*, produced by boiling down grape must, is added with brandy to wine from the Catarratto, Grillo and Inzolia grapes to produce a dark golden sweet wine, of 17% vol. alcohol, which after four months' aging is *fine* and, after two years in cask, is *superiore*. Marsala Vergine must have been in *solera* for five years and have had no *vino cotto* added: it is lighter and drier.

A good dessert wine, Moscato di Pantelleria, strong and golden in color, comes from the Mediterranean island of Pantelleria, which lies closer to Tunisia than to Sicily. This wine is made from the Zibibbo grape.

The wine industry of Sardinia concentrates around Alghero, on the west coast. Cannonau, named for the grape and having at least 13.5% vol. alcohol, is a typical red wine in which part of the sugar is left unfermented. It can be fortified with brandy to make a Port-style drink. Vermentino di Gallura, Malvasia di Bosa and Vernaccia di Oristano all have DOCs for strong white wines that are rather like Sherry, although they are unfortified. With 14% vol. alcohol, or even more, they are usually dry and share a bitterness noticed in many Italian wines.

Vines for the production of Corvo *(above)*, the most famous of all Sicilian wines, on display at the Sicilian Trade Center. Well over half a million cases of wine — mostly Corvo Bianco and Rosso, and the white Colomba Platino — are marketed each year by Corvo (Duca di Salaparuta) from Casteldaccia, near Palermo.

Vineyard terraces intermingle with dwellings on the steep hills of Casteldaccia *(right)*, where the Corvo winery was founded in 1824 by the Duca di Salaparuta. The winery is now managed for the region by Benedetto Migliore, the winemaker being Franco Giacosa.

# GERMANY

## Rheingau ♦ Rheinhessen ♦Rheinpfalz ♦ Nahe ♦ Mittelrhein and Ahr Mosel-Saar-Ruwer ♦ Baden and Württemberg ♦ Hessische Bergstrasse and Franken

The vineyards of Germany lie at the most northerly latitudes at which the natural ripening of grapes is possible. In fact, only white grapes can be brought to full ripeness (and even then only with infinite care); black grapes, even if from famous French vines, yield undistinguished wines at these latitudes. However, although the white wines are low in alcohol and high in acidity, they rank as the best of their kind in the world; this is the result of human assiduity in adapting to and harnessing nature in a continental climate renowned for its inconstancy. Cold winters may be relied upon, and they are generally preceded by long hot falls; also, Whitsuntide in the northerly vineyards is nearly always fine, helping fertilization and setting of the vine flowers, and the summers are hot. This pattern would seem acceptable; however, the weather tends to vary not by the week or the month but by the year, so that the qualities of successive vintages vary very widely. In Germany the vineyards are often on the steep sides of river valleys where the soils lack nitrogen for agricultural crops. With uncertain climates and poor soils, the growing of grapes for wine is doubly logical, despite the difficulties of viticulture and transport that arise.

Some 90,000 growers own between them about 100,000ha (386sq mi) of vineyards, although the trend is for the number of growers to decrease and the areas of individual vineyards to increase: the disaster of 1803, albeit slowly, is, thankfully, being purged. Two-thirds of these growers together own nearly 40% of the vineyard area, but do not make wine. Their average holding is less than one hectare (2½ acres), insufficient to support the smaller owners, who must therefore have other means of livelihood: the vast majority sell their grapes to the cooperatives, who have now established a chain of excellently equipped and managed wineries (largely independent of each other) throughout Germany's wine regions. The other two-thirds (approximately) of the vineyard area belongs to the remaining one-third of the growers, all of whom make wine. Half sell their wine in bulk to the wine trade. The rest sell either solely in bottle or partly in bulk and partly in bottle; of their produce, over two-thirds is sold direct to the consumer.

The noble grapes of Germany are few. Riesling is the classic, because it gives the best wine; it is, however, low-yielding and late-ripening. The Silvaner grape performs the opposite role, prolific in yield and early to ripen, but failing to give quite such superb quality in the wine. It was perhaps natural, therefore, that a century ago a scientist called Müller, from Thurgau in Switzerland, crossed these two vines to produce the Müller-Thurgau, hoping to produce a vine incorporating the better qualities of each. The attempt was largely successful, but the grape displayed a predisposition to rot, and so further crosses were attempted by German viticulturists; however, Germany's "perfect grape" never emerged. The Müller-Thurgau gained in popularity, replacing Silvaner to a marked extent, and today it is the most frequently planted vine, with Riesling second and Silvaner third; between them they account for over two-thirds of Germany's vineyard area.

West Germany's vineyards are centered on the banks of the Rhine and its major tributaries, the Mosel, Maine and Neckar *(below)*. Outstanding among the wine regions are three bordering the Rhine — Rheingau, Rheinhessen, and Rheinpfalz — and Mosel-Saar-Ruwer, which produces wines characteristic of the deep slate valley in which the vines grow.

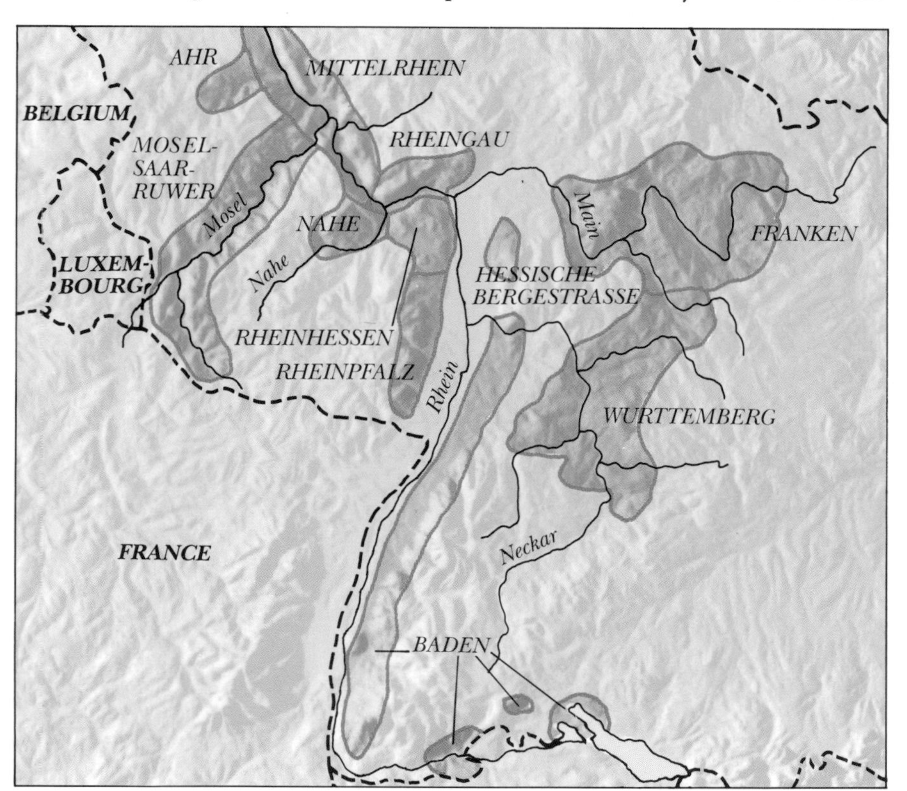

Bernkastel *(above)* is the acknowledged center of the Mittelmosel, between Trittenheim and Ürzig. In the foreground, Einzellage Bernkasteler Doktor has a slope as steep as that of the rooftops below.

The Johannisberg Riesling *(right)* is held by many to be the world's finest white grape, although Chardonnay lovers may disagree. The crisp, fruity wine, with perfect acid balance, which it yields is unchallenged for excellence.

Bereich Johannisberg nestles between the Taunus mountains and the north bank of the Rhein from Hockheim up to Lorch. The famous Schloss Johannisberg *(far right)* is planted solely with the true Riesling.

Other vines planted to a significant extent in more than a single German wine region are Morio-Muscat, Scheurebe (these two named for enologists who tried to improve on the Müller-Thurgau), and Ruländer, for white wines, and Portugieser and Blaur-Burgunder, for red wines.

## GERMAN WINE LAWS

To grasp the system of wine-making in Germany it is necessary to understand not only the national regulations devised to interpret the EEC standards that came into force in 1971 but also the "German way of doing things" — regimentation and documentation combined with rigid chemical and physical precision.

German wine laws differ from those of other EEC countries. They deal principally with wine regions of specified quality production and with labeling regulations; notably, they do not specify the grapes that are to be used, and there is no equivalent of an AC or DOC for recognition of individual vineyard or commune qualities.

The country is divided into 11 quality wine regions and four regions for table-wine and Landwein. Only the quality regions may make Qualitätswein, which can be either (a) Qualitätswein mit Prädikat (QmP), the best wines having one of six "Prädikats" of increasing quality and distinction, or (b) Qualitätswein-bestimmte-Anbaugebiete (QbA), wines of the next best quality that do not rank for any of the Prädikats. A quality wine region may also produce any of the lesser grades that are otherwise made in the four table-wine and Landwein regions. These grades are: Deutscher Tafelwein (DTW), made exclusively from German-grown grapes vinified in Germany; Tafelwein, which is blended in Germany but contains also wines from other EEC countries; and the new Landwein, literally "country wine" (created as a category by the amending legislation in 1982), which is a superior Deutscher Tafelwein, with a potential extra 0.5% vol. alcohol.

The six Prädikats (best translated as "distinctions") and their legal requirements are shown in the table. The term "Oechsle," used in the table, refers to a German measure of the amount of sugar in the wine must. Degrees Oechsle are defined by the number of grams by which one liter of must is heavier than one liter of water at 20°C (in short, the system provides a measure of the must's Specific Gravity). Approximately 25% of the Oechsle reading is the sugar content of the must in grams per liter.

The Kurfürstenhof vineyards of the Seip family at Nierstein *(below)*. Here modern techniques are used in the winery to produce sweet aromatic wines.

Grapes are collected from the pickers' tubs into a larger container *(top)* during vintage at the Niederberg-Helden vineyard at Lieser. On the left bank of the Rhein between Branne Berg and Kues, Lieser has its own Grosslage of Beerenlay, covering about 200ha (495 acres). The soil here gives the wines a stony flavor.

The vineyards of Weingut Dr Bürklin-Wolf at Wachenheim, Forst and Deidesheim are among the best in the Rheinpfalz; they have been in the family for 400 years. Here Riesling grape pulp is being fed into a press *(above)* at Wachenheim. Many of the world's winemakers have learned their skills here.

*Kabinett* the lowest Prädikat: must weight 70-81° Oechsle

*Spätlese* made with late-gathered and hence sweeter grapes: 76-90° Oechsle

*Auslese* made from riper whole bunches of grapes that are free of rot: 76-91° Oechsle

*Beerenauslese* made from individual overripe grapes picked successively to give a wine in the Sauternes style: 110-125° Oechsle

*Eiswein* (created as a category in 1982) made from ripe grapes naturally frozen when pressed, which concentrates the grape acids and sugar; this Prädikat may be used only in conjunction with another Prädikat, usually Kabinett or Auslese: 110-125° Oechsle

*Trockenbeerenauslese* made from individual overripe grapes heavily infected with *Botrytis cinerea*; a very sweet wine with low yield and high production costs: minimum 150° Oechsle

The enrichment of musts with sugar (now called *Anreichern*, equivalent to *chaptalisation* in France) is strictly forbidden for all QmP wines, but is permitted to the extent necessary to bring German QbA wines, Deutscher Tafelweins and Landweins up to the minimum alcohol level (which for Tafelwein is 5.5-8.5% vol. alcohol).

Recently the practice of adding *Süsswein* to fully fermented wines has been adopted. *Süsswein*, or *Süssreserve* (sweet-reserve), is grape-must that has had all yeasts killed or filtered out and has therefore not fermented. This is not a substitute for *Anreichern*, as no fermentation can take place after its addition, but rather a method of sweetening and thus balancing wines that would otherwise be too harsh and acid.

To qualify as QmP or QbA, wines must be submitted to an official state testing-station, where—upon approval—a national certification or *Amtliche Prüfungsnummer* is granted; this *must* appear on the label of every bottle so approved. This number consists of up to 11 figures—for example, 55271702885—of which the first is the reference number of the testing-station (5), the next two are the village code (52), the next three are the bottler's code (717), the next three are the bottler's serial application number in that year (028), and the final two are the year (85).

"Sekt" is the name for the sparkling wines of Germany—over 20 million cases per year are produced, and it is made in all regions. To qualify as QbA or QmP, it must be made entirely from grapes grown and vinified in Germany; otherwise it may contain up to 40% of imported wine while still retaining the name "Sekt." Its advantages are, firstly, that it may use grapes that fail to ripen in poor years (and the late-ripening Riesling is no exception), and, secondly, that the best-quality Sekts, although made by the *méthode champenoise*, have quite different characteristics from Champagne. Such Sekt retains the flowery flavor and distinct aroma of the Riesling, compared with the fuller fruity qualities of Champagne. Among the best producers are Deinhard at Koblenz, Henkel and Söhnheim Rheingold at Wiesbaden, Herres at Trier, Müller at Eltville and Fürst von Metternich at Johannisberg.

The German wine label, which usually incorporates a confusing number of polysyllabic words, contains relatively few details that are mandatory. QbA and QmP wines are required by law to state the *Anbaugebiet*, or "quality wine region," which may be Ahr, Baden, Franken, Hessische Bergstrasse, Mittelrhein, Mosel-Saar-Ruwer, Nahe, Rheingau, Rheinhessen, Rheinpfalz, or Württemberg; they must also quote the Amtliche Prüffungsnummer (A.P.Nr). QmP wines must state also their Prädikat. Every other detail on the label is optional and intended to be helpful(!), and may include the *Bereich* (a main subdistrict of the *Anbaugebiete*), the *Grosslage* (a collective site); the *Weinbauort* (wine-producing village), the *Einzellage* (single vineyard), vintage year of production of at least

All the wines of Hermann Freiherr von Schormeler are made and matured in oak; 90% of them come from the Riesling grape. Here, in the cellars at Zeltingen *(below)*, the wine is in the process of being racked off its lees.

The Weingut Reichsrat von Buhl is one of the biggest and most famous wine-producers in Germany, with vineyards in Forst, Deidesheim, Ruppertsberg, Wachenheim and Königsbach. Here in the center of the Bereich Mittelhaardt the Pechstein vineyard of the Buhl family announces its boundary *(left)*.

The five-story tower of the Rheingau Schloss Vollrads *(below)* was built in or around the year 1300. The Greiffenclaus family had already been there for some 200 years; the present owner is 29th-generation Count Matuschka Greiffenclaus.

The estate of Schloss Vollrads *(below)* predates the *Grosslage* and *Einzellage* classifications, and has its own personal identification, or *Ortsteil*, instead. Schloss Vollrads is one of the very few unified tracts on the Rhein, where mostly the vineyards still remain in the small parcels required by law early in the nineteenth century. The late-gathered grapes — all Riesling — produce exquisite wines that are heady and heavy in aroma.

RHEINGAUER
RIESLING
ROUTE

SCHLOSS
VOLLRADS

This notice *(left)* is more of a command than a direction! If the visitor fails to make the last mile up the hill from Winkel, his mission has failed.

The elegant tasting-room at Schloss Vollrads *(below)*. Here a range of the estate's wines may be sampled.

85% of the contents, and the principal vine variety if it has contributed at least 85% of the grapes used.

For Deutscher Tafelwein and Landwein the only mandatory detail on the label is the *Weinbaugebiet*, or "Tafelwein region," which may be Bayern (subdivided into Donau, Lindau and Main), Nahe, Oberrhein (subdivided into Burgengau and Römertor), or Rhein-Mosel (subdivided into Mosel, Rhein and Saar). To this may be optionally added the *Bereich* and *Weinbauort*. Many extra optional items, such as the fact that the wine is red, white, rosé or sparkling, may be added—as may, of course, brand-names.

### THE QUALITY WINE REGIONS

The regions bordering the Rhine from the Palatinate to Bonn are unquestionably the most important simply because they produce the best German wines. Here is Rheinpfalz, west of the Rhine in the south. To its north, in the angle of the river as it turns sharply to the west, is Rheinhessen. North again, but across on the right bank, is Rheingau, where nature has provided the conditions, superbly utilized, for the production of perfect wine. Nahe is to the west of Rheinhessen, straddling the river Nahe, while Mittelrhein runs on both sides of the Rhine as it turns north again to reach up to the city of Bonn; the small region of Ahr is just beside it.

At Koblenz, halfway up the Mittelrhein, the river Mosel flows into the Rhine from the southwest. The amazing Mosel-Saar-Ruwer region, producing wines of incredible delicacy, is acknowledged to be second in importance only to the regions bordering the Rhine.

Only 3% of Germany's vineyards lie within the Bereich Johannisberg *(below)*, the single *Bereich* that spans the Rheingau. The vineyards' south-facing aspect under the Taunus mountains and the sun's heat reflected from the Rhine insure full late harvests.

The remaining four quality regions of Germany are Baden, in the south, bordering the right bank of the Rhine opposite the French region of Alsace; Hessische Bergstrasse at Baden's northern tip; the enormous region of Franken, which has the serpentine river Main running through it; and, watered by another twisting river, the Neckar, Württemberg, renowned for its red wines.

## RHEINGAU

Most of Rheingau shelters in the wooded slopes under the Taunus mountains which run west from Weisbaden. The Rhine is joined by the river Main before turning west in a valley from Walluf to Bingen. There it curls north again to the Rhine Gorge. The whole of Rheingau comprises one *Bereich*, named Johannisberg for the town in the hills above Winkel. There are ten *Grosslagen*—Daubhaus at the eastern end, on the river Main by Hochheim; then, running east to west, come Steinmächer, Heiligenstock, Deutelsberg, Mehrhölzchen, Gottesthal, Erntebringer, and Honigberg in the center; Steil, hugging the right bank of the Rhine as it turns north to Assmanshausen; and Burgweg, which passes Geisenheim and Rüdesheim on the Rhine before it sweeps north to Lorch. Of these *Grosslagen* the more important are Daubhaus, Steinmächer, Deutelsberg, Erntebringer, and Burgweg. The whole region accounts for only 3% of Germany's vineyard area yet, with three-quarters of that area planted with Riesling, it produces unsurpassed, delicate wines, balancing strength with acid and a perfect finish. The

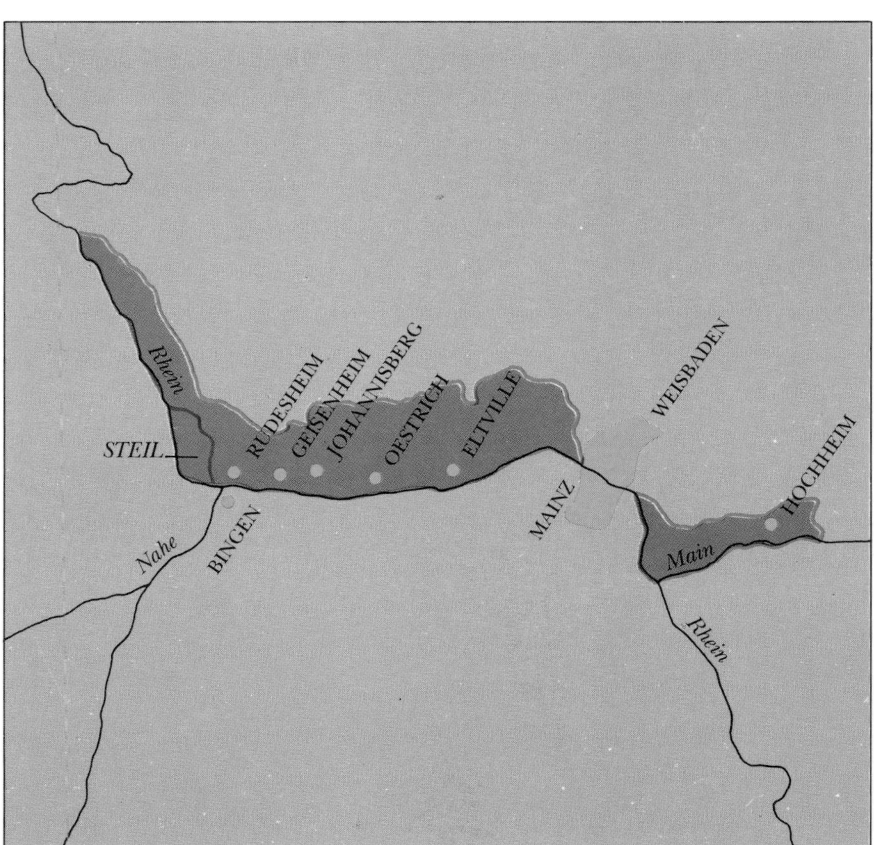


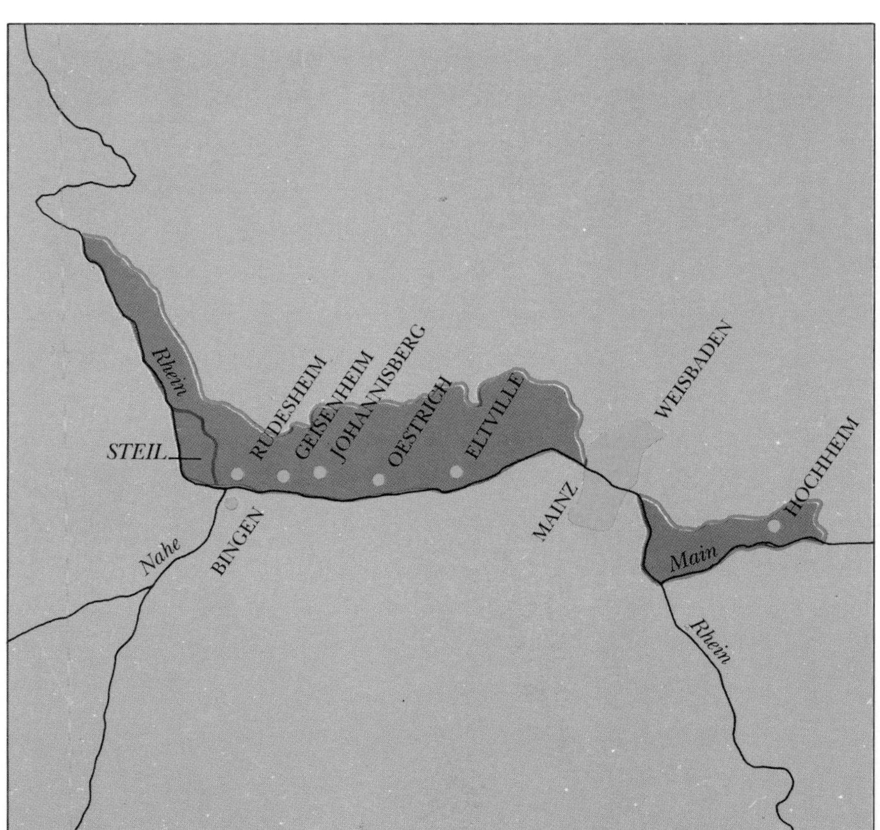

The State Domain, centered at Eltville *(above)*, owns a number of properties along the north bank of the Rhine in the Rheingau. A sizable monolith *(left)* in Schloss Johannisberg indicates the path of latitude 50°N that cuts through the vineyard.

Taunus mountains protect the vineyards from cold north winds, and the heat of the sun is reflected from the Rhine's surface.

Daubhaus is most famous for some 600ha (1,480 acres) of vineyards at Hochheim. Here the soils vary considerably—even from vineyard to vineyard—and the wines differ accordingly. The best vineyard is Domdechany, and the most famous Viktoriaberg, named for Queen Victoria, who created a fashion for German wines by drinking them with soda water. The Queen would ask for "mein Hock," thus creating for any still German wine a word that means nothing in Germany or, for that matter, anywhere else outside the UK. According to Hugh Johnson, however, "hock" originated as a contraction of "hockamore," an early and clumsy English attempt at saying "Hochheimer."

Wines from the Wiesbaden area are bottled under the *Grosslage* Rauenthaler Steinmächer. Out of the produce from 150ha (370 acres) of vineyards, that from the 4.5ha (11 acres) of Neroberg is the most likely to be quoted. Sharing the same *Grosslage* are the wines of Walluf, which are full-flavored and long-lasting.

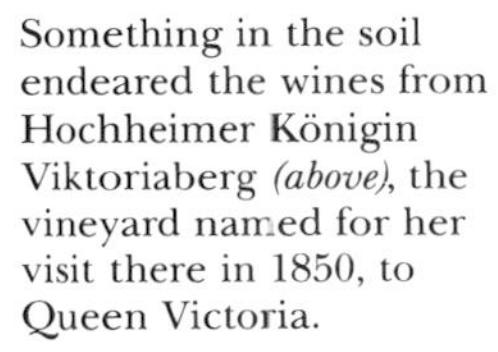

Something in the soil endeared the wines from Hochheimer Königin Viktoriaberg *(above)*, the vineyard named for her visit there in 1850, to Queen Victoria.

The huge Schloss Johannisberg above the Rhein *(left)*. The hill it caps was originally the Benedictine Mons Episcopali.

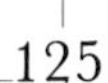

Medieval gate at Kloster Eberbach *(below)*, the beautiful and perfectly preserved Cistercian abbey dating from 1135. Here the 40ha (99-acre) vineyard of Steinberg, near Hattenheim, produces wines considered supreme in good years but overpriced in others.

The entrance to the cellar *(top)* at Schloss Johannisberg. Secularized by Napoleon, the Schloss first became the property of Napoleon Prince of Orange and then of the Emperor of Austria, before being awarded to the Metternichs.

The wines of Schloss Johannisberg, despite fierce competition, are still acknowledged as the model of all that the Rheingau and the Riesling stand for. They owe much to the quartzite and loess soil that outcrops on the hill *(above)*.

Every year the vintage brings manual workers into thousands of vineyards that defy mechanical methods of harvesting. Schloss Johannisberg is no exception. Here grapes cut by hand are tipped into a mobile crusher *(left)*.

Line upon line of Riesling vines *(right)* curl around the hill under Schloss Johannisberg. The aspect of Johannisberg is perfect for drawing all the heat of the summer sun.

The effect of botrytis *(inset)* on Riesling grapes at the State Domain. The beneficent form of *Botrytis cinerea* concentrates the sugar, and grapes so affected are picked individually for *Beerenauslese* and *Trockenbeerenauslese* wines.

The mobile crusher brings the grapes on their stalks to the winery, where the mass is pumped as a pulp into a vaslin-type press *(left)*. The stalks help to lighten the sticky mass of skins and pips as the juice is expressed.

By the time grapes are picked for the making of *Eiswein*, winter has descended on the vineyard of Viktoriaberg *(left)*. Prädikat Eiswein is reserved for grapes picked in winter when frozen and crushed before unfreezing.

In the vineyards of Königin Viktoriaberg, bunches of Riesling grapes *(below)* approach ripeness. Riesling plantings amount to about 78% of all vines growing in the Rheingau.

A little down the Rhine is Rauenthal, known for its Auslese wines, which are smooth and spicy and superior to its Kabinetts. The name of Rauenthaler Rottenberg refers to the "red hill" where the vineyards lie, higher in the Taunus foothills. Near the river in Deutelsberg is Hattenheim, home of the full-flavored Wisselbrunnen and Nussbrunnen "hocks," reminiscent of those from Erbach a little upstream. Higher in the hills is Kloster Eberbach, the Cistercian monastery belonging to the State Domain, used as the ceremonial headquarters of the German wine industry. Above Hattenheim in *Grosslage* Mehrhölzchen is Hallgarten, at the highest point of Rheingau, some 210m (700ft) above the Rhine. It enjoys warmer days and cooler nights than the vineyards below, and exchanges the riverside mists and frosts for windier conditions. The wines, mostly made from the Riesling, grown on clay soil, are full-bodied and slow to develop.

Oestrich, on the Rhine in Gotesthall, is the largest Rheingau *Grosslage*. Here top-quality Ausleses are produced. Oestricher Lenchen is the name to look for.

Downstream again are Mittelheim, Winkel, Johannisberg and Geisenheim, four place-names to conjure with: all have added to the Riesling reputation. Mittelheim wines are usually marketed as "Johannisbergers" at a higher price; those labeled simply "Mittelheim" are reasonably priced for good QbA Rieslings. Winkel harbors the famed Schloss Vollrads: the vineyard of Winkeler Hasensprung (hare spring) produces wines of delicacy and distinction.

Johannisberg, higher up the Taunus slopes, is a small village with the Schloss Johannisberg nestling below it. Everyone expects the Schloss that gave its name to the sole *Bereich* of Rheingau to produce magnificent wines, and they do in fact live up to that expectation, although wines of ample delicacy, spice and subtlety abound around them. Schloss Johannisberg has belonged to the family of Prince Metternich since 1816.

Geisenheim, on the river bank, is noted rather for its Weininstitut, the center of Germany's viticulture, than for its wine, but there is no such thing as a bad Riesling, and, even if there were, it wouldn't be found here.

Deeper into the *Grosslage* Burgweg is Rüdesheim, clinging to the slopes where the Taunus mountains rise rapidly from the north bank of the Rhine. Here the vineyards were once terraced, so that mechanization was impossible, but bulldozers have achieved a compromise that has brought the hillside into the twentieth century. The vines, grown on slaty soil, collect all the sun, giving early ripening and sometimes a lack of acid. One of the best vineyards, Rottland, is named for the red schistous soil.

A view of Schloss Johannisberg *(below)*, cockpit of Bereich Johannisberg, from the east. In 1775, the Abbot's messenger was once late to arrive with the designated date of vintage, so that the grapes were already overripe when harvested. The wines were accordingly sweet, and the word "*Spätlese*," for noble rot, is said to date from this incident.

# RHEINHESSEN

Although differing in so many ways from Rheingau, Rheinhessen is regarded by many as the second in importance of the German regions. It lies in the crook to the west of the Rhine as it flows north from Worms to Wiesbaden and then west to Bingen. The soils vary considerably. Slate occurs in the most northerly area, around Ingelheim, and red wines are accordingly made in the villages. Over most of the region marl and quartzite persist, but the soil turns to sandstone on the Rheinfront —the steep slopes of the Rhine as it flows north past Nierstein. Here the Riesling grape is planted, producing the noble wines for which Nackenheim, Nierstein, Oppenheim and Dienheim are famous.

In contrast with the Rheingau, the most heavily planted grape in Rheinhessen is the Müller-Thurgau, well supported by Silvaner. There is an increasing tendency to improve the crop and the bouquet and balance of the resulting wines by introducing experimental varieties in addition to known vines from the German list. Thus new crossings of Bacchus, Faber, and Huxelrebe, and of Scheurebe, Kerner, and Ehrenfelser are under trial; and there is a new grape, Jübiläum, which ripens early—a boon to makers of the better Prädikat wines.

Rheinhessen is divided into three *Bereiche*—

Bingen, Nierstein, and Wonnegau, which occupy the northwest, northeast, and south of the region respectively; altogether there are 24 *Grosslagen* and some 450 *Einzellagen* in the region. The average holding in the 24,500ha (60,500 acres) of Rheinhessen vineyards is minimal, and many small growers operate on a ''weekend'' basis, bottling their wines in their own cellars; by law these wines must pass all the state tests if they are to be offered for sale.

Liebfraumilch, known throughout the world, is possibly a mixed blessing so far as Rheinhessen's reputation is concerned, since it occupies a position in the limelight which it barely deserves. The wines known as Liebfrauenmilch or Liebfraumilch came originally from the vineyard of Liebfrauenstifte owned by the Liebfrauenkirche, the Church of Our Lady in the city of Worms. However, the name was widely plagiarized, so that now the law decrees that Liebfraumilch must be a quality wine, that it must come from Rheingau, Rheinhessen, Nahe or Rheinpfalz, and that it may not have any Prädikat. So far so good—but the law decrees also that its labels may not bear the name of a grape, district, village, or vineyard; which means that the Wormser Liebfrauenstifte may not call its wine ''Liebfaumilch''— the name it gave to the world—unless it gives up its original vineyard name.

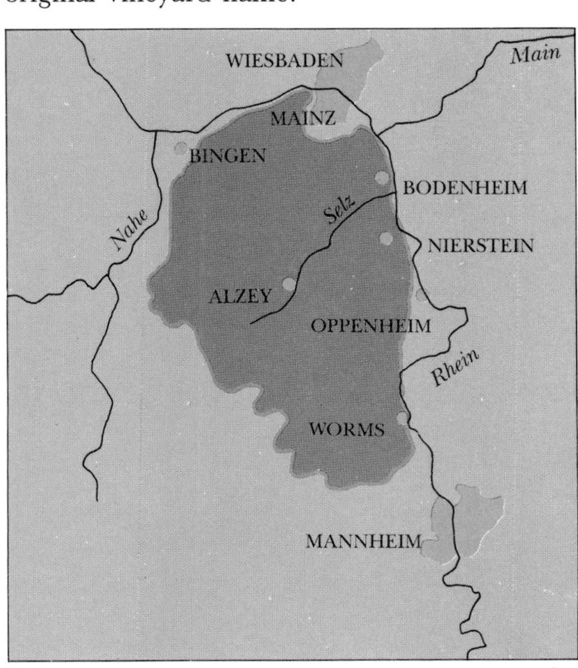


Rheinhessen *(above)*, in the triangle between Bingen, Mainz and Worms, has the largest share (25%) of Germany's vineyard area: the region generally favors the Müller-Thurgau grape. The soils vary: slate in the north, quartzite and marl in the west, and sandstone on the Rheinfront. Bordering the Rhein between Worms and Mainz, the Rheinfront produces the best of the wines from the Riesling.

In the Weinbauort Nierstein, the best central area of Rheinhessen, the Goldene Luft vineyard *(top right)* is planted with Sylvaner and Riesling grapes true to the Rheinhessen tradition.

When the grapes are to be late-harvested, birds become a double menace. At Kurfürstenhof on the Rhine *(right)*, flares are fired from the tower and nets are draped over metal hurdles.

Herr Bohn *(above)*, the present owner, holds a portrait of Bürgermeister Anton Balbach, one of a long line of Nierstein Bürgermeisters.

The famous Pettenthal slope *(below)* of the Anton Balbach Erben vineyards above the Rhein at Nierstein.

This insignia *(right)*, dated 1696 with the coat of arms of the Seips, is painted on a caskhead in the cellars at Kurfürstenhof in Rheinhessen.

Winzermeister Heinrich Seip *(right)* holds a bottle of Niersteiner Klostergarten. The Klostergarten vineyard is in the Rheinfront, where the best Rheinhessen wines are made. An outcrop of stone at Nierstein *(below)*, reflecting the soil of the area, which has 50% sandstone and schist, with 20% limestone and some loess.

# RHEINPFALZ

Rheinpfalz lies about 15 to 25km (9-15½mi) west of the Rhine and runs parallel to it from *der Deutscher Weintor*, "the German winegate," 75km (46½mi) south, at the French frontier, up to its border with Rheinhessen. East of Rheinpfalz are the Haardt hills, the northern remnants of the Vosges mountains, and these act as a rain shadow, helping to give this wine region the best weather of all Germany for ripening grapes. The region is divided into two *Bereiche* by an east-west line just south of Neustadt an der Weinstrasse; below it is *Bereich* Südliche Weinstrasse and above it *Bereich* Mittelhaardt.

The soil varies in the region, tending to improve as one goes from south to north. The Südliche Weinstrasse has soil of chalk and lime with some clay, producing most, but not the best, of the region's wine. The upper Haardt district is, geographically, a continuation of the lesser-quality Bas-Rhin district of Alsace. The wines change suddenly here from the dry crisp wines of France to the sweeter, fuller wines of Germany, due mainly to the change from Riesling to a preponderance of Müller-Thurgau and Silvaner grapes, but the soil is the same, keeping the quality down. The long hot falls do, however, enable excellent sweet Auslese and Beerenauslese wines to be made in the vineyards closer to the Haardt foothills.

The city of Landau was until 1935 the center of Germany's wine-dealing, but the marketing system was then changed to the Deutsche Weinstrasse, whereby each German city nominated its own wine village for bulk wine supplies. Today, much of the upper Haardt crop is vinified by cooperatives, and a high proportion of output is shipped in bulk—although Alsace now imports significant quantities of wine from the upper Haardt in bottle.

All the glory of Rheinpfalz wines belongs to the Mittelhaardt, where the soil, especially in the center around Forst, turns to black basalt which stores the sun's heat for radiation at night. Leading estates between Kallstadt and Ruppertsberg, planted mainly with Riesling, produce wines of the finest quality. In good years they are beefy, full of flavor and deep in color, reaching their best after maturing for eight to ten years.

The most famous vineyards in the Mittelhaardt include the diminutive Jesuitengarten at Forst and, close by, Freundstück, Kirchenstück and Ungeheuer. Deidesheim, which must epitomize in character and architecture everything the wine-loving tourist may seek, is a

The estate of Weingut Dr Bürklin-Wolf *(below)*, the showpiece of the Rheinpfalz. Dr Bürklin-Wolf, Germany's great enologist, died in 1979: now his daughter Bettina is the owner.

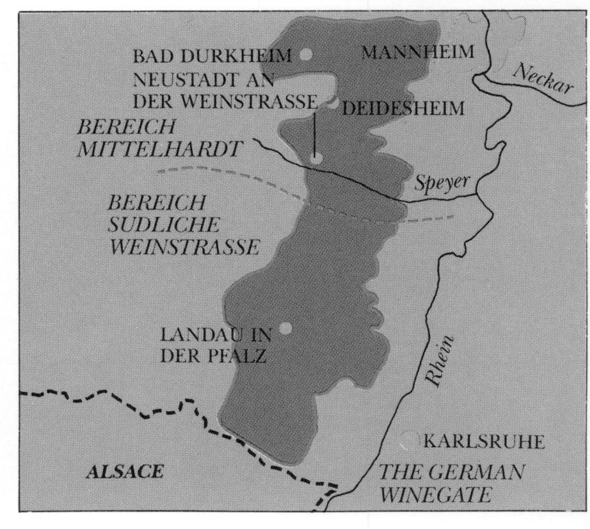


Rheinpfalz *(above)*, up-river from Rheinhessen, stretches 75km (47mi) from the German winegate, near Karlsruhe, down to Worms.

Georg Raquet *(top)* of Bürklin-Wolf, who is upholding a tradition for superb semidry Riesling Kabinetts and full late-vintage wines of immaculate style and balance.

contender with Forst for the wine accolades of the Rheinpfalz, but only after spreading quantities of potassium-rich basalt quarried at Forst. Its best vineyards lie in the *Grosslage* Mariengarten. Just to the north are Wachenheim, Ungstein and Kallstadt, all producing worthy full-bodied noble wines typical of the *Bereich*. As the "Pfalz" reaches its northern extremities, the wines become insignificant.

The region produces more red wine than either Rheingau or Rheinhessen: it is all made from the Portugieser grape; Bad Dürkheim, just north of Forst, is noted for the best of it, but no more than for its white Rieslings.

# NAHE

There are only 4,550ha (11,250 acres) of vineyard plantings in this comparatively large region. The river Nahe rises in the Hunsrück (dog's back) hills which separate Nahe from Mosel-Saar-Ruwer, to its west. The region is divided into two *Bereiche*, the greater of which, *Bereich* Schloss Böckelheim, is in the south; *Bereich* Kreuznach tapers northward to reach the Rhine at Bingen, where four German wine regions meet. Thus Nahe has the Mittelrhein to its north, Rheingau to its northeast, and Rheinhessen to its east.

The vineyards of *Grosslage* Paradiesgarten, along the higher Nahe reaches, yield light fragrant wines, similar to those of the Mosel, from sandstone soils.

Downstream, toward Bad Kreuznach, the river runs through the *Grosslage* Burgweg, where most of the prize wines of the region are made. Schloss-Böckelheim not only gives its name to the *Bereich*, its village houses the Kupfergrube vineyard of the State Domain, possibly the most famous of all Nahe properties.

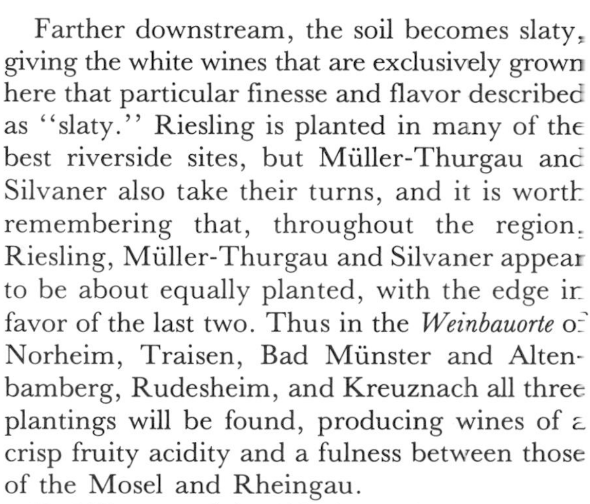

Farther downstream, the soil becomes slaty, giving the white wines that are exclusively grown here that particular finesse and flavor described as "slaty." Riesling is planted in many of the best riverside sites, but Müller-Thurgau and Silvaner also take their turns, and it is worth remembering that, throughout the region, Riesling, Müller-Thurgau and Silvaner appear to be about equally planted, with the edge in favor of the last two. Thus in the *Weinbauorte* of Norheim, Traisen, Bad Münster and Altenbamberg, Rudesheim, and Kreuznach all three plantings will be found, producing wines of a crisp fruity acidity and a fulness between those of the Mosel and Rheingau.

Bad Kreuznach itself is the capital and nerve center of Nahe. Wine experts throughout the world know the town for the Seitzwerke, a factory specializing in wine-filtering techniques and equipment. No less than 100ha (247 acres) of vineyards lie within its commune; Brückes, Kahlenberg, Krötenpfuhl, and Steinweg are the best sites.

Between Bad Kreuznach and Bingen there are a number of good vineyards, some on south-facing slopes along the left bank of the Nahe river. The Riesling becomes less prominent in favor of the Müller-Thurgau and the Silvaner as the slate is left behind and sandy loam soils appear. The wines accordingly become more full-bodied, lacking in some of the mystery of the noble wines made higher up the river. Rothenberg wines, from *Grosslage* Sonnenborn, are typical. Burg Layen and Rümmelsheim, in *Grosslage* Schlosskapelle, and Weinsham, in *Grosslage* Rosengarten, are communes with better-than-average sites west of the river, where the land rises with stonier soils.

If any red wine is made in the Nahe, little is said of it, but the white wines are never less than good and are generally available at a reasonable price.

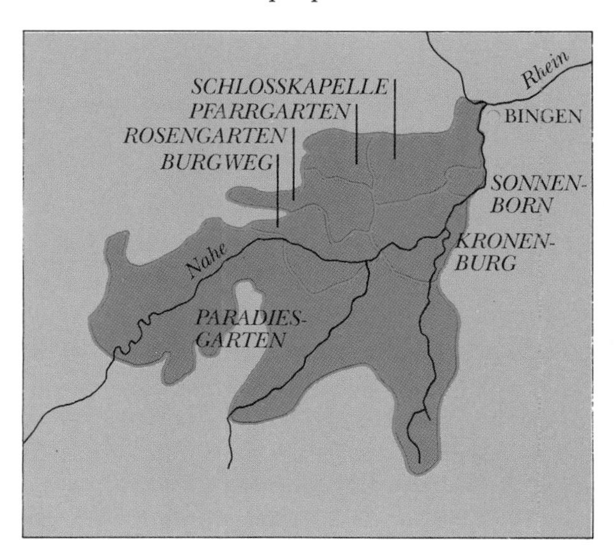


The bulk of the Nahe lies west and north of the Nahe river *(above)*, and is wedged between the north Mosel region and Rheinhessen. Its wines reflect the character of each.

Schlossböckelheim, *Bereich* and village, is the star of the upper Nahe. Here is its best vineyard, the Kupfergrube *(right)*, owned by the Estate Domain at Niederhausen.

The steep-sloping Kupfergrube vineyard of the Estate Domain at Schlossböckelheim *(below)*. In the background the river Nahe may be seen flowing through its valley to join the Rhein at Bingen.

The dividing line between the Kupfergrube and Hermannsberg vineyards *(right)* on the Niederhausen-Schlossböckelheim estate. In front of the precipitous Hermannsberg vineyards on the right are the State Domain buildings.

The State Domain's vineyards in Schlossböckelheim *(left)* are among the best of the Nahe, producing Rieslings reminiscent of the neighboring Mosels and Rheinhessens.

Riesling grapes on the vine at Hermannsberg *(inset left).* The upper Nahe originally specialized in Riesling plantings and the lower in Sylvaner, but the Müller-Thurgau has encroached on both.

The soils in the middle reaches of the Nahe river tend to be slaty, and at Schlossböckelheim there are outcrops of pink-to-mauve porphyry crystals *(inset right)* in finer soil derived from sandstone and slate.

Dr Werner Hofäcker *(right),* successor to Dr Bürklin-Wolf as the winemaker at the State Domain estate of Schlossböckelheim.

# MITTELRHEIN AND AHR

The Mittelrhein wine region, hugging the fast-flowing lower Rhine, as it runs north through the Rhine Gorge from Bingen to the seven hills of Bonn, has a medieval atmosphere. On each side cliffs of slate and schist are topped with castles that recall a past when survival was by the sword, and when heraldic banners alone distinguished friend and foe.

There are three *Bereiche*: Bacharach, at the southern tip; Rheinburgengau, covering nearly the full length of the region; and Siebengebirge, at the northern tip. *Bereich* Klosterberg covers the whole of the neighboring "mini-region" of Ahr, which runs west-to-east along the banks of the river Ahr, a Rhine tributary, close to the northern extremity of the Rheinburgengau.

South of Koblenz the vineyards are mainly on the left bank; north of this city they are mostly to be found on the other side. All make white wines from the Riesling. In good years they are pleasing, with an unusual flavor of peach kernels, but in poor years they are destined for conversion to Sekt.

The soil remains schistous in the Ahr valley, where strangely—even extraordinarily—red wines are made at this most northerly point of any of Germany's wine regions. Heat reflected from the cliffs at each side of the narrow valley does its best to ripen the Spätburgunder grapes, but only in a good year is the wine better than thin and light-colored. It does not usually reach the outside world: as Glühwein it is an acceptable mixer in punch for the winter skiers, while in summer natural soda water bubbling from the Apollinaris spring in the Bad Neuenahr spa may be added to make it a cooling drink. Of the grape crop, 60% is Spätburgunder and Portugieser and 40% Riesling and Müller-Thurgau. From these are made attractive wines that fail, however, to compare with those from farther south.

# MOSEL-SAAR-RUWER

Here is a region that captures the imagination and romance not only of wine-lovers but of all who yearn for a make-believe land of turreted castles, sleepy valleys above a winding river, twinkling lights under the moon, and wines that help to dim reality! Few of the millions who set out each year along the Mosel fail to imprint that very scene on their minds forever. Here, from where the cherry and plum trees intermingle with the vineyards of Luxembourg to the confluence of the Mosel with the Rhine at Koblenz—some 130km (81mi) as the crow flies and over twice that distance by river—is to be found an enormous industry second to none in its task of marrying the perfect grape with perfect natural wine-making conditions.

The river Moselle rises on the western slopes of the Vosges mountains and has already flowed half its length before it leaves France to serve, for 50km (31mi), as a natural border between Luxembourg and Germany. A few kilometers later the river Saar flows into the Moselle from the southeast, and immediately the river assumes its German identity as the Mosel; after flowing another 16km (10mi) the river Ruwer comes in, also from the southeast, to join the Mosel on its long journey downstream.

Mosel-Saar-Ruwer is divided into five *Bereiche*. The uppermost, starting at the frontier with France, is *Bereich* Moseltor, and then comes *Bereich* Obermosel. Just before the confluence with the Saar, *Bereich* Saar-Ruwer begins. This *Bereich* is carefully charted so that it may incorporate the vineyards on the banks of both the Saar and the Ruwer. It runs downstream to Probstberg, where the beautiful *Bereich* Bernkastel of the middle Mosel begins. At a point lower down the river, close to Zell, *Bereich* Zell takes over; it covers the remainder of the Mosel's course to the Rhine.

To discover the secret of the middle Mosel gorge, and to understand the anomaly that the greatest of Mosel wines all belong essentially to this one district, it is necessary to turn to geology. In prehistoric times the Devonian Sea covered the whole area of the Mosel; as it subsided it left sedimentary layers which have since become soft slate. The Mosel river, over countless centuries, has cut its way down through this slate to form a deep gorge, revealing fossilized sea-life in the slaty shale of its steep banks. The canyon is too deep to feel the effects of any wind, and the river twists so tortuously that many reaches, often several kilometers long, are bound to receive the rays of the sun at ideal angles. Furthermore, since the canyon has been canalized (with eleven locks) the waters have risen and widened, so that the broad surface of the Mosel reflects and intensifies the sun's heat. As a consequence the valley is warm and humid long after the surrounding hills have been frozen solid.

The superlative wines of the Mosel are made near the center, which may be taken as Bernkastel; upstream beyond Trittenheim and downstream beyond Traben-Trarbach the vineyards rely increasingly upon the season for their finest wines. The best estates all grow Riesling, but in the *Grosslagen* Obermosel and Saar-Ruwer the Riesling can need encouragement to ripen, so the Müller-Thurgau and the sharp Elbling are often used to produce wines that may sometimes excel or, at other times, may warrant marketing only under the name of "Moselblümchen"—the Mosel's equivalent of Liebfraumilch. Wines from the Elbling grape in a bad year have been called "Dreimännerwein" ("three-man wine")—it takes two men to hold the third one down and force him to drink it! But that should not

The Egon Müller estate under the Scharzhofberg hill at Wiltingen *(right)*. Originally a monastery, the estate was confiscated following the French Revolution and sold to the great-great-grandfather of Egon Müller, the present proprietor. Inheritance has hived off two-thirds of the original estate since then; only 11ha (27 acres) remain.

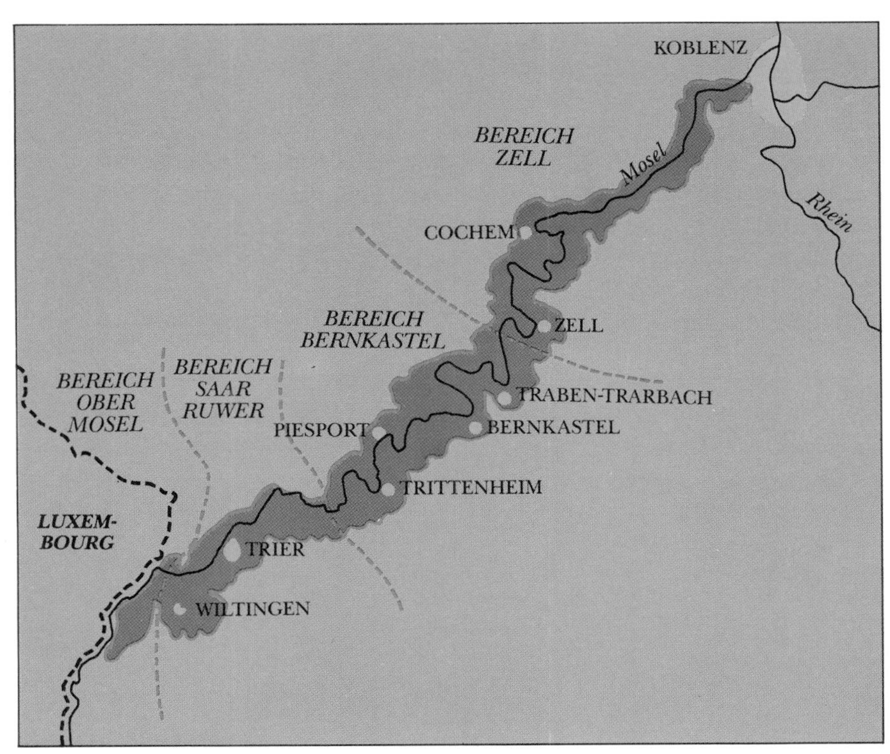


Second in size to Rheinhessen, Mosel-Saar-Ruwer *(above)* is famed for its supreme and gently different Riesling wines. North of Trier, where the Saar and Ruwer have already joined the river, the Mosel runs through a deep valley cut into the slate. In the summer the sun is trapped, and in the winter the warm river and the steep slopes above it give protection. Bereich Bernkastel in the Mittelmosel has beauty of world renown, and produces the best of Mosel's wines, principally from the Riesling grape.

Egon Müller, proprietor of the Scharzhof Manor at Wiltingen on the Saar *(center)*, is dedicated to producing "late-picked" wines of the highest quality: they top the prices at the annual Trier auctions.

Der Bischöflichen Weingüter Trier, the biggest estate combine in the Mosel-Saar-Ruwer, formed by joining three religious charitable properties *(above)*. The wines, which are light, medium-dry, and superbly made, are fermented centrally at Trier.

Just above the bridge from Kues, Bernkastel *(above)* is seen hugging the right bank of the Mosel. Above the town is the Doktor vineyard, whence come Mosels held to be the best of all Bernkastel wines.

The soil of the Doktor is mainly a schistous slate and has a subtle moist quality that has been likened to that of demerara sugar. The slate is clearly identifiable *(right)* in this picture.

Before bottling, wines are racked during fermentation and fined with a gelatinous substance such as isinglass. They are then said to "fall bright". Just how bright this can be is demonstrated in this unusual photograph *(right)* of a glass of wine from the Doktor vineyard at Bernkastel.

The great Bischöfliche Weinguter estate in the Saar and Ruwer is famous for the Riesling wines it produces. Here the town of Kasel on the Ruwer is seen skirting the foot of the great Nieschen hill *(above)*. The Bischöfliche Weinguter has a long history of church proprietorship centered on Trier, where its offices and cellars are located today.

The total vineyard area of the Bischöfliche Weinguter is 95.5ha (236 acres), spread through some 20 vineyards in the Saar, Ruwer and Mittel-Mosel. These Riesling grapes *(right)* are being held late on the vine for QmP *Kabinett* and *Spätlese* qualities.

distract us from the exquisite wines of the region.

The Saar has several worthy *Grosslagen*. In Ockfen are found the Bockstein vineyards, owned partially by the State Domain, and lower down the river, around Wiltingen, center of the subregion, are vineyards including Scharzhofberg which make well balanced wines that age well. Nearer the Rhine is Filzen, with some 60ha (148 acres) of worthy vineyards which, together with Falkenstein and Menning, comprise the *Grosslage* of Konz. Trier, between the Saar and Ruwer, is famous for its essentially light Riesling wines, and the vineyards of Avelsbach, now in the *Grosslage* and operated jointly by the State Domain and Hohe Domkirche, give delicate wines of intoxicating perfume. Kasel, the small wine "capital" of the Ruwer, contains the Nies'chen property, making wines in the same tradition.

From the Ruwer downstream there are many bends in the river that offer superior vineyard sites, and the wine improves all the way down to Bernkastel. From Trier to Longuich, Longen and Lörsch, all in *Grosslage* Probstberg, the Riesling takes over and the real Mosel characteristics start to appear. By the time Klüsserath is reached, in the *Grosslage* St Michael, the true Middle Mosel begins; in the next *Grosslage*, Michelsberg, Trittenheim, Neumagen, and the famous Piesport with the celebrated Goldtröpfchen vineyard on the north bank. Then comes the outstanding Juffer vineyard of Brauneberg (once selling the most expensive Mosel of all, and worth it), and Bernkastel is but a few kilometers away.

The little town of Bernkastel and the larger town of Kues on the opposite (left) bank of the river, are literally and otherwise, the center of the Middle Mosel. Vineyards cling to the precipitous hill rising behind Bernkastel; the Doktor is the most famous of them. The hill stretches downstream for 9km (5 ½ mi) and rises to 250m (820ft). Along it are the finest of all properties, one merging into the next, through Graach, past Wehlen and on to Zeltingen; they offer the best wine that Riesling, nature and mankind can put together. Wehlen, across the river, has its best vineyard, the Sonnenurh, on this amazing hill. Among the growers are names of international renown, like Burgweiler-Prüm (and other Prüms), Deinhard, Josephshof, Meyerhof, Schneider, and Selbach-Oster.

Riesling plantations continue downstream, taking in Urzig, Kröv, Traben-Trarbach, and Reil, all famed for their Mosels; and then *Bereich* Bernkastel melts into *Bereich* Zell. Zell itself is the best known commune, it makes light, flowery wines marketed always with a black-cat label to reflect the name of the *Grosslage*, Schwarze Katz. There is no *Grosslage* where Riesling is deserted, although the Muller-Thurgau is increasingly bringing more bouquet and less nobility to the wine.

The river straightens out after the hairpin bend at Cochem, but the gorge continues through softer slate with lowering slopes past Winningen to the confluence of the Mosel and Rhine at Koblenz.

Of all the Prüms in the Mittel-Mosel, the Weingut Joh Jos Prüm is the most important, although all branches of the family stem from Herhardus Hermann Prüm who planted a vineyard in about 1100. The Riesling grapes in this bunch *(right)* are ready for conversion to sweet *Prädikat* wines.

The Wehlener Sonnenuhr vineyard of J. J. Prüm, opposite Wehlen on the left bank of the Rhein, is regarded as equal in quality and consistency with the Doktor. The sign *(center right)* is used to mark the vineyard row at the limit of the Prüm property.

The giant sundial *(far right)* that gives the Wehlener Sonnenuhr vineyard its name and keeps the town of Wehlen on the opposite bank well informed — on a fine day. Note the high training of the vines on individual stakes. The QmP wines made here are superb.

7
8
9
10·11·12·1·2
3
4
5
6

The imposing Schloss Lieser *(left)* towering above the Mosel a few kilometers upstream from Bernkastel. Lieser's 208ha (514 acres), although next to Grosslage Bernkastel-Kues, have their own Grosslage Beerenlay, shared by many growers, including the noble domain of Freiherr von Schorlemer.

Casks in the cellars of Meyer-Horne *(right)*, at Zeltingen. A valve to release carbon dioxide without letting air into the cask, during the process of "reductive" aging, is seen on the nearest cask.

A worker in the vineyard at Lieser *(left)* collects grapes in a small tub to avoid crushing the fruit. The height above the Mosel can be gauged from this view looking upstream to the small village of Lieser. There are 120ha (297 acres) in the *Grosslage.*

Schlossberg, at Lieser *(above)*, looking downstream to the intricate pattern of hills through which the Mosel threads its way to the Rhein at Koblenz. In the foreground, debris marks the aftermath of the harvest. The wines can be lively but are rarely above average.

241

## BADEN AND WÜRTTEMBERG

To the east of the upper Rhine is the large scattered region of Baden, hugging the right bank of the Rhine from Basel to Heidelberg, with two isolated *Bereiche*, one by the Swiss border at the Bodesee (Lake Constance) and the other near Franken. In the last 20 years the vineyards have been remodelled and modernized by the Government, under the Flubereinigung policy, doubling their size and quadrupling their output.

Baden's wines are beefy and varied, cooperative wineries processing practically all of the crop. Müller-Thurgau is the leading grape for white wines and Spätsburgunder for reds and rosés; but Ruländer, Riesling, Silvaner, Gewürztraminer and Weissburgunder are all planted. The EEC has recognized the warmth of this southerly region by classifying it in wine-producing Zone B. All other German regions are in Zone A.

Württemberg, lying east of Baden and contiguous with it for some 25km (15½mi), produces good wine—but the Württembergers drink it all, and so it has little national, let alone international, significance. The white wines are generally Rieslings, while the reds and rosés are made principally from Württemberg's own Trollinger vine. Black and white grape plantings are about equal; the black Spätsburgunder is used to make Weissherbst, a rosé QbA wine. The rosé, mixed with white wine, produces Schillerwein, a specialty of the region.

## HESSISCHE BERGSTRASSE AND FRANKEN

Hessische Bergstrasse is Germany's smallest wine region, with only 380ha (940 acres) under vine. It is surrounded on three sides by the Rhine and Main rivers and their confluence. Fruity wines with a delicate acidity are made in Starkenburg, the larger of its two *Bereiche*, using the Riesling grape, while Müller-Thurgau is planted in *Bereich* Umstadt, to its east around

The slopes of the flat-topped hill of the Kaiserstuhl *(below)* northwest of Freiburg in Baden are a perfect illustration of the German Government's *Flubereinigung* policy of remodeling and modernizing the vineyards.

Darmstadt. About 90% of the harvest is processed by the cooperatives at Heppenheim and Gros Umstadt.

In the north of Bavaria the river Main struggles through the Spessart hills in two mighty loops—the first from Schwein down to Kitzingen and up to Lohr, the second down to Wertheim and up to Frankfurt—before running steadily west to meet the Rhine. The wine region of Franken surrounds the Main, north and south, on this journey. It is divided into three *Bereiche*: Steigerwald, taking in Castell and Iphofen in the east; Maindreieck, including all the river towns in the center from Volkach to Wertheim; and Mainviereck, covering the area north of Wertheim and west along the Main to Aschaffenburg.

At the center of the region is the old cathedral and university city of Würzburg, where the famous Würzburger Stein vineyard has given the name Steinwine to Franconian wines in general (although this is contrary to German wine law, which reserves the name for the original vineyard only). These quality wines are dry and flinty and tend to become acid; they are bottled in the flagon-shaped *Bocksbeutels*. Though most of the harvest in *Bereich* Maindreieck is converted by cooperatives, three of the greatest wine estates of Germany are here—the Bürgerspital, Juliusspital, and Staatliche Hofkeller.

The climate in Franconia is an inland-continental one, with harsh winters and late springs, and the vineyards are scattered on south-facing slopes where they can find the sun and if possible avoid the hard frosts. The vintage yields of the 1980s have already produced a low of 31hl/ha and a high of 170hl/ha. The soils vary considerably: upstream in *Bereich* Steigerwald the soil of the better vineyards is a heavy mixture of marl and clay; in the center it is limestone, the ideal for German wines; and in *Bereich* Mainviereck the soil is loamy with a sandstone base.

Good wines made in this region from a variety of the Silvaner grape are often compared with white Burgundy, being full-bodied and suitable for drinking with rich foods; and Rieslaner (a Riesling-Silvaner cross) in a good year will produce excellent Ausleses. Müller-Thurgau vines are now much planted to produce wines of low acidity that are softened somewhat by use of the Bacchus grape (also gaining in popularity), which can add body and flavor. Frankenwein is overpriced, but this does not stop the inhabitants of this beer-producing region from drinking most of it in the big-city bars of Bavaria.

The center of Heppenheim village in Hessische Bergstrasse *(above)*, home of one of the two cooperatives that between them convert nearly all of the region's grapes.

The Neckar and its tributaries wind through the hills of Wurttemberg affording ample sites for vineyards with south-facing aspects. Here the small Klingenberg property of Graf von Neipperg at Emzellagen clings to the river's north bank *(right)*.

# IBERIA

## Spain ♦ Sherry ♦ Portugal ♦ Port ♦ Madeira ♦ Setúbal

The Iberian Peninsula measures some 1,250km (775mi) both down and across. One-half of her coast juts into the Atlantic, and one-third borders the Mediterranean; the remaining one-sixth of her perimeter separates her from France along the Pyrénées. Her climate accordingly varies dramatically. In the west and north a maritime climate brings winds to the coastal mountains with rainfall at double the annual rate experienced in Britain. Beyond the mountains, in the body of Portugal and in southwestern Spain, the weather is temperate with only half as much rain. The central plateau of Spain is dry and may be extremely hot in summer and bitterly cold in winter.

The rivers of Spain are vital to her wine industry. Four important rivers rise some 200km (124mi) inland from the Mediterranean and flow across to the Atlantic. The most northerly are the Douro and the Tagus, which run on through Portugal into the ocean at Oporto and Lisbon respectively. The Guadiana runs west to cross the border into Portugal at Badajoz, where it turns due south to flow into the Gulf of Cadiz at the Spanish border. The Guadalquivir flows through Cordoba to Seville before turning south to Jerez de la Frontera. A fifth river, the Ebro, rises in the Cantabrian mountains at Reinosa and flows east-southeast through northern Spain to the Mediterranean.

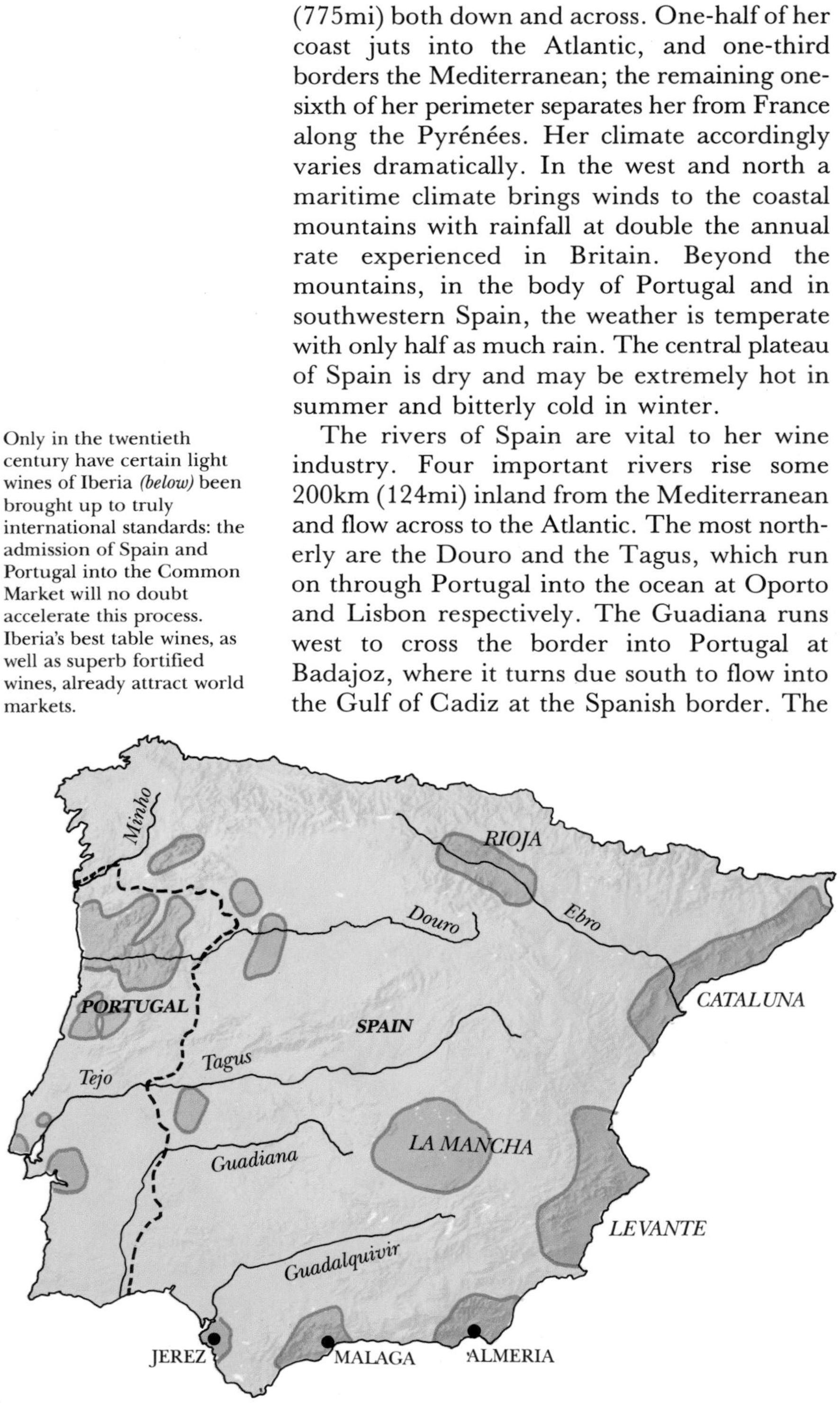

Only in the twentieth century have certain light wines of Iberia *(below)* been brought up to truly international standards: the admission of Spain and Portugal into the Common Market will no doubt accelerate this process. Iberia's best table wines, as well as superb fortified wines, already attract world markets.

Minho
RIOJA
Douro
Ebro
PORTUGAL
SPAIN
CATALUNA
Tejo
Tagus
Guadiana
LA MANCHA
LEVANTE
Guadalquivir
JEREZ
MALAGA
ALMERIA

## SPAIN

The poor reputation of the light wines of Spain stretched back far beyond the Christian era. Even during the Napoleonic wars neither side had a good word to say for them. They were stored in a *cuero* (pigskin) daubed internally with tar, and so for obvious reasons there was little chance of finding an export market: the contents were safely secured for the Spaniards. In this century, however, the government has taken a hand, so that now certified "fine" wines are made instead of the red "tinto" or white "blanco" of yesteryear. Although the trade—through several organizations—had started to improve the better wines, it was 1970 before the Ministerio de Agricultura introduced its "Statute of Vines, Wines and Spirits," giving powers to regional *consejos* or committees (a few of which had existed since the 1920s) to regulate a system of Denominaciónes de Origen, a fair and welcome copy of the preexisting French AC and Italian DOC systems. This does not mean that the Spaniards have yet brought all their wines up to standards of international acceptance, though their membership of the EEC may accelerate this process.

Spain has the largest area of vineyards in the world, but areas of mixed planting are included, so that her average yield of only 20hl/ha may be misleading. More than half her two million hectares of vineyards are delimited by Denominacióne de Origen; while this figure includes the vineyards of Jerez, one must nevertheless wonder about overall quality.

The wines of Spain are generally heavy in alcohol, especially those of the central plains, and this situation seems likely to continue. Only in the north and northeast do the wines have the character and balance to appeal to the inter-

To the east of the La Mancha plateau is a group of regions that have earned Denominaciónes de Origen; jointly they are known as the Levante. Valencia and Alicante dominate the Mediterranean coastal area, and lying in hilly country inland are Uliel-Requena, Almansar, Yecla, and Jumilla, the last two being in the province of Murcia. These vineyards in Jumilla *(above)* are representative of the region.

The best of the wines of Navarro, although not so well known as those of Rioja, share with them the style that engenders comparisons with those of Bordeaux. The bodegas of Señorio de Sarria produce superb wines based mainly on the Tempranillo grape (60%), their best being the full-bodied, well balanced Viña del Perdon. The green bottles of Señorio de Sarria *(right)*, cleansed and inverted, are seen here waiting to be filled.

national market: the red wines of Rioja and the mainly white Penedés of Catalonia are quality table wines now exported in bulk; Riojas have attained one-third the volume of Sherry exports.

## RIOJA

This region of the upper Ebro is named for the Rio (river) Oja, a tributary joining the Ebro at Haro. Rioja is divided into three districts, Rioja Alta, Rioja Alavesa and Rioja Baja.

The Rioja Alta lies along and to the south of the Ebro, from the province of Burgos (where several Oja tributaries assemble) down to the province of Lograno. Three important wine centers, Cenicero, Fuenmayor, and Lograno, all lie along the Ebro's south bank. Rioja Alavesa is in the province of Alava, above the north bank of the Ebro, and Rioja Baja straddles the Ebro to the southeast, from the straight north-south boundary of the Alta and Alavesa districts down to Alfaro.

There is a remarkable change in climate between the Alta and Alavesa districts, on the one hand, and the Baja, on the other. The higher districts lie in the lee of the Cantabrian mountains, and enjoy a temperate climate with moderate rainfall, while the Baja is hot and dry, with less rainfall. From subhumid the climate becomes suddenly semiarid, and the wine suffers accordingly.

The grapes of Rioja are the Tempranillo and Garnacho, for red wines, and the Viura, for white wines. The Garnacho is identical with the Grenache of France; the Viura is known in Cataluña, to the southeast, as the Maccabeo. The soil is basically clay with plenty of gravel and limestone, and throughout the region the vines are trained in bush fashion.

Although DO Valdepeñas is the one superior wine from the vast La Mancha sea of vines, it is not of great class. Known as *aloque*, it is made by adding about 10% of the near-black Tempranillo (locally Cencibel) grapes to the white Airén, to give a claret-color. Here *toneles (below)* are being made at Ciudad Real.

The wines have character and strength, and the full-bodied ruby-red *tintos* and green to gold dry *blancos* have been likened to Burgundies, although they are low in alcohol. The *claretes* are subtler and lighter, with a good bouquet, and are more worthy to be compared with those of the Médoc. This may be logical: when phylloxera ravaged Bordeaux in the 1870s the French intensified their interest in the Rioja region, and Bordeaux methods—including the use of the oak *barrique* of 225-liter (59½ gal) capacity for maturation—were introduced. Although Rioja was to suffer from phylloxera at the dawn of the twentieth century, the French influence has remained, and brought DO status to the whole region.

## CATALONIA

Catalonia is the fruit-garden of Spain: nestling on the coast and in the hills above the northeastern Mediterranean, this independent province of Spain breathes welcome to the wine-lover in an almost endless array of reds, pinks and whites. There are seven districts of Catalonia, each making its individual claims to DO quality recognition.

### Alella and Ampurdán

The quality of the wines produced in these districts is at best acceptable rather than notable. Were it not for the Alella Vinecola Cooperative, which vinifies most of the grapes in the valley north of Barcelona, the fruity, acid dry and semisweet whites of this district would lack what uniformity and character they achieve. The wines are matured in oak for up to two years and sold after three. Blanco Seco is a dry fresh wine with the right acidity; Blanco Abbocado is sweeter. The vines are Garnacho, Maccabeo, Malvasia and Picpoul. Ampurdán touches the French border around Perelada in the province of Gerona. Production is mainly of rosé, although some red and white wines are produced, too; some of the latter are sparkling. None reach the true quality of Penedés wines.

### Conca de Barberá

With 10,000ha (24,700 acres)—double the area of vineyards in Alella and Ampurdán—Conca de Barberá is almost entirely devoted to the production of sparkling wines made by the *méthode champenoise*. The Chardonnay grape is used in their manufacture, and this accounts for a similarity with the product of the Côte des Blancs of Champagne.

### Penedés

This is the most important district of Catalonia, centering on the town of Villafranca del Penedés. Great strides have been made to bring the quality of Penedés wines up to international standards. The deep red wines are darker and somewhat fruitier than those of the Rioja, but have less finesse. The limestone soil of the upland vineyards produces fine dry white wines from the Parellada and Maccabeo grapes; they have a recollection of Muscadet about them. Down at Sitges, on the coast, is produced the sweet Malvasia de Sitges, a fortified wine in the tradition of the French Vins Doux Naturels to the north across the border; it is made from Malvasia and Sumoll grapes dried in the sun.

Three grapes combine to produce the must for *vinos espumosos*, latterly also called *cava*, after the name that may be adopted by a bodega using the *méthode champenoise*: they are Parellada, Xarel-lo, and Viura. These sparkling wines compare favorably with anything except Champagne. Annual production is not immense, between 1,000hl and 1,500hl (26-40,000gal), and a similar quantity of sparkling wine is made by *cuve-close* or impregnation. Spanish sparkling wines are labeled *bruto, seco,* or *semiseco,* for extradry, dry or semidry, and *semidulce* or *dulce* for semisweet or sweet.

Priorato, named for the Priory of Scala Dei in the Sierra de Montsant, is watered by the Montsant, a tributary of the Ebro. The soil is volcanic slate. It lies inland to the west of the coastal town of Tarragona, and has a DO for a dry red wine, almost black in color, looking like and (if it is not just an association of ideas) tasting slightly like blackberry juice. Some 50 to 60 thousand hectoliters (1,320-1,585 thousand gallons) are produced annually. Made from Garnacho, Negro and Cariñena grapes, the wine is full-bodied, with up to 18% vol. alcohol. Another interesting wine is the sweet white dessert wine made here from Garnacho Blanco, Maccabeo and Pedro Ximénez grapes. A quantity of *mistela* (grape-must inhibited by grape spirit before fermentation) is made here for blending into dessert wines and Vermouths.

DO Tarragona (which contains Priorato) covers an area within and without the Penedés district. Its claim to fame is the range of sweet fortified dessert wines generically bearing its name.

Finally, Gandesa Terra Alta is a mountainous subdistrict to the west of the Ebro, with some 16,000ha (39,500 acres) of vines producing "blending" wines in the Tarragona tradition.

## LA MANCHA

This region to the south and southeast of Madrid is a vast plateau, some 600m (1,970ft) above sea-level, which has considerable variations of temperature every day and also through the seasons. The soil, a strong red over a subsoil of chalk and slate, is suitable for vines that have to fend for themselves, short pruned vines stretching kilometer after kilometer, planted three meters (10ft) apart, that rely on the occasional olive tree for shelter from the sun. There are still windmills and wheat to remind us of Don Quixote. Miraculously, the grapes ripen well, to give the cafés of Madrid and northern Spain—and even the borders of France—reasonable carafe wines. The area of vines is almost astronomic—nearly half a million hectares (1 ¼ million acres)—and nearly all are planted with the white Airén grape, yielding

Sheltered to the north by the Pyrénées and looking down on the blue Mediterranean, the vineyards of Catalonia are renowned for grapey dessert wines and heavy reds, although unexpectedly crisp white wines may be found as well. A picking of the native white Parellada grapes *(above)* is being loaded into a trailer.

The DO region of Cariñena in the province of Aragon lies south of Rioja Baja, and has given its name to the Carignan grape, pride of the French Midi. The grape of the region is, surprisingly, the Garnacha Tinta; here *(left)* row upon row of *barricas* at Bodegas Vincente Suso y Pérez are oak-aging its strong red wine.

At Logroño in the Alta Rioja the Bodegas Franco-Españolas *(right)* produce almost a million cases of wine yearly, of which one-quarter is exported. Their range includes oak-aged white wines, the full-bodied Royal *reservas*, and Excelso *gran reservas*.

The Catalans may be only half Spaniards, but they have the knack of drinking *vino en porrón (far right)* with never a drop wasted! Penedés is the major DO of Catalonia, where a number of French noble vines are now being introduced: *cava*, or sparkling white wine made by the *méthode champenoise*, is a Catalan specialty.

An artisan at Ciudad Real *(left)* is seen making *botas* from the skin of goats. Students of Cervantes will recall that Don Quixote spent much time lancing the *cueros* (pigskins) that were then the standard containers for the wines of Spain.

This view of the Valle de Abalos in La Rioja *(below)* gives a general impression of the irregular spread of vineyards. The territory opens out to wider valley land as the river Ebro flows east from the heights of the Sierra Cantabrica.

wines which have about 14% vol. alcohol and little flavor. Exceptional is DO Valdepeñas, from an area about 160km (100mi) south of Madrid, where the Airén is blended with a small but strong fraction of Cencibel (Tempranillo) and Garnacho grapes, darkening the color but adding no significant acid or tannin. Fermentation in the *tinajas* used since the days of ancient Rome still may be seen, although some wine is aged in the barrel. Mostly the result is a light wine with a touch of the *solera* about it, as the *tinajas* are never quite emptied before being recharged.

## EXTRAMADURA AND LEON

This region in the west of Spain surrounds the town of Almendralejo in the province of Badajoz and is watered by the Duero. Here 40,000ha (99,000 acres) of vineyards are planted mainly with the Cayetana vine to add yet more low-acidity, high-strength wines to what is already a Spanish surplus of them. There are exceptions, however. There is a good white from the Cañamero as well as two reds, the Salvatierra de Barros from the Portuguese border and the Montánchez from Cáceras. The grapes are Almendralejo, Garnacho and Morisca. To the south of Extramadura is Toledo, where the Garnacho grape produces strong red wine under the DO Méntrida.

## LEVANTE

On the eastern slopes of La Mancha is a composite region embracing Cheste, Utiel-Requena and Valencia in the north, Almansar in the middle, and Alicante, Jumilla and Yecla in the south. This is an area of coastal hillsides along the Mediterranean where over 1½ million hectoliters (39½ million gallons) of DO wine is produced each year. The Bobal grape is used to produce light red and rosé wines of up to 12% vol. alcohol. In Jumilla and Yecla, where the climate is hotter and drier, stronger wines, up to 17% vol. alcohol, come from the Monastrel grape. The soil becomes alluvial and too rich for the production of wines as the plateau drops gently to the coastal plain.

## OTHER SPANISH REGIONS

Navarra lies between Rioja and the Pyrénées and has its own DO for wines matured for two or more years. A robust red wine is made from the Garnacho vine, and red wines comparable with those of the Rhône are made near Pamplona from Cerasol and the Secano grape (known as *ojo de gallo*—"partridge eye"). They are lighter than Riojas, and have a distinctive bouquet.

Between Madrid and Barcelona is Cariñena, lying south of Sierra de la Muela. Here wines

Bodegas Olarra at Logroño in the Rioja Alta *(below)* is an important winery, founded in 1972; it is superbly equipped, and already produces a Reciente white wine and an excellent full-bodied dark red *reservas*, the latter under the Cerro Añon label. Here *barricas* are drawing wine from giant fermentation tanks.

generally appreciated throughout Spain are made from Bobal, Cariñena, Garnacho Negro, and Juan Ibanez vines. They are red wines and *claretes*, of 18% vol. alcohol. A sweet *licorosa dulce* is also made, similar to the Malvasia de Stiges.

The region of Montilla Y Moriles lies south of Cordoba in Andalusia; here the Pedro Ximénes grape gives big white wines. Although not fortified with spirit, these wines reach a strength of up to 19% vol. alcohol and fall into the fortified-wine tax-class. Their popularity at one time threatened Sherry's to such an extent that the Jerezanos named one of their styles of sherry "Amontillado," "like the wine of Montilla." However, such is the power of the Jerezanos that, when later the Montilleros tried to call one of their own wines "Amontillado," the attempt was rapidly quashed, and today the Montillas must be satisfied with the simple descriptions "dry," "medium" and "cream."

Malaga is another wine in the Sherry style that uses the *solera* system (see page 160) but is not fortified with spirit. Wherever the grapes are grown in the surrounding area of the Costa del Sol, they must come to Malaga to mature. The grapes may be dried in the sun or the must may be boiled down to *arrope*. The result varies, according to method, between a wine similar to Montilla, a semisweet aperitif wine called Pajarete, and a rich aromatic Moscatel.

The Alvear bodegas were founded 250 years ago by the present proprietors, the Alvear family. The wine of Montilla pursues its old rivalry with Jerez, and traditional Jerez methods are used in certain stages of its production. At Alvear, Pedro Ximénez grapes, preferred to Palomino in Montilla, are being loaded into the *lagar (left)*.

The fermentation room of Alvear *(below)* is also true to tradition, holding a vast number of *tinajas*. These tall clay vessels, in the shape of giant Roman amphoras, are used for fermentation; there are some 1,700 of them at Alvear. *Flor* develops within them and the wine is processed through a *solera* system, as in Jerez.

The grapes used in the production of the wines of Malaga are grown 40km (25mi) from the city but have to be brought to Malaga to be converted to wine. The two main grapes of the region are the Moscatel, which is concentrated to produce sweet dark wines, and Pedro Ximénez *(above left)*, which gives a dry white wine similar to a Montilla *fino*.

The vintage at Vilafranca del Penedés in Barcelona brings pickers — including many women — into the vineyards to gather in the harvest *(above)*. The main grapes of the region are the Tempranillo (shown here and known in Penedés as the Ull de Llebre); the Monastrell, another black grape grown especially in Penedés, the Levante and Valdepeñas; and the white Parellada for pleasant fruity whites and sparkling wines.

The giant *tinajas* stand in line at Ciudad Real in DO Valdepeñas *(left)*. The bodega is that of the cooperative La Invencible, considered to be one of the best cooperatives in the region. La Invencible is known for a *clarete;* the Cooperativa del Campo La Daniel is a principal producer of white wine marketed as Clavileño; and the Cooperativa Virgen de la Viñas, at Tormelloso, produces a popular Reserva de Cencibel.

The *vendimiadar* at Bodega Alvear in Cordoba is testing a Montilla wine for color *(right)*. The main vine is Pedro Ximénez, which produces smaller crops in Andalusia than it does in Jerez because of the hotter climate; the resulting wines lack the balance of Sherries. Alvear is reputedly the oldest bodega in the whole of Spain: in 1979 it celebrated 250 years of continuous production.

# SHERRY

The Sherry region centers on Jerez de la Frontera, near the river Guadalete, which runs into the Bay of Cadiz 50km (31mi) northwest of the Straits of Gibraltar. "Jerez" is a name derived from "Xera," the name given to the town by the Greeks before the 500-year Roman occupation; "de la Frontera" is a reminder of the shifting frontier during the drive by the Moors through Spain and into France against the barbarian Visigoths and Vandals who had ousted the Romans. Strangely, the Moors continued to tend the vineyards although allegedly abstainers themselves; they made Sheris sack and boiled down the grape-must to make *arrope*, used to this day for sweetening. Sack was known and appreciated in England in the late medieval period; and Christopher Columbus, on his second voyage to America, embarked from Puerto de Santa Maria carrying the wine of Jerez as ballast. Jerez de la Frontera and Santa Maria are today the only ports from which Sherry may be shipped in barrels or bulk containers.

The region forms an irregular circle some 70km (43½mi) in diameter, and the vineyards occupy about 15,000 ha (37,000 acres). There is hardly a tree to be seen in the blinding white plain. Here there are three types of soil. The best, Albariza, has up to 80% chalk which, being water-absorbent, dries out in the summer to make a hard pan; it has to be forcibly broken up again to give a winter tilth. The largest area of Albariza embraces the low hills of Macharnudo, Carrascal, Anina, Balbaina, and Los Tercios, surrounding the town of Jerez almost entirely. There are smaller outcrops from the northwest, by Sanlucar de Barrameda, through north to southeast. The triangle between Sanlucar, Jerez and Santa Maria is known as Jerez Superior. Local rules demand that every bodega must buy a proportion of its grapes from Jerez Superior, although this area itself now represents almost 90% of the whole region.

The other two soils, Barros and Arenas, contain only 10% chalk: the Barro, with more clay, grows weeds and produces coarser wine; a Barro with 25% chalk is found near Trebujena in the north and Chiclana in the south. It is an in-between soil which produces medium-quality wines. Arena soils are sandy and largely weed-free, but are good only for growing sweet-wine vines. The region is hot and dry between May and October, followed by persistent rains from mid-October through November—the annual rainfall is about 550mm (21½in). These rains must not be lost, and so trenching systems are devised to collect the water and avoid erosion. The prevailing winds from the Atlantic bring rain and, exceptionally, the Levante—a south-easterly wind from the Mediterranean—blows damagingly hard but dries up the land again. The winters are mild enough to avoid frosts but hard enough to rest the vine, and grafting may therefore be done in the vineyard. The white Palomino is the grape of Sherry, growing perfectly in the Albariza soil to produce the best finos. Two other vines, the Pedro Ximénes (PX)

The modern interior of the Gonzalez Byass bodega in Jerez *(right)*. The great Sherry house was created by a partnership of Don Antonio Gonzalez y Rodriguez and Robert Blake Byass, his London agent, starting in 1855, and their descendants run the business to this day. As well as extensive holdings in Jerez, Gonzalez Byass own Bodegas Beronia in Rioja and Gonzalez y Dubosc in Catalonia.

The vineyards of Jerez *(far right)* are highly prized properties, especially those that lie on the *albariza*, a brilliant white soil of some 80% chalk and 20% clay. *Albariza* reflects the heat of the sun up into the bush-trained vines, yet has high water-retention that carries the vines safely through the summer drought. *Barro*, a darker soil with a higher clay content, produces inferior wines.

In contrast with the vineyards in many parts of Spain, those of Gonzalez Byass in Jerez are the ultimate in orderliness *(left)*. Longitudinal corridors give access to thousands of short rows of Palomino vines. The chalk soil of the *albariza* is clearly seen. Gonzalez Byass own 15% of the 15,000ha (37,000 acres) of vines in Jerez, producing roughly two million cases of Sherry and four million cases of brandy each year.

Pickers in the Finca Macharnudo of Domecq in Jerez *(above)* selecting ripe bunches of grapes in the vineyard to go forward for drying in the sun. The carefully folded sheeting and hoops are there to cover the vines when hail showers are imminent: hail during the ripening of grapes on the vine can be disastrous.

At Cadiz, Jerez de la Frontera, bunches of Moscatel grapes are placed to dry on circular mats of esparto grass *(inset)*. They will be made into sweetening wine, used to give added sugar and a fruity taste to the sweeter blends of Sherry. Sweetening and coloring wines are added after Sherry has been drawn from the *solera*.

The bodega of Antonio Barbadillo *(right)* is the largest in Sanlúcar de Barrameda and has the lion's share of the market for the Manzanilla for which the district is famous. In the cellars, Manzanilla is aging in oak *barricas*. Barbadillo have 800ha (1,975 acres) of vineyards in the areas of Balbaina, Cadiz, Carrascal, Gibaldin, and San Julian. Their offices are in a former bishop's palace in the town center.

and the Moscatel are planted on the lesser soils and the resulting wines are used mainly for sweetening and coloring.

The vines of Jerez are grown as single bushes in the Guyot Simple style—one main branch with a shoot for next year's growth. Increasingly, the vines are being trained on wires with rows 2m (6ft 7in) apart for machinery access. The mechanical auger is much in evidence: it makes holes for replanting and for fertilizing, which is needed every five years. Also the now ubiquitous helicopter is used for spraying weed-killer. The vines crop heavily and those not trained on wires need props. The yield ranges between 24 and 120hl/ha, averaging about 70hl/ha. The vintage takes place during the first three weeks of September.

Vinification in Jerez is, in its opening stages, similar to standard wine-making practices. No longer are the grapes trodden in the original *lagares*; they are first lightly crushed, although not destalked, and the acidity of the crushed grapes is then increased by adding gypsum, to produce tartaric acid, which helps settle the lees. The grapes are then pressed in cylinder-screw presses in the bodegas. The must is run into a tank oak barrels, where it ferments furiously for a few days, after which fermentation continues less dramatically for about three weeks until all the sugar is converted into alcohol and a still white wine results. The new wine, confusingly called *mosto*, is run off its lees into butts where it is left to mature, *without* any sealing (with bungs) and topping-up to counteract ullage. Now the first fortification is made to bring the alcoholic strength up to about 15%.

Pedro Domecq is the oldest firm producing Sherry. Don Jose Ignacio Domecq *(right)*, head of the Domecq Company, acclaimed worldwide as "the nose of Sherry", is seen here classifying the wines in one of his Jerez bodegas.

An important and unusual development then occurs. At random, some butts—but not others—develop *flor*, a kind of cream-colored yeast that floats on the top of the butts and covers their surface. The aerobic *flor* takes oxygen from the air and feeds on the wine. The flavor of the wine changes and, in the process, the wine gains in strength. Now the *catador*, or wine-taster, inserts a *venencia* (a cup on the end of a long stick) through the bunghole of the butt to gather a specimen of *mosto*, which he samples, or "noses," and then classifies. Those butts with *flor* are classified as potential *finos* and are cut with identifying *palma* marks. Those without *flor* are marked with a stroke (*raya*), and are classified as *rayas*. This is the first step in the classification of Sherries.

The diagram shows the division of Sherry from this stage into *finos* and *rayas*, and the eventual styles under which they are marketed. All *finos* and *rayas* are subject to blending with sweetening and coloring wine as well as to further fortification with brandy. The *finos* are finally separated into Amontillados, Finos and Manzanillas, the latter having a salty tang acquired during maturation at Sanlucar de Barrameda, by the sea. The *rayas* become Olorosos or may be relegated to "burning wine," used in the production of brandy. The Olorosos may sell under that name or, by blending, may be made "cream" or "brown." A rare Sherry type is Palo Cortado, from an Oloroso that has converted to a *fino*.

It is usual for a further fortification to be given to the *rayas* immediately after classification; this stops them becoming *finos*, which cannot stand a strength greater than 18% vol. alcohol. The wines of any one year are examined in their individual butts for several years, during which time they are regularly inspected to determine their suitability for further treatment. They are, in fact, preparing for the *solera* system of blending that gives Sherry its guarantee of quality and consistency. There are no vintages in Sherry.

If a small amount of similar though younger Sherry is added to a larger quantity of older Sherry, the young wine will assume the characteristics of the older. A small quantity of the *añada* (this year's vintage) wine is therefore added to a butt—a *criadera* (literally a nursery)—four-fifths full of wine of similar characteristics from the previous year; thence it progresses through the scales of the *solera* to the shipping *solera*, which contains blended mature wine. The shipping *solera* is called the first *criadera*, and the earlier *criaderas* are numbered backwards from it—for example, if there were five scales in the *solera*, the *añada* would start in the fifth. There would, of course, be a considerable number of butts holding wine at each of the five *criadera* stages, and likewise there would be several or possibly many separate *soleras* for wines of different qualities separated by the *catador*, to include all *fino* and *raya* derivatives.

Sherry from the shipping *solera* is not yet ready for marketing, for it may need sweetening, coloring or both to satisfy the precise requirements of a shipper's customer. Grapes from the Pedro Ximénes and Moscatel vines are shriveled in the sun for about three weeks and then vinified to produce an extremely sweet wine; this has low alcohol, because the high sugar content inhibits fermentation. "Coloring" wine, or *vino de color*, is made by fermenting one part of unfermented must with two parts of grape-syrup (grape-juice boiled down until it caramelizes). When this blend has aged in the butt it has a strong aroma and is dark-brown. Both sweetening and coloring wines are added to accord with the customer's wishes, and the final blend may also require further fortification with brandy to reach the correct shipping strength. After this it is stored in refrigerated stainless-steel vats where tartrates and other soluble salts are removed by precipitation to give permanent clarity and brightness to the wine.

The traditional treading of Sherry grapes by foot in *lagares* is now largely superseded by modern presses **(1)** of various types. The grapes, always the Palomino, are pressed gently so that there is no danger of the grape-pips being crushed.

The juice, or *mosto*, is pumped from the press into new oak barrels or a tank **(2)** where it ferments furiously for three or four days; fermentation then continues for three weeks. By then the yeasts have converted all the sugar to alcohol, producing a dry, still white wine of some 11 to 12% vol. alcohol.

The wine, also called *mosto*, is pumped **(3)** into a series of butts each of 600-liter (159gal) capacity. Only 500 liters (132gal) are fed into each butt so that an oxidative aging of three to four years begins. Early in the aging period, an addition of spirit **(4)** is made to bring the alcoholic strength of the *mosto* up to 15% vol.

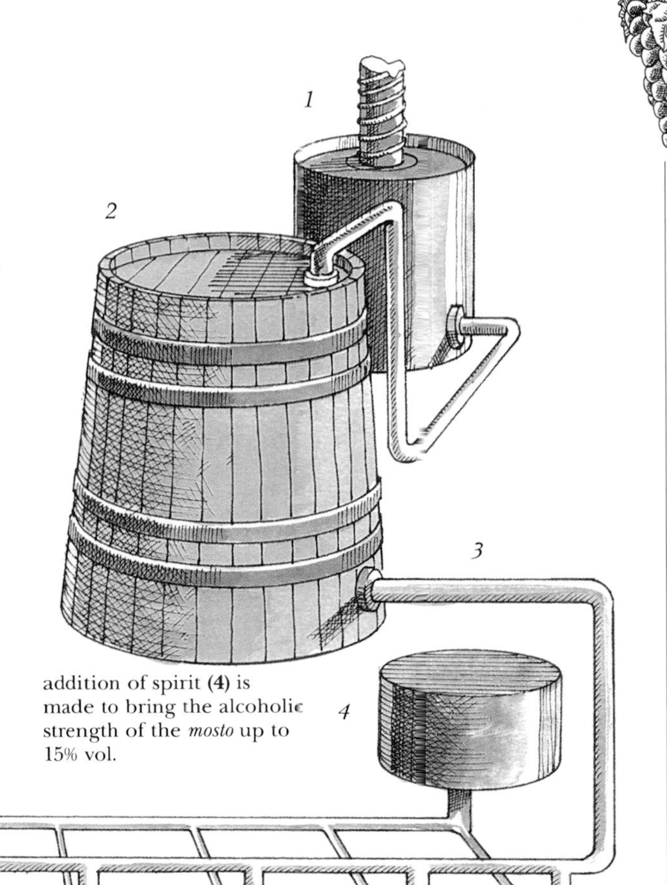


5
a b c d e f g h i j
6 7

In some of the butts **(5)** a substance called *flor* forms, entirely at random. *Flor* is a creamy aerobic yeast that floats on the surface, feeding on the wine, which it shields, preventing further oxidation; it also slightly increases the wine's alcoholic strength. Now the *catador*, or wine-taster, enters the process, sampling the wine of each butt regularly by inserting a *venencia*, a small cup on the end of a long handle, through the bungholes, withdrawing it, and tasting wine from it. Those with *flor* are identified as *finos* and those without **(6)** are called *rayas*.

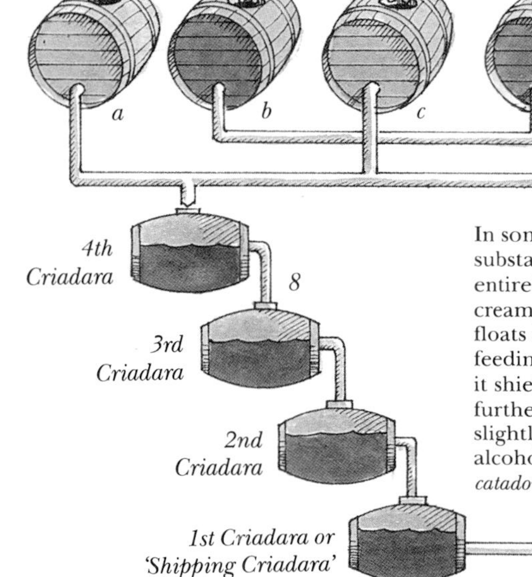


Finos
Olorosos
8

Wines for sweetening Sherry are made from Pedro Ximénez and Moscatel grapes. Dried in the sun, they shrivel and are fermented to produce an extra sweet wine, low in alcohol. *Vino de color* is made by fermenting one part of grape-juice with two parts of grape-syrup. After slow fermentation and aging a dark and highly aromatic *vino de color* results. The *finos* and *olorosos* finally have to be blended **(9)** with sweetening and coloring wines, and perhaps also fortified with additional spirit to bring them to the precise specifications of standard brands, or those required by wholesale customers.

9

The permutations that happen in the styling of sherries at this stage cannot be illustrated in chart form. Finos go into the three resulting types on the left; olorosos into those on the right.

Some *rayas* turn sour **(7)**, and the contents of such butts (e.g., J) go for distillation. The remaining *rayas* are then called *olorosos*. The new wines, whether *finos* or *olorosos* are called the *añada* (or new wines of a single year): they now enter the *solera*, or "nursery" system **(8)**, which gradually changes their character into that of the older wines with which they are to be mixed. The *solera* may have six or seven scales called *criaderas*. The first *criadera*, or "shipping scale", holds wine ready for sale (after further treatment to meet customers' requirements).

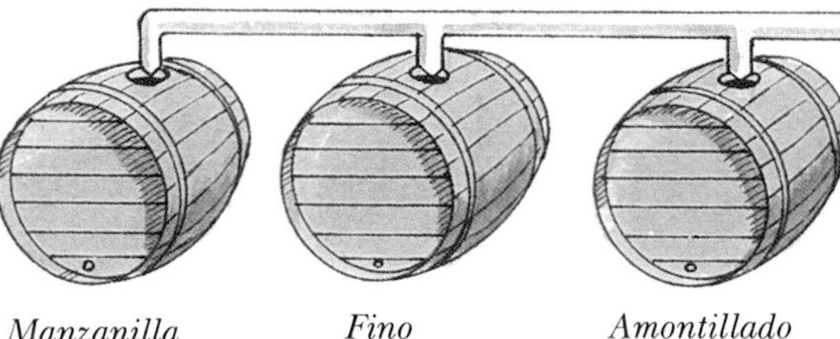


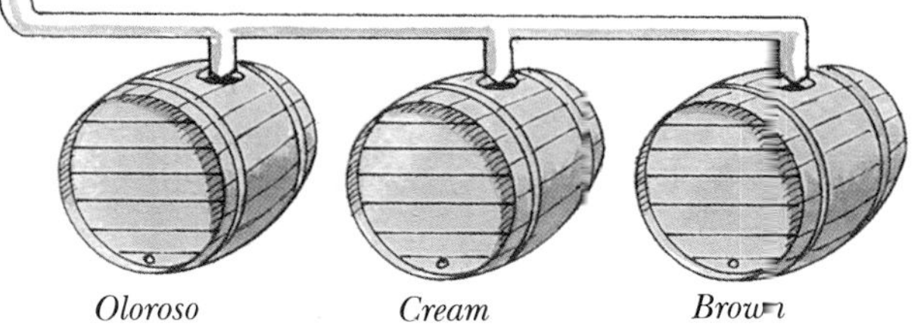

Valencia, on the Mediterranean coast of the Levante, has always been famous for its range of sweet wines, including *blancos, tintos, claretes,* and *mistelas*; the bright red wines, big and heady, have up to 16% vol. alcohol. Here vineyards at Requena *(right)* are seen at the beginning of the growing season.

The Canary Islands have a small wine industry. Among its vineyards are these excavated in the volcanic La Geria Las *(below)*, where protective stone walls contain the powdered lava. Over 50,000hl (1.32 million gal) of wine is produced each year, including Vidueno and dry Palma, both white, and a little *clarete.*

# PORTUGAL

The partition of Portugal and Spain took place at the end of the twelfth century. Up to that time there was a single wine history of Iberia; but afterward Spain became an unfriendly neighbor, which was one of the reasons that Portugal allied itself with England in the Treaty of Windsor, of 1353. Thereafter the English had considerable influence in shaping the character of Portuguese wines.

East of a narrow coastal plain, the wine regions of Portugal are located in the sierras of this predominantly mountainous country. The Atlantic brings in cloud that turns to heavy rain as it is carried up and over the sierras by strong southwesterly winds. Except from June to September, the weather is consistently bad. The vineyards need terracing, and indeed the whole vineyard year is labor-intensive; it is fortunate that the vineyard areas are well populated. In certain regions the vines have to vie with root crops for space.

Considerable improvement in the quality of Portuguese wines has been made in recent years since the adoption of controls parallel to the French AC system. Portuguese wines are described generically as either *verde* or *maduro*. *Vinhos verdes* are not, however, wines green in color but wines from underripe and unaged grapes, whether still or sparkling. They are the product of northwest Portugal; in fact, the term is now legally restricted to the northern Minho province. "*Maduro*," meaning mature, refers to the wines aged in barrel or bottle, or in other words wines made in accordance with standard practice in Portugal and elsewhere. For reasons of national taste they tend to be made from ripe grapes, producing astringent wines full of color, tannin and strength, but needing time to acquire the smoothness and finish normally looked for on the export market.

The demarcated regions of Portugal are Entre Minho e Douro, Douro, Tras os Montes, Beira Alta, Dão, and Agueda/Bairrada—plus three diminutive areas around Lisbon, collectively called Estramadura, and Setúbal, which is demarcated for fortified wine only.

## ENTRE MINHO E DOURO

This is the land of the *vinhos verdes*, and over 75% of the wines are red or rosé. The "Minho" and "Douro" of the region's name are rivers, the Minho forming part of the northern border with Spain and the Douro running due west from Spain to the Atlantic at Oporto, 100km (62mi) to the south. Here the grapes grow 2.5m (8ft) above ground, providing cover for food crops beneath; thus the grapes hang in paradise, between the vine foliage above and the crops below, drawing little direct or reflected heat from the sun. As a result, at harvest, the grapes have less sugar and more malic acid than normal, and there is a resultant tendency to create a secondary malolactic fermentation which is allowed to complete in the bottle, after the wine has first been racked. The resulting light sparkle gives a zest to these wines, which have relatively low alcoholic strength—under 10% vol. However, the standard practice in the bigger wineries is to process them to dryness and stability, adding the sparkle by carbonation and sweetening the wines by the addition of unfermented must, if required.

The black grapes of Entre Minho e Douro are the Vinhão (predominantly), Azal Tinto, Borracal, and Espadeiro; here the pips and stalks as well as the skins are fermented with the juice. The white grapes, Alvarinho, Azal Branco, and Doudaro, are the first to be harvested, late in September.

The region is divided into Monção in the north, Amarante, Basto, Braga, Lima, and Penafiel. In the hills the vineyards are terraced, so that mechanical methods are impracticable. Throughout the region the soil is granite, reflected in the flinty astringency of red wines that offset local fatty seafood dishes such as large grilled sardines; the green-golden white wines make good aperitifs when suitably chilled.

## DOURO, TRAS OS MONTES, AND BEIRA ALTA

Apart from Port, which has made the Douro region famous, there is an enormous production of light wines in the Douro valley, accounting for two-thirds of total output. Here grapes from Tras os Montes, to its northeast, and from Beira Alta, to its south, contribute to those converted on a massive scale into Mateus, a pink rosé, which now sells annually over 3½ million cases, almost worldwide. The rosé industry in the Douro, being undemarcated, has the advantage of using grapes from anywhere in the country, so that production is virtually unlimited. The process is normal, in that the pink color is obtained by short contact with black grape skins; fermentation is then stopped by sulfuring when approximately 18g per liter (2½oz/gal) of sugar remains unconverted. The wine is finally bottled and carbonated to give the light sparkle characteristic of Portuguese rosés. The grapes used include the Alverelhao, Bastardo, Tinta Pinheira, and Touriga.

The Douro and its neighboring districts make make good red table wines of medium strength, many of which sell as *garrafeira*, ready-matured wines for drinking when sold.

## DÃO AND AGUEDA/BAIRRADA

The region of Dão lies 60km (37mi) inland from the Atlantic: it is a high plateau of granite encircled by hills, and takes its name from the Dão tributary of the Mondego river. Over 15,000ha (37,000 acres) of vineyards, on soil of granite sand, are to be found at altitudes between 200m and 2,000m (660-6,600ft) above sea-level.

Of the region's three subdistricts, the outer

surrounds and protects two central districts, northwest and southeast of the Mondego, which produce superior wines more through better techniques than because of any natural advantage. Here the vines are trained low, in contrast with the practice in the Minho. The grapes for red wine are the Preto Mortágua, Tinta Pinheira, and Tourigo, the last being a descendant of the Pinot Noir. At four years, the wines are smooth with a fine bouquet; they have been likened to Rhône wines. White wines from the Arinto (using the Riesling) and Doura Branca need to be drunk young.

Agueda/Bairrada, a small region further down the Mondego river, produces similar wines to those of the Dão. The region stretches out towards the coast and has a limestone soil. Red wines predominate; they include Baga, from a local grape, which is an excellent wine but slow to mature. A sparkling white from the Bical is outstanding.

## ESTRAMADURA

Around Lisbon there are three small wine regions which each have a *selos de origen*; they now exist as little more than tokens of the past. The region of Carcavelos, in Estoril, is down to a single vineyard of some 7ha (17½ acres) which produces a mere 3,000 cases of a dessert or aperitif wine each year: it is medium-sweet, moderately fortified wine of amber hue, likened sometimes to a dry Madeira. Bucelas, several kilometers north of Lisbon, has under 200ha (494 acres) of vineyards which yield dry white wines of a fair character that are mostly dispensed to local inhabitants. Colares, one third the size of Bucelas, makes a special red wine from the small ungrafted black Ramisco grape: the wine is dark, astringent and increasingly rare. Here, close to the Atlantic, the sand drifts over the vineyards, so that measures are taken to plant the vines deep down and protect them by windbreakers of reed or bamboo: eventually their roots can reach 10m (33ft) below the surface, where the *Phylloxera* louse cannot penetrate.

Two huge regions, the central coastal area of Torres Vedras, north of Lisbon, and Alentejo, south of the Tagus, remain undemarcated; they are regarded rather for the quantity than the quality of their wines, which are rarely if ever seen outside Portugal. The red Periquita wine is produced in the undemarcated vineyards of Azeitao, and (this must be unique!) the wine gave its name to the grape from which it is made.

# PORT

Port is with little doubt the first in quality of all Portuguese wines. Both Portuguese and UK law now give Port wine an identical definition: "Port is wine of the Cima Corgo and Baixo Corgo regions of the Douro valley which has

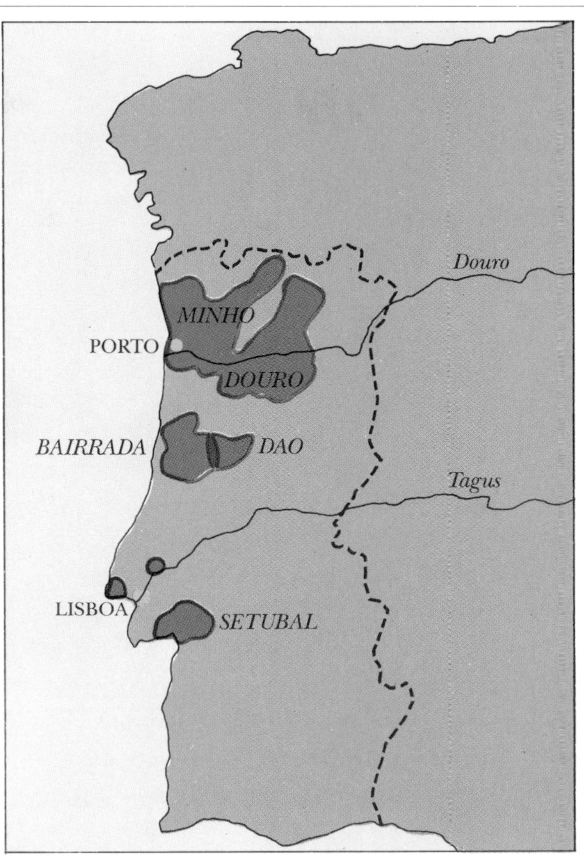


been fortified by the addition of grape brandy, matured in shippers' Lodges in Vila Nova de Gaia, and bottled there before shipment." The definition, has, however, an interpretation whereby the bottling restriction applies only to dated Ports. Under earlier trade methods a vast quantity of Port, much of it as yet unconsumed, entered England in pipes to be stored in bond in the cellars of London docks and elsewhere, so that even more anomalies abound.

The town of Oporto lies on the north bank at the mouth of the river Douro; its suburb, Vila Nova de Gaia, is on the south bank, facing it. The history of the unique wine that must first come to Vila Nova de Gaia is unlikely but true. The development of Port is a story of the liaison and cooperation between Britain and Portugal that started with the Methuen Treaty of 1703, which opened a market for English woolens in exchange for Portuguese wines. This was a direct result of increased taxes levied on the clarets of Bordeaux. The red wines of the Douro were then unsuited to the British taste, and a number of English wine merchants who settled in Oporto altered the coarse and heavy Portuguese wines to produce the fortified wine we know today. A strange happening: out of all of their wines, the Portuguese like Port least.

Nothing but the vine will grow in the stony territory of the Upper Douro valley. The soil is an igneous schist that keeps its underlay of compressed clay well out of sight on the mountainous slopes of the valley. In this territory the sole virtue of the soil, which lacks nitrogen, lime and organic matter, is a richness of potassium.

The Port region starts where the river Douro enters Portugal from Spain and reaches down to Regua (about 65km—40mi—from Oporto), where the Corgo tributary of the Douro comes in from the north. The region has cold wet

Portugal has made Port for some six centuries. Other wines, however, such as the semisparkling *vinhos verdes* and the wines of Dão, have long enjoyed an international reputation.

The Douro river *(left)* winds in a deep valley from the Spanish border down to the Atlantic at Oporto. The impossible conditions of the Upper Douro defy any crop other than vines; and because of the barrenness of this rocky territory the vine is admirably suited. Rich in potassium, the soil lacks lime and has little nitrogen and organic matter.

The seasonal demand for pickers brings many women into the vineyards. The grapes for Port wine are varied, although the most important are Roriz and Malvasia Preta, which give sugar and good color to the wine, and are resistant to heat: others are Sousão, Tinto Francisca, Touriga, Mourisco Semente, and Rufete, an early ripener.

No animal or machine can negotiate the steep slopes of the Douro valley, and traditional tall baskets are used by the pickers. The vineyards are planted and tended on manmade terraces in extreme conditions: summers at 41°C (105°F), bitterly cold winters, and rainfall of 132cm (52in) in the opening months of the year.

winters with 1,300mm (51in) of rainfall each year. Yet the summers are torrid and dry, with temperatures up to 41°C (106°F), so that explosives have sometimes to be used to make holes in which to plant the vines.

The Douro valley is so steep that the vineyards are terraced to give workable areas. Maintenance is hard, and olives are planted with the vines to hold the schistous soil together; even so, the torrential rains wash soil to the bottom of the valley, whence it has to be returned to the vineyards. Vines for Port may not be grown above a 400m (1,312ft) contour, and even below it the grapes must be specially chosen, the balance going for production of light wines.

The best vineyards are in the Pinhão area, about 30km (19mi) above Régua. The Roriz and Malvasia Preta black grapes are most widely used—they give good color and sugar—while the Sousão is also grown for its exceptional red juice. Others of note are Mourisco Semente, Rufete (an early ripener), Tinto Francisca, and Touriga. White grapes, used to make white Port, are Malvasia Corada, Malvasia Fina, and Robigato. The Port vineyards continue along the valleys of tributaries discharging into the higher reaches of the Douro; they include the Tavora, Torto, Tua, Teja, Sabor, and Coa rivers.

When the vintage comes, the grapes are gathered by hand and brought into the hillside *quintas* (wineries) for processing. At a few *quintas* the grapes are still trodden as they have been for centuries in lagares. In these broad troughs, made now in stone, the villagers work in four-hour shifts, usually to an accompaniment of rustic music, to crush the grapes and start the process of fermentation: this process of "cutting the *lagar*" warrants a premium. When the must has acquired its full color from the grapeskins, and half the sugar has been fermented, it is run off into *toneles*, large barrels that have previously been charged with brandy to one-fifth of their capacity. The alcoholic level of the mixture left to mature exceeds 17% vol. alcohol, at which strength further fermentation is automatically inhibited. In contrast with Sherry, where the sugar is fermented to dryness before the brandy is added, Port is thus left with 50% of its sugar unfermented, and is therefore a sweet wine.

The modern method of converting the grapes to wine is totally mechanical. First a crusher-destalker is used, as in the making of still wines; then the grapes are pumped into *cubas*, or large vats. It is important to extract quickly as much color as possible from the skins, and a technique of auto-vinification has been devised (see page 45). The grapes are pumped into the auto-vinifier, a sealed syphon vat. Under the pressure of the $CO_2$ gas being produced, the auto-vinifier forces fermenting liquor from the base of the vat onto the top of the *manta* (floating grapeskins and stalks), beating more color from it and circulating the liquor continuously until the required color is obtained. Alternatively, a circulatory vat may be used to achieve the same result; this forces the *manta* to the bottom of the vat continuously by means of a central, rotating Archimedean screw.

After this the half-fermented wine is drawn off into a vat containing the same proportion of brandy as in the treading process. The brandy must by law come from the Casa do Douro—the winegrowers' cooperative.

After racking in the new year, the young Port is run into pipes of 522-liter (138 gal) capacity ready for its mandatory journey to Vila Nova de Gaia, where it will mature in the shippers' Lodges. In times past the pipes traveled down the Douro in the single-sail *barcos do rabelos*; it was ever a hazardous journey, because of numerous rapids, but today it is impossible: the river is broken by the dams of hydroelectric plants. So, like most other freight, the pipes now travel in trucks.

Maturation at Vila Nova de Gaia may take an indefinitely long time; it depends on individual blending and other treatments to meet the specifications of the market and the shippers. Wines of differing types in the Lodges are divided into *lotes* and are blended using two measures, the *almude* of 25 liters (6⅔ gal) and the *canada* of 2 liters (2 quarts): blends consist of 537 liters (142 gal) using 21 *almudes* (139 gal) and 6 *canadas* (3 gal).

Rules introduced in 1975 decree that four categories of dated Ports must be Oporto-bottled, while undated Ports, including ruby, tawny and white Ports, may be shipped in bulk and bottled in the country of destination. The four dated Ports are "Vintage," "Late-bottled Vintage," "Date of Harvest," and "Ports of Indicated Age." There is only one Vintage Port: it must be bottled during the second or third year after harvest. It follows that this young Port, bottled for vintage, must throw a considerable sediment in the bottle; it will therefore mature on its lees, and so careful decanting is necessary before serving.

"Late-bottled Vintage" Ports must be kept longer in cask and be bottled between the fourth and sixth year after harvest. The system suits Ports from lesser years that can be softened by concentrated aging before bottling. Although they have less lees in the bottle, fourth-year bottlings still need careful decanting: they mature slowly and are good for laying down. Those left until the fifth or sixth year have thrown most of their deposit in the cask and are ready for drinking immediately.

"Date of Harvest" Ports must rest in their casks until the eighth year after harvest: they will then be practically free of deposit when bottled. Even though they represent a single year, which may be stated on the label, they may not be described as "Vintage Port." Finally, there are "Ports of Indicated Age." Here the wine is a blend of different vintages and may only be described on the label as being 10, 20, 30, or "over 40" years old. These are fine old Tawny Ports, tawny through having, necessarily, aged in the wood. Oxidation in cask through the years has two effects: it dulls and pales the original color, and it changes the fruitiness to a nutty flavor, so that a vintage bottled wine of similar age would be readily distinguishable.

Ports shipped in bulk (Wood Ports) fall into three classes entirely distinguished by their age when bottled. Young Ruby and White Ports are usually matured for four years in wood before bottling for immediate drinking: Young Tawny is a blend of them. Ruby is simply matured for another three years in cask. Old Tawny has acquired its color by oxidation before bottling at 10 years: three years before this it was Old Ruby. Whatever descriptions are attributed to Ports marketed by a shipper, he may ship only one-third of his stock each year.

The controlling bodies of the Port industry are the Ministerio de Economia, the Instituto do Vinho do Porto, the Casa do Douro, and the Gremio dos Exportadores do Vinho do Porto. Although total annual production of the base wine in the Douro is about 180,000 pipes, only one-third is authorized for Port production, and of this only 10% is consumed in Portugal.

## MADEIRA

The fortified wines of Madeira have a romantic story dating from the early fifteenth century. Prince Henry the Navigator ordered Captain João Gonçalves to claim the uninhabited island for Portugal. This he did, landing in the Bay of Funchal. Finding the land above the cliffs dense with trees, he lit a fire to make a clearing—an early example of overkill, for the fire took hold, raged for seven years, and consumed every tree on the island. Ironically, the name "Madeira" in Portuguese means "forested." The igneous soil of Madeira thus became rich in potash and even more suitable for vines. Prince Henry ordered the Malvasia vine of Greece to be planted, together with Sicilian sugar cane; each were to be vital to Madeira's future.

Madeira is about 650km (400mi) west of Morocco in the Atlantic. It rises gaunt out of the sea, and at its inland peak has an altitude

A picker returns with a fully loaded basket of grapes *(left)* that will be converted to Port in the *quintas* or wineries in the Douro region: the best vineyards are around Pinhão, some 32km (20mi) above Régna. In the spring the crude Port will be taken down to mature in shippers' Lodges at Vila Nova de Gaia.

Most of the vineyards of Portugal are concentrated in the north in mountainous territory, making them highly labor-intensive. Between the Minho and Douro rivers is the land of *vinhos verdes* or "green wines", made from underripe or "green" grapes: 80% of them are made into red wine.

Baskets of Touriga grapes *(bottom)* in the Dão region. This region is on a high granite plateau surrounded by hills. Originally the product of a cottage industry, these wines have been sought-after since standards were raised under the Federacão dos Vinicultores do Dão, formed in 1942.

Treading the grapes *(right)*, otherwise known as "cutting the *lagar*" (trough) is now rare, although still practiced in a few *quintas*. Chains of treaders of both sexes work in four-hour shifts, carrying out the exhausting process to the accompaniment of rustic music.

A scene among the wine lodges of Funchal *(top)*, where must from grapes trodden in *lagares* around the coast is brought for conversion into the famous Madeira wine. Fortified by spirit and produced by the *estufagem* process, Madeira is the only wine known to be unaffected by oxidation.

Collecting grapes for treading *(above)*. In the old days each of the four varieties of Madeira was made from a different grape. But since replanting after the phylloxera scourge, the all-purpose Tinto Negra Mole grape, believed to be a Pinot Noir variety, is mainly used for all four.

of over 2,000m (6,560ft) above sea-level. The hinterland remains inaccessible, and the vineyards, of manmade terraces, cling to the crags and fissures of the steep coastal cliffs, themselves between 400m and 600m (1,300-2,000ft) high.

The island became known among merchantmen as a source of water, and ships bound for the southern Atlantic and Indian oceans called at Funchal for supplies before entering the tropics: there they might lie becalmed in the doldrums for weeks or even months. The ships, which were mostly empty of freight, needed ballast as well as water; instead of stones, barrels of Madeira wine were shipped, to be sold in the East Indies and, later on, in Australia. When they reached the tropics, the wines slowly heated to a maximum temperature of about 45°C (113°F), afterward cooling again equally slowly during the six-month voyage.

It was discovered that this natural cooking process (*estufagem*) gave a new character to the wine, which stabilized yet continued to mature —it now seems almost indefinitely—and to improve all the time. It was patently only a matter of time before the process of *estufagem* was duplicated in the winery. In the early days, small quantities of brandy had been added to Madeira wines, more to preserve them than to give flavor or strength. But, as the island's crop of

sugarcane increased, cane spirit became much cheaper than brandy, and is now the sole fortifying agent—presenting a conundrum that will no doubt be regularized under EEC law now that Portugal has joined the Market.

The wine-making process still starts with the treading of the grapes in *lagares*. Because of the terrain, the resulting must goes first in goatskins, then in barrels, for conversion in the wine lodges at Funchal. After fermentation the wine is kept for a period of six months in the *estufa*, a heated store in which the temperature is gradually raised to 45°C (113°F) before being allowed to subside. This is followed by *estagio*, a recovery period of 18 months, and then maturation in a *solera* system similar to that used for Sherry (see page 161). True to the *solera* principle, young wines are still being added even to *soleras* with an average age approaching 100 years.

The Treaty of Methuen (1703) revived the spirit of the earlier Treaty of Windsor between England and Portugal and gave preferential rates of duty to Portuguese wines. As a result, English wine-merchants settled in Madeira as well as Oporto, and built up an export trade with Europe and America. In the American War of Independence, 75 years later, the British endeavored, with only partial success, to restrict American wine-shipments to British ships, but the trade survived. A century later two plagues attacked the vines of Madeira: *Oidium tuckeri* and, 20 years later, phylloxera between them killed all the island's vines; it was left to those British shippers who remained on Madeira to salvage the wine industry. American vines were first planted, but unsuccessfully, and then the new method of grafting European scions onto American stocks was adopted.

The Sercial vine, named for the village of Seixel, on the north side of the island, where it was grown, is a relation of the Riesling, and produced Sercial, one of the two drier types of Madeira wine: the other is Verdelho. These two varieties have spirits added after *estufado* whereas Malmsey and Bual retain much of their unfermented sugar by having spirits added before *estufado*. The Malvasia or Malvoisie grape was used for making Malmsey (a corruption) Bual and Verdelho were likewise vine names With the replanting of the vineyards these vines were supplanted almost entirely by the Tinta Negra Mole, seemingly an all-purpose vine that by suitable adjustment can produce commercial qualities of all four Madeira wine varieties—another matter that could attract the attention of the EEC. Originally the Tinta, said to be a variety of Pinot Noir, was used to make the strong red Tent.

Two further grapes were used for still wines the Terrantez made a dry full-bodied wine with a bitter finish, while Bastardo, today being made in small quantities, gave a medium-dry light-bodied wine. Another variety of Madeira that is still produced is "Rainwater," allegedly gaining its name from a type of "accident" more frequently attributed to dishonest milkmen. Apparently the mistake, so far from being noticed by the customer, brought forth compliments, and the style went into history.

A market for all Madeira wines, today covering nearly all the western European countries as well as the United States and Canada, has been created by the Madeira Wine Association, formed by many of the shippers for control and promotion purposes.

## SETUBAL

This region of 20,000ha (50,000 acres) lies to the south of the Tagus river, on the Arrabida peninsula. Here the famous aromatic Moscatel del Setúbal is produced from a blend of black and white muscat grapes. Fermentation is arrested by the addition of brandy, and the grapeskins are steeped in the macerated wine to intensify and enhance the muscat bouquet and flavor. The strength varies from 16% to 20% vol. alcohol, and the wine ages for six years in barrel, for earlier consumption, or, if aged for 20 years, may be sold as Setúbal Superior. The long maturation process darkens the wine from amber to brown.

# THE MINOR EEC WINE COUNTRIES

**Greece ♦ Luxembourg ♦ United Kingdom**

At the start of 1985 three EEC countries besides France, Italy and Germany had their own wine-making industries: Greece, with the largest annual production; Luxembourg; and the UK, with the least. (At the time the entry of Spain and Portugal, two important wine-making countries, into the European Community was undecided, but was ratified in 1985 and is effective from the beginning of 1986).

## GREECE

Greece and wine are locked together in both mythology and history. The ancients had their own wine-god, Dionysus, to guard its interests, and, to their credit, it was the Greeks who brought to the people the precious commodity previously reserved for royal lips. Furthermore, the Greeks spread vines to their colonies around the Mediterranean, while their wines from Chios and Lesbos even challenged Latium's *Falernum* in its home city of Rome.

The shape and number of the Greek islands tell of the volcanic eruptions through geological time that have given them their rugged form and their outcrops of igneous soil; likewise, the limestone of Macedonia is sedimentary proof of past ages when Greece was submerged in the sea. As legacies, Greece today has all the soils needed to produce beautiful wine. Much of this remains merely a potential, however, for her primitive viticulture stood still for 2,000 years. Her vineyards were mostly areas of free-standing bushes rather than of neatly regimented rows trained in shapes suited to their microclimate.

Wisely, when the EEC came into being, Greece foresaw that her export markets would require products whose standards were commensurate with those set up by the Community. The government therefore introduced controls for the wine industry, and enforced them as law in 1963. In the previous year the industry had formed its Institute of Tasters, parallel in its purposes with the *consorzi* of Italy, but having an equal lack of authority. By 1970 price controls for wine were introduced. Much earlier, work had started to restore the damage done by phylloxera and mildew after the Second World War, and to reconstitute the run-down vineyards and bring them, as it were, into the twentieth century. In the early 1980s the Greek vineyards in the wine industry (as opposed to those growing grapes for dried fruit) reached over 100,000ha (247,000 acres), making Greece the ninth largest wine producer in Europe and the thirteenth largest in the world.

Now that Greece is a member of the Common Market, wines for export are produced under modern hygienic conditions, and go mainly to Benelux, the USA, West Germany, Sweden and Switzerland. At the head of the industry are well over 50 cooperatives and some 250 private wine companies all producing wines of "appellation" quality. At a lower level, innumerable peasant farmers make wine of "country" quality in enormous volume for immediate consumption. The per capita consumption of wine by some nine million Greeks is between 40 and 50 liters (10½-13¼ gal) each year; wines of "appellation" quality so far represent only 12% of national production.

Before we look at individual quality wines, it is worth considering the generic forms of wines that are known throughout Greece.

About half of all Greek wines become Retsina, by the addition of pine resin: Retsinas may be either white or rosé, but never red. Retsina most probably had its origin in the use of pine resin to preserve the wine, either covering the whole interior surface of the *amphorae* in which it was stored, or to help seal the stoppers to avoid oxidation. Today Retsina is made throughout the land, but the best comes from around Athens. It has an aroma and flavor that is overwhelming to most visitors, but is much loved by the Greeks. It does not improve with age, and has 12.5% vol. alcohol or a little over. Another resinated wine is Kokkineli.

The style of these two casks *(above)*, dating from 1882, surely betrays the Bavarian taste of the founder of Axaïa-Clauss, although the reference to Trieste suggests that he may have developed interests in the northern Adriatic region on his journey to Patras. Many generations of aging wine have left their mark on the casks.

The Peloponnese is the most important wine region of Greece, producing over one-third of her wines. The wine-center is Patras, at the western entry to the Gulf of Corinth. An important feature of the town is the headquarters of Greece's largest wine producer, the Axaïa-Clauss company *(left)*.

Beyond the vineyard, the Patras plant of Axaïa-Clauss *(left)*. The company was founded 125 years ago by a Bavarian, Gustav Clauss, who developed vineyards in the Peloponnese; later they were extended to Crete. Peloponnesia has four appellations, Mavrodaphne, Muscat, Muscat of Rion, and Patras. Mavrodaphne is the best known: it improves with long aging.

A third generic name in Greece is Monemvasia, now used for wines approximating to the Malmseys of renown toward the end of the English medieval period (known then in Spain as Malgavia, in Italy as Matvasia, and in France as Malvoisie). The name ''Monemvasia'' derives from that of the little port at the toe of the Peloponnese from which it was exported (although it was not made here).

The quality wines of Greece come from 26 areas delimited by the EEC; some are too small really to call ''regions,'' some are on little Aegean islands, and a few are on Crete.

## THE PELOPONNESE

Here the vineyards spread over nearly 70,000ha (173,000 acres); they produce roughly one-third of the wines of Greece. Patras, in the Corinthian Gulf, is the wine center. The appellations are for: Mavrodaphne, a sweet and fortified wine that matures well, is dark red in color (Mavro means ''black-haired''), and is heavy with 16% alcohol (it comes from the Mavrodaphne grape); Patras, a straightforward red wine for drinking young; and Muscat from Rion. The Aghiorghitiko grape names a strong red wine in Nemea, where the cooperative makes also the supple Mantinea white wines, which are satisfying but unexceptional, and good Rhoditis rosé.

## ATTICA

This region accounts for 15% of Greek wine production. Retsina dominates production, and it is necessary to look hard for the saving graces of quality wine. The best white wine of all Greece comes from a small estate called Pallini; and the Mandilaria and Mavroudi grapes produce red wines that are worth finding—the latter at Delphi.

## MACEDONIA

This area, stretching from the Turkish border to the Adriatic sea, has only some 18,000ha (45,000 acres) of vines, but earns several appellations. West of Thessaly, in the northwest corner of the Aegean, Naoussa has an appellation for a well balanced tannic red wine; in Epirus, to the southwest, are appellations for Aminteion, a light red wine; Metsova is a wine worthy of its origin—the Cabernet Sauvignon grape; and Sista is a light white wine from the Debina grape. Cabernet and other French grapes are being planted by the Domaine de Porto Carras in an exciting attempt to bring the Khalkidhiki peninsula, in the north Aegean, into prominence. Thessaly, in the adjacent area, has the appellation Rapsani for a medium red wine from Mount Olympus.

## CRETE

Third largest producer of Greek wines, this island specializes in dark, sweet red wines, for which it has four appellations: Archanes, Daphnes, Peza, and Sitia. These come from Kotsiphalo, Liatico, and Mandilari grapes, any of which can be found under the name ''Mavro

The Imperial Cellar at Patras *(right)*. The range of Axaïa-Clauss wines includes Château Clauss, a long-lasting red wine; Mavrodaphne of Patras; a Muscatel; and Santa Rose rosé.

Romeiko." These wines can be big and fleshy, rich in alcohol, and mature to a considerable finesse. Efforts to protect the appellations have been worthwhile.

## CEPHALONIA

This western isle has 10,000ha (24,700 acres) of vines for winemaking, and is known chiefly for its red Mavrodaphne and Muscat wines, similar to those made in nearby Patras. There is also a dry white wine, Robola, that is earning a good reputation.

## THE AEGEAN ISLANDS

These islands have volcanic soils and produce notable wines of character. Rhodes, once the stronghold of the Hospitallers, has made wine for many centuries; best known is the white Lindos, grown by the ruins of the Parthenon, although strangely it has not achieved appellation status, despite the fact that the island's Malvasias and Muscats have.

The Muscats from Samos and Lemnos share this honor. Samos is a place-name delimited by law, so that no wine made elsewhere may use it, nor may Samos wines be blended with any other wine. To make assurance doubly sure, no other Greek wines are allowed on the island.

From the vineyards of the volcanic remnants of the still beautiful island of Santorini (Thēra) comes the fruity sweet Vino Santo, which has up to 15% vol. alcohol, and the dry Santorin; both are worth finding.

The vine often shares pride of place with the olive in the eastern countries of the Mediterranean *(above)*. Crete despite its often rural atmosphere, is second only to the Peloponnese in Greek vineyard area, although Attica, with a smaller area, makes more wine.

These low bush-trained vines *(left)* have been pruned hard for the winter, which can be cold. Crete's wines, made from Liatico, Mandilari and Romeiko grapes, are made big and fleshy; Peza is the biggest cooperative.

# LUXEMBOURG

The wine industry of the Duchy of Luxembourg is largely a domestic affair; in order to find token quantities to export to Belgium, Holland, and Germany, the Luxembourgers have to import wine from France and Italy to make up their per capita consumption of nearly 30 bottles a year. The wines are all produced from 1,200ha (2,960 acres) of vineyards that share the left bank of the Moselle with cherry and plum orchards; these provide fruit for Kirsch, Mirabelle and Quetsch distilled in the Duchy. Since the country was French at the time of the Revolution, Luxembourg's vineyards suffered the national fate of partition into diminutive allotments, so that even today there are roughly 1,670 vineyards. To some extent the situation is compensated for in modern practice: between them the cooperatives, of which there is one in each main town along the river, convert two-thirds of the grapes to wine.

However, this was not the solution which Luxembourg found first. At the turn of the century Luxembourg wine was blended with German wines to produce Moselblümchen—a practice doomed to terminate with the First World War. By 1926 the government had stepped in to form a Viticultural Station at Remiche, and wine soon became a quality product, complete with government financial aid

Not even an escarpment of marly chalk can disturb the placidity of these vineyards above the Luxembourg reaches of the river Moselle *(far right)*. The soil is excellent for light wines; half the vineyards are planted with Rivaner, a Riesling x Sylvaner cross.

As with many other countries, Luxembourg's wine-making history goes back many centuries (her records start at AD809), yet her vines and wines did not amount to anything until the 1920s, when the Remich Viticultural Station was built *(right)*.

The vineyards of Luxembourg all lie along the west bank of the Moselle *(above)*, opposite Germany. Each year these 1,200ha (2,950 acres) of vineyard produce about 150,000hl (4 million gal) of wine in the tradition of the Alsace Rieslings, rather drier than the German Mosels.

Looking down onto the parade at the Grevenmacher Wine Festival *(right)*. There is great national pride in the wines of Luxembourg, which are regarded as a quality rather than a quantity product.

and instruction. The von Rundstedt counter-offensive of 1944 overran the vineyards, but they recovered within a year. Since then the wines have remained light and fruity, similar to those of Alsace.

The vineyards on the Moselle are east-facing and protected from the seemingly eternal west wind by the hill forests behind them. The best soils of the region are the chalk and marl at Remiche, roughly in the center, and the chalk and clay at Grevenmacher, near the northern extremity; the former is ideal for the Riesling grape and the latter for the Pinot varieties. The Müller-Thurgau does well along the whole distance.

In 1935 the Luxembourg government introduced the Marque Nationale which, as a small label affixed to the neck of certified bottles, indicates that the wine has been subjected to tasting tests and bottled under government supervision. Since the formation of the Common Market, Luxembourg has the Appellation Complète, sometimes called Appellation Contrôlée, for fine wines; the label must indicate the vintage year, locality, vineyard site, grape variety and grower's name and domicile. In descending order below AC, the wines may be designated by a locality name and grape, without a vineyard site—for example, Wellenstein Riesling—or as Vin de la Moselle Luxembourgeoise with the grape variety added. The same title may be given, without the grape variety, to wine exports in cask or to describe *grâchen* (ordinary wine); this practice is, however, rare.

# UNITED KINGDOM

The most southerly point of England, the Lizard, has a latitude of roughly 50°N, so that growing grapes for wine in England is at the best a risky business. The uncertain climate will give the grower two or perhaps three fair vintages every five years, and therefore the choice of grapes is largely controlled by the need for early ripening and resistance to rot. However, on the other side of the ledger, there are two advantages. England has all the soils most suitable for viticulture: granite, gravel, clay, limestone, and chalk; and the British Isles are surrounded by the Gulf Stream, a moderating influence on winter temperatures. All but one or two of the 25 largest vineyards of England, between them cultivating 125ha (309 acres), are within 60km (37mi) of the sea, between the Wash and the Bristol Channel.

The vineyards, laid down by the Romans and sustained later by the church, were lost to history when Henry VIII dissolved the monasteries. There were 130 of them; some, but not many, are included in about the same number of commercial vineyards now registered with the English Vineyard Association. Most are owned by families whose lifestyle does not depend upon their success as vintners, but this reflects in no way upon their skills: they are highly professional in their knowledge and practice of viticulture and vinification. The considerable

The manor house at Brympton D'Evercy in Somerset, England *(below)*. The village's ancient "Vineyard Lane" proves that vines have been grown on this site for several centuries. Müller-Thurgau and Reichensteiner are the main vines under cultivation.

revival of interest in wine in the last 25 years has encouraged about 1,000 growers to lay down smaller vineyards, the majority simply as a hobby. They, like all but 20 of the larger growers, send their musts to cooperatives for vinification.

In 1974 the EEC issued a list of recommended and authorized vines for cultivation in the UK; other vines were to be considered "experimental." Of the three recommended vines, Müller-Thurgau, Pinot Meunier (Wrotham Pinot), and Auxerrois, the first is mainly used; all of the eight authorized varieties are in general use but to a lesser extent (they are Bacchus, Chardonnay, Huxelrebe, Kanzler, Madeleine Angevine, Ortega, and Seyval Blanc). With the paucity of sun, the English grower concentrates on white-wine production from vines resistant to grey rot. They are planted in well spaced rows and trained to the Guyot, Lenz Moser, or Geneva Double-Curtain styles. The young shoots are endangered by frost in April and May but, if they survive this, will produce grapes ready for picking from the last week of September to the end of October. Delay in transporting the grapes to cooperatives causes oxidation, although this is offset to some extent by the methods employed by the Germans for reducing ill-effects.

The distinction between "English wines" and "British wines" is worth noting. The former are table wines of the EEC made from fresh grapes in England. The latter are made in Britain from imported dried grapes or concentrate musts and are categorized as "made wines:" in quantity these far outstrip the volume of English wines produced each year.

Six English vineyards, chosen for their size and/or location. Müller-Thurgau, expectedly, is the most used vine, followed by Seyval Blanc and Reichensteiner. All the authorized vines and a number of others have been tested by each of these vineyards, and those now blended in small quantities include Huxelrebe, Schonberger, Riesling, Bacchus, Pinot Noir, and Ortega. None use the recommended Auxerrois vine. These vineyards have an average yield of between 6,500 and 7,500 bottles per hectare (2,600-3,000 bottles per acre) in a fair year.

The Biddenden vineyards at Ashford *(above)*, in Kent, are sited in country that does well for grape-growing – subject to the overall *caveat* that England cannot rely on enough sun to guarantee a good harvest in more than three years out of every five. This tends to restrict wine-making to those who can afford to treat it as a hobby, albeit a serious and businesslike one. At Biddenden Mr R. Barnes has 6ha (nearly 15 acres) of vines which are a credit to the small English industry.

| Vines | Lamberhurst Priory, Kent 12ha (30 acres) | Adgestone, Isle of Wight 10ha (25 acres) | Highwaymans, Suffolk 10ha (25 acres) | Three Choirs, Gloucestershire 7ha (17½ acres) | Cavendish, Suffolk 4ha (10 acres) | Wraxhall, Somerset 2.5ha (6 acres) |
|---|---|---|---|---|---|---|
| | % | % | % | % | % | % |
| Müller-Thurgau | 44 | 48 | 33⅓ | 33⅓ | 100 | 40 |
| Seyval Blanc | 19 | 22 | — | 20 | — | 40 |
| Reichensteiner | 16 | 22 | — | 25 | — | — |
| Pinot Noir | 4 | — | 33⅓ | — | — | — |
| Madeleine Angevine | — | — | — | — | — | 20 |
| Schonberger | 7 | — | — | 5 | — | — |
| Kerner | — | 8 | — | — | — | — |
| Huxelrebe | — | — | 5 | 5 | — | — |
| Others to balance | 10 | — | 28⅓ | 11⅔ | — | — |

The vineyard at Flexern Fruit Farm, Fletching Common, East Sussex *(right)*, is a model of viticultural exactitude. Typical of many such properties of 1-2ha (2-5 acres) under vine, Flexern is adding to the knowledge of the English wine industry.

The 8.5ha (21 acres) of vines at Westfield, Hastings, Sussex *(bottom)*, puts the Carr Taylor vineyards among the six largest in the United Kingdom. The vintage has attracted villagers into the vineyard.

Winter pruning *(below)* — work undertaken by the proprietors themselves — is in progress at Brympton D'Evercy.

# COUNTRIES AROUND THE COMMON MARKET

The Chablais district of the French-speaking canton of Vaud is centered on the ancient town of Aigle *(below)*: the Swiss wine museum, Schloss Aigle, has a superb setting high on the slopes above the north shore of Lake Geneva. White Chablais wines are mainly from the Chasselas, reds from Pinot and Gamay.

A ring of countries almost surrounds those of the Common Market: it runs from Switzerland through Austria to the countries of eastern Europe; past Turkey and Russia to the Levant; and along the north African coast to Morocco. Each of these countries has a wine history and a modern wine industry. (To the north of the EEC it is too cold for grapes to ripen for wine production.)

The land-locked countries of central and eastern Europe have discovered that geography and ethnology make stronger boundaries than the divisions of war and politics, which have failed to alter the language, customs and tastes of the races within those natural boundaries; thus, for example, the three Swiss cantons have separate languages, while the six republics of Yugoslavia share four languages. In this context, it is hardly surprising that the types of wine produced remain faithful to tastes that are primarily racial rather than political.

With the exception of Switzerland, all the eastern European countries share the great river Danube, which flows east from the Black Forest to the Black Sea: its importance will become obvious in succeeding pages. Wines have been made by these countries for 20 centuries or more, although the Muslim laws of the Turks intervened to stop wine production wherever they ruled in southeast Europe during the millennium following the eighth century. Today the joint production of these countries is some 20 million hectoliters (530 million gallons) each year.

The Levant and the countries of northwest Africa have a similar (comparatively recent) history of Muslim prohibition of wine-drinking; but it was certainly in the Levant, probably around Shiraz in ancient Persia, that the *Vitis vinifera* was first cultivated. The Assyrians then spread the vine and its precious product northwest to the shores of the Black Sea, south through Lebanon, and round into Egypt. In turn, the Phoenicians, Greeks, and Romans planted the vine wherever their conquests or colonizations took them, and so Europe, excepting only the northern countries where the vine would not ripen, became a vast vineyard.

The Romans were the most thorough in converting rudimentary wine-making into a skill. Pliny was responsible for planting acclimatized vines to resist frost in the Bordeaux region, and he was also among those recognizing the quality of Egyptian wines—though today it still remains to be discovered who was clever enough to unearth the sole, minute, part of Egypt where the soil can produce grapes for wine-making.

The three wine-producing countries of northwest Africa had another "intervention" which affected their wines. This was the period when, for roughly 130 years, the French dominated colonies on the south border of the Mediterranean. France brought many benefits to the wines of Tunisia, Algeria and Morocco, both by planting European vines there and by introducing European wine-making methods and skills.

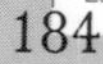

# CENTRAL AND SOUTH-EASTERN EUROPE

**Switzerland ♦ Austria ♦ Czechoslovakia ♦ Hungary ♦ Yugoslavia ♦ Romania ♦ Bulgaria**

With the solitary exception of Switzerland, the seven countries of southeastern Europe which we shall consider in this chapter all share the blessings of the Danube river. Rising in the Black Forest, it flows across northern Austria, passing through Vienna, and then forms the boundary between Czechoslovakia and Hungary for 150km (93mi) before turning south through Budapest, dividing Hungary in two. After crossing into Yugoslavia, it is joined by four other rivers, the Drava from Austria, the Tisa from eastern Hungary, the Sava which flows in at Belgrade, and the Morava, flowing north from Serbia. Thereafter the Danube runs east, forming the border between Romania and, to the south, Bulgaria. When only 200km (124mi) from its mouth, the Danube turns north into Romania and then east to create a delta flowing into the Black Sea: the USSR borders this delta for about 125km (78mi).

The importance of the Danube and its tributaries to the vineyards of eastern Europe is inestimable. Not only do they water the plains, but the increasing width and strength of the Danube has provided essential transportation from Central Europe to the outside world for at least 2,000 years.

## SWITZERLAND

The Rhône and the Rhine rise in the Bernese Alps within about 20km (12½mi) of each other. The Rhône flows west through Lake Geneva, turning south and eventually reaching the Mediterranean. The Rhine curls in a semicircle east, north and then west to Basle before flowing north through Germany and the Netherlands to the North Sea. The story of the rivers and their significance continues, for their geography was largely responsible for dividing Switzerland into French-, Italian-, and German-speaking cantons, each having separate national characteristics in the wines they produce.

The best areas for both climate and soil are in the French-speaking cantons of the west. They include: Valais, between the Bernese Alps and the Italian border; the Vaud, north of Lac Léman (Geneva); and Neuchâtel, the most northerly, encompassing Lake Neuchâtel. Around Lake Geneva are the small cantons of Lavaux, between Lausanne and Montreux; Aigle, in the foothills of the Alps, south of the lake's eastern tip; and La Côte, on the western shore of the lake from Geneva up to Nyon.

Valais, known for its sunny although overdry climate, is surrounded by the Alps, and here white Fendant wine, from the Fendant (Chasselas) grape, is delimited under the appellation Sion, the name of its principal town. Half the wine from the Valais is Fendant, a robust wine, high in alcohol and low in acidity. Good red wines of the Valais include Dôle, a blend of Pinot Noir with rather less Gamay grapes, making a wine of 12% vol. alcohol. Chaptalisation is accepted throughout Switzerland; the permitted sugar addition is up to 5% for red wines and 3% for white.

The Vaud canton spans the north shore of Lake Geneva and runs down to the border of the Valais. There are three zones in the Vaud: Lavaux in the centre, La Côte, between Lausanne and Nyon, and Chablais in the southeast. The wines of the Côte tend to be light. The best of the Lavaux wines come from Dézaley and Marsens, whose white wines, made from the Chasselas, have their own appellation and are exceptional. Dorin is the appellation for wines similar to, but not so firm as, Fendant; the same may be said of Chablais Chasselas wine.

The Vaud Canton borders the north shore of Lake Geneva and in its center is the small zone of Lavaux *(above)*. Although Pinot Noir grapes hang in this vineyard, Lavaux is better known for its exceptional white wines from the Fendant (Chasselas) grape.

Looking over the vineyards of Lavaux to Lake Geneva *(right)*. The zone, which lies between Lausanne and Montreux, enjoys an ideal climate for wine-making, and so its specialization in light, dry white wines is something of a paradox.

To the north of Lake Neuchâtel the influences of the Jura mountains and their limestone soil are apparent. Here mainly the Chasselas is planted, providing the base for light sprightly wines and for sparkling wines. The red Cortaillod Oeil de Perdrix, made from the Pinot Noir, is considered one of the best Swiss wines. The wines made close to Geneva are light and dry, often slightly *pétillant*, and matured *sur lie*; most are consumed locally.

Italian Switzerland is confined to Ticino, the canton east of the Valais running down to the shores of lakes Maggiore and Lugano. Here wine-making is less serious. Merlot is replacing Italian vines, although the Bondola survives and is used to make red Nostrano. More popular is the fruity red Viti from the Merlot, at 12% vol. alcohol.

There are eight cantons in the German-speaking region of Switzerland. The two of importance are Zurich and Schaffhausen, where the vine for red wine is principally the Blauburgunder (or Pinot Noir). The Herrschaft canton near Lichtenstein produces the best Blauburgunder, a full wine with good color. Here also white Completer wines, named for the rare vine, are made to Auslese standards with late-picked grapes; they are hence high in price. The other German cantons are Aargau, Basel, Grisons, St Gallen, and Thurgau, all of which produce insufficient wine for local needs.

# AUSTRIA

Austria has nearly 60,000ha (150,000 acres) of vineyards compared with only 10,000ha (25,000 acres) in Switzerland. Her important wine industry is concentrated in the east, where the Danubian valley runs through mountains on all sides. In 1972, following the German example of 1971, Austria introduced her own wine laws, under which four regions were delimited: Lower Austria, or Niederösterreich, is by far the largest, with 35,000ha (86,000 acres) of vineyards straddling the Danube north and south of Vienna; Burgenland, to its south and bordering Hungary, is next, with just over 20,000ha (50,000 acres); Steiermark, in the extreme south touching the border with Yugoslavia, has 2,500ha (6,200 acres); and Vienna, sometimes thought of more as a district, has a mere 800ha (2,000 acres). The wines are divided into *Spitzenweine* or quality wine, and *Tischweine* or table wine.

The Grüner Veltliner vine, from which nearly one-quarter of Austria's wines are made, the Wälschriesling (Italian Riesling), and Müller-Thurgau account for practically all of the white wines of Lower Austria. Exceptionally, Gumpoldskirchen, a medium-dry strong white wine, is made from the Rotgipfler grape. The Blauer

The finest wines of Austria come from the Burgenland, a region of some 20,000ha (49,400 acres) to the southeast of Vienna. On the eastern shore of the Neusiedler See is the district of Seewinkel, where the Lenz Moser estate is run by the two sons of the late Dr Lenz Moser. Here *auslese* wines are shown aging in casks *(above).*

Steiermark, or Styria, forms the southeastern boundary of Austria with Slovenia in Yugoslavia. Südsteier is the most fertile area, making good-quality wines from Rhine Riesling, Sauvignon Blanc and Wälschriesling grapes. Scattered vineyards *(left)* hug the hills; Steiermark's total area under vine is only 2,600ha (6,400 acres).

Langelois *(right)* lies in the Kamp valley, north of Krems in the Wachau region. The soil is loess and rock, producing mainly German-style white wines from the Rhine Riesling. The surrounding Niederösterreich region is the largest in the country, with some 34,000ha (84,000 acres).

A series of superb carvings *(above)* on the heads of fermentation tanks at the Lenz Moser estate, Mailberg, symbolize the hunt, the *vendange*, and other scenes of Austrian life. The carvings are one of many features that attract thousands of visitors each year to the estate.

Where once the Knights of Malta lived, the Lenz Moser estates today have their headquarters *(above right)*. The style of the raised entrance reflects that earlier age and epitomizes the heritage of superb Austrian architecture that complements the beautiful countryside.

The wine region of Wachau *(right)*, west of Vienna, has scenery to match the gorges of the Rhine and Mosel rivers. Small vineyards such as those that struggle on the steep north bank at Weissenkirchen are planted mostly with Grüner Veltliner and Rhine Riesling.

Vöslau in Styria *(far right)* produces the best red wines of all Austria, made from the St Laurent (60%), Cabernet Sauvignon, Merlot, and Blauer Portugieser grapes. The Vöslau vineyards of the Weinwirtschaftsfonds show the low style of training adopted where reasonably level land permits.

Portugieser (Merlot) and Gamay grapes are used for red wines, which amount to only about 12% of Austria's total output. The soils of Lower Austria include chalk gravel, loess, sand and schist, contributing to a wide variety of wines, mostly whites.

The wines of Burgenland are exceptional. They come from two districts: Rust, which is west of the Neusiedlersee, and Eisenberg, between the Neusiedlersee and the Styrian border. Noble rot enables late pickings of the Furmint grape to produce Trockenbeerenauslese-quality wines marketed as Ruster Ausbruch. White wines from east of the lake come from vines including the Muscat-Ottonel, Neurburger, Traminer, and Wälschriesling grapes.

The volcanic soils of Steiermark contribute to the quality of excellent white wines made from the Wälschriesling, Traminer and Ruländer grapes in Klöch and East Styria.

The Viennese consume more wine than is made in the small region of Vienna. The custom of serving locally produced *heurige* (young wines) in the *Heurigen* (winebars) of Vienna is happily surviving, for the tourists like it so much that these days *heurige* wines from outside the region are brought in by special permit.

## CZECHOSLOVAKIA

The vine-growing propensities of Czechoslovakia are restricted—thanks to the wholly mountainous character of the country—to the valleys of three rivers, the Elbe, Danube and Oder. The soil in the valleys is mainly loess and well suited to viticulture. The industry is limited to some 53,000ha (131,000 acres) of vineyards, producing about one million hectoliters (26½ million gal) of wine annually. Under the country's system, the varieties of vine planted are classified as: 20% Class A white-grape varieties; 50% Class B white-grape varieties; and 30% black-grape varieties. Class A includes Gewürztraminer, Muscat-Ottonel, Rhine Riesling and Pinot Blanc; Class B includes Müller-Thurgau, Grüner Veltliner and Wälschriesling. The black grapes include Cabernet Sauvignon and, to a greater extent, Frankovka (Limberger).

The white and red wines of Czechoslovakia are now produced to good modern standards in the style of German and Austrian wines. The fact that they are marketed in poor bottles with cheap labels does not affect the outside world, for the 16 million or so Czechoslovaks account for all home-produced wine and much imported wine as well.

Perhaps the star billing on Czechoslovakia's wine-list should go to her own Tokay, made near the border close to the Tokai vineyards of Hungary. Here a blend of two-thirds Furmint, a quarter Hárslevelü, and the balance of Muscat de Frontignan is processed by the Hungarian Tokay method.

The national planting of vines of all kinds consists of 1,000ha (2,500 acres) in Bohemia (the western province), 15,000ha (37,000 acres) in Moravia (the center), and 37,000ha (91,000 acres) in eastern Slovakia.

## HUNGARY

Hungary has a wine history going back to the days when the Greeks were spreading the vine around the Mediterranean shores. But it was the nomadic tribes from the Caucasus who drove their cattle into central Europe and brought their vines with them. The vast plain of Hungary, entirely surrounded by mountains and containing Balaton, the largest lake in central Europe, was a good place to settle. The Danube runs north to south, cutting Hungary in two, and the wine industry is divided into four regions, two each side of the river. On the west the Small Plain (Kisalföld) lies in the northwest corner of the country; and Transdanubia, in the neck of the Danube and Drava rivers, stretches down to the border with Yugoslavia. East of the Danube is the Great Plain (Alföld), which occupies most of the country; yet farther to the east, in rising country, are the Tokaj and Eger vineyards, sheltering under the North Massif of the Carpathians.

The whole of the Small Plain is one district, registered as Sopron, and here mainly red wines are produced from Kékfrancos, a local name for the Gamay vine. The diminutive region has a mere 1,100ha (2,700 acres) of vineyards.

Transdanubia is a different matter. Here some 15,000ha (37,000 acres) of vineyards surround Lake Balaton and many wines of outstanding quality are produced. The white wines of Badacsony are exceptional; they are grown from the indigenous Szürkebarat and Kéknyelü vines (now with some Wälschriesling added) on basaltic rock under loess topsoil. Beautiful wines are produced also at Balatonfüred-Csopak on a soil of red sandstone over slate. Made from the Furmint, Silvaner and Wälschriesling, they are gentler than those of Badacsony, and have been compared with the finest white wines of France and Germany. Also in Transdanubia are the vineyards on the small volcanic mountain of Somto, where white wines judged second only to Tokay have been made since the eleventh century. The best, a dessert wine, comes mainly from the Furmint vine, with Riesling and Traminer added.

East of the Danube, Alföld, the Great Plain, has almost 120,000ha (296,000 acres) of vineyards stretching over sandlands that have been reclaimed by the Magyars through the centuries; the sand makes the vines phylloxera-resistant. Here red wines, mostly from the Kadarka vine, and white wines, from the Olaszrizling (Wälschriesling), are made in equal quantities. Largely produced on huge State

In Veszprém county, western Hungary, the Csopak Tája (District) cooperative has formed an exporting organization for Balaton highland wines. A winery with a holding capacity of 40,000hl (1 million gal) has been built to process and store these wines. The huge container tanks (left) are shown here.

farms, the wine is of only average quality, and is exported in qualities suitable for making Sekt in Germany, for making Vermouths, and for distillation.

The northern Massif of the Carpathians dominates the northeast of Hungary, beyond the Great Plain. In the foothills, the town of Tokaj lies at the confluence of mountain streams that become the river Tisza. Here the famed Tokay of Hungary is produced. Although known at the time of the Crusades, the discovery of *aszú* was not made, according to contemporary Hungarian literature, until around the middle of the seventeenth century. Voltaire described it as a wine "that in vigorates every fiber of the brain and brings forth an enchanting sparkle of wit and good cheer from the depths of the soul." There are those who would put Tokay above d Yquem, Trockenbeerenauslese and Champagne, and the Hungarians even claim it has magical life-giving and restorative powers. It is sufficient to say that Tokays are unique. Tokay is now made from three permitted grapes, Furmint (by far the most important), Hárslevelü, and Sárgamuskotály, and conversion takes place exclusively in the State cellars at Satoraljaujhely. The vineyards, of about 6,000ha (15,000 acres), lie at an altitude of on average 600m (1,970ft) and are cultivated on a loess topsoil over igneous rocks.

*Aszú*, meaning "dried out," is the name for over-ripe, late-gathered grapes rotted by *Botrytis cinerea* to reduce natural acids and concentrate their sugar. The *aszú* mass, by virtue of its weight alone, oozes a relatively small quantity of precious syrupy juice, and this is collected in *gönci*, small casks that remain in the cellars for many years. Eventually it is bottled as Tokaji Eszencia, an extremely rare product seen only occasionally in Hungary and practically never outside.

For the famous Tokay Aszú, the *aszú* grapes are next trodden gently into a paste; the rotten skins dissolve but the pips remain whole. The

Yeasts, molds and damp combine in the ancient cellars of Tokay to produce this scene *(right).* The bottles age standing up, and the corks are changed after 15 to 20 years. Tokay is all made in the cellars of Tokajhegyaljai, the state farm at Satoraljaujhely. 9,000ha (22,000 acres) of vines grow on volcanic soil near the Soviet border.

The better vineyards around Lake Balaton have a soil of basalt, and lie along the 80km (50mi) northern shore of the lake. Here the vineyards around Mount Badacsonyi *(below),* with some 2,400ha (5,900 acres), produce the excellent dry Kéknyelü and other white wines.

The Olaszrizling (Wälsch-riesling) is the most widely grown white vine in Hungary *(inset).* Its grapes are blended with Furmint and Sylvaner to produce the best wines of Balatonfüred-Csopak. Magyar Mézesfehér and Ezerjó grapes are blended in small percentages into the lesser white wines of the Balaton region.

*aszú* paste, taken from buckets (*puttonyi*) of 35-liter (9¼ gal) capacity, is then blended with must made from grapes of the same harvest, but unaffected by botrytis, that have been macerated with their stalks for a few hours. The strength of this blend depends upon the number of *puttonyi* added to one *gönci* of 140-liter (37 gal) capacity. This blend is fermented in open vats for a few days, after which the enriched must is drawn off into *gönci* for a slow fermentation and maturation of six to seven years. The *gönci* are not made airtight so that, aided by storage in damp cool caves or cellars cut into the hillside, a fungus similar to the *flor* of Sherry forms on the wine's surface, and through ullage spreads to the cellar walls. In this atmosphere the wine slowly oxidizes to give the supreme Tokay bouquet. Tokay Aszú is eventually bottled after vatting, and the neck label of each bottle will state its strength in terms of the number of *puttonyi* that were added to one *gönci* of wine must: 3 *puttonyi* is the least concentrated, 6 *puttonyi* the most—and hence the most expensive. The alcohol varies between 14% and 15% by volume. It is not possible to crop grapes for *aszú* in every year, for it requires the same natural conditions as those needed for Trockenbeerenauslese and Sauternes.

Tokaji Szamorodni is a wine made from bunches of grapes that are not suitable for *aszú*, and is therefore plentiful in years when *aszú* is scarce, and vice versa.

About halfway between Budapest and Tokaj is Eger, where Hungary's best known red wine, Egri Bikavér or "Bull's Blood of Eger," is made from a blend of mainly Kadarka grapes, with Pinot Noir and Merlot added. The soil is clay over igneous rock, and good white and dessert wines are also made.

# YUGOSLAVIA

Yugoslavia, the largest of the Balkan countries that surround her, is a land of six republics, four languages, and two alphabets: she stretches from Italy and Hungary in the north down to Greece, and from the Adriatic east to Romania and Bulgaria. Fortunately, none of her political or linguistic complications affect her wine industry, which may be as much as 4,000 years old. It was defunct during five centuries of Turkish rule; it revived in the nineteenth century, but collapsed once more during the Second World War. Since then there has been considerable advance, notably the adoption of western-European vines in place of indigenous vines, and a tendency in the north and northwest to model their wines on the German and Italian styles. Yugoslavia has over 250,000ha (617,500 acres) of vineyards, from which some seven to eight million hectoliters (185-211 million gal) of wine are produced each year, with a sufficient proportion exported to put her firmly on the world scene. Most of the grapes are converted to wine at State cooperatives, although the vineyards are mainly in private hands.

The wine regions divide into Slovenia, Slovania, Croatia, and Dalmatia in the north and west, Bosnia-Herzegovina in the center, and Serbia and Macedonia in the east and south.

Slovenia (home of the Wine Institute, which works to improve technology) produces the best white wines of Yugoslavia from a variety of vines including Furmint, Müller-Thurgau, Silvaner, Traminer, and Wälschriesling: the soil is mainly lime and marl. Lutomer white wines are widely exported. To the east Slavonia, with a smaller vine area, also produces white wines of average quality, although the autonomous Vojvodina in the far northeast corner makes excellent Plemenka from the Bouvier grape and, from Kadarka and Pinot Noir, blending wines for export. In the beautiful Istrian peninsula of Croatia, strong well balanced red wines are made from Pinot Noir, Cabernet, Merlot, and Gamay vines, and good sweet dessert wines from Malvasia and Muscat. Further south, in Dalmatia, red and white wines are made but warrant only local drinking.

The river Sava, which flows down from the Julian Alps through Slovenia and Slavonia, joins the Danube at Belgrade and together they form the northern boundary of Serbia; with the regions of Kosmet and Macedonia, a good one-half of Yugoslavia's wine total is produced here from over 150,000ha (370,000 acres); most is consumed at home. The soil turns from loess in the north to limestone. Smederevka grapes name a good white wine; Prokupac, a full red, and Ružica, a good rosé, are also produced. Amselfelder Spätburgunder, a notable wine made from the Pinot Noir, is exported to West Germany from Kosmet, where the vineyards were replanted only 15 years ago. "Cabernet from Kosova" is also exported to the UK from this area.

A scene in the precipitous valleys *(right)* of the river Sava north of Belgrade, where unworkable land for vineyards is used as a nursery for the propagation of scions from western European vines. Yugoslavia, one of the world's oldest wine countries, suffered almost total annihilation of her wine industry during centuries of Turkish dominion and again during World War II. Despite all she is the tenth largest wine exporter in the world today.

# ROMANIA

Romanians are enthusiastic wine drinkers: they consume seven-eighths of the country's annual production, leaving a mere one million hectoliters (26½ million gal) for export, principally to Austria, Czechoslovakia, East Germany, and Poland, with lesser quantities for Belgium, France, Holland, Sweden, and the UK. The white wines of Romania are generally superior to the reds, although three red wines are worthy of mention.

The Cotnari vineyards in the northeast produce a well known pale dessert wine of about 14% vol. alcohol, made from the Grasa de Cotnari vine. It has a suggestion of Sauternes about it, but is not of the same class. Due south, the Dealul-Mare vineyards, 100km (62mi) northeast of Bucharest, are planted with Cabernet, Merlot, and Pinot Noir to produce full, velvety wines with deep color, and also white table wines that come from Feteasca, Muscat, and Riesling grapes. South again is the Banat vineyard, which makes full-flavored red Kadarka de Banat, from the Kadarka vine, and white Riesling de Banat. Chardonnay with Pinot Gris, Pinot Noir, and Cabernet Sauvignon grapes produce a sweet dessert wine in the Murfatler Hills above the Black Sea. This wine has a distinct bouquet of the orange flower. Northeast of Banat, in the Foscani region (the largest in Romania), red wines are made from Pinot Noir and Babeasca de Nicoresti vines and white wines from Aligoté, Feteasca, Muscat-Ottonel and Riesling vines: both are good quality table wines. The remaining vineyard of note is Tirnave, on the Transylvanian plateau in the midwest, where Perla de Tinarve white wine is a satisfactory blend.

Romania is the sixth largest wine producer in Europe (after France, Italy, Spain, Russia, and Portugal) but the enthusiastic Romanians spare only 1 million hl (26 million gal) of their 8 million hl (211 million gal) production for export. The huge Banat vineyard *(right)* lies in the plain between the Carpathians and the Transylvanian Alps.

The Kadarka vine is used for the production of Kadarka de Banat, a red wine of considerable character and rounded flavor. This Romanian picker *(far right)* is taking Kadarka grapes from vines trained high on wires. Northeast of Banat is Focşani, the largest region in Romania, where Pinot Noir is the leading grape for red wines and Riesling for whites.

# BULGARIA

The Bulgarian wine industry, which shared the fate of those in other Balkan states under the Muslim Turks and again in the Second World War, managed to double her 1940 product of two million hectoliters (53 million gal) by 1975. A program of expansion by Vinprom, the State wine organization, to double that figure again within 10 years has successfully met this target.

Bulgaria is divided into four main wine regions, mainly determined for her by nature as one-half of her area is mountainous, leaving only the plains of the Danube and Meritza valleys for cultivation. The northern and southern regions are divided by the Stara Planina (Balkan mountains), north of Sofia, and each produces one-third of the country's total red and white wine. The eastern region, accounting for the other one-third, covers the area east of the mountains down to the Black Sea; the fourth region is tucked between the Rodope mountains and the Yugoslav border.

The better red wines of Bulgaria have been made from the native Mavrud, Pamid and Saperavi vines; more recently the Cabernet Franc and Sauvignon have been planted in considerable quantity to introduce the style of French clarets. White wines are made more conventionally from indigenous vines, the Rkatziteli being heavily planted with lesser quantities of Dimiat, Red Misket, and Muscat-Ottonel. Steps to introduce Chardonnay, Sauvignon Blanc, and noble German varieties may soon lead to wines more acceptable to the export market.

Some two-thirds of Bulgaria's wines are exported, West Germany being the largest customer. Among those exported by the State Vinimpex are the dark red Mavrud; Gamza, a red wine for drinking young; Klosterkeller from Dimiat grapes; Misket, a white wine tasting of grapes from the Danube valley; Muscats from Karlovo; Melnik, a very full red wine from the Rodope area; and Perle, a dry white wine from Feteasca grapes. Some good sparkling wines are made in the northern region, including Iskra, or Bulgarian champanski, which is made by either the tank or by the champagne method.

The vineyards of Bulgaria are concentrated in the valleys of the Danube and Meritza rivers *(below)*. Today Vinimpex, the commercial state agency, is exporting over 5 million hl (132 million gal) of a variety of red, white and sparkling wines each year.

There are a number of state wineries in Bulgaria. Asenovgrad, near Plovdiv, produces an excellent red Mavrud and at Karlovo, in the Valley of Roses, good Muscats are made under the brand name "Hemus". These state wineries conform to a conventional pattern, as may be seen from this fermentation room at Karlova *(left)*.

# THE LEVANT

**Cyprus ♦ Turkey ♦ USSR ♦ Syria and Lebanon ♦ Israel ♦ Malta**

The countries bordering the Mediterranean from Turkey to Israel have here been grouped for convenience with the Russian vineyards (which lie mainly between the Black and Caspian seas) and the islands of Cyprus and Malta. Russia's exports are relatively small, but it has been policy to encourage the drinking of wine within the USSR to cut down the inordinate quantity of Vodka consumed there. Whether or not this has been successful, some 17-20 liters (4½-5¼ gal) of wine is now the average consumption per capita, and a considerable quantity of North African wine is imported to add to the total of an expanding home industry.

## CYPRUS

Cyprus stands some 100km (62mi) off the coast of Lebanon and enjoys an excellent climate (and an excellent reputation) for her wine production. The wine industry has a long history, going back into Greek mythology, and it has survived and improved through the centuries despite the proximity of the Muslim world of forbearance. Today Cyprus produces around 1.5 million hl (39½ million gal) of wine yearly from 50,000ha (123,000 acres) of vineyards in the Troodos mountains and the hills of Marathassa and Afames to the south, with a few others in the Makheras mountains further east. Cyprus entered an agreement to bring her industry into line with EEC standards and practice as from the beginning of 1975.

The soil is mostly volcanic and, exceptionally, the island has so far remained free of phylloxera, a credit to the care taken to keep imported vines in quarantine for long periods.

One of the oldest of her wines was renamed Commandaria by the Knights Templar; originally it was made by the Mana system, not dissimilar to the *solera* system of Jerez (see page 160). The grapes have always been dried in the sun for 10 days before pressing and today the wine-making process is thereafter mostly normal. The villages above Limassol specialize in Commandaria production: they include Kalokhorio, Zoopiyi, and Yerassa, where Xynisteri and Mavron grapes are standard. Commandaria reaches 15-16% vol. alcohol without fortification.

Cyprus sherry (which must be thus labeled under a High Court ruling) is an important export, and is made in a wide range, from very dry *finos* through creams to sweet dark types simulating *olorosos*. The process for Cyprus sherry is to cultivate *flor* separately and to cover the surface of white wines with it in American oak butts. Each year half the butt is replaced with young wine, while the wine withdrawn is transferred for further aging in wood.

For table-wine production, the black Mavron grape is by far the most generally planted, with about 15% of the white Xynisteri and a little Muscat. Some of the best red wine comes from Afames, in the hills due north of Limassol: the indigenous Maratheftika and Ophthalma grapes may be added for acidity, balance and color. The Mavron is used also for Kokkineli rosé. Aphrodite and Arisnöe are medium-dry white wines; they are full-bodied with a flavor said to be unique.

Limassol *(below)* is the chief port on Cyprus's south coast from which "Sherries" are exported. "Sherries" represent nearly 40% of the island's wine production of a quarter-million hectoliters (6.6 million gal) each year; the UK is a major importer.

The vineyards of Cyprus *(left)* are mostly on the slopes of the Troödos mountains in the west, with some nearer Nicosia and the Makheras mountains in the center. The black Mavron grape is traditional for red wines and the Xynisteri and Alexandria Muscat for whites.

Local yeasts ferment strongly, producing full-bodied dry wines. Left to weather in cask in the sun *(below)*, the wines develop a mellow, Sherry-like flavor. As the modern taste is for lighter Cyprus "Sherries", *flor* is introduced to produce *fino* styles.

# TURKEY

Turkey has over 300,000ha (750,000 acres) of vineyards from which only 3-4% of the grapes are used for wine-making, the remainder mostly going to the dried-fruit industry. The wine industry is said to date back to the third millennium BC; it collapsed entirely when, in the eighth century AD, the Turks were converted to Islam. Through subsequent centuries the industry has slowly returned, although the process of revival was reversed by the First World War.

The state monopolies wine industry was started in 1927, and in the following year a Turkish decree finally removed the Muslim faith as the country's established religion. Any tendency to drink wine was slow to start, but the industry has steadily revived, and recently a number of European vines have appeared on the scene to broaden the appeal of Turkish wines outside the country. Most grapes are sent to the cities for wine-making by Tekel, the state monopoly. With 20 wineries, Tekel dominates the industry and controls the country's exports. There are, however, over 100 private wineries which contribute a diversity of wines that are included in the mainstream of state production.

The country is divided into four main regions: Thrace-Marmara on the western side of the Bosphorus, the Aegean coast, Central Anatolia around Ankara, and eastern Anatolia. Trakya Kirmisi, meaning "red," made from Papazkarasi and Adakarasi grapes, and Trakya Beyaz, meaning "white," from Semillon grapes, are good quality wines, the latter being exported in worthwhile quantities. They are made in Thrace and around the Straits of Marmara near Istanbul. Here also Cinsault and Gamay grapes are used for red wines and Semillon with Clariette for whites; both make excellent quality wines.

The Muscat grape produces a good white wine of its type at Izmir, bordering the Aegean; it is superior to reds made from Irakara and Tokmak grapes. In Central Anatolia a dry white wine from the Emir grape is made at Nevşehir-Ürgüp, and another from Narince grapes at Tokat. The strong red Buzbag (pronounced "Boozhwar") is made by Tekel from the Bogazkarasi grape at Elâzig, opposite Cyprus in eastern Anatolia.

# USSR

It is difficult to substantiate information available on the wines of the USSR, but what is certain is that the superpower is the world's third greatest wine producer. It probably now has over 1,500,000ha (4 million acres) of vineyards concentrated in the only part of the Union which lies within the northern wine band and is capable of vegetation—the republics of Moldavia, Armenia, Azerbaijan, and Georgia, and the Crimea. In addition to an estimated 35 million hl (925 million gal) of home-produced wine, Russia has net imports of about another 8 million hl (210 million gal) each year to balance her home consumption—and that excludes spirits. The Russians already drink more spirits per capita than any other nation, and at present wine-consumption must work out at about 18 liters (26 bottles) per capita each year. Included in these estimates, based on known but outdated statistics, is the Soviet plan for sparkling-wine production; now well over 7,000 hl (185,000 gal) and perhaps nearer

Russian wine-production has increased with her territorial gains, and the extensive vineyards of the Prut State Farm in Moldavia (formerly Bessarabia and part of Romania) are a good example *(right)*. Large quantities of wine have been produced around Kishinev, capital of Moldavia, for centuries.

Another basket of grapes is checked in at a collecting point on a cooperative farm in Moldavia *(above)*. The state of Moldavia is the largest producer of wines in the USSR. The grapes, glowing in the sun, are a variety of Muscat.

Stephen Bolbochanu *(above left)*, a prominent Moldavian viticulturalist, selecting grapes that have been affected by noble rot on the Michurin collective farm. Much of the wine comes from hybrid vines, but plantings of Pinot, Aligoté, Riesling, and Traminer are increasing.

The region of Krasnodar *(left)* lies east of the Black Sea and the Sea of Azov. The Kuban valley has always been famous for sparkling wines, and the vineyards of the "Champagne" distillery in Abrau-Dyurso, shown here, produce two sparkling wines: Krasnodar itself and Isimjanskoje Igristoje.

The Bekaa valley *(right)* is 900m (2,950ft) above sea-level at the foot of Mount Lebanon, and here the best wines of Lebanon are produced. Château Musar, at Ghazir, 24km (15mi) north of Beirut, is the finest winery; others are the Kefrega, Naquad and Domaine de Tournelles.

In Syria and Lebanon the vineyards are found away from the coast in hilly country. The custom of walling-in small plots of land precludes mechanization in viticulture, and the donkey is a classical substitute *(below)*. The grapes are grown for the fruitbowl as well as for wine.

Gaston Hochar founded the Château Musar *(inset)* 50 years ago, and has proved that Lebanon can produce, from Cabernet Sauvignon blended with a little Cinsault and Syrah, noble red wines similar to the Médocs. Here *barriques* are seen in store at Musar.

14,000 hl (370,000 gal) are made each year. The best is Kaffia, from the Crimea; another excellent one is made at Krasnodar near the Sea of Azov.

About three-quarters of Russian-produced wine is sweet, with 15% sugar and an average of 15% vol. alcohol. Even their use of noble European vines is not to make their wines drier but to improve their sweet wines. The great problem for Russian viticulture is the winter temperature which can register -40°C (-40°F). For protection the vines must be released from their supports, bent down and covered with soil, and then, in the spring, unearthed and remounted before they come into bud. This is all now done by huge machines, and in many areas this is followed, later in the year, by mechanical harvesting.

In the Crimea, production is not vast but the quality of wines, including both still and fortified varieties, is the best. The most famous are the red and dry white Massandra. Muscat with Cabernet, Riesling, and Pinot Gris grapes from Europe are common throughout the Crimea. Indeed, in Moldavia, Georgia, Armenia, and the Ukraine, these and other European vines are now in general use. Authorized vines for use in named districts throughout the regions have created disciplines similar to but not as far-reaching as Appellations d'Origine: whether these have been updated to include the European vines is doubtful.

## SYRIA AND LEBANON

This is probably the area in which wine was first made; certainly Damascus was an important wine center in Biblical history, already exporting to the limits of charted lands. Little is said of the intervening period, and naturally Islam had its effect. By the early nineteenth century white wine was being made and marketed in amphoras, and today Syria has about 75,000ha (185,000 acres) under vines, in the Latakia region near the coast and in the hills of Aleppo, Damascus, and Homs. More significant are the 25,000ha (62,000 acres) of vineyards near Mount Lebanon, mostly in the prized Bekaa valley. However, the majority of grapes grown here and in the Syrian vineyards are for the table and the dried-fruit industry, so that wine production is relatively small.

The Bekaa valley, to the north of Beirut, produces excellent red wines from Cabernet Sauvignon with Cinsault and Syrah grapes; unfortunately, the light soil enables the *Phylloxera* louse to defy attempts to eliminate it by grafting. The wines are aged in barriques; they last well and are fairly likened to good Bordeaux. The best Bekaa properties are Château Musar at Ghazir, Domaine de Tournelles, Naquad, and Kefraga.

## ISRAEL

A thriving wine industry has been built up in Israel in the last 100 years; previously wine had been made there for at least 5,000 years. In 1906 Baron Edmond de Rothschild gave to their growers two vineyards (with their wineries) that he had earlier laid down at Richon-le-Zion, near Tel-Aviv, and Zikhron-Yaacov, at Mount Carmel, south of Haifa. In the same year the Societé Coopérative Vigneronne des Grandes Caves Richon-le-Zion et Zikhron-Yaacov was formed: this development laid the foundation of an important export business, conducted to this day principally with the USA, Canada, and the UK through the Carmel Wine Company of New York and London.

Zionist immigrants had been arriving in Palestine before the creation of the Jewish State in 1948. Vines introduced from Europe already included several from France and the Riesling from Germany. Rapidly the vineyards for wine-making more than doubled to 7,500ha (18,500 acres).

From the original sweet Muscat-style sacramental wines, the industry has now broadened to produce a full range of dry red and white wines and sparkling wines made by the *méthode champenoise*. The principal grapes selected in the last 30 years have been Carignan, Grenache and Semillon, although other varieties are being introduced experimentally. In 1957 the Israel Wine Institute was established at Rehovot to improve the quality of the whole new range of sweet wines and to monitor the quality of exports. The vineyards today have increased to over 15,000ha (37,000 acres) in Upper and Lower Galilee, the coastal area of Haifa, and in Tel-Aviv, Jerusalem, and the Negev. The product is over 450,000hl (12 million gal), of which about 100,000hl (2⅔ million gal) is exported.

## MALTA

Although some 2,000ha (5,000 acres) of vineyards are spaced around the south coast of Malta, with a few on the neighboring island of Gozo, the Maltese have some dilemma about their role in the wine industry. Close to the southern extreme of the northern wine-band, the grapes are scorched in the summer yet the vineyards are drenched with heavy rains earlier in the year. This results in production of no better than ordinary red and white wines that tend to lack character or finesse. For this reason, a sweet dessert wine has been developed using the Muscat grape. The better vineyards are at Burmarrad, Rabat, and Siggiewi, and the vines most planted are Dun Tumas, Gannaru, Gellewza, and Nigruwa.

Hazor in Upper Galilee *(below)* was once a major Canaanite sanctuary. Vineyards may be seen in the distance: this area of Galilee is now producing commendable red Cabernet wines.

Today Israel is making good dry and sparkling wines from European vines *(left)*, including Carignan, Grenache and Semillon; the *méthode champenoise* is used for the sparkling wines. Current yearly production in Israel is approaching 500,000 hl (13.2 million gal).

# NORTH AFRICA

## Egypt ♦ Tunisia ♦ Algeria ♦ Morocco

All of the countries bordering the Mediterranean coastline of North Africa produce wine. The critical latitude 30° North runs west from the southern end of the Suez Canal, and brings a strip of northern Egypt and the most northerly three to four hundred kilometers (190-250mi) of Tunisia, Algeria, and Morocco into the wine-producing zone. All these countries' wine industries suffered the same fate under 1,000 years of Muslim abstention.

## EGYPT

Virgil, with Horace and Pliny, extolled the virtues of Egyptian wine, but no samples survive of the wine of those far-distant days; only the friezes of ancient Egypt tell of the method by which it was produced. However, at the beginning of the twentieth century an Egyptian, Nestor Gianaclis, decided to find and unearth the vineyards where it had been made. With faith akin to folly the task was tackled—successfully. At Mariout, on the edge of the desert, west of the Nile, Gianaclis discovered deep under sand a chalk soil almost identical with the chalk of Champagne, and entirely different from the alluvial soils flowing endlessly into the Nile Delta. Experimental vines were planted in 1903, but it remained to be discovered which vines were the most suited to the sun, soil and microclimate of the desert. Over 70 vines were tried and tested with the assistance of experts from France, Germany, and Hungary; and 20 new crosses developed by Gianaclis were added to the trials. Almost 30 years went by before he was able to place before the Chambre Syndicale des Courtiers Gourmets of Paris wines that were judged equal to the white Meursaults and Montrachets of Burgundy and the finest wines of the Rhine. Experience has proved the climate to be capable of developing great wines with an international appeal. Today over 15,000ha (37,000 acres) of vineyards have been restored, and an export market, especially with the Russians, has been developed.

## TUNISIA

Wine-making returned to Tunisia when it became a French possession in 1881. Vines were planted in the peninsula on the east side of the Gulf of Tunis, in the Medjerdah and Oued Miliane valleys and around the city of Tunis. In the early 1930s production of wine rose to an annual average of almost 1.25 million hl (33 million gal). In 1936 the *Phylloxera* louse reached Tunisia, however, and by 1946 the vineyard area had been halved and wine production reduced to one-third. In the mid-1970s the vineyards had recovered to 25,000ha (62,000 acres) and wine-production to over 750,000hl (20 million gal) annually.

Since the wine industry restarted, the Carignan, Alicante-Bouschet, and Cinsault vines have been used for red wines, with Beldi, Clairette de Provence, and Ugni Blanc for whites. The wines, particularly the reds, tend to maderize, so that Sauvignon and Semillon from France and Pedro Ximénez vines from Spain have been introduced for white wines, and Cabernet, Nocera Noir, and Pinot Noir for red wines. One of the best light rosés from North Africa is made from the Alicante-Grenache grape, although it is best drunk young—with the additional advantage that thereby maderization is avoided.

The appellations introduced when Tunisia was a French possession are to some extent academic, now that she is independent, but they are still used. AC Vin Muscat de Tunisie is a strong sweet dessert wine, fortified to give 17% vol. alcohol, having 70g of sugar per liter (9½ oz/gal), and made from the Muscat varieties Alexandrian, Frontignan or Terracina. The level of unconverted sugar is controlled either by adding spirit, to prevent the must from fermenting, or by adding brandy or completely rectified spirit to arrest fermentation. The product of the former method is rightly a *mistelle*. The two types may not be mixed; the best result comes from arresting fermentation with brandy.

The classification AC Vin Supérieur de

The vineyards of Tunisia are spread around the cities of Tunis and Carthage, in the typical sandy soil of North Africa. *Phylloxera*, which struck in 1936, has halved the vineyard area to about 35,000ha (86,500 acres). Workers in the vineyards *(above)* are harvesting Alexandria Muscat, one of the three mandatory grapes for producing AC Vin Muscat de Tunisie.

Tunisie discounts place-names and grape-types, but indicates that each batch has been tested and accepted for purity and taste, and gives the date of harvest on the label to show that it is at least one year old. Today 13 state-owned wineries, another 13 cooperatives, and 10 private wineries have standardized wines for export. The main producer, Union des Cooperatives Viticoles de Tunisie, makes Magon, a good quality red wine of 12% vol. alcohol, using Cinsault and Mourvèdre grapes from Tébourba in the Medjerdah valley. The Union produces also Muscat de Kelibia, an aromatic dry white wine of 11.8% vol. alcohol, from Cap Bon in the northeast; Château Mornag red and rosé wines from the Mornag hills; and Sidi Rais, a Muscat-scented rosé. The state-owned Office des Terres Domaniales makes red Château Thirbar, from the Medjerdah valley. There are a number of creditable red wines to be found, but the white wines do not have the same quality.

# ALGERIA

During Algeria's 130 years as a French colony, her wine production grew to be the third largest in the world: in a vineyard area of 350,000ha (865,000 acres), 15 million hl (396 million gal) of wine was produced. Today that area has been reduced to more like 160,000ha (400,000 acres) and her production to less than 5 million hl (132 million gal).

After independence, with the French market almost disappearing and local consumption banned, Algeria needed to find a new market for her wines. Previously they were exported in vast quantities to the Midi and other parts of France, largely for blending, but also as a cheap wine to accompany everyday meals; substantial exports also went to other EEC countries. Now, however, Russia absorbs all Algeria's bulk wine exports for blending and strengthening, and shares with other smaller markets her export of quality wines.

Algeria's vineyards have always been found some 80km (50mi) inland from the Mediterranean; since 1962, while those in the foothills of the Saharan Atlas mountains have been retained, those beneath them in the plains have been given over to agricultural crops. Six of the seven quality regions are spread between the central province of Alger and the western province of Oran; they include most of the 12 districts which earned VDQS status.

Red wines have always dominated the Algerian scene. They are high in alcohol, varying from 11% to 15% vol., with low acidity, and tend to be heavy, soft, and fat, with deep color. The main grapes planted for them are Alicante-Bouschet, Aramon, Carignan, Cinsault, Grenache, Monastrel, and Mourvèdre. The Office Nationale de Commercialization des Produits Viticoles (ONCV) has now produced standard labels naming only the region of origin of wines which are otherwise described by type or brand name.

Oran has always been responsible for three-quarters of Algeria's wine production, and in the Coteaux de Tlemcen on the Moroccan border are produced strong dry red, rosé and white wines. The whites do much for the lesser reputation of Algerian white wines generally; they are made from blends of Clairette, Faranan, Listan, Maccabéo, Merseguéra, and Ugni Blanc grapes.

Two other quality regions in Oran are Monts du Tessalah at Sidi-bel-Abbès, producing lesser quality wines, and the Coteaux de Mascara, whose red wines were formerly notorious as a base for some shippers' burgundies. They are dark and strong, with good texture and an aroma of oak from the barrels in which they are now matured. Here the white wines are excellent and have been described as the best made in North Africa.

Close to the Oran-Alger border at Dahra, three red wines are now called Taughrite, Aïn Merane, and Mazouna; each previously had VDQS-quality ranking. They are full-bodied and typically dark in color. A good rosé is made here, rather more fruity than another made in the Coteau du Zaccar, further east. In the Medea hills, inland and above the plain, blends of red wines are made using Cabernet and Pinot Noir grapes; they are firmer than traditional Algerian wines, with considerable finesse. In the eastern province of Constantine, lighter red wines with 11.5% vol. alcohol are produced at Aïn Bessem Bouira, together with very good rosés, and are perhaps among Algeria's best wines.

# MOROCCO

Morocco has the shortest modern wine history of the North African countries and the smallest area of wine vineyards, about 23,000ha (57,000 acres). Although the French slowly colonized Morocco from 1830, their dominion dates only from 1912 until 1956; they started the development of vineyards after the First World War. The area at its maximum was some 80,000ha (200,000 acres). Phylloxera may have been partially responsible for the present concentration of vineyards away from the north of the country. Exceptionally for a Muslim country, half of the wines produced are consumed domestically, a situation for which the presence of some remaining French settlers may in part account.

The pattern of Moroccan wine exports since independence is interesting for, while her markets are mainly France and other EEC countries, they also include the USA. This came about chiefly when Algeria sought a new market outside Europe. The Moroccan Ministry of Agriculture substituted its own system of Appellation d'Origine Garantie (AOG) when the French left, and this is strictly enforced. Moroccan wines cannot be exported unless they are sound and salable with 11% vol. alcohol, or more, and made from permitted vines. A central organization, SODEVI, is responsible for wine-production; the Comptoir des Vins du Maroc in Brussels bottles and sells Moroccan wines for the table in Europe.

The vines used for both red and white export wines are mainly the same as those used in Algeria. The Cinsault and Carignan make the best red wine and also give an excellent rosé—possibly the most popular type of wine for domestic drinking. Local table wines are made from native grapes, such as the Rafsai white grape of the Rif mountains, although here and on the Zerhoun and Great Atlas slopes the vines fell victim to phylloxera. Mechanization has now taken over from the plow on soil that is necessarily sandy.

The principal wine region of Morocco is the Meknès-Fez on the northern skirts of the central Atlas mountains. Here excellent, smooth long-lasting red wines from Carignan, Cinsault and Grenache grapes are made in the Beni M'Tir and Guerrouanne districts; they are marketed domestically as Les Trois Domaines and for export as Tarik and Chantebled.

An AOG *vin gris* is also made at Guerrouanne, a pale vin rosé made from the Cinsault and Carignan grapes. Three other designated districts, Beni Sadden, Sais, and Zerkhoun, all lie within the Meknès-Fez region. At Fez-Meknès SODEVI markets non-AOG red and rosé wines as Aïn Souala.

To the northeast, nearer the Algerian border, is the Oujda-Taza region, where the muscats of Berkane and presentable rosés exceed the quality of average red wines made at Taza, which are good for blending.

The third region is Rabat-Casablanca. South of Rabat is Sidi Larbi, an important red-wine area, and around Rabat are Chellah, Gharb, Zaer, and Zemmour, districts that have now given their names to soft red wines previously known by their brand names.

The wines of Casablanca are said to be swallowed before they have been allowed to mature. From Zennata comes a full red wine of 12% vol. alcohol, which is marketed as Ourika, and south of Casablanca the Gris de Boulaouane is produced by Sincomer: pale, dry, slightly fruity and faintly orange in color, it is (according to Hugh Johnson) the archetypal refresher of North Africa.

A farm near Rabat *(far right)*, the center for several important wine regions of Morocco, including Chellah, Gharb, Zaer, and Zemmour. These regional names are now being used for good full red wines made to Appellation d'Origine Garantie standards from vines including the European Carignan, Cinsault, and Grenache.

# NORTH AMERICA

This panorama *(below)* takes in most of the 70ha (170 acres) of Joseph Phelps' vineyards in the Napa Valley. Phelps and Walter Schug, his winemaker from Geisenheim in the Rheingau, have developed late-harvest botrytized Johannisberg Rieslings and other fine vinifera wines from grapes grown on selected plots of widely varying soil.

Today the North American continent has a rapidly expanding wine industry. In Canada only a small strip below the 50th parallel, in the west, and the area down to the Great Lakes, in the east, have the climate to ripen grapes for wine-making; but the industry there, although small, is growing as fast as it is in the USA.

The continent has always had wild vines growing in profusion; they include the *Euvitis* varieties *labrusca, riparia, rupestris* and *berlandieri*, all of which make wines described as "foxy," meaning wild and strange. But the wine-making *Vitis vinifera* was not native to America. It arrived thanks to the Jesuit evangelists who came to the Spanish dominions in Central and South America early in the sixteenth century. Wherever the missions were established their vine, appropriately renamed the Mission (from the Spanish Criolla grape), was planted to provide sacramental wine. The vine traveled north through Baja and Upper California during the seventeenth and eighteenth centuries.

Not until they discovered San Francisco Bay in 1769 did the Mexicans lay serious claim to Upper California, although even then neither Spain nor Mexico took steps to lay firm hold upon it. Two years previously Pope Clement XIV had suppressed the entire Jesuit movement under pressure from the Bourbon monarchies and Italian states; as a consequence some 20 Jesuit missions throughout Baja and Upper California survived in only an informal association until the Mexican government, having achieved independence in 1821, secularized the missions in 1830.

By this time American settlers were reaching the West Coast via Cape Horn as well as by overland trails from the east. Increasing American interest led to the Mexican War of 1846-8, which settled the USA's claim to California within its present boundaries. The discovery of gold in Sutter's Mill-race in the Sacramento valley led to the Gold Rush of '49, and the population of California increased dramatically: the resulting wine boom was followed by a wine slump. However, among the many natural advantages that the pioneers were quick to appreciate was the Californian climate: it was, and is, perfect for producing wine. For the wine-makers the next 100 years were to be packed with both successes and disasters; yet their weight of empiric and scientific knowledge was constantly growing, so that the development of the enormous wine industry of the 1980s was inevitable.

While the Jesuit vineyards in California had been falling into disuse, Joseph Chapman, an early settler, had planted the first commercial vineyard with Mission vines at Los Angeles in 1824; and Jean-Louis Vignes from Bordeaux had arrived on the scene with cuttings of French vines to prove that *Vitis vinifera* varieties other than the Mission would grow equally well.

Around 1850, an extraordinary newcomer arrived from Europe. Colonel Haraszthy, a Hungarian nobleman, brought with him 100 cuttings and six rooted vines which he planted in San Diego. One was the famous Zinfandel, now the most used vine in the state, and by 1880 large areas of Zinfandel were already planted. Haraszthy worked to identify the vines best suited to different areas in the state, and in 1861 he was commissioned by Governor John Downey to gather from Europe all the varieties of vine that he (Haraszthy) thought suitable. He returned with 100,000 cuttings from 300 varieties, most of which were planted around San Francisco, primarily to prove that fine wines may be made from non-irrigated grapes. Haraszthy is rightly acclaimed as the father of Californian viticulture.

The European varieties were soon tested in the eastern states, and it was concluded that *Vitis vinifera* vines would not grow east of the Rockies. As a result, hybrids were bred from the native *Euvitis labrusca*, which in nature contains an odorous ester that spoils wines made from it. The hybrids were grouped under a new species name, *Vitis labruscana*; they include the white Noah, black Concord, and red Catawba grapes. These vines, like all native American vines, had the advantage of being resistant to the *Phylloxera* louse, which was indigenous to them, and had first been carried to Europe on vines sent from America. The louse reappeared in California in 1870 and by 1879 had ravaged the vineyards around San Francisco, as it had most European vineyards. The remedy, discovered in France, of grafting *V. vinifera* scions onto American rootstocks eventually saved the wine industry.

By this time, and with the science of enology or oenology progressing by the hour, the wine industry of the USA should have been set for uninterrupted success and expansion. But, from the early days of the twentieth century, the concept of total abstinence by everyone in the country was growing, and the Volstead Act of 1919 brought Prohibition to the USA; the Act was repealed in 1933. Although the slump after the Gold Rush, the impact of phylloxera, the period of Prohibition and the financial crash of 1929 have all left their scars, the US wine industry has now reached the point where, through exports of worthy wines, it is taking its rightful place in the world scene.

Canada's wine history has not been without its share of disasters, for phylloxera also reached the young vineyards in the Dominion, and Prohibition in Canada antedated Prohibition in the USA by seven years. Since repeal, the system of state-monopoly liquor-store selling has not helped Canadian wine and spirits to compete with other liquors.

Mexico, which runs far up into the North American continent, has a wine industry with a history of disasters ranging over a much longer period. Her independence, followed by the war with the USA and the Mexican Revolution of 1910-20, left the remnants of her old wine supremacy in tatters. However, since 1929 everything has gone right, so that the wine industry of Mexico, too, has an excellent future.

# THE UNITED STATES

## California ♦ The Northwest ♦ The Eastern States ♦ The South and Southwest States

With the predictability of a young man's fancy in Spring, talk of wine in the USA will swiftly turn to California. However, although this is far and away the most important wine state in the Union, there are others that must be recognized in order to appreciate the modern wine industry of the USA.

In the north west, three states have considerable wine industries: they are Washington, Oregon, and Idaho. All the other wine areas of any consequence fall east of a north-south line drawn down the western boundaries of Minnesota, Iowa, Missouri, Arkansas, and Louisiana. In this half of the Union the more important wine regions are centered in the states bordering or near the Atlantic and the Great Lakes: exceptional are large wine centers in Indiana and Missouri. California dwarfs them all individually, and exceeds them all collectively.

The taste for wines in the USA continues to vary dramatically, and accordingly the producing areas, including California, seem at some loss to know the direction they should take. But two points should be considered. First, every kind of wine known to man can be produced somewhere in the USA: it is a matter of purposeful selection of the right microclimate for a particular product. Second, the general direction of wine-production in the USA has already belied the statement made 125 years ago by a critic who said: "We shall not make our best wines till we cease to strive for foreign imitations." The USA is as much entitled to import foreign vines as any other country — and just as much as Europe is entitled to import American rootstocks! "Foreign imitation" starts only when the names of foreign wine regions or wine products are used. Fortunately, labeling in the USA is moving away from such plagiarism towards varietal and brand names. The international market has already praised and accepted the subtleties of US wines from Chardonnay, Sauvignon and other exotic vines, and the US industry must now teach its customers at home to appreciate those same subtleties — texture, aroma, strength, acidity, and finish — of fine American wines. Experience has certainly shown that, whatever wine the USA produces, it will be consumed, so the US wine industry should now go on to lead native fashion, not follow it.

In 1983, the US Government introduced new rules to bring definition to the wine industry. Two main areas are covered: mandatory and other information that shall be or may be printed on the label; and the setting up of "approved" viticultural areas (parallel to the delimited areas in EEC countries).

Five mandatory statements must be printed on the label:

○ **The wine type** which may be *fortified, sparkling* or *still*. Sparkling wines must state how the bubbles were produced (that is, "in this bottle" for *méthode champenoise*, and "in the bottle" for all other methods). Still or table wines are classified as *generic, varietal* and *proprietary*, and if varietal must be made from a blend including at least 75% of the named grape.

○ **The brand name**, which may be, and usually is, the name of the winery.

○ **The region of origin**, defined separately for:

**Estate Bottled**, when the winery is in an "approved viticultural area". Here the grapes must come from vineyards owned or directly controlled by the winery that lie within that approved viticultural area.

**Proprietor or Vintner Grown**, which applies to wines made from grapes grown outside the approved viticultural area.

**Viticultural Area**, for wines not labeled "Estate Bottled," having a blend where at least 85% of the grapes must come from the approved area named.

# THE UNITED STATES

For a continent unblessed by nature with the species *vitis vinifera* the "wine-growing" areas of North America have made unbelievable advances in the last century. The United States is today using natural resources and modern technology to produce wines equalling the world's best, mainly from the classic noble vines of Europe.

**Political Subdivision**, for wines naming, for example, a state or county in which at least 75% of the grapes were grown.

**Multiple Subdivision**, for wines naming more than one political subdivision, and the percentage of grapes from each.

○ **Bottler**

**Produced and Bottled by**, for wines of which at least 75% of the must was fermented by the winery.

**Made and Bottled by**, for wines of which at least 10% of the must was fermented by the winery.

○ **Alcohol Level** The alcohol content must be stated as a percentage content, with a permitted variation from the stated level of ±1.5%. Alternatively the term "Table Wine" may be used to indicate an alcohol level not exceeding 14%.

Three optional statements may be printed on the label:

○ **Vintage Date** If used, 95% of the grapes must be from that year's harvest.

○ **Individual Vineyard** If used, 95% of the grapes must be from that vineyard.

○ **Specific Character**, for statements such as "dry" or "sweet." If the label says "Late Harvested" or "Late Picked," the sugar content of the grapes at harvest and the amount of residual sugar after fermentation must be stated on the label.

In January 1985 the work of defining *Approved Viticultural Areas* had not been completed by the Bureau of Alcohol, Tobacco, and Firearms. In California, 14 such areas had been approved and a further 23 had been filed. In other states, six had been approved, while seven for single states and four for multi-states had been filed.

In all, some 325,000ha (800,000 acres) of vineyards are now under cultivation in the USA, and this area is still growing rapidly, for supply has by no means reached demand. The output, perhaps in the region of 25 billion bottles a year, makes the USA sixth in world production after France, Italy, the USSR, Argentina, and Spain. The tendency is for the number of bonded wineries to decrease as fewer firms produce more wine; in 1985 there were between 1,100 and 1,200 bonded wineries in the USA, of which one-half were in California, where a few giant firms account for most of the wine product.

The Phelps vineyards in the Napa Valley *(overleaf)*. Joseph Phelps was a Colorado builder specializing in winery construction who in 1973 became gripped by the romance of winemaking; he was joined by winemaker Walter Schug from Geisenheim.

# CALIFORNIA

The State of California lies between latitudes 43° and 33° north. For 1,300km (800mi) from Crescent City in the north to San Diego in the south, the country rises from the Pacific Ocean to the Coastal Range of hills, some 600m (2,000ft) in height. To the east of this range is the Great Central Valley, separating it from the Sierra Nevada, the border of neighboring Nevada. The Coastal Range breaks at San Francisco Bay and two rivers, the Sacramento from the north and San Joaquin from the south, flow into the bay. These rivers, each fed by many tributaries from the Sierra Nevada, water the Central Valley and add to a climate perfect for viticulture.

Down the Pacific Coast from the Aleutians runs the Humboldt Current — another contributor to California's amazing climate. This cold current cools the air above it, forcing the hot summer air upwards and creating a white fog below it. The fog drifts inland through the coastal gaps and fills the valleys, giving much needed moisture to the vineyards, and protecting them from the intense summer temperatures, which reach 27-32°C (80-90°F) every-day in the summer.

The sun must be the most important determining factor of all in any climate. Variations in temperature in California have been analyzed by the Enological Laboratories of the University of California at Davis to produce a formula of "degree-days" whereby specified areas of the state may be readily assessed and classified for effective sun-strength. The formula is simple and logical. The vine will not grow at a temperature under 10°C (50°F), and there are in California 214 critical days from April 1 to October 31 during which the vine-growing cycle is completed. The formula therefore takes the mean daily temperature (High plus Low ÷ 2) for each of the 214 days, adds them together, and subtracts 214 × 50 degrees (the formula is worked in Fahrenheit). The answer is the degree-day total for that area, which falls into one of five "degree-day regions."

| | |
|---|---|
| Region I: | less than 2,500 degree-days |
| II: | 2,501-3,000 degree-days |
| III: | 3,001-3,500 degree-days |
| IV: | 3,501-4,000 degree-days |
| V: | 4,001 and over degree-days |

Thus, for example, Napa and Sonoma counties vary between Regions I and II; Livermore Valley is in III; the northern San Joaquin Valley is in IV; and Sacramento Valley is in V.

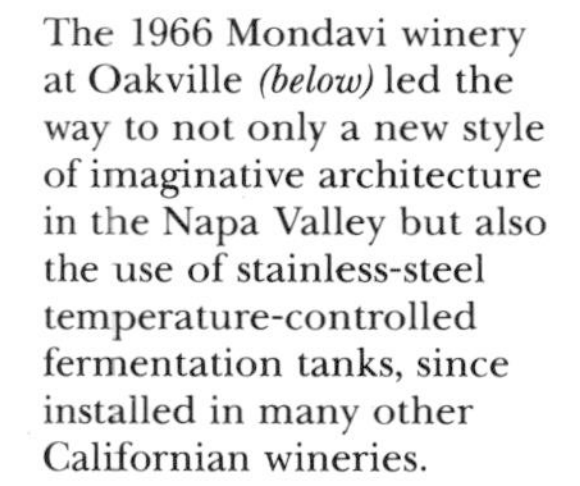

The 1966 Mondavi winery at Oakville *(below)* led the way to not only a new style of imaginative architecture in the Napa Valley but also the use of stainless-steel temperature-controlled fermentation tanks, since installed in many other Californian wineries.

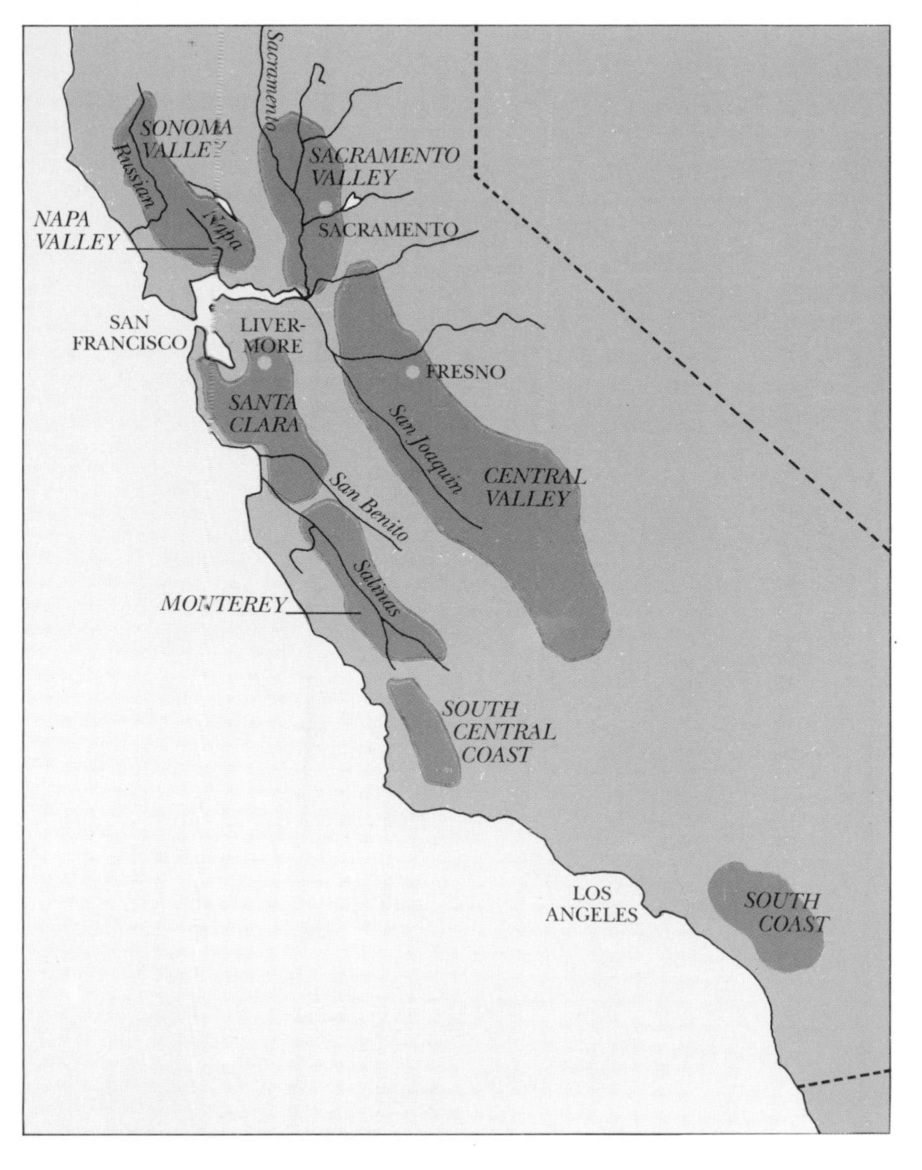

The vineyards *(top)* of the internationally famous Paul Masson wine organization have grown to over 2,000ha (5,000 acres), mainly in Monterey County. Started in 1852 by Etienne Thée, a *vigneron* from Bordeaux, the company was handed down to Paul Masson, and from him to Martin Ray. In 1942 Ray sold it to the House of Seagram.

California *(left)* stretches for 800km (500mi) down the Pacific Coast between northern latitudes 42° and 33°, thus enjoying ideal temperatures and sunlight to produce wines of most, if not all, known kinds. Matters are assisted by the offshore Humboldt current, which brings moisture and humidity, and by the most fertile valleys of the western states.

Mondavi has remained a family concern since its inception; Robert's son Tim is winemaker. Among their whites Fume Blanc from the Sauvignon Blanc is probably the most famous; here Robert Mondavi *(above)* is nosing a sample of the new vintage.

Spring Mountain Vineyards came into being in 1968 when Michael Robbins decided to give up a career in real estate and make wine. His first venue was north of St Helena, but in 1974 he bought Miravelle, the old Tiburcio Parrott estate, high above the Napa Valley. The old winery was torn down and rebuilt into the hillside *(above)*, using gravity-flow to bring the wine down to the bottling line at ground-level.

The pride of the Robert Mondavi Winery are Reserve Cabernet Sauvignons, with small quantities of Cabernet Franc and Merlot in the blends according to the vineyard conditions of the year. The Beaujolais Gamay grapes *(top)*, are grown for wines of character and distinction.

The clinical appearance of the fermenting tanks at the Oakville Mondavi Winery *(center)* tends to belie the subtlety of the wine they produce. Although many wineries still ferment their wines in wood, the Mondavis use stainless steel and draw the benefits of wood in the maturation and aging stages.

Tasting is a ceremonial at Mondavis, and regular sessions *(above)* are held with the staff for many purposes; for instance, the body and flavor of a wine will determine the type of barrel in which it will mature — or, during aging, show which barrels are developing suitably for reserve blends.

The new winery of Spring Mountain Vineyards was built in the style of the original estate house; it sits in front of a 27m (90ft) tunnel, dug beneath the mountainside in the nineteenth century and now incorporated into the cellars. Intended perhaps to emphasize that Chardonnay is the best white on the Spring Mountain tariff, this stained-glass window *(inset)* adorns a wall in the cellars.

The estate house of Spring Mountain Vineyards *(right)* was erected late in the nineteenth century. Michael Robbins set about a thorough restoration of the building, retaining the external heavily featured decor, but letting the light and air of the twentieth century into its dark high corridors. The period architecture was retained for new buildings.

Napa has been called the "winiest county in the United States". Today it has 52,000ha (128,000 acres) of vineyards and over 130 bonded wine cellars. There are more huge fans and sprinklers to fight spring frosts in the Napa Valley *(opposite)* than in the rest of the world.

From this information it is possible for planters to determine the kind of wine most suitable to their degree-day region and the vines that are best for its production, using *inter alia* available information on European vineyards falling in equivalent degree-day regions and the vines that are planted there (the Rhône valley and Tuscany, for example, would equate to Livermore Valley, in Region III).

The growing season for grapes in California is exceptional, at over 200 days, and in other parts of the United States (and in Europe) it may be much shorter. Rainfall is no longer regarded as a crucial element in grape-growing. Winter rainfall of between 41cm and 76cm (16-30in) is necessary and may be relied upon, coming mostly from cyclonic storms; but little rain is wanted in the summer, and can be damaging at flowering and harvest. If necessary, rain can easily be replaced by irrigation.

Attitudes towards soil and its value in viticulture are different in the USA than those in Europe. Instead of the distinctions of limestone, gravel, schist, clay, and igneous and other rocks, held to be so important in Europe, in California soil is either "residual" or "transported;" "residual" implies that the rock was formed *in situ* whereas "transported" rocks have been deposited by wind or water. It is, however, conceded that vines "stressed" in poor soils produce high-quality grapes with strong varietal characteristics, although in lesser quantity, while good soils produce greater quantities of poorer grapes. But the US conclusion is that transported soils are the best for wine-making — in sharp contrast to European views. "Transported" soils should not be confused with substitute soils imported by man, which may be laid down in a new vineyard.

The climate of California is mild and sunny, and the microclimates in vast areas of the state bring together every element for which the viticulturist could ask. The grape varieties planted are too numerous for a list to be meaningful, particularly as many relate to widely varying types of wine (dealt with below according to their districts of production). Some vines, developed from crossings of European grapes at Davis, have been designed to withstand the Californian temperatures. The most-planted vines for wine in the state are Zinfandel, Carignan, Cabernet Sauvignon, Barbera, Grenache, and Ruby Cabernet, for red wines; and French Colombard, Chenin Blanc, Chardonnay, White Riesling, and Sauvignon Blanc for white wines — all in the descending order stated. A list of vines suitable for planting in the degree-day regions (see table) is also significant in identifying California's most important grapes.

| | |
|---|---|
| Region I: | Pinot Noir, Chardonnay, Riesling |
| Region I and II: | Cabernet Sauvignon, Chenin Blanc, Gamay Beaujolais, Napa Gamay |
| Region II: | Grenache, Petite Sirah |
| Region II and III: | Sauvignon Blanc, Semillon |
| Region IV: | Barbera, French Colombard, Ruby Cabernet, Emerald Riesling |
| Region V: | Palomino and other dessert-wine grapes |

The vineyard regions of California are in two vast areas: the first is Coastal Counties, embracing the two cooler regions nearer the Pacific coast, stretching from Mendocino County, north of San Francisco, down to San Diego County in the extreme south; the second is the Great Central Valley, east of the Coastal Range, extending from Sacramento County down to Kern County, northeast of Santa Barbara. The Coastal Counties produce about 15% of California's wine, including many of the best "Estate Bottled" wines, while the hotter Central Valley contributes the remaining 85%.

The vineyards of the Paul Masson winery at Pinnacles *(below)*. These vineyards were laid down in the early 1960s to feed the winery built at Soledad in 1966. As a result Massons were ready for the "wine boom" of the late 1960s.

When the "wine boom" came to the USA, the Paul Masson vineyards were able to benefit from test-plantings *(below right)* made in the early 1960s at Pinnacles, matching varieties of soil and microclimate conditions to each vine.

Warren and Barbara Winiarski abandoned a career in teaching at the University of Chicago to fulfill a dream, and built the Stag's Leap Wine Cellar, named for the rocky outcrops on the eastern ridge of the Napa Valley; the vineyards were laid down in 1972 on the Silverado Trail *(far left)*. Winiarski, the winemaker, is seen *(above)* transferring carbon dioxide gas from a tank of fermenting Chardonnay to a tank of Pinot Noir which requires carbon dioxide but, having fermented fully, can no longer produce it. "Pumping over" from the bottom to the top of the tank during fermentation *(left)* is necessary to give color and strength to red wines. Only by painstaking cellar work *(below)* can the casks of wine reach their optimum during aging and racking.

## THE COASTAL COUNTIES

The main wine subregions of Coastal Counties are Napa County, Sonoma County (including Valley of the Moon and Russian River), Mendocino and Lake Counties, Bay Area, and the North Coast, South Central Coast, and South Coast regions. Yields in the USA are always expressed in short tons (2,000 lb) per acre.

**Napa County**

The Napa Valley produces a wide variety of wines in an area that is, by US standards, minute. Wedged between the Mayacamas mountains to the west and the Howell mountains to the east, the valley is no more than 50km (30mi) in length, and has 125 bonded wineries within its boundaries: no wonder it has been called the "winiest county in America." The valley, about 80km (50mi) to the northeast of San Francisco, draws upon coastal and inland influences to broaden the range of its wine products. The river Napa flows down it in a southeasterly direction; the higher up the valley (centered on Highway 29—"the wine road"), the hotter it gets, all the way to Mount St Helena. Altogether, there are some 10,500ha (26,000 acres) of vines in the valley.

Its southern area runs from Carneros Creek up to Yountville and across from the Mayacamas to Stag's Leap; it enjoys a cool Region I climate, more accentuated at the valley's sides than in the center. The cool air is ideal for growing Pinot Noir and Chardonnay. The Californians were not immediately successful with Pinot Noir, producing heavy, lifeless wine, but the more recent vintages are showing great promise. The Chardonnay is undoubtedly California's most successful white grape, giving wine that improves with age, and with fermentation in oak. Wines from both grapes now show up well in the Burgundy tradition. Pinot crops only 3 to 4 tons per acre but Chardonnay is more prolific, with 4 to 6 tons.

For 15km (10mi) north of Yountville, the mountains close in on the valley, reducing the

The Heitz Wine Cellars in the Napa Valley started in 1961 with a patch of Grignolino grapes; a tasting-room now stands on that site, south of St Helena. In 1964 proprietor and winemaker Joe Heitz bought the old stone winery built in the valley in 1898. White oak tanks *(above)* installed there are today used for clarifying all Heitz wines.

Heitz now have 12ha (30 acres) of Chardonnay vines in addition to 8ha (20 acres) of Grignolino planted around the winery *(above)*. "Martha's Vineyard," 6ha (15 acres) in size, has been put down to Cabernet Sauvignon, which produces a popular dark-colored, full-bodied, well balanced red wine. A wind-machine is used to avoid frost damage.

Surrounded by Grignolino vines of a selected strain, the old stone winery of Heitz Wine Cellars in the Napa Valley *(right)*. The cellars of Joe Heitz have rapidly gained an international reputation as a result of the unerring acuteness of his palate in blending wines; his Cabernet Sauvignons and Chardonnays speak eloquently for themselves.

Not far from the Silverado Trail and approached by the steep Pritchard Hill is the 40ha (100-acre) vineyard of Don Chappellet *(right)*, developed in 1967 when he abandoned the food-vending business to enter the Napa Valley wine industry. The winery is contained in a unique pyramid-shaped building.

The policy of Chappellet is to produce wines from grapes grown on the estate. Fine white wines are made, and the Chappellet Bordeaux-style Cabernet Sauvignon, made with a blend of 10% Merlot, is a sound wine. A tipper *(below)* is offloading grapes into a screw-fed crusher-destalker.

The Archimedean screw *(center)* carries a charge of Merlot grapes towards the crusher-destalker. The Merlot was first seriously put to the task of winemaking in Bordeaux, and has since performed well all around the world to balance other black grapes. It ripens earlier than Cabernet Sauvignon, and softens the wine.

One corner of the Chappellet pyramid's interior is given to modern equipment, including stainless-steel tanks of various sizes, jacketed for temperature-control, in which the wines may be fermented, blended or stored. These two *(above)* are open for cleaning-down.

In another corner of the vast and airy Chappellet pyramid, wines are put to mature in French oak barrels *(right)*. The dry Chenin Blanc made here is reckoned to be the best in California, and the Chardonnay, fermented partly in barrels, is a firm wine of full flavor.

At the northern end of the Napa Valley is the Sterling Vineyards winery *(left)* described by Leon D. Adams as "the most spectacular in America and quite possibly in the world."

Sterling Vineyards, now owned by Seagrams, make "Champagne," in association with Mumm's, as well as fine varietal wines, seen here *(below)* aging in oak casks.

The Schramberg Champagne Cellars *(left)*, beneath Mount Diamond, were founded in 1862 and immortalized in Robert Louis Stevenson's *Silverado Squatters*; in 1880 Stevenson found Schramberg "the picture of prosperity."

In the cellars of Sterling vineyards, illuminated by stained-glass panels, over 20,000 hl (600,000gal) of wines age in oak tanks and barrels *(above)*; they include strong Cabernet Sauvignon and Merlot wines, a dry Sauvignon Blanc, and an equally good Chardonnay.

maritime influence, and the temperature rises to Region II levels. Above it is Zinfandel Lane, just north of Rutherford, and here the Zinfandel grape is king: this grape, on its distinctive red stems, produces well balanced wine that ages almost indefinitely. Zinfandel is heavily planted, some 12,000 ha (30,000 acres) or more already being under cultivation throughout California; the crop is 4 to 6 tons per acre. Deriving possibly from the Primitivo of Umbria in Italy, it gives wine similar in flavor to the Riojas of Spain.

The Cabernet vine is also heavily planted in this neck of the valley, which is one of three areas making the best Cabernets of all California. They are fragrant, full-bodied and tannic, and are ready after four years in bottle. The area of Cabernet-planting has more than quadrupled in the last seven years (to 1985).

All the way up the valley beyond Zinfandel Lane to St Helena the heat rises, and here Petite Sirah is planted with rather less Cabernet, although Zinfandel is still the most used. The Petite Sirah grape is good for blending-in color and tannin, and is also a heavy cropper, at 4 to 8 tons an acre.

Christian Brothers (the Catholic Order of La Salle) own four wineries in Napa Valley: with a total of 500ha (1,250 acres) of vineyards, and marketing four million cases of wine each year, they are the largest producers in the county. The hilltop Mount La Salle winery, for its beauty, and the Greystone winery, for its age (founded 1920) and size, are notable, and their dated wines come from Cabernet, Chardonnay, and Gamay Noir vines.

The Charles Krug Winery at St Helena and another situated at Oakville, run independently by the Mondavi Brothers, are also big producers. Krug is the oldest winery in the valley, dating from 1861, and here Peter Mondavi has a reputation for exceptional white wines. At the Robert Mondavi Winery the aim is perfection in quantity, and the best is Cabernet Sauvignon Reserve. Other big properties in the valley are Domaine Chandon at Yountville (the first Californian enterprise by a Champagne producer) and Louis M. Martini at St Helena.

A worker in Mondavis' magnificent aging cellars *(below)*. Company policy is to give total responsibility for each stage or section of the winery to the operative, thus securing his or her dedication to the high standards maintained throughout.

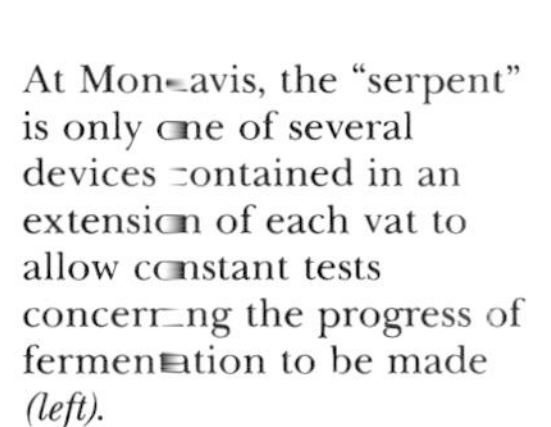

Mounted above the top of a vat during fermentation, a glass "serpent" *(far left)*, a simple and efficient device, enables carbon dioxide gas to be released but prohibits air from entering.

At Mondavis, the "serpent" is only one of several devices contained in an extension of each vat to allow constant tests concerning the progress of fermentation to be made *(left)*.

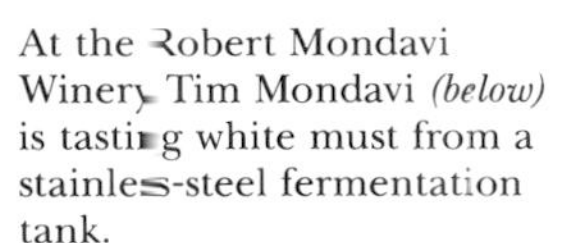

At the Robert Mondavi Winery, Tim Mondavi *(below)* is tasting white must from a stainless-steel fermentation tank.

John Luper *(left)*, who graduated in enology from Fresno State University and who succeeded the Croatian Milenko Grgich as winemaker at Montelena in 1977. He was succeeded in turn in 1981 by James P. "Bo" Barrett, who maintains the Grgich and Luper wine tradition.

The Napa Valley's Château Montelena, built in 1882, did not become a serious wine cellar until 1970. The Chinese gardens, lake, and summerhouse were built by Chinese non-winemaking owners in the period after Prohibition. A junk on the lake completes the illusion *(above)*.

Château Montelena has some 24ha (60 acres) of Cabernet Sauvignon, 9ha (22 acres) of Chardonnay and 4ha (10 acres) of Zinfandel. The Zinfandel grapes *(inset)* have been ripened evenly and are in excellent condition. The wine is made in a fresh, fruity style.

The medieval character of the Montelena estate buildings is carried, with dubious logic, into the oriental gardens *(left)*.

Depite the castellations and turret of the estate house at Château Montelena *(top)*, the building was constructed as a winery in the closing years of the nineteenth century.

A stenciled board proclaims a bin-number in the annals of Château Montelena *(above)*. In red-wine production the free-run wine is fermented separately and not blended with the pressed wine until just before malolactic fermentation.

**Sonoma County**

This county lies between the Pacific Coast and the Mayacamas mountains, which separate it from Napa County. Its wines are held by many to equal those made in the Napa Valley. The county is subdivided into "Valley of the Moon," from the title of a Jack London book, and the Russian River Valley, named for the Russian trappers who sought fur and fortune here before the land was settled by Americans. There are nearly 100 wineries in the county.

The Russian River winds south from Cloverdale and turns west at Forestville to Guerneville and on to flow into the ocean. There are five areas of concentration in the Russian River Valley wine region. In the north the area of Cloverdale-Asti is the warmest, with a Region III to IV climate and a good deal of Zinfandel grapes. Below it the Dry Creek area, between Geyserville and Healdsburg, is slightly milder, and to its west the Alexander Valley straddles the serpentine river. Dry Creek has Zinfandel planted, with Cabernet Sauvignon, Chardonnay, and some of the low-cropping Pinot Noir; Alexander Valley adds Johannisberg Riesling and Gewürztraminer, each cropping 4 to 6 tons per acre, in a Region II to III microclimate. Southeast of Alexander Valley is Knights Valley, farther inland and hence warmer still. The final subdistrict is the Santa Rosa Plain, a triangle with Healdsburg in the north, Santa Rosa at the southeast, and Guerneville at the southwest. The vines here are mostly Chardonnay, to suit the Region I microclimate, with Pinot Noir, Gamay Beaujolais, and some of the still scarce Gewürztraminer. With Chardonnay and Pinot Noir in abundance, the Korbel wineries at Guerneville produce excellent wines by the *méthode champenoise*. To a range of Brut, Dry, and Demi-Sec wines, Blanc de Blancs and Blanc de Noirs have now been added.

The reputation of Russian River Valley wines is steadily rising; of the five subdistricts, at least three expect to gain their own individual "appellations."

Sonoma Vineyards at Windsor are producers of reliable wines, principally from Cabernet Sauvignon, Chardonnay, and White Riesling. Here Sonoma Vineyards have 485ha (1,200 acres) under vines, and in a new joint enterprise with Piper-Heidsieck that produced its first champagne-type wines in 1982, have established an instant reputation for Brut and Blanc de Noirs. The Alexander Valley Vineyards of Healdsburg are known in the USA and UK for a full dry Chardonnay in the Burgundy tradition. Also in the Alexander Valley, the Field Stone Winery have perfected a pink Spring

Château St Jean *(below)* stands in large grounds and is tucked under the Sugarloaf Ridge in the Sonoma valley. Richard Arrowhead was told to construct the winery, the concept of three San Joaquin Valley winemakers, brothers Edward and Robert Merzoian and Kenneth Sheffield, on a "money-no-object" basis.

Cabernet, a rose ideal for picnic drinking.

The Gundlach Bundschu winery at Vineburg recreates one lost to the earthquake of 1906; since 1973 it has once more been making its own wines rather than merely selling the grapes. Wines from Cabernet, Merlot, and Gewürztraminer have great character.

The "Valley of the Moon" lies immediately to the southeast of Russian River Valley, and will always be remembered because Agoston Haraszthy planted the first vines he brought back from Europe at Buena Vista, just outside the town of Sonoma. The Buena Vista and Hacienda companies at Sonoma now share the original Haraszthy vineyards. Buena Vista has excellent white Fumé Blanc and Zinfandel wines, while Hacienda does best with Gewürztraminer and Chardonnay.

The microclimate warms from Region I conditions near the Bay to Region II at Kenwood, east of Sonoma. At Valley of the Moon Vineyards the white blending grape, French Colombard, is planted with Pinot Noir, Semillon and Zinfandel to produce mainly jug wines. From Windsor good Cabernet and Chardonnay wines are marketed under brand names. At Kenwood, Jack London Ranch Cabernet is made close to the author's ranch, which remains as a tourist attraction.

Richard Arrowhead *(left)*, winemaker at Château St Jean, believed that late-harvest Johannisberg Riesling wines in the German style could be made in California — and proved it: the winery is a showplace of white-wine production. The new sparkling-wine installation has brought annual capacity to over 150,000 cases.

As soon as grapes arrive at the winery they are sprayed with $SO_2$ to kill the wild yeasts and acetobacters *(left)*. After crushing, a select yeast culture is added to start fermentation.

An operative at St Jean *(below)* about to release pomace into a pneumatic horizontal press that will gently crush the grapes (but not the pits. The pressure will release the free-run juice before extraction of the pressed wine.

The Parducci Wine Cellars, established at Ukiah in 1933, was the first winery in Mendocino County *(above)*. It is now run by fourth-generation John A. Parducci. Winemakers are J. and T. Monostori.

The oak shield *(inset)* depicts grapes and their journey through press, barrel and bottle. True to Italian origins, Parducci make wines that are mostly big and red. They come from Cabernet, Zinfandel, Carignan, and Pinot Noir.

In the extensive Châ eau St Jean cellars all white wines are transferred from stainless steel to oak to complete their fermentation *(left)*. The oak will give added flavor and, if the barrels are new, tannin and a deeper color.

Ripe Pinot Noir grapes *(right)*, used classically in Burgundy and in Champagne where, exceptionally, they are blended. This grape is sweeter and smoother than Cabernet, and the wines ready to drink earlier.

It is not unusual to see temperature-controlled fermentation tanks in the open air. At Ridge Vineyards, Cupertino, Santa Clara, wine is being pumped over to break up the cap of skins and bring maximum color to a red wine *(top)*. Ridge Vineyards was founded in 1959.

The Paul Masson plant at Soledad was laid down to process grapes grown in plots of about 0.4ha (1 acre) each. Both vines and soils were varied so that Massons knew just how to achieve the best results when the "wine boom" came. Today racks of sample wines under test fill this cellar *(above)*.

**Mendocino and Lake Counties**

These are the most northerly wine districts in California. The Mendocino vineyards lie along the young Russian River and surround the town of Ukiah. The district is mountainous and registers a cool Region I sun-count in Anderson Valley to the west. Potter and Redwood Valley, to the north of Ukiah, have Region III sunshine; the new district of McDowell Valley is near Hopland to the south. The whole of this region fell into decay in the past, but revival has taken place quite rapidly over the last decade. Typical are the McDowell Valley Vineyards, where solar energy and night harvesting combine to produce excellent wines from Chardonnay, Sauvignon Blanc, Cabernet Sauvignon, Grenache, Zinfandel, and other grapes. Potential expansion here is enormous. Cresta Blanca at Ukiah is a cooperative for local growers. Parducci, the first Mendocino winery, makes big red wines from Cabernet, Carignan, Petite Sirah, and Zinfandel grapes, and semisweet white wines from Riesling, French Colombard, and Chenin Blanc; grapes from other growers in Mendocino and Lake Counties are blended with their own. The new Weibel Vineyards north of Ukiah make good sparkling wines usually marketed under merchants' labels. Five wineries in Lake County, adjacent to Mendocino and to its east, are now developing 1,000ha (2,500 acres) of vineyard in a Region III microclimate. The grapes are mainly Cabernet Sauvignon, Gamay, and Zinfandel.

**The Bay Area**

This area around San Francisco Bay includes the Alameda, Santa Clara, and Santa Cruz counties. The vineyards are restricted by urban sprawl, and some wine-makers have had to abandon their local vineyards and develop them in more economical areas, where there is room for expansion, while retaining their town wineries. It is more for the wineries than for the vineyards, therefore, that the Bay Area is important today.

Despite this, the famous Livermore Valley in Alameda, in the hills east of San Francisco, survives as the county's vineyards center. Although close to the bay it has a Region III microclimate. Alameda is primarily a white-wine county, and Chardonnay, Chenin Blanc, Grey Riesling, Semillon, and Sauvignon Blanc vines fill most of the 800ha (2,000 acres) of vineyards. Sheltered from the coast by the Santa Cruz mountains is Santa Clara, at the foot of San Francisco Bay. In the mountain area the climate is Region I but the Hecker Pass/Morgan Hill area in south Santa Clara has a Region III climate and 525ha (1,300 acres) of vines.

Here the giant Paul Masson Vineyards, now owned by Seagram, have their headquarters at Saratoga, and part of their 1,800ha (4,500 acres) of vineyard is in the county. The main Masson wineries are in Monterey and the San Joaquin Valley, but their huge sparkling-wine and bottling plant is a feature of Saratoga. Much

The fabric of the imposing façade of the old La Cresta Masson winery *(left)* came from the church of St Patrick's in San José, destroyed in the 1906 earthquake. The winery building had been started by Paul Masson in 1905, and the purchase of the church fabric was typical of the extravert Masson.

One approach to the problem of hills: bring your "big machines" either to remove them or, as in this instance, to create quarries for the development of wine cellars *(left)*. The Paul Masson organization is constantly expanding its acreage and plant.

White grapes are transported from the vineyards in two-ton gondolas *(left)*; to prevent oxidation en route, the grapes may first be given a light dusting with sulfur dioxide. Paul Masson's white wines, with the exception of Chenin Blanc and the generic "Chablis", are produced entirely from Monterey County grapes.

Approaching the equipment used to remove the MOG *(right)*. The fresh green leaves indicate that this consignment has been reaped with a combine-harvester.

Use of the combine-harvester is restricted to reasonably flat, open territory and to vineyards that have been laid down with space for mechanical harvesting equipment. Elsewhere traditional pickers are still worthy of their hire *(below)*.

In Paul Masson's sterile bottling plant, a vacuum is created in the head-space above the bottled wine before the cork is inserted *(bottom)*. Masson's storage capacity for wine awaiting bottling in stainless-steel tanks runs into tens of millions of gallons.

Stripped of fruit and foliage, the vineyard after harvest and tidying up looks bare, lonely and spacious. In the weakening fall sunlight, vines of some 20 years' growth are being pruned in a Masson vineyard *(above)*.

A large wooden vat *(right)* proclaims 1852, the date when Etienne Thée, a *vigneron* from Bordeaux, purchased 140ha (350 acres) of land 8km (5 miles) east of Los Gatos, near San José, and planted vineyards there. Charles LeFranc became Thée's partner, and LeFranc's son Paul Masson built the business.

Neither a bar nor a canteen queue, but a tasting — or rather a testing — of wine at Paul Masson's Soledad winery *(inset)*. The test plantings for the huge Masson organization are still largely confined to Soledad.

W
PAUL MASSON
21
1280
EST. 1852

Johannisberg Riesling which reaches Massons here as grapes or must is converted into champagne-type wines.

Another giant of Santa Clara is the Almadén Vineyard at San Jose, founded (as Massons were) in 1852. This property belongs to the National Distiller and Chemical Corporation, ranked among the four largest wine companies in the USA. From a total of 2,800ha (7,000 acres) of vineyard spread between Santa Clara, Monterey, and San Benito, the Corporation produces and markets over 50 varietal and branded wines; those in the medium-price range are marketed under the Almadén label and the more expensive under Charles LeFranc. Pinot Noir Eye of the Partridge is a pale pink sparkling wine with refreshing fruitiness for unserious occasions; a Blanc de Blancs based on the French Coteaux Champenois is more important. The climate of Santa Clara has encouraged considerable plantings of Cabernet Sauvignon, Carignan, Chardonnay, French Colombard, and Zinfandel among about 35 wine properties in the county.

Santa Cruz County lies south of Santa Clara along the Pacific Coast, and the "Santa Cruz Mountain" appellation is shared by a dozen small wineries. Chardonnay and Cabernet Sauvignon grapes grow well on the steep mountain slopes in a Region I climate.

**North Central Coast**

This region takes in Monterey County, south of Santa Cruz, and, next to it inland, San Benito County, south of Santa Clara.

Monterey County lies between the ocean and the Coastal Range; south of Monterey Bay the Sierra Santa Lucia rises close to the coast to form the west side of the Salinas Valley, along which the Salinas River flows north to the bay. In this valley is centered practically all of the Monterey wine industry. The growth of the industry has been dramatic—from only 40ha (100 acres) of vineyard in Monterey County 20 years ago, there are now over 14,000ha (35,000 acres) shared by a handful of important properties.

At Gonzalez, where wine-making begins in the Salinas Valley, the Monterey Vineyards (founded in 1973) produce white wines from Gewürztraminer, Riesling, Sauvignon Blanc, and Sylvaner vines. Late-harvested Riesling produces "Thanksgiving," a good wine at five years, and "December" Zinfandel, a dry, full red. Here also Taylor California Cellars, a successful western development of Taylor's New York State Wines, market some 5.5 million cases of blends from Cabernet Sauvignon, Chardonnay, Chenin Blanc, Riesling and Sauvignon Blanc. The blends are made for Taylor at a number of wineries.

Higher up the valley are Ventana Vineyards and the Chalone Vineyard. Ventana Vineyards have the larger production—30,000 cases of wine annually—and also supply grapes to other wineries for conversion. Among their own full ranges of wines is a Sauvignon Blanc "botrytis" of some renown. The Chalone vines, planted in 1920, made little headway on a water-starved outcrop of limestone, but lately Pinot Noir and Chardonnay grapes have been used to emulate the tradition of red Côte d'Or Burgundies and white wines of the northern Rhône. This progressive winery should be kept in mind.

At Greenfield, Jekels added a winery in 1978 to the vineyard laid down in 1972. Already over 30,000 cases of wines go out each year: a white Riesling is exceptional and the Cabernet Sauvignon is faultless but somewhat expensive.

The Salinas Valley continues down to King City, where Almadén have vineyards.

Just one vineyard, complete with winery, owned by the Durneys, constitutes the Carmel Valley district of Monterey, facing the ocean; their Chenin Blanc and Cabernet are well made. Another district with one winery is the Pinnacles area to the east of the Salinas Valley. In the north of Monterey County is River Run, a small but promising vineyard at Watsonville, now in its seventh year and doing well with Cabernet Sauvignon, Chardonnay, Pinot Noir, and Johannisberg Riesling grapes. The Monterey Peninsula Winery at Monterey concentrates on single-vineyard wines made from grapes (mainly Zinfandel and Cabernet Sauvignon) drawn in from Monterey and adjacent counties.

The vineyards of San Benito County are dominated by Almadén—they own all but 80ha of the 2,250ha (200 out of 5,600 acres) of vines in the county. The climate is Region III and the grapes are principally Cabernet Sauvignon, Chardonnay, Gewürztraminer, Pinot Noir, White Riesling, and Zinfandel. Two sub-districts, Paicines and La Cienega, house the remaining vineyards.

A scene in the early stages of the growing season in the Chalone Vineyards *(above)*, 10 miles east of Soledad and 600m (2,000ft) above the Salinas Valley. Richard Graff, a Harvard music graduate, took over the half-built winery in 1965, and brought in his younger brothers John and Peter.

Pumping over Pinot Noir wine during fermentation at Chalone Vineyards *(right)*. In the early 1970s the Graff family increased production substantially, although it remains at a level suitable for wines of the high class made here. A feature of their winemaking technique is that they do not use $SO_2$ at this stage.

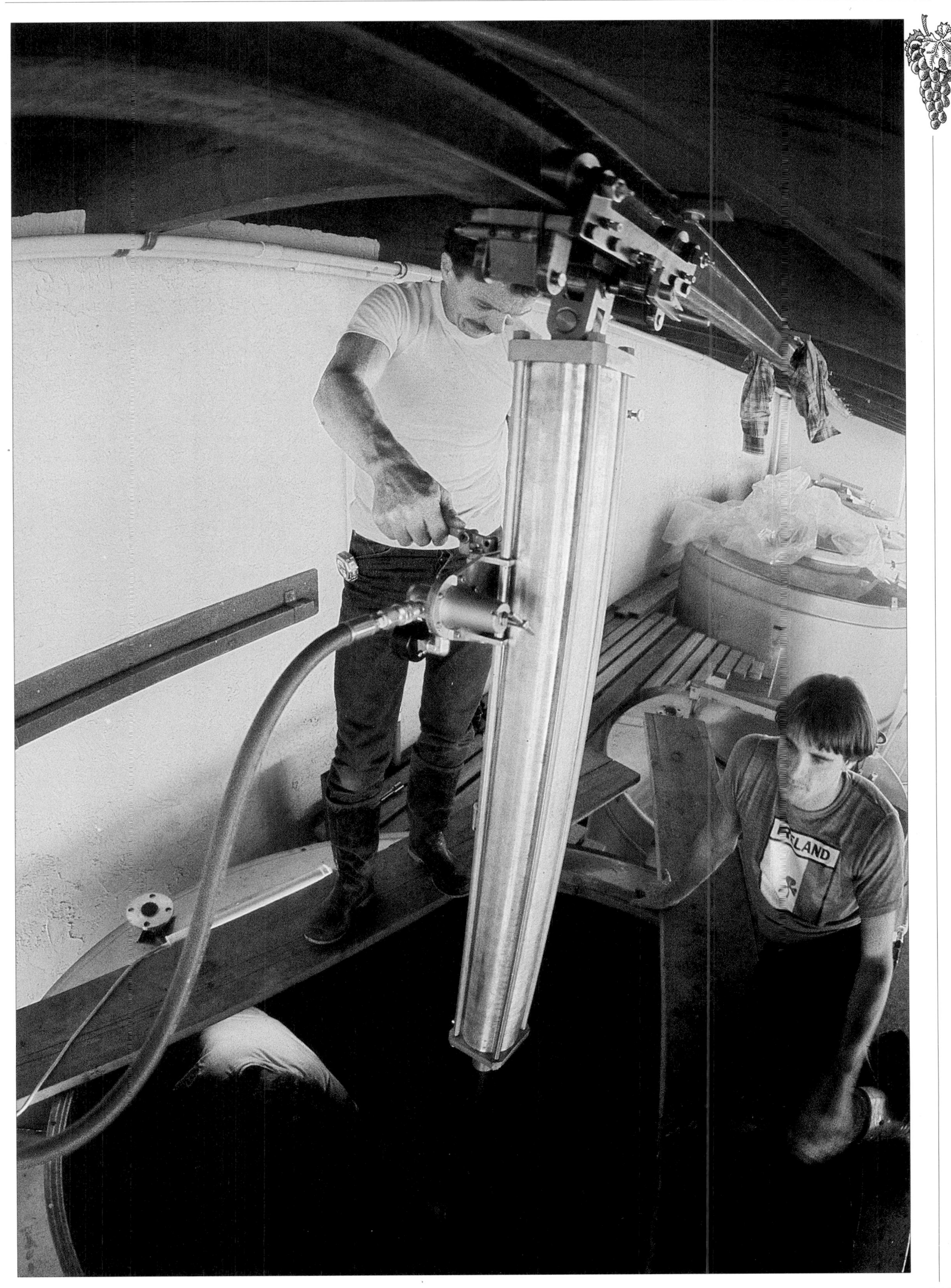

Gavilan Vineyards Inc., who own Chalone Vineyards in the Gavilan mountains, have interests in two other wineries, Edna Valley Vineyards and the new Carmenet Vineyard in the Sonoma valley. Here Pinot Noir grapes are being picked and packed into wooden trays of the type more often seen in apple orchards *(top).*

The vine flower is small and relatively unattractive to the bee, which often needs to be lured to the area by the growing of flowers such as roses nearby *(above).*

Chardonnay, Pinot Blanc and Chenin Blanc are the vines for white wines at Chalone Vineyards, with Cabernet Sauvignon and Pinot Noir *(right)* for reds.

Much of the mechanical harvesting work at Chalone *(left)* is done on contract; the contract system enables smaller vineyards, who could not absorb the heavy amortization involved in purchase, to take advantage of the speed and efficiency of the "big machine".

Boxes of Pinot Noir grapes at Chalone are being unloaded directly into the fermenter *(above)*, a practice that is unusual if not unique: picked black grapes would usually be crushed and destalked before fermentation. The apparent illogicality fits in, however, with the equally rare Chalone practice of using no sulphur dioxide.

**South Central Coast**
Next down the Pacific Coast is San Luis Obispo County, where the wine industry has shown rapid growth. Today about 1,900ha (4,750 acres) of vineyard are under cultivation by a dozen companies.

In the north of the county, the Paso Robles district has a Region III climate; it stretches south to Templeton and east to Shandon. The biggest property is the Estrella River Winery, founded in 1973, which already has 280ha (700 acres) of vineyard and produces 70,000 cases of wine annually. The French varieties used in California are all planted, together with Zinfandel, Muscat, and White Riesling, and the Estrella wines are quickly gaining a good reputation.

Hoffman's Mountain Ranch is high up the slopes, at 300m (1,000ft), and here limestone soil helps to produce Chardonnay and Pinot Noir at their best. There are 50ha (120 acres) of vineyard, supplying grapes for most of the 30,000 cases marketed each year.

The enologist Max Goldman now owns the York Mountain Winery at Templeton, and good wines from Zinfandel, Riesling, and the French varieties are currently enjoying widespread recognition.

South of the town of San Luis Obispo is the Edna Valley district, where Chardonnay and Pinot Noir yield well in a slightly cooler climate nearer the ocean. The Lawrence Winery, with vineyards in the Edna Valley (and more in Santa Barbara County), was founded as recently as 1979 and is producing 300,000 cases of wine annually; Chardonnay and Riesling are heavily planted in the Edna Valley. A smaller property is Edna Valley vineyard, which produces 20,000 cases of wine from the Chardonnay and Pinot Noir.

Santa Barbara County borders the Pacific to the south of San Luis Obispo, and its wine industry dates only from the mid-1960s. Already it has 2,400ha (6,000 acres) of vineyard and 11 wineries. There are two vineyard areas, about 80km (50mi) apart: a small area in the valley of the Santa Maria river in the north of the county and the other in the valley of the Santa Yuez river, further south. Each district has a Region II climate near the coast rising to Region III inland. The vines mostly grown in Santa Barbara are Cabernet Sauvignon, Chardonnay, Pinot Noir, and White Riesling.

In the Santa Maria Valley, which runs from Sisquoc to Santa Maria, the Rancho Sisquoc Winery, built in 1978, has 78.5ha (194 acres) of vineyards that were laid down in 1972. Here some Sylvaner and White Riesling vines have been added to the main French varieties that flourish in the climate.

The valley of the Santa Yuez river forms the southern boundary of the Santa Yuez subdistrict, and several good wineries are to be found slightly to the north, at Los Olivos and around Lompac. The Santa Yuez Valley Winery, from 57ha (140 acres) of vineyard, produces 10,000 cases of wine each year, mainly of their celebrated Sauvignon Blanc. Vega, at Buellton, is a vineyard of the early 1970s to which a winery has recently been added; also at Buellton are Brander's, making another good Sauvignon Blanc, and Ross-Keller, marketing under the brand names San Carlos de Jonata and Zaca Creek. Ballard Canyon, at Solvang, produces red and white Cabernet Sauvignon, and some late-harvest wine from White Riesling. The Firestone Vineyard at Los Olivos, a joint enterprise of the tire company and the Japanese Suntory distillers, have 120ha (300 acres) under vines, and produce excellent wines, including the sweet Ambassador's Vineyard Riesling.

**South Coast**
Although the Californian wine industry started in the South Coast region, urban sprawl has for practical purposes killed all the vineyards of Orange and San Diego counties, and in Los Angeles County production is from only two wineries, both of which convert grapes from outside the county boundaries. This leaves two important subdistricts, in the counties of San Bernardino and Riverside, where limited production continues.

The first is Cucamonga, at the southwest corner of San Bernardino County (and lipping the border of neighboring Riverside County). Here the sun is hotter than in any other wine region of America—a solid Region V—and it is amazing that the arid country, backing into the Mojave Desert to its east, can grow grapes for wine at all. It is therefore no surprise to find that mainly dessert wines are produced, to satisfy what is now a diminishing taste for this type of wine.

Brookside is the largest company, with an annual production of about 850,000 cases of wines marketed under brand names including Brookside, Guasti, and (for Zinfandel and Petite Sirah) Assumption Abbey. Brookside is important historically, for it was founded in Monterey in 1832 and moved to Guasti in 1916. Today its wines are distributed throughout the USA and in Canada, Central America, and Japan. The J. Filippi Vintage Company at Mira Loma specializes in dessert and table wines, and is now capable of an output of approximately 200,000 cases.

The wine industry of Riverside County centers on Temecula, in an area known as Rancho California. A few good wineries share between them some 1,000ha (2,500 acres) of vineyard, growing mainly Cabernet Sauvignon, Chardonnay, Grenache, Petite Sirah, and White Riesling. The climate is between Regions III and IV. Callaway is a pioneer and major producer of varietal wines in southern California; these include "Sweet Nancy," made from late-harvested overripe Chenin Blanc grapes (US, "botrytized"). Cilurzo & Piconi and Filsinger are among the other makers of good wines in Temecula.

At the Callaway Vineyards at Temecula, southern California, there are two unusual vineyard practices: weeds between the rows of vines are encouraged, and the soil is not cultivated *(left)*. To judge by the resulting varietal wines, the combination of the two "heresies" works! The wines include a "botrytized" Chenin Blanc and a dark fruity Zinfandel.

Harvesting by hand at Callaway Vineyards *(below)* is another elected discipline of the process, whereby the grapes come in entirely free of MOG. Ely Callaway started planting vines in 1969 but only in 1973, after experimental wines had been made from his grapes at the University of California and elsewhere, did he decide to build his own winery.

Steve O'Donnell (right), the winemaker at Callaways, discussing carbonic maceration with John Moramarco, the estate manager *(center)*. Moramarco controls the vineyards personally, doing all the pruning and even cluster-thinning the individual bunches.

O'Donnell and Moramarco checking the Brix in the must at the crusher-press *(above)*. Brix (also called "balling") is the amount of sugar in the juice: in terms of the "potential alcohol" scale used in Europe, 10% vol. alcohol equals 19.3 Brix.

Seen from Callaways' Temecula Winery, the coastal mist coming through the Rainbow Gap, halfway between Long Beach and San Diego *(right)*. Without this mist, generated as the Humboldt current flows down the western seaboard of North and South America, there might be little or no wine in California, for it moderates the heat of the sun and provides much needed moisture for the growing vines.

A bottle of Callaways' Fume Blanc from the Sauvignon Blanc *(above)*. "Vinified and bottled" at their own winery, this wine therefore has appellation status under Federal law.

## THE GREAT CENTRAL VALLEY

This valley, through much of which flows the San Joaquin, is the largest area east of the Rocky Mountains that is consistently less than 180m (600ft) above sea-level. Surrounded by mountains, the valley experiences intense heat, which may account in some measure for the fact that the San Joaquin Valley produces most of the USA's everyday drinking wine, dessert wine, and brandy.

**The Sierra Foothills**

To the east of Sacramento is the territory where the "forty-niners" arrived during the Gold Rush, one and one-quarter centuries ago. The region rises into the foothills of the massive Sierra Nevada, and here it was that the boom wine industry of those far-off days was to slump when the lodes ran out; it took almost a century to recover. The wine region runs from Placerville in the north to Sonara in the south, but the principal vineyard areas are in the counties of Amador, El Dorado north of it, and Calaveros south of it.

In terms of both vineyard area and its product, Amador County is the most important subdistrict. The wineries are mainly located in the Shenandoah Valley, east of Plymouth, and the grape varieties now planted include Zinfandel (for red and white wines), Cabernet Sauvignon, Sauvignon Blanc, Chardonnay, and Barbera. Zinfandel was the original grape and is still the most heavily planted. Santino Wines at Plymouth specialize in a sweet near-white Zinfandel of excellent quality, and the neighboring Montevina Wines, with 73ha (180 acres), produce strong Zinfandels, both red and white. D'Agostini in the Shenandoah Valley have 50ha (125 acres), mostly growing Zinfandel, from which they produce "traditional rustic wines" for local drinking. The Amador Foothill Winery has its winery sunk into the ground to combat the heat.

Eldorado County is not yet a large wine region, but three wineries, each faithful to the Zinfandel vine, are worthy of mention. Boeger, at Placerville, produces around 9,000 cases annually of wines including the brands Sierra Blanc and Hangtown Red (the latter is indeed capital although, it is to be hoped, not terminal). Madrona, at Camino, east of Placerville, annually produces 8,500 cases, with some German-style wines from White Riesling and Gewürztraminer included; and Sierra Vista, at Placerville, has a smaller output from the Californian French varietals.

The vineyards of Calaveros are now being replanted after a long period of procrastination. The few vineyards surround the town of Murphys, where the Stevenot Winery bottles 11,000 cases annually of fine wine from an estate vineyard, specializing in Zinfandel and Chenin Blanc wines. There are so far no wineries in Placer County, although a good deal of Zinfandel is grown in its vineyards. Both Calaveros and Placer counties have the opportunity and space to enlarge their wine industries, and radical developments may be expected in the next few years.

**The Central Valley**

The San Joaquin river, from Fresno up to its confluence with the Sacramento river northeast of San Francisco, gathers strength from a number of tributaries running down from the Sierra Nevada to the east and from the Coastal Range to the west. South of Fresno the Central Valley contains other rivers from the mountains; these are absorbed into lakes and reservoirs, or simply fade out in the heat of the sun after watering the southern end of the valley, down to Bakersfield. The wine industry in the valley is organized somewhat differently from that in the coastal areas, as some 50 companies making wines draw their grapes from any, or even all, of the nine counties in the valley: they are San Joaquin in the north, through Stanislaus, Merced, Mariposa, Madera, Fresno, Kings, and Tulare, to Kern in the south. Only in the area around Lodi, in San Joaquin, are grapes grown and processed into wine by individual companies, and for this reason Lodi alone has its own identity as a subdistrict. The vines mostly planted in the nine counties are Barbera, Carignan, Chenin Blanc, French Colombard, Grenache, Ruby Cabernet, and Zinfandel. The climate of the valley is hot, changing slowly from Region IV in the north to Region V in the south.

The Lodi area is cooled by air from the ocean sweeping up the broad mouth of the Sacramento river, and it therefore has a mild Region II to III climate. Among the wineries of the subdistrict are the Barengo Winery at Acampo, founded in 1934, marketing 800,000 cases annually from 260ha (640 acres) of vineyard spread between Lodi, Modesto, and Fresno; the Cadlolo Winery at Cadlolo, founded in 1913, distributing 100,000 cases (mostly in bulk) of dessert and generic wines; and the cooperative East Side Winery, founded in 1934, marketing about one million cases under the Conti Royale, Royal Host, and Gold Bell labels (Conti Royale also appears on the labels of some dessert wines and brandies). The new Turner Winery, with 235ha (580 acres) in Lake County, is producing fine wines from Zinfandel, Cabernet Sauvignon, Gamay Beaujolais, Chardonnay, Chenin Blanc, Sauvignon Blanc, and White Riesling.

Away from the Lodi subdistrict, Franzia Brothers, owned by the Coca-Cola Bottling Company of New York, have 1,600ha (4,000 acres) of vines at Ripon and market 9.6 million cases of wine annually—about half in bulk. Franzia French Colombard, slightly sparkling, is a well known label. Delicado Vineyards, with a production approaching 6 million cases of many varietal and generic wines, satisfy their customers with the description "Northern California."

In Stanislaus County is the world's most

prolific wine-making company, the E. and J. Gallo Winery. The two sons of an Italian immigrant grape farmer, Ernest and Julio, started making and selling wine in 1933, in the town of Modesto. Here the vast plant of the Gallo business has grown from a diminutive winery built on the same site in 1935. Today, Gallo are said to grow or buy one grape in every three grown in California, and the present-day statistics of their concern are awe-inspiring. Every working day of the year they produce, bottle and pack on average 250,000 cases of wine. Two wineries supply a tank farm having a storage capacity of 10 million hectoliters (an amazing 265 million gal), and there is a 10ha (25-acre) warehouse. It is hardly surprising that the bottling plant starts with its own glass factory. There are few wines—if any—that do not come into the Gallo production range. From 1964 their reputation was built on Chablis Blanc and Hearty Burgundy, but sparkling and sherry-type wines came into the list together with E. & J. Brandy, and within the last decade or so a number of French varietals have been introduced. Now there are Barbera, Cabernet, Chardonnay, Colombard, Gewürztraminer, Riesling, Sauvignon Blanc, and Zinfandel wines in a variety of blends to suit all tastes. Building a 0.8ha (two-acre) warehouse to age Chardonnay and Cabernet wines in oak was a simple matter of logic to the brothers, who are dedicated to the continual improvement of their produce. Brand names include Gallo, Paisana, Thunderbird, Carlo Rossi, Ripple, Madria-Madria, Tyrolia, Spanada, and Night Train Express. The contribution made by the Gallo brothers in research and technology has benefited not only California but the entire US wine industry.

In the whole of the Central Valley there are some 90,000ha (225,000 acres) of wine grapes, and another 100,000ha (250,000 acres) of Thompson seedless, of which about one-third goes to wine production and two-thirds to the market for fruit for the table. The counties of Merced, Mariposa, and Kings contribute substantially to this vineyard area, but have no important winery centers of their own. In Madera County the Papagni Vineyards, founded in 1920 as growers only, have a variety of vines planted at Clovis and Bonita ranches; more recently, in the first decade of their wine-making experience they have produced first-class wines, including a light Alicante Bouschet red wine and a refreshing Chardonnay aged for six months in French oak. About 150,000 cases are marketed each year. Also at Madera are the Ficklin family, growing Portuguese grapes to produce one of California's best port-type wines which, although non-vintage, has some vintage characteristics and ages indefinitely. A third winery at Madera is Quady, making small amounts of port-style and Essensia dessert wine.

At Sanger in County Fresno is a large growers' cooperative, turning out over 225,000hl (nearly 6 million gal) of bulk table and dessert wines. In the town of Fresno, A. Nonini, founded in 1936, has 80ha (200 acres) under vines and produces about 40,000 cases of table wines each year.

Moët Hennessy, the great French Champagne-Brandy-Dior perfume combine, was the first French firm to make an important investment in Californian wines in 1973, building Domaine Chandon in the Napa Valley. Out of deference to their French connections, their wines, seen here in bottles, are called "sparkling" and not champagne, but there the difference begins and ends.

California Growers is a large winery at Tulare converting grapes grown in the Sierra foothills around the Fresno/Tulare borders. Annual production runs at over 600,000 cases, marketed under several brand names including Growers, Bounty, and Setrakien (Robert Setrakien is the proprietor). The principal vines are French Colombard, Ruby Cabernet, Cabernet Sauvignon, Riesling, and White Riesling, and the quality of the wines and their prices are "middle of the road." At Exeter in Tulare, Anderson Wine Cellars, a small winery started in 1980, produces good wines from Ruby Cabernet and Chenin Blanc.

Kern County, at the south end of the valley, has three huge wineries. The oldest (founded 1894) is Perelli-Minetti, which now produces over six million cases, mainly of varietal and jug wines, each year. The company name is used

Moet-Hennessy's mighty fermentation tanks at Yountville *(above).* Count Frédéric Chandon de Briailles visited the Napa Valley two years before Chandon was built: in jocular commemoration, a still white Chardonnay was called "Fred's Friends". A Pinot Noir Blanc of the same name followed: both remain popular.

Cabernet Sauvignon grapes in the Mirassou vineyards *(left).* The dynasty started in 1853 when Pierre Pellier arrived in San José with French vines. After Pierre came his son-in-law Pierre Mirassou, succeeded in turn by his son Peter and by Peter's sons Edmund and Norbert. Now fifth- and sixth-generation Mirassous are taking control.

The single word "Vynyard" appears on the Ridge Vineyard license plate *(above),* which appears wherever Ridge buy in their grapes — Cabernet Sauvignon and Petite Sirah from the Napa Valley and York Creek, and Zinfandel from Sonoma and Fiddletown, Amador. Ridge produce over 30,000 cases of wine annually.

Inside one of the large stainless-steel fermentation tanks at Joseph Phelps Vineyards, a bubbling must of Sauvignon Blanc *(right).* After fermentation white wines are filtered and racked to a series of large German "ovals" for maturation.

to brand good wines from coastal regions: other brands include Ambassador, Eleven Cellars, and Greystone. LaMont Winery, at Di Giorgio, markets even more wine each year—around 8½ million cases. A number of table, sparkling and dessert wines are labeled M. LaMont or Mountain Gold. The Giumarra Vineyards Corporation at Bakersfield has 1,600ha (4,000 acres) of vineyards; in the last decade or so good varietals have been added to bulk wine production, and the brand names Giumarra, Breckinridge, and Ridgecrest are now meaningful.

## THE NORTHWEST

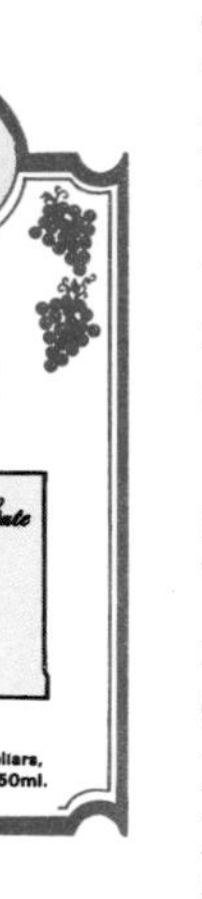


The states of Washington, Oregon and Idaho have a long-standing wine industry that is small but important. Like California to their south, these states are fertile areas separated from the rest of the continent by the Rocky Mountains and the high arid plains that stretch for over 1,500km (1,000mi) to the east. The Cascade mountain range runs north and south through Washington and Oregon, affecting the climate much as the Coastal Range does along the Californian coast. A break in the Cascades at Point Disappointment provides access to the Pacific for the important Columbia river and its many tributaries. West of the Cascades the ocean modifies the climate to produce Region I conditions, and here the vineyards of Oregon are centered, while most of the Washington vineyards and the inland Idaho vineyards lie between the Cascades and the Rocky Mountains in a sunnier and drier Region II climate.

The early settlers brought hardy indigenous vines over the Oregon Trail in the 1870s, so that Concord, Delaware, Diamond, and Campbell Early were the first planted. The earliest vineyard in Washington was laid down by Lambert B. Evans in 1872, and plantings continued intermittently until the Cascade watershed opened up the Yakima Valley between the Cascades and the Columbia river in 1906. Idaho already had a small wine industry before the turn of the century, as evidenced by prizes taken by Idaho wines at the Chicago World Fair of 1898.

Whatever production was achieved in the northwest during the early years of the twentieth century, it was unequal to local demand; nevertheless, although wines came in from other areas, the original vines continued to be used until Prohibition had come and gone. *Vitis vinifera* vines were slow to reach the area, and by 1963 there was only one winery using European vines in the northwest. Today there are over 50 wineries, and although the *V. vinifera* grapes favored most are Cabernet Sauvignon, Chardonnay, Pinot Noir, and Riesling, chosen for their performance in cool climates, the indigenous vines are still far more heavily planted.

A great advance has been made since the mid-1960s, both in viticultural and vinification methods, and in the eruption of a great and growing industry. In Washington, the vineyards are concentrated in the south-center of the state, where the climate is best and essential irrigation is available. In the Grandview-Sunnyside area of the lower Yakima Valley the sandy loam is free from phylloxera, enabling ungrafted vines to be planted on south-facing slopes. There are now about 11,300ha (28,000 acres) under vines, of which only some 2,000ha (5,000 acres) are planted with *V. vinifera* grapes. The considerable fruit industry culls the state's pickers at harvesting time, so that mechanical harvesting is a necessity.

Château St Michelle, northeast of Seattle, is by far the largest winery in the three states, owned by the United States Tobacco Company. Its vineyards of over 1,000ha (2,500 acres) are mainly in the Columbia basin at Cold Creek and Grandview; about half the area is shared between seven French varietals and the White Riesling. In 1985 production was only a little less than one-half million cases, and wineries were opened at Grandview and Paterson to share the load with St Michelle.

Associated Vintners, an organization which has no vineyards, makes some 30,000 cases of wine annually from Yakima Valley grapes, mainly Cabernet Sauvignon, Chardonnay, Pinot Noir, Semillon, Gewürztraminer, and White Riesling. The skills of David Lake, MW, the wine-maker, are apparent in a variety of beautiful wines. Washington's second largest winery is Preston Wine Cellars at Pasco in the Yakima Valley, with about 80ha (200 acres) of vineyards producing some 60,000 cases of fine wines each year.

In Oregon there are three main areas of vineyard cultivation. Close to the border with California in the west is the Rogue River Valley; above the Rogue River is the Umpqua Valley; and in the northwest of the state, 50km (30mi) west of Portland, are the Willamette and Tualatin valleys. Altogether 485ha (1,200 acres) of vines are planted in the three areas, so the potential for development is vast. In Yamhill County, west of Portland, a Burgundy-style Pinot Noir is being made in the cool Region I climate.

The Hillcrest Vineyard at Roseburg in the Umpqua Valley was the pioneer winery of the state, founded in 1961. Taking advantage of a slightly warmer climate than Willamette has 80km (50mi) to the north, late-harvested Riesling grapes here give sweet wines aided by some noble rot. Hillcrest were prime movers in forming a wine-growers' association in the early 1970s. The majority of Oregon's wineries have been laid down in the Willamette Valley: the state's largest is the Knudsen Erath Winery in Yamhill County, with 40ha (100 acres) under vines, which already has a reputation for Pinot Noir and White Riesling products. Chardonnay vines complete the vineyard plantings here, and this triumvirate of vines is common to most

other wineries in the Willamette Valley, including the Tualatin Vineyards at Forest Grove, Amity Vineyards at Amity, Sokol Blosser at Dundee, and Elk Grove at Gaston. In addition to estate-bottled wines from grapes grown in their 34ha (85-acre) vineyard, Tualatin import grapes from Washington for white wines. Amity Vineyards are best for Pinot Noir, using grapes from Washington as well as their own grown on 28ha (70 acres) of mixed plantings that include also some Gewürztraminer.

Oregon has laws for *V. vinifera* vines that do not apply to native vines. Generic names (for example, "Bordeaux" and "Burgundy") are banned, and wines labeled as viniferas require 90% minimum of the content to come from the named vine (except for Cabernet Sauvignon, which must have 75% minimum), with the balance coming from other red Bordeaux grapes. The labels must also show appellations of origin and the grapes must have been grown in the designated region. The three delimited regions are Willamette Valley, Umpqua Valley and Rogue Valley.

Idaho has as yet only some 120ha (300 acres) of vines, mostly in the southwest corner of the state, near to the Oregon border and north of the Snake river. Here the original Concord grapes have given way to European vines; Chardonnay and White Riesling have been successful since first planted in 1976 at St Chapelle (Caldwell), then the state's only commercial vineyard. By 1985 two more wineries had been laid down, the Facelli Vineyards at Wilder, where Chardonnay and White Riesling have been planted, and the Troy Winery, making quality wines from Pinot Noir, Aurora, and Riesling vines.

## THE EASTERN STATES

The first known suggestion that wines should be made from European grapes in the New World was contained in a letter from Lord Delaware, Governor of Virginia, to the London Company in 1616. Many attempts, all unsuc-

Hard winters hit the vines in Washington's Yakima Valley, although the annual heat units in the lower end of the valley are the same as for Beaune. After pruning (*left*), many of the vines are therefore buried in the earth from December until March.

cessful, were made not only by Delaware but also by Lord Baltimore in Maryland, William Penn in Pennsylvania, Thomas Jefferson at Monticello, and many others. It was finally assumed that east of the Rockies the *V. vinifera* vines would not grow, and the native grapes ruled the day.

James Alexander (William Penn's gardener) of Pennsylvania was the first to domesticate the indigenous Labrusca grape and Alexander, the grape named for him, was planted liberally in the eastern states. However, 50 years were to pass before the first winery was established. The Pennsylvania Wine Company was formed in 1793 with a vineyard and winery at Spring Mill on the Susquehanna river. Nicholas Longworth made the first US "Champagne" at Cincinnati in 1842 and, by 1860, one-third of all US wine was made in Ohio; at that time California was producing only one-sixth. Cincinnati was "the Queen of the West" and the Ohio river "the Rhine of America." In New York State, indigenous grapes were cultivated by Deacon Elijah Fay at Chautauqua in 1818, and in 1827 Dr Richard Underhill established a vineyard in the Hudson Valley to which the Croton Point Winery was later added. At about the same time the Rev. William Bostwick started cultivating grapes around the Finger Lakes.

In all these enterprises, mainly *Euvitis labrusca* hybrids were used for experiment and development. The name *Vitis labruscana* was given to such hybrids. Examples of white labruscanas are the Diamond (bred in 1870), the Elvira (1863), and the Duchess and Niagara (1868); red labruscanas of note are the Catawba (1823) and the Delaware (popularized by Abram Thompson of Delaware in 1850); black labruscanas include the Concord (1854) and the Steuben, Isabella, and Lenoir vines. Viticulturists were in a large degree responsible for the term "labruscana," claiming that these vines were originally labruscas crossed with *V. vinifera* or other species and that their mixed parentage should be identified. Their wines are high in acid and low in sugar.

In the 1860s black rot and *Oidium tuckerii* overtook many eastern vineyards and destroyed them, just as *Phylloxera vastatrix* was devastating the vineyards of Europe. The *Phylloxera* louse had been exported accidentally from the eastern states, carried on the US species *E. riparia*. By the end of the century most of the vineyards of Europe had been destroyed and uprooted. European *vignerons* were tempted to plant the US *E. riparia*, *E. rupestris*, and *E. berlandieri*, as they were resistant to the louse, but found the resulting wines to have an unacceptable pungent flavor; they became known as "fox wine." With their hybrids, these vines were, and still are, banned in many regions.

French biologists next produced hybrids by marrying French noble varieties to the phylloxera-resistant US species, but eventually found a better solution, for a cutting or scion of a *V. vinifera* species grafted onto a resistant

Wineries like the 20,000 hl (600,000gal) Franz Wilhelm Langguth Winery, built in 1982 on the Wahluke Slope north of the Columbia and east of Mattawa, brought with them to the northwestern states German-style vats fermenting Rieslings and other white viniferas *(below)*.

Keuka, in the Finger Lakes district of New York State *(left)*, is known as the "crooked lake" for its irregular yet distinct Y-shape; it has vineyards on its east and west banks from Branchport and Penn Yan in the north down to Hammondsport.

The Taylor Wine Company, the largest winery in the Finger Lakes district, also owns the Pleasant Valley Winery *(inset)*. Pleasant Valley's brand-name "Great Western" reflects Colonel Marshall Wilder's comment that the wine was "the greatest in the West."

US rootstock was found to be resistant to phylloxera. The French hybrids (called "direct producers") were later found to be highly suitable for planting in the eastern USA, where their hardiness and productivity have helped to offset these weaknesses in the native vines.

In the first two decades of the twentieth century, the eastern US wine industry progressed steadily, and wines from Ohio claimed medals at expositions in Paris and Rome. But in 1918 Prohibition, enforced under the Volstead Act, brought the industry to a 14-year standstill. Only after the industry had recovered from Prohibition did Philip Wagner start planting the French hybrid vines in his Boordy vineyards in Maryland; from this beginning the hybrids were rapidly planted throughout the eastern and midwestern vineyards. It remained for a German immigrant, Dr Konstantin Frank, to graft true *V. vinifera* vines onto hardy Canadian rootstocks successfully in 1957; at last here were vines able to withstand the winters of the eastern states. But, even today, vineyards in the east are mainly planted with *V. labruscana* and French hybrid vines.

New French hybrids will continue to appear on the market in the perpetual search for better or characteristically different vines. The New York State Agricultural Experiment Station at Geneva, NY, developed the Cayuga white vine, one of the first of these hybrids to appear on the scene after World War II.

Another group of native North American grapes are the muscadines, from which the first US wines were made. They grow in the southeastern states and west to the borders of Texas. They belong to the species *Vitis rotundifolia*, and the Scuppernong is the oldest and best known of them. This bronze-colored grape grows profusely in the Carolinas, Florida, Georgia, Tennessee, and Virginia. Newer varieties such as Creek are becoming less important.

Thus the industry in the eastern states is still looking critically at three options: the mainly native *V. labruscana,* the French hybrids, and the true *V. vinifera*, now proved hardy when grafted onto Canadian rootstocks. The climatic differences between states in the north and south, and between those on the Atlantic seaboard and those far inland, will ensure continued research and experiment to bring out the best. But no one grape, be it for red, white, rosé, still, sparkling, or fortified wine, can ever suit all the wine industry of the eastern states.

## NEW YORK STATE

Several identifiable regions lie within the state boundaries. The most important of them is the Finger Lakes region, but other regions, such as Hudson Valley and Long Island, are making notable progress.

The western corner of New York State which borders Lake Erie has been included here in the discussion of the Lake Erie region (see page 265), for viticultural reasons.

**The Finger Lakes**

The aptly named Finger Lakes lie a little south of Lake Ontario, between Rochester, 50km (30mi) to the northwest, and Syracuse, to the east. The lakes hang like the fingers of a glove, Lake Seneca and Lake Cayuga in the middle, each about 70km (45mi) in length and no more than some 15km (10mi) in width. They lie in beautiful rolling country. Center of the wine region is Lake Keuka, having Hammondsport at the north and Penn Yan at the south.

The Finger Lakes region of New York State is the oldest wine-producing region in the eastern states: the Pleasant Valley Wine Company, producing both sparkling and still wines, won a Gold Medal at the Paris Exposition of 1867 for US "Champagne;" and the Urbana Wine Company (now the Gold Seal Vineyards), also producing sparkling and still wines, received awards in Vienna in 1873 and Paris in 1878.

The soil, drainage and microclimate of the Finger Lakes are remarkably similar to that of Champagne in France, which may account in some measure for the distinguished sparkling wines made there so long ago. The older wineries have recently been updating their equipment and employing highly qualified winemakers; and in the area of Lake Seneca, which has a slightly milder microclimate than Lake Keuka, *V. vinifera* vines have recently been planted. As a result, the Finger Lakes are building a reputation also for noble table wines.

The Pleasant Valley Wine Company, founded in 1860 and now trading as Great Western, is one of two wineries owned by Wine Spectrum, a subsidiary of the Coca-Cola Company. Great Western "Champagne," although fermented in the bottle, is disgorged and clarified by the transfer process. Wine Spectrum also own the Taylor Wine Company, Inc., at Hammondsport, whose 465ha (1,150 acres) of vineyard are filled with labruscanas and French hybrids—indeed, it was they who introduced these hybrids to New York State. Their wines are marketed under Taylor and Lake County labels.

Widmer Wine Cellars, with 96ha (237 acres) of vines at Naples, were founded in 1888 and are now owned by Reckitt & Colman. Labruscanas, mainly Niagara, Foch, and Delaware, are converted to produce over 400,000 cases of wine each year, including good wood-aged sherries. Vinifera Wine Cellars at Hammondsport are largely experimental, marketing only 6,000 cases of vinifera wines from vineyards of 40ha (100 acres). The owner is Dr Konstantin D. Frank, who proved *V. vinifera* will grow in the east before establishing this business in 1962.

Recent additions to the growing list of Finger Lakes wineries are Glenora Wine Cellars at Glenora-on-Seneca, with 200ha (500 acres) only partly planted with hybrids and *V. vinifera* for wine-making, founded in 1977; Heron Hill Vineyards at Hammondsport, also founded in 1977, with 16ha (40 acres) shared between

The modest sign at the entrance to the estate of one of the world's largest wine companies *(top)*. Taylors have concentrated on labruscan and hybrid wines at a time when other companies have been introducing viniferas.

The Pleasant Valley Winery headquarters at Hammondsport *(above)*. Founded in 1860, this is the oldest winery in New York State. Great Western "Champagne" is made by the transfer process, not the true *méthode champenoise*.

The imposing front door of the Taylor Wine Company *(above right)*.

A selection of still wines marketed under the "Great Western" label *(right)*. In the center is Pink Catawba, made from a native grape: on its right the two generic names, "Chablis" and "Burgundy," may be used to indicate the use of French varietals but not of Chardonnay or Pinot Noir.

On this and the facing page are six photographs underlining the skills of modern wine-making.

Only human hands can detect the presence of unripe or rotten grapes fed into the press *(right)*.

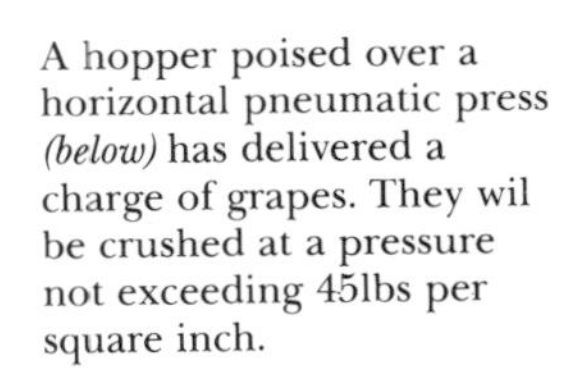

A hopper poised over a horizontal pneumatic press *(below)* has delivered a charge of grapes. They wil be crushed at a pressure not exceeding 45lbs per square inch.

Initially the must ferments rapidly *(below right)*, causing a substantial release of carbon dioxide and a rising temperature. Control of the temperature is vital at this stage.

Black grapes are discharged onto an Archimedes screw *(left)* that will feed them into a destemmer-crusher before fermentation.

Here cloudy red wine drawn by pipette from a cask *(below)* is tested to see whether the particles will fall naturally or whether filtration will be necessary.

At every competent winery worldwide, the wine will be tasted and tested *(bottom)* at regular stages during manufacture so that the necessary corrections may be made.

Chardonnay and Riesling (70%), Aurora and Seyval Blanc (25%), and Ravat 51 (5%); and Herman J. Wiemers Vineyard at Dundee on Seneca Lake, founded in 1979, where 10ha (24 acres) of Riesling and 4.5ha (11 acres) of Chardonnay fill the vineyard. The move towards *V. vinifera* vines at Heron Hill and Weimers vineyards is encouraging, and their superb crisp white Chardonnays and Rieslings may encourage others to follow suit.

**Hudson River and Long Island**

The Hudson River wine region is one of the nation's oldest vineyard areas. Marlboro, close to the right bank, is the center; the region reaches up to Kingston and down to Washington. At its widest it includes Walker Valley in the west and Millerton in the east. The Hudson Valley Wine Company has been trading since 1907 from Highland, where 130ha (325 acres) of potential vineyard is so far about half-planted with labruscana vines, including Catawba, Delaware and Concord, and the French hybrid Chelois. Over 100,000 cases are marketed each year. The Royal Kedem Winery produces labruscana wines mainly from Concord and about one-third as much varietal wine from Aurora, Seyval, and de Chaunac. Royal Kedem have 70ha (170 acres) of vines at Milton.

At Marlboro the Benmarl Wine Company is an unusual cooperative of the "Société des Vignerons," with some 400 wine-loving members who help finance the business, pick the grapes and swallow the product. Practically all of the 17ha (42-acre) vineyard is planted with French hybrids, and the wines are much respected in New York. Perhaps "*vigneron*" is a heavy word for grape-picker, but it is a happy thought. Also at Marlboro is the small Cagnasso Winery, converting French hybrid grapes and a small proportion of labruscanas. The red wines are heavy and smooth and the white wines fully fermented to dryness.

Cascade Mountain Vineyards at Amenia have 18ha (45 acres) of hybrids, principally Seyval and Léon Millot. The produce generally is described as being "Spring" wines, by no means unfitting for these crisp dry whites and rosés, and reds for drinking young. Over to the west, at Walker Valley, Valley Vineyards have an interesting range of vines in their 10ha (25 acres). It is divided as to 55% white hybrids, 20% red hybrids, 15% Riesling, and 10% Chardonnay, and the wines succeed in conveying the European tradition.

New York's own Monarch Wine Company in Brooklyn produces in all 200 million cases of wine each year. Their products include the Kosher Manischewitz from Concord grapes, and three New York State "Champagnes."

When in 1973 Alexander and Louisa Hargrave put down over 20ha (50 acres) of vines on the North Fork of Long Island, almost surrounded by the Atlantic, many interested eyes turned to watch their progress: more especially because every grape was true *Vitis vinifera*. The project has been a complete success: the vines are principally Sauvignon Blanc and Chardonnay, making white wines that compare with the best the USA can produce, and Cabernets and Pinot Noir, which are aged in new American oak barrels to make red wines worthy of Bordeaux.

In 1976, New York State law was varied to encourage small wineries producing less than 50,000 gallons (1,893hl) of wine each year to open up in the state. The restrictions on sale were also eased in their favour. This has already resulted in the creation of some 40 new businesses.

**New England**

There are now wineries in the states of New Hampshire, Massachusetts, Rhode Island, and Connecticut, as well as (and why not?) on the island of Martha's Vineyard, off Cape Cod. As yet the industry in New England is still at the experimental stage, and two schools of thought divide their faith between French varietals and *V. vinifera*; the labruscanas do not seem to have made an appearance, although it is far too early to say whether this is coincidence or a trend.

Hardy-type viniferas do better near the coast, and the Chicama Vineyards on Martha's Vineyard (adjacent to Nantucket) have Cabernet Sauvignon, Chardonnay and Riesling vines. Prudence Island Vineyards, in Naragansett Bay, have 8ha (20 acres) of viniferas including Chardonnay and Gewürztraminer. The state of Rhode Island now has several small vineyards; Sakonnet, the largest, is divided between hybrids and *V. vinifera*. Haight Vineyards, 65km (40mi) inland at Litchfield, is Connecticut's first winery, and successfully grows Chardonnay and Riesling, for white wines, with the hybrid Marechal Foch for its red wine.

North of Rhode Island the varietals are favored. The Commonwealth Winery at Plymouth, Massachusetts, uses Seyval, Vidal Blanc and Cayuga for excellent white wines, with Foch and de Chaunac for reds. All are hybrids that are also well planted in the Finger Lakes region. White Mount Vineyards, in up-country New Hampshire, has since 1969 drawn grapes locally as well as from farms in Maine to its east and Vermont to its west to complete a range of hybrids for making good white and red wines.

The pending multi-state appellation "New England South Coast" includes Rhode Island, Connecticut, and Massachusetts, but excludes New Hampshire.

## THE MIDWESTERN STATES

Where the midwest of the USA begins and ends is debatable. Here it is arbitrarily taken to include the area bounded by Minnesota, Iowa, and Missouri in the west, Kentucky and West Virginia in the south, and Pennsylvania in the east, all these states being included. To the north this area is bounded by the Great Lakes.

### Lake Erie

Three states have boundaries running along the southern and eastern shores of Lake Erie: they are Ohio, Pennsylvania, and the western extremity of New York. The Ohio wineries reach from Sandusky, in the west, through Cleveland to Conneat: Pennsylvania has only 65km (40mi) of the lakeshore and here the industry centers on North East City. The New York wineries are in the Chautauqua area, south of Buffalo. The pending multi-state appellation for the Lake Erie region will permit grapes from any or all of the three states to be sold separately or blended under the "Lake Erie" label, so that in the wine trade the whole is regarded as a viticultural region, rather than as three separate parts according to the three states.

### Lake Michigan

The important vineyards around Lake Michigan, and there are many of them, are grouped from its south near Chicago and along its east coast. The lake provides warmth to protect the vines in a northern climate and allows prevailing westerly winds to bring snow cover to protect the vine-roots from frost. Fennville in the south and the Leelanau peninsula to the north have already been delimited with their own appellations. Bronte, at Hartford, and St Julian and Warner at Paw Paw, three of the biggest wineries in the south, have all planted hybrids; Bronte was the first company to produce a French hybrid, the Baco Noir. At Tabor Hill, close to the Indiana border, Chardonnay and Riesling have been flourishing for over a decade alongside hybrids—and producing great wines. Château Grand Travers, in Travers county close to the lake's north, has also experimented successfully with Chardonnay and Riesling.

### Other Midwestern Wine Regions

The states of Minnesota, Iowa, Wisconsin, Illinois, and Indiana have wineries in sufficient numbers to justify regarding them as areas ready for potential development. The Iowa wineries are in the Amana and Boone areas. Missouri has an important wine industry, and had the distinction of receiving the first appellation granted for any of the 50 states, declaring Augusta a delimited region. Here the Mount Pleasant vineyards make a range of excellent red and white wines from hybrid grapes, including Münch, a light red Beaujolais-type wine from the Cynthiana grape, and a claret-like Cordon Rouge. The valley of the Ohio River, in the southwest of Ohio state, has attracted many wineries, and the river runs on through southern Indiana and Kentucky where more wineries are situated. The Ohio Valley industry goes back to Nicholas Longworth, who started wine-making around Cincinnati 150 years ago. The industry lapsed after his death and did not revive until the repeal of Prohibition. Today a central Ohio wine region is growing around Columbus and Springfield.

## THE MIDATLANTIC STATES

These states include New Jersey, a small part of eastern Pennsylvania, Maryland, and Virginia, and—were there any viable vineyards there today—should also include Delaware, named for Lord Delaware (De La Warr), who was planting grapes in the region 350 years ago. Philip and Jocelyn Wagner are remembered for planting the first French hybrids at Boordy Vineyards near Ryderwood in Maryland in the 1940s, and for making their stock available to other growers. Their success led to a resurgence of wine-growing throughout the eastern states. Since Dr Konstantin Frank grafted *V. vinifera* scions onto Canadian rootstocks, Hamilton Mowbray at his wine cellars at Westminster near Baltimore has been experimenting with viniferas successfully, despite set-backs from equinoctial gales and hurricanes coming in from the Atlantic. Chardonnay and Riesling are being introduced also by Meredyth Vineyards at Middleburg, Virginia, but as in Baltimore the viniferas as yet have a poweful backup of hybrids beside them. Several other vineyards in Virginia and over the border in Pennsylvania are experimenting with the same vinifera varieties, but with the same *caveat*. It remains to be seen whether the customer is sufficiently impressed to pay the necessarily higher price.

# THE SOUTH AND SOUTHWEST STATES

Arkansas and Texas both show a lively promise for the future. The Arkansas wine industry has been established for many years in the western half of the state, near Altus in the Arkansas river valley. Here immigrants from Switzerland and neighboring countries of central Europe settled in the 1870s. "At home" at altitudes of up to 600m (2,000ft), the settlers have reared a successful crop of viniferas, sheltered from the north by the Ozark Mountains. Texas is even more businesslike, with a 285ha (700-acre) State University project near Lubbock in West Texas, planted in conditions similar to those of the Californian Central Valley. Here the McPherson family are pioneering 70ha (170 acres) of Cabernet, Chardonnay, Chenin Blanc, Sauvignon Blanc, and Riesling. Arizona and New Mexico vineyard-owners are also starting to experiment with viniferas. Two problems in the south are high humidity and Pierce's disease, which first attacks the vine's leaves and goes on to kill the vine within five years.

Every state in the continental union has at least one bonded winery, and many states have thriving wine industries. The areas east of the Rocky Mountains that show little or no current promise of success, however, are the northern plains of the Dakotas, the Mississippi Delta, and parts of the Gulf Coast.

# CANADA

## Ontario ♦ British Columbia ♦ Nova Scotian and Other Wineries

Jesuit evangelists were in Quebec as early as 1636, making sacramental wine from native grapes on the banks of the St Lawrence river, but the start of the wine industry of Canada really took place in 1811 when John Schiller, a German, settled in Cooksville near Toronto, planted a vineyard and built a winery, Clair House. By 1867 Clair House wines were receiving honorable mention at the Paris Exposition, and Schiller's lead had caused others to create vineyards whose area, by the 1890s, totaled 2,000ha (5,000 acres). However, there was growing public sentiment against drinking alcohol in any form, and during the First World War all the Canadian provinces except the French-blooded Quebec voted for Prohibition. To save the grape-growers of Ontario, at that time the only province producing wine, the embargo was restricted to beers and spirits: wines could be bought, but only from the wineries and in quantities of not less than 5gal (19 liters) or a case at a time.

Prohibition was repealed in Canada in 1927, but repeal was not heralded with the enthusiasm that would later be shown by people in the USA. In place of Prohibition, the provinces all established government-monopoly liquor-stores, and purchasers of any alcoholic beverage had first to possess an annual license, costing $2. Ontario had an advantage over the other states, for it already had some 50 wine stores owned by the wineries, the smaller of which were promptly bought out by the bigger ones for the sake of their licenses. However, what the Ontario wine industry gained at this time was soon offset by the loss of clandestine "exports" across Lake Erie into the USA, which rose to a substantial trade before its collapse in 1934.

Canada *(below)* has two fast-developing wine regions: Ontario and the smaller, less-important, British Columbia.

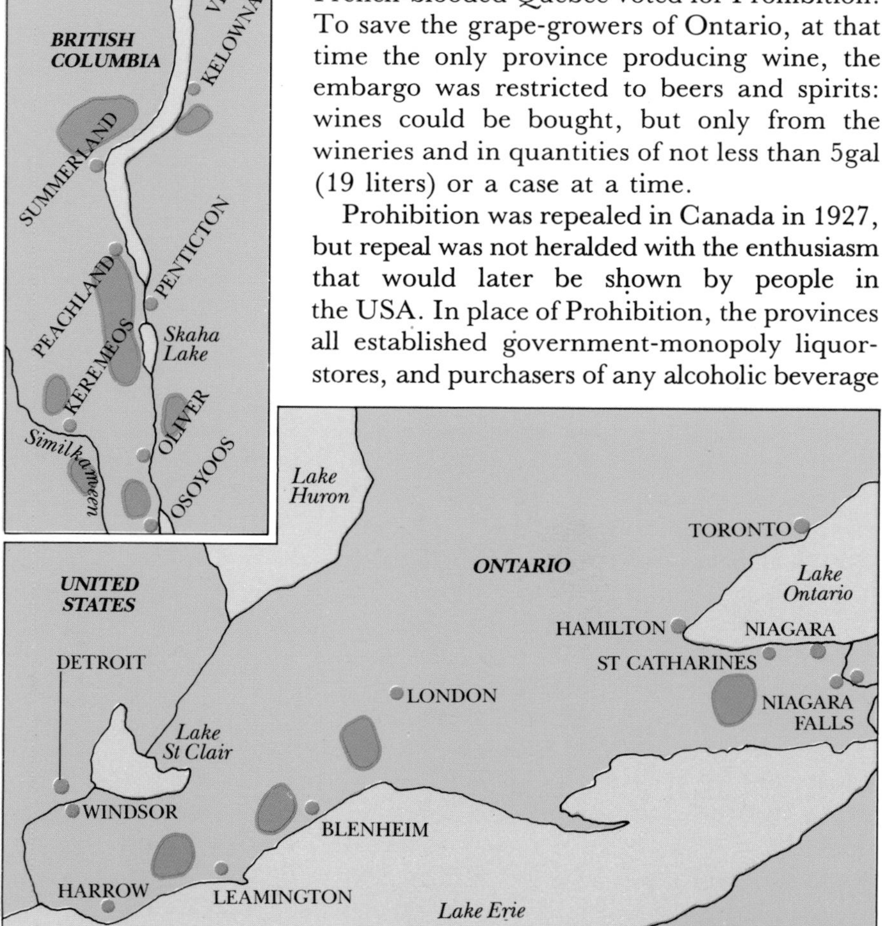


Although a number of new wineries opened after repeal, the Canadian industry made little appreciable headway until after the Second World War. Postwar immigration then brought vast numbers of Europeans to Canada; they, with the returning soldiers, all had a taste for wines made from the *V. vinifera* vines of France, Italy, Germany, and Spain. The consumption of wine in Canada quadrupled by 1964, from a level of 2.37 liters (5 pints) per capital annually to over 8.71 liters (2.3 gal), a slightly higher level than in the USA. Partially due to the influx of immigrants, this may also have reflected a slow beginning of a switch to the planting of *V. vinifera* grapes, in place of the labruscanas which had dominated the Ontario vineyards for over one hundred years.

Before the war a young French chemist, Adhemar de Chaunac, had already set the great firm of Brights, at their Niagara Falls Winery, on the way to making dry table wines. In 1946 he brought back from France 100 *V. vinifera* vines and one-half as many French hybrids. This led to the production of Canada's first "Champagne" in 1949 and to many other wines of noble class; but, more importantly, it was the start of a slow move towards the replanting of Canada's vineyards with viniferas — a slow process because Dr Konstantin Frank had not yet discovered the system of grafting vinefera scions onto Canadian rootstocks. The big changeover to viniferas and hybrids came with the international wine revolution that took place in the 1970s.

Ontario was joined by British Columbia as a grape- and wine-producing region in 1934, and in 1980 Nova Scotia staked a claim to become a third recognizable wine region.

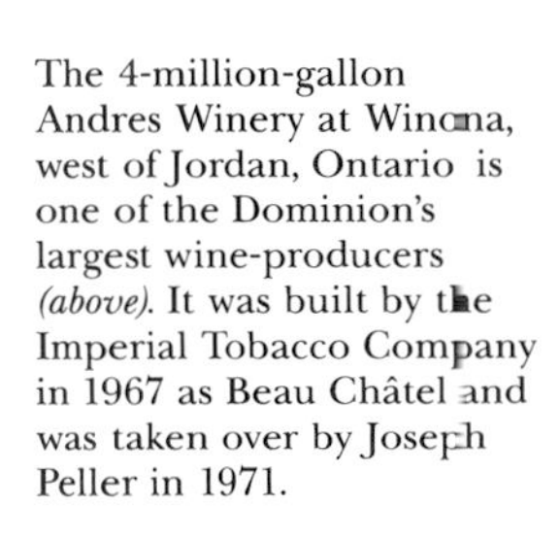

The 4-million-gallon Andres Winery at Winona, west of Jordan, Ontario is one of the Dominion's largest wine-producers *(above)*. It was built by the Imperial Tobacco Company in 1967 as Beau Châtel and was taken over by Joseph Peller in 1971.

Frost has to be respected in Ontario, although the Great Lakes make the climate milder than average at these latitudes. Earthing-up in October or November to protect the vinifera roots is customary; in March the soil is removed *(right)*.

## ONTARIO

The center of the Ontario wine region is the Niagara Peninsula, between Lake Ontario and Lake Erie, bounded on the east by the Niagara river. Today about 10,000ha (25,000 acres) of vineyards are planted on the peninsula which stretches westward from Niagara-on-the-Lake for 65km (40mi) to the area south of the city of Hamilton. Further west there are a few important vineyards near the coast of Lake Erie.

On latitude 43°N, the Niagara Peninsula is on roughly the same parallel as the Pyrénées. The climate is strongly affected by the waters of lakes Ontario and Erie, which give the region more frost-free days than are experienced, for example, in West Virginia, 500km (300mi) to the south. The winter temperatures are mild, usually averaging between −4°C (25°F) and −1°C (30°F), and the average growing season is 175 days. There is a long and reliable fall for ripening and harvest.

The peninsula produces one-quarter of all Canadian wines, mainly from four giant plants. T. G. Bright and Company is the largest winery in the country and the second oldest. 416,000hl (11 million gal) of wine are made annually at this winery outside the city of Niagara Falls. Originally Brights were manufacturers of "ports" and "sherries," and today their President "port," named for a little known Munson grape from Texas, is still an award-winning brand. Other wines, like Bright's Baco Noir, continue to win medals wherever they are shown. Today Brights is owned by the Hiram Walker Distillery.

Almost as large, at St Catherines on the Ontario lakeshore, are the Jordan and St Michelle Cellars owned by Carling O'Keefe Breweries, where 380,000hl (10 million gal) of wine are produced each year. The Château-Gai winery at Niagara Falls, founded in 1890, and now owned by the John Labatt breweries, was the first to make "Champagne" in North America by the Charmat process (see page 44); it is also said to have been, in 1965, the first exporter of Canadian wines to the UK. In 1967, Château-Gai lost a case brought by the French Government, who obtained damages and an injunction stopping Château-Gai from calling their sparkling wines "Champagne," which they had been doing in contravention of the French-Canadian trade agreement of 1933, which had specified that Champagne should come only from France. But in 1980 Canada finally had her way, by simply canceling the 1933 agreement!

Outside St Catherines is the winery started by George and Thomas Barnes a century ago; it is now definitely more of a winery than a vineyard. About 57,000hl (1.5 million gal) are produced here each year, including Grand Celebration "Champagne" and Ontario Red, the latter entirely from Ontario grapes. The small vineyard is now planted with French hybrids in place of the old labruscas.

North of Queenston is Inniskillen, Ontario's first estate winery. Here the partnership of Donald Ziraldo and Karl Kaiser, which started in 1971, is devoted to the technical and practical study of enology. Their first vintage brought them the first winery license to be granted in Ontario since 1929, and since then a modern winery with a capacity of 6,800hl (180,000gal) a year has been developed. Their wines include Chambourcin, Gewürztraminer, Merlot, Riesling, and blends marketed as Brae Blanc and Brae Rouge. A bottle-fermented "Champagne" was first marketed in 1984.

Nearly 150km (90mi) west of the Niagara Peninsula is the London Winery, which produces 133,000hl (3.5 million gal) of wine each year; and to its southwest, at Blenheim, are the Charal Winery & Vineyards, named for Charles and Allan Eastman who have over 15 years created from scratch 40ha (100 acres) of vineyards producing 2,600hl (70,000gal) of wine annually. Their Light Wine Spumante sells well at the state-monopoly stores.

The Vin Villa Vineyard cellar, set up 100 years ago on Pelèe Island in Lake Erie, was closed down during Prohibition. Now the vineyards have been replanted successfully with *V. vinifera*, but the winery is being rebuilt near Leamington on the lakeshore.

At Harrow, not far west of Leamington, Colio Wines of Canada built a 9,500hl (250,000gal) winery in 1980. The wine descriptions confirm the Italian interest in the company. They include dry and semidry table wines called Rosso and Bianco, each with Secco versions, and a semisparkling ("crackling," in Canada) wine.

Wine research in eastern Canada is the responsibility of the Horticultural Experiment Station at Vineland. Positive results from this imaginative establishment have included a system of working *flor* yeasts to develop *fino* "sherries" in days instead of years, discovered by Ralph Crowther; and the breeding by Oliver Bradt of many hybrid grapes that have contributed materially to improvements in the character of wines from the USA as well as Canada.

## BRITISH COLUMBIA

In 1934 British Columbia started to produce wine seriously, although at first it was made partly, or in bad years even wholly, from Californian grapes with some from the young vineyards in Washington State. The wine region lies in the Okanagan Valley, between the Trepanier Plateau and the Monashee mountains, 250km (150mi) east of Vancouver. The climate here, tempered by the deep waters of Lake Okanagan, gives a growing season of over 180 days. The latitude is just within the northern wine-band and conditions are excellent for vines in the

rising plain by the lake. Irrigation provides ample water to supplement the rainfall, which rarely reaches more than 25cm (12in) annually.

The first wine made from British Columbian grapes was from those grown in a small vineyard south of Kelowna; they were vinified in the Growers' Winery at Victoria. During the Depression of the early 1930s, apples, the principal crop in the Okanagan Valley, were unsalable, and this prompted two teetotal traders in Kelowna to make wine from them. William Bennett, from the hardware-store, and his Italian neighbor Pasquale Copozzi, the grocer, built the Calona Winery. However, their apple wine could not compete with grape wine, and so they switched to the conversion of Californian grapes. Several new wineries joined in to form an industry selling "Canadian Wine" made from imported grapes. In 1960 Bennett, now Premier of British Columbia, caused the Liquor Board to decree that certain percentages of British Columbian grapes should be incorporated in wines produced in the province: these mandatory figures were 25% for 1961, rising to 50% in the next year and to 65% by 1965. As a result, the vineyard plantings grew from 250ha (600 acres) to about 1,000ha (2,500 acres) in four years. The quota had to be rescinded in 1965, because subzero temperatures and gales in December 1964 had frozen the vines, but by the mid-1970s it had risen to 80% and the vineyard area had increased to 1,400ha (3,500 acres).

The Calona Winery was eventually sold to Standard Brands of Montreal, a subsidiary of their US company, in 1971, when its annual capacity was raised to 150,000hl (4 million gal). Calona produce a wide range of still, sparkling and dessert wines; their brands include Haut Villages, Schloss Laderheim, and Sommet Blanc and Rouge. Some 65km (40mi) south of Kelowna at Penticton the Casabello Winery, now owned by Labatt Breweries, has a yearly capacity of over 95,000hl (2½ million gal). When permission was granted in 1976 for wineries to incorporate visitors' tasting rooms, Casabello was the first to benefit. Here a wide range of proprietary brands are promoted, together with varietal estate wines from vinifera vineyards planted at Osoyoos by Walter Davidson, son-in-law of the Casabello founder-president, Evans Longheed.

A great winery with an annual capacity of 30,000hl (800,000gal) has been set up at Oliver, south of Skaha Lake, by the Bright organization of Ontario. It has some 120ha (300 acres) of its own vineyard under development to supplement supplies of grapes bought from local growers. This new winery is named Brights Wines of BC.

The St Michelle Winery, 40km (25mi) southeast of Vancouver, was built by Carling O'Keefe Breweries in 1977 to carry on the business of the old Growers' Winery, which had operated for over 50 years at Victoria on Vancouver Island. Joseph Zimmerman, who was trained at the Geisenheim Institute in the Rheingau, is wine-master of the new winery as well as of their Jordan and St Michelle wineries in Ontario. Also in the Vancouver region, at Port Moody the Andrés Winery has reached an annual production of 115,000hl (3 million gal). The name of Guy Baldwin, the wine-maker, is one to conjure with on three continents, through his previous connections with the Paul Masson and Seagrams groups—not to mention the quality of the Andrés wine selection.

Both St Michelle and Andrés have visitors' tasting rooms, and it may not be realized abroad

Casks for aging "Sherry" stand high in the sun at Andrés Winery, Winona *(below)*. They are a familiar landmark on Queen Elizabeth Way. Andrew Peller, father of proprietor Joseph, started the first Andrés Winery in British Columbia in 1961.

A notice on the Niagara peninsula leaves little to the imagination *(right)*. It has been estimated that half of Canadian wine is made outside its wineries: many Canadians prefer to ferment their own wine from grapes produced on farms in the peninsula.

how important this development has been in a country where the government-monopoly liquor-stores have such tight control. The newly licensed estate wineries in British Columbia may each sell up to 30,000gal (1,136hl) yearly directly to consumers and restaurants. This wine must be made solely from grapes grown in the province at a rate of 150 gal per ton (about 6001/tonne) of grapes, compared with 250 gallons per ton (about 1,0001/tonne) allowed for Ontario's commercial wines.

## NOVA SCOTIAN AND OTHER WINERIES

Nova Scotia has a mild sheltered shore along the Bay of Fundy to the southwest. Dr Roger Dial came here, to Annapolis Valley, from California, where he had helped to manage a winery, to lecture at Dalhousie University; the vineyard and Grand Pré winery which he founded in 1977 were perhaps an afterthought. The Annapolis valley is between latitudes 44°N and 45°N, which Dial claims gives the valley a climate similar to that of Mosel in Germany. In fact, the Mosel valley is 650km (400mi) further north even at its southern extreme, and so there is every reason to support the doctor's view that excellent estate wines will be produced here. Others must follow in his footsteps.

In a dozen big cities of Canada there are large wineries which have no vineyards but make and sell wines of all descriptions from grapes, grape musts or concentrates bought in from numerous sources. Some come from Canada, most come from California, and many come from Europe. (Grape concentrates, or condensed unfermented grape juice, are usually used for sweetening wines, and their flavor can often be detected.) The reasons for the establishment of these wineries in the 1960s were two. First, their produce, plus the output from the Ontario and British Columbia wine industries, is easily absorbed into the dominion's huge wine consumption; and second, by creating local employment, the owners were entitled to have their wines listed in their province's monopoly liquor-stores. These wineries are to be found in Calgary, Dorval, Lachine, Laval, Moncton, Moose Jaw, Morris, St Hyacinthe, Selkirk, Truro, and Winnipeg.

A system now operated by the state-monopoly liquor-stores tells customers in a new way the sweetness of each wine they sell. Instead of the confusing "brut," "sec," "extra dry," "demi-sec doux" and other indications which mean different things in different countries or on different labels, the new system classifies each wine for its sweetness with a number between 0 for very dry and 25 for very sweet. The system is said to be working well, in which case perhaps the number could find its way onto the label. Every bottle of Tokay from Hungary already has one.

# MEXICO

The Rio Grande separates the USA and Mexico from El Paso all the way to the Gulf. West of El Paso the border runs almost in a straight east-west line to the Pacific Coast at San Diego, some 3,200km (2,000mi) from Mexico's southern border with Guatemala. Although the missionaries accompanying the conquistadores carried the vine to this huge country 450 years ago, the present-day wine industry of Mexico is no more than 30 years old. The reasons stand out in history: Spain, jealous of her own wine industry, forbade the planting of vines when she saw a rival industry growing. Over the centuries, however, there has always been some wine being made in Mexico.

Only after Mexico gained her independence in the nineteenth century did her will to progress stir, faint though that stirring was: during that century just two new wineries were built, the Bodegas Ferriño at Cuatro Ciénegas in Coahuila, and the Bodegas de Santo Tomás in Baja California. Both sustained the Criolla or Mission grape tradition. Mexico's big step forward came in 1889 when James Concannon, from Livermore in California, persuaded President Porfirio Díaz that he could develop Mexican wines to commercial standards using *V. vinifera* vines from Livermore. Concannon promptly imported several million cuttings, and these were distributed throughout Mexico with suitable instructions in the vernacular. Hacienda Roque, near Celaya, owned by the father-in-law of Díaz's son, was chosen for the major planting: the whole operation, throughout Mexico, was completed by 1904. Díaz also assigned to the son of the Hungarian ambassador the task of insuring that at least one bodega would be established in every state. Concannon returned home to be replaced by another Californian, Antonio Perelli-Minetti, who had just lost a wine fortune in San Francisco. With authority from the President, Perelli-Minetti went on to plant nearly 400ha (1,000 acres) of vines near Torreón at Rancho El Fresno, Mexico's largest vineyard. But all was in vain, for in 1910 the Mexican Revolution began: it lasted for 10 years, cost one million lives and wrecked most of the vineyards. During the revolution, Perelli-Minetti left the chaos of Mexico; he returned to the San Joaquin Valley in 1916, and made another fortune in wine. However, he visited Mexico often after the revolution, and was partly responsible for establishing the modern wine industry there.

After the revolution, the vineyards of Mexico were to get worse before getting better: the wines were adulterated and diluted, so that during the 1920s and early 1930s the best way to consider them was with abject mistrust. The Association Nacional de Vitivinicultores wisely took the decision in 1929 that the revolution and its aftermath had severed Mexico from its past vinicultural history. The youngest wine industry in the Americas was about to develop.

In the same year, Don Nazario Ortiz Garza, a grocer in Saltillo, the capital of Coahuila, on a hunch started a winery. He became progressively Governor of Coahuila, a member of the Mexican Senate, and Secretary of Agriculture. Not only did he develop vineyards at Saltillo, Mexico City, Aguascalientes, Coahuila, Durango and Chihuahua, but he spread the gospel of the vine throughout Mexico, distributing cuttings just as royalty might distribute largess. He built a distillery for brandy at Torreón in 1966, by which time he was converting one-quarter of all Mexico's grapes in his own plants. The Mexican Government had given an enormous fillip to her wine industry after the Second World War by raising duties and putting quota restrictions on imported wines, so that the prices of US, French and Spanish wines rose to five times that of the Mexican ones. As a result, the area of Mexican vineyards has increased since the war from 1,600ha (4,000 acres) to 71,000ha (175,000 acres), while as yet the Mexican consumption of wine per capita is under one-half liter (1 pint) per annum, compared with 7.6l (2gal) in the USA. No wonder that Martell Cognac, Pedro Domecq, Osborne, and Seagrams have all purchased part of the action.

A strange law in Mexico prevents wineries from owning vineyards: often, however, families achieve dual ownership by sharing the two functions among themselves.

# THE WINE REGIONS

It is no accident that the majority of Mexico's vineyards are in the centre of the country, away from the east and west coasts. The northwestern border of Mexico is at latitude 32°N, so that practically all the country is in the hot sub-equatorial region normally detrimental to successful grape production. But the Central Plateau of Mexico is on average some 1,500m (5,000ft) above sea level, and every 300m (1,000ft) of elevation will cause a drop of 1.7°C (3°F) in temperature, so that the altitude of the plateau compensates in some ways for the unfavorable latitude.

The grape will grow well during the warm fall days, which are shorter nearer the equator; but the drop in temperature at night is dramatic, creating the danger of frost damage. Rainfall is not consistent in Mexico, so that some grapes may need irrigation from scarce water supplies while others may be flooded during the growing season. Nine-tenths of Mexico's grapes are used for brandy production, for which this climate is generally well suited.

Mexico's vineyards are grouped in eight regions. From north to south these are: Baja California; Hermosillo-Caborca, on the Sonora river; Delicias, in Chihuahua; La Laguna and Torreón, on the border of Coahuila and Durango; Parras and Saltillo, in Coahuila; the Fresnillo-Ojocaliente region in Zacatecas; Aguascalientes; and San Juan de Rio, north of Mexico City.

Baja California, where Pacific breezes contribute to an excellent climate, is one of the more important regions. Here the biggest winery is the historic Bodegas de Santo Tomás, with an annual yield of nearly 75,000hl (2 million gal). In 1972 Pedro Domecq added their 37,500hl (1 million gal) winery northeast of Ensenada to others in the Guadalupe Valley. Here also is the enormous Vinícola la Cetto, owned by Angelo Cetto who, with his family, contributes greatly to the wine industry's welfare in Baja California and elsewhere. There are now some 10,000ha (25,000 acres) under vine in the region.

Some 500km (300mi) south and close to the Gulf of California, brandy has been distilled at Hermosillo for 20 years. The grape-growing region has spread north as far as Caborca, so that Sonora has become the main vineyard of Mexico with five large factories crushing brandy grapes. Across the Sierra Tarahumare in Chihuahua, there is one winery at Ciudad Delicias producing table wines, and a distillery making brandy from extensive vineyards in the province.

The regions of La Laguna, Parras, and Saltillo lie roughly in line west to east from the Durango border across Coahuila province. Substantial vineyards have been planted in the La Laguna

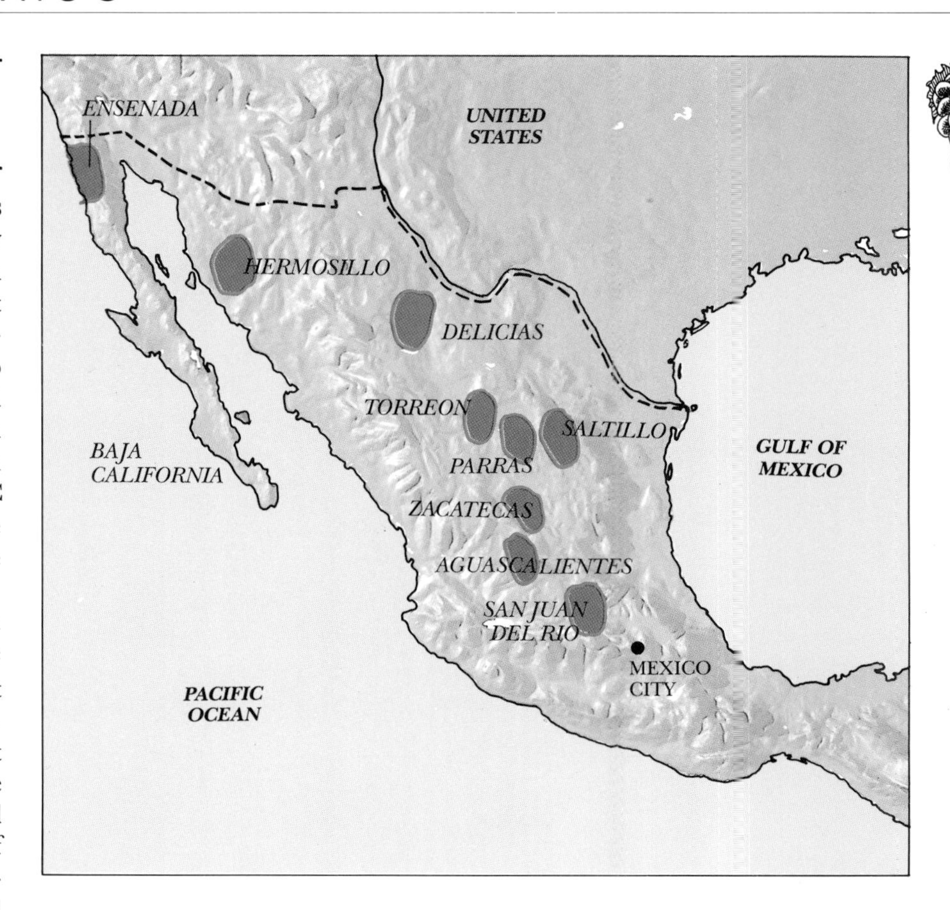


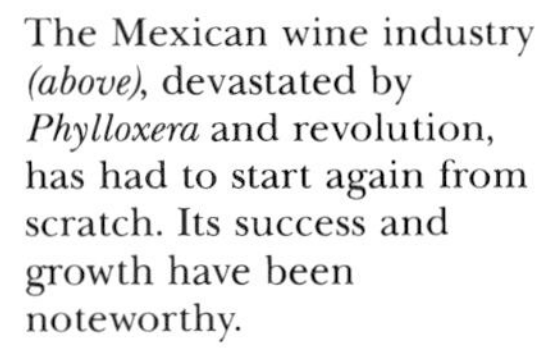

The Mexican wine industry *(above)*, devastated by *Phylloxera* and revolution, has had to start again from scratch. Its success and growth have been noteworthy.

Most of Baja California's vineyards lie in the most northerly 240km (150mi), between San Diego, on the US border, and Rosario, close to the Punta Pireta on the Pacific coast *(below)*.

South of Mexico City the heat is intense, but although the vine disappears the Agave cactus still thrives. The Agave is fermented to produce *pulque*, the national native drink, which is then distilled to produce tequila. This vista of the Oaxaco region *(main picture)* is typical of southern Mexico territory.

Popocatépetl, the extinct volcano at Mexico's highest point, near Mexico City *(below)*. An east-west line through Popocatépetl represents the southern limit of Mexico's vinegrowing propensities. Some of Mexico's best wine is made just north of Mexico City.

A copper canyon in the Zacatecas region of the Central Plateau of Mexico *(bottom)*, where most of the country's vineyards are sited. In time the economic importance of the wines may begin to challenge that of the minerals found here.

district, and at Torreón there is a state vineyard planted with virus-free vines from Davis. Brandy practically monopolizes production, but about 12% is table wine, which is now being made with care at the Vinícola del Vergel.

The oldest vineyards of Mexico are to be found in the unspoiled *adobe* area of Parras de la Fuente, and possibly the first vines sent to Argentina, Chile, and Peru started from here. Now the family of the late President Madero have a 375,000hl (10 million gal) brandy distillery, the Bodegas de San Lorenzo, at Parras. Exceptionally, the early haciendas of Parras grew grapes *and* made wines. At the Hacienda Alamo are the headquarters of de Nazario, whose vineyards spread over four states. Mexican brandies for the Spanish Gonzalez-Byass organization are also produced here.

By contrast, the newest vine-growing district of Mexico lies over 160km (100mi) south in Zacatecas, no less than 2,150m (7,000ft) up in the Sierra de Nayarit. Between Fresnillo and Ojocaliente to its south, thousands of hectares of vineyard have been planted since the early 1970s in open country begging for cultivation. Viñedos don Luis is the largest vineyard of Ojocaliente; Bodegas de Altiplano was the first Zacatecas winery, and Vides de Zacatecas at Luis Moya the most beautiful.

Spanning the highway between El Paso and Mexico City is Don Nazario' Viñedos San Marcos, immediately recognizable by the mammoth wine bottle dominating the winery. Alamo and San Marco are the brands for the main brandies and wines. Bodegas Brandevin, dating from 1948, is the oldest wine in Aguascalientes, and here sangria is included in the range.

In the state of Querétaro, 160km (100mi) north of Mexico City, the valley of Rio de San Juan, at some 1,850m (6,000ft), is almost as high above sea-level as Ojocaliente. Here some of the most delicate of Mexican table wines, now gaining a fine and reliable reputation, are produced at several wineries. Cavas de San Juan, just east of San Juan de Rio, produce wines branded Hidalgo, a range that now includes a vintage-dated Cepa Cabernet Sauvignon, and a family of "Champagnes" made by the Charmat (see page 44) process. Other important wineries here are Cruz Blanca and the Madrileña winery. The enormous Martell establishment near Tequisquiapan produces excellent *V. vinifera* wines from Cabernet, Merlot, Grenache, and Sauvignon Blanc, and the brandies come from Ugni Blanc.

Perhaps our short survey of Mexican grape-brandy and wine production should end where it all started. In neighboring Guanajuato state are the Bodegas San Luis Rey, where wines and spirits dating from the revolution are still stored in tunnels below the cellars. The tunnels were dug hundreds of years ago by Jesuit priests, who hid there with their Mission wine to avoid capture by warring Mexicans.

# SOUTHERN HEMISPHERE

Most of the world's landmasses lie north of the equator; the southern wine-belt crosses only six countries in which wine industries of any consequence can exist: Argentina, Brazil, and Chile, in South America, and Australia, New Zealand, and South Africa. Argentina is the world's fourth largest wine producer, South Africa the 10th, Chile the 13th, Australia the 17th and Brazil the 19th. So far, New Zealand has not been ranked in the world list, but her importance is established by other criteria: she shares with California the ideal climate for growing grapes for wine; her industry is growing rapidly; and her wines have recently improved amazingly in quality.

Argentina has over one-half the vines of South America at her disposal, and should assume her full importance on the world wine scene once she has recovered from the Falklands war and her political and financial affairs are stabilized.

Chile can and does produce beautiful wines, but something seems to be lacking. It is not the heat of the sun and it is not manana—she has enough of each. Although her wine-making equipment is mostly out-of-date, her home market is satisfied with what it produces and the unprepossessing País grape grows in abundance to make it. During her period of junta rule, politics added to the disadvantages of the Chilean wine industry, but since then things have improved and, if the industry will look farther than South America for new sizable export markets, it has a great future.

International interest in the relatively small Brazilian wine industry has been attracted by the home market potential existing there. The country is vast; although the equator runs through her northern forests, there is ample room in the latitudes south of São Paulo for excellent wine production.

Australia has known far more about wine production for much longer than is generally imagined. Politics has not always helped her wine industry forward; nor for that matter did phylloxera. But without adequate central direction, the industry seems to have "muddled through perfectly." Australian consumers are now developing an increasing and increasingly discerning taste for wine, despite the mild chaos of the country's labeling methods; if they can decode them they will find that Australia's best wine now compares with the best anywhere.

In New Zealand the situation is even more electric. Cut off from the outside world during the Second World War, she turned seriously to home-production of wines for the first time. As so often happens, however, the doldrums had to be weathered (and the ubiquitous phylloxera came, too) before the recent surge forward began. Now the growers have invaded South Island, and the possibilities are chartless, for the climate, latitude, and soils are perfect, and of space there is plenty.

South Africa has taken a giant leap forward in the last decade, even though her industry is controlled to ensure that all her wines released for sale shall be safely disposed of at fixed minimum prices. In spite of this and the long quarantine period that has delayed arrivals of exotic varietals for many years, the new wines are now appearing and quality is steadily improving. Even the thirsty South Africans are at last being weaned from brandy and dessert and fortified wines onto selective table-wine drinking.

All in all, much is going to be heard from all these countries in the southern hemisphere.

Evening sun highlights these vineyards in the Barossa Valley flats, 55km (35mi) northeast of Adelaide *(right)*. The valley was originally settled by German immigrants about 150 years ago. The vineyards today have a reputation for fine Rieslings, Gewürztraminers, Shiraz and dessert wines. Penfolds, their subsidiary Kaiser Stuhl, Orlando and Smith's Yalumba are among the principal growers.

# SOUTH AMERICA

## Argentina ♦ Chile ♦ Brazil ♦ Other South American Countries

The wine industry of South America *(below)* dates from the arrival of the Spanish conquistadors; it was sustained by the Jesuits until the growth of the international wine market. Argentina produces the greatest volume, and supports some 300,000ha (740,000 acres) of vineyards.

Wine has been cherished in South America from the days of Spanish dominion in the sixteenth century. The wine industries of her three main wine-producing countries have grown, despite various setbacks, until today Argentina has over 300,000ha (740,000 acres) of vines, Chile over 110,000ha (270,000 acres) and Brazil about 80,000ha (200,000 acres). In a sentence, it is Chile for quality, Argentina for quantity, and Brazil for a future promise that has attracted several of the world's wine giants to invest there.



## ARGENTINA

The recognizable wine industry of Argentina was established little more than a century ago, despite the fact that the Jesuit Father Cedron planted the first of the country's vineyards in the Cuyo region in 1556. The Criolla grape survives from that time and still flourishes today.

The story of the modern industry is concerned rather with Italian than with Spanish settlers, and paradoxically Argentina's wineries today are far better equipped than those of Chile. Emulating the Californians, who had irrigated the Central Valley mechanically, the Italians drew the snow-waters of the Andes out over the arid Mendoza desert to create a vineyard of 200,000ha (500,000 acres). The Mendoza province runs from the foothills of the Andes to within 1,000km (620mi) of Buenos Aires, and today produces three-quarters of Argentina's wine. The potential for high-quality wine-production here is largely negated by mass-production methods: one winery in Mendoza town processes one million hectoliters (26½ million gal) of wine every year.

The best Argentinian wine is produced to the west of north Mendoza, where the Malbec grape is planted; in the east Criolla, Malbec, and a variety of Pedro Ximénes grapes produce wines of only average qualities. In the central zone the Uco River Valley is planted with Malbec, Tempranilla, and Semillon vines; and in the south better wines come from the Malbec and Criolla as well as Muscatel Rose and Chenin vines.

North of Mendoza, in San Juan province, the same grapes are used in a warmer climate to make big, richer wines of good quality. Irrigation is paramount here, too, and has proved to be a mixed blessing, as the water flushes out the *Phylloxera* lice and can carry them from one region to another. Conversely, however, the Argentinians will dam and flood an infected region for a short period, so drowning the louse

Activity in the vineyards east of the Sierra de Cordoba in Argentina *(left)*. This vast plain, east of the Andes foothills, has many enormous wineries fermenting staggering quantities of wine. Two-thirds of Argentina's wines are red; white, rosé, sparkling and fortified wines account for the balance.

Although the Italian influence is greater, white viniferas from France have been planted in reasonable quantities in Argentina. Chardonnay, shown cropping heavily here *(above)*, as well as Chenin Blanc, Ugni Blanc, and Riesling are gaining in popularity.

The vineyards of Argentina are just south of latitude 30°S, where temperatures are equivalent to those of Mediterranean Africa. The vines are therefore trained high on wires *(right)*, as in the Italian trellis system, so that the grapes are shaded and avoid reflected heat from the soil.

in its lair. One-fifth of Argentina's wine is made here, from some 60,000ha (150,000 acres) of irrigated vines, almost entirely Palomino and Pedro Ximénes.

The third most important region is Rio Negro, south of Mendoza, where good dry white wines and sparkling wines are made. Here, farther from the equator, the climate is colder and harder. About one-twentieth of Argentina's wines are made in the region. Other significant regions are Occidente (divided into La Rioja and Catamarca) and Norte, above it, in the far north (divided into Salta, in the south, and Jujuy). East of La Rioja is Cordoba, and east again is Litoral (divided into Buenos Aires and, above it, Sante Fé). East of Santa Fé is the small province of Entre Rios.

Red wines account for two-thirds of Argentina's produce. Italian grape varieties are in evidence, including Barbera, Bonarda, Lambrusco, Nebbiolo, and Sangiovese; and French varieties, including the Cabernets, Merlot, Pinot Noir, and Sirah, have also been planted, although so far with little positive effect. However, the Malbec wines, aged well in oak, remain the country's best so far. For white wines the French *V. viniferas* are in array; they include Chardonnay, Chenin Blanc, Semillon, and Ugni Blanc, together with Silvaner, here called Riesling. Proviar, a subsidiary of Moët & Chandon, provides an excellent sparkling wine. Rio Negro, although in the Andes rain-shadow, has increasing plantings of white grapes in its 18,000ha (45,000 acres) of vineyards, making crisp white wines already sampled liberally in Europe and elsewhere. In the hotter provinces, from San Juan northward, sherry-type wines are made from Palomino and Pedro Ximénes, with surplus production being used for distillation or converted into various concentrates for export.

The Argentine National Wine Institute has done good work to encourage expansion of the industry and the planting of more European vines, but the home consumers remain solidly in favor of low-quality, high-volume wines. This gives rise to a dilemma, for the Argentinians like old-fashioned wines, tending to sweetness and aged for too long to be at their best (as opposed to the situation in the USA, where red wines are inevitably consumed before they are allowed to reach their peak). Also, there are no laws governing place-names, vintage dates, or varietal wine contents. As a result, there arises what would elsewhere be called fraud. Generic titles such as Chablis, Beaujolais, and Rioja are used indiscriminately, and false varieties are attributed, so that a wine labeled (say) Chardonnay may well have been made from Semillon grapes. Foreign importers of these wines, therefore, regard them as no better than run-of-the-mill. Argentina must remain in her own wine-shadow, or introduce laws to define areas, ban false generic titles, and standardize wine qualities and labels, if she wants to develop and benefit from a trusting export market.

Despite financial problems that have overtaken some important state and private wineries, there is sufficient confidence for Seagrams and Moët & Chandon to have invested in Argentine wines. Seagrams have 1,000ha (2,500 acres) of vineyards at San Rafael Mendoza, where the Suter company's Etiqueta Maron Pinot Blanc is the brand-leader, Pinot Blanc being the local name for Chenin Blanc. Also at San Rafael, Seagrams' subsidiary, Bianchi, farm 100ha (250 acres) to produce Chardonnay Particular and Bianchi Borgogna, a misleading name for the country's top-selling red wine. Seagrams' third Argentinian subsidiary, Crillon, with no vineyard of its own, markets 20,000 cases of sparkling Crillon and 130,000 cases of still Embajador each year.

At Florida, Buenos Aires, Moët & Chandon produce top-quality Baron B. and lesser grades of Champaña as well as a number of first-rate still brands from Cabernet Sauvignon, Malbec, Pinot Noir, Sauvignon Blanc, Semillon, and Ugni Blanc.

Peñaflor is the country's largest wine company. The Pulenta family owns its four modern bodegas in Buenos Aires province; among many products, these specialize in the Andean export brand. Also owned by the Pulentas is Trapiche, with 300ha (740 acres) of various vines producing top-quality refreshing wines. Bodegas Lopez in Buenos Aires province have 1,000ha (2,500 acres) of vines; their Cabernet Château Vieux is exported as Casona Lopez, and Château Montchenot as Don Federico. Good wood-aged wines come from Malbec and Merlot grapes. Angel Furlotti at Maipu, also with 1,000ha (2,500 acres) of vineyards in the province, are well known for their blend of Cabernet, Lambrusco, and Merlot. Norton, with 500ha (1,236 acres), make oak-aged Perdriel Cabernet and well balanced white wines from Chardonnay, Riesling and other vines. Goyenechea, with a family-owned estate of 300ha (740 acres) in Buenos Aires, market big red wines under the familiar Aberdeen Angus label.

Orfila, in Mendoza, is a family estate of 275ha (680 acres) planted with Cabernet, Chardonnay, and Sauvignon; the best wines from here are sold under the brand name Cautivo. Flichman, also in Mendoza, market a white wine as Caballero de la Cepa. Here, too, Bodegas La Rural make light Rieslings and Gewürztraminer with commendable care; their wood-aged reds are heavier. Giol is a huge cooperative run by the province of Mendoza, and markets various wines, with Canciller as the principal brand.

In Cordoba, Esmeralda market good Cabernet, Malbec, Sauvignon and other wines; Felicien Cabernet is their chief label. Also in Cordoba, at the Bodega la Rosa, Michel Torino have planted three-quarters of their 300ha (740-acre) estate with white Torrontes to make a fruity white Don David brand.

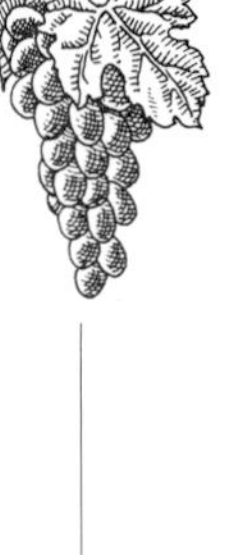

Worldwide, the grape harvest provides full-time work for women in the fall, and Chile is no exception *(left)*. The terrain is not naturally adaptable to mechanical harvesting and none of the international giants, other than the Spanish company Rumasa, has interests here that might lead the way to automation.

# CHILE

Like most of the South American countries, Chile had to wait for the arrival of Italian immigrants to lay the foundations of a recognizable wine industry, despite the fact that the missionaries, following the conquistadors of the sixteenth century, had laid down vines to provide sacramental wines. Two vines provided the nucleus of Chile's earliest vineyards, the Muscat and the País, the latter probably coming from Spain and given this name by the Chileans. By 1556 the vines were well settled around Santiago, and had spread across the mountains into present-day Argentina. Little progress was chronicled over the next 300 years or so, but then, in 1851, came Silvestre Ochagavia, who imported a variety of cuttings from the classic French grapes. With him came French viticulturists who laid down these grapes in the central valley. Now the industry started to grow, and immigrants started to arrive. Today the industry is divided into more than 30,000 small vineyards and relatively few large ones. The government, by making loans, established cooperative wineries and this may account for the old ideas and equipment remaining in the small vineyards, where nearly all growers sell their grapes.

Today the vineyards of Chile are unique. Her 110,000ha (270,000 acres) of vines are stretched over 1,500km (950mi) along the Pacific seaboard between latitudes 25° and 40°S. With the Andes to the east and onshore winds prevailing from the ocean, she has climates ranging from arid in the Atacama desert, in the north, to one of high rainfall around Valdivia, in the south. The polar Humboldt Current produces coastal fogs, just as it does in California, while the Andes mountains and the Atacama desert have successfully prevented the *Phylloxera* pest from attacking Chile's vineyards. Nature has given Chile every possible advantage for growing wine grapes, and—naturally—she makes the best wines of the South American continent. Annual production of wine is roughly 5 million hectoliters (132 million gal), of which a mere one-hundredth is exported. In an endeavor to curb alcoholism some years ago, a limit of 60 liters (15¾ gal) per inhabitant was set as a yearly maximum intake, but average consumption remains well below the limit.

Chile is divided into three main regions. The northern region runs down from the Atacama desert to the river Choapa, in all some 600km (375mi), and what irrigation there is comes from a few rivers flowing down from the Andes; the vineyards are set in these transversal valleys. Here the vines for wine-making are largely Muscat, and the wines are high in alcohol, some being fortified to produce simulated Sherries, Ports or Madeiras. The country's best grapes for the fruitbowl are grown here in the northern region. Rainfall is negligible, except when the Humboldt Current varies its course, bringing warmer water to the coast; then catastrophic rains result, devastating the region and with it the vineyards.

By far the most important wine-making region is the central region, between the Aconcagua river, north of the capital Santiago, and the Maule river, roughly 400km (250mi) south. This embraces the counties of Aconcagua, Santiago, O'Higgins, Colchagua, Curicó, and

This bunch of Sauvignon Blanc grapes *(above)* has ripened to perfection in the Chilean sun. The largest Chilean bodega, owned by Concha y Toro, markets wine from this grape under the brand-name Casillero del Diablo.

Talca, amply watered by the Maipo, Chachapoal, Tinguiririca, Lontué, and Maule rivers. Here there is more limestone and less of the sand and slate found in the other regions. Helped by irrigation, the yield is as high as 60hl/ha. The two best subdistricts of the central region are the Maipo Valley (the best) and the Aconcagua Valley above it. Cabernet Sauvignon and Cabernet Franc are the best red grapes, producing strong, stable wines, deep in color and with a powerful nose. Merlot and Malbec also do well. Although Chilean white wines have not equaled the reds for quality, Sauvignon Blanc and Semillon, the most planted vines, produce good table wines, and the rarer Riesling is even better.

The best part of the southern region lies between the Maule river and the Bio-Bio river, 200km (125mi) to the south. The wines are less interesting here, possibly because the bulk-giving País grape is the most widely planted. Cabernet, Malbec and Semillon are also planted, however, and much of Chile's wine for everyday drinking is produced by blending here.

It is noticeable that the international wine companies have not tested the Chilean potential, probably because of the mercurial political scene, although this is now more stable than for many years past. The National Council of External Commerce has decreed that exports must have at least 12% vol. alcohol for white wine and 11.5% for red wine, and the wines must be clear, healthy, and not less than one year old. By another law, Chilean growers each have a maximum production figure and any surplus has to be disposed of, either by export or by conversion to industrial alcohol. Also, if the national permitted production of wines is exceeded, wineries which have overshot their maximums must dispose of their excesses and declare how such disposal has been effected.

The largest bodega in Chile is owned by Concha y Toro, a public company with 1,600ha (4,000 acres) at Pirgue, south of Santiago. Here Marqués de Casa Concha is the best known brand for Cabernet Sauvignon, and Casillero del Diablo for other wines, including Riesling and Sauvignon Blanc. Concha y Toro produce 1.1 million cases annually here, and have opened another bodega in Maipu; they also control Tocornal, an estate of 150ha (370 acres) in the Puente Alto.

Undurraga, in Santiago province with 250ha (620 acres), produces annually just under half a million cases of oak-aged wines labelled Viejo Roble ("old oak") and sparkling wines in the Champagne tradition; one-third of the produce is exported. Consiño Macul, a family-owned bodega in the province with 375ha (925 acres) of vines, produces excellent light-red Don Luis and dark-red Don Matias and Antiguas Reservas Cabernets. One-third of its annual output of 300,000 cases is of white wine from French varietals and Palacio Consiño vines. Santa Carolina, one of the biggest bodegas in Chile, grows Cabernet, Merlot, Cot, Semillon, Sauvignon and some Chardonnay at Santiago to satisfy an immense market for reasonably priced wines.

In Talca province, José Canepa have 500ha (1,250 acres) of vineyards in Isla de Maipo Ciricó and in Lontué, and make excellent varietal wines including red Gran Brindis Cabernet and white Gran Brindis Semillon. 500,000 cases of these and other fine wines are marketed yearly. In the Maipo Valley is Viña Linderos, founded as early as 1865, a small bodega making excellent Cabernet Linderos para Guarda and other branded wines for selected clients in Chile. Exports are mainly to the northern countries of South America, but also to the UK. Founded in the same year in Talca province, the San Pedro bodega sells Gato Blanco, a reliable and popular white wine, and a Gato Negro red. The company is controlled by the Spanish giant Rumasa.

The official classifications for Chilean wines are: Courant at one year old; Special at two; Reserve at four; and Gran Vino at six and over. Reserve is thought to be the best, Gran Vino tending to develop an oak-barrel taint.

## BRAZIL

With only 80,000ha (200,000 acres) of vines as yet developed in Brazil, the international wine groups have already claimed their stakes in the huge domestic-market potential. The vineyards are in the most southerly states, for almost all of Brazil is too near the equator for quality-wine production. Rio Grande do Sul is the principal wine region, while Santa Catarina has vineyards on a smaller scale. The modern industry dates from the years after World War One, when Italian settlers brough *V. vinifera* vines with them to add to the labruscanas, particularly Isabella, Niagara, Delaware, and Concord, used by earlier Portuguese settlers. Rio Grande do Sul, at the southern tip of Brazil, is bounded by Uruguay to the south, Argentina to the west, and the Atlantic Ocean. Immediately north is the province of Santa Catarina. The warm wet Atlantic climate is unhelpful for growing *V. vinifera* grapes: the labruscanas tolerate this climate better.

The name of the largest wine producer in Brazil, at Caxias do Sul, is more staggering than its volume product: Industria Comércio e Navegação, Sociedade Vinicola Rio Grandense, Ltda, which is generally shortened to Rio Grandense; its wines, both red and white, sell under the Granja União label.

International companies that have already invested in Brazilian bodegas include Cinzano, Domecq, Heublein, Martini & Rossi, Moët & Chandon, and National Distillers. Hugh Johnson reports that the four best wines of the country selected at a 1981 Brazilian Wine Olympiad were Champagne M. Chandon (Profivin), white Lejou (Dreher/Heublein), rosé

Moscato Adega Medieval (Viamão), and red Vinho Velho do Museu (Vinhos Finos Santa Rosa—Château Lacave).

## OTHER SOUTH AMERICAN COUNTRIES

Four other South American countries produce wine: of them only Uruguay is seriously in business. The others are Peru, Bolivia, and Colombia.

Uruguay, between latitudes 30° and 35°S, is well placed to produce good wine. Included in her annual production of 900,000hl (23⅔ million gal) are all types of wine—red, white, pink, sparkling, fortified, and vermouths. The sparkling and fortified wines, unfortunately, use the generic styles "Champagne" and "Port." The vines used are Tannat, from Madiran in the French Pyrénées (locally called Harriague); Vidiella, of unknown origin; and Cabernet. Some Barbera and Nebbiolo from Italy complete the red portfolio. White wines are made from Semillon and Pinot Blanc. Isabella is also planted, but lowers the quality of Uruguayan wines.

Physically, Uruguay is an extension of the Brazilian plain, and her *cuchillas* (volcanic hills) rise to a mere 600m (2,000ft). Moderate temperatures of 22°C (72°F) in the summer (January and February) and 10°C (50°F) in the winter (July) are experienced in the vineyards, which are mainly in the departments of Montevideo, Canelones, San José, and Maldonado, along the river Plate, and in Soriano and Paysandú, next to Argentina. Uruguayan wines may occasionally reach Brazil, but are otherwise totally accounted for by the local thirst.

Peru has been wine-making ever since 1566 when Francesco de Carabantes planted vines near Ica, south of the capital, Lima. Since Peru touches the equator in the north and reaches only 18°S at its southern extremity, it is not surprising that her vineyards are limited to 8,000ha (20,000 acres); they produce mainly fortified wines as well as some table wines in the Spanish style. The vineyards remain around Ica and Lima and near the Inca cities of Cuzco and Arequipa: a few vineyards in the south are in the department of Moquega.

Bolivia, lying mainly between latitudes 10° and 20°S, is not a wine producer by definition and only 2,000ha (5,000 acres) of vineyards are planted with grapes for fermentation. The total annual wine production—a negligible 6,000hl (159,000 gal) of sweet wine—tells its own story.

Colombia, on the equator, has only one-tenth as many hectares under vines as Bolivia. The product is almost entirely of sweet wine fortified with brandy, miscalled "Manzanilla" and "Port."

Peru is not a serious winemaking country: it is too far north, with the northernmost tip of the country actually touching the equator. Beyond the vineyards in this picture *(below)* is the coastal town of Ica. Most of the wine produced here is fortified in the Spanish style, a practice that started in Ica in the sixteenth century.

# AUSTRALIA AND NEW ZEALAND

## AUSTRALIA

The wine history of Australia is almost precisely as old as the settlement itself. In 1787 Captain Arthur Phillip and his fleet set out from the Thames with a cargo including "plants for the settlement," and among these were the first vines to enter Australia. Planted in 1788 in the damp climate too near the ocean at Sydney, they developed anthracnose, or "black spot," and died. Three years later Governor Phillip planted 1.2ha (3 acres) of vines 20km (12mi) inland on the Parramatta, where there was a drier climate. At the turn of the eighteenth century, Captain John McArthur became the first man to plant vines on a commercial scale: this he did on land he had been granted, which he named Camden Park, near Sydney. But a feud between McArthur and Governor Bligh led McArthur through many vicissitudes before he lived to become established in affairs of state as well as in Australian viticulture.

Australia *(below)* has made wine ever since the late eighteenth century. Today many of her wines excel in world markets.

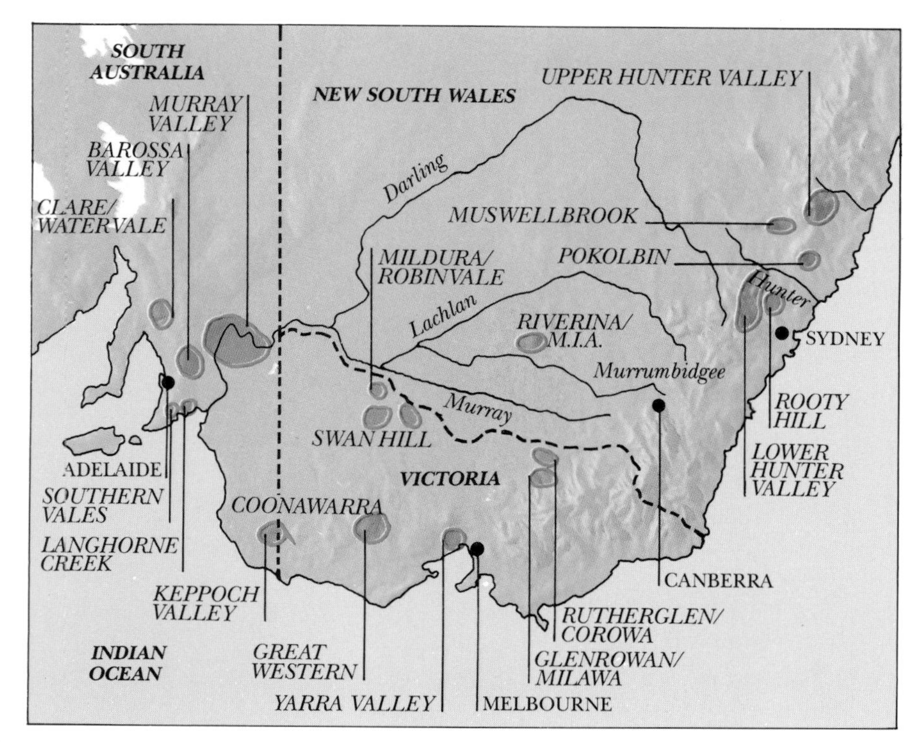


More important was the arrival of James Busby, an enterprising young Scot, who received a grant of 800ha (2,000 acres) of land in the Hunter River district in 1824; he named the area Kirkton, and it was later to be famed for its wines. Busby's great project was his tour of the vineyards of Europe, from which he returned with nearly 700 vine specimens. These he offered to the government, which set up the Botanical Gardens at Sydney, where over half the vines were struck successfully in 1833. They became the strain and source of Australia's vineyard propagation.

The industry did not flourish, however, until P. B. Burgoyne & Company in 1872 started marketing a Burgundy-type tonic wine for export. In England the wine was popular, and several shippers made fortunes from it: Burgoynes, with the brands Harvest and Tintara; Gilbeys, with Rubicon; Stephen Smith, with Keystone; and Powells, with Emu.

The first of two disasters to attack the wine industry affected the state of Victoria alone. In 1890, Victoria produced 72,000hl (1.9 million gal) of wine, compared with 31,000hl (820,000 gal) from New South Wales and 23,000hl (608,000 gal) from South Australia. Then phylloxera attacked the vines of Victoria, first in Geelong, next in Bendigo, and finally in the northeast of the state. The vineyards were devastated and the cost of replacing them with phylloxera-resistant grafts was prohibitive. The land was converted to other uses, and Victoria's wine industry could only slowly regenerate itself over the next three-quarters of a century. Her lead has never been recovered, so that today, while South Australia produces 2,000,000hl (53 million gal) of wine and New South Wales 700,000hl (18½ million gal), Victoria produces only 350,000hl (9¼ million gal) in an average year.

Disaster again visited the industry when the

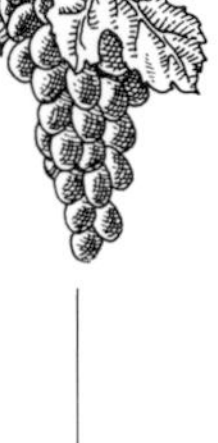

Bruce-Page Government overplanted grapes in Australia under a scheme for the employment of repatriated soldiers after World War One. This led to a surplus and a subsequent slump. The industry was finally saved by the government, who subsidized the making of brandy, so that in due course a massive export market for fortified wines was built up. The old-style tonic "Burgundy" was forgotten, as the trade in fortified wines rose to over17,000,000hl (450 million gal) in 1927 and then slowly subsided; today exports are nearer 100,000hl (2⅔ million gal) annually.

Through all the changes, the Australian vineyards have mostly stayed in the families of original settlers, and slowly a tradition of fine-wine production in small quantities but in many varieties, has developed—wines that are splendid yet different. Big strong red wines have a flavor redolent of their native soil, and white wines of remarkable character and zest, yet low in acidity, are now produced. The beginnings of a modern industry can be recognized.

Australia has been quick to appreciate her advantages. A remarkable consistency of climate frees her from the vintage problems experienced in Europe; and her soils are such that the yield of a single vine may be processed to make wines of widely differing types; in fact, "type" is today a key word in Australian wine language. Up-to-date methods have helped to make Australian wines equal to the wines of California and a constant challenge to those of Europe.

The best Australian red wines come from Cabernet Sauvignon and Shiraz (Hermitage) grapes, which in fact blend well together. Merlot, Cinsault, and Pinot Noir are also prominent, mainly for blending. Rhine Riesling and Semillon are completely adaptable to both climate and soils and produce superb white wines, flowery and dry, that age well. Chardonnay seems set for success, too, just as in California, but it has not yet been fully tried. The Portuguese Verdelho, Italian Trebbiano, and Marsanne from the northern Rhône are used for fuller white wines, and also for blending. The brown Frontignac and Muscadelle grapes are used for dessert wines.

There is as yet no steadying influence on Australian wine labels, which may use names of grapes and their growers, their vineyard or district (or both) their vinifier, their vintage (which in the equable climate is rarely meaningful) and (presumably for the real enthusiast) their bin numbers. Happily, generic names are not as frequent as they were.

## SOUTH AUSTRALIA

The vineyards of South Australia are all contained between the north-south state boundary, east of Adelaide, and the Spencer Gulf to its west. The vines were first planted in 1837 and since then the region has suffered virtually no setback peculiar to itself: many families have remained to celebrate the centenary of their ancestors' vineyards. South

In the open territory of the Barossa valley northeast of Melbourne, the Orlando Wine Company has over 100ha (250 acres) of vineyard and one of Australia's largest and best equipped wineries *(top)*.

A corner of Brown Bros Winery at Milawa, Victoria *(above)*. This family business is now in the hands of John Brown and his four sons: John Jr, winemaker; Peter, *vigneron*; Ross, sales; and Roger, technical development.

A battery of stainless-steel tanks in the Barossa valley at Penfolds' Tanunda plant *(left)*, famous for its red wines. Penfold's Grange Hermitage is acknowledged as the supreme red wine of the southern hemisphere; it is made from Shiraz with some Cabernet.

After 18 months' maturation in small wood casks, Penfold's Grange Hermitage is matured for a further three years before being sold. The bottles are kept in these wooden bins *(above)* in the bottling warehouse.

Such was Grange Hermitage's unique style that at first — in the early 1950s — it was ridiculed; however, its amazing fruit and oak flavors have prevailed *(above right)*.

The famous Grange vineyard is close to the city of Adelaide *(right)*. Penfold have over 400ha (1,000 acres) of vineyards in the Barossa valley. The Grange Hermitage production process is a secret.

Max Schubert is the chief winemaker at Penfold and it was he who created the Grange Hermitage classic *(right)*. His object was to create wines that would last and improve for 20 years or more.

To give its best performance, every machine requires regular attention and service. Here Penfold engineers are surveying the "wet end" of a crushing machine *(far right)* used for red-wine production.

Rhine Riesling, grown in the Barossa valley near Rowlands Flat, on a soil of clay, loam and limestone, is the source of Orlando's "Prädicat"-style wines, marketed as "Auslese Rhine Riesling" and "Steingarten Spätlese" *(above left)*.

Gunter Prass *(above)* is the winemaker at Orlando, duly proud of the "Auslese" vintages that have appeared almost annually since 1972. This wine is bottled early and is best for drinking after five or six years.

One of Orlando's vineyards *(left)* is devoted to grapes for "Steingarten Spätlese". Though famed for these white wines, Orlando also produce an excellent Jacob's Creek Claret and a range of other red and white wines.

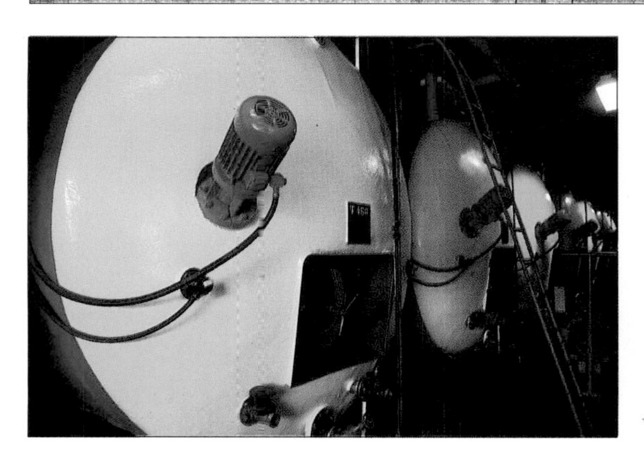

The heads of a row of fermentation tanks at Orlando's Rowlands Flat winery *(far left)*. Cold fermentation in specially jacketed tanks is used for white wines, with great benefit to the ultimate wine quality.

White wine travels through the bottling process at Orlando *(left)*. The company, owned by Reckitt & Colman, is renowned among Australian wine-producers for its advanced technology.

PETALUMA
1979 RHINE RIESLING
750ml
PRODUCE OF AUSTRALIA BOTTLED AT PICCADILLY SA

Australia now produces two-thirds of all Australia's wine.

The Barossa Valley, 50km (30mi) north of Adelaide, is the largest and most important region; fine Rieslings, produced in the easterly Eden Valley and Pewsey Vale, bear witness to the German settlers of 1840 who opened up this area. Penfolds, now owned by brewers Tooth & Company, have the largest property in the valley, with over 400ha (1,000 acres). Mostly they concentrate on red wines, although Kaiser Stuhl, the Barossa Valley cooperative recently acquired by Penfolds, has a well established reputation for Rhine Rieslings, marketed as Green, Gold, or Purple Ribbon. Penfolds have many brands for red wines, notably Grange Hermitage for Australia's best wine, aged in American oak from the Shiraz grape. Henri Claret, Bin 707 Cabernet, and, from Penfolds' estate in the south, Bin 128 Coonawarra Shiraz, are among their best brands.

The interior of a 275hl (7,150gal) stainless-steel fermentation tank at Penfold's Nuriootpa winery *(below)*. This red-wine tank has a central chute through which pass the crushed grapes to enter the vat at a level below the screen that keeps the cap of skins submerged.

Seppelt, with offices in Adelaide and headquarters at Barossa, is a public company with 650ha (1,600 acres) of vines in South Australia, 365ha (900 acres) in Victoria and 120ha (300 acres) in New South Wales; yet these vineyards supply only one-third of the grapes needed for the company's huge variety of wines. Great Western is their brand leader in Australian "Champagne." Other brands include Chalambar, for their Bin "Burgundies," Moyston Claret, Black Label for Shiraz, Cabernet, and Rhine Riesling, and Para Liqueur port.

The Orlando wineries, started in 1847 at Rowland Flat, Barossa, by Johann Gramp, is now owned by Reckitt & Colman. Some 225ha (550 acres) of vines are spread between Barossa, the Eden Valley and Ramco Riverland. Orlando is recognized as one of the most technically advanced companies in Australia. White wines are its speciality, with firm Rhine Rieslings, well made Spätleses and Ausleses, and a spicy Eden Valley Gewürztraminer. Jacob's Creek is a good dry claret. A William Jacob label is used for exports.

The Tollana company, original producers of brandy, has come into prominence in the last 15 years for Tollana-branched Rhine Rieslings and Gewürztraminers. These come from their vineyards at Woodbury Estate, Eden Valley and Waikerie, probably amounting in all to nearly 400ha (1,000 acres). Equally good red wine from Eden Valley is marketed as Eden Valley Shiraz.

Smith's Yalumba Company, with 250ha (600 acres) in the Barossa area and another 250ha at Waikerie, now specialize in a range of white wines, especially their Pewsey Vale Rhine Riesling and a drier Carte d'Or Riesling. Their Signature brands of Cabernet/Shiraz, Cabernet/Malbec and other barrel-aged red wines sell as well as any in the country. Over 100 years of "port" production should convince their customers that Galway Pipe is a worthy bottle. Perhaps one wine-lover who described Smith's Yalumba as an uppercrust winery was making a Freudian slip?

Saltram, with 100ha (250 acres) in the Barossa valley, are now owned by Seagrams. Most grapes are bought in; they make some good red and white varieties. Mamre Brook Cabernet remains an excellent red wine, and the more recent Chardonnays are better than good-value white wines. Henschke, at Keyneton in the Barossa valley, market the famous Hill of Grace and Mount Edelstone brands of Shiraz, the former fuller and the latter more subtle in character. Rhine Riesling, which is also planted on the 100ha (250-acre) estate produces an excellent crisp dry Riesling wine.

The McLaren Vale area lies immediately south of Adelaide and has a name for powerful red wines and excellent dessert wines, all of which benefit from the warm climate. However, newcomers—Chardonnay together with Riesling plantations in the eastern Lofty Hills—are making their mark. Thomas Hardy is the largest producer: grapes from 130ha (320 acres) of vineyards and twice as many bought in give an annual production of 750,000 cases. Some of Australia's best fortified wines come from Thomas Hardy's McLaren Vale winery, and blends from plantings in the cooler Keppoch area to the south produce Siegersdorf Rieslings. Nottage Hill Claret is strong for its type but excellent, and Eileen Hardy red wines, mainly from Shiraz, are expensive but worth it. Hardy's have recently bought the Reynella company in Southern Vales, as well as Houghton in Western Australia.

D'Arenberg have 60ha (150 acres) of mixed vines at McLaren Vale: a red "Burgundy" from Grenache with 25% Shiraz is a specialty, and a dry white Palomino figures well in their list.

The small Clare/Watervale region, some 65km (40mi) north of Barossa, grows good Rhine Riesling vines on hills ranging to 380m (1,200ft), as well as having Shiraz and Cabernet plantings for fine red wines. Stanley's are the leading wine-makers, buying in most of their grapes and marketing Leasingham Cabernet, Bin 56 Cabernet/Malbec, and Bin 5 and Bin 7 Rhine Rieslings (Bin 5 is the sweeter). Quelltaler, after being bought by Rémy Martin of France, are producing new-style Rieslings and reds from Cabernet Sauvignon and Shiraz that have taken their prices into the top range, where they certainly belong. Andrew and Jane Mitchell run a new winery, Mitchells, concentrating on Rhine Riesling at Watervale and Seven Hill, with some Cabernet Sauvignon at the latter: their wines are interesting and promising, especially those from Seven Hill.

The remaining vineyard regions of South Australia are Coonawarra, 400km (250mi) southeast of Adelaide; the irrigated Riverland vineyards on the Murray river, northeast of Adelaide; and the diminutive but historic Langhorn Creek, making dessert and strong red wines a few kilometers southeast of Adelaide. Coonawarra leaders include Katnook, founded in 1979, with 200ha (500 acres) down to Cabernet Sauvignon, Rhine Riesling, Gewürztraminer, Chardonnay, and Sauvignon Blanc. Their Chardonnays and Rieslings clearly come from fully ripe grapes, while their Gewürztraminers are somewhat lighter; their Cabernet is also on the big side. Redman's winery concentrates on red wines from Cabernet Sauvignon and Shiraz. The Cabernet is excellent and their claret, from straight Shiraz, is equally good after long bottle-aging. In the Riverland Irrigation Area the Angove family markets the well known Bookmark brand of Rhine Riesling wine; Tregrehan claret is another of theirs. All Angove wines sell at everyday prices.

## NEW SOUTH WALES

Sydney, on the border of the Tasman Sea, is the pivotal point from which to measure distances in New South Wales.

Hunter Valley, the most important wine region in the state, is 160km (100mi ) north; here the red wines stem from Shiraz and Cabernet Sauvignon and the whites from Semillon ("Riesling") and Chardonnay. Cloud tempers the hot summer sun, but unwanted rain can fall at vintage. There are many substantial wineries in the Lower and Upper Hunter valleys. Dominant are the Lindeman, McWilliams, Arrowfield, and Saxondale companies.

The Lindeman organization has successively acquired the wine properties of Ben Ean (1912), Leo Buring (1962) and Rouge Homme (1965), and were themselves taken over by the Philip Morris Company in 1971. They own 150ha (365 acres) of vines in Corowa and the Lower Hunter Valley, and extensive vineyards in Victoria and South Australia. Australia's third biggest wine company, they have about 400 labels and a substantial share of the cask market. Perpetuating a name dating back to 1870 is Ben Ean Moselle, Australia's most popular wine.

McWilliams have 180ha (450 acres) in the Hunter Valley and more in the Riverina

Red-wine fermentation tanks at Orlando are not jacketed *(below)*. Cabernet Sauvignon, Cabernet Franc, and Merlot grapes with some Malbec are grown. The brand-name "William Jacob" is used for a number of these lines for export.

The Petaluma Winery is a newcomer to the Australian industry; its winery at Piccadilly, near Adelaide, therefore has modern equipment *(left)*. In the foreground is a cooler for must and behind it is the initial crushing equipment.

The shallow, skeletal nature of the shale base to the soil at Piccadilly *(right)* means that the vines have to be planted well apart to give each as much soil moisture as possible. However, gaps of 3.5m (11½ft) between rows and 2.5m (8¼ft) between plants result in a 50% reduction in yields.

Seppelt have vineyards *(inset)* totaling about 1,200ha (3,000 acres) found in Victoria (Great Western, Drumborg, and Rutherglen) and South Australia (Keppoch, the Barossa valley — shown here — and Partalunga), with a few small lots elsewhere.

The Petaluma vineyard *(below)* is over 500m (1,650ft) above sea-level on the side of the Mount Lofty range: with a southwest aspect and the lowest night temperatures in Australia, the Rhine Riesling grapes ripen slowly and develop extra flavor in the process.

Irrigated Area, where they have three wineries. Philip Hermitage and Mt Pleasant Elizabeth Riesling are their best known brands, together with Mark View "Champagne." In the Upper Valley Arrowfield have over 400ha (1,000 acres) of Cabernet Sauvignon, Shiraz, Chardonnay, Gewürztraminer, Rhine Riesling, and Semillon.

Saxondale vineyards have over 325ha (800 acres) in Fordwich and Pokolbin, mostly planted with Cabernet Sauvignon, Shiraz, Chardonnay, and Semillon. So far the white wines exceed the red, and more varieties, both red and white, are expected from the energetic Stanlee management. The Rosemount Estate in the Upper Hunter Valley specializes in Rhine Riesling and Gewürztraminer, which have each won gold medals. Also made are great Semillon and Chardonnay wines matured in wood; and a Riesling Trockenbeerenauslese appeared in 1982 to delight both manufacturer and customer.

In the Mudgee region, some 160km (100mi) northwest of Sydney, the growers have developed their own appellation system, such is their pride in the local wines. Craigmoor, established in 1858, is the oldest Mudgee vineyard: 52.5ha (130 acres) are planted with seven vines, mainly Chardonnay, Semillon, and other white grapes. However, their Shiraz "Port," matured in rum casks, represents a tradition predating the Van Heyets, who took over in 1980; they are showing an ability to make subtle wines.

Two Italian engineers, Salteri and Nettis, own the Montrose vineyard of 45ha (111 acres), and have added Sangiovese, Nebbiolo, and Barbera to a standard list of French and German viniferas. Their wines, red and white, have the strength that would be expected of them in far-off Italy. The tank-fermented Montrose Brut is a good buy.

Excellent Cabernets and Chardonnays at modest prices come from the 40ha (100-acre) Huntingdon estate owned by Bob and Wendy Roberts. Miramar vineyards, with much the same grape varieties on their 32ha (80 acres) at and near Miramar, have a name for true Chardonnays, Cabernets, and Shiraz.

The Riverina or Murrumbidgee Irrigation Area (MIA), 500km (300mi) west of Sydney, is renowned as a flat fertile region for fruit-growing. McWilliams (see page 289) are biggest in the area, with wineries at Hanwood, Yenda, and Beelbangera. Huge quantities of grapes are bought in to supplement grapes from their 81ha (200 acres) of vines near Griffith; the product is mostly bulk and flagon wine, together with some good dessert wines.

Three small districts complete the New South Wales contribution to Australian wines. Rooty Hill is the remains of an area on the outskirts of Sydney. Here the Richmond State winery survives with 9ha (22 acres) shared between Shiraz and Cabernet Sauvignon, making good red wines at bargain prices, and incidentally taking the occasional gold medal to boot. Cowra is a small, new region 320km (200mi) west of Sydney: so far it has earned renown for its Chardonnay, and there is potential for expansion here. And Corowa, on the Victoria State border, is the southernmost of the New South Wales vineyards, close to Rutherglen; it is known chiefly for Lindeman's Corowa Muscats.

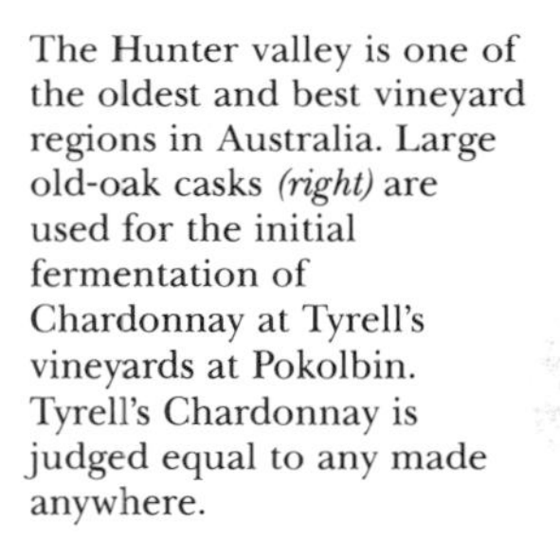

The Hunter valley is one of the oldest and best vineyard regions in Australia. Large old-oak casks *(right)* are used for the initial fermentation of Chardonnay at Tyrell's vineyards at Pokolbin. Tyrell's Chardonnay is judged equal to any made anywhere.

Rothbury Estate is close to Tyrell's in the Hunter valley. It is renowned for excellent, rich and powerful white wine made from the Semillon; Rothbury's red wines have great promise, too. Young white wines, fermenting in these stainless-steel tanks *(left)* are being film-cooled.

An assistant winemaker at Rothbury Estate checking a sample of Semillon for clarity *(below left)*. The wine ages well and is at its best after five years. Rothbury have nearly 365ha (900 acres) of vineyard shared between Shiraz, Cabernet Sauvignon, Semillon and Chardonnay vines.

Before fermentation the Semillon grape-juice is cooled and the solids are removed in a high-speed centrifuge *(below)*. This is one of several stages at Rothbury's designed to ensure that the finished wine retains its regional and varietal characteristics.

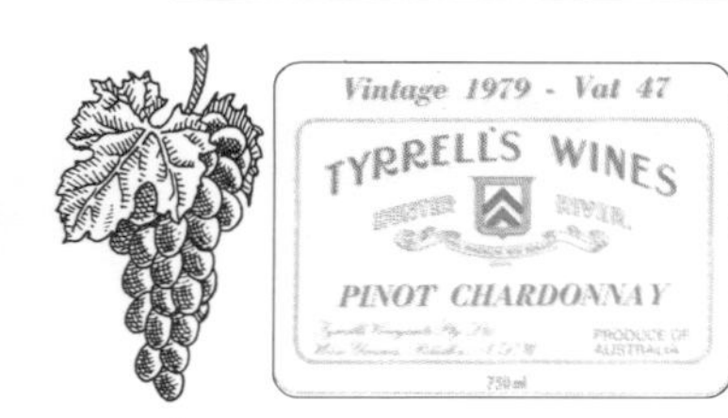

1979 was a good vintage for Tyrrell's Chardonnay *(top left)*, one of Australia's premier white wines. Although best known for Chardonnay, Tyrrell's also produces Pinot Noir *(left center)*.

Wine tastings may be combined with staff conferences at Rothbury *(right)*, but if great decisions have to be made they may be restricted to a few experts. Each year distinctive white and red parcels are held to be sold, if they subsequently mature successfully, as "Individual Paddock" wines.

Rothbury produce distinctive red wines under various vineyard names; their plantings are mainly of Hermitage (Shiraz) and Cabernet Sauvignon, which may be blended or otherwise, according to the year. These Hermitage grapes are in their final ripening stage *(below)*.

A view across the Lower Hunter valley in New South Wales *(below right)*. The microclimate here provides the essential characteristic of all major wine regions: a slow ripening cycle. Rothbury vineyards are seen in the foreground.

Seen in the halflight of the cellars at Milawa is John Brown Jr *(left)*, winemaker son of proprietor John Brown. He is nosing a Noble Riesling of the 1976 vintage, which was best for drinking in 1985.

A comprehensive view of the Brown Bros vineyards and winery at Milawa *(above)* The vineyard is in one of the few areas of Australia where noble rot occurs enabling Browns to produce Noble Riesling in most years. It is luscious, aromatic and sweet, with great finesse.

## VICTORIA

Melbourne, at the top of Port Phillip Bay, is central to most of the state of Victoria. The two most important wine regions are the Valley of the Murray river, 240km (150mi) to Melbourne's north, where the Mildura Irrigated Area plays a dominant part in Victoria's wine industry; and northeast Victoria, between Milawa and Rutherglen on the New South Wales border.

The Lindeman organization owns 160ha (400 acres) of vineyards at Karadoc in the Sunraysia district; these are mainly planted for the production of cask wines. The Mildara vineyards at Merbein, near Mildura, founded in 1891, have 30ha (75 acres) at Irymple, Mildura, and buy in most of their grapes; they produce excellent "Sherry." Mildara also have 240ha (600 acres) of vines just over the state border at Coonawarra growing grapes for table wines—especially well balanced Cabernets. Tisdall of Echuca is a new company owned by Dr Peter Tisdall, with 80ha (200 acres) of vines at Rosbercon, Echuca, and another 80ha at Mt Helen in the Strathbogie hills of central Victoria. Cabernet, Chardonnay, and Rhine Riesling, marketed under the Mt Helen label, are creating considerable interest, and Merlot from Echuca grapes is a sound red wine.

Between Milawa and Rutherglen is the northeast Victoria region, long renowned for dessert Muscats and excellent full Hermitage wines; a number of wineries are more recently building a reputation for white wines as well. Four brothers of the Brown family have now added vineyards in the hills to their 120ha (300 acres) at Milawa and Mystic Park; the original vineyards are famed for Cabernets and Shiraz, and particularly for Liqueur Muscat, a specialty of the region. Now the new vineyards, 760m (2,500ft) up, at Whitelands are planted with white grapes, and the first-class wines emerging include Chardonnay, dry Muscat, and Late Harvest Rhine Riesling. St Leonards winery, at Wahgunyah, also owned by the Browns, is likewise making a success of white wines, using Chardonnay and Semillon. Morris Wines, at the Mia Mia vineyards in Rutherglen, have turned a hand to good white-wine production since being absorbed into Orlando Wines (see page 288) of South Australia. The Morris business was founded on superb old Muscats and Tokays, the latter from vines at Balldale, New South Wales.

All Saints, established in 1864, have 105ha (260 acres) of vineyards at Wahgunyah; the grapes include Palomino for Old Tawny "Port." Very Old "Madeira" and some good Muscats are made, with red wines, from Shiraz and Cabernet blends, tending to be big with little delicacy. Baileys at Glenrowan produce another strong red, the well known Bundarra Hermitage, which can improve for 20 years. Campbells at Rutherglen, already known for their sweet Muscats, Tokays and 'Port', have recently introduced refreshing dry white wines. Chambers Rosewood, also at Rutherglen, remain true to their old liqueur Muscat and Tokay, together with red wines for which the

Rhine Riesling grapes from the extensive vineyards of Brown Brothers at Milawa are fed into this hopper *(right)* before being discharged into a destemmer. Destemming is unusual for white wine, but necessary here because of the high (sticky) sugar content of late-picked grapes affected by noble rot.

district is famous. Stanton & Killeen there market excellent red wines from Cabernet and Shiraz under the Moodemere label.

Goulburn Valley, named as a wine region mainly because of its isolated location 160km (100mi) north of Melbourne, has but two wineries, Château Tahbilk and Mitchelton, both on the banks of the beautiful Goulburn river. Tahbilk, dating from 1860, complements these surroundings with a winery like a nineteenth-century farm, its recessed tower, ample barns, and tall trees standing as though created only to epitomize the serenity of a settlers' paradise. It is also one of Australia's best wine producers. Under the direction and ownership of Eric Purbrick, superb dry white Marsanne wine starts crisp and fruity to round off with age into incredible subtleness. Cabernets and Shiraz are matured for six to seven years. The prices are fairly, almost too fairly, held down. Mitchelton, owned by the Dorado Wine Company of Melbourne, is also an unusual edifice but in the modern manner. Marsanne and Semillon wines aged in wood and an excellent Riesling bear the Mitchelton label, while lesser wines are branded Thomas Mitchell

The Great Western and Avoca region, 240km (150mi) west of Melbourne, has the old winery used by the Seppelts company for making fine sparkling wines. A few newcomers are also going for sparkling-wine production, not without success. North of this area is the central Victoria region, surrounding the gold-mining towns of Ballarat and Bendigo. Balgownie was the first winery in the area, built in 1969, and the wines aged since then and now appearing on the market include a beautiful Cabernet Sauvignon and promising wines from Hermitage, Chardonnay, and Pinot Noir grapes. Other newcomers include Château le Amon, Taltarni, and Yellowglen.

Finally, the Yarra Valley, 50km (30mi) east of Melbourne, is reviving after a relapse as a vineyard area; it is cool and well suited to light dry-white wine production. Yarra Yering was the first winery, established in 1969. Mount Mary, St Huberts, and Yerinberg are all making good wines, including fine reds. There is a small wine activity at Geelong to the west of Port Phillip Bay.

## WESTERN AUSTRALIA

There are four wine regions in the state, of which Margaret River, 320km (200mi) south of Perth, now seems established as the most important and go-ahead. The Swan Valley region, outside Perth, is also important, and can justifiably be proud of its firmly established wines of white and red Burgundy types, and its well finished dry white wines. Indeed Evans & Tate and Sandalfords both have a very firm foot in each region. The former have vineyards at Redbrook, Margaret River, and at Gnangara and Bakers Hill in Swan Valley. Shiraz produces softer and fuller wine at Gnangara than the reds from Margaret River. Sandalfords make a white Burgundy-style wine at Swan Valley, using a blend of Chenin Blanc, Semillon, Muscadelle and Verdelho to produce an aromatic wine which attains great character after aging for seven years.

At Margaret River, Riesling Auslese, Verdelho and a fruity Cabernet are the best wines. Another notable winery at Margaret River is Leeuwin, founded in 1974, making wine in a superclass of its own from Rhine Riesling and Gewürztraminer grapes grown on a 90ha (222-acre) estate close to the ocean; Hermitage, Cabernet, and Pinot Noir are all promising here. The smaller Moss Wood company, with their long-aging Moss Wood Cabernet, set the style that has made the Margaret River famous, and their Chardonnay and Pinot Noir are equally good. Vasse Felix, at Cowaramup in the Margaret River Valley, have also specialized in a dark Cabernet that will age well, and in excellent late-picked Riesling and Gewürztraminer.

Houghton/Valencia, owned by Thomas Hardy, at Swan Valley, have huge vineyards at Houghton and Valencia, and more at Moondah Brook, north of Perth. They are reckoned to have the best Cabernet in Western Australia. Their white "Burgundy" is lighter but more subtle.

## QUEENSLAND AND TASMANIA

Just north of the New South Wales border is the only wine-producer of Queensland, with 10ha (25 acres) of vines at Ballandean. The Robinson Family Winery has planted Cabernet with Shiraz and Chardonnay, Gewürztraminer, and a little Rhine Riesling. So far north, the red wines have more than enough sun, but they are well made. Not surprisingly, the white wines are not up to the same standard.

Tasmania, comfortably in the wine-growing grape-band, has attracted growers of French and German vines which so far do much better in the north around Launceston than further south near Hobart. At Pipers Brook, Launceston, Heemskerk have 20ha (50 acres)—and more for development—so far planted with Cabernet, Pinot Noir, Chardonnay and Gewürztraminer. The red wines may need a little more warmth or later harvesting, but are nevertheless promising. The Pipers Brook Company, in the same locale overlooking the Bass Strait, have the same plantings with Rhine Riesling, Merlot, and Cabernet Franc added, and here Dr Andrew Pirie, the wine-maker, has selected the nearest to the ideal, cool moist climate that he could find. The results are excellent Riesling and Chardonnay and full flavored Cabernet wines. The Launceston area is set for success.

Moorila, at Berridale, Hobart, have 8ha (20 acres) down to Cabernet Sauvignon, Pinot Noir, and Rhine Riesling. The Riesling does well, but the Cabernet and Pinot are problematic, tending to greenness. Frost, birds and underripeness complicate the wine-maker's cycle. Possibly it is all a matter of microclimate.

# NEW ZEALAND

The vine was introduced to New Zealand some 160 years ago by Samuel Marsden, chaplain to the New South Wales government, and James Busby (see page 284), said to be the first British resident in New Zealand. In 1840 French settlers planted vines at Akaroa, and three years later Germans planted vines at Nelson, but phylloxera killed them all off. Right up to World War Two there is no record of there being more than 270ha (670 acres) of vines in the country; then, however, the war cut off overseas supplies of wine and New Zealand had to look to her own resources.

The country's dilemma had been the fashion for fortified wines, which could be made in the cool New Zealand climate only by the addition of up to 30% cane sugar. But, thanks to an educated interest in table wines that started slowly but has recently intensified, New Zealanders are producing, from vines grown in the perfect soils and equable climate of their country, red, white, and sparkling table wines challenging the best of Europe and California. The country has some 200 licensed wine-makers today.

The industry developed first in North Island, where the present wine regions are Auckland with the Waikato valley, Hawkes Bay, and Gisborne with Poverty Bay. Only in the late 1970s did the industry move to South Island, where developments are current at Marlborough, in the extreme north, and at Canterbury, 240km (150mi) to its south.

## NORTH ISLAND

Montana Wines, in which Seagrams have a large interest, is New Zealand's biggest wine company; it has vineyards at Auckland and Gisborne, and on South Island. Most of their white wines, including Benmorven Riesling/Muscat, are semisweet. Other proprietary names are Blenheimer and Ormond, with Fairhall River and Lindauer for sparkling wines.

Cooks' New Zealand Wine Company have 160ha (400 acres) spread between Waikato and Hawkes Bay, and buy in further grapes from the Hawkes Bay and Gisborne areas. Their oak-aged Chardonnay, firm Gewürztraminer, and sweet Chenin Blanc, together with a light fruity Cabernet, have secured a solid export trade to the UK. Müller-Thurgau vines, which were popular early plantings in New Zealand, make good wine which is generally for drinking young and locally.

Corbans Wines, who export mainly to

Only during the Second World War did New Zealand *(right)* turn seriously to wine production. In the center of the southern wine band, with a climate considered similar to Germany's, a prosperous wine industry with substantial exports has rapidly developed.

Pioneer missionary Samuel Marsden and four of the earliest settlers in New Zealand, bartering with Maoris for title to land *(top)*. Marsden planted some 100 vines at his Kerikeri mission in North Island in 1819.

The German viticulturist, Professor Helmut Becker, noticed that the climate and growing conditions for vines in New Zealand were nearest to those of Germany. Unsurprisingly, the Müller-Thurgau grape *(above)* yields half of all New Zealand's harvest.

A combine-harvester at work *(above)* in the Te Kauwata vineyards of Cooks' New Zealand Wine Company.

This truck and trailer *(left)* are taking grapes gathered by mechanical harvester to the winery at Te Kauwata. The big transport has stainless-steel trays for bringing in large loads from vineyards at Hawkes Bay and Gisborne as well as at Te Kauwata.

Canada, have nearly 400ha (1,000 acres) in Auckland, Gisborne and Tolaga Bay, mostly planted with white vines. Brand names are Tolaga Chenin Blanc, Gisborne Gewürztraminer, and Henderson Müller-Thurgau Auslese. Premium wines are marketed as Robard, Butler, and Riverlea. Babich Wines, at Auckland, make excellent fruity whites that reach the UK as well as a good wood-aged Cabernet. At Huapai Valley, north of Auckland, the Nobilo family concentrate on red wines, including a well balanced and satisfying Private Bin Claret from the Pinotage grape.

McWilliams Wines (NZ), partly owned by McWilliams of Australia (see page 289) are the biggest producers at Hawkes Bay and second largest in the country. Cresta Dore Müller-Thurgau and Bakano red hybrid brands are household names in New Zealand; their Cabernets and now Chardonnay are among the best made in the country. Glenvale Vineyards, founded in 1933, have expanding vineyards in Eskdale, Hawkes Bay; best known for dessert wines, they have new plantings which will produce varietal wines to balance production. Other producers at Hawkes Bay include Mission Vineyards, owned by the Catholic Society of Mary and making excellent Sauvignon Blanc and Tokay d'Alsace; Te Mata, the oldest winery in the country (founded 1896), producing an exceptional Cabernet/Merlot blend; and Vidal Wine Producers, with good Chasselas, Chenin Blanc, and Müller-Thurgau wines.

At Gisborne, Matawhero, run by the Irwin family, produce a dry Gewürztraminer, and have created much interest in a blend of Müller-Thurgau with Gewürztraminer that really outstrips Müller-Thurgau alone. Most activity in Gisborne and Poverty Bay is in the contract-growing and sale of grapes.

## SOUTH ISLAND

Developments in South Island proceed apace. While Auckland has subtropical weather with fall rains, and Hawkes Bay has dry summers and falls; Marlborough has more sun, cooler falls and low rainfall; it does have wind, however, but this may in due course be counteracted with tree windbreaks.

Corbans have a big project at Blenheim in Marlborough county. Montana have 400ha (1,000 acres) that in fact pioneered the Marlborough region in the 1970s; now varietal wines marketed under the Marlborough brand include a firm Cabernet, a spicy Riesling, and a dry Sauvignon Blanc.

All eyes are on South Island as an area for future expansion, and many pleasurable surprises are anticipated. Marlborough is well ahead in wide-row planting, allowing mechanical vine cultivation and harvesting. It must be said, however, that North Island, too, although its capabilities are better known, has not nearly reached its potential capacity for vineyard plantings.

Cooks' winery *(above)* was built in 1971 and is said to be the finest installation in Australasia. The stainless-steel tanks seen here each have a capacity of over 1,100hl (30,000gal). Cooks have spearheaded the export of excellent still wines to Europe.

Both Cabernet Sauvignon and Chardonnay wines are oak-aged at Te Kauwata *(right)*. Of all New Zealand vines, 6.5% are now Cabernet Sauvignon and 5% Chardonnay: Müller-Thurgau is the runaway leader with 38%. Only 9% are non-viniferas.

At the end of the line of the bottling plant at Cooks *(far right)*. Many of the bottles moving through the plant contain a wine labeled for export as New Zealand Dry Red Wine, which recently won a Gold Medal in international competition in Britain.

# SOUTH AFRICA

**Paarl ♦ Stellenbosch ♦ Tulbagh**

Vines were imported into Cape Province from as early as the mid-seventeenth century. The first came from the German and Dutch settlers, in the early 1650s; among those, from Holland, was South Africa's miracle grape, the Steen. Johan van Riebeeck is credited with producing the first wine, in 1659, and 20 years later Governor Simon van der Stel made wine on his farm at Groot Constantia outside Cape Town. At the end of the century French Huguenots arrived bearing vines from France, and settled at Paarl and Stellenbosch to the west of the Drakenstein mountains. South African wines improved in quality rapidly and materially as a result of their arrival.

When in 1805 the British seized the Cape, a great trade with England developed. But in 1861 Gladstone abolished preferential tariffs, ruining the trade and, even worse, in 1851 phylloxera arrived, eventually to destroy the vineyards entirely. Vines grafted onto resistant US rootstocks were then planted in such quantities that the even greater disaster of overproduction followed. By 1917 wines sold for as little as one penny per bottle, which led to the founding of the Kooperative Wijnbouwers Vereniging (KWV), or Cooperative Wine-Growers' Association of South Africa. In 1924 the Wine and Spirit Control Act empowered the KWV to fix the minimum price for all South African wines converted to spirits; it also brought non-member winery-owners under the same legal restraints as members. Trade with the UK and Holland was resumed, and in 1931 the South African Wine-Farmers' Association (London) Limited was formed with the KWV as an equal partner.

The purpose, and indeed the effect, of this association was to maintain supplies, distribution, uniformity of quality and stability of prices. An amending Act to that of 1924 was passed for the fixing of the annual price for good wines sold by the producer, and empowering the KWV to limit the volume of wine reaching the market by declaring a surplus according to each year's total crop. It remained for the KWV to pick up the other half share of the London company in 1950, and accordingly the KWV alone controls the South African wine industry for all these purposes. This has obvious advantages, but it has acted as a brake on the growth of an industry that today has enormous potential for development—not only in volume but also in variety and technique. In effect, it means that in 1985 South Africa is 10 years behind California and Australia.

The wine regions of the Cape fall into two groups, separated by the Drakenstein mountains, which run southeast to northwest 100km (60mi) east of Cape Town. To the west, the Coastal Belt has Tulbagh at the northern tip of the mountain range, and from there down to the coast, the regions are Swartland, Malmesbury, Durbanville, Paarl, Franschhoek, the Cape Division, Stellenbosch, and Walker Bay. To the east and close to the Drakensteins are Ceres, Worcester, Robertson, Montagu, and Swellendam, all following the valley of the Breede river. They lie in the Little Karoo, which stretches out to the east for 500km (300mi), taking in two more regions: Ladismith, 100km (60mi) northeast of Montagu near the Gouritz river, and Oudtshoorn, along its Olifants

Cape Province *(below)* has produced wine and brandy for almost 300 years, although government policies have retarded her winemaking progress. However, the next few years may see the results of the introduction here of the noble vines of Europe in commercial quantities. The vineyards are free of frost and hail, producing fine wines.

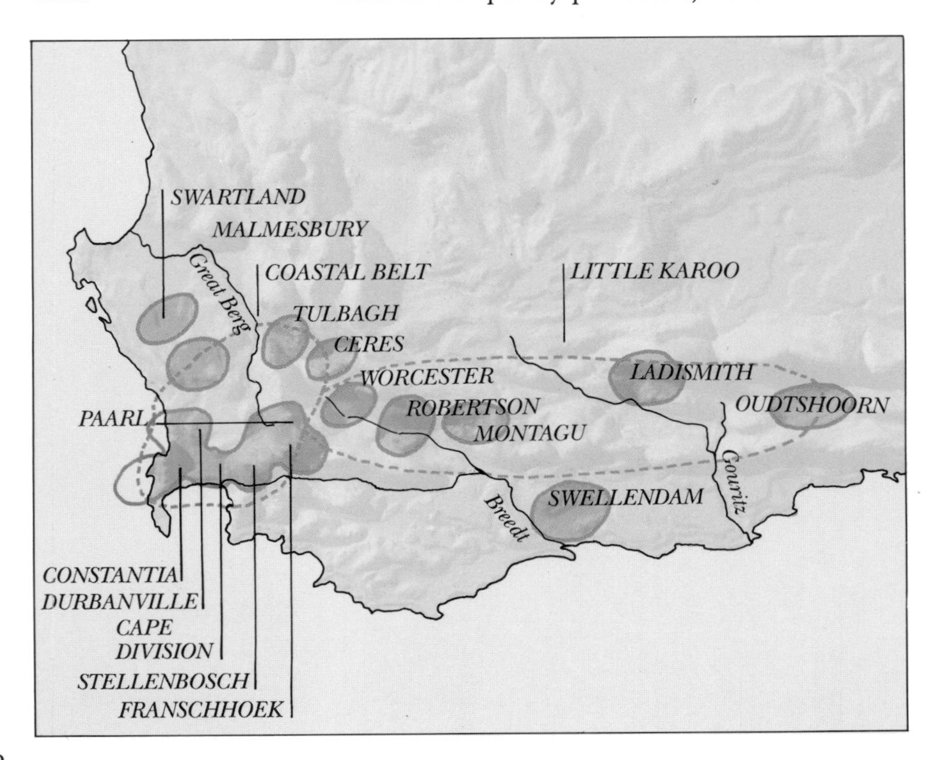

The Boschendal estate at Groot Drakenstein is in the newly recognized region of Franschhoek, previously part of Paarl. The highly technical Boschendal administration have devised their own "wine library" *(below)* in which records of every step in the progress of each vintage is chronicled.

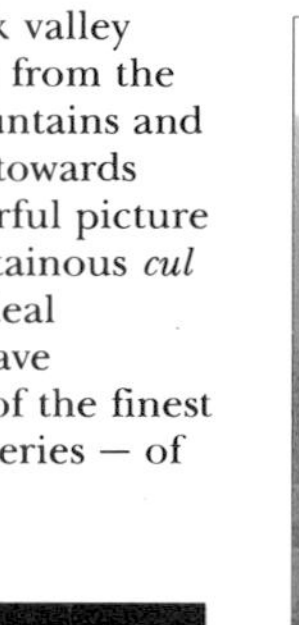

The Franschhoek valley *(right)* runs down from the Drakenstein mountains and turns northwest towards Paarl. This powerful picture shows the mountainous *cul de sac* in which ideal vineyard areas have produced some of the finest wines — and wineries — of the Cape.

The homestead of the Boschendal estate *(above)*, built in classical Cape Dutch style, is set among vineyards stretching along the slopes of the Simonsberg for 13km (8mi). The original 240ha (600-acre) vineyard here is in the process of being doubled in area.

The Boschendal homestead, dramatically lit by the midday sun *(left)*. The faultless detail seen here is typical of the care taken by winemaker Achim von Arnim and his staff to strive for perfection in everything on the estate.

tributary, another 110km (70mi) east.

In September, 1973, the Wines of Origin (WO) seal system, largely equivalent to the French *Appellation d'Origine Contrôlée* system, was introduced in South Africa. The seal guarantees that the bottle bearing it contains wine of the stated vine variety, of the vintage year, and from the place of origin stated on the label. The WO seal is now applied to the bottle-capsule of all bottles bearing any one of these three features. Vine varieties (cultivars) have to be approved by the State Wine and Spirit Board, and the designated Wine of Origin regions have been given the force of law. The contents of a bottle of wine claiming WO quality must be 80% derived from the named region, and it is planned that this figure will increase to 100% for table wines. Wines of Origin Superior (WOS) must contain only wine from the specified cultivar, made and bottled in the named region.

The designated regions for Wines of Origin number about 25. The main ones are Breede River Valley (for fortified wines from Worcester, Robertson, and Swellendam), Coastal Region (for wines from grapes grown in Constantia, Durbanville, Paarl, Franschhoek, Stellenbosch, and Tulbagh WO districts), Constantia, Durbanville, Franschhoek, Little Karoo, Paarl, Robertson, Stellenbosch, Swartland, Swellendam, Tulbagh, and Worcester.

The principal grapes used in South Africa are: for red wines, Cabernet Sauvignon, Cabernet Franc,* Cinsault* (Hermitage), Gamay, Merlot, Shiraz* (Sirah), Tinta Barocca, Zinfandel; for white wines, Blanc Fumé (Sauvignon Blanc), Bukettraube,* Chardonnay, Chenin Blanc, Clairette,* Colombard, Gewürztraminer, Hanepoot, Kerner, Müller-Thurgau, Fransdruif* (Palomino), Pinotage, Pinot Noir, Rhine Riesling (Weisser), Riesling (Crouchen), Semillon, Steen, and Silvaner (those marked * are for wines commonly used for blending). The long period of quarantine enforced on imported vines has held up the development of new vines for 10 or more years, but they have now finally been planted, although the government has restricted their quantities.

Soils in the Coastal Belt are sandy with heavy loam; in the Little Karoo deep, rich alluvial soils are mostly found. These soils are intensely fertile. The climate through all the Cape regions is perfect or near-perfect for growing grapes. There is an incredibly long growth season of eight months; the days are hot and the nights are cool; there is no frost and the rainfall is low (Little Karoo has only half the rainfall experienced in the Coastal Belt). And the lower slopes of the mountain ranges offer innumerable superb sites for the vineyards in latitudes 33°-34°S.

As so many grapes are converted at cooperatives, it will be seen that the area of vines in each designated WO region is not directly relevant to its wine production. The regions with the largest areas of vineyards are Paarl (including Franschhoek) (22,250ha; 55,000 acres), Worcester (18,500ha; 46,000 acres), Stellenbosch (16,200ha; 40,000 acres), Swartland (16,200ha; 40,000 acres), Robertson (8,900ha; 22,000 acres), Olifantsrivier (7,300ha; 18,000 acres), Tulbagh (4,450ha; 11,000 acres), and Little Karoo (3,850ha; 9,500 acres). The number of individual vine growers in these and smaller regions is well over 6,000, yet 75% of all grapes are pressed, vinified or collected for vinification by 70 cooperatives; the balance is converted by private wineries, producer-wholesalers, and the KWV.

From the grapes vinified, 36% are distilled for home-consumed spirits and a further 16% for export; 34% are sold in the form of still and sparkling wines; and 14% are converted into fortified wines. The national product for sale as wine amounts to over 80 million cases—in the region of seven million hectoliters—in an average year, making South Africa the 10th largest producer in the world. The structure of the wine- and spirit-manufacturing industries in South Africa is therefore unusual if not unique.

# PAARL

The town of Paarl is the wine center of the Cape. Here the KWV, controller of the industry, has its headquarters. As we have seen, each year the KWV fixes the minimum price for "good wines;" every grape farmer in the Cape is now an obligatory member and under the Wine and Spirit Control Acts must each year, to avoid a market excess, deliver to the KWV the declared surplus percentage of his production—an amount often totaling as much as one-third. The KWV may only export its wines or sell them back to other South African producers, and it therefore distills an enormous volume of wine for brandy, the majority of which is sold and consumed in the country, the balance being exported.

The KWV has one of its five massive winery/distilleries at Paarl. Apart from brandy, its range of products is mostly restricted to "Sherries," "Ports" and some table wines not available directly in South Africa. The best (and they are excellently made) "Sherries" are marketed under the Cavendish Cape label. Red wines include Roodeberg (a blend of Cinsault, Pinotage, and Shiraz), Tinta Barocca, and an estate wine, Vergenoegd. KWV Chenin Blanc, several Rieslings, and a sweet special Late Harvest Steen are all good-value white wines.

Nederberg Wines at Paarl are a branch of the Stellenbosch Farmers' Winery, and have a justified reputation for their quality cellars. Here the annual Nederberg auction is held in March —vintage time in South Africa—at which buyers attend from Europe, North and South America and, latterly, Australia. Nederberg Wines have 750ha (1,850 acres) of vines in Paarl and the Groot Drakenstein valley, and buy in grapes from the coastal regions. Much of the vinification is done by the parent company. None of Nederberg's wines is average: they are all excellent. They include Edelkeur, a rich, raisiny dessert wine from the Steen grape (occasionally blended with "botryfied" Riesling) which is best aged for several years; Gewürztraminer and Paarl Riesling; and sparkling wine made by the continuous Charmat process (see page 44). The Baronne label is for a worthy

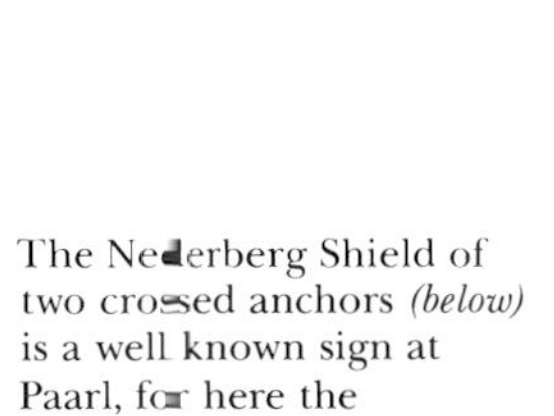

The Nederberg Shield of two crossed anchors *(below)* is a well known sign at Paarl, for here the internationally famous Nederburg wine auction is held every March.

Nederberg often blend the Steen *(below left)*, South Africa's own vine, with Riesling infected with noble rot to produce Edelkeur.

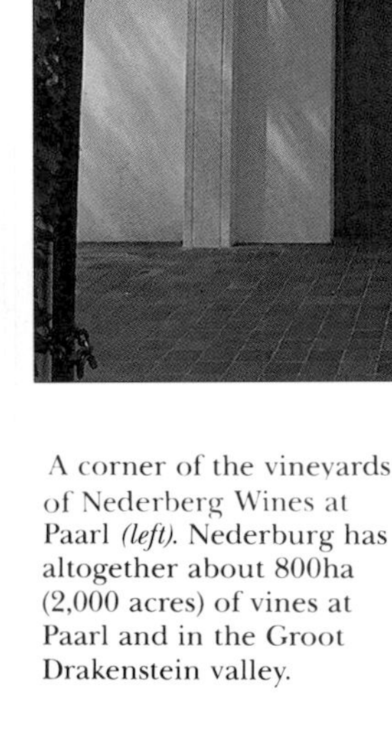

A corner of the vineyards of Nederberg Wines at Paarl *(left)*. Nederburg has altogether about 800ha (2,000 acres) of vines at Paarl and in the Groot Drakenstein valley.

The entrance to Nederberg *(above)*. Cellarmaster Günther Brözel welcomes experts from all over the world not only to discuss his own methods and skills but to learn theirs.

The vineyards of Boschendal *(left)* are planted with Cabernet Sauvignon, Merlot, Pinot Noir, and Shiraz for red wines, and a great area for whites, including Chardonnay, Chenin Blanc, Gewürztraminer, Pinot Gris, Sauvignon Blanc, and Semillon.

Workers in the Boschendal vineyards, tending young vines, are equipped with protective clothing for the job *(left)*. Early care in shaping the vines will repay its cost in the years when good vine-training enables perfect bunches of grapes to be grown.

Maturation vats and casks in the cellars at Boschendal *(left)*. Although von Arnim has said that "grapes picked at ideal ripeness look after themselves," there is a little more to it than that — as this expert winemaker will readily concede.

The Backsberg estate *(right)* of 160ha (400 acres) at Simondium, Paarl, is owned by Michael and Sidney Back, who helped to set the fashion for high-density planting in the Cape. The vineyards are set on the sunny north-facing slopes of the Kanonkop.

Cabernet blend, oak-aged for 15 months.

Union Wine, a member of the Picardi Group, markets three-quarters of a million cases of wine every year under the brand names Bellingham and Culemborg. Union have 100ha (250 acres) of vineyards in the Paarl valley, and buy in grapes locally (as well as wines from all over the Cape). Prize-winning wines are made at the Simonsvlei Cooperative at Suider Paarl from grapes gathered from the whole Paarl valley. The range of fruity, well flavored wines includes Grand Cru Dry Steen and Silvaner; Late Vintage Bukettraube and Chenin Blanc; and Late Harvest Cabernet Sauvignon, Cinsault, Pinotage, and Riesling. All are best for early drinking.

The newly created region of Franschhoek Boschendal, founded in 1977, has over 240ha (600 acres) of vineyards under cultivation and another 300ha (750 acres) under development. They stretch for kilometers along the eastern slopes of Simonsberg. The grapes are cropped at 65hl/ha, which is less than average for the Cape, being harvested carefully when the grapes reach ideal ripeness. A selection of varietals and blends is made from Cabernet Sauvignon, Merlot, Shiraz, Pinot Noir, Cape Riesling, Rhine Riesling, Chardonnay, Chenin Blanc, Gewürztraminer, Sauvignon Blanc, and Semillon. Their Lanoy Cabernet Sauvignon blend is an unusual light and fruity wine, and is still reasonably priced.

The Backsberg vineyards occupy some 160ha (400 acres) on the north-facing slopes of Kanonkop, where Sydney Back has planted Chardonnay, Chenin Blanc, Sauvignon Blanc, and Steen vines above the red Cabernet Sauvignon and Shiraz, using high-density planting. The white vines have produced some of the best-yet dry wines for early drinking. Chardonnay is cask- and bottle-aged for two years before marketing. Another important vineyard is the 200ha (550-acre) estate of Landskroon on the southwest slopes of Paarl mountain. The owner is Paul de Villiers; the wine-maker is his son Paul. They are direct descendants of the Huguenot family who settled in Franschhoek 300 years ago. Cabernet Franc and Chardonnay are sold separately. In addition to the usual vines, they have Tinta Barocca, which produces big red wines much appreciated in the Cape.

The clean Cape Dutch style is retained for the portals of the Backsberg winery (*below*). Sydney Back's 1982 Chardonnay, Chenin Blanc and Sauvignon Blanc vintages are now on the market after two years' aging.

# STELLENBOSCH

The Stellenbosch Farmers' Wineries are a subsidiary of Cape Wine and Distillers Limited. They press some grapes, but these are few compared to the huge volume of blending wines bought in from cooperatives and private cellars. Their best products are those marketed as Nederberg (see page 305); other brands include Autumn Harvest, Château Libertas, Capenheimer, Kellerprinz, La Gratitude, Lanzerac Rosé, Oude Libertas, Virginia, and Zonnebleom. KWV have another of their five cooperative wineries at Stellenbosch.

Spier, founded in 1969, has an estate of about 285ha (700 acres) at Lynedoch in the Stellenbosch WO region on slopes above the Eerste river valley. Its output is 60,000 cases annually of good-quality wines. The white wines include Chenin Blanc and Colombard, which have good flavor, and the Pinotage from here is one of the best examples in the Cape of wine from this dubious vine.

The Bergkelder is a merchant business owned by the Oude Meester Group. The chief executive, Dr Julius Laszlo, was formerly in charge of the Romanian state wine industry, and has brought radical ideas for improving still farther the wines of the Cape. Hoffie Hoffman, the wine-maker, blends some of the wines bought in from a number of top estates with grapes bought in Paarl and Stellenbosch and vinified by him. Others of the estate wines are bottled by The Bergkelder. Their Fleur du Cap Cabernet Sauvignon is considered to be one of the Cape's supreme red wines. Grunberger Steen is an excellent white for everyday drinking, and a range of Stellenryk wines bearing that label are well worth the money.

Gilbey's, at Stellenbosch, owned jointly by IDV (UK) and the Rembrandt South African Corporation, have nearly 325ha (800 acres) spread between Kleine Zalze and Devon Valley. Grapes from these vineyards and from other Stellenbosch growers are used to make wines of solid reputation which have been developed over the company's six-year existence. At the head of an impressive range of labels, Bertram's red wines have already been selected to take many awards. The 1979 Cabernet is full and tannic, and a Shiraz of the same year is also marketed. For the mass market, the Festival and Valley labels are used. Gilbey's also own Montagne Estate, which, because Montagne is quoted in the WO region structure, will have to change its name. Montagne have marketed good Cabernets, Shiraz, and white blends.

Meerlust has been in the Myburgh family since 1776. This is a 230ha (575-acre) estate at Faure, sited on southwestern slopes which overlook False Bay. The white manor house, one of the oldest and most beautiful in the Cape, was the center of a wine business 80 years before

The Neethlingshof homestead *(left)*. Although only 5,000 cases of its wine are estate-bottled, the reputation of the Neetlingshof property at Vlottenburg, Stellenbosch, has been enhanced by a well balanced Cabernet Sauvignon from their 280ha (690 acres) of vineyards.

A trailer-tipper of Cabernet Sauvignon grapes *(left)* at the Neetlingshof winery being harnessed to the crusher-destalker. The grapes have been hand-picked on the slopes running down to the valley of the Eerste river. Some Cinsault and Pinotage (a Pinot Noir × Cinsault cross) are also planted.

Geared to the crusher-destalker, the tipper disgorges the grapes onto an Archimedean screw *(left)*. Neetlingshof produce a crisp white wine from Weisser Riesling grapes; other white grapes in their vineyards include Gewürztraminer, the new German Bukettraube, and Kerner.

Looking north in the Neetlingshof vineyards *(main picture).* The Stellenbosch region is divided between mountains and their foothills with occasional level spaces. The foothills and flat areas are occupied by many of the best vineyards in the Cape.

Looking down on Neetlingshof *(inset);* the winery and farm are in the foreground. On the horizon are the Hottentot-Holland mountains, and to their right the Helderberg mountain. The vineyards lie in the middle distance.

A load of black grapes being scaled on arrival at the Neetlingshof winery *(inset right).* Some of the grapes that arrive here are destined for conversion at the winery, while others are shipped out to other wineries which take much of the crop under contract.

Supported on a bracket, a Neetlingshof curiosity *(right)*: an intricately wrought hand-operated bottle-opener. This object dates from the early twentieth century.

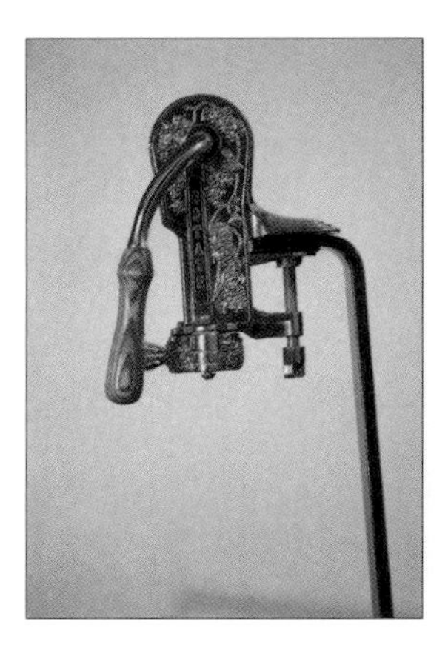

This plaque *(far right)* commemorates the opening of the Neetlingshof vineyard.

A wall cabinet devoted to samples from notable Neetlingshof vintages *(right)*. Neetlingshof was one of 14 original estates qualifying for the "Estate Wines of Origin" classification granted by the South African Wine and Spirit Board in 1973.

the Myburgh occupation. Today Meerlust is given over to red-wine production: it started with Cabernet Sauvignon 20 years ago, and now Cabernet Franc, Merlot, and Pinot Noir have been brought in. The resulting Rubicon blend has been designed to please in the Bordeaux fashion, but straight wines from the three grapes are made, if only to prove how much better and more subtle is the blend of all three. In 1980 Meerlust won the "top estate" award and Nico Myburgh the award for "top wine-maker." In the same year the Cabernet was South African Champion. Maturing the wine in wood in his own cellars, Myburgh leaves the marketing to The Bergkelder.

Schoongezicht Rustenberg, at Simonsberg, is another beautiful estate with white Dutch buildings fit for a calendar under an umbrella of huge trees. Mostly vines for red wines are planted on the 80ha (200-acre) estate in the south-facing foothills of the Simonsberg mountain. The Cabernet Sauvignon has an enviable reputation throughout the Cape; Rustenberg Dry Red is the better for maturing. Schoongezicht white wines, from Rhine Riesling, and a rosé blend from red and white grapes round off a good collection. The cellars were enlarged a few years ago.

Another important estate here is Delheim, marketing some 60,000 cases of red and white wines made from grapes from over 120ha (300 acres) of vines at two vineyards and more bought within the WO region. All the wines are well spoken-of, and the Cabernet Sauvignon and Sauvignon Blanc have an excellent reputation. The estate's range of wines is extensive, including Shiraz, Gewürztraminer, Heerenwyn (made entirely from Steen), Rhine Riesling, and sparkling white blends.

The harvest at the Neetlingshof vineyards is brought in by manual labor in March *(right)*. In the distance, the Hottentot-Holland mountains rise out of a morning mist.

# TULBAGH

Three well known estates in the Tulbagh WO region account for 13% of its vineyard acreage. They are Twee Jongegezellen (familiarly shortened to "TJ"), Theuniskraal, and Montpellier.

TJ have experimented with all the possibilities on their 240ha (600-acre) estate at the foot of Obiekwa mountain. The proprietor is N.C. Krone, and his son Nicky is wine-maker—hardly an impulse of nepotism, for the family have been in the wine business for over 200 years, handing down knowledge, ideas and incentives to their descendants. New ideas abound. In 1982, for instance, they cropped the harvest by night and found that the resulting wines had improved characteristics and strength; and their Schanderl white vine is strained from an isolated red clone of Frontignac which was bred in their nurseries. TJ 39 is a Riesling blend, and the range includes also Gewürztraminer, Steen, and red wines from Cabernet Sauvignon. Gilbey's handle 14% of the TJ production for export.

Theuniskraal have 160ha (400 acres) along the Klein Berg river, and have planted Gewürztraminer, Cape and Rhine Riesling, Semillon, and Steen to gain a reputation (and many awards) for their range of dry white wines. Some of these wines reach the UK and Holland. Montpellier, also on the Klein Berg river, produce 35,000 cases, mainly of white wines, on their 150ha (375-acre) estate. The warm Tulbagh climate seems to favor white-wine production, although the tendency is for fermentation to lead to dryness, hampering the balance of these wines. Gewürztraminer has been a success, but other wines, including the Rieslings and Steen, have lacked acidity. Sweet Tuinwingerd Rhine Riesling is generally better balanced.

Between the Tulbagh region and the west coast is Swartland, a substantial vineyard area whose grapes go mostly to cooperatives. The best winery there is Allesverloren, at Riebeek West, with 160ha (400 acres) of vines laid down for the production of red wine and "Port." Cabernet Sauvignon is taken towards its limits by the warm dry climate, and a full raisiny wine results. Allesverloren have an older reputation for their "Ports.'

KWV have another of their cooperative wineries in the Robertson WO region. Much of the remaining wine crop is sold out of the region, but a few important private wineries support a reputation for the potential of the Robertson region. Zandvliet vineyards, with 220ha (550 acres) of grapes on both banks of the Kogmanskloof river, have specialized in a strong Shiraz which has been certified "Superior" in each of its five vintages. De Wetshof, owned by J.J. de Wet, has a substantial influence in the Cape, arising from the enthusiasm of wine-maker Danie de Wet, who brought back from Germany new ideas for South African white wines. The De Wetshof plantation of 60ha (150 acres) lies along the Breede river and is planted with Chardonnay, Rhine Riesling, and Sauvignon Blanc. The Chardonnay '82 is rather expensive but the others are reasonably priced. Sweet Edeloes, from noble-rot grapes, is in a class of its own, and has really focused attention on Robertson.

Worcester and Montagu, on the Breede river in the Little Karoo, have cooperative cellars converting grapes to dry white and dessert wines; KWV has a winery/distillery in each of these regions. The small Swellendam, most easterly of the Breede-river regions, concentrates on producing wine for distillation.

Twee Jongegezellen, at Tulbagh, has been in the Krone family for 200 years *(below)*. The family started winemaking only in 1950, and quickly made a name for good white wines. The estate, of over 275ha (680 acres), is under the towering Obiekwa mountain.

Theuniskraal *(left)* is an award-winning company at Tulbagh owned by Rennie and Kobus Jordaan. White wines are produced from Gewürztraminer: they are full with a fruity flavor. Other vines on the estate are Cape and Rhine Rieslings and Steen.

The KWV Paddagang wine-house at Tulbagh *(far left)* is one of a number of wineries of this great state cooperative, to which 6,000 grape farmers in the Cape belong.

The Krone family at Twee Jongegezellen work adventurously to develop new white wines *(left)*. Experiments have included cloning and the harvesting of grapes by night.

The grace of the wine-house of KWV's Paddagang vineyards and winery is enhanced by a broad lawn *(left)*. The principal products of the KWV, whose headquarters are in Paarl, are brandies, sherries and ports.

The Paddagang vineyards are seen against a backdrop of the northern end of the Drakenstein mountains *(right)*; the buildings of the KWV plant nestle between them. KWV may produce wines for export or sale to Cape winemakers but not for retail sale in the Cape.

# SOCIAL AND AFTER-DINNER DRINKS

Wherever nature has provided the right climate, human beings have cultivated grapes and converted them to wine. And, as we have seen, wherever there are wines spiritous liquors have been distilled from them and their by-products. So far, however, we have been talking in terms of the fundamental fact that grape sugars fermented with their natural yeasts produce alcohol. But many fruits besides grapes have sugar, and many plants have starch that may be converted to sugar, so hundreds if not thousands of spirits, flavored before, during or after distillation, have been devised and perfected during the last 2,000 years.

These drinks can bring to many of the more civilized experiences of life a conclusion that is at once subtle, mellow, and deeply satisfying. It was Dean Aldrich of Christ Church, Oxford, who said some two and one-half centuries ago:

If all be true that I do think
There are five reasons we should drink
Good wine—a friend—or being dry
(Or lest we should be by and by)
Or any other reason why . . .

If the dean had not been inspired by a brandy or Benedictine to write his verse, it was not for the want of opportunity, for every Fellow of Oxford and Cambridge was a resident bachelor, cloistered over cellars filled with the best and rarest wines and spirits of Europe. The colleges, all church foundations, carried on the traditional link between religion, learning, and wine. The deans and their dons were following and promulgating a pattern of gracious living that had spread during a period of some 10 centuries to the castles, manor houses and homes of England's ruling class, and thence through the professions and industry to the nation's bourgeoisie. After all, you may ask, for what did young men go to Oxford and Cambridge, if not to learn to appreciate the best and disseminate their knowledge to the less fortunate?

Perhaps the culmination of a successful week is the entertainment of one's close friends to dinner at home on a Saturday night, or, if those friends are weekend guests, the relaxed pleasure of lunch on Sunday. Not all social drinking is done at the weekend, however. A glass of Sherry or Madeira before lunch will put an edge on your appetite, while those who are young enough (and perhaps still learning) may prefer a martini cocktail so dry that the vermouth is indiscernible and the alcohol electric.

That assumes that the morning is not for celebration! Champagne *très frais* at 11.00am for an anniversary, or a ratafia (should you be fortunate enough to find a waiter who knows what that is!) to consummate a deal, can add another pleasant memory to be cherished for ever.

Again, there is the drink taken to melt away the harassment and cares of the day when what remains of it belongs solely to yourself and your family. Not only will it do you a power of good, it will ensure relaxation, stimulate appetite, invite deep sleep, and restore vigor and courage for the challenge of tomorrow. And knowing not only what one is drinking but where it comes from, its ingredients, and how it is made adds greatly to your enjoyment.

This brightly colored array of bottles, glasses and sliced fruits *(right)* gives just a hint of the variety of drinks that may be taken single, mixed, shaken, stirred, iced, long, short . . . to meet the mood of the moment. Cognac, Brandy, Scotch, Tennessee whiskey, Dutch gin, Russian vodka and Italian vermouth are seen here.

D.GENEVER
VERMOUTH
MARTINI
EXTRA DRY
FINE
CHAMPAGNE
V.S.O.P.
EMY MARTIN
JACK DANIEL'S
Old No.7
ONE
Quart
Tennessee Whiskey
Genuine
Russian Vodka
STOLICHNAYA
70° PROOF

# DISTILLATION

## Facts Relevant to Distillation ♦ The Strength of Distillates ♦ Distilling Techniques ♦ Maturation

Aristotle wrote: "Sea water can be rendered potable by distillation: after it has been converted to humid vapors it returns to a liquid." If the translation is literal, not only did Aristotle observe the result, but he clearly understood the physical process involved. The Greeks used the principle of distillation not for the isolation of alcohol, however, but in the preservation of scents, spices, and balms in water or wine, sealed tightly to trap fugitive aromas and other qualities. The science of distillation had been known earlier to the Egyptians; however, it was not applied to the derivation of alcohol from wine until about the tenth century. The Arabs are credited with the discovery.

Three centuries passed before "eau-de-vie" came into the language; it referred to a distillate from pomace, consisting of alcohol and many of the by-products of distillation, much later called "congeners." The first treatise on wine and spirits was written by Arnáu of Vilanova, a professor at the University of Montpellier, who died in 1313. Arnáu rhapsodized about eau-de-vie, describing it as a long-sought panacea and the elixir of life itself, and as "the dream of alchemists." His pupil and successor Raimundo Lulio was slightly more guarded, calling it "an emanation of the divinity, newly revealed to men but hid from antiquity." Like most of their kind, these two men merely thought their discovery was the greatest ever made for mankind, and there are many today who would support that view!

But the original distillate had an obnoxious smell and a vile taste. Known as *aqua vitae* (the "water of life") from the earliest times, it was doctored with herbs to disguise the taste and cure the sick: for centuries it was regarded simply as an unpleasant alchemists' draft. By the Middle Ages, however, *aqua vitae* was becoming appreciated for what it was, an alcoholic drink more powerful than wine: the problem was how to eliminate the odious flavor. Many different methods were tried, and the distilled wines of the Charentes, an early success, were exported from France by Dutch, Danish, and English merchantmen. These distillates were called *brandewijn* (burnt wine), which the English promptly corrupted to "brandy." The Germans call it *Weinbrand*, and the Spanish call it *aguardiente* (ardent water). It was the original version of the spirit we call "Cognac" today.

As early as the fifteenth century malt whisky was being distilled in the Highlands of Scotland, while in Ireland it was already being made as *uisge beatha* (a corruption of *aqua vitae*) from a barley beer. The Scots had like-sounding names for their product including *usquabau*, from which the word "whisky" has been derived. (Variant spellings of both Gaelic names exist.) Scotch whisky slowly filtered south to the Scottish court in the Lowlands, and on to England. It was only a matter of time before this new spirit would attract taxes and duties, and the kilted distillers promptly took to the hills when the Hanoverian kings took the predictable step. They concentrated principally in Glenlivet where some 200 illicit stills openly made their whisky as a thriving industry, heavily armed and guarded against customs officers.

In 1800 some 750,000 gallons (2.25 million

An illicit still in the Highlands of Scotland *(below)*. The primitive methods used in the second and third decades of the nineteenth century made it little wonder that the Scots alone were addicted to malt whisky.

The modern malt whisky plant at Glenfiddich, with its row of shining copper stills *(far right)*. Color dynamics identify the flow-lines of the process.

LOW WINES
G

liters) of Scotch whisky was being distilled illegally, while practically none was subject to tax—mainly because any distiller who deigned to pay tax promptly had his still burned by those who didn't. The Glenlivet ring ignored a lowering of duty in 1823 (which the English government thought would encourage payment), but the ring slowly disintegrated after an honest trader, George Smith, set up in their midst with adequate self-protection. The number of known illicit stills in all Scotland dropped to 177 by 1835 and to 6 by 1884.

In North America the distillers of whiskey took equally badly to the idea of paying duty on spirits. The distilling of fermented brews from rye and barley had become commonplace by the 1870s. In 1874 the Whiskey Rebellion in Pennsylvania erupted as an armed revolt by illicit distillers against the payment of duty. Like their Scots counterparts, they took to the hills; they went west, and joined the distillers of Bourbon County, Kentucky, who had started making corn whiskey (which eventually took the generic name of Bourbon). Certainly the production of illicit whiskey in Kentucky was already rife when the eastern settlers arrived, for the price of whiskey in Jefferson County had been fixed 12 years earlier at 240 dollars a gallon. The call to order of illicit distillers in the Union was a slow one. If the hatchet was ever decently buried, the distillers certainly knew where to find it when Prohibition started.

The principle of rectification of spirits had been known from the beginning of the nineteenth century, and slowly a revolution in distilling techniques took place. Even where the pot-still method was retained for its special features, the method of distribution had to change: in competition with rectified spirits, even Cognac brandies started to be shipped in bottles rather than barrels, because of the knowledge that the barreled Cognac could be diluted or adulterated at the end of its journey. The labeling of the bottles also enabled the brandies of the Charentes to become known as Cognac for the first time.

Rum has its own story. Distilled mainly from the sugarcane of the West Indies, it became not only the drink of the Senior Service but also of Britain's American colonies. It would be hyperbole to suggest that the residents' disapproval of paying duty levied at Westminster on rum consumed in the colonies caused them to break away and found the United States of America, but no doubt the rum question was a catalyst in sparking their diverse objections into action. Rum now sells in many forms, some of which lack the pungency and fire of the original Demerara and Jamaica varieties. Less strong rums are made in Cuba, Trinidad, Barbados, Puerto Rico, and Martinique.

Finally, the flavored gin and the tasteless vodka of today are the perfect products of the continuous still. Ideal for blending with mixers for long drinks or with vermouths and cocktail ingredients for shorts, both are produced and sold in gigantic quantities.

So much for the history of distillation: now for a more clinical study of its physics and chemistry.

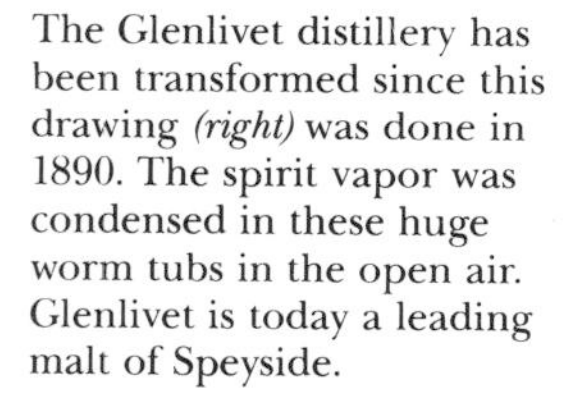

The Glenlivet distillery has been transformed since this drawing *(right)* was done in 1890. The spirit vapor was condensed in these huge worm tubs in the open air. Glenlivet is today a leading malt of Speyside.

## DEFINITION OF DISTILLATION

The wide range of liquors that we call "spirits" includes fruit spirits, grain spirits, vegetable spirits, flavored spirits, and liqueurs—and, of course, fortified wines have spirits added to them. In one form or another, spirits represent an important contribution to the pleasures of social drinking. If we had to define the term "spirits," we might say that it referred to alcoholic distillates that are potable and (taken in moderation) unharmful to health. However, for practical purposes—that is, from the legal point of view—definition is not so simple. The legal definitions of terms like "liquors" and "spirits" vary from country to country, sometimes including fortified wines as well as mixtures, compounds or preparations made with spirits—except for methylated spirits. Note the "m" in methylated; the methyl radical is $CH_3$, found in poisonous, non-potable wood alcohol ($CH_3OH$). In fact, legal definitions might be more explicit were they to restrict spirits positively to ethyl alcohol (with the radical $C_2H_5$) which, subject to careful treatment during preparation, is potable.

Even then, the definition would be far from adequate in its description of the products made by the spirits industry. The process of making spirits is obviously distillation from a base material which already contains alcohol. But, out of a vast range of materials capable of fermentation, the spirits industry deals with only a few. The most important are grape and grain; but there are other fruits (categorized as pip, pit, and soft fruits) and vegetables that will ferment to produce a base material for distillation. The trade therefore defines spirits as a liquid of high alcoholic content obtained by the distillation of such fermentable materials.

# FACTS RELEVANT TO DISTILLATION

The process of distillation, if carried to completion, would produce pure ethyl alcohol, a colorless, odorless and tasteless liquid, *whatever* base material had been used. It is therefore necessary to take distillation only to the point where the product is purified yet retains sufficient by-products to characterize the original base material. Controlled distillation therefore not only separates alcohol from water: it is carefully balanced, removing poisonous lighter alcohols (fusel oils) that were present in the base material in safely diluted quantities, but stopped at a critical point so that flavoring agents are retained. The principle of distillation depends entirely upon the application of heat to a base material, so that (at known temperatures) the ingredients separate. Water boils at 100°C (212°F) and freezes at 0°C ( – 32°F); ethyl alcohol boils at 78°C (172°F) and freezes

Akvavit has been the national drink of Denmark for over 400 years. This equipment *(top)* from one of the early distilleries at Aalborg is now preserved in the old Town Museum at Aarhus.

Another exhibit at the Aarhus Town Museum, Denmark *(above)*. The long-handled wooden shovel or *skip* was used for turning barley on the malting floor before the introduction of the automated saladin box.

at −133°C (−207°F). The process of distillation is one of vaporization, not boiling. When the temperature of the base material, or "wash," is raised even slightly, vaporization of both water and alcohol will start (water vaporizes at any temperature; even ice does so). However, when the temperature reaches 78°C (172°F) and is held there for some time, *all* the alcohol will change to vapor; this is taken over and down through a cooling system to condense and be collected in a cask (see diagram, page 326). This is precisely what the alembic of olden days did in a more primitive way.

Parenthetically, it should be noted that the alcohol *could* also be separated by cooling to below 0°C (32°F), at which temperature the water can be removed in the form of ice. This process is called "congelation," and for practical reasons is not used in the spirits industry; it is, however, unfortunately used sometimes in Canada for the home manufacture of "apple-jack." Cider is put outside at night in open containers, and the resulting ice is removed in the morning. After the same cider has been subjected to this treatment for several nights, the residue is concentrated—and so are its dangerous fusel oils. It is for this reason (not the implicit evasion of duty) that this practice is illegal. Sadly, freezer-owners in the rest of the world have discovered the same trick.

Alcohol is produced by the fermentation of sugar in the presence of yeast. The original sugar may come from fruit such as grapes, apples, plums, strawberries, and many more; it may be in honey, or it may be processed from sugar-cane or -beet. But the grains, wheat, oats, rye, barley, and corn (in Europe, maize), contain starch, which has to be converted to

Distillation requires precise heat control, so that the alcoholic wash is held at 78°C, at which the spirit will vaporize. Here aquavit is being distilled *(right)* and a bright light is beamed onto the thermometer and other instruments.

At Sissach in northern Switzerland, the H. Nebiker distillery produces fruit brandies. The volume of production depends upon the fruit: Kirsch from cherries, with Mirabelle and Quetsch from plums, are plentiful; raspberries and strawberries distil to much smaller quantities.

Pulverized flavoring agents are assembled in an alembic in readiness for the preparation of an elixir by percolation *(left)*. The agents will be distilled with a mixture of alcohol and water.

Although *brannvin* means literally "burnt" or distilled wine, by the eighteenth century in Sweden it had come to be a synonym for akvavit and vodka; in other words, a grain- rather than a grape-based spirit *(above)*.

sugar before fermentation can occur. Barley is the only one of these grains that can do this for itself. It contains a mixture of enzymes, *diastase*, which turns the starch of barley into a sugar called maltose. In nature, the diastase is created when rain and sun cause the barley grains to sprout, and the resulting maltose will then feed the plant and be consumed. In the malting process, however, the grain, artificially moistened and heated, is allowed to sprout until most of its starch is converted to sugar; it is then "screened" to remove the culm (small green roots), and finally dried in a kiln. (This is a much shortened description of an essential and critical stage occurring also in the brewing of beers.) The processed diastase is so strong that it will convert the starch in the other grains to sugar, thus making them fermentable by yeast.

Joseph Louis Gay-Lussac (1778-1850), the French scientist, described the process of fermentation chemically. One metric system of measuring alcoholic strength (by percentage volume) is named for him. His hydrometer is shown here *(below)*.

## THE STRENGTH OF DISTILLATES

In different countries around the world, varying standard strengths exist for grain, vegetable and fruit spirits when bottled for retail sale. For example, in the US whiskeys are bottled at not less than 80° proof, and in the UK whisky is usually bottled at 40% vol. alcohol (though some "cheap" spirits are marketed at 37.5% vol. alcohol in smaller bottles.) An essential difference between the US and UK systems for taxing all alcoholic drinks is that in the US the rates of federal excise and customs duty are peculiar to each of the many individual types of drink (eg. various beers, wines and cordials,) whereas in the UK there are duty bands for rising strengths by percentage volume alcohol, regardless of type. The alcoholic strength and bottle capacity must always be shown on the label, not only because the appropriate duty must be paid on withdrawal from bond but also because the customer must know what he or she is buying.

The instrument of measurement of the strength of alcohol in a spirit solution is the hydrometer. Originally the current scale was devised in the 1870s by a customs officer called Sikes; he introduced the "Proof" reading, which runs from 0 for pure water to 175 for pure alcohol. The Proof system still operates in the USA (although the units are different—see below) but has been superseded in Europe and elsewhere first by the Gay-Lussac system and then by the OIML (Organisation Internationale de Metrologie Legale) system. Both systems measure alcohol by percentage volume, the only difference being that OIML measures this at 20°C (68°F) whereas Gay-Lussac measures it at 15°C (59°F), and therefore gives a marginally higher reading (the difference is insignificant to anyone not in the trade). Proof is expressed in degrees equal to twice the percentage volume Gay-Lussac value: for example, 40% Gay-Lussac is equal to 80° Proof (or 70° Sikes Proof). The scales are illustrated on page 325.

Twenty-six states in the USA levy taxes on table wines at rates from 50 cents to $2.25 per gallon, to which Federal excise duty is added, making wine-drinking an expensive occupation.

| Gay Lussac | American proof | British proof |
|---|---|---|
| 10% | 20 | 17.50 |
| 20% | 40 | 35.00 |
| 30% | 60 | 52.50 |
| 40% | 80 | 70.00 |
| 41% | 82 | 71.75 |
| 42% | 84 | 73.50 |
| 43% | 86 | 75.25 |
| 44% | 88 | 77.00 |
| 45% | 90 | 78.75 |
| 50% | 100 | 85.50 |
| 57% | 114 | 100.00 |
| 60% | 120 | 105.00 |
| 70% | 140 | 122.50 |
| 80% | 160 | 140.00 |
| 90% | 180 | 157.50 |
| 100% | 200 | 175.00 |

# DISTILLING TECHNIQUES

The process of distillation is effected in a still. The original type, the pot still, works on a batch principle, while the more recently developed Coffey still is continuous. The two processes both remain in everyday use for reasons that will become apparent, for their capabilities are by no means identical. Each technique requires careful consideration; however, in order not to delve too deeply into biochemistry, scientific as well as mathematical proofs are here merely accepted rather than explained in depth: for those needing such proofs there is a surfeit of textbooks.

## THE POT STILL

The pot still, in its simplest form, is illustrated on page 326. A boiler heats a container of alcoholic wash, which partially vaporizes. The vapor passes up through a pipe containing a head, and over into a cold bath in which the pipe, shaped as a coil (a "worm"), condenses the vapor once more to a liquid, which pours into a cask. By virtue of the differing boiling points of water and alcohol, the distillate that enters the cask will be mainly spirit, but there will also be a proportion of distilled water and a small residue of other substances.

A number of spirits are produced in pot stills today; they include brandy, Scotch malt whisky, Irish and Bourbon whiskeys and rum. The specification of the still and method of manufacture may vary, but the principle of the pot still is common to them all.

When wine is made, the sugar in the grapes is converted (defining the original sugar content as 100%) to 48% ethyl alcohol (ethanol), 49% carbon dioxide and a soluble 3% residue, made up of many compounds, which gives flavor to the wine. In the resulting wine, that 48% of the original sugar represents only about 10% alcohol by volume, and the 3% residue is also reduced proportionally to only about one-fifth, or approximately 0.6% by volume. What happens to this 0.6% of residual compounds in the distillate is now crucial, for it undergoes a number of chemical changes. Jointly these compounds—as opposed to ethanol, the primary

The hydrometer, seen measuring the alcohol by volume in akvavit *(above)*, is scaled to read the strength of the distillate after it has been diluted to commercial strength. 100% American Proof equals 50% alcohol by volume (Gay-Lussac).

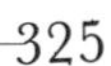

substance—are called "secondary substances." Known also as "congeners," they vary according to the origin of the sugar. They fall into four groups. The most important comprises higher alcohols, fatty alcohols whose molecules are more complex than that of ethanol: the more common are propanol and butanol, although neutral grain spirit, used for gin, contains little of any higher alcohol. The second group contains esters formed during the fermentation period, resulting from the action of fatty acids on ethyl or amyl alcohols, the principal ester involved being ethyl acetate. The third group are acids, of which acetic acid is the major component, accompanied principally by tartaric and butyric acids. And, finally, there are aldehydes, which result from oxidation of the ethanol. The main aldehyde involved, furfural, develops during distillation but may increase or diminish during aging, according to the original base material. Generally, however, all of these secondary substances tend to increase during aging and, together with tertiary constituents plus minute quantities of essential oils, terpenes and volatile materials, will add to the spirits' flavor.

The conditions of aging are important. For Cognac the spirit is aged in casks of oak made out of wood from the nearby Limousin Forest near Limoges; Armagnac is made in casks from the now rare Armagnac oak. These oaks give brandies their color, flavor and finesse during a maturation period of up to 20 years or more. During the first year, brandy will absorb 2kg (nearly 4½lb) of oak products from its cask, and will continue to evaporate through its pores during the whole period of its maturation.

But what of those poisonous fusel oils that we noted as being dangerous in applejack? Infinite care is taken to make sure that these and other poisons are removed during distillation. The pot-still method first requires three successive charges of alcoholic wash to be heated until all the alcohol has been vaporized. The resulting primary distillate therefore has a volume equal to approximately one-third that of the original

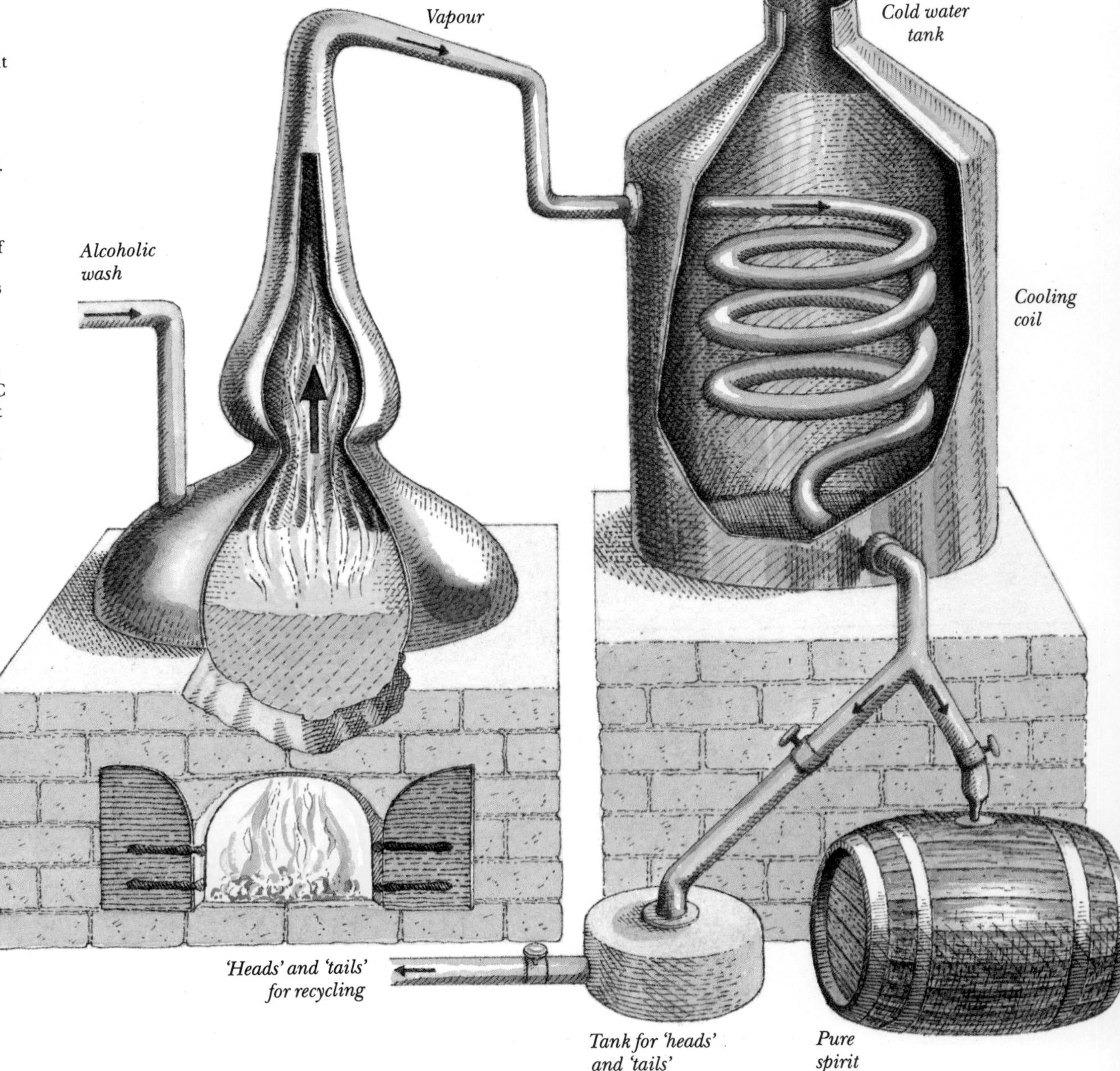


THE POT STILL

The pot still, in which malt whiskey is distilled, is charged with an alcoholic wash in which the proportion of alcohol by volume is about one-third. After three such charges, the total of spirit distilled ("low wines") is therefore equal to one full charge of the still; the spirit is then redistilled, and during this secondary distillation poisonous materials are extracted from the spirit. The more volatile poisons ("heads") evaporate at 28°C (82°F) and are drawn off at the beginning of this distillation, while the fusel oils ("tails"), being less volatile than alcohol, are drawn off at the end.

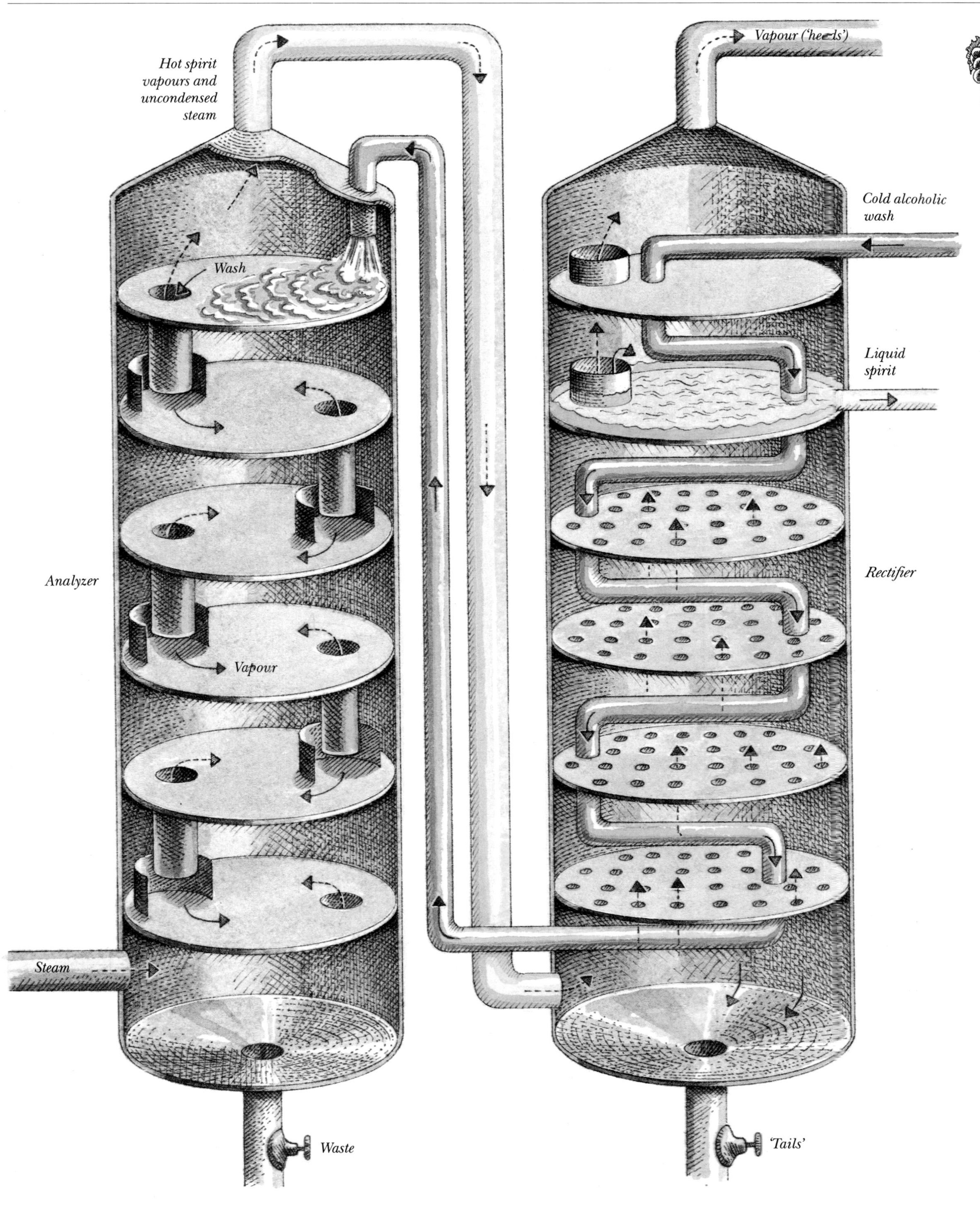


THE CONTINUOUS STILL

While the pot still has the advantage of leaving more flavor in the spirit, it is labor-intensive and has a small throughput. The continuous (Coffey) still produces purer spirit in far greater quantities and by a cheaper automated process. It consists of two tall columns, the analyzer and the rectifier, each divided into a number of chambers by copper plates. The cold alcoholic wash enters high in the rectifier and flows down through a worm. Steam and alcoholic vapors rising in the rectifier heat the wash, which is then pumped from the bottom of the rectifier to enter the top of the analyzer. Steam pumped into the bottom of the analyzer rises and converts the hot wash to a spirituous vapor. The vapor rises, is drawn out of the analyzer, and enters the foot of the rectifier where, by heat exchange, it is cooled and condenses. The less volatile "tails" condense at the foot of the rectifier; the spirit vapor condenses near its top and collects on the spirit plate; and the more volatile "heads" rise to the top and are extracted. Both "heads" and "tails" are recycled with subsequent washes.

wash, or to one full charge of the boiler, and is ready for secondary distillation.

This distillate, now about 35% vol. alcohol, is called *"brouillis"* in Cognac or, in malt-whisky distilleries in Scotland, "low wines." The first vapors coming from the *brouillis* contain a high proportion of volatile poisons, mainly acetaldehyde, which boils at 28°C (82°F). These poisons condense in the worm and are drawn off into a special receiver; being lighter than alcohol, they are readily detected by the hydrometer. When the hydrometer reading—and the stillman's practiced nose—indicates that purer alcohol is coming over, the stream of condensate is directed into the receiving cask. A second time, towards the end of the process, the hydrometer reading plus a rank smell will indicate that poisonous fusel oils (this time the ones less volatile than alcohol) are again present in significant concentration, and the stillman will accordingly direct the stream back into the first receiver. During this secondary distillation the stillman has effectively separated the poisonous "heads" and "tails"—or "foreshots" and "feints" in Scotland—from the good "heart." Nothing is lost, for the heads and tails will be recycled with the next batch of alcoholic wash.

There are good reasons for the use of the pot still in the preparation of certain fruit and grain spirits: these will be explained in succeeding chapters. However, the pot still has disadvantages, too. Firstly, it is a batch process, requiring the still to be recharged four times to produce less than half a charge of alcohol. Secondly, the product retains some of the volatile and non-volatile poisons, while the removed "heads" and "tails" contain some of the alcohol. For speed, especially in relation to spirits produced for the mass market, the continuous Coffey still is therefore far quicker and more efficient.

### THE CONTINUOUS STILL

The pot still remained the sole method of distillation until a customs officer named Aeneas Coffey designed his patent still in 1830. It has been used up to the present day, and there would seem no reason to change the basic design, which is illustrated diagrammatically on page 326. It utilizes the principle of heat exchange in two tall columns, each about 18m (60ft) in height, known as the "analyzer" and the "rectifier." The function of the analyzer is to break down the alcoholic wash into its constituents as vapors; that of the rectifier to condense these vapors selectively, so that the resultant alcohol is separated and purified, or "rectified." The cold basic wash is piped into the still at a point near the top of the rectifier, and from here it flows down a coiled pipe by gravity. Around the pipe is a rising current of steam and hot spirit vapors so that, on reaching the base of the rectifier, the wash is already hot. It is then pumped over and released into the top of the analyzer. A constant stream of steam enters at the foot of the analyzer; the ascending steam vaporizes the descending wash, which flows down through a maze of plates and bubble caps until its temperature reaches that of the boiling point of alcohol. Some steam is condensed by heat exchange in this process, and collects with any unvaporized part of the wash at the foot of the analyzer (in the same way as the spent wash is left in the boiler of the pot still after the primary distillation). Much of the steam, together with vapors of alcohol and impurities, rises and passes out through a pipe at the top of the analyzer and is pumped down into the bottom of the rectifier.

By heat exchange, these vapors are cooled as they rise in the rectifier and condense near the top, as the temperature drops below 78°C (172°F). At this level they are collected on the spirit plate and are pumped out of the rectifier in the form of fairly pure alcohol.

The impurities, or congeners, separate themselves in this process by their differing volatility. The less volatile fusel oils, or "tails," condense near the base of the rectifier and fall to the bottom, where they either revaporize or are collected. The more volatile "heads" rise to the top of the rectifier where they are either piped away for condensation elsewhere or collected as condensate on a plate above the spirit plate (placed there to stop the congeners from dropping down and contaminating the finished product). All the congeners are eventually recycled with a fresh alcoholic wash.

Although there are many designs of the continuous still, these fundamental principles are common to them all.

Alcohol obtained through either the pot-still or continuous-still process has a small proportion of remaining impurities: at this level, however, the concentrations are not dangerous and will contribute to the flavor and character of the product during maturation or, alternatively, may evaporate having first done so.

## MATURATION

Something has already been said of maturation, or aging, but not enough to indicate the dramatic changes (described in more detail in the sections on fruit spirits and liqueurs) in the volume and physical characteristics that always occur. Brandy, for instance, picks up some 2kg (nearly 4½ lb) of oak products from the new barrel in which it is stored, and loses bulk by evaporation through the oak barrel's pores. Transferred to an old barrel after one year, the brandy continues to evaporate and to change through differing chemical processes for the next three to 25 years. It has been calculated that the annual evaporation loss in Cognac is equivalent to all the brandy consumed in France—the French call this "the angels' share." In the Scotch whisky process, as much alcohol is lost each year during maturation as is consumed in the whole of the United Kingdom. What the Scots call that is unprintable!

Continuous stills work in tandem to produce spirit for akvavit at the giant De Danske Spritfabrikker *(left)*. Made from potatoes or grain, according to season, the spirit is flavored with, usually, caraway seed.

The malt distilleries of Scotland are a constant attraction for tourists, seen here in the lofty hall of the Pitlochry distillery *(below)*. Stairways lead down to the peat-fired furnaces beneath the gleaming copper stills.

# FRUIT SPIRITS AND LIQUEURS

**Cognac ♦ Armagnac ♦ The Prorate ♦ Eaux-De-Vie-De-Marc ♦ Calvados ♦ Other Fruit Spirits ♦ Liqueurs**

The finest brandy in the world comes from the Charentes, near the French coast north of Bordeaux. Known as Cognac, and made from comparatively poor wine, its quality depends primarily upon the chalk soil (best in the region's center) on which the grapes are grown.

A fruit spirit is, by definition, an unsweetened spirit made by distilling fermented natural fruit juice. No sugar may be added during fermentation, and therefore only fruit containing its own sugar can produce the required alcoholic wash; moreover, no sugar may be added to that wash. By far the most important fruit capable of conversion to spirits is the grape, from which brandy is the prime spirit derivative; not to be underrated, however, is the considerable world production of various eaux-de-vie-de-marc, distilled from the marc, or pomace, left after the grape juice has been pressed out for wine-making.

Brandies are made throughout the world of wine; inevitably they vary in quality and price, and some are developed purely as the strengthening agent for fortified wines. At the top end of the scale, the brandy made from the unlikely, poor-quality wine of the départements of the Charentes is unquestionably the finest in the world: it is Cognac. From the départements of Gers and Landes, further south, the second brandy of world renown, Armagnac, is made in a timeless atmosphere among medieval reminders of D'Artagnan and the Three Musketeers.

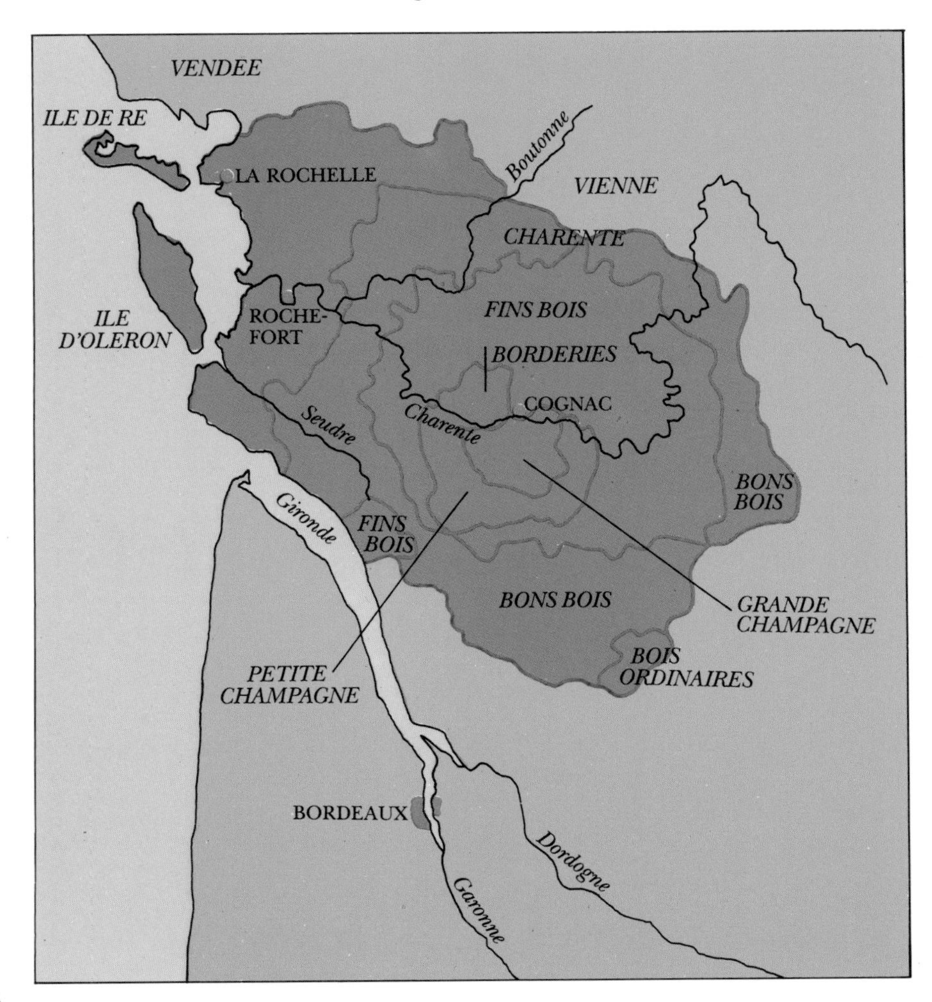


## COGNAC

The Folle Blanche was the grape of the early white wines of Charente, which were sour and acid; however, a trade in this doubtful wine grew during the fifteenth and sixteenth centuries with England and later the Low Countries. There developed the practice of boiling the wine down to strengthen it for its journey and to reduce tax, which at that time was levied on bulk. The product was not yet "brandy," however, for in the boiling of the wine most of the spirit was lost. The concentrated wine was intended to be diluted with water before consumption. The change was remarkable: the quality of the "burnt wine" was noticeably superior to the wine from which it was made.

When distillation was adapted for industrial production in the early seventeenth century, the Charentais went over to the use of the pot still, and immediately produced a natural brandy that was at that time unique, for all other early brandies had such bad tastes that herb and fruit flavors had to be added to conceal them. Word of the product spread abroad, or at least to the Channel Islands, Ireland, and Dorset in England, from which parts four gentlemen, Martell, Hennessy and two Englishmen, Hardy and Hine, made their way to the little town of

A variety of modern Cognac labels bearing some of the finest names *(right).* The standards generally adopted for export are a strength of 80° Proof (40% vol. alcohol) in a 23fl oz (68cl) bottle, although this is not yet enforced by EEC regulations.

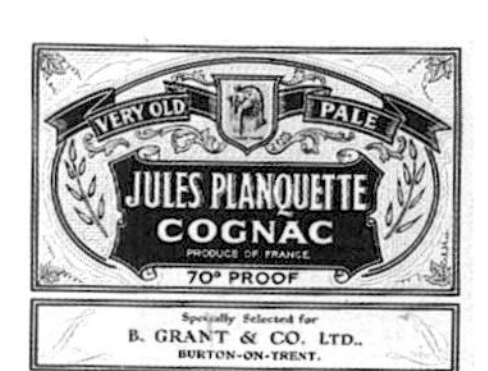

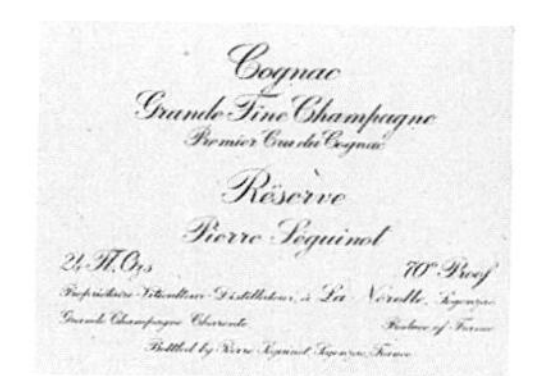

The white St Emilion grape *(above)* used for the making of some 90% of all Cognac is a heavy cropper, low in sugar and high in acidity. Paradoxically, its poor wine provides the basis of the world's finest brandy.

France has a mighty array of spirituous drinks to offer, in addition to her almost infinite variety of superb wines. Brandies from Cognac and Armagnac are deservedly among the best-known around the world *(right).*

Cognac on the Charente river, never to return home. They were largely responsible for founding the massive industry centered there today.

When the brandy of the Charentes had been made with the pot still for two farther centuries, a significant change of its character came about. To the east of Cognac in the foothills of the Massif Central, surrounding the town of Limoges, is the forest of Limousin, consisting mainly of oak trees. Around the beginning of the nineteenth century, the brandy distillers adopted this Limousin oak for their barrels. Up to that time Charente brandies were light in color, even after aging, which no doubt accounts for the early description under which the best of them were marketed, "VSOP," which stands for "Very Superior Old Pale." During maturation the tannin in the Limousin oak barrels gives these brandies an increasingly dark appearance, while other oak chemicals add to the flavor and finesse of the brandy as they dissolve in it.

The nineteenth century had other developments in store for Charente brandy. In 1860 a French geologist called Coquand arrived in Cognac with a professional wine-taster. Independently they visited all the vineyards and distilleries of the Charente and Charente — Maritime départements, one making a geologic survey and the other sampling the product. They discovered an affinity between soil and brandy that varied precisely with the quality of the soil. In the center of the region, south of the Charente river, is the rolling, open, soft chalky downland, which the French call *campagne*. This has soils similar to those of the great Champagne area in the north. The further the distance from this center, the less chalk there is to be found in the soils.

As a direct result of this survey—geologic and enologic—the six famous districts of the Cognac region were identified and delimited. The vineland was divided into geographical proportions as follows:

| | |
|---|---|
| Grande Champagne | 14.5% |
| Petite Champagne | 16.0% |
| Borderies | 4.5% |
| Fins Bois | 38.0% |
| Bons Bois | 22.0% |
| Bois Ordinaires et Communs | 5.0% |

Grande Champagne has the best soil and the most heavily planted vineyards; thereafter, as one goes down the list, the soils are progressively inferior, and plantings in the Bois areas are thin and well scattered. The quality and value of the brandy decline accordingly.

There were two other consequences of Coquand's work. From 1860 onward the name "Cognac" was given to these brandies, and the method of marketing also changed. Historically brandy had been shipped out in the barrel to mature in the cellars of the buyer. But, with the advance of multiple distillation, competition was mounting from neutral spirits, and their sale in bottles was creating a vogue. Also, the brandy manufacturers feared dilution and adulteration of their product from barrels beyond their reach and control. Brandy in bottles could be labeled and hence guaranteed under seal for origin, quality, and variety, and so the change came about. The cost of financing it, measured in terms of stocks maturing for up to 25 years, and being sold even at 40 years, can be imagined: the brandy casks, or *tierçons*, each hold between 350 and 450 liters (90-120gal) and a stock of about 50,000 such casks would be held by the larger producers.

In the early 1860s all seemed set for the future, but it may well be guessed what next befell. Phylloxera struck and wiped out the vineyards of the Charentes; they had to be purged of the louse and replanted with grafted viniferas on American rootstocks.

Saint-Émilion is now the vine of Cognac. Folle Blanche and Colombard represent only 6% or even less of the vineyard plantings; and there are five other varieties which may be blended-in under certain conditions, but not to more than 10% of the whole. Since 1955, any grower in one of the six subregions of Cognac who plants an unauthorized vine will have his whole crop refused. There is no restriction on the yield of the heavy-cropping Saint-Émilion, but it is essential that the wine is sound, for distillation exaggerates imperfections and Cognac from tainted wine would be undrinkable.

Though heavy-cropping, the Saint-Émilion thrives better in hotter regions. It is the same vine as the Trebbiano of Italy and the Ugni Blanc of Southern France and California, which ripen fully. But Saint-Émilion rarely ripens properly in the Charentes—hence the high-acid, low-alcohol hard and sour wine that is perfect for brandy-making, passable with shellfish, and otherwise grimace-making. Among viticulturists who designate growing zones for vines, Saint-Émilion is a Third Epoch grape, unlisted for the Bay of Biscay.

The climate is similar to that of Bordeaux, immediately to its south, giving warm summers and cool winters, but without the forests of the Landes to protect the region from moist salt air from the Atlantic. The land is rolling and misty, and the soils are sandier towards the coast, turning to marl and clay before reaching the limestone and chalk of the central areas. In all, over 30,000 growers have vineyards in the Charentes, although less than 1% of them distill brandy—and even this is a contracting fraction. They and their forebears have cleared the forests (*bois*) to create their vineyards. The larger rural

The Charente grape harvest begins before the crop is fully ripe in order to produce the acidic wine ideal for distillation *(below)*.

establishments, unlike the châteaus across the Gironde, are relics of the Saracens—a walled enclosure, complete with courtyard, house, sheds, stables, and farmyard livestock.

The grapes are gathered in and converted to wine by normal methods, except that the continuous screw press may not be used, nor may any sugar be added when making wine for Cognac. When the year's wine is fully fermented it goes to the stills; and distillation must be complete before March 31 to obtain a certificate of age.

Cognac must by law be produced in the Charantais still. This still, or *chaudière*, may not have a capacity of over 30hl (790gal), nor contain a charge of more than 25hl (660gal); it looks much like a giant copper kettle. By law, the still must be heated by a "naked flame," interpreted these days to include gas-heating or coal fires using briquets. The *chaudière* is capped with a head, of which there are two shapes, the Turk's Cap and the Olive; from here a swan-necked pipe leads the vapors to a water-cooled condenser. The alcoholic wash has about 10% vol. alcohol. Three charges of the wash are run through the still successively, as a primary distillation, and the resulting distillate, or *brouillis*, is then sufficient to make a full charge for the secondary distillation (or *bonne chauffe*). The "heads" and "tails" (see page 328) are separated from the "heart" during this process, to be recycled with the next charge of *brouillis*. The *brouillis* going to the secondary distillation has a strength of 30-35% vol. alcohol, and the final "heart" must be taken at a strength of 72% vol. alcohol, or less.

The raw and fiery water-white "heart" is then run into barrels of 350- to 450-liter (90-120gal) capacity made from Limousin oak, or now very rarely from Tronçais oak, found farther to the north in the Allier département. These oaks have a low tannin content and the wood is porous, both qualities being essential to the production of Cognac; moreover, to ensure mellowness in the brandy, the trees from which the barrels are made should be at least 100 years old. During the first year in a new barrel the brandy needs to be in contact with oxygen, and so the barrel is not completely filled. During this time the brandy picks up weight in various oak products and losses bulk by evaporation. After one year it is transferred into an old barrel which has less tannin, and there it will remain for its long period of maturation—between one and 15 years as either mandatory or desirable, or, exceptionally, up to 40 years.

During this time the loss by evaporation will be considerable, and there will be lesser chemical changes involving oxidation, hydrolysis and

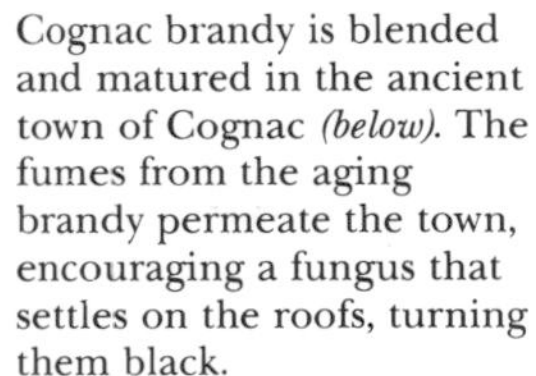

Cognac brandy is blended and matured in the ancient town of Cognac *(below)*. The fumes from the aging brandy permeate the town, encouraging a fungus that settles on the roofs, turning them black.

The acronym "VSOP" appearing on the labels of many Cognac brandies *(left)* stands for "Very Superior Old Pale." The words are in English, reflecting the fact that England was the principal market originally developed for Cognac.

Armagnac does not have as great an export market as Cognac, and much of it is bought near the points of production. Thanks to the lead of the Marquis de Montesquieu, scientific controls *(below)* now guarantee the consistency of standard Armagnac types.

acetylization, while the brandy will continue to darken from tannin absorption. A manifest sign of the evaporation is a black fungus which grows in the *chais* and indiscriminately on roofs in the vicinity. The evaporation loss each year has been reckoned to equal all the brandy consumed in France, equivalent to one-fifth of world consumption. The barrels need to be topped up from *chanteaux*, or partially empty barrels, as evaporation occurs.

The blending of fully matured brandies in the shippers' establishments is a long and slow process, for several reasons. The brandy has to be reduced from 70% vol. alcohol to the required shipping strength of 40%, and in effect this is done by the addition of distilled water. However, to achieve the shippers' required specification different brandies have also to be blended at the same time. All this takes some while, because the differing brandies and the water have to be given time to marry. To reduce the shock of these additions, *faible*, a weak brandy prediluted at 27% vol. alcohol, is often stirred in instead of distilled water, and even then the reduction is made in stages of 8% or 9% vol. at a time. According to shippers' requirements, caramel may also be added during blending to correct color.

There are separate appellations for Grande Champagne, Petite Champagne, Borderies, Fins Bois, and Bons Bois. Each must be matured in a warehouse in which no other district's Cognac is ever present; for the lower AC Cognacs the warehouse must simply never have a spirit of any kind other than Cognac in it. Any "foreign" spirit—say, a single bottle of gin—discovered by an inspector means that all the brandy in the warehouse has to be relegated to nameless eau-de-vie-de-vin.

There are two other appellations, Fine Champagne for a blend of at least 50% Grande Champagne with Petite Champagne, and Grande Fine Champagne, synonymous with Grande Champagne, but possibly superior in some way claimed on the label or obvious to the consumer.

Grande Champagne needs to mature for at least 15 years to bring out its superb bouquet and finesse; Petite Champagne, less distinguished and lighter than Grande Champagne, matures more quickly. Borderies brandies have more body than any other Cognacs. Up to a maximum of 40 years, these three brandies will improve with maturation in barrel: over that period they may tend to acquire barrel taint. For the Bois appellations, 10 years is considered the maximum maturation period to reflect improvement. AC Cognac, for consumption in France, must have matured for one year: after three years it may bear a marque (usually ★★★), and after four years this marque may be VSOP. In the old days shippers used to add another V or O at whim to VSOP, until one topped out at VVVSOOOP which M. Martell thought was overdoing it, whereupon his Cognac was renamed "Cordon Bleu" — which name it still bears.

Maturation (and evaporation) ceases when Cognacs and other brandies are bottled—which raises the question of the validity of Napoleon brandy. Since brandy deteriorates after 40 years in barrel, and from the day it is bottled becomes static (if properly stored), no claim to maturity of more than 40 years can be made for *any* brandy. And it is virtually impossible for this to apply to Napoleon's brandy, as no brandy was bottled until after 1860. Brandy purporting to contain any minute fraction contemporary with Napoleon is therefore fraudulent. But Napoleon-*style* brandy is, by French law, brandy of twice the normal age, generally taken to mean at least six years old, or if it is labeled VSOP (that is, having less caramel added for color) it should be at least eight years old.

"Old Brandies," a term for blends with an average maturation period of 15 years, are

The pillars of the modern Cognac industry have been in the Charentes since the beginning of the seventeenth century. The Courvoisier headquarters *(left)* are at Jarnac, on the river Charente. Martell, shippers of perhaps the best known of the three-star export brandies, have their offices in the center of Cognac itself *(above)*.

sometimes called Liqueur Brandies. But as liqueurs by definition have sugar added, and brandies by definition do not, this must be a misnomer, and the intention no doubt is simply to suggest that they make good after-dinner digestives.

Two further subjects concerning the definition of brandies should be mentioned: they are type and age. Every worthwhile brandy producer has his own interpretation of the three types, of which the cheapest is a young raw brandy for drinking with soda. Next is Three-Star brandy—the stars do *not* indicate its age, although it is older than the inferior type: usually Three-Star will have aged in the barrel for about five years. The third is VSOP, which varies in maturation-time from distiller to distiller. It may be up to 20 years old, but each distiller by careful blending will repeat the style from year to year. VSOP will undoubtedly be a blend of different areas and different years, and will tend to be far better value than the Three-Star, which is much inferior but costs only a little less.

There are four relevant age indications for the Cognac that reaches the US and UK markets. In the US, Cognac may not be sold unless at least two years old; in the UK, at least three years old. VSOP for export must be at least four years old by French law. The fourth indication is for a Cognac shipped to the UK in casks and matured domestically, called "British Bonded" or "Old Landed" (because it is landed before bottling). A record of the years is kept, as a result of which British Bonded Cognac has attracted a US market, being the only Cognac bearing a date indication beyond the US legal minimum. Since World War Two, however, shipments in cask to the UK have dwindled dramatically.

The *charentais* still *(above)*. The fermented wine is stored in the *chauffe-vin (center)* before entering the still *(right)*, above its furnace. The vapor is piped through the *chauffe-vin* (preheating the wine) on its way to the condenser *(left)*.

## ARMAGNAC

In one of the few fairy-tale districts remaining in the civilized world, the second most famous brandy has been perfected during the twentieth century. Armagnac is produced in the heart of Gascony, the southwest corner of France. There you may encounter the blessings or curses of witches still lurking in the countryside, or on the right day you might bump into D'Artagnan and the musketeers, or even Cardinal Richelieu and the King of France, robed in the fineries of yesteryear. The Company of Musketeers is at it again, attracting tourists from all over the world and putting in a word for Armagnac on the side. The locale and the people who live there are as exciting and as fiery as the brandy they produce.

The vineyards of AC Armagnac lie in the département of Gars, with one good enclave in neighboring Les Landes. The territory falls west to the Atlantic from the lower slopes of the Pyrénées, and the region is divided into three: in the Pyrénées is the Haut-Armagnac; in the

Thousands of barrels *(left)* are made each year for the new season's spirit from Limousin or Tronçais oak; they are built to last for up to 50 years. The oak staves are seasoned for several years before being made into casks, which then mellow the young brandy for 18 months.

center is Ténarèze; and in the west is the Bas-Armagnac, where the best brandies are produced. These regions were in 1909 marked out specifically to convert the fragmentary production of Armagnac into an industry and a product as well known as Cognac.

The similarities between Armagnac and Cognac are outweighed by the differences. Where there is chalk in Haut-Armagnac, the brandy is rough, and is used mainly as a basis for liqueurs; the soil in Ténarèze is clay, and the brandies are light and develop quite quickly; but the brandies of great character and finesse come from the Bas-Armagnac, where the soils are essentially sandy. All of this reverses the findings of Cognac. The climate in AC Armagnac differs from the moist maritime climate of Cognac: Armagnac is farther from the ocean and has a more continental climate—a searing summer sun that burns up the rolling plains, tempered by cold easterly winds from the Pyrénées in winter.

The Folle Blanche (Picpoul) grape is steadily giving way to the Saint-Émilion, as in Cognac. But the Colombard and Jurançon are also permitted and heavily planted, together with a few others that are rarely encountered. In Gascony, however, the sun brings the Folle Blanche and Saint-Émilion to full ripeness, so that the brandies of Armagnac have more fire and strength, are richer and have a stronger bouquet, than the Cognacs. The hybrid Baco 22A, a cross between Picpoul and the American labrusca Noah, has been used with some success in Bas-Armagnac; this practice may yet attract the attention of the EEC, which forbids hybrids for making wine in AC regions but has so far done nothing about the anomaly of using hybrids for spirits.

The growers in Armagnac are rustic and their vineyards tend to be small. The Armagnac grape-growing industry's kernel is the Château de Marsan, where the Marquis de Montesquieu laid down a model farm and experimental station to maintain high standards and protect the interests of the small growers. The pressing of grapes is an individual matter; but a traveling still converts the must to raw brandy. It has been likened to "an ancient black locomotive drawn backward." Drawn by a team of blond oxen, it moves slowly around the region.

Since 1936 Armagnac must be made in a native continuous still that defies detailed description. Broadly, it is a cross between the pot and continuous stills, and combines the unique feature of causing the vapors to be refined by the wine from which they have been separated. The still has three boilers, one above the other; at the beginning of a charge, each contains cold wine. The bottom boiler is heated by a furnace below and, as the vapors come off at 78°C (172°F), they bubble up through the wine in the central boiler, heating its contents and condensing at the same time. When the central boiler has heated to 78°C (172°F), the vapors rise and bubble up through the top boiler

Armagnac is the oldest brandy in France, predating Cognac by 200 years. The Château Ravignon *(left)* is one of hundreds where skills in maturing and blending have been passed down from generation to generation.

in like fashion. Eventually vapors from the top boiler rise and pass through a fractionating column to a condenser from which the partially rectified spirit is drawn. The process absorbs all the "tails" in the spent wine, while the "heads" are retained in the finished spirit, where they slowly leach out during maturation. The still may be charged with only two fillings of wine in one day.

The wine entering the still has 9% to 10% vol. alcohol, and the spirit from the condenser must have an alcoholic strength not exceeding 63% vol. In this way Armagnac is made in a single distillation and immediately has a strong flavor and aroma, although maturation is required to make it truly potable. It is aged in barrels of native Armagnac oak which play a great part in giving color (through tannin) and flavor to the brandy. Tests have been made to see whether Limousin oak could be used instead, but it was proved that Armagnac oak, although now scarce and expensive, is essential to the dark, smooth smoldering spirit universally recognized as Armagnac.

These brandies are made to "types," as in Cognac, among them Three-Star, VSOP, and Extra, which respectively claim five, 20 and 40 years' maturation. The types are known to contain blends of younger and older dated brandies, but now, if a date is printed on the label, it must by law be the date of the youngest brandy in the blend. Armagnac will improve for 50 years in wood before passing its best, and nearly all Armagnacs are safely transferred to glass at that stage, if not earlier. The weight of opinion favors blending Armagnacs from year to year, rather than producing vintages, which are rare (and somewhat pointless) in both Armagnac and Cognac.

## THE PRORATE

Brandies are now made anywhere in the USA that good wines are produced. An incident of almost 50 years ago is the key to the founding of the brandy industry in California.

When Prohibition was repealed on December

Armagnac is wholly different from the smooth, soft, dry-flavored Cognac; the dancing fire of the pungent, earthy Armagnac is appropriate to the sand and heat of its Pyrenean climate. Here *(opposite)* the cellar-master noses the new season's spirit with approbation.

31, 1933, over 700 wineries were bonded overnight in California, many by bootleggers who had been granted amnesty. Even though much wine was condemned, there was suddenly a "wine lake" in California, a situation exacerbated by a succession of three bumper grape crops and two good ones. In 1938, the fifth year after repeal, a record crop of some 2¾ million tons of grapes was grown, and, under the state's farm law, a Grape Prorate was voted: this required every grape farmer to convert 45% of his harvest into brandy and not to sell it for two years. The measure was hotly contested, but half a million tons of brandy was made. With another heavy crop in 1939, 20 San Joaquin Valley wineries formed a combine, the Central California Wineries (CCW), to keep surplus wine off the market; this act nearly led to indictment of the CCW and their bankers under Federal antitrust laws.

The advent of World War Two cut off supplies of wines from Europe, so that the indigenous wine trade's surplus suddenly turned into a shortage, bringing with it financial success. However, the old stock of Prorate brandy still lay dormant. During the war, wine experts from Europe settled in California and sampled these Prorate brandies; from them they blended a new type of brandy, much lighter than Cognacs and Armagnacs and with a "different" bouquet. In 1946, new designs of distillery were built to produce this Prorate blend, and in the succeeding 25 years brandy consumption—three-quarters of it the new Prorate blend—quadrupled in the USA.

Eau-de-vie-de-marc is made from the residue of skins and stalks left after fermentation. Seen here as a dried product *(below)*, the marc is next soaked in water, so that the remaining sugar ferments, and the alcohol is extracted by steam.

As a bonus, the same enologists from Europe discovered that the Thompson Seedless grape, if cropped when the acid-sugar ratio was in balance, was an excellent grape for processing to brandy.

The Prorate had proved to be a success much against the odds.

## EAUX-DE-VIE-DE-MARC

Cognac and Armagnac are the only two French AC eaux-de-vie-de-vin. All others have the lesser classification AR (Appellation Réglementée, which has been described loosely as a "spiritous VDQS"). The difference between eau-de-vie-de-vin and eau-de-vie-de-marc is that the former is a distillation of wine and the latter a distillation of marc (pomace), the mass of grape-skins, pits, and stems left after pressing. There are some excellent eaux-de-vie-de-vin with AR status, including those of Aquitaine (from Bordeaux), Faugères (from Languedoc), Burgundy (Bourgogne), and Champagne.

Eau-de-vie-de-marc is a cheap universal spirit, known by other names in different countries: it is *grappa* in Italy, *aguardiente* in Spain, and *bagaçeira* in Portugal. It is usually made by soaking the marc in water in an open pit to allow the remaining sugar to ferment, and then extracting the alcohol with steam. Although the method is crude, the resulting spirits can be extremely palatable, although strong in tannin and tending to bitterness. They have sufficient character to reflect the grape, soil, and climate of origin, however: they are really brandies under a different name. The best marcs come from the Hospice de Beaune, Nuits-Saint-Georges and Montrachet, in Burgundy, and from Champagne and Aquitaine. Eaux-de-vie-de-marc do vary, however, and the poor ones can dramatically affect the liver.

Strict licensing laws apply to the production of eaux-de-vie-de-marc in France, for the wine-maker is not primarily a distiller, and the product is virtually a government monopoly until released under license.

## CALVADOS

Apple orchards take the place of vineyards in Normandy, for it is too far north to ripen grapes. Instead there is annually a massive crop of apples and pears in an area some 150km (95mi) square between the Somme and St Malo. The crop is first converted into cider and perry, the cider being acid, green and unpalatable by comparison with most ciders. But it is used mostly for distilling into the dry fruit spirit Calvados. AC Calvados du Pays d'Auge, from the center of the region, is the best; it must be made from fruit fermented for at least one month, and distilled twice in a *charentais* pot still.

Other spirits with Appellation Réglementée include Calvados-du-Calvados and Calvados-de-la-Vallée-de-l'Orne, and these may be made in a continuous still. The legal minimum maturation period for Calvados is one year, although the raw, fiery liquid is usually matured in oak casks for four, by which time it has the character of a brandy with the flavor and aroma of apples.

The pears of Calvados, when fermented and distilled, make a spirit marketed as eau-de-vie-de-poiré, "*poiré*" meaning perry or fermented pear juice. When distilled the spirit is marketed also as Poiré Williams in France and as Birngeist in Germany.

# OTHER FRUIT SPIRITS

The number of fruit spirits distilled around the world is vast and probably not accurately known: every country is at least capable of making many of its own, even if it does not in fact do so.

Several of the better European fruit spirits are made around the Vosges mountains, either in Alsace to their east or Lorraine to their west. Mirabelle, distilled from the yellow plum of that name, has AC Mirabelle de Lorraine, for which the plums must be grown in the region of Metz and Nancy. Mirabelle Fine du Val de Metz comes from the better, Metz, plums. The plum juice is fermented with yeast and, after two months, is twice distilled in the *charentais* still before maturation in casks. Mirabelle is distilled also in Alsace. Quetsch is another fruit spirit from the plum—the blue plum, which flourishes between the Ill river and the Rhine, close to the vineyards of Alsace. Rhein-Claude, named for the daughter of Louis XII, comes from the greengage and is rarely distilled: it has an overwhelming bouquet.

Among spirits made from soft fruits, Frais, from wild and cultivated strawberries, is very expensive; Framboise, from raspberries, is even more so (35kg of fruit make only one litre of spirit—about 37 lb per pint); Mûre comes from blackberries; and Myrtille from bilberries.

Kirsch is better known, being distilled from cherries on their pits in vast quantities. It is more reasonable in price than Framboise, for 35kg (77 lb) of cherries will produce 15 liters (4gal) of spirit. The wild cherry grows abundantly halfway up the Vosges mountains, around Trois-Épis. Kirsch is always pure white, and accordingly the casks for maturation are lined with paraffin wax—or earthenware containers are used instead. Kirsch made in Germany is marketed as Schwarzwalder, and Swiss Kirsch made near Basel is called Basler Kirschwasser. For cooking, Kirsch Fantaisie, a milder version diluted with neutral spirit from grapes, is substituted.

Slivovitz is Serbian and Bosnian plum brandy from Yugoslavia, where it is called *rakija*; the

Kirsch *(left)* is distilled from wild cherries, and is also flavored with their stones; the cherries grow in the foothills of the Vosges mountains to the northwest of Colmar. About 2kg of cherries produce 1 liter of Kirsch (2lb per pint).

From the village of Steinhagen in Westphalia comes the juniper-flavored spirit called Steinhäger *(left)*; wheat and barley are also added to the wash. The colorless liquor is usually marketed in stoneware crocks which preserve the penetrating juniper aroma.

Fürst Bismarck *(left)* is a popular German Korn, distilled from rye and wheat that have been fermented into a mash; after distillation it is matured in ash vats. Named for the first chancellor of the Reich, it is still made by the Bismarck family.

Most eaux-de-vie are stored in either earthenware jars or glass-lined casks *(right)*, as their color and flavor would change in wood. Meyblum of Betschdorf hand-make their own traditional pottery containers with matching cups.

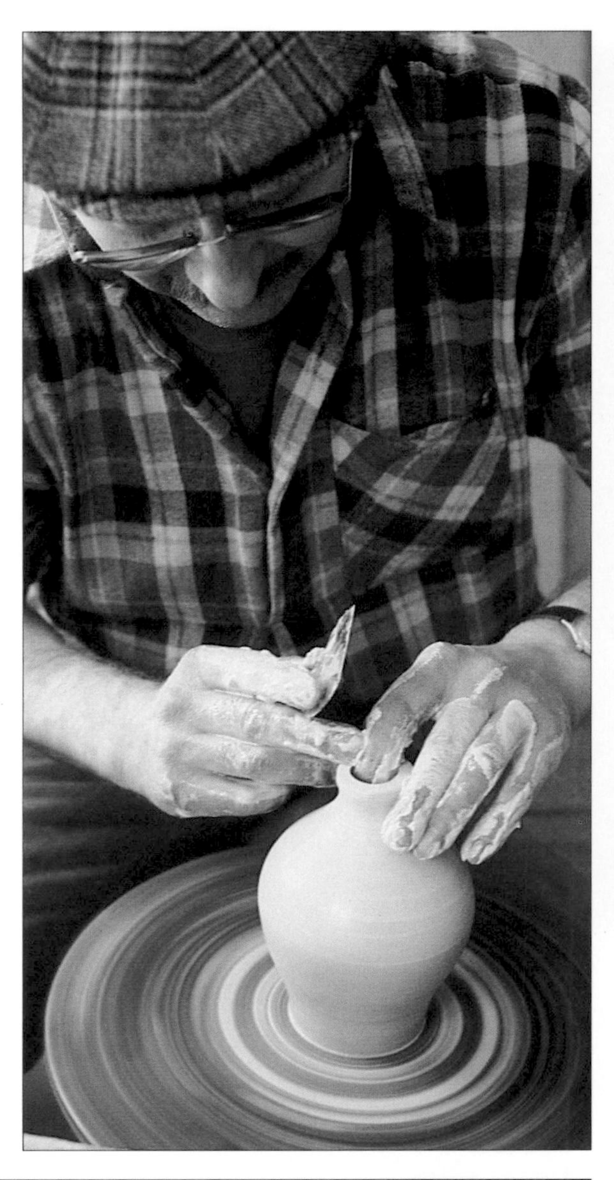

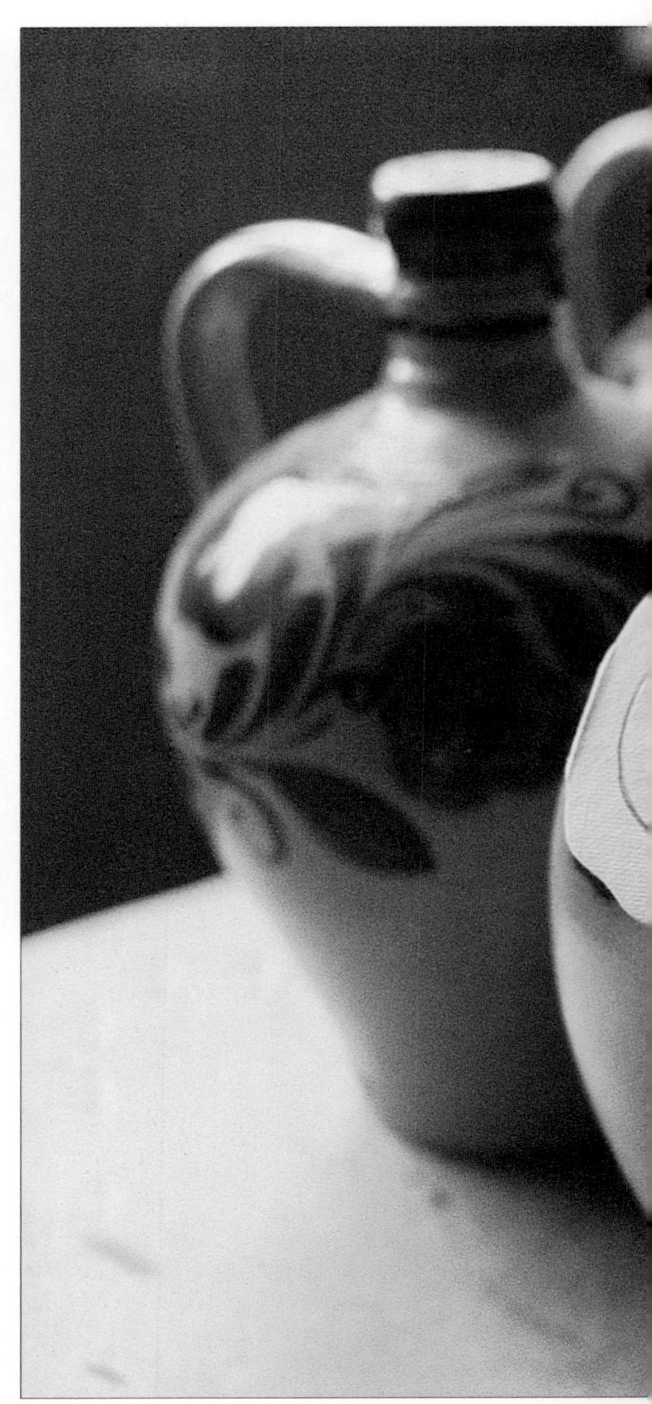

Ergolsthaler Apfel-Brand *(below)* is a leading Swiss fruit brandy, here shown among the apples from which it is distilled. The distillery is in the northern town of Ormalingen.

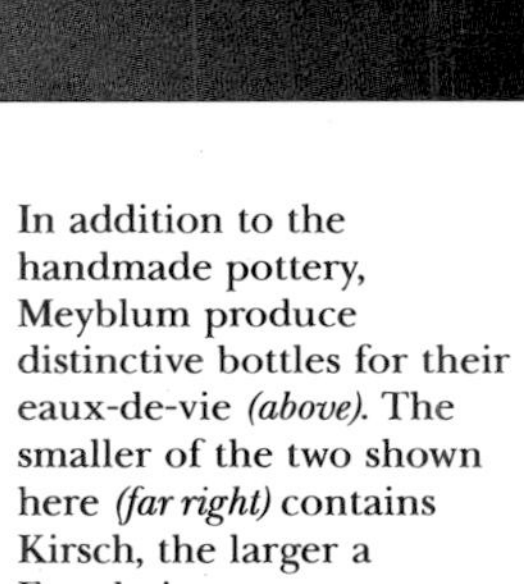

In addition to the handmade pottery, Meyblum produce distinctive bottles for their eaux-de-vie *(above)*. The smaller of the two shown here *(far right)* contains Kirsch, the larger a Framboise.

The Hans Nebiker distillery of Sissach has named a brand of Kirsch *(right)* for the Swiss-born General Johann Sutter, one of the founders of California's wine industry.

Fruits of the anise, drying preparatory to infusion *(left)*. Aniseed has carminative properties and is the base for many liqueurs, including Brizard's Anisette and the drier Greek Ouzo.

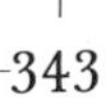

blue plum is grown in the second largest plum-growing area of the world. Slivovitz is double-distilled and exported at 80° and 100° Proof to markets in the USA, UK, Australia and western Europe.

# LIQUEURS

The essential definition of a liqueur is a spirit that has been sweetened and flavored. The spirit component may be any potable spirit: brandy is the base for many French liqueurs; malt whisky for some Scottish liqueurs; and rum for liqueurs from the West Indies. Also, plain spirits from grain, sugar, molasses, potatoes, and other vegetables form the base for many liqueurs throughout the world. The sweetening agent is usually sugar, in one form or another, refined or unrefined, or sometimes in the form of honey. It is the flavoring, however, that gives each liqueur its individuality: one liqueur has no less than 130 herbs, peels, roots, spices, and other constituents which combine to give a flavor renowned and appreciated everywhere.

Hippocrates, the "Father of Medicine," recorded that the distillation of aromatic plants for medicinal purposes was practiced in the fifth century BC, and even today a liqueur, to be genuinely "digestive," is reckoned to need curative as well as aromatic ingredients. In 1847 François Vincent Raspail invented a liqueur that (in his judgment) would "destroy the parasites held to be the cause of most human sickness."

Some fruit liqueurs require many kilograms of fruit to the bottle, especially of soft fruits such as strawberries *(right)*. In the infusion method the strawberries are pulverized and hot spirit is circulated through the mash in a continuous circuit. The expensive Crème de Fraise that results is exquisite.

As ever, the Church played a considerable part in creating and popularizing liqueurs (a name derived from the Latin *liquefacera*, to dissolve). Taken as they usually are after dinner, liqueurs, whose elements are already dissolved and blended together, were believed to dissolve and blend the meal just eaten. The monks knew that alcohol could dissolve the medicinal elements in herbs, and set about preparing them to ease the burdens of comfortable living—developing an appetite, eating too well, and then suffering the next day. They therefore created the *apéritif*, the *digestif,* and the *correctif*. For the first they produced vermouth or flavored wine; for the second a liqueur or flavored spirit; and for the third bitters, of which Angostura, Fernet Branca, and Underberg are modern examples. For the Lord's vineyard, laymen have much to be thankful.

Individual flavoring agents in liqueurs may enhance either (or both) of two qualities in the finished product, aroma and flavor—important elements in the mystery, exhilaration and soul-subduing qualities that round off the mood of the satisfied diner. Aromas (imagine them, for a moment, "disembodied" from their solids) may be soluble in water, oil, or spirits, and they may or may not be harmed by heating. The method of their extraction from base materials is therefore crucial to their survival, and the choice of the correct one of three methods will guarantee this. These three are cold maceration over a long period, hot infusion (which is quick), and distillation to produce an elixir.

Maceration is a slow process in which the flavoring agent is soaked in alcohol or water, perhaps for only 24 hours but more usually over a period of up to a year. It is essential for aromatic plants if the retention of their fragrance, freshness, and natural color is to be secured, or if their flavor would be lost by heating.

In hot infusion, or percolation, the flavoring agent is pulverized and hot spirit is cycled in a closed circuit through a filter containing the mash. For this fast method to be used, the agent must of course be stable to heat.

Making an elixir can be a little more complicated. Alcohol vapor is passed through a filter of one or possibly many pulverized flavoring agents, all impervious to heat; alternatively, the agents may be distilled with a mixture of alcohol and water. Delicate agents may be treated by the latter process, as the temperature of distillation can be lowered under vacuum. "Heads" and "tails" are eliminated by normal methods during distillation, as the strength and purity of the water-white heart is essential.

Certain types of ingredients, including citrus fruits, may yield their flavor simply by use of mechanical pressure; and nonvolatile compounds, such as fat, can be used to absorb bouquet for later extraction by alcohol.

Whichever process is used for the extraction of aroma and flavor from these agents, spirit and

sugar have yet to be added—as well as coloring materials where appropriate—to balance the product as a salable liqueur.

So well guarded are the secret formulas of the great liqueur recipes that few of them have ever been committed to writing. But it is well established that the major ingredients fall into four categories—fruit liqueurs, citrus liqueurs, herb liqueurs, and bean and kernel liqueurs.

## FRUIT LIQUEURS

There are several reasons why fruit liqueurs are often confused with fruit spirits. They may look alike, even taste alike, and are consumed on similar occasions, or used similarly in the preparation of sweet dishes. But the two types of drink *are* different: fruit spirits are unsweetened, both fermentation and distillation

An array of the labels of a few dozen of the many eaux-de-vie and liqueurs made in France *(left)*. Although many are disappearing because of the prohibitive cost of production, there are still varieties available for every taste and occasion.

The colorful stone jar in which Doornkaat, one of Germany's best Korns, is occasionally seen *(top left)*. The company was founded by Jen ten Doornkaat at Norden in northwest Germany. The triple-distilled Korn has a high reputation for its purity.

A character study of the distiller at the H Nebiker distillery in Sissach *(top right)*. Some of the fruit brandies and eaux-de-vie Nebiker produces are made in very small quantities.

This montage representing the distilling process *(above)* stands in the Town Museum at Aarhus. The chocolate Dalmatian appears to be sampling the ferment — normally made from potatoes in the winter, grain in the summer.

Tanks of akvavit at Aalborg in Denmark *(right)* bear the distinctive Maltese Cross of De Danske Spritfabrikker, DDS. The DDS Taffel Akvavit, flavored with caraway, has been made since 1846.

having been generated by natural fruit sugar, and have flavors which likewise come from their original fruits, so that they are in fact eaux-de-vie. By contrast, apricot brandy, cherry brandy, and peach brandy are all fruit liqueurs, "brandy" being in each case a misnomer: they are not eaux-de-vie but flavored and sweetened spirits.

Crème de Cassis is made near Dijon from blackcurrants and grape brandy, and the flavor of Maraschino, from Italy, comes from sour maraschino cherries and their crushed kernels, with sugar and flower-blossom perfumes added. Crème de Banane, with a strong banana aroma and flavor, is popular in Australia.

## CITRUS LIQUEURS

Curaçao probably leads the group of liqueurs made from citrus fruits. The term, originally describing liqueurs made from oranges grown in Curacao, is now generic for all liqueurs derived from orange peel. As the liqueurs are water-white when made, colored variations include orange and blue, as well as the white triple-sec variety which has 45% vol. alcohol. Cointreau is a triple-sec Curaçao, and Grand Marnier, made in the Bordeaux wine region with a Fine Champagne Cognac base, is another excellent Curaçao: it is marketed as Cordon Rouge, the red variety (which has higher strength), or as the yellow Cordon Jaune. Van der Hum, the South African liqueur made from nartjies, a type of oranges, was made in the Cape by settlers to imitate the much loved Curaçaos of their homes. Forgetting after many years who had discovered it, they renamed the liqueur "Van der Hum," or "Mr What's-his-Name."

In the USA, Southern Comfort, with peach and orange flavors overriding a base of Bourbon whiskey, is in much demand. Other favorites are Forbidden Fruit, made from shaddock, a type of grapefruit, with a resulting bitter-sweet citrus flavor, and Rock and Rye, named for its base spirit and its unusual bottle, which has crystallized rock candy on its side: it has citrus flavors.

Other citrus liqueurs reaching export markets

A range of bottles from the House of Balkamp, Rheinfelden *(below)*. On the left are two eaux-de-vie-de-marc (Grappa and Branntwein being Italian and German synonyms). The other three are fruit spirits, 'Eau-de-Vie-de Prune' being a strange misnomer.

are Aurum from Italy; Bergamot and Citroneneis Likör from Germany; Filfar from Cyprus; Kitron from Greece; Mersin, from Turkey; and Sabra from Israel.

## HERB LIQUEURS

These liqueurs may be divided into those having the mixed flavor of many herbs and those having the flavor of one: all have a remarkable subtlety about them.

Benedictine and Chartreuse, from the monasteries of France, are the best known liqueurs with mixed herbs. Benedictine was invented and made at the Abbey in Fécamp by Don Bernando Vincelli in the sixteenth century. When the Abbey was destroyed during the French Revolution, the Abbey's *Procureur Fiscal* saved the recipe. So grateful was the wine merchant who was given the recipe that, ever since, every bottle has borne the initials DOM, for *Deo Optimo Maximo*—"To God most good and great."

The monks of Chartreuse, where the Carthusian Order was founded, kept for many years the secret of their *digestif*, but by the mid-nineteenth century its existence had been discovered, and in 1860 a distillery was built at Fourvoirie to meet a demand for Green Chartreuse, at 55% vol. alcohol, and Yellow, at 43%. Trappistine, made at the Abbey of Grace-Dieu, is flavored with herbs from the Doubs mountains; and La Vieille Cure, from the Abbey of Cenon in the Gironde, is made from 50 root and aromatic plants steeped in Cognac and Armagnac.

Two Scotch whisky liqueurs have mixed herbs added. The recipe of Drambuie is supposed to have been given to Mackinnon of Strathaird by Bonnie Prince Charlie after the unsuccessful rebellion of 1745, since when the Mackinnons have produced and marketed it up to the present day. The other notable Scots herbal liqueur is Glen Mist, made with a blend of herbs, spices, and honey.

The French liqueur Pernod replaced the original Absinth when the constituent of poisonous wormwood stalks caused Absinth to be banned before World War One. Pernod continues to be taken in the same way with water and ice, which turns it milky.

Aniseed is also a good example of a herb used for single-herb liqueurs. Anisette is one such: it is made by Brizard, a firm that did much to establish the French liqueur industry. Another aniseed liqueur of renown is the Greek Ouzo.

Cumin is even better known as a single-herb flavoring agent for liqueurs. Lucas Bols was the first to make Kümmel (literally "cumin") in Amsterdam in 1575, and Bolskümmel remains popular today. After Peter the Great came to Amsterdam in 1696, the production of Kümmel travelled east to Riga, from where the Wolfschmidt family now ship it back to the West. From Danzig comes Danziger Goldwasser, flavored with both aniseed and cumin, and containing gold flakes—a reminder of the days when gold was alleged to have curative properties for certain conditions. Danziger Silberwasser has flakes of silver. Finally, Crème de Menthe is the common example of a single-herb liqueur, made solely with mint.

## BEAN AND KERNEL LIQUEURS

Liqueurs in this group may be made from cocoa, coffee, or vanilla beans, or from fruit kernels and nuts.

Crème de Cacao, produced by the maceration of Venezuelan cocoa beans, is the best known. Tia Maria is produced using Blue Mountain coffee extracts in Jamaican cane spirit. The similar Kahlua, from Mexican coffee, is successfully marketed in the USA. From vanilla beans comes Crème de Vanille; from peach and cherry kernels Crème de Noyau; from hazelnuts Crème de Noisettes.

## ADVOCAAT

Advocaat, with a strength of only 17% vol. alcohol, is the weakest of all liqueurs and one of two which does not fall into any preconceived category. It looks like custard, and is made from egg yolks and grape brandy. The other is Bailey's Original Irish Cream, whiskey already blended with cream, also at 17% alcohol.

## SOME LIQUEUR DEFINITIONS

The French have classified their liqueurs as shown in the table (*below*). Other definitions, applying either in the relevant countries of origin or internationally, include:

- **Triple-sec**, for Curaçaos that have been double-rectified.
- **Ratafias**, now for liqueurs having wine-based spirits. (Originally the term applied to liqueurs drunk at the ratification of treaties and other international agreements.)
- **Kristal-Liköre and Millefiori**, for liqueurs (respectively German and Italian) containing sugar crystals.
- **Eis-Liköre**, for German liqueurs intended for drinking "on the rocks."
- **Double liqueurs**, for liqueurs theoretically containing double the quantity of flavoring agents, but more often containing only 50% more (because the full increase causes certain oils to cloud the liqueur when water is added).

| Classification | Standard strength in degrees GL | Kg of sugar per 100 liters |
|---|---|---|
| Simple | Less than 23° | 20 |
| Demi-fines | 23° | 20-25 |
| Fines | 28° | 40-45 |
| Surfines | 30° | 45-50 |

# GRAIN AND OTHER SPIRITS

**Malt Whiskies ♦ Grain Whiskies ♦ Maturation, Blends, and Storage ♦ Whiskeys ♦ Gin ♦ Akvavit ♦ Vodka ♦ Rum ♦ Tequila**

The Highland Malt distillery at Knockando, in Strathspey *(opposite).* Featured on the drum in the foreground are a few of the artifacts of the distiller's art.

Malt whiskies have been produced in Scotland *(below)* from time out of mind: only since the invention and commercial introduction of the continuous still 120 years ago have grain whiskies been made to temper their fire. Nearly all grain whiskies are made north of the "Highland Line" from Greenock to Dundee.

The oldest grain spirit in the world is whiskey: it has been made for over 1,000 years.

Until the 1830s all whiskeys were Scotch malt whiskies, strong-flavored spirits, made in a pot still, which only the Scots appreciated. The patent or continuous still was invented in 1830, and was soon in use to make grain whisky. It was inevitable that malt and grain whiskies would be blended to give variety for all tastes. When blends produced this milder spirit in the 1860s, there was an immediate overseas market which rapidly extended to become worldwide. Today there are about 120 malt distilleries in Scotland, each with an annual production of between 13,500hl and 90,000hl (360,000-2,400,000gal) of spirit. Each has its own characteristics, but all have a standard strength of 70% vol. alcohol when put into cask; grain whiskies have the same standard strength. There are only 14 grain-whisky distillers in Scotland: their spirit production is used for making gin and vodka as well as whisky. Each of these distilleries produces several hundred thousand hectoliters of spirit each year.

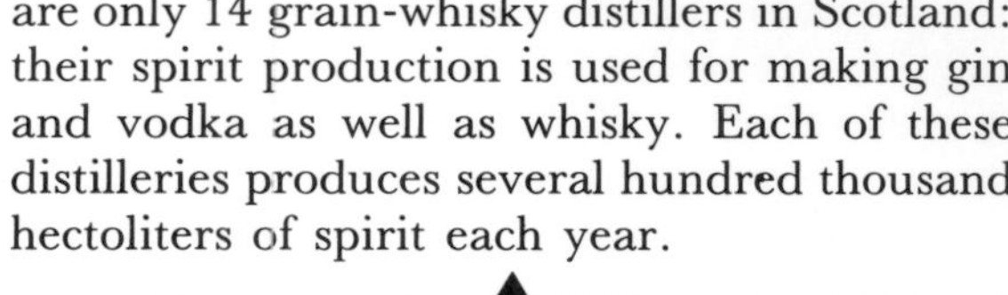

## MALT WHISKIES

All malts are made from malted barley and no other grain.

There are four groups of malt-whisky manufacturers, normally distinguished by geographic location, although a professional would easily distinguish them by their taste. The first group are the Highland malts, made north of a line drawn between Greenock and Dundee. Also from north of this line come the Islay malts, made on the isle of Islay. All malt whiskies made south of that line are described as Lowland malts, with the exception of Campbeltown malts, made at Campbeltown on the Mull of Kintyre. The malt whisky produced by every single distillery is distinctive, although there is a "family" resemblance within each of the four groups which may be attributed to the quality of local water, the peat used in malting, the type of pot still used, the location of the warehouse in which the whisky was matured, and of course the craft of the stillman.

The making of malt whisky falls into four main stages: malting, mashing, fermentation, and distillation. The barley is first screened to remove any foreign matter, after which it is steeped in water tanks for 60 hours. It is then spread out over the concrete floors of "maltings" (buildings especially erected for this process), where it will germinate within eight to twelve days, according to the season. As the barley germinates, the enzyme diastase is secreted, and as this happens the temperature of the barley rises. The barley must be turned

by raking to insure even humidity and thus control the rate of fermentation. During fermentation, the barley's starch is being converted to maltose. When germination is sufficiently advanced, the malt is first screened to remove the green shoots that have grown and then dried in peat-fired kilns. The reek of the peat impregnates the malt and gives it flavor. The dried malt is then ground in a mill, ready for mashing. Many breweries and distilleries today prefer to draw ground malt from centralized maltings which are fully automated and under the control of biochemists, the process taking place in drums, or saladin boxes.

The malt is now mixed with hot water in the mash tun, a circular vat with stirrers. Here any remaining starch is converted to maltose and the soluble maltose sugar is dissolved, producing a "sugary wort" that is drawn off, leaving the "draff" to be processed into cattlefood (see below). The wort is "sparged" with hotter water, and then cooled to blood-heat before being discharged into washbacks, tanks that may hold up to 450hl (12,000gal).

Here the yeast is introduced. Within 48 hours the wort will be converted into an alcoholic wash of 11% vol. alcohol. (The original weight of barley grain and the volume of water added in the mash tun and during sparging are all critical if the resulting wash is to have the requisite 11% vol. alcohol.) The wash now also contains unconvertible solids in suspension and chemical by-products of fermentation.

The alcohol has next to be purified and condensed by the process of distillation in the pot still, the principle of which has already been described previously (see page 326). In malt-whisky making, the distillate is known as "low wines," and the residual two-thirds of the original batch of wash is known as "pot ale." The pot ale is malodorous but full of valuable proteins; it is therefore mixed with the draff to produce cattlefood which is finally dehydrated and known as "dark grains"—a product so valuable that highly taxed whisky has been called its by-product!

The batch of low wines passes into a second still, sometimes called a low-wines still, for further concentration, and it is here that the first and last runnings (the foreshots and feints) in this secondary distillation are drawn off and collected: any usable potable alcohol in them is recovered by redistillation. The residue left in the low-wines still has no value and is sprayed over the countryside.

The "heart" of refined alcohol passes directly into a Crown-locked spirit safe, for measurement by customs officers. The impure fraction in the heart will leach out during three years' maturation—the legal minimum—in oak casks. What comes from the still is officially "British Plain Spirits," and not until after three years may it be called whisky.

## GRAIN WHISKIES

Diastase, which is essential in the process of converting starch to sugar, comes only from barley, and in the form of dried malt must be added to the starches of corn, wheat and millet (and sometimes unmalted barley) if grain whisky and other spirits are to be made from them.

Before corn, the grain most often used, can be treated with diastase it requires pretreatment by milling and cooking under steam pressure for 3½ hours to burst the starch cells. The resulting mash is mixed with diastase and water in the mash tun, for conversion into sugar. The wort so produced has a low specific gravity, and is less concentrated than that for malt whisky. In the whisky distillery the process of distillation of the wort now becomes a continuous process, using the Coffey-type patent still. The

The primitive worm shown here *(right)* was an early step in the evolution of the clinical methods used in modern whiskey manufacture.

Malt whiskies are made almost entirely from barley *(far right)*, the only grain which produces the enzyme diastase during germination. The diastase from barley is an essential catalyst in every distillation process.

supply of wort therefore has also to be continuous process.

The principles of the Coffey still have been described earlier (see page 328). Like that from the pot still, the spirit coming from the patent still needs three years'' maturation in wood before it is ready for blending. This spirit is much stronger than that from the pot still, but it is diluted to 70% vol. alcohol before the maturation process.

# MATURATION, BLENDS, AND STORAGE

Whether from pot or patent still, British Plain Spirits are put into cask at 70% vol. alcohol. Sherry butts are often used to give more color, or new wood, possibly American oak, may be preferred. Volatile impurities will evaporate through the wood pores, and damp Scottish air will replace them. Alcohol will evaporate also, so that the spirit loses strength, although little is lost in bulk. The congeners that do not evaporate will form compounds with elements from the air in the cask, and it is these compounds which will give the eventual whisky much of its flavor. Malt whiskies may be left to mature far longer than the legal minimum of three years; they have many highly flavored constituents to digest, and will improve for 15 years in wood. Grain whiskies will not improve after three years.

Although a ''single-grain'' whisky—from one distillery—is palatable, it is rare; single malts are more popular, but mean more to the dedicated Scot than to anyone else. Most branded whiskies are therefore malts blended with grain whisky. Up to 50 single malt whiskies may be included in any one blend, two-thirds of which by volume will be grain whisky. Each blending company has highly secret formulas for its brands, which must above all else be consistent, and be recognizable for color, flavor, and strength. As with brandies, whiskies must be left for a period of months before bottling to marry the ingredients of the blend. The whiskies are finally reduced to shipping strength with mains water, usually in Glasgow or Edinburgh, at the time of bottling. The usual strength for home and continental sales, declared by law on the label, is 40% vol. alcohol; whisky for the USA, however, is shipped at 85° US Proof, or 42.5% vol. alcohol.

Newly distilled spirit going into cask is described volumetrically as the ''original gallonage:'' what remains after maturation is the ''regauge gallonage.'' The loss, or difference, is ''ullage,'' reckoned to account for over 450,000hl (12 million gal) of whisky annually.

The Finance Acts of 1969 and 1980 decree, *inter alia*, that ''Scotch whisky'' by definition must be distilled and matured in Scotland, and, if maturation applies to a blend, the minimum

The malts of Islay are "peated" heavily to give the pungent spirit that characterizes the product of this and seven other distilleries on the island *(top)*. There is a hint of salt, too, in these deep-flavored malts.

Peat is the essential fuel in the malting process for the production of diastase. Fifty years ago peat was cut out of the moorland by gangs of manual workers *(above)*; now machines have taken over.

Most blending and bottling of Scotch takes place around Glasgow and Edinburgh. Here in Dunfermline *(left)*, bottles are being checked for accurate weight of contents.

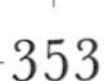

A stack of traditional 100-gal (455-liter) butts on Islay. The duties of a resident cooper *(above)* include the maintenance of these casks, which are shipped with their precious contents to the mainland.

Barley in the maltings has to be raked constantly *(left)* so that the temperature is kept even throughout the mass of grain. The barley starch is converted to maltose by the action of the enzyme diastase.

The distant malt distillery of Dalwhinnie is set off by the thistle — no less! — in bloom *(right)*. This distillery is isolated in the heart of the Highlands, not far from the source of the river Spey.

legal period of three years' maturation (or any longer period stated on the label) shall apply to the most recently distilled of the spirits in the blend. Moreover, Scotch whisky exported in cask and blended with whiskey other than Scotch shall not be labeled or sold as Scotch whisky.

Many of the companies distilling, blending and bottling Scotch whisky, gin, and vodka today are incorporated in the International Distillers and Vintners Group, now itself a subsidiary of Grand Metropolitan Hotels. Despite the hierarchy, the individual member-firms are left to apply their knowledge and skills independently.

# WHISKEYS

Distillers around the world, except in Canada, give Scotch the sole use of the word whisky without an "e," and spell theirs with one. It is a trade custom, touched perhaps with a little reverence. "E" or no "e," the drink so named must start with diastase from a mash of malted barley.

## IRISH WHISKEY

This pot-still whiskey usually uses unmalted barley, rye, and wheat. It has three distillations; the heads and tails are drawn off during the second distillation and those remaining are drawn off during the third distillation. Naturally some congeners remain, but fewer than otherwise would. "Irish" is matured for not less than three and up to 15 years. It has a distinct smoky aroma which is in fact a result of the use of rye: Irish malt is kilned without smoke.

Poteen is roughly the same product, made in remote country areas by independent manufacturers unknown to Customs officers.

## RYE

Canadian rye whisky is light in body and remarkable for the attention paid by government officers to every stage of its production. This starts with approval of every batch of grain and ends with payment of duty on release of the product from bond.

Rye is made in a continuous still and therefore lacks the smoky aroma typical of Irish whiskey. Corn is added to rye in the mash, which is ground down and heated with live steam before the barley malt is added. After fermentation and distillation, the resulting spirit is reduced to barrel-strength for aging from four to 12 years, and is bottled at 40% vol. alcohol (or at the Proof strength of the country of destination).

Canadian rye must be made from the alcohol potential in its cereals alone, whereas in the USA blended rye may have neutral spirit added from other sources. "Straight" US rye must have at least 51% rye in the grain mix and be distilled at not more than 80% vol. alcohol (160° Proof), bottled at not less than 40% vol. alcohol (80° Proof), and be aged in new charred oak barrels for not less than two years. Corn whiskey, with at least 80% corn, is a fiery drink of the backwoods that gets little chance to mature at all. This "white lightning" should be left to the natives. In the USA rye whiskeys are made mainly in Pennsylvania and Maryland, and are often taken with mixers. They enjoy a better social image than gin does in England, although generally used for very similar purposes.

## BOURBON

A development from the illicitly distilled spirits made in Arkansas, Kentucky, and Tennessee, the recognized Bourbons of today have emerged since US Customs officers finally prevailed in the fight against large-scale illegal distillation almost 100 years ago. Kentucky is today the centre of US whiskey production, with over half the nation's distilleries in the state. Here Bourbon whiskey was first made in Bourbon county, although it may now be made anywhere in the USA. Bourbon, by definition, is now any whiskey made from a sour mash having at least 51% corn, distilled at not more than 80% vol. alcohol (160° Proof), but usually at between 62½ and 70% vol. alcohol (125-140° Proof), and aged in new charred oak barrels. (A sour mash is one in which the residue of a former

distillation, called "spent beer," is used for fermentation.) Aged for two years and unblended it is Straight Bourbon; blended with other Straight Bourbons it becomes Blended Straight Bourbon. These two are the USA's largest-selling whiskeys.

## GIN

Today gin is perhaps the cleanest spirit sold, but it was by no means always so. The change in drinking habits in England came about through prohibitive duties levied on French wines in the closing years of the seventeenth century. As duty was levied on bulk, spirits, with their greater strength-to-bulk ratio, attracted proportionally less duty than wine. French brandy became popular under James II, but, when William of Orange displaced the francophile James in 1688, Hollands gin was introduced. In its worst form Hollands gin then had no preliminary rectification, and even the poorest could afford to buy it. Cheap gin was made in England, too, and the almost penniless poor took to the oblivion it brought as their only escape from their life of poverty, neglect, and sickness.

Social conditions were still appalling in the nineteenth century when the dangers of poisonous gin were first recognized as a social evil Gladstone waged a war against it with only moderate success; the Salvation Army and the Band of Hope joined in, the former campaigning for total abstinence and the latter calling for temperance. Temperance was, and still is, the keynote, for wines and spirits in moderation never did anyone any harm, and have done many much good.

Two major steps to correct the social misery that spirits were exacerbating came during the nineteenth century. In 1830 the Coffey continuous still with its rectifier (see page 328) was designed, and the Sikes hydrometer for measuring the strength of alcoholic drinks was later adopted by Gladstone. These two factors meant that duty could be assessed relative to strength, not bulk, and that congeners which had been present at dangerous levels in spirits could be reduced by rectification to safe levels. Although the principles of both inventions have much broader application, their development is particularly relevant to the history of gin, which as a result was raised in quality as well as priced out of reach of the poor, whose plight was at last being relieved in other ways by more socially conscious governments.

The Dutch were the first to disguise the taste

Time was when Irish whiskey was served across the bar from oak casks *(left)*. Indeed, when the Old Bushmills distillery in County Antrim was first licensed in 1608, bottling of alcoholic drinks had not been introduced on a commercial scale.

Coates' trademark *(center)* is, predictably, a Black Friar.

The blue-black berries of the juniper bush *(bottom)* provide gin's main flavoring agent; indeed it was the supposed medicinal value of juniper that led to the discovery of gin. Coriander is also used in its flavoring.

The historic refectory of the Black Friars Distillery in Southside Street, Plymouth, the home of Coates' Plymouth Gin *(right)*. The Black Friars were the building's original occupants until Henry VIII dissolved the monasteries. The Pilgrim Fathers slept in this room on the night before sailing to America in 1620. After serving as a debtors' prison, the building became Coates' distillery in 1793.

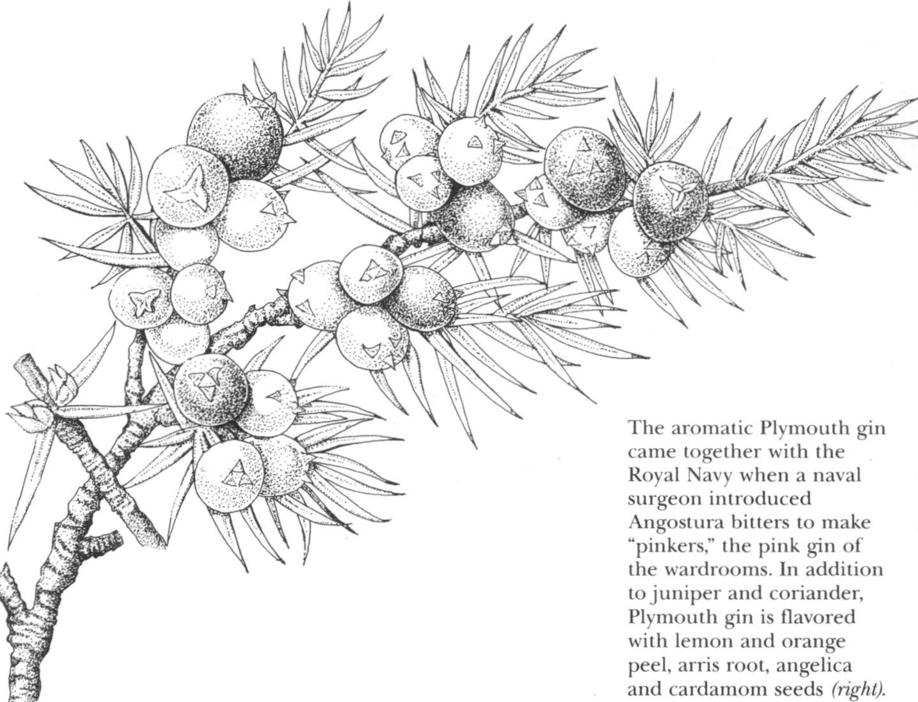

The aromatic Plymouth gin came together with the Royal Navy when a naval surgeon introduced Angostura bitters to make "pinkers," the pink gin of the wardrooms. In addition to juniper and coriander, Plymouth gin is flavored with lemon and orange peel, arris root, angelica and cardamom seeds *(right)*.

A 'twenties flapper getting her feet very wet indeed to publicize dry and Old Tom London gins *(left)*. Old Tom is the base for Tom Collins, dry London gin that for John Collins.

of the insufficiently purified gin they distilled from rye. They did so with berries of the juniper, which they call *genever* and which the English shortened to "gin." The gin of today may be made from any sugar- or starch-based vegetable, including sugarcane, grains and root vegetables such as potato and sugarbeet. However, modern gin still requires flavoring to offset rank flavors from these spirits. The main agent remains the juniper berry, and other herbs are now added to particular gin brands. The substantial list of these herbs and spices used for gin and other flavored spirits includes aloes, angelica, aniseed, arrowroot, camomile, caraway, cardamon, cassia, centaury, cinnamon, citrus peels, cloves, coriander, fennel, gentian, ginger, hyssop, liquorice, marjoram, mint, orris root, quinine, rosemary, sage, vanilla, and wormwood.

The bad name that gin earned will probably linger for some while yet, but today the compounders of gin buy twice-rectified spirit of 70% vol. alcohol from patent-still distillers: this is redistilled through fractionating columns to remove the harmful fractions and leave a spirit of 96% pure ethyl alcohol. This is odorless, tasteless, pure spirit, and is ready for gin, vodka, and liqueur production. The spirit is poured into a pot still and powdered herbs are added; after maceration the still is heated, mainly by steam

coils immersed in the spirit. The heads and tails are taken off, for they have gained too much pungency from the flavoring agents. The good heart alone is taken for gin. It remains only for the gin to be diluted to market strength with pure water before bottling.

"London gins" may vary, but are generally dry and light-flavored; juniper and coriander are the most usual flavoring agents, but as many as 20 may be added. Plymouth gin is similar to London gin. Dutch genevers today are of two types: Oude (old) genever starts with malted barley and rye, is pot-distilled, and is usually put up in stone bottles; and Yonge (young) genever is patent-distilled from grain or cane, and is similar to London gin in flavor.

## AKVAVIT

In Denmark akvavit is distilled from grain or potatoes in continuous stills. The main flavoring agent is caraway seed.

Akvavit is the most obvious of all corruptions of *aqua vitae*—the name given to the first distillation from wine in thirteenth-century Italy. But akvavit is the flavored spirit of Scandinavia, and of Sweden in particular, where it is also called "snaps," meaning "a mouthful." The basic spirit comes, during the winter, from potatoes, which are pretreated with heat to break down the tough starch granules; in summer it comes from corn flour from which the corn oil has first been extracted. From either source, the starch is saccharified by synthetic diastase before being fermented by baker's yeast into an alcoholic wash: today most akvavit is produced at potato distilleries and rectified to remove congeners and the taste of potatoes.

In Sweden, caraway seed is the almost universal flavoring agent, but aniseed and fennel are occasionally used, as in the export brand of O.P. Anderson. Akvavit is served as cold as possible, like vodka, and is taken traditionally with *smörgasbord*. Next to Sweden, Denmark is the largest producer of akvavit, generally known there as "schnapps;" it accounts for over 70% of Denmark's spirit consumption. Norway is a smaller producer.

With akvavit, which tends to be more of a way of life than just a flavored spirit, there are many variations. There is Danish Jubileumsakvavit, to celebrate the Jubilee of the monopolistic State Distillery; there is one for the ceremony of "crossing the line;" and so on. The Norwegians maintain an aged theory that akvavit benefits from a sea voyage by giving it a return trip to Australia.

## VODKA

Russian vodka is available there from many distilleries and in a wide range of bottles. Zubrovka is a leading export brand.

Vodka is the spirit of Russia, Poland,and the Baltic states. In the years since the Second World War, however, it has become an international drink, now made throughout the western world, from California through the rest of the USA and across the Atlantic to Western Europe.

In Russia there is a dramatic variation in the production of grain and root crops from year to year, and vodka has been produced there mainly from any surpluses which might occur. Rye and potatoes figure most noticeably as available crops under this system, and the disagreeable flavors from each need to be disguised. Peach- and cherry-flavored vodkas are therefore to be found, and the Polish Zubrowska (or Buffalo) vodka is famous for its green color and the flavor of the coarse grass which feeds the buffalo; you may find a bottle actually containing a sample blade.

The vodkas made in the USA, UK, Germany, and elsewhere are entirely colorless, tasteless, and odorless, however, and may be made from cane spirit as well as from grain crops or potatoes. To ensure that every trace of color or smell has been removed, the spirit is filtered through activated charcoal of vegetable origin, usually from coconut shells, which has been heated to over 1,000°C (1,832°F) in a vacuum, then canned and sealed. Reactivating the charcoal is extremely expensive and so, to offset this cost, vodka is reduced from 96% vol. alcohol after rectification to a shipping strength of 37.4% vol. alcohol (in the UK) using demineralized water; less duty is thus levied than on the 40% in other plain spirits. Elsewhere, vodkas range from 37 to 56% vol. alcohol (74-112° Proof). Vodka now competes with gin as a popular spirit for incorporating with various mixers in short and long drinks.

## RUM

The UK defined rum in 1909 as "the spirit produced by distillation of fermented sugar-cane products, distilled in sugar-cane producing countries." That hardly does justice to the spirit that so influenced the behavior of the Royal Navy that it was nicknamed "Rumbustion" or "Rumbullion." The British Navy fell upon it in the West Indies, adopted it, and have been splicing the mainbrace with it ever since.

Rum originated in the West Indies, but is also produced in a number of other countries where sugarcane grows, including North and South America, Indonesia, and Australia. It is made from molasses, a glutinous black liquid by-product in the extraction and refining of sugar from the sap of the sugarcane. The cane is a fast-growing grass that will yield two or three crops each year; it is possible that Columbus may have brought it from the Azores on his second voyage. Propagated simply by planting a short length of cane into the plowed soil, it will grow to 2-2.5m (6-8ft) in height, and the ripe cane will be 10cm (4in) thick.

Canals surrounding the sugarcane plantation provide a means of transport for the finished crop, but equally important is their value as fire-

breaks when the fields are set alight at harvest. This is done primarily to burn off the leaves, but it also adds potash to the soil and rids the plantations of snakes.

After cutting with sharp knives, called "cutlasses" in the West Indies and "machetes" in Guyana, the cane is gathered in to go through a series of refining stages. First it is crushed to extract the sap, which is boiled to evaporate the water content and then centrifuged to separate the sugar crystals. Further extractions will separate golden syrup and black treacle, finally leaving a residue incapable of being refined any further. This is molasses, the raw material of rum.

The molasses is diluted with water and fermented with yeast or with dunder, the residue from a previous distillation, to produce an alcoholic wash of about 10% vol. alcohol: cultivated yeasts are the more often used. The wash goes forward to distillation, which can be effected through either the pot still or the continuous still; the product from the former will be pungent and from the latter much lighter. All rum is water-white when it leaves the still; the color in pungent rums comes either from the addition of caramel, which does not affect the taste, or from maturation in wood casks. The difference in flavor arises rather from the length of fermentation and the addition (if any) of dunder, each of which will produce more highly flavored rum. Slow fermentation in the pot still may take up to 12 days, whereas rapid fermentation in the continuous still may be completed in as little as 12 hours, although 24 to 36 hours is more usual.

Distillation was all done originally in the pot still, with two fermentations, the heads and tails being separated during the second fermentation. The pot-still method is the same today, but the product is too pungent for popularity and so the continuous still has also come into use. As with malt whiskey, the pot-still rums have many variations depending upon climate and soil as well as on water, which in the West Indies is reckoned to be as pure as may be found anywhere.

Rums are made in a number of different countries, and they are generally recognizable by their individual styles. The US Federal Alcohol Administration maintains somewhat awkwardly that a list of rums including those from Barbados, Cuba, Demerara, Haiti, Jamaica, Martinique, Puerto Rico, St Croix, St Thomas, Santo Domingo, and the Virgin Islands are not distinctive types of rum. "Such names," it says, "are not generic but retain their geographical significance. They may not be applied to rum produced in any other place than the particular region indicated in the name."

It is obviously satisfactory that each country, island, or region has the exclusive use of its own name attached to its rum, but many will disagree on the matter of distinctive types, which in the international spirits trade most certainly are identified with certain areas. The old Jamaica-style rum, for instance, is the prototype for pot-still rums of greater body; Barbados rums are soft with a smoky flavor, and the Mt Gay distillery there produces one rum that may be taken neat like a fine brandy. Cuban rum is treated with charcoal to help make it lighter and more delectable. The extremely light-bodied White Label and less light Gold Label rums are made in Puerto Rico. Rhum Barbancourt from Haiti is medium-bodied with perfect balance: it is not the one poured on the ground at Voodoo ceremonies so that the gods may first be satisfied.

Export rums are usually sent to more temperate climates to mature, thereby avoiding too much evaporation; the period of maturation may be only two years before sale, a short period allowed because the original sugarcane develops fewer congeners than do grain spirits.

Arrack (which can be spelled "arack," "arrak," "arraki," and so on) is made from native spirits. The word is Arabic for "juice" or "sweat;" the drink is produced from the former and may cause the latter. Arrack is made variously from fermented palm sap and rice in the East Indies, from grain spirits in Greece, and from dates in Egypt and the Middle East. Batavia arrack, distilled in Java, is a highly aromatic form of rum. The French proverb, "He who has once tasted arrack never forgets it," sums up the situation. This coarse spirit of the people, from whatever source material, should be strictly left for the people.

Rum, made throughout the Caribbean, ranges from a dark potent liquor to the white Bacardi. Here two Jamaican rums bottled in the UK are shown.

# TEQUILA

Mexican tequila is the most civilized of three alcoholic drinks that come from the same plant: the agave cactus, whose spiky leaves grow from a tuberous ball of roots that beds itself on the scorched surface of the Mexican sierras. The agave is known variously as the century plant, maguery, mezcal, and American aloe. From its milky juice tequila and mezcal are distilled, and obtained from it also is pulque, a fermented beverage of between 4% and 6% vol. alcohol. Pulque was known to the Aztecs, and is now very popular among Mexicans; it is usually drunk when freshly made. Sales reach millions of gallons each year, mainly to country farms *pulquerías* in the cities.

When the root of the agave has grown to a diameter of some 25cm (10in), it is dug out and the spiky leaves are sliced off. The white center is cut up and steam-cooked in an autoclave. Pulque is the filtered ferment from this base material, which is then distilled throughout Mexico to make mezcal; tequila is in fact superior mezcal made only in Tequila County, some 325km (200mi) northeast of Mexico City. Several modern distilleries now produce this high-quality spirit, which is popular also in the USA.

Two similar Mexican drinks from the Agave cactus are tequila and mezcal. The former, from Tequila county, is the better.

# WINE AND THE CONSUMER

As we have seen, drinking habits have changed with fashion, discovery, and the disciplines of history over the centuries. Canada and the USA in turn even went so far as to prohibit the consumption of alcohol for eleven years, although in both cases Prohibition defeated its own ends. In terms of satisfaction, there has never been an effective challenge to the drinking of good wines and spirits, and, when it has been impossible or impolitic to obtain one liquor, there has always been another to take its place. Although the population of the world is as always rising, the consumption of alcoholic drinks, and especially of wines, is rising even faster. Improved communications have made the world smaller; as people of all nations have traveled, so knowledge has spread. New sciences have been developed, and nothing is any longer taken for granted. Old methods of producing wines have been examined anew, and much that was classic and standard has been replaced. Aided by new materials, technology, and research, a revolution in viticulture and vinification has come about in the last 25 years, and a new and excited generation of wine-lovers has shown its appreciation.

In the closing chapters of this book we shall look at not only the structures of the modern wine and spirit industries but also the methods used by the experts to create and perfect the various products. Nothing happens by chance: from international level down to regional and even district level there are organizations working to give the public a constant supply of wines and spirits of guaranteed quality from all over the world. There are comparatively new industries rising in countries such as Canada and New Zealand, whose wines are or soon will be comparable with the superb wines of Europe. And, in many of the world's centuries-old vineyards and wineries, new methods are being tested against the old—then often adopted.

Subjects such as wine-tasting and wine-selection are not simply for the experts, and even a fundamental knowledge of them will help the wine-lover to buy more wisely and more purposefully than before. Equally useful is information about storage of wines in the home; moreover, in all the stages of broaching and serving them, there is a right and a wrong way of going about things, and it is well worth knowing which is which.

The use of storage space to the best advantage is a matter for planning in the quiet of the home, rather than in a rush at the point of sale, for the selection of wines and spirits to occupy this premium space should be made carefully and with forethought. This raises the questions of choosing wines for everyday use, as opposed to those reserved for special occasions, and of selecting wines for drinking with different kinds of foods, for wines can complement certain dishes perfectly and ruin (or be ruined by) others.

Parties—why, when and where to hold them, and how to entertain the guests—are another subject where forethought can often generate new ideas and be thoroughly worthwhile. Notes on this subject will be found on pages 327-380, together with instructions for mixing some of the world's most famous long drinks and cocktails. The "coda" to all the drinks of the day is the liqueur or flavored spirit taken with coffee after dinner. How to stock a selection of these *digestifs* reasonably and effectively is a final matter for serious thought.

Bottles stored in a typical wine rack *(right)*. Home storage of wines discussed on page 380, needs great care if the wines are to be at the right temperature and in perfect condition when required for drinking.

CHATEAU PONTET-CANET
PONTET-CANET CHATEAU
CHATEAU
PONTET-CANET CHATEAU
CHATEAU

# THE WORLD WINE AND SPIRITS INDUSTRIES

## National and International Regulations ♦ Distribution and Licensing ♦ Wine-Tasting

It is a matter of history that England traded in the import and export of wines in a substantial way long before it became common policy among other nations to do so. Certainly the Phoenicians, Greeks and Romans had taken the vine and wine with them on their voyages of discovery and conquest—indeed, had they not done so, the vineyards of Bordeaux would not have been thriving in the twelfth century—but it was the marriage of Henry, Duke of Anjou, later King Henry II of England, to Eleanor of Aquitaine in 1152 that brought the provinces of Gascony and Bordeaux—all of France south of the Loire—under English control: in those days a dowry was something to be reckoned with. As the French needed wool, England's main export, the English were paid in wine from Bordeaux; and, as England's small population could not consume wine in such quantity, re-exports were made to the Hanseatic states of Germany and to the Baltic. England was onto a good thing and she never let go.

As the French wars and differences in foreign policy divided England and France, the English wine trade swung to Spain, Portugal, Germany, and Italy during the fourteenth and fifteenth centuries. Although trade with France eventually recovered somewhat, the pattern was changing, and duty on wine exports and imports became a determining factor. Late in the seventeenth century, when alcohol was taxed on bulk, poisonous Hollands gin displaced French wine on the British market: England's lowest classes resorted to the oblivion of cheap gin, and their social plight further deteriorated until Gladstone's reforms came to their rescue.

But then a remarkable turn of fate came to the aid of the British wine industry. The Liberal party, with their newly acquired power, introduced the policy of free trade. This did nothing to help Britain's exports, but it did allow wines and spirits from all over the world to be imported freely at a time when every other wine- or spirit-producing country put up huge tax barriers on imports to protect the home industry. The Liberals were therefore—unconsciously—responsible for making the British the world experts on wines and spirits.

The USA is not in the front line of wine-exporting nations (although this situation is changing, and she probably soon will be). In fact, only a small fraction of the world's total wine product is exported, and only about a dozen countries are significant exporters. This is due primarily to the levels of consumption within the individual countries, as well as to the fact that wines that keep perfectly well at home often lack the stability to travel. The countries that export quality wines in substantial quantities are France, Italy, Spain, West Germany, and Portugal from Europe, and Argentina, South Africa, Australia, Cyprus, Chile, and more recently the USA from outside Europe. If the wines of countries other than these are to be found anywhere away from home it will be in the UK. The significant exporters of spirits include France, Scotland, the USA, Canada, South Africa, Sweden, and Holland—and there are many others.

The world output of wine alone is today nearing the equivalent of some 50 billion bottles (350 million hectoliters) every year and is still increasing. If you add the world output of spirits and beers it is several times greater. The mammoth industries that produce these quantities are headed by giant companies: some are international combines, some are state-owned, and many more have enormous public funds invested in their operations. Yet there are, in addition, tens of thousands of experts growing grapes, and of these a significant proportion also convert their grapes to wine, with many others

having invested in cooperatives whose intake of grapes is sufficient to warrant purchase of the best and most modern equipment so that fine wines can be produced in substantial quantities.

# NATIONAL AND INTERNATIONAL REGULATIONS

In bringing wines and spirits to the marketplace, the industries share and uphold a trust to sell pure products delivered in good condition. In any single country the various branches of the wine, spirits, and associated industries are close-knit, but at world level there is only one organization—only one is necessary—that works for the betterment of international standards and relationships; this is the International Federation of Wine and Spirit Merchants (FIVS), whose concerns include labeling and bottling, freights, permitted additives to wines and spirits, education of everyone engaged in the merchant industries, and a host of ancillary matters. In the EEC there are more wine-importing than wine-producing countries, and consequently there is an EEC wine-importing group responsible for rationalizing such activities throughout the Community; the EFTA countries also have a wine merchants' group.

Here we shall look at the control of the wine and spirits industries by government regulations and trade associations in the UK, USA, Canada, Australia, New Zealand, and South Africa, and the thoroughness with which matters of quality, purity, research, and marketing are dealt. There are of course similar organizations, regulations and relationships in all wine- and spirit-producing countries, and constant liaison with them is maintained by the FIVS.

## UNITED KINGDOM

The national association to which all responsible manufacturers in the UK belong is the Wine and Spirit Association of Great Britain, which represents to the government the views of the UK trade on such matters as customs and tax procedures, and liaises with individual government departments on a variety of matters affecting the trade: on such subjects the association reports to its subscribing members. The association is also in close contact with the Scotch Whisky Association, the Brewers' Society, and the National Federation of Off-Licensees, so that uniform policy and opinion may be presented to government.

Exceptional in the hierarchy of trade organizations are four of the ancient livery companies of the City of London; these are the worshipful companies of Vintners, Distillers, Brewers, and Innholders, each of which has taken an active part in the affairs of their trade for many centuries, and continues to do so today. The Vintners' Company was responsible for setting up, with government approval, the Wine Standards Board, which has responsibility for controlling the proper documentation of imported wine. The Vintners also, with the Wine and Spirit Association of Great Britain, founded the Wine and Spirit Education Trust to train those engaged in the wine, spirits, and associated trades. Founded 14 years ago, the trust already trains some 8,000 students yearly; many pass out eventually with diplomas, having taken two intermediary examinations. The trust and the Wine Standards Board, together with the trade's benevolent society and the Wine Development Board (which promotes public interest in wines and spirits, and helps to educate the consumer), are all housed in the complex of buildings surrounding Vintners' Hall in the City of London.

In the UK the Ministry of Agriculture, Fisheries and Food, the Home Office, the Treasury, and the Department of Trade are all concerned with the conduct of the wine and spirits industries in relation to various Acts of Parliament, such as the Food and Drugs Act (1955) and its amending orders, the Licensing Act (1964), the Customs and Excise Act (1952), and the Trade Descriptions Acts (1968 and 1972)—these and many other Acts are administered by trading standards officers, the commissioners of customs and excise, commissioners of inland revenue, local government officers the police, and others, all with the object of protecting the individual or the community from malpractices of any type.

Among the more important controls to which the wine and spirits industries must conform are those on weights and measures, analysis of contents, labeling requirements, and licensing—the latter affects on the one hand the manufacture and separation of alcohol by fermentation and distillation, and on the other its sale. In addition, there is the Treaty of Rome, to which the UK acceded on January 1, 1973 and under which she is bound by appropriate EEC regulations and directives (see page 47).

## UNITED STATES OF AMERICA

The consumption of wines in the USA was some 20 million hectoliters (529 million gal) in 1983, compared with 16.7 million hectoliters (440 million gal) of spirits and 216 million hectoliters (5,700 million gal) of beers. Wines and spirits therefore represented only 8% and 6.6% respectively of liquors being consumed by the US public.

### Wines

California produces the majority of US wines—13.4 million hectoliters (353.7 million gal) in 1983, the other states together producing only 1.7 million hectoliters (44.6 million gal). In 1983 the wines were divided principally between table wines (76.5%), sparkling wines (8%), and dessert wines (7.5%). Imports, at 4.9

million hectoliters (130.2 million gal), were bolstered by the strength of the dollar, and provided nearly one-third of table wines and one-quarter of sparkling wines; it is interesting that Italy supplied the lion's share of them, 54.5%, against 19.5% from France, 12% from Germany, 6.2% from Spain, and 3.6% from Portugal. The USA exported just over 280,000hl (7.5 million gal) of wine in 1983: Canada took 136,000hl (3.6 million gal) and the UK 45,000hl (1.2 million gal); West Germany, Japan, and Belgium (combined with Luxembourg) each took somewhere around 9,500hl (¼ million gal).

The domestic US market for wines (and for spirits) is mainly through off-premises liquor-stores, as well as through the hotel, restaurant, and catering industries. The retail value of all wines reaching the market in 1983 was nearly $8 billion; the market shares of six of the production leaders, with their average price per 75cl bottle, were:

| | | |
|---|---|---|
| Gallo | 27.4% | ($1.70) |
| Seagram | 10.8% | ($3.55) |
| National Distillers | 5.1% | ($3.15) |
| Heublein | 4.9% | ($3.95) |
| Allied Grape | 3.4% | ($2.15) |
| Brown Forman | 2.4% | ($4.85) |

The loaded average price per bottle of the 10 production leaders was $2.95.

Per capita annual consumption of wine in the USA is 8.33 liters (2.2gal) per adult, and has remained at that figure since 1981. At this level the USA is not a serious wine-drinking nation: compare the Italian rate of 91 liters (24.15gal) per capita per annum, a consumption which puts it at the head of the list of the 15 nations which drink over 23 liters (6gal) per capita each year. Threats of a federally mandated minimum drinking age for all 50 states of 21 years could slice 190,000hl (5 million gal) off the market. Already 22 states have imposed this minimum drinking age.

Here is an interesting fact which must reflect an underlying social problem—or perhaps its solution? Analyses have been done in the USA to find out how much of each category of wine is drunk by people of different occupational status. Whatever the category of wine, the various employed groups are each responsible for the consumption of between 21% and 28% of it, with those from the professional/managerial classes leading the field in all categories. However, there is one group whose wine consumption outstrips even that of the professional/managerial group: the unemployed, who are responsible for drinking between 29.5% and 40.5% of the wine produced in each category.

**Spirits**

Spirits are divided by the liquor trade into whiskeys, known as brown goods, and vodka, gin, rum, and tequila, known as white goods. Brandies, with fruit and flavored spirits, liqueurs, and cocktails are included in a separate classification, "specialty mixed drinks." The total of brown goods distributed for sale in 1983 was 7.16 million hectoliters (189 million gal) or 42.9% of total spirits consumption; Bourbon (12.8% of overall spirits consumption), Canadian (11.9%), Scotch (10.4%), and blends (7.6%), together with a small fraction of Irish whiskey, made up this total. Vodka, taking 22.6% of the market, is easily the most popular of the white goods; gin at 9.2%, rum at 7.7%, and tequila with 2.2% make up the white-goods consumption of 6.85 million hectoliters (181 million gal), or 41.6% of the spirits market. The specialty sector, at 2.6 million hectoliters (68 million gal) is responsible for 15.5% of the total, with brandies at 4.9%, cordials and liqueurs at 8.7%, and cocktails and mixed drinks at 1.9% accounting for this figure.

Included in the figures for spirits consumption are 5.35 million hectoliters (141 million gal) of imports, made up as follows:

| | thousand hl | million gal |
|---|---|---|
| Canadian whisky | 2,000 | 52.5 |
| Scotch whisky | 1,750 | 45.8 |
| vodka | 102 | 2.7 |
| rum | 57 | 1.5 |
| tequila | 364 | 9.6 |
| brandy | 284 | 7.5 |
| liqueurs | 568 | 15.0 |

The nation is divided into 32 License States, where consumption totalled 12.4 million hectoliters (326.8 million gal) in 1983, and 18 Control States, in which only certain counties are licensed to sell spirits, where consumption was 3.95 million hectoliters (104.3 million gal); the Control States are Alabama, Idaho, Iowa, Maine, Michigan, Mississippi, Montana, New Hampshire, North Carolina, Ohio, Oregon, Pennsylvania, Utah, Vermont, Virginia, Washington, West Virginia, and Wyoming.

The philosophy of the industrial USA looks for a steady Consumer Price Index—in 1983 it rose by only 3.2%, a modest increase after the disasters of 1979-1981. Low inflation means disposable income rises and hence increased consumer purchasing-power: when this comes about, economic growth is sustained and unemployment figures should decrease. Accordingly, it was hoped that the 1983 US unemployment level of 9.6% would reduce toward 7.5% in the years to 1986.

Early in 1985 the spirits industry remains energetic but undecided, with an eye to the impact of possible farther drinking-age restrictions and the effect on interest rates if the Federal Reserve Board clamps down too heavily on inflation. Also they see the need to introduce changes in the production-mix to compensate for the shortfall in the consumption of whiskeys and other standard lines. A projection of sales to 1995 sees whiskeys declining from a volume indicator of 7.16 million hectoliters (189 million gal) in 1983 to 5.83 million hectoliters (154

million gal) in 1995: over the same period the projection increases white-goods sales from 6.9 to 7.3 million hectoliters (from 183 to 193 million gal), with an increase of specialty drinks from 2.6 to 3.1 million hectoliters (from 68 to 82 million gal). In total, this gives an annual volume decrease in spirits sales from 16.7 to 16.3 million hectoliters (from 441 to 430 million gal) between 1983 and 1995.

## CANADA

The annual consumption of wine in Canada is approaching 2.3 million hectoliters (60 million gal), and the per capita annual consumption throughout the country is about 8.7 liters (2.3gal). The sale of wines and spirits in Canada is still confused: the country has never had an effective nationwide rethink since the provincial government-monopoly liquor-stores were set up after Prohibition ended in 1927. Generally these monopoly stores supply wines and spirits to the public, as in countries operating an off-license system. After Prohibition, Ontario also allowed its wineries to sell wines at their 51 existing stores, and since 1976 has permitted those wineries to open as many stores as they like—although still only to sell their own wines. But all restaurants in Canada have to buy either through the monopoly liquor-stores at full retail prices or from local estate wineries at prices fixed by the provincial government, with the result that wines in Canadian restaurants are necessarily expensive. Since 1978 groceries in Quebec have been able to sell wines, and sales in the province have doubled, but lobbies to get similar authority elsewhere have so far been unsuccessful. Ontario wineries have, however, opened a number of ministores close to the food sections of department stores. Wine is easier to purchase in Ontario than elsewhere, but the per capita consumption remains in line with the country's average. The heavier drinkers are to be found in British Columbia, where the annual per capita consumption is 13.5 liters (3.57gal).

## AUSTRALIA

Consumers in Australia purchase their wines and spirits in bottle-shops licensed for off-sales In the big cities a limited number of large bottle-shops carry an exhaustive stock of home-produced and imported wines and spirits. Away from the city centers and in more minor communities several thousand smaller bottle-shops give the same service but with less variety.

The "bag in box" package for medium-quality domestic wines is very popular in Australia. Bars in hotels and restaurants and in places of public entertainment usually serve cask wines in addition to spirits and other drinks.

The Wine and Brandy Corporation, created by the wine and spirits industries, is the vehicle for trade representation in all matters affecting government relations and regulations as well as trade standards, methods, and techniques.

## NEW ZEALAND

The distribution of wines and spirits in New Zealand is divided between wholesale lincenses and lincenses held under the New Zealand Wine Resellers system. Supermarkets and groceries are not licensed to sell alcoholic drinks. Two breweries groups, Lion with 55% of the market

Wines can pass through many hands on their way from the producer or blender to the consumer. One such "stop" is the warehouse of a wine-broker *(left)* who may deal in bin-ends and in surplus stocks as well as in bulk.

and Dominion with 45%, are the wholesale licensees with all off-lincenses and all branches of the catering industry as their main customers; they may also supply the public with "wholesale" quantities of not less than one case (9 liters) of wine.

The off-lincenses, or "bottle-stores," are attached to the public houses in the two brewery chains. The trade holds 40% of New Zealand wine resellers lincenses and the remaining 60% are in independent hands, and the system now permits sale of both New Zealand and imported wines. The breweries are the sole producers and sellers of spirits, which are mainly grain-based.

The coordinating organization set up by the trade to deal with production policy, government and industrial relationships, licensing, exports, and standards throughout the wine and spirits industry is the Wine Institute of New Zealand, not to be confused with the Viticultural Research Station near Te Kiauwhata. The labeling system in New Zealand is simple and straightforward, favoring varietal rather than brand names and based on EEC requirements, which must in any event be incorporated on labels for shipments to EEC member states.

### SOUTH AFRICA

Although there is a substantial element of government control in the production, administration, and sale of wines and spirits in South Africa, the areas of control are well defined and nothing is left to doubt. A situation of overproduction and uneconomic prices brought about the formation in 1918 of the Co-operative Wine Growers" Association of South Africa (KWV). In 1931 the South African Wine Farmers Association (SAWFA) was set up in London to ensure standards of quality, distribution, and price. Today KWV owns SAWFA, and exercises the powers derived from the South African Wine and Spirit Control Act of 1924, as amended.

The KWV declares each year a price for "good" wine and also declares a surplus above which all wine or grape production must be sold to the KWV. It has a monopoly on the distillation of spirit from grapes or wine made in South Africa, and also on its sale, both at home and for export. Finally, it may make wine for one of three purposes only: for export, for conversion to spirit, or for sale back to the privately owned wine producers of South Africa; the KWV may *not* release such wine for sale and consumption in South Africa, either wholesale or retail, or to any catering organizations, such as hotels or restaurants. The traveler will thus find no abnormality in the wholesale and retail branches of the South African wine and spirit industries, despite the unusual character of their hierarchies.

### OTHER COUNTRIES

Every country that produces wines and/or spirits has its own individual variations in one or other of its methods of distribution, government control, quotas, exports, and so on. Should you wish for any reason to pursue these matters, including the supply of wines or spirits from a particular country, you should first write to the nearest office of the trade or commercial commissioner of that country, or, failing that, to the embassy or other chief representative office of the government of the country concerned. Answers sometimes take a few weeks to arrive, but on the whole you will find a friendly willingness to help.

## DISTRIBUTION AND LICENSING

The marketing of wines, spirits and other alcoholic drinks involves many allied industries and professional associates. Between the producer and the eventual retailer there are barrel-makers, bottle and cork manufacturers, packagers, land- and sea-transportation and warehousing operators, insurance brokers, accountants, and lawyers. All these services are called upon *after* the manufacture of the product; but the producer has to know the markets for wines and spirits intimately in order to know what to make in the first place.

In the wine and spirits industry, practically every manufacturer is represented by a broker. In France it is the broker's responsibility to assess wines and spirits and introduce them to *négociants*, members of the Courtiers Picquet en Vin, who received their charter from Philippe le Bon in the fourteenth century; it is the *négociant* who actually purchases the produce, the broker merely taking his commission on the deal. The *négociant* is responsible not only for buying but also for storing, maturing and, if necessary, blending wines before marketing them. His full title is *négociant-éleveur*: the "*éleveur*," "teacher," part of the name indicates that his main skill is looking after or raising young wines like children.

The *négociant* may receive wines into his cellars from bulk containers, rail tankers, or a variety of other metal or wood containers. Those wines that will not stand in the market on their own will be blended, with the object of balancing the faults and virtues of two or more insufficient wines to produce a better, viable wine that will sell; this blending demands a critical and highly trained palate. Eventually the wines will be shipped (a term that may or may not imply sea transportation) to customers at home or abroad, in bulk or in bottle.

The *négociant* acts as agent for many of the shippers who buy his wines or spirits; with them he tastes the wine and discusses prices and details of shipments, and, given the remit by the shippers, he may even seek what they require elsewhere. It may be gathered that the *négociant* is a highly skilled and well informed professional.

The shipper (who may be described as the second purchaser of the wine, even though it may have changed in character or substance since leaving the producer) may be buying for domestic resale or be an importer who will use the expertise of shipping and forwarding agents to effect documentation, entry, clearance, and insurance of the goods. The shippers or their customers in the importing country may be the wine divisions of large brewing groups, off-license chains, hotels, restaurants, or caterers; however, many shippers are also themselves wine-merchants, some having been established for well over a century. Some wine-merchants have the great shippers of Champagne, Médoc, and other superb wines as their partners.

When a liquor is admitted under import license it will be received into bonded warehouses. Wines and spirits are rarely if ever bought, sold, and passed on immediately, and it is more likely that years will elapse before they are withdrawn from bond—and even that may involve a number of separate transactions. On arrival, therefore, the wine is examined for any imperfection. It will need to settle down, because no wine likes the vibration or shake-up of travel. It may have suffered as a result of damage to its container: damaged casks inflict a "woody" taste on the wine, while damage to a Safrap or other metal container may produce a smell of bad eggs or a greyish haze; such disorders may be diagnosed and cured. If wines bottled at source show signs of secondary fermentation the whole consignment will need to be disgorged, filtered, and rebottled in sterile bottles. Finally, the wine may yet need to be blended according to the requirements of any or every customer down the line.

At every stage from lying in bonded storage onward, licenses of one kind or another are required by the owner or dispenser of wines and spirits (and of other alcoholic drinks). In the UK, for example, the wholesaler requires a dealer's excise license for selling quantities to retailers. In the UK this is required for quantities of over 9 liters (one dozen bottles, 19 pints). Establishments selling alcohol, whether it is for consumption on or off the premises, require a magistrate's license. The name of the licensee of an on-license, the hours when alcohol may be sold, and the minimum age of the persons to whom it may be sold are all specified in the UK license. Orderly behavior is required, which eliminates the presence of criminals and prostitutes, while drunkenness may likewise cost the manager his license.

Special licenses may be obtained for an extension of hours, and there are also club licenses, restaurant licenses, and residential licenses for hotels and boarding houses. For a dance or "wine and cheese party" an occasional license is required if wines, spirits or beers are to be sold. Such on-licenses may specify not only the premises but also the room in which alcohol shall be served.

Distillers must have an excise license and brewers a brewer's license. Home wine-makers, however, require no license so long as they produce alcohol only for their own households.

In the western world, although there are now many instances of large groups that encompass the whole range of production and sales functions under central control, they still require separate licenses at each stage of their activities, and at each individual establishment.

A wine-tasting at Christie's in London *(left)*. Such tastings precede all major auctions in the world's wine centers. Note the candles for testing brightness, the schooners for testing aroma, and the funnels for discarded samples. No one smokes or wears perfume.

# WINE-TASTING

Whenever wines and spirits change hands there is a gathering of experts; these may include wine-makers or distillers, brokers, and *négociants*, shippers and importers, and wholesalers and retailers, gathered together to discuss quantities, terms and delivery. But no deal is ever consummated until the wine has been tasted. Wine is tasted by the experts on other occasions, too; there are, for example, tastings during manfuacture, and preceding monthly wine and spirit auctions in the world's capital cities.

However much time you spend studying the skill of the wine-taster, it will not be wasted, for everything you learn in the process will increase your future enjoyment of wine. Professional tasting is the key to the purchase prices of wines at auctions, and the amateur is advised to attend and watch the procedures for some time before joining in the bidding.

The first objective of potential buyers at an auction is to see that the wine offered is precisely what they need, whether it be for blending or to suit a particular customer. They will also want to compare it for quality with samples they have tasted in the vineyard region, and so will take a tasting from each cask individually on arrival. "Tasting" is hardly an adequate word to cover the range of tests to which they will now subject the wine, but the term is used because there is not another one that describes these tests better. The purchasers are about to satisfy themselves as to the color, brightness, clarity, life, aroma, and feel of the wine, as well as its taste, balance, texture, and strength.

Before letting the wine touch their lips they will examine its color and brightness. If the wine has an unnatural color or is clouded or hazy, it is unlikely to taste good, and will be approached with great caution. The color will help to tell its age, for wines darken with age; white wines tend to deepen to gold or onion-skin color, while red wines generally lose their purple-redness and turn through garnet to mahogany. Moreover, color gives an indication of strength, which increases with deepening color, especially in light white wines. Any color that may be described as "dirty" or "misty" indicates that all is by no means well, and the wine is unlikely to have freshness and life.

Aroma is not to be confused with smell: aroma is what the taster seeks, and it may indicate all that is good—or better—in a wine of known class. Beautiful strong aromas have a bouquet of fruit and spices underpinned with the vapors of a sound clean ferment. Smells that have been identified with sick wine include those of cabbage, rotten eggs and something between old socks and soiled towels. (Soiled towels can indeed be the cause of such a smell, but not at an auction—the taster will ensure that his glass is freshly polished and free of any taint before using it.) Wines with foul smells are useless, with one exception: if there is a chemical smell that catches the nose in the sinus region, the wine may be cured by exposure to air.

After testing the color and aroma of the wine, it is time to taste it, to make sure that the taste confirms the diagnoses of eye and nose. Tasters will take a generous mouthful of wine, and do everything with it except swallow it. They will hold it in their mouths; they will wash their tongues in it, chew it, and swish it through their teeth to bring out the aroma.

Grapes start their life with too much acid and no sugar; however, as the sugar develops the acid is neutralized, and so there is a *right* time, when acid and sugar are in optimum balance, to pick the grapes. The wine-maker can, however, manipulate matters by stopping fermentation before all the sugar is converted to alcohol, so that the final balance between sugar, alcohol, and acid in a fine wine can be adjusted to conform with the ideal. Sadly, this does not always happen. A wine may be judged too sweet, too acid, too light (lacking in alcohol), or too heavy. Perfect balance means that the wine is faultless in all these respects.

The sensory organs in the mouth are distributed between the tongue, gums, lips, palate, and throat; they vary in sensitivity and position for different people. A sweet wine, even though well balanced, may taste too sweet on the tip of the tongue and too acid at the back of the throat. Tannin, mostly in red wines, impinges on the sides of the mouth, especially around the saliva glands; and alcohol will produce a prickly sensation on the gums thanks to its slightly astringent effect.

Having made their judgment, wine-tasters spit out the wine to remove its memory from their palates (a dry biscuit may be taken to help do this). At a wine-tasting this is essential so that the palate is ready for the next assault.

There is one further quality in a wine that has to be detected. It is known as "finish," and it is acknowledged to be the most difficult to describe in words, yet it is the quality by which the Lafites, Latours, and Mouton Rothschilds of this world are rated above all others. Finish has been described as the *character* of the wine, and is best appreciated by answering the question: "How long did I *remember* the wine?" The "memory" of a great wine will linger on the palate for some time—possibly as long as 24 hours—and will not be removed in spite of foods and other wines taken in the meantime.

At a wine-tasting the experts will take notes as they go along. The language will be restrained and orderly, noting from the eye the brightness, clarity, haziness, and deposit of each wine; white-wine colors from white through green or straw to deep gold, and red-wine colors from purple through garnet to mahogany. From the nose they will record the bouquet of fruit or flowers, or the spicy fragrance and peppery charm of wines made in hot countries; or they may note the sickly sweet or acetic smell of wines turning to vinegar, or the musty metallic smells caused by damaged containers. From the palate they will note alcoholic strength, and from the tongue and gums acidity, sweetness, and tannin. Alcoholic strength will be noted as "luscious" or "heavy" if too great and "light" if insufficient, and acidity as making the wine "sharp" if too great and "flat" if inadequate. Red wines with too much tannin will be called "hard" or, if they have too little, "soft."

Then the tasters will attempt to anticipate finish, although they may have to act fairly quickly if they have decided to bid. Finally, they must mentally price the wine in accordance with their own conclusions, so that they know when to stop bidding.

It will be seen why the amateur should look, listen and learn before entering into the auction-room fray. Many of those present will be Masters of Wine, people who can normally name an unlabeled wine simply by applying the routine of tests listed here to their vast and intimate knowledge of all the world's wines. The MW of the Institute of Masters of Wine in England is the highest accolade accorded anywhere in the world to members of the wine and spirits industries; it is not surprising that Masters of Wine may be found, thinly spread, in every major wine region of the world.

Before the auction *(above)* the buyers will have decided what they hope to buy and how much they are prepared to bid for it. They are a somewhat elite class, some buying privately, others representing various facets of the worldwide wine-marketing industry.

The warehouse of the important London Wine Brokers *(left)*. Every day is one of deals and special offers: sellers and buyers are expert, and the instincts of each determine the true market value of the day.

# WINES, SPIRITS AND THE CONSUMER

**Drinking Out ♦ Wines that Match Foods ♦ Cocktail Parties ♦ The Wine-Label ♦ Drinking at Home**

The variety of wines and spirits available is almost limitless, and many people are therefore driven to select their purchases more or less at random, without any clear idea of what they are letting themselves in for, or, perhaps as bad, they stick to a few labels or brands which they know they like, paying little heed as to whether a trusted favorite is in fact the right choice for a particular occasion. In this chapter we shall look for some of the "reasons why" consumers purchase wines and spirits, for every selection that you make should be both informed and with a specific reason in mind.

## DRINKING OUT

Drinking can be done either on or off the premises where the drink is purchased. Within a premises suitably licensed for "on" drinking, the drinks may be dispensed by the measure, or glass, or they may be purchased by the bottle for immediate consumption. Premises in the "on" category include inns, hotels, restaurants, winebars, clubs, places of public entertainment, public houses, road houses, and licensed canteens.

Occasionally, in restaurants, the drinks may sometimes be consumed partly in a bar and partly at the dining-room table; the bill for the former may be carried forward and added to the dining-room account, and the wine to be consumed during the meal may be selected from the wine-list and ordered in the bar beforehand (although *after* the orders for food have been given to the head waiter). Giving this service is a small part of the duties of an efficient *sommelier* or head wine-waiter, and the host should remember what food has been ordered by each guest before ordering the most suitable wines, or types of wine, to go with it. The host should also see that the wine is presented at the table unbroached, and is exactly the one (or ones) previously ordered. When staying at hotels, the host must expect to sign numerous "checks" presented by the wine-waiter and these will be presented with and charged in the final check.

If a meal is not to be taken, drinks from the bar are usually consumed by the glass or measure, and in either case may have mixers added. "Short" drinks, aside from spirits, are divided into two categories: fortified drinks, as for example sherries, madeiras and ports, which may be served as singles or doubles or by the glass; and cocktails, which will be mixed and then shaken or stirred and poured by the bartender. (Aperitifs are discussed later in this chapter.)

Occasionally, two or more people in a bar may order a bottle of wine, and this is usually served at a table away from the bar; quite often it may already be broached. This is not strictly correct but the practice is rarely challenged, for two reasons: firstly, wines served for such purposes are unlikely to be either rare or particularly expensive, or chosen from an extensive list; and secondly the bartender is usually working under considerable pressure.

## WINES THAT MATCH FOODS

Before approaching the subject of matching wines to foods, it is worth noting a warning. "Starters" at lunch or dinner, especially in the summer, may include fruit dishes such as melon and citrus fruit mixtures. These dishes have an

astringent effect on the palate so that even fine wine will taste terrible. You can avoid this aftereffect by cleansing the palate with a piece of dry wafer-thin crispbread, without butter or any addition, after finishing the starter. There is little point in drinking any wine while actually in the process of eating these fruits.

Formal meals are these days usually restricted to a few courses—say three at lunch and three to five at dinner. The first course or courses may, according to the time of year, include soup or fish. Strong soups such as mulligatawny and chowder give you little opportunity to appreciate any accompanying wine, but the cloudy sediment that remains after decanting bottles of heavier red wines, which should never be thrown away but kept for making sauces, may also be used to give added flavor to these soups. Consommés, including turtle soup, are improved enormously by a soupspoonful of Fino Sherry stirred into them on the plate—although you must remember that the spirit in Sherry will evaporate at temperatures above 78°C (172°F). With many cold soups a glass of Manzanilla is excellent. For hors d'oeuvres, Muscat is a good accompaniment, and with eggs Chasselas or Sylvaner from Alsace is right: the sulfur in eggs makes most red wines an unsuitable choice. Sauternes or other noble-rot wine is fine with pâté de foie and most other pâtés.

There is a wide selection of wonderful wines for drinking with shellfish and lighter white fish: they include Muscadet, Sancerre, and Pouilly Fumé from the Loire, and white Graves, Chablis, Riesling, and Brut Champagne (in fact, one or other of the Champagnes, according to taste, may be selected to accompany a meal from start to finish); the Mosels of Germany and Verdicchio and Frascati from Italy round off this short selection.

Heavier and oilier fish, such as salmon, sole, and halibut, need a full-bodied white wine to stand up to the food. Suitable wines include Meursault and other white wines from the Côte de Beaune, fuller white Graves or Entre-deux-Mers wines from Bordeaux, Condrieu and Hermitage from the Rhône, Rheingau and Rheinhessen wines from Germany, and Soave and Orvieto Secco from Italy. The *vinhos verdes* of Portugal cut through the oil in the large grilled sardines eaten there, and red Graves is traditional with the lampreys and eel-like sucker fish of the Gironde coast.

The wines suggested for the stronger white fish are suitable also to complement pork, veal, ham, and chicken. The contrefilet Entrecôte Bordelaise, however, is both cooked in and accompanied by red Graves, and the French drink Chablis with ham that has also been cooked in Chablis. Similarly, in Alsace, Coq au Vin is cooked in Riesling; in the Jura, Poulets de Bresses (chicken that have their own AC) are cooked in the rare local *vins jaunes*; and Escalope de Veau Marsala is eaten with the fortified wine Marsala.

For roasts and game the wines have to be full and big to hold their own. The strong red wines of Burgundy, the Rhône Valley, and Rioja Alta come instantly to mind, as do the Barbarescos and Barolos of Italy. Any of these may continue to be drunk afterward with the cheeses. The French always take cheese before the dessert (many do not bother with a dessert course at all) because the dessert course would ruin the palate for reversion to wine afterward. Dry white wines, too, go well with most cheeses, although the soft creamy cheeses such as Camembert and Brie will give Rieslings and similar wines a decidedly "off" taste.

With the dessert course, Sauternes and the whole range of Beerenausleses and Trockenbeerenausleses come into their own; the Ausbruch wines from Austria and the fabled Tokays from Hungary are among those reserved for special occasions. Port is a dessert wine, but will do well also with cheese; it is certainly the most popular fortified wine to take with fruit and nuts, although others of the sweeter fortified wines, such as Bual and Malmsey madeiras are also right for the occasion.

Digestif spirits and liqueurs may be offered to guests with their coffee, which may be taken, at the host's suggestion, either at the table or in the drawing room. A change of scene may be virtually obligatory when dining out, alas: a move to the coffee room may be "suggested" by the management because the dining table is required for another party. By this time it is too late for the host to do anything about his or her mistake—dining where two sittings are booked by the management. Nothing will more rapidly destroy the relaxation that the meal should have inspired than this enforced removal.

For two reasons no reference has been made to the wines from outside Europe suitable for drinking with the different types of food. Firstly, for practically every category of wine mentioned above there is an equivalent to be found among the excellent wines of vinifera origin now being made in the USA, Canada, Australia, New Zealand, South Africa, and South America. Secondly, the main diet varies considerably from continent to continent and local palates are accustomed to widely varying dishes and flavoring agents; there is little purpose, therefore, in giving here a précis of information available in considerable detail in magazines and books of national origin.

## COCKTAIL PARTIES

Cocktail parties, of which there are many variations, may be held almost anywhere and for a number of reasons. Many are organized by businesses for launchings or other occasions, and there are constantly recurring cocktail parties put on by trade associations. Private parties are arranged for anniversaries, or at climacterics in life's changing pattern, or just for the fun of it —or because it is high time to return hospital-

That a good wine tastes better when properly and elegantly served is universally agreed. What better container could there be for a vintage Port than this superbly decorated decanter *(above)*.

ity received.

The selection of liquors served on such occasions varies enormously. At the best, it will be Champagne all the way, with fingers of smoked salmon and diminutive baskets of caviare to freshen the palate; at the worst it will be "wine and cheese" where a cheap blended still white wine of mixed origin will be expected to accompany all the cheeses offered, some of which will undoubtedly kill the wine stone dead —assuming it was alive in the first place. Between these two extremes, however, there are many elegant variations on the theme. At a Sherry party it is ideal to have two Sherries, one dry but not the driest and the other sweet but not heavily so, say a Manzanilla and a Cream Sherry served with fingers of mature Cheddar. Always have a bottle of gin and a bottle of scotch on hand for those who cannot take Sherry, which some people find liverish.

At Christmas or the New Year, a hot punch-bowl will entice your friends to drop in to exchange greetings for a half-hour or longer, its warming heat and rich aroma making a welcome change from traditional, but cold, eggnog. From an old recipe, a formula for making punches suggests "One sour, two sweet, four strong, eight weak," which may be interpreted to mean the juice of one lemon, double the same quantity of sugar or honey, double the "sweet" quantity of rum, whiskey or brandy, and double the "strong" quantity of wine, beer, cider or water (16 instead of eight "weak" can in fact be recommended). All the ingredients *except the spirit* should be heated to near boiling-point (*not* boiled) with spices—say, cinnamon, ginger, nut-meg, or allspice, to taste. Then you should add the spirit, stir and ladle into heat-proof glasses (preferably in holders with handles). A reserve of the ingredients is desirable so that the bowl can be replenished with fresh hot punch: possibly the answer is to have two bowls.

The party at which mixed drinks are served is popular among the young and middle-aged, but short drinks are not too popular with the elderly. There should therefore be available straightforward grain spirits to be served with mixers as long drinks, such as gin or vodka and tonic with ice and lemon, or scotch with soda or cold water; other long drinks could include chilled punches and cups. Beyond these there is a wealth of cocktails, of which a few are also noted below.

○ **The Collinses** Usually a large gin with soda and fresh lemon or lime. Tom Collins is made with sweetened Old Tom gin, and John Collins with London or Dutch gin.

○ **Horse's Neck** Gin or whiskey, ice and ginger ale (in the British Navy the spirit is more usually brandy).

○ **Planters' Punch** Rum, fresh limes and soda.

○ **Sangria** Red wine with sweetened orange juice.

A good cocktail deserves an individual glass *(opposite)*. Here are a John Collins with a slice of orange; an Americana in the cone-shaped glass; a Manhattan and a Dry Martini; and a Planters' Punch.

○ **Black Velvet** One-half chilled Champagne and one-half Guinness.

○ **Buck's Fizz** One-half chilled Champagne, one-half fresh orange juice, and a dash of brandy.

○ **Mint Julep** Fill a tall tumbler with alternate layers of crushed ice and shredded mint leaves. Fill up the tumbler with Bourbon whiskey and keep it full by replenishing with Bourbon. As the drink gets stronger the nose gets colder.

○ **Old-Fashioned** Place a slice of orange and sugar in a tumbler and crush together with a pestle. Fill the tumbler with crushed ice. Then add Bourbon whiskey until the tumbler is full. Keep it full by replenishing with Bourbon.

The classic cocktails number about a dozen, of which one-half are gin-based.

○ **Gin and French** Half dry gin, half dry French vermouth.

○ **Martini** Two parts dry London gin to one part dry French vermouth. (Named for a US bartender, not for the Italian wine company.)

○ **Dry Martini** Dry London gin with just a dash of French vermouth.

○ **Bronx** Two parts dry gin to one part each of sweet Italian vermouth and dry French vermouth, with a dash of orange bitters and a tablespoonful of fresh orange juice.

○ **White Lady** Two parts dry gin to one part each of Cointreau and fresh lemon juice.

○ **Gimlet** Half gin, half concentrated lime juice. (A dash of Angostura Bitters added to the Gimlet—and to many other cocktails—will sharpen the flavor of the various ingredients.)

○ **Screwdriver** Two parts of vodka to one part of fresh orange juice and half a teaspoonful of powdered sugar.

○ **Bloody Mary** One part of vodka to three parts of tomato juice with a teaspoonful each of Worcester sauce and lemon juice: add a shake of celery salt and Cayenne pepper.

○ **Manhattan** Two parts of Bourbon or rye whiskey to one part each of sweet Italian vermouth and dry French vermouth. (This is the whiskey equivalent of the Bronx.)

○ **Sidecar** Two parts of brandy to one part each of Cointreau and fresh lemon juice. (This is the brandy equivalent of the White Lady.)

All these cocktails are served ice-cold, often in frosted glasses. Be warned that none of them mix readily with beers or lagers. However, for those who insist on mixing, or on simply drinking a little too much, here are a few potions that may ease the burden of the following day:

○ **Prairie Oyster 1** 30ml (1 fl oz) of Cognac and one teaspoonful each of wine vinegar and Worcester sauce: add a dash of Cayenne pepper. Stir and pour over a raw egg in a small tumbler, and drink without breaking the yolk.

○ **Prairie Oyster 2** One can of tomato juice in a wide tumbler with four dashes of Angostura Bitters and a dash of Worcester sauce added. Float a whole raw egg on top and get the sufferer to drink it before it looks at him.

○ **Enzian** A measure of this spirit (flavored with the bitter root of the giant yellow gentian found in the Jura mountains) will be found most effective, and will not be habit-forming!

## THE WINE-LABEL

Whether ordering for immediate consumption, for a planned party, or for putting down in a cellar or wine-rack, the most important features of the bottle are firstly the wine-label and secondly the price. For you need to know that what is in the bottle is what you want to buy, and that you are paying the right price for it. Unfortunately, there is no universal bottle-size, nor are there any universal laws governing the mandatory information that must appear on the label. Happily, there are within the EEC laws standardizing these matters for wines produced in the Common Market; but outside the Market there are far more exceptions than rules. Prevailing rules in some of the major wine-producing countries are noted here to help you when examining the label of a bottle you are thinking of buying. In other countries the rules, if there are any, are in a state of flux: you should look up the main discussions of the countries concerned where they appear earlier in this book (see Index).

### THE EEC

The EEC categorizes wines as either "EEC wines" or "imported wines," with some rules applying to both categories and some applying only to one. For EEC wines there are eight essential items that must appear on the wine-label: the words "table wine" or other quality indication (for example, Appellation Contrôlée); the specified region of origin within the EEC; the country of origin when shipped from one country to another within the EEC; the words "wine from different countries of the European Community" where applicable; the indication "EEC" where the grapes were grown in one member country and converted into wine in another; the name and address of the bottler and the consigner; the nominal volume of contents; and the "e" mark indicating that the container size is EEC-approved. German wine-labels must also contain their quality-control number, or *Prüfungsnummer* (see page 121).

For wines imported into the EEC the five essential entries are: the word "wine;" the country of origin and the geographical unit within the country of origin; the name and address of the importers; the nominal volume of contents; and the "e" mark.

For both EEC and imported wines the following optional details may be added: whether the wine is red, white, or rosé; the alcoholic strength, either actual or total; any indication to the consumer such as "serve chilled;" sweet/dry description; indications of vine varieties, vintage year, vineyard name; indication of production method; indication of where bottled (for example, "château-bottled"); brand name; distributor's name and address; any citation award (for example, "By Appointment to . . "); and details of history and aging. The alcoholic strength does not yet have to appear on labels of ordinary wines.

Two points concerning blending are worth comment. It is possible for a customer to find that a branded wine which he last purchased as "produce of France" may on the next bottle be described as "produce of Algeria, Yugoslavia and France," or some other combination. This is no matter for complaint, but indicates that the shipper has needed to blend the wine differently in order to maintain the standard brand, for no blender can guarantee to be able to produce a standard brand from the same sources each year. Another important point is that a blend of quality wines may show only the highest classification to which *every* wine in the blend is entitled, and not any higher classifications applicable only to some. Thus a blend of Médoc and Pomerol quality wines could only be called AC Bordeaux (up to 10% vol. alcohol) or Bordeaux Supérieur (if over).

Labels on spirit and liqueur bottles also have to indicate essential information. These details are: an "appropriate description" (for example, "gin," "whiskey"); the name and address of the shipper or bottler; the strength, as percentage vol. alcohol OIML in the UK or as percentage vol. alcohol Gay-Lussac (see page 45), which is only marginally different, in the continental countries of the EEC.

### NORTH AMERICA

A survey of some 40 labels of US wines shows a pattern of universally supplied information. The following details were standard: grown, produced and bottled by (name and address); grown in (county, state or region) shown separately where appropriate; the grape or grapes from which the wine has been made, or the type of wine in the bottle; and the percentage vol. alcohol.

On many labels there was a description of the wine as well as of the grape—for example, "A soft fruity white wine from the noble Pineau de la Loire grape"—and advice on service—for example, "serve chilled." Moreover, the type of wine was often preceded by the words "American," "Californian" (or other state description), or the name of the region in which the wine was made. Where appropriate, a "dry"/"sweet" classification was included, although the interpretation of the various terms varied between manufacturers. Two "champagne" labels stated the bottle capacity as four-fifths of a quart (which is 75.7cl).

### CANADA

In Canada the existence of the monopoly-liquor-store system has tended to result in standardization of the label details relating to wine descriptions, origins, and producers. In certain provinces you may have more difficulty in finding somewhere to buy your wine than in understanding the label descriptions once you have the bottle in front of you.

### AUSTRALIA

Labels in Australia have been described by Hugh Johnson as a "pathless jungle." Basic details concerning growers, wine-makers, grapes, regions, individual vineyards, vintage dates, bin-numbers, and so on could be helpful but, with a philosophy of "distance no object" and what might be called a cross-pollination of proprietorships, grape consignments, and regional identities, the result is a label which is confusing; intervention by the government to systematize the matter has yet to come. The details on labels of bottles for export are, naturally, those required by the countries of destination.

### SOUTH AFRICA

The interrelationships between the KWV and the private-sector wine-makers of South Africa, coupled with the need to conform to EEC regulations for exports, have already done much to standardize South African label details as well as bottle shapes and capacities. The authorities in South African are constantly investigating these and all other means to bring the country's wine and spirit industries into increasing international prominence.

## DRINKING AT HOME

With a knowledge of wine gained from labels experiences of dining out, and of selecting wines from wine-lists, wine-lovers should already be fully capable of ordering their wines from a liquor-store or wine-merchant; in the last 15 years wines have also taken their place on the shelves of many stores, supermarkets, bars, and taverns. Yet the selection of wines does need careful thought. For instance, wines may be purchased for cellaring or for shorter-term storage in a wine-rack, or specifically for a planned dinner party. Storage space in the home is usually at a premium, and it is necessary to find some way of using that space to store a representative selection of wines. In addition to the question of storage space, however, the

capacity of the pocket comes into the reckoning, too, and each wine-lover must decide what capital he or she can lock up in wine, spirit and liqueur stocks.

The chief questions to ask yourself are: what proportion of my stocks should be wines as opposed to spirits and liqueurs?; how should the wine stock be subdivided between red, white, rosé, sparkling, and fortified wines?; what grain and fruit spirits, liqueurs and flavored spirits do I want to include?; how many of each do I want to carry?; and should I include half-bottles among them? For most people it is probably best to stock wines at two quality levels and to restrict the varieties to a comparative few, with a reasonable stock of each (say one case, possibly more). The advantage of having some good-quality wines in store is that they carry on improving until they are wanted, leaving you a range of cheaper yet admirable wines for everyday drinking. The true wine-lover's philosophy and pleasure is to share good wines with friends who will really appreciate them, and it is for those people that such wines should be reserved. Generally half bottles are more expensive and do not keep so well as whole bottles; if any, stock only a few.

You could do worse than select your wines from the following suggested types, but individual selection will depend upon personal taste.

**Red Wines**

○ *Better-quality*
- Médoc
- St Émilion
- Pomerol
- Côte de Nuits
- Côte de Beaune
- Barolo
- Rioja Alta

○ *Medium-quality*
- Bordeaux Rouge
- Rhône
- Chianti Classico
- Beaujolais Villages

**White Wines**

○ *Better-quality*
- Champagne
- AC Chablis
- Sancerre *or* Pouilly Fumé
- Meursault
- Montrachet
- Bernkasteler

DECODING THE LABEL

Although the primary purposes of a wine-label are to attract the customer and identify the contents, laws have been introduced to make certain that those contents are honestly and adequately described and that the consumer can identify the producer. The laws of the major wine-producing countries specifying both the mandatory information that *must* and the additional information that *may* appear on the label are described on pages 376-7. There are anomalies in the French, German and US labels shown here. The French label from 1981 fails to show the "e" mark for a bottle of standard 75cl (25⅓fl oz) capacity. The German label from 1971 (two years before the EEC was formed) was not then required by law to display the "e" mark; nevertheless, as we can see, Germany was well prepared for the EEC. The US label shows the alcoholic strength but not the volume — in Europe, EEC law has yet to make alcoholic strength a mandatory feature of labeling.

○ *Medium-quality*
Vouvray *or* Asti Spumante (sparkling)
Niersteiner
Gewürztraminer (Alsace)
Soave *or* Orvieto Secco
AC Cassis *or* AC Seyssel

Grain and other spirits should be stored according to the rate of turnover in the home—usually one quart broached and six quarts in stock for the most used ones and two quarts of each of the others.

Of fruit spirits, brandy at both levels is necessary: at better quality you should have two large bottles of Petite Champagne Cognac (one broached) and one large bottle of Armagnac, and at lesser quality two bottles of export Cognac ★★★ should be to hand. One bottle each of Kirsch, Mirabelle or Quetsch, and Fraise should be sufficient among the flavored spirits.

The range of liqueurs is considerable. Here the leading liqueurs (in roughly descending order of popularity) in each of the four categories are listed for you to make your selection from according to your individual taste.

○ **Fruit Liqueurs**
Maraschino
Crème de Cassis
Cherry Brandy
Apricot Brandy
Crème de Banane

○ **Citrus Liqueurs**
Cointreau
Grand Marnier
Curaçao (water-white)
Van der Hum
Southern Comfort

○ **Herb Liqueurs**
Benedictine
Drambuie
Chartreuse
Kümmel
Crème de Menthe

○ **Bean and Kernel Liqueurs**
Crème de Cacao
Tia Maria
Crème de Noisettes
Crème de Noyau
Crème de Vanille

○ **Unclassified**
Advocaat

## STORAGE OF WINE AND SPIRITS

The three enemies of wine in storage are temperature variation, light, and vibration. Cellar temperature should ideally be between 10°C and 15°C (50-59°F), and should be kept constant. Where wine is stored anywhere else it should be kept away from the roof, fires, and radiators: preferably it should be stored in a cupboard, and certainly it should be protected from the light by some means. Wherever possible vibration should be avoided.

Wines must be stored lying on their sides, so that their corks do not dry out, which can be fatal, and the labels should be uppermost so that the bottle does not need to be turned as it is carefully withdrawn either to read the label or for use. In a large cellar it is useful to number the racks vertically and to note the wines stored in each vertical row. Bottles of spirits are usually stored standing upright, but the contents are inert and so the bottles may be kept on their sides if this is more convenient; this should apply in any event to unbroached bottles with corks (as opposed to sealed caps)—fruit spirits, flavored spirits, liqueurs, and so on. Some of these, however, may be in bottles whose shapes will not fit into a standard winerack.

The advantages of buying wine by the case are several. Usually it is possible to obtain a discount, and a further economic advantage arises because prices increase not only when rates of duty go up but also with age, especially if the wines of subsequent vintages prove to be inferior. It is irksome to find that a vintage that has been particularly enjoyable is sold out or unavailable when you want more. Finally, it may be "after hours" or some kind of holiday at your usual point of purchase when you need service.

It is worth bearing in mind that vintage charts reflect only the *general* experience of wine-makers in each year: there are some good wines in poor years and some poor wines in good years. It is as well to discuss matters with a reputable wine-merchant or retailer.

## SERVING WINES

Wines need different treatment when they are taken from storage according to whether they are red, white, or sparkling.

Red wines that need decanting (some do not) should if possible be taken carefully from storage to stand upright for a day before decanting: the sediment will then fall to the bottom of the bottle. (However, for immediate drinking the bottle should remain horizontal until decanted.) The capsule—usually of lead but sometimes of plastic—should be cut at least half a centimeter (¼ in) below the lip of the bottle, and the bottle should be held firmly to avoid disturbing the wine as the cork is drawn. The shoulders and neck of the bottle should then be wiped, so that the wine when poured may be observed; a lamp placed behind the bottle before decanting is most helpful for this purpose. Holding the bottle label-side up, pour the wine in one steady movement into the decanter, stopping when the sediment is seen climbing into the neck. The wine that is left in the bottle is undrinkable—but invaluable in the kitchen for making sauces. It might seem unnecessary to say that the decanter should be brilliantly clean before filling, but decanters do tend to become stained if all the wine in them is not used at once. These stains may easily be removed by quarter-filling the decanter with warm water and carefully adding some pellets from a sporting cartridge—the bore does not matter, but the smaller the pellets the better. You then lift the decanter and swirl the contents around in a continuous circular motion. In no time at all the most obstinate stains will be removed. The pellets may be kept carefully for further use, as otherwise they will inevitably be spilled, lost or thrown away.

Red wines should be served at room tempera-

*Paris goblet (Burgundy)*

*White wine*

*Claret (large)*

*Claret (small)*

ture, or between 16°C and 22°C (61-72°F). The wine should rest in the dining room for several hours either before or after decanting: it should *never* be placed in an oven, near a fire, or in hot water, for such treatment will damage the bouquet and probably make the wine too hot. If the wine is not at the right temperature at mealtime it is best to warm your glass in the palm of your hand, and to serve a lesser amount of wine per glass until the temperature in the decanter is right.

Glasses for red wine should be large and thin and should be only half-filled—two-thirds at the most. They should be clear to show the color of the wine and tulip-shaped to conserve the aroma.

White wines should be cooled gradually from storage temperature to chilled temperature. An hour in a wine-cooler is better than a few minutes in the bottom of a refrigerator—and *never* put white (or any!) wine in a freezer. The wine-cooler is often an ice-bucket, but this is frequently misused, with the bottle being plunged into a mass of crushed ice. Wine-coolers of whatever sort should be deep enough to contain the whole bottle and half-filled with cold water to which have been added some fairly large pieces of ice. Remember that white wines (and rosés) should be served *frais*—that is, at 10°C to 15°C (50-59°F), equivalent to cellar temperature.

Glasses for white wine should have long stems and should be held by these, so that the hand does not warm the wine nor the wine cool the hand.

Sparkling wines should be opened with care; they should be chilled or *très frais*, between 4°C and 10°C (39-50°F). Even at this temperature the pressure in the bottle is up to four atmospheres, which can eject a cork fast enough to lose you the sight of an eye and certainly, assuming no other catastrophes, some of the precious contents will be wasted. The horseplay beloved by successful sports enthusiasts should be left to successful sports enthusiasts: wine-lovers have more important things in mind.

First remove the gold foil and, while holding the left thumb firmly on top of the cork, release the wire muzzle that holds the cork down and lift it away. Using your right hand to hold the bottle at its base at an angle between 30° and 45° from the vertical, take a cloth and put it over the cork. Grip the cork through the cloth firmly in the left hand. Now, with the right hand, slowly turn the *bottle* on the *cork*—which, being restrained by the left hand, will ease out, allowing the pressure to escape gently: a discreet "pop" will be heard as the cork finally exits.

The colder the wine when opened, the lower the pressure in the bottle and the less risk of losing any wine. However, if the wine is colder than *très frais* it will retain its bubbles in solution and explode like a bomb in a warm stomach. For obvious reasons of comfort this should be avoided.

The shapes of wine glasses generally favored by knowing wine drinkers are illustrated below. Note that the Champagne saucer has largely gone out of use as unsuitable, and that the Champagne flute retains the bubbles longer. Often you will find a line drawn on a wine-glass to indicate the level for filling, especially when you are buying wine by the glass, but in fact there is as yet no laid-down measure for dispensing wines of any kind, anywhere—in direct contrast with the laws on spirits and beers, which in many countries must be sold in mandatory quantities, if by the glass, or in sealed containers. In the home the measure given is at the discretion of the host, however; for most purposes half a glass at a time is safe for wines and up to half a gill for spirits, including brandy. The liqueur glass, being so small, is usually filled to three-quarters capacity.

*Champagne flute*

*German and Alsace wine*

*Sherry schooner*

*Sherry copita*

# GLOSSARY

The countries in which special terms are used, or words in foreign languages originate, are indicated by the letters *Fr* (France), *Ger* (Germany), *It* (Italy), *P* (Portugal), *Sp* (Spain), *UK* (United Kingdom) and *USA* (United States of America) after the headword.

SMALL CAPITALS indicate cross-references within the Glossary.

Readers are advised to use this Glossary in conjunction with the Index.

## A

***Abbocato*** *(It)* Sweet.
**Acetic Acid** A VOLATILE ACID (vinegar) produced among the CONGENERS separated in the FERMENTATION process. It is the acid produced most prolifically among the secondary products of fermentation.
**Acetobacter** An aerobic (oxygen-breathing) bacterium (genus *Acetobacter*) present in the skin of the grape. Acetobacters in the presence of ethyl ALCOHOL produce ACETIC ACID.
**Acidity** The presence of acid in wines is essential to their BALANCE. VOLATILE ACIDS are produced by interaction with ACETOBACTER. The FIXED ACIDS include the natural fruit acids — tartaric, malic, lactic and citric acids. The sum of the volatile and the fixed acids is described as the **total acidity** of the wine.
***Adega*** *(Sp)* Cellar.
**Aftertaste** The taste that lingers in the back of your throat and indicates COMPLEXITY in a good wine.
***Aguardiente*** *(Sp)* Spirits, mainly brandy or whisky.
**Alcohol** In wine-making and in brewing, the main product of the FERMENTATION of liquid sugar compounds. It is **ethyl alcohol** (ethanol), formula $C_2H_5OH$, and should not be confused with methyl alcohol ($CH_3OH$), which is poisonous. The **actual alcohol** content of a wine is the percentage alcohol by volume (% vol. alcohol) actually present in the wine. The **potential alcohol** is either (a) the % vol. alcohol that could be produced by complete FERMENTATION of sugars in the MUST, or (b) those remaining unfermented after the fermentation process has been stopped. The **total alcohol** is the sum of the actual and the remaining potential alcohol.
**Alcohol levels and measurement** Methods of measuring the sugar content of grape-must and alcohol levels in wine vary from country to country. The PROOF systems have been replaced in most parts of the world by % vol. alcohol systems, either GAY-LUSSAC or OIML. Other measurements relate to the wine's SPECIFIC GRAVITY (water = 1.0); examples are shown in the box below.

| *Specific Gravity* | 1.060 | 1.080 | 1.100 | 1.120 |
|---|---|---|---|---|
| OECHSLE | 60.0 | 80.0 | 100.0 | 120.0 |
| BAUMÉ | 8.2 | 10.7 | 13.1 | 15.2 |
| BRIX/Balling | 14.7 | 19.3 | 23.7 | 28.0 |
| potential vol. alc. | 7.5 | 10.0 | 12.5 | 15.0 |

**Aldehydes** Secondary substances among the CONGENERS caused by the oxidation of alcohol during the FERMENTATION process.
**Alembic** Originally a glass beaker having roughly the shape of an inverted comma and used to separate out the alcohol from spirituous compounds by application of carefully controlled heat — in fact, a very crude form of DISTILLATION. A copper flask with a swan neck was later used in the same way, and a version came to be incorporated in the POT STILL. The French for alembic is *alambic*. The ***alambic armagnaçais*** is a modified still incorporating features of both the pot still and the CONTINUOUS STILL, and is used in the production of Armagnac. The ***alambic charentais*** is a modified pot still used in the production of Cognac.
***Amabile*** *(It)* Sweeter than ABBOCATO.
***Amaro*** *(It)* Bitter.
**Amontillado** *(Sp)* A full *fino* Sherry developed in oak and having a nutty mellow flavour.
***Amoroso*** *(Sp)* A medium-dry *fino* Sherry.
***Amtliche-Prüfungsnummer*** **(AP)** *(Ger)* The government certificate number for tested quality of all QbA and QmP wines in Germany (see QUALITÄTSWEIN SYSTEM). This number must be printed on the label of every bottle of wine so certified.
***Añada*** *(Sp)* The wine from a single year. The term is usually used for the source from which the SOLERA wines develop. See page 160.
***Anbaugebiete*** *(Ger)* Any one of the eleven major German wine regions for the production of QbA wines.
***Annata*** *(It)* Year of vintage.
***Anreichern*** *(Ger)* The enrichment of the must with sugar to increase its potential ALCOHOL, permitted in Germany for all wines except those of QmP quality. It is equivalent to the French CHAPTALISATION.
**Anthocyanines** Chemicals resulting from the degradation of TANNIN and coloring substances during maturation. They give rise to haze and deposits which must be removed by FINING.
***Apéritif*** *(Fr)* An appetizer taken before a meal. *Apéritifs* are traditionally a short drink; for example, a FORTIFIED WINE (other than Port) or a cocktail.
***Appellation d'Origine Contrôlée*** **(AC) system** *(Fr)* The mandatory system used to classify French wines as laid down by the Institut National des Appellations d'Origines des Vins et Eaux-de-Vie (INAO) in 1935, as subsequently adopted and adapted by EEC law. The best-quality wines are *appellation contrôlée* (AC); the second category is *vins délimités de qualité supérieure* (VDQS); the third contains *vins de pays*; and the fourth *vins de table*. Infractions of the decrees of the Institut are dealt with by the Service de Répression des Fraudes.
**Areometer** Another name for HYDROMETER.
**Aroma** A word used among wine experts to describe the grapy smell of young wine. See page 370 for a fuller explanation and, for contrast, see BOUQUET.
***Arrope*** *(Sp)* Wine reduced by being boiled down to one-fifth its original volume. Black and extremely sweet, it is used only for coloring and sweetening blends.
***Asciutto*** *(It)* Very dry.
***Assemblage*** *(Fr)* A term used to describe blending wines of different origins, characteristics or ages. Fine wines are not usually blended, although fine wines from different casks may be "assembled" to avoid cask-to-cask differences within a single shipment. VIN DE GOUTTE and VIN DE PRESSE may be blended in this way.
**Astringency** The quality of drying the mouth found in highly tannic wines.
***Auslese*** *(Ger)* Means literally "selected." Such wines are third in the rising order of *Prädikats* of German QmP wines (see pages 120-21).
***Azienda*** *(It)* Wine estate.

## B

***Baixo Corgo*** *(P)* See CORGO.
**Baked** A term applied to the cooked and earthy AROMA and BOUQUET of wines made in hot countries.
**Balance** The blend of alcohol, acids and sweetness in a wine, described as "perfect" when correct or as "lacking" if it is deficient in any particular.
**Balling** See BRIX.
***Ban de vendage*** *(Fr)* The proclamation date when the harvest is permitted to start, an expression used especially in Bordeaux and Champagne. (Literally, "prohibition of the harvest.")
**Barrel-aging** The changes that occur to a wine as it ages in the barrel. The barrels impart character to the wine as it clarifies and matures, and therefore the type and age of the timber used are important. Wine is often rotated between new and old barrels so that it can gain the desired characteristics from the wood.
**Barrel types** The names and capacities of the barrels used vary from region to region. Some important examples are set out in the chart below.

**Barrel types**

| Region | Name | Capacity (liters) |
|---|---|---|
| Alsace | *Foudre* | 1000 |
| Beaujolais | *Pièce* | 212 |
| Bordeaux | *Barrique* | 225 |
| Burgundy | *Pièce* | 228 |
| France (generally) | Hogshead | 272 |
| Portugal | Pipe | 522 (Port) |
| | | 418 (Madeira) |
| Rhine | *Stück* | 1200 |
| | *Halbstück* | 600 |
| Scotland | Hogshead | 249 |
| | Butt | 490 (Whisky) |
| Spain | Butt | 490 (Sherry) |

***Barrique*** *(Fr)* See BARREL TYPES.
**Baumé** *(Fr)* A hydrometer scale named for Antoine Baumé (1728-1804) and used to measure the density of grape-must in order to establish its sugar content. See ALCOHOL.
***Beerenauslese*** *(Ger)* Fourth in the rising order of *Prädikats* of German QmP wines. (Literally, "selected grapes.")
**Bentonite** Aluminum silicate, a clay used as a FINING agent for precipitating the protein solids in new wine.
***Bereich*** *(Ger)* A main subregion of an ANBAUGEBIET.
***Bianco*** *(It)* White wine.
**Binning** The laying-down of bottled wine for aging. The term is usually reserved for wines in makers' cellars laid down under strictly controlled conditions. A special vintage or batch may therefore acquire an identifying **bin number**.
**Bitters** Herb-flavored drinks originally used medicinally but now used as additives in mixed drinks or as DIGESTIFS.
**Blending** The mixing of liquors of different origins to produce a desired product. For wines, see ASSEMBLAGE. Spirits — e.g., malt and grain whiskeys — are also blended. Generally blending must be done gradually and slowly so that the liquids have time to "marry."
***Bodega*** *(Sp)* See CELLAR.
**Body** A term used in tasting to describe consistency in a wine in terms of, especially, taste, alcoholic strength and "mouth-filling" qualities.
***Bonde de côte, bonde à côte*** *(Fr)* Term used to describe the position of barrels used for aging wines when the bung is not to the top. When the bung is to the side less wine evaporates.
***Bonne chauffe*** *(Fr)* Raw and immature Cognac.
**Bora** *(It)* See KATABATIC WINDS.
**Bordeaux mixture** Copper sulfate and lime, a mixture widely used for spraying vines to protect against pests and diseases.
***Botrytis cinerea*** A fungus that feeds on grapes. In maleficent form, in cold, wet conditions, it produces a grey mold called **grey rot** or ***pourriture grise***. However, in beneficent form, in warm, humid conditions, the fungus sucks water from the grapes, so concentrating the sugar: in white grapes this gives rise to **noble rot *(pourriture noble)***. This effect is undesirable in black grapes, which are therefore not left to overripen.
***Bottiglia*** *(It)* Bottle.
**"Bottled in Bond"** *(USA)* A 100% straight whiskey at least four years old.
**Bottle sizes** Regulation EEC bottle sizes (indicated by the letter "e" on the label) contain 75cl (25.4fl oz) — 37.5cl (12.7fl oz) for the half-bottle. However, the Champagne bottle contains 80cl (27fl oz). Larger bottles for Champagne are:
- **Magnum** 2 bottles
- **Tappit-Hen** 3 bottles
- **Jeroboam** 4 bottles
- **Rehoboam** 6 bottles
- **Methuselah** 8 bottles

The even larger sizes — **Salmanezah** (12 bottles), **Balthazar** (16 bottles), **Nebuchadnezzar** (20 bottles) — are no longer produced.
**Bottling, cold-sterile process of** Technique used for fine wines that need to age in bottle. The bottles are sterilized using sulfur dioxide and are then filled with wine in an inert carbon-dioxide atmosphere.
**Bound $SO_2$** Sulfur dioxide that has been added to wine and has combined with sugar or ALDEHYDES, or has converted to sulfuric acid. See SULFURING.
**Bouquet** The smell given off by a wine when the bottle is opened. It arises from the slow oxidation of alcohol and fruit acids into esters and aldehydes. Wines high in acids usually have a stronger bouquet. Compare AROMA.
**Breed** A loose term, meaning approximately "distinctive and distinguished," applied to such factors as the origin, soil and winemakers' skill in producing a fine wine.
**British wines** See MADE-WINES.
**Brix** *(USA)* A scale used to determine sugar-density in grape-musts. Also called **balling**.
***Brouillis*** Synonym for BONNE CHAUFFE.
**Brown Sherry** A blend of OLOROSO and RAYA sherries, sweeter than CREAM SHERRY and considerably darker in color.
***Brut*** *(Fr)* Very dry. Term applied to Champagne and other French sparkling wines.
***Bual*** *(P)* The less sweet of two MADEIRA wines to which spirit is added before ESTUFAGEM (the other is MALMSEY). Two other types — Sercial and Verdelho — are fermented to dryness.
**Bubble cap** A valve which permits the escape of carbon dioxide ($CO_2$) from a sealed tank or cask during fermentation but which excludes air. This valve may not be incorporated with the BUNG when the bung is BONDE DE CÔTE.
**Bung** Made of wood, earthenware or glass, the stopper of a barrel in which wine is being aged.
**Burgundy mixture** A solution of copper sulfate and calcium carbonate used to spray on vines to protect them against pests and diseases.
**Butt** *(Sp)* See BARREL TYPES.

## C

***Cantina*** *(It)* Wine CELLAR.
***Cantina sociale*** *(It)* Growers' cooperative winery.
**Cap of skins** In the fermentation of red wines, the mass of black grape-skins and their pips which rises up to a submerged screen. See page 37.
**Capsule** Metal or plastic protector sealed over the neck and cork of a bottle.
**Cask** See BARREL TYPES.
**Casses** Several wine maladies. **Iron casse** and **copper casse** affect the wine's smell and taste. The cure is by blue fining with potassium ferrocyanide (an overdose poisons the wine). **Oxidic casse**, a discoloring through oxidation, has no certain cure. **Protein casse**, common in fortified wines, is cured by FINING with BENTONITE.
***Cave*** *(Fr)* Place for the storage of wine, usually an underground cellar, where the temperature may be maintained at 11°C (52°F).
**Cellar** (1) See CAVE. (2) Building for the vinification and manufacture of wine. European equivalents are *chai (Fr), Keller (Ger), bodega (Sp), adega (P)* and *cantina (It).*
**Cellarmaster** (French ***chef de cave***.) Manager responsible for cellar operations, possibly including vinification.
**Centrifuge** Device using centrifugal force to draw suspended particles out of liquids. It may be used on MUST or wine.
***Cépage*** *(Fr)* A selection of one or more vines for planting in a vineyard; e.g., the *cépages nobles* — Chardonnay, Riesling, Cabernet Sauvignon and Pinot Noir — recommended by the University of California for planting in California's Coastal Counties.
***Chai*** *(Fr)* See CELLAR.
**Chaptalisation** Addition of sugar during winemaking to strengthen the alcohol potential; forbidden in Italy, but permitted under strict conditions for some wines in France and Germany. Named for the French scientist Jean Chaptal (1756-1832).
***Château*** *(Fr)* Vineyard or property, usually with an impressive main building — anything from a castle to a modest house.
**Château-bottled** Also **mis du château** and **mis en bouteilles au château**. Made from estate grapes only (not necessarily a guarantee of quality).
***Chef de cave*** *(Fr)* CELLARMASTER.
***Chef du culture*** *(Fr)* Vineyard manager. See also VIGNERON.
**Chromatography** Analysis of the substances present in a solution by color-separation on special filter papers.
**Cima Corgo** *(P)* See CORGO
**Claret** Originally, light red wine originating from Bordeaux Clairet, but now adopted as a generic term. Use is limited to wines with AC Bordeaux, although Australian and South African Claret are also permitted.
**Clarification** Clearing wine of protein matter or until it **falls bright**. See FINING.
**Classed growth** (French ***cru classé***) A property that has been awarded an official classification; see APPELLATION CONTRÔLÉE.
***Classico*** *(It)* The center, usually the best wine-producing area, of a DOC wine region.
**Clean** Term used to describe a wine that is "refreshing."
***Climat*** Burgundian term for a vineyard.
***Clodosporium cellare*** A fungus that develops in cellars and is said to give the wine a "sealing-wax" tone.
**Clone selection** Establishment of a vine variety by repeatedly grafting scions from vines of desired characteristics.
***Clos*** *(Fr)* A walled vineyard, or one that was once walled, especially in Burgundy. The word *"clos"* may not appear on a label unless the vineyard actually exists and produced the wine. The vineyard must also be surrounded by an enclosure, unless the existence of the *clos* has been recorded for over 100 years.
**Coarse** Description of a crude or badly made wine.
***Cocks et Féret*** Edited and published every 4-5 years, the definitive listing of Bordeaux vineyards.
***Collage*** *(Fr)* CLARIFICATION or FINING of wine using a coagulant such as eggwhite, ISINGLASS or BENTONITE.
**Commune** Administrative unit comprising a town, parish or village and the surrounding land. The commune name is often adopted as that of an *Appellation Contrôlée* area, in which case the wine produced by all the vineyards in the commune must be of standard quality.
**Complete** Description of a balanced and mature wine.
**Complexity** Tasters' term used in discussing the scents-within-scents of a fine wine, redolent of flowers, fruit, and herbs.
**Congeners** The toxic impurities in spirituous compounds whose levels have to be reduced by RECTIFICATION during distillation. The small quantities that remain contribute to the spirits' flavor and character. See also FORESHOTS AND FEINTS and HEADS AND TAILS.
***Consejo*** *(Sp)* Official governing body of a wine region. Not to be confused with the similarly pronounced ***conseho***, meaning "vintage" or "harvest."
***Consorzio*** *(It)* Association of producers who control quality, promotion and legal and other matters affecting the wine produced in their region.
**Continuous still, Coffey still or patent still** Invented in 1830 by Aeneas Coffey, a customs officer, a device for the distillation of spirits incorporating the separation and RECTIFICATION of alcohol in a continuous stream, so making possible the mass-production of spirits (especially grain spirits). It is still used today in a variety of modified forms. See Index.
**Cooperage** General term for wooden casks, barrels or vats used for storage in a particular cellar or winery. Used also to mean the storage capacity and repair of these containers.
**Cordial** A sweetened and flavored spirit, described in most parts of the world as a **liqueur**. See Index.
**Corgo** *(P)* River flowing into the Douro from the north at Regua. Cima Corgo is the area east of the Corgo stretching to the Spanish frontier, and produces a small quantity of superb grapes. Baixo Corgo, west of the Corgo, is a small area producing a large quantity of grapes.
**Corky** Description of the smell and taste of a wine contaminated by a moldy cork.
***Côte*** *(Fr)* A slope with vineyards, often above a river valley.

***Coulure*** Partial or total failure of the grape crop when bad weather (usually rain, wind or both) stops the bees from pollinating the vine flowers. The newly formed clusters of small green berries fail to develop into grapes.
***Coupage*** *(Fr)* BLENDING of wines of different years and/or origins.
***Courtier*** *(Fr)* Broker acting between a vineyard owner and a NÉGOCIANT; the full term is *courtier piquet-en-vin.*
**Cream Sherry** A blended and sweetened OLOROSO.
***Criadera*** *(Sp)* The nursery stage in the blending and maturation of Sherry. See page 160.
**Cross** A new variety of vine resulting from the cross-pollination of two varieties of *Vitis vinifera*; e.g., Riesling × Silvaner = Müller-Thurgau. Compare HYBRID.
***Cru*** *(Fr)* (1) A growth or crop of grapes. (2) A vineyard and the wine it produces.
***Cru classé*** Classed growths of the Médoc have five categories: *Premier Cru, Deuxième Cru, Troisième Cru, Quatrième Cru* and *Cinquième Cru.* (The last three are nowadays ranked with *Cru Bourgeois.*) Other Bordeaux regions have *Premier Grand Cru Classé* and *Grande Cru Classé.*
**Crust** Heavy SEDIMENT. The term is usually applied to vintage Port.
***Cuvage*** *(Fr)* Literally vatting, or the loading of a vat with grape-must.
***Cuvé*** *(Fr)* Large vat or tank in which wines are fermented.
***Cuvée*** *(Fr)* The contents of a CUVÉ; i.e., all the wine made at one time.
***Cuvier*** *(Fr)* A winery.

## D

***Débourbage*** *(Fr)* In the making of white wine, delaying the fermentation of newly pressed MUST for 24-48 hours, so giving it time to stand and clarify. Fermentation is postponed by keeping the must at a low temperature.
**Decanting** Transferring red wine that has thrown a DEPOSIT from the bottle to a decanter. See pages 373 and 380.
***Décuvage*** *(Fr)* The devatting of red wine after fermentation, involving the separation of the wine from the CAP OF SKINS, which sinks to the bottom of the vat as it empties.
***Dégorgement*** *(Fr)* Removing sediments from the necks of inverted bottles of sparkling wines. ***Dégorgement à la volée*** is extraction by hand without freezing; ***dégorgement automatique*** is the extraction by machine of the frozen capsule containing the sediment.
**Degree-day regions** or **heat-day regions** *(USA)* System of identifying regions by use of a formula based on hours of sunshine. See pages 220 and 224.
***Denominazióne de Origine Controllata* system (DOC)** *(It)* The Italian wine-laws of 1963 created the DOC award, broadly equivalent to the APPELLATION CONTRÔLÉE, for wine made in a specific vineyard and produced and bottled according to the laws. A higher award (DOCG) adds the words *"e garantita"* for top-quality wines, but only Brunello di Montalcino has so far received this.
**Deposit** The fall-out of SEDIMENT as wines (especially red) mature in bottle. Deposit collects along the lower side of the horizontal bottle, which should therefore be stood upright for 24 hours before DECANTING.
**Diastase** The enzyme formed as the barley-grain sprouts and in MALTING. Diastase catalyzes the conversion of starches to MALTOSE.
***Digestif*** *(Fr)* Any spirit, often sweetened and flavored, taken after a meal to aid the digestion. *Digestifs* were originally developed in the monasteries as CORDIALS.
***Dolce*** *(It)* Very sweet, having 5-10% residual sugar in the wine.
***Domaine*** *(Ger)* A state-owned wine property, of which there are six in Germany.
***Dosage*** *(Fr)* Sweetened wine *(liqueur d'expedition)* added to disgorged bottles of sparkling wine to make up the loss. See POIGNETTAGE.
**Draff** By-product remaining when the sugary WORT is removed from the GRIST in the production of MALTOSE. Draff is a major component of a valuable cattle-food produced as a by-product of grain-spirit distillation.
**Dry** Description of wines in which all sugars have been converted to alcohol.
***Dulce pasa*** *(Sp)* Sweetening wine made from Sherry grapes (Pedro Ximénez or Moscatel) which have been left in the sun to shrivel and concentrate their sugar.
**Dunder** The residue from a previous distillation of rum, sometimes used instead of yeast in the fermentation of molasses.

## E

**Earthy** Describes the taste of soil characteristic of big red wines.
**Eaux-de-vie** Spirits similar to brandies. **Eaux-de-vie-de-marc** are made from MARC, the residue in the fermentation of wines: eau-de-vie-de-marc-d'Aquitaine and eau-de-vie-de-marc-de-Champagne are of excellent quality, but not all others are. Other eaux-de-vie are: **eau-de-vie-de-cidre**, made from cider, Calvados being the most famous example; **eau-de-vie-de-poiré**, distilled from perry (known as *Poiré Williams* in France and *Birngeist* in Germany); and **eau-de-vie-de-vin**, an early name for brandy still used in France.
***Edelfäule*** *(Ger)* Noble rot. See BOTRYTIS CINEREA.
***Égrappage*** *(Fr)* In the making of red wines, the removal of the grape-stems before they are pressed or fed into the fermentation vat. This is now done mechanically by the *égrappoir* or destemmer. (For white wines the stems are not removed.)
***Einzellage*** *(Ger)* An individual vineyard of not less than 5ha (12.4 acres); this area may take the form of several smaller, separated parcels of land.
***Eiswein*** *(Ger)* Wine made from grapes gathered in midwinter and pressed while still frozen solid. The juice is separated from the ice, so that the sugar is concentrated. The wine is extremely sweet with exaggerated flavor and low alcohol.
**Elegance** A complimentary term applied to a wine of BREED, finesse and style.
**English wines** As distinct from British wines (see MADE-WINES), English wines are made in England from English-grown grapes.
**Estate-bottled** Produced and bottled by the estate owner solely from grapes grown on the estate. Synonyms are *"mis en domaine," "mis du proprietaire," "mis en bouteilles par le proprietaire"* and *"mis à la propriété."*
**Esters** Compounds of alcohol and organic acids which give flavor and bouquet to wines and spirits.
**Estery** Describes the fruity odor developing from the slow formation of esters in wine.
***Estufagem*** *(P)* Process by which Madeira wines are raised gradually to a temperature of 45°C (113°F) and then cooled down again over a period of six months. This is done in the ***estufa***, a heat-store which simulates the conditions experienced by early Madeira wines, which were discovered to derive beneficial effects from being heated while passing through the tropics on their way to the East and Australia.
***Etichetta*** *(It)* The wine-label.
***Euvitis*** The genus or subgenus of vines native to North America which includes the species *E. labrusca, E. riparia, E. berlandieri, E. rupestris, E. californica* and *E. arizonica.* All these species are hardier than the Old World *Vitis vinfera*, but their wines have an unpleasant pungency, being known as "fox wines." Planting of *Euvitis* vines has been banned in many regions.
**Extract** The nonvolatile soluble solids in a wine which give it body and substance. In sweet wine, the main soluble solid is sugar; in dry wine the extract is mostly composed of ESTERS and ALDEHYDES.
**Extra dry** Term used to describe a slightly sweet Champagne!

## F

**Fat** Describes a fleshy wine, too alcoholic and rich in GLYCEROL and EXTRACT.
***Fattoria*** *(It)* A wine estate in central Italy.
**Fédération Internationale des Marchands du Vin, Spiritueux, Eaux-de-Vie et Liqueurs (FIVS)** The vital federation of national associations concerned with the production and marketing of wines and spirits in all aspects, including education, labeling, promotion, quotas, social aspects, standards, laws and treaties, and all other matters where international understanding and cooperation are desirable. An annual congress is attended by all member nations.
**Feints** See FORESHOTS AND FEINTS.
**Fermentation, alcoholic** The process by which sugar is converted into alcohol and carbon dioxide. See pages 28-32.
**Fermentation, malolactic** A secondary fermentation that can take place at any time after the primary (alcoholic) fermentation. The MALIC ACID in the wine is converted into the milder lactic acid and carbon dioxide. It takes place in white wines of high acid content, notably Champagne, and is usually regarded as desirable in the fuller red wines.

***Fiasco** (It)* Flask, including the famous raffia-covered Chianti bottle no longer produced because of the cost.
**Filtration** The clarifying of wine prior to bottling by passing it through a filter (there are many kinds of filter). Many German wines are sterile-filtered to remove all bacteria so that the wine can be bottled earlier.
**Fining** One of three methods of clarifying wines (the others are FILTRATION and by use of the CENTRIFUGE). Fining, the traditional method, uses an organic agent such as gelatin or eggwhite, for red wines, or isinglass, for whites, to coagulate and precipitate out the particles held in suspension in the wine. Fining is still used for the finest wines.
**Finish** An ultimate quality in good wines: the taste that remains on the palate for some length of time, even if other foods and drinks are consumed in the interim.
**Fino** *(Sp)* Sherry made from wine that has developed FLOR during maturation. Fino is the best and lightest of all Sherries.
**Firm** Said of a wine that has youth and style.
**Fixed acids** See ACIDITY. In wine, the principal fixed acids are tartaric, malic, succinic and lactic acids.
***Flor*** A yeast that develops haphazardly on some butts of Sherry during fermentation, whereupon they are classified as FINOS.
**Flowery** Describes an attractive BOUQUET.
***Flurbereinigung** (Ger)* Government-sponsored scheme for remodeling vineyard areas by converting steep slopes into plateaus capable of development and the mechanical harvesting of the grapes.
**Foreshots and feints** Scottish terms for the HEADS AND TAILS.
**Fortified wines** Wines to which spirit has been added to increase their natural strength. Brandy is added to Sherry *after* fermentation is complete, to give a dry wine of 15.5-18% vol. alcohol. Brandy is added to Port *during* fermentation, inhibiting the conversion of further sugar; Port is therefore sweet. Four styles of Madeira have spirit added, two during fermentation, two after it. Other fortified wines are Moscatel de Setúbal and Marsala. See Index.
***Foulage** (Fr)* The gentle crushing of grapes to start the juice running in preparation for fermentation. This is now mechanized, the device used (which combines destemming) being the stemmer-crusher, or *égrappoir-fouloir.*
**Foxiness** The pungent scent of EUVITIS wines.
**Free-run wine** Also ***vin de goutte.*** The must that runs from the crushed grapes before they are pressed. It is of better quality than the PRESS WINE.
**Free $SO_2$** Unbound sulfur dioxide active in wine as a bactericide.
***Frizzante** (It)* Slightly sparkling wine.
**Frost** A hazard to the vine, especially at the colder limits of the WINE-BANDS. The main danger is in spring when the buds have formed: frost can affect one year's crop and the next year's vintage. Fans and heating apparatus are used to protect the vines; another technique is water-spraying, which gives the vines a layer of ice and so protects them from the colder frost.
**Fusel oils** Toxic higher alcohols, present in wines in safe quantities. In distillation they must be separated as "tails" or "feints" during RECTIFICATION. See page 326.

## G

**Gay-Lussac system** See page 45.
**Glycerol** Also **glycerin** or **glycerine** An important component in wine, a colorless syrupy hygroscopic liquid (formula $CH_2OH.CHOH.CH_2OH$) resulting from the alcoholic fermentation of glucose in the presence of sodium sulfite.
***Goût de terroir*** Distinctive earthy taste in wines, specific to their soil or origin.
***Governo** (It)* Winemaking process in which 5% of a mixture of four grape varieties is dried out and added after fermentation of the other 95% is complete. This causes a slow second alcoholic fermentation. The wine gains more body and a higher GLYCEROL content — beneficial in, for example, the aging of Chianti Classico.
**Grafting** The joining of a scion (or shoot) of one vine variety onto a rootstock of another variety. This became the solution to the scourge of PHYLLOXERA VASTATRIX which almost wiped out the vineyards of Europe in the 1860s. See pages 20 and 258-60.
**Grain spirits** Spirits made by distillation of the ferment produced from a mash of GRIST, grain and YEAST.
***Grand vin** (Fr)* Meaning a "great wine," this term has no legal definition.
**Grape** The genus *Vitis* has over 20 species, of which *Vitis vinifera,* the wine-bearing vine, is one. *V. vinifera* flourished in Europe and around the Mediterranean. No other species produces wine-grapes of equivalent quality and attraction. See pages 21-4 and Index.
**Grappa** Brandy distilled in Italy and California from grape-musts.
**Green** Describes a very young, immature wine.
***Greffe** (Fr)* A graft of a scion onto a rootstock. ***Greffe anglaise*** is a grafting style of English origin (see page 20); ***port greffe*** is a phylloxera-resistant rootstock.
***Grêle** (Fr)* Hail — a danger to the grape; it breaks the skin and leaves and gives the resulting wine (especially red) an off-taste of rot called ***goûte de grêle.*** A heavy storm can destroy a crop in minutes. Growers use aircraft in their endeavors to make hail-clouds disperse their contents as rain, or, less extravagantly, nets can be used to cover the vines; but there is no certain way to avoid this natural disaster.
**Grey rot** See BOTRYTIS CINEREA.
**Grist** Kilned and crushed MALTOSE. Grist is used as a catalyst to convert the starches of grains other than barley into maltose. See WORT.
***Grosslage** (Ger)* A collective vineyard area consisting of a number of EINZELLAGEN of equal quality. There are 150 *Grosslagen* in the 32 BEREICHE.
**Gunflint** Describes the flinty flavor of extra-dry white wines.

## H

**Hail** See GRÊLE.
**Hard** Describes a tannic young red wine.
**Head and cold-mix systems** Methods of flavoring gin.
**Heads and tails** During distillation in the pot still the more volatile poisons (heads) evaporate at 28°C (82°F) and are drawn off at the beginning of the distillation, while the FUSEL OILS (tails), being less volatile than alcohol, are drawn off at the end.
**Heat-day regions** See DEGREE-DAY REGIONS.
**High wines** The refined spirit obtained in distillation after the HEADS AND TAILS have been eliminated.
**Hybrid** A variety of vine obtained by cross-pollination of *Vitis vinifera* with a wild vine, such as *Euvitis labrusca* or *E. riparia.* For example, Cinsault × Noah = Baco 22A.
**Hydrometer** Instrument used to measure the Specific Gravity of a liquid. Synonyms are areometer, *mustimètre* and saccharometer. See ALCOHOL LEVELS AND MEASUREMENT.

## I

**Improvement of musts** See CHAPTALISATION.
**INAO** See APPELLATION CONTRÔLÉE.
**Informing grape** *(USA)* The principal grape that gives a VARIETAL WINE its particular character.
**Inoculation** Introducing a special YEAST culture into a grape MUST, usually after the wild yeasts have been destroyed by sulfur dioxide
**Isinglass** Purified fish glue. The usual FINING agent for white wines.

## J

**Jeroboam** See BOTTLE SIZES.

## K

***Kabinett** (Ger)* The lowest in the rising order of *Prädikats* of German quality wines, being superior to QbA but inferior to *Spätlese.* See pages 120-21.
**Katabatic winds** Winds caused as cold air moves downwards by convection, as when cold air from glaciers flows down into a valley. Velocities can reach 60-80kph (37½-50mph). Examples are the mistral of southern France and the bora of northern Italy and Yugoslavia.
***Kellermeister** (Ger)* Cellarmaster.
**Kieselguhr** An absorbent earth with which wine is mixed to clear protein haze it then has to be filtered through fine filters.

## L

***Landwein** (Ger)* A 1982 addition to the categories of TAFELWEIN, *Landwein* must not have more than 18g/l (about 2oz/gal) of residual sugar, and must be made in one of 20 designated areas.
**Late-picked** Certain grapes — e.g., Riesling — may be left on the vine after the vintage proper. Such grapes accumulate sugar. The earliest to be picked are called *Spätlese* in Germany and *vendange tardive* in France. In Germany, the later the picking (meaning higher sugar content), the higher the *Prädikat* awarded.
**Lees** The coarse sediment remaining in the barrel when wines are racked (see RACKING). It consists largely of dead yeast cells and solid protein matter.
**Liqueur** See CORDIAL.
***Liqueur de tirage** (Fr)* A mixture of sweetened wine and yeast used to induce a secondary FERMENTATION.
***Liquoroso** (It)* Strong wine with any residual sugar content.
**Lively** Describes fresh wine that shows signs of lasting.
**Lodges** *(P)* Warehouses at Vila Nova de Gaia where Port is stored and matured. The same term is used for warehouses in Madeira.
**Loess** A soil type: a mixture of lime, loam, sand, and mica — one of the most fertile soils for vine-growing.
**Low wines** The first distillate in the production of malt whisky.

## M

**Maceration** Extracting flavor and color from grapes by steeping them in their own juice before fermentation.
***Macération carbonique*** Fermentation process in which carbon dioxide is retained under slight pressure. In red-wine production, this releases color from the skins more quickly and tends to shorten the aging period.
**"Made and Bottled by"** In legal terms, this means that up to 90% of the wine has been bought in bulk.
**Made-wines** Strictly speaking, these are not wines at all, because they are not made by the fermentation of newly gathered grapes in their district of origin. They are produced using preserved musts or dried raisins which are fermented after export. **British wines** are a famous type.
**Magnum** See BOTTLE SIZES.
***Maître de chai** (Fr)* The cellarmaster responsible for wine-making.
**Malaga** *(Sp)* An extra sweet wine made in Andalusia. It is not fortified, but is sweetened with boiled-down must called ARROPE.
**Malic acid** A tart fruit acid converted into lactic acid during malolactic FERMENTATION.
**Malmsey** *(Sp)* The sweetest style of Madeira. The name is a corruption of that of the Malvasia or Malvoisie vine, originally brought from Cyprus.
**Malting** The controlled germination of barley, during which the enzyme DIASTASE is produced. This catalyst is essential in the conversion of all starches to MALTOSE.

**Maltose** or **malt sugar** A sugar which is produced by the action of the catalyst DIASTASE on starch during the germination of barley. Its formula is $C_{12}H_{22}O_{11}.H_2O$.
**Malts** Unblended Scotch whiskies produced in the POT STILL are known as single malts. They may be blended with other malts and with grain whiskeys under strict legal conditions. See pages 350-52.
**Manzanilla** *(Sp)* Sherries matured near the sea in the bodegas of Sanlucar de Barrameda: they pick up an attractive salty tang. Basically, Manzanillas are pale FINOS which darken with age to gain a nutty richness.
**Marc** The grapeskins, stems and pips left after pressing out the wine MUST. It is the raw material of EAUX-DE-VIE-DE-MARC.
**Mash** Malted grain, ground and steeped in hot water at the beginning of the FERMENTATION stage of distillation.
**Metallic** Describes a taste noticeable in strong red wines that cannot be otherwise described! It is not detrimental to the wine.
***Méthode champenoise*** *(Fr)* (Italian, ***metodo champenois***) The only permitted method of making Champagne, and one used also in the production of sparkling wines in other regions and indeed countries. See pages 88-9.
**Mildew** Fungal disease which attacks the vine during persistent wet weather.
***Mistelle*** *(Fr)*, ***mistella*** *(It)*, ***mistela*** *(Sp, P)* Grape juice that has been inhibited from fermenting by the addition of alcohol. It is used for sweetening, especially in APERITIFS and CORDIALS.
**Mistral** See KATABATIC WINDS.
**Molasses** The residue (or final by-product) in the progressive extraction from sugarcane of sugar, syrup and treacle by boiling and centrifuging. Molasses can be diluted with water and fermented with yeast and/or DUNDER to produce an alcoholic wash for distillation to rum.
***Muffa nobile*** *(It)* Noble rot. See BOTRYTIS CINEREA.
**Must** (1) Grape juice pressed for FERMENTATION. (2) The term can also be used for the contents of a vat during fermentation.
***Mustimètre*** See HYDROMETER.
**Musty** Describes a wine odor caused by fungal growth, probably as a result of an unsound barrel or other fault in the controlled conditions of aging.

## N

**Nastoika** Flavored Russian vodkas.
***Négociant*** *(Fr)* Wine-merchant or -shipper. A ***négociant-éleveur*** is a purchaser, stockist and blender of young wines for eventual sale or shipment.
***Nero*** *(It)* Literally, "black." A term used for dark red wines.
**Neutral spirits** Spirits, from whatever base, which have been distilled to 100° Proof (50% vol. alcohol) or more.
**Nobile** A grape condition which gives sweetness to wines such as the Italian Orvieto, Ausbruch in Austria, and, as *aszú*, to Tokay Eszencia. It occurs also in California, and sometimes elsewhere.
**Noble rot** See BOTRYTIS CINEREA.
**Nose** Describes a wine's BOUQUET, especially when it is in a glass ready for TASTING — or just for drinking.

## O

**Oenology** The UK spelling of enology.
**Oechsle scale** *(Ger)* A measure of the SPECIFIC GRAVITY of a must: 1° Oechsle = SG 1.001, 2° Oechsle = SG 1.002, and so on. If you divide the number of degrees Oechsle of a must by 8 you get its potential vol. alcohol (see ALCOHOL LEVELS AND MEASUREMENTS). The system is named for its inventor, Ferdinand Oechsle (1774-1852).
***Oidium tuckerii*** Fungal disease, known also as Powdery mildew, which attacked European vineyards just before PHYLLOXERA. It covers the grapes, splitting and rotting them, and is native to the USA. See page 25.
**OIML system** See page 45.
**Oloroso** *(Sp)* A full dry Sherry from a RAYA butt that has not developed FLOR. Olorosos pick up color and oak flavors before, during and after passing through the SOLERA system. See pages 160-61.
**Overproof** A spirit of over 100° Proof (50% vol. alcohol).

## P

**Palo Cortado** *(Sp)* A rare Sherry having both FINO and OLOROSO characteristics. It is not blended in the SOLERA with other Sherries.
**Palus** Rich alluvial soil, unsuitable for growing wine-grapes.
***Passito*** *(It)* Sweet strong wine made from grapes that have been dried to concentrate their sugar.
**Pasteurization** Process devised by Louis Pasteur (1822-1895) to inhibit bacterial development. It is *never* used for fine wines, as it arrests the development and improvement of the wine in the aging process.
**Patent still** See CONTINUOUS STILL.
**Percolation** Process whereby spirit is forced in a closed circuit through herbs or fruit to pick up their flavor.
***Perlwein*** *(Ger)* TAFELWEIN carbonated under pressure so that it has a slight sparkle.
***Phylloxera vastatrix*** A vine louse, native to North America's eastern regions, that destroyed many of Europe's vineyards between 1862 and the end of the nineteenth century. It can be countered only by GRAFTING *Vitis vinifera* scions onto resistant rootstocks from those regions, by quarantine, or by planting in sand. For various reasons, a few areas of the world are phylloxera-free.
***Pièce*** *(Fr)* See BARREL TYPES.
**Piges** Wooden poles used to keep the CAP OF SKINS submerged.
**Pineau de Charentes** *(Fr)* A MISTELLE produced in Cognac for drinking (rather than for sweetening).
***Plafond limite de classement*** **(PLC)** *(Fr)* Ceiling production yield, expressed in hectoliters per hectare.
***Poignettage*** *(Fr)* Gentle shaking of bottles to which DOSAGE has been added, in order to mix the contents.
**Pomace** *(UK)* MARC.
**Pop wines** "Wines" of various fruit flavors, of strength 8-10% vol. alcohol (16-20° Proof), with a permitted carbonation level of 14.7 pounds per atmosphere. They give a slight "pop" when opened.
**Portacask** A shipping container of capacity 26.4hl (580 gal) made of fiberglass and lined with stainless steel.
**Poteen** Illegally distilled Irish whiskey.
**Pot still** A batch still used in the production of Scotch whisky, brandy and other spirits. See pages 325-8.
***Pourriture grise, pourriture noble*** See BOTRYTIS CINEREA.
**Press wine** or ***vin de presse*** The wine expressed when the MARC is pressed after the FREE-RUN WINE has been drawn off. It may be added to the free-run wine to give more body, or may be processed to completion separately.
**"Produced and Bottled by"** When this appears on a label it means, according to US law, that at least 75% of the contents are wine fermented at the winery.
**Proof** A measure of the degree of alcohol by volume present in wines and spirits. The **Sikes Proof scale** runs from 0° Proof for pure water to 175° Proof for pure alcohol; the **US Proof scale** runs from 0° Proof for pure water to 200° Proof for pure alcohol. 2° US Proof = 1% vol. alcohol.

## Q

***Qualitätswein bestimmte Anbaugebiete*** **(QbA)** *(Ger)* Quality wine from one of 11 designated regions. See page 120.
***Qualitätswein mit Prädikat*** **(QmP)** *(Ger)* Quality wine with special distinctions or attributes. See pages 120-21.
***Qualitätswein system*** *(Ger)* See page 120.

## R

**Racking** Drawing wine from one cask to another, leaving the LEES behind.
**Racy** Describes a wine that is exciting and fresh.
***Raya*** *(Sp)* The contents of all Sherry butts before they are divided into FINOS, OLOROSOS, and "burning wine." Finos (butts developing FLOR) and olorosos (butts not developing *flor*) go forward separately to the SOLERA system to produce Sherries. Butts that go bad ("burning wine") are sent for conversion to brandy or industrial alcohol.
***Rebêche*** *(Fr)* Juice from the final intense mechanical pressing of MARC in a hydraulic or screw press. Containing constituents of stems and pips, it is too bitter for use in wine and goes for distillation.
**Rectification** The purification of spirits by distillation. The CONGENERS are removed before and after the "good heart" (i.e., the rectified spirit) is condensed and collected.
**Reducing** Lowering the alcoholic strength of spirits by the addition of water from production to selling levels.
**Refreshing** Adding new wine to older wine in the cask.
***Régisseur*** *(Fr)* Manager of a wine estate.
***Remontage*** *(Fr)* "Pumping over"; i.e., taking wine from the bottom of the fermentation tank out and back into the top of the tank. This helps cool the ferment and, with red wines, also helps keep the CAP OF SKINS mobile and submerged, so that more color can be extracted from it.

***Remuage*** *(Fr)* The slow and laborious process of bringing the SEDIMENT from the secondary FERMENTATION down onto the cork of the inverted bottle. Part of the MÉTHODE CHAMPENOISE, this is performed manually by a ***remueur***. See page 88
***Rendement*** *(Fr)* A cropping measure, given in hectoliters per hectare, or the hectoliter measure of grape juice permitted for conversion to Grand CRU and Premier Cru wines. ***Rendement de base*** is the basic yield.
**Residual sugar** (German ***Restsüsse***) Sugar that is not converted to alcohol during FERMENTATION. One per cent residual sugar means that a wine is sweet.
***Riserva*** *(It)* DOC wine that has matured for the mandatory period applying to its district. ***Riserva speciale*** implies a longer aging period, often an extra one or two years.
**Robe** The film of color left in a glass from, especially, a red wine.
**Rootstock** See GRAFTING.
***Rosato*** *(It)* Rosé.
***Rosé*** Light pink wine made by removing red grapeskins early in the fermentation process. In some countries it is made by mixing red and white wines.
***Rosso*** *(It)* Red wine.
**Rotation** (1) Wine may be rotated between new and older casks. (2) Rarely, vine-crops may be rotated in vineyards in a regular order.
***Rotwein*** *(Ger)* Red wine.
**Ruby Port** An undated blended Port shipped in bulk. **Young Ruby** is bottled and ready for drinking after four years; **Old Ruby** is bottled and ready for drinking after six.

## S

**Saccharometer** See HYDROMETER.
**Saki** or **Saké** Japanese rice wine.
**Schnapps** German and Dutch term for spirits.
***Schaumwein*** *(Ger)* Wines of lower than QbA quality that have been made sparkling, usually by carbonation.
***Schloss*** *(Ger)* A castle or building of noble origin, or an estate on which such a building once existed.
**Sealed-tank method** A method of producing sparkling wines; see page 44.
***Secco*** *(It)* Dry wine.
**Sediment** A deposit (rare in white wines) composed of TANNIN, pigments, and small quantities of mineral salts; in white wines crystals of cream of tartar may also form, often at the base of the cork. Neither indicate a fault; indeed, they are a guarantee of careful preparation without over-refinement. Crystals may be ignored, but red wines throwing deposits should be decanted (see DECANTING).
***Sekt*** *(Ger)* Sparkling wine of QbA quality made by the Champagne, transfer or sealed-tank method.
***Semisecco*** *(It)* Literally, "semidry"; actually medium sweet.
***Solera*** System used for the blending and maturing of Sherry and Madeira. See pages 160-61.
***Sommelier*** A head wine-waiter.
**Sour mash** A combination of mash from a previous FERMENTATION and new mash with fresh yeast, used to induce fermentation in the process of distilling whiskeys and whiskies, especially Bourbon.
***Spätlese*** *(Ger)* The second-lowest *Prädikat* in the German Qualitätswein system.
**Specific Gravity** (or **relative density**) The ratio of the weight of a given volume of a substance to the weight of the same volume of water at 4°C (39.2°F). Obviously, water's own SG is 1; liquids of alcohol content 7.5-15% have SGs in the range 1.06-1.12.
***Spumante*** *(It)* Sparkling wine.
**Stalks** (or **stems**) The sprigs on which individual grapes grow in bunches, usually left attached in fermenting white wine, but not for red wine.
**Steeps** Tanks used for the MALTING of barley prior to fermentation in the production of malt whisky and other grain spirits.
**Stemmer-crusher** (French ***égrappoir-fouloir***) Used before fermenting red wine, a rotating cylindrical machine which in a single operation removes the stems and lightly crushes the grapes.
***Stück*** *(Ger)* See BARREL TYPES.
**Sulfuring** Sulfuric acid, sulfur dioxide or sulfides may be added to grape MUST to delay or prevent fermentation; later, selected yeasts may be required to start fermentation. In the form of sulfur dioxide ($SO_2$), sulfur is in many countries the only permitted antiseptic and deoxidant treatment for wines. Because of the smell, total sulfur is limited to 450 parts per million.
**Sulfury** The eggy odor of white wine in which sulfur has been used as a preservative. The bottle will usually lose this odor within a half hour of being broached.
***Superiore*** *(It)* Wine that is superior in one or more of several possible ways, according to the particular DOC award.
**Supple** Describes wines that are neither hard nor soft, usually having a good finish.
***Süssreserve*** *(Ger)* Unfermented grape-juice, used for sweetening or balancing fully fermented dry wines to meet required marketing specifications. Its addition lowers the wine's alcohol content.

## T

***Tafelwein*** *(Ger)* The lowest quality of German table wine, for everyday drinking. *Tafelwein* is fully classified by law. ***Deutsche Tafelwein*** is of solely German origin.
***Tailles*** *(Fr)* Used in Champagne, must from later pressings, after the marc has been dug-over or cut (*taillé*).
**Tails** See HEADS AND TAILS.
**Tannin** Group of organic compounds found in wood-bark and in the roots and stems of many plants. Astringent, it is more pronounced in red wines, where the tannin from the grape-skins adds to that from the oak barrels (especially new ones). Tannin helps development during aging and gives longevity to many wines.
**Tartaric acid** The principal acid (see ACIDITY) in wine made from ripe grapes. It is precipitated in the form of potassium bitartrate crystals in cask, bottle, or both. See SEDIMENT.
***Tastevin*** *(Fr)* Silver tasting cup, most commonly found in Burgundy.
**Tasting** Wine-tastings are held so that experts and potential purchasers may sample and assess the value of wines and spirits offered by producers, agents, shippers, wholesalers, merchants and others prior to their sale. Such sales may be made through the wines and spirits trades or at auction or other occasion. For the methods used in tastings see pages 370-71.
**Tawny** Undated blended Port shipped in bulk; the color comes from aging in wood. **Young Tawny** is bottled and ready for drinking at four years; **Old Tawny** is bottled and ready for drinking at ten years, when it has a light tawny color and a nutty flavor.
***Tirage*** *(Fr)* A bottling. Several casks may be assembled in a vat for one *tirage*.
***Tonneau*** *(Fr)* Old French cask of 900-liter (238gal) capacity. No longer found, it was equal to approximately four *barriques*. See BARREL TYPES.
**Topping up** Filling casks to replace wine lost through ULLAGE and to prevent oxidation.
**Total acidity** See ACIDITY.
**Transfer method** (or ***cuvé close***) A method of making good sparkling wine. It follows the principle of the MÉTHODE CHAMPENOISE up to the point of DÉGORGEMENT, at which stage the wine (including sediment) is sucked from the bottle, filtered, and transferred to and sealed in a new bottle. See page 44.
***Trocken*** *(Ger)* Literally dry, for wines having less than 9g/l (about 1oz per gal) of unfermented sugar.
**Tufa** Rock of volcanized chalk. Found in the Touraine district of the Loire and in areas of southern Italy, it could have been designed with wine-makers in mind: it is easy to cut into for *caves*, full of minerals, porous, and water-retentive.

## U

**Ullage** The natural process of wine- or spirit-loss by evaporation during aging in casks. When bottled under airtight conditions these liquids do not ullage perceptibly.

## V

***Valinch*** *(Fr)* "Thief-tube" or pipette, used to draw samples of wine from cask.
**Varietal** A wine named for its grape, or principal grape. Under US wine-laws, at least 74% of a labeled **varietal wine** must be from the named grape.
**Vats** Containers made for fermentation, aging and storage of wines and for several other major purposes, including stages of MALTING and DISTILLATION. They may be of wood, stainless steel, concrete, glass-lined concrete, or stainless-steel-lined fiberglass.
***Vecchio*** *(It)* Old wine.
**Verdelho** *(P)* One of the two Madeira wines to which spirit is added after ESTUFAGEM, making them dry. The other is Sercial.
***Vigna*** (or ***vigneto***) *(It)* Vineyard.
***Vigneron*** *(Fr)* The vineyard chief or *chef de culture*.
***Vin de cuvée*** *(Fr)* MUST of the first pressing — i.e., FREE-RUN WINE — particularly for Champagne, unmixed with PRESS WINE.
***Vin de goutte*** *(Fr)* See FREE-RUN WINE. ***Vin de presse*** *(Fr)* See PRESS WINE.
***Vino Cotto*** *(It)* Process of boiling down grape MUST, which is then added with brandy to normally fermented wine to produce Marsala.
***Vino da pasta*** *(It)* Wine for everyday drinking.
***Vino da tavolo*** *(It)* Italian table wine of less than DOC standard.
***Vino de color*** (or ***paxarete***) *(Sp)* Coloring wine; e.g., ARROPE.
***Vino novello*** *(It)* New season's wine: like Beaujolais *nouveau*, it is for drinking as young as possible.
**Vinosity** Describes the character of a wine — its balance, body, flavor, and bouquet.
***Vins de Liqueur*** **(VdL)** *(Fr)* Fortified wines having, before the addition of spirits, a lower potential alcohol than VINS DOUX NATURELS. Only some VdL have AC.
***Vins Doux Naturels*** **(VDN)** *(Fr)* Fortified wines flavored with Muscat grapes and chilled to make excellent APÉRITIFS. Roussillon, in the southwest corner of France, is most famous for them. All VDN have AC.
**Vintage** (1) The annual grape harvest. (2) The wine made from those grapes. (3) A wine year; for example, you can say that "1978 was a good vintage for Bordeaux and Burgundy."
***Vite*** *(It)* Wine.
**Viticulture** The science of cultivating the vine and producing grapes from it. It requires many skills, and knowledge of other sciences such as biology and meteorology.
***Vitis vinifera*** The "wine-bearing vine" species, from which all the finest strains of GRAPES come. Of these there are about 40; nearly all others (over 2000) are crosses bred from them. In addition there are HYBRIDS resulting from crosses with other species.
**Volatile acid** ACETIC ACID, acceptable as a by-product of alcoholic fermentation up to a level of 600-800ppm.

## W

**Wash** (or **beer**) A fermented liquid prepared for distillation; the term is usually used in connection with Scotch-whisky production.
**Weeper** A leaking bottle, usually a result of a faulty cork.
***Weingut*** *(Ger)* A wine estate. The term is reserved for growers who use only self-grown grapes in their wine-production.

**Wine-bands** The bands, encircling the Earth between parallels 30° and 50° north and south of the Equator, in which the annual reception of sunlight is sufficient in duration and strength to bring grape-crops to full ripeness. Nearer the poles there is not enough **heat** (nearer the Equator there is too much) to produce firm wines with definitive characteristics.
***Winzergenossenschaft*** *(Ger)* Wine-growers' cooperative.
**Woody** Describes the taste acquired by wine that has been too long in the wood.
**Wort** The liquor produced when GRIST and grain are infused in hot water. Wort is the base material fermented with YEAST and then distilled to make GRAIN SPIRITS.

## Y

**Yeasts** Single-celled plant organisms that react with the sugar in the grapes to produce alcohol and carbon dioxide.
**Yeasty** Describes a wine odor indicating partial bottle-fermentation.

# INDEX ◆ GRAPES AND VINES

This index is divided into three parts:
**1** Grapes and Vines
**2** Wines and Other Drinks
**3** General

Page numbers in *italics* indicate the sites of relevant illustrations and captions; those in **bold** refer to major discussions. The letter G indicates that the keyword is defined in the Glossary.

Where confusion might otherwise arise, wines are distinguished from regions (or districts) of the same name by the appearance of (w) or (r); for example, "Champagne (w)" refers to the wine, "Champagne (r)" to the region. Where wines and grapes have the same name, (w) and (g) are used; for example "Riesling (g)" refers to the grape rather than the wine. Where a wine has the same name as its vineyard, château, etc., the listing is only under the wine unless there is a specific discussion of the vineyard or château in the text. (R) stands for "river".

Where two proper names are synonymous, the = symbol is used together with, where helpful, an indication of the country of origin of the lesser known synonym; for example "Cariñena (Sp) = Carignan" indicates that Cariñena is the Spanish name for the Carignan grape, the main entry for which is listed under Carignan. In similar references, (var.) signifies "variety".

## A



## B



## C

## R



## S



## T

# INDEX ♦ WINES AND OTHER DRINKS

# INDEX ♦ GENERAL

## N



## O



## P

# ACKNOWLEDGEMENTS


*l* left; *r* right; *t* top; *b* bottom; *m* middle.

All photographs are by Colin Maher, Jon Wyand and Michael Freeman, except for the following: **19** *tl* Matter of Fact; **19** *bl* Champagne Bureau; **19** *br* AISA; **23** *tr* Wine and Spirit Education Trust Limited; **23** *bl* Wine and Spirit Education Trust Limited; **25** *l* and *r* Wine and Spirit Education Trust Limited; **27** *bl* Wine and Spirit Education Trust Limited; **30** Food and Wine from France; **81** *m* Denis Hughes-Gilbey; *b* Wine and Spirit Education Trust Limited; **82** Denis Hughes-Gilbey; **85** C.I.V.A.S.; **90** *mr* Food and Wine from France; *bl* Food and Wine from France; **117** *l* Italian Trade Centre; *r* Hedges and Butler; **144-5** Deutsche Wein Institut; **147** AISA; **148** AISA; **149** AISA; **150-1** AISA; **152-3** AISA; **154-5** AISA; **156** Gonzalez Byaz; **157** AISA; **158** Gonzalez Byaz; **158** *inset* AISA; **159** AISA; **160** H.P. Bulmer Ltd; **162-3** AISA; **162** AISA; **166-7** Matter of Fact/Deinhard; **169** Matter of Fact/Deinhard; **170-1** Matter of Fact/Deinhard; **172** Hedges and Butler; **175** Axaia-Clauss Ltd; **176** Axaia-Clauss Ltd; **177** Robert Est; **178** *br* J. Allan Cash Ltd; **178-9** Luxembourg Wine Company; **180-1** British Tourist Authority; **182-3** British Tourist Authority; **184-5** Robert Est; **187** Swiss National Tourist Office; **188** Weinwirtschaffsfunds; **189** *t* Lawlers Heidsieck; **189** *b* Weinwirtschaffsfunds; **190** *t* Lawlers Heidsieck; **190** *b* Weinwirtschaffsfunds; **191** Weinwirtschaffsfunds; **193** Interfoto MTI, Hungary; **194-5** Counsel Limited; **194** Counsel Limited; **197** J. Allan Cash Ltd; **198-9** Fruitexport; **200-1** Bulgarian Vintners; **202-3** Cyprus Trade Centre; **204-5** Novosti Press Agency; **206-7** Chateau Musar; **211** Tunisian Tourist Office; **213** J. Allan Cash Ltd; **267** *t* Robert Est, Ontario House; **273** J. Allan Cash Ltd; **276-7** Australian Tourist Commission; **279** Stevens Garnier Ltd; **298-9** Cooks New Zealand Wine Co; **303** Alastair Campbell; **318** Mansell Collection; **319** Scottish Tourist Board; **320** Mansell Collection; **329** *b* Scottish Tourist Board; **335** Vernon East; **351** Scottish Tourist Board; **352** *r* Scottish Tourist Board; **353** *t* and *b* Scottish Tourist Board; **354-5** Scottish Tourist Board; **362-3** Hugh Olliff; **367** Hugh Olliff; **369** Christies; **371** *t* Christies; **371** *b* Hugh Olliff; **374** Martini and Rossi; **375** Hugh Olliff